Research Anthology on Implementing Sentiment Analysis Across Multiple Disciplines

Information Resources Management Association
USA

Volume II

Published in the United States of America by
IGI Global
Engineering Science Reference (an imprint of IGI Global)
701 E. Chocolate Avenue
Hershey PA, USA 17033
Tel: 717-533-8845
Fax: 717-533-8661
E-mail: cust@igi-global.com
Web site: http://www.igi-global.com

Library of Congress Cataloging-in-Publication Data

Names: Information Resources Management Association, editor.
Title: Research anthology on implementing sentiment analysis across
   multiple disciplines / Information Resources Management Association,
   editor.
Description: Hershey PA : Engineering Science Reference, [2022] | Includes
   bibliographical references and index. | Summary: "This reference book of
   contributed chapters discusses the tools, methodologies, applications,
   and implementation of sentiment analysis across various disciplines and
   industries such as the pharmaceutical industry, government, and the
   tourism industry and presents emerging technologies and developments
   within the field of sentiment analysis and opinion mining"-- Provided by
   publisher.
Identifiers: LCCN 2022016823 (print) | LCCN 2022016824 (ebook) | ISBN
   9781668463031 (h/c) | ISBN 9781668463048 (ebook)
Subjects: LCSH: Sentiment analysis.
Classification: LCC QA76.9.S57 R47 2022 (print) | LCC QA76.9.S57 (ebook)
   | DDC 005.1/4--dc23/eng/20220622
LC record available at https://lccn.loc.gov/2022016823
LC ebook record available at https://lccn.loc.gov/2022016824

British Cataloguing in Publication Data
A Cataloguing in Publication record for this book is available from the British Library.

The views expressed in this book are those of the authors, but not necessarily of the publisher.

For electronic access to this publication, please contact: eresources@igi-global.com.

Editor-in-Chief

Mehdi Khosrow-Pour, DBA
Information Resources Management Association, USA

Associate Editors

Steve Clarke, *University of Hull, UK*
Murray E. Jennex, *San Diego State University, USA*
Ari-Veikko Anttiroiko, *University of Tampere, Finland*

Editorial Advisory Board

Sherif Kamel, *American University in Cairo, Egypt*
In Lee, *Western Illinois University, USA*
Jerzy Kisielnicki, *Warsaw University, Poland*
Amar Gupta, *Arizona University, USA*
Craig van Slyke, *University of Central Florida, USA*
John Wang, *Montclair State University, USA*
Vishanth Weerakkody, *Brunel University, UK*

List of Contributors

Table of Contents

**Section 2
Development and Design Methodologies**

Volume II

Section 3
Tools and Technologies

Volume III

Section 4
Utilization and Applications

Section 6
Critical Issues and Challenges

Preface

Sentiment analysis is a field that is gaining traction as more organizations and fields discover the myriad benefits and opportunities it offers. Regardless of industry, it is always useful to know what consumers think, whether that be about a product, a service, or a company in general. With sentiment analysis technology, it has never been easier to understand what audiences want and need. Organizations must embrace this technology and integrate it into their business strategies and tactics in order to successfully reach and communicate with their audience.

Staying informed of the most up-to-date research trends and findings is of the utmost importance. That is why IGI Global is pleased to offer this four-volume reference collection of reprinted IGI Global book chapters and journal articles that have been handpicked by senior editorial staff. This collection will shed light on critical issues related to the trends, techniques, and uses of various applications by providing both broad and detailed perspectives on cutting-edge theories and developments. This collection is designed to act as a single reference source on conceptual, methodological, technical, and managerial issues, as well as to provide insight into emerging trends and future opportunities within the field.

The *Research Anthology on Implementing Sentiment Analysis Across Multiple Disciplines* is organized into six distinct sections that provide comprehensive coverage of important topics. The sections are:

1. Fundamental Concepts and Theories;
2. Development and Design Methodologies;
3. Tools and Technologies;
4. Utilization and Applications;
5. Organizational and Social Implications; and
6. Critical Issues and Challenges.

The following paragraphs provide a summary of what to expect from this invaluable reference tool.

Section 1, "Fundamental Concepts and Theories," serves as a foundation for this extensive reference tool by addressing crucial theories essential to understanding the concepts and uses of sentiment analysis in multidisciplinary settings. Opening this reference book is the chapter "Fundamentals of Opinion Mining" by Profs. Ashish Seth and Kirti Seth from INHA University, India, which focuses on explaining the fundamentals of opinion mining along with sentiment analysis and covers the brief evolution in mining techniques in the last decade. This first section ends with the chapter "Sentiment Analysis in Crisis Situations for Better Connected Government: Case of Mexico Earthquake in 2017" by Profs. Rodrigo Sandoval-Almazán, Asdrúbal López Chau, and David Valle-Cruz from the Universidad Autónoma del Estado de México, Mexico, which adapts the methodology of sentiment analysis of social media posts to an expanded version for crisis situations.

Section 2, "Development and Design Methodologies," presents in-depth coverage of the design and development of sentiment analysis for its use in different applications. This section starts with "Integrating Semantic Acquaintance for Sentiment Analysis" by Profs. Rashmi Agrawal and Neha Gupta from Manav Rachna International Institute of Research and Studies, India, which focuses on semantic guidance-based sentiment analysis approaches and provides a semantically enhanced technique for annotation of sentiment polarity. This section closes with "An Extensive Text Mining Study for the Turkish Language: Author Recognition, Sentiment Analysis, and Text Classification" by Profs. Durmuş Özkan Şahin and Erdal Kılıç from Ondokuz Mayıs University, Turkey, which provides theoretical and experimental information about text mining and discusses three different text mining problems such as news classification, sentiment analysis, and author recognition.

Section 3, "Tools and Technologies," explores the various tools and technologies used for the implementation of sentiment analysis for various uses. This section begins with "Tools of Opinion Mining" by Profs. Neha Gupta and Siddharth Verma from Manav Rachna International Institute of Research and Studies, India, which examines how opinion mining is moving to the sentimental reviews of Twitter data, comments used on Facebook, videos, or Facebook statuses. This section closes with the chapter "Opinion Mining for Instructor Evaluations at the Autonomous University of Ciudad Juarez" by Profs. Abraham López, Alejandra Mendoza Carreón, Rafael Jiménez, Vicente García, and Alan Ponce from the Universidad Autónoma de Ciudad Juárez, Mexico, which considers how opinion mining can be useful for labeling student comments as positive and negative and, for this purpose, creates a database using real opinions obtained from five professors over the last four years, covering a total of 20 subjects.

Section 4, "Utilization and Applications," describes how sentiment analysis is used and applied in diverse industries for various applications. The opening chapter in this section, "A Survey on Implementation Methods and Applications of Sentiment Analysis," by Profs. Sudheer Karnam, Valarmathi B., and Tulasi Prasad Sariki from VIT University, India, compares different methods of solving sentiment analysis problems, algorithms, merits and demerits, and applications and also investigates different research problems in sentiment analysis. The closing chapter in this section, "Communicating Natural Calamity: The Sentiment Analysis of Post Rigopiano's Accident," by Profs. Nicola Capolupo and Gabriella Piscopo from the University of Salerno, Italy, aims at understanding the dynamics that led to the exchange and value co-creation/co-production in the interaction between P.A. and citizens during natural calamities and proposes a horizontal communication model in which both actors cooperate to respond to a crisis.

Section 5, "Organizational and Social Implications," includes chapters discussing the impact of sentiment analysis on society and shows the ways in which it can be used in different industries and how this impacts business. The chapter "Open Issues in Opinion Mining" by Profs. V. Uma and Vishal Vyas from Pondicherry University, India, explains the various research issues and challenges present in each stage of opinion mining. The closing chapter, "eWOW of Guests Regarding Their Hotel Experience: Sentiment Analysis of TripAdvisor Reviews," by Profs. Zelia Breda and Rui Costa from GOVCOPP, University of Aveiro, Portugal; Prof. Gorete Dinis from GOVCOPP, Polytechnic Institute of Portalegre, Portugal; and Prof. Amandine Angie Martins of the University of Aveiro, Portugal, focuses on sentiment analysis of comments made on TripAdvisor regarding one resort located in the Algarve region in Portugal.

Section 6, "Critical Issues and Challenges," presents coverage of academic and research perspectives on the challenges of using sentiment analysis in varied industries. Opening this final section is the chapter "Multimodal Sentiment Analysis: A Survey and Comparison" by Profs. Ramandeep Kaur and Sandeep Kautish from Guru Kashi University, India, which provides a full image of the multimodal sentiment analysis opportunities and difficulties and considers the recent trends of research in the field. The closing chapter, "A Sentiment Analysis of the 2014-15 Ebola Outbreak in the Media and Social Media," by Prof. Nilmini Wickramasinghe from Swinburne University of Technology, Australia & Epworth Health-Care, Australia; Prof. Blooma John of the University of Canberra, Australia; and Dr. Bob Baulch from the International Food Policy Research Institute, Malawi, analyzes news articles on the Ebola outbreak from two leading news outlets, together with comments on the articles from a well-known social media platform, from March 2014 to July 2015.

Although the primary organization of the contents in this multi-volume work is based on its six sections, offering a progression of coverage of the important concepts, methodologies, technologies, applications, social issues, and emerging trends, the reader can also identify specific contents by utilizing the extensive indexing system listed at the end of each volume. As a comprehensive collection of research on the latest findings related to sentiment analysis, the *Research Anthology on Implementing Sentiment Analysis Across Multiple Disciplines* provides social media analysts, computer scientists, IT professionals, AI scientists, business leaders and managers, marketers, advertising agencies, public administrators, government officials, university administrators, libraries, instructors, researchers, academicians, and students with a complete understanding of the applications and impacts of sentiment analysis across fields and disciplines. Given the vast number of issues concerning usage, failure, success, strategies, and applications of sentiment analysis, the *Research Anthology on Implementing Sentiment Analysis Across Multiple Disciplines* encompasses the most pertinent research on the applications, impacts, uses, and development of sentiment analysis.

Chapter 26
Sentiment Analysis of Game Review Using Machine Learning in a Hadoop Ecosystem

Arvind Panwar

(iD) https://orcid.org/0000-0001-9957-6365

Research Scholar, Guru Gobind Singh Indraprastha University, India

Vishal Bhatnagar

Ambedkar Institute of Advanced Communication Technologies and Research, Delhi, India

ABSTRACT

Internet, & more unambiguously the creation of WWW in the early 1990s, helped people to build an interconnected global platform where information can be stored, shared, and consumed by anyone with an electronic device which has the ability to connect to the Web. This provides a way of putting together lots of information, ideas, and opinion. An interactive platform was born to post content, messages, and opinions under one roof, and the platform is known as social media. Social media has acquired massive popularity and importance that why today almost everyone can't stay away from it. Social media is not only a medium for people to express their thoughts, moreover, but it is also a very powerful tool which can be used by businesses to focus on new and existing customers and increase profit with the help of social media analytics. This paper starts with a discussion on social media with its significance & pitfalls. Later on, this paper presents a brief introduction of sentiment analysis in social media and give an experimental work on sentiment analysis in a social game review.

INTRODUCTION

The discovery of computers, digital electronics, social media, and the Internet has really accompanied us from the industrial age into the information age. The Internet, and more unambiguously the creation of WWW at the starting of the 1990s, facilitated folks to form an organized worldwide stage where data and information can be kept, consumed and shared by everybody with an electric gadget that has the ability

DOI: 10.4018/978-1-6684-6303-1.ch026

to connect to the Web. This provides the way of putting together the vast amount of information, ideas and opinions which people, brands, organizations and businesses want to share with everyone around the world. So, an interactive platform was born, to share ideas, to post content, to share messages and opinions under one roof, and the platform is known as social media.

This paper will take you on a journey to understand social media, analyzing rich data produced by media and gaining precious insights. The author will focus on social media which serves to audiences in different forms, like micro-blogging, social networking, software collaboration, news and media sharing platforms. The main purpose is to use standardized data access and retrieval techniques using APIs (application programming interfaces) for social media platforms to collect data from these websites and apply different data mining, and machine learning, statistical, deep learning and NLP (Natural Language Processing) methods on the data.

This paper is divided into a different section. Section two presents related work in sentiment analysis. In section three the author presents research methodology followed in this paper. Section four presents a brief introduction of social media with its significance and pitfalls. Section five gives the answer about social media analytics with the help of a framework and also present its challenges and opportunity. In section six author describe sentiment analysis in social media platform. Section seven presents experimental work on the game review dataset. The last section gives a conclusion and future research on this topic.

RELATED WORK

Social media is fuel for business nowadays and a daily basic need for every person to share the life moment, memories and views. Moreover, social media applications from daily life, numerous research papers on these applications have also been available. For example, authors in (Liu, Cao, Lin, Huang, & Zhou, 2007), suggested a model for sentiment analysis forecast sales of an organization. In the research paper(McGlohon, Glance, & Reiter, 2010), authors used for company merchants and their products. This (Hong & Skiena, 2010) research paper, shows relations within the community opinions and NFL betting, using twitter and blogs. In the study(Marvell Solutions, n.d.), authors linked civic view and Twitter opinion polls. A research paper written by (Cerezo, 2004), used Twitter opinions poll to predict election results in a country. In (B. Chen, Zhu, Kifer, & Lee, 2010), the study considered political perspectives. In (Yano & Smith, 2010), authors present a method for sentiment analysis to forecasting statement measurements of political blogs. In (Asur & Huberman, 2010; Joshi, Das, Gimpel, & Smith, 2010; Sadikov, Parameswaran, & Venetis, 2009), authors used blogs, Twitter reviews, and public opinions of a movie to predict box-office collection. In (Miller, Sathi, Wiesenthal, Leskovec, & Potts, 2011), social media networks were examined using sentiment flow. In (Mohammad, Tony, & Yang, 2013), the authors show a study, to find how genders fluctuated on emotive axes, using sentiments and opinions in emails. In (Mohammad, 2012), authors analyze and track emotions in stories and tales. In (Bollen, Mao, & Zeng, 2011), the author studies the Twitter data and forecast the stock market using sentiment analysis. In (Bar-Haim, Dinur, Feldman, Fresko, & Goldstein, 2011; Le Caillec, Itani, Guriot, & Rakotondratsimba, 2017), (Zhang & Skiena, 2010), Authors study trading strategies by using the blogs sentiment and news website sentiments. In (Sakunkoo & Sakunkoo, 2009), the authors present societal impacts by study reviews in an online book store. In (Groh & Hauffa, 2011), societal associations were described and shows using sentiment analysis(Castellanos et al., 2011).

As deliberated above, universal real-world problems and applications are the prime motivation for sentiment analysis is a widespread research focus. It is also largely researched in text mining, Web mining, data mining and information retrieval. In fact, it's not limited to computer science only, it had extended to management science also. (Brown, Broderick, & Lee, 2007; Y. Chen & Xie, 2008; Das & Chen, 2007; Ghose & Ipeirotis, 2007; N. Hu & Pavlou, 2006; Nikolay, Anindya, & Panagiotis, 2011; Park, Lee, & Han, 2007)

DIFFERENT TYPE OF ANALYSIS

The author now stretches a momentary overview of the foremost research complications constructed from the available research in the area. In wide-ranging, sentiment analysis has been primarily divided into three parts or levels.

Document Type: The job at this stage is to categorize the complete document or the opinion document articulates a positive or a natural or negative sentimentality (Cerezo, 2004; Yano & Smith, 2010). Such as in a goods product review system, the system analyzes a comment and present a positive or negative emotion about the product.

Sentence Type: The analysis work carried out at this stage to find out sentiment whether it is negative, neutral or positive, at the sentence level. This stage of analysis is narrowly allied to subjectivity classification (Bar-Haim et al., 2011).

Entity and Aspect Type: The above-discussed analysis methods do not conclude what individuals adored and did not adore. Aspect and entity-level achieve better-quality analysis. The previously aspect level is known as feature level analysis (M. Hu & Liu, 2004). As an alternative of considering at language creates (paragraphs, phrases, clauses, sentences, or documents), aspect level unswervingly considers sentiments itself.

To create additional interest and challenge, here we discuss two different types of opinions one is regular and the second is comparative describe in(Koellner & Müller, 1989). A regular opinion states a sentimentality only on a specific characteristic of the object, e.g., "Pepsi flavors are good,". In comparative sentiment analysis, we compare various things depends upon some of their common characteristics, e.g., "Pepsi better than Coke.".

RESEARCH METHODOLOGY

As the research in social media and sentiment analysis is tough to restrain to precise disciplines, the related things, resources and tools, are distributed through countless journals. KDD (Knowledge Discovery in Data), BI (Business Intelligence), and opinion mining or social network mining are the utmost collective academic area for sentiment analysis research in social media. Consequently, the subsequent online journal databases were searched to offer a complete catalog of the academic works on social media and sentiment analysis.

- ACM digital library Database;
- Springer;
- IGI-Global;

- Science Direct;
- Scopus;
- IEEE Transaction and
- Wiley

Figure 1. Article selection and research methodology flow chart

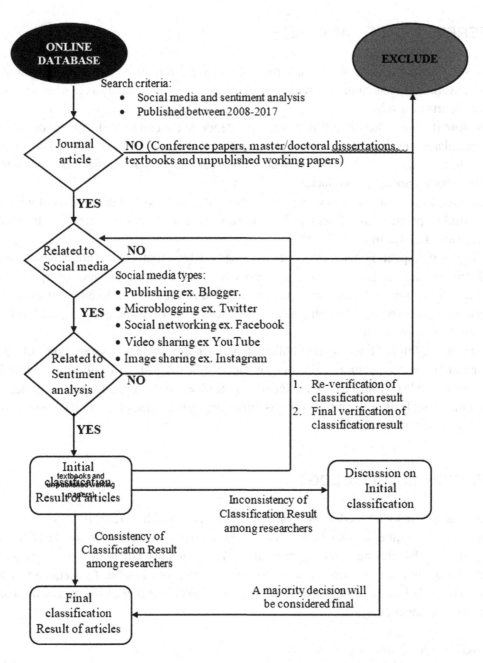

The database search was depending upon the search keyword, "social media and sentiment analysis" and "opinion mining and opinion analysis", which formerly created approximately 600 editorials. The complete text of separately editorial was studied to remove those that were not truly allied to the application of social media and sentiment analysis or opinion analysis. The individual editorial was cautiously studied and distinctly classified according to the diagram, as shown in Figure 1. Even though this examination was not complete, it assists as a wide base for a thoughtful reading about sentiment analysis in social media.

Understanding Social Media

The Internet age has been accountable to transform the approach to how individuals communicate with each other in the 21st Century. Nearly every person has some habits to use any kind of electric device to communicate with others, it can be a laptop, smartphone, tab or a PC. Social media is constructed on the idea of a place where users use CMC (computer-mediated communication) approaches to interconnect with others. They can use any method like as emails, instant messaging, and chat rooms to forums and social networking. Traditional media usually follow a one-way communication system. For example, always read some books or magazines, watch a television show or get an update about the news from television news channels or newspapers. The communication mechanism in the various forms of social media is a two-way street, where audiences can share information and give ideas and others can take them and provide their own ideas, opinions and feedback on the same, and they also share their own material based on what they see. Traditional based media, like radio or television, now use social media to give a two-way communication mechanism to support their communications, but it's much more seamless in social media where anyone and everyone can share content, communicate with others, freely give their ideas and opinions on a huge scale.

One can now properly explain social media as collaborative platforms depend upon the fundamental of CMC and Web 2.0, who empower handlers to be originators as well as trades, to generate and share thoughts, feelings, information, sentiments, and words in countless methods. While various and diversified arrangements of social media platforms available in the world, they consume several crucial attribute and common characteristics, some of them stated as follows:

- Web 2.0 Internet-based applications
- Content is produced as well as consumed by users
- Profiles give users have their own unique identity
- Social networks help connect different users, similarly to communities

In fact, social media give users their own universal identity and the freedom to show themselves in their own user profiles. These profiles are maintained as accounts by social media vendors. Features like what you see are what you get editors, emoticons, photos and videos help users in creating and sharing rich content. Social networking potential enables handlers to join other handlers to their own contact or friend lists and create groups and forums where they can share and talk about likeminded interests. The figure 2 shows some of the social media used today across the world:

Social media is used in various ways and can be grouped into distinct buckets by the nature of its usage and its features.

Figure 2. Social media framework

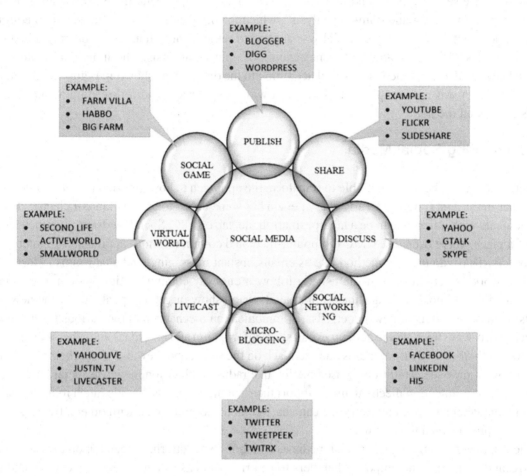

The above figure does not show the complete list of social media because there are so many applications and platforms out there. The author expresses regret in advance in case, he missed out mentioning your favorite social media! Figure clarify the different forms of communication and material sharing process that are available for users, and that they can choose any of these social media to share content and connect with other users. We will now discuss some of the key benefits and significance which social media must deliver.

Advantages and Importance

It has acquired massive popularity and importance that why today almost everyone can't stay away from it. Social media is not only a source for people to prompt their thoughts, moreover, but it is also a very powerful tool that can be used by businesses to focus on new and existing customers and increase profit. Now, the author will discuss some of the main advantages of social media as follows:

- **Cost Savings:** One of the biggest challenges for business is to do marketing or advertising on traditional or legacy-based media, to reach out to the customers and clients, which can be expensive.

On the other side, social media gives the facility to user to make business pages and post content and advertising at a minimal cost. Thus, social media is helping in cost-saving and increasing the visibility of a business.

- **Networking:** With the help of social media one can form their own network, in terms of social life and professional life with the public through the world. This has unlocked a great number of prospects and opportunities where folks from various countries and places can labor collectively on cutting-edge inventions.

- **Ease of Use:** It is very easy to get started with social media. A person who wants to use social media only needs to create an account by registering his details in the application or website and within a few minutes, he is ready to go! Apart from this, it is very easy to navigate through any social media website or application without any specific technical knowledge. A person only needs an Internet connection and an electronic device, which can connect to the internet, like a smartphone or a computer. Perhaps this could be the reason that a lot of parents and grandparents are now connecting to social media to share their moments and link with their friends.

- **Global Audience:** With the help of social media, a person can also make their content reach out to a global audience across the world. The reason is very simple: social media applications are available openly on the web, users across the globe can use it. A person who has their Businesses that engage with customers in different parts of the world have a key advantage to push their promotions and new products and services.

- **Prompt Feedback:** Businesses and companies can get quick feedback on their new product launches and services being used directly from the users. Tweets, posts, videos, comments and many more features present in social media to give instant feedback to companies by posting generally or conversing with them directly on their official social media channels.

- **Grievance Redressal:** One of the big advantages of social media is that users can now give any grievances or inconveniences, like electricity, water supply or security issues. Most government department and organizations, including law enforcement, have public social media channels which can be used for instant notification of grievances.

- **Entertainment:** This is surely the most popular advantage used to the maximum by all the users. Social media give us an unlimited source of entertainment where you can spend your time playing online games, watching videos, and participating in competitions with users across the world. In Fact, the possibilities of entertainment in social media are endless.

- **Visibility**: Anyone can hold their social media profile to gain visibility in the world. Professional social networking websites like LinkedIn are the best way for people to get noticed by recruiters and also for companies to recruit great talent. Even now a day's small startups or individuals can develop inventions, build products, or announce discoveries and grip social media to go viral and gain the necessary visibility which can propel them to the next level.

The significance and importance of social media are quite obvious from the preceding points. In today's interconnected world, social media has almost become crucial and while it might have a lot of disadvantages, including distractions, if we use it in the right direction, it can indeed be a very important tool or medium to help us obtain great things.

Disadvantages and Pitfalls

Even though the world has been roared the broadcast about social media and its importance, but some of us already thinking about pitfalls and disadvantages, which are directly or indirectly caused by social media. We want to cover all possibilities of social media including the good and the bad, so let's look at some negative side of social media:

- **Privacy Concerns:** this is a major aspect with respects to use social media is a deficiency of confidentiality and privacy. All our individual and private datastore on the social media platform have a threat of being unlawfully retrieved, however regularly assured to be protected by companies that host it. Additional, some companies charged from others for retailing or using users' private data without user permission.
- **Security Issues:** sometimes users share some personal information on their social media profiles which can be used by hackers and some other bad entities to gain insights into their personal lives and use it for their own personal gain.
- **Addiction:** This is applicable to a huge percentage of people on social media. Social media addiction is indeed real and a thoughtful apprehension, especially among teenagers. Now a day there are so many forms of social media and you can really get occupied in playing games, trying to do with what others are doing, or just sharing some moments from your life every other minute. A lot of us have a habit of regularly checking social media applications every now and then, which can be interference, especially if you are trying to meet the time limit. Few of us keep using social media while driving, due to this there are lots of accidents that happened in fatal results.
- **Negativity:** It consents user to prompt their self spontaneously and this is habitually miss-used by individuals, extremist, and other radical crowds to share terrible speech, horrible advertising, and negativity. Folks frequently post mocking and harmful responses depend upon individual thoughts and state of mind. However, users can report such actions, there is a cybercrime cell, but it is not sufficient, because it is not possible to observe massive users on the social network.
- **Risks:** There are quite a lot of possible risks of using social media for your personal use or business promotions and movements. One wrong post can possibly prove to be very costly. Above and beyond this, there is the persistent risk of hackers, fraud, security attacks, and unwanted spam. The nonstop practice of social media and habit to it also poses a potential health risk. Officialdoms must have appropriate social media use strategies to confirm that their workforces do not end up being unproductive by wasting too much time on social media, and do not leakage company secrets or confidential information on social media.

In the above section, we discussed numerous drawbacks attached to using social media and some of them are very thoughtful concerns. Suitable social media usage strategies and rules should be borne in mind by everyone because social media is like a telescopic glass: anything you post can be used a counter to you or can possibly prove harmful later. Be it tremendously sensitive personal information, or private information, like the blueprint of your product or your next invention launch, always think carefully before sharing anything with the rest of the world.

Though, if you know what you are doing, social media can be used as a suitable tool for your personal as well as professional gain.

SOCIAL MEDIA ANALYTICS

At this point, readers have an exhaustive outline of social media, its consequences, drawbacks, and numerous aspects. Now it's the time to deliberate social media analytics and advantage it delivers for, scientists, data analysts and industries in over-all considering to collect valuable perceptions from it. It can be well-defined as the procedure of collecting data from social media platforms and investigating the data by means of various analytical strategies to excerpt valuable insights, later used decision making for the business. A vital thing to recall is that the procedures involved in social media analytics are generally domain-specific and you can put on them on data belonging to any company or business in any area.

Figure 3. Social media analytics framework

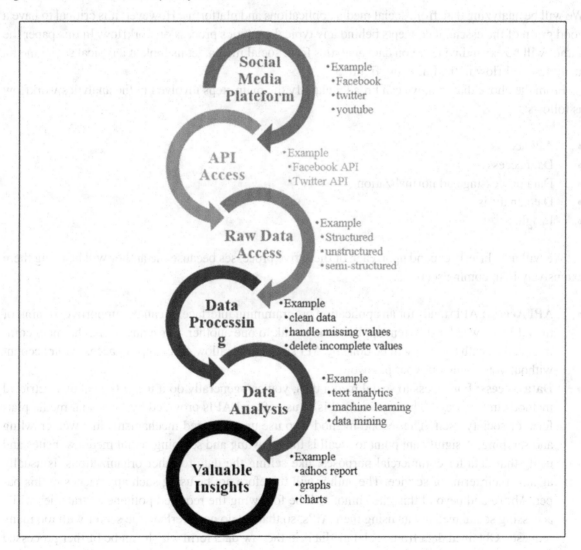

The most significant phase in going forward with any social media analytics-based workflow or progress is to govern the business goals or purposes and the insights that we want to gather from our analyzes. These goalmouths are generally in the form of key performance indicators (KPIs). For example, the total amount of likes, size of followers, the total figure of comments and shares can be KPIs to measure product engagement with customers using social media. Every so often data is not structured, and the end aims are not very concrete. Methods like NLP and text analytics can be used in such cases to extract insights from noisy unstructured text data like understanding the sentiment or attitude of customers for a specific service or product and trying to understand the key trends and themes based on customer tweets or posts at any point in time.

A Typical Social Media Analytics Workflow

We will be analyzing data from social media applications and platforms. However, it is critical to have a good grasp of the essential concepts behind any typical analytics process or workflow. In this paper the author will be expanding more on data analytics from social media, let us look at a typical social media analytics workflow in the following figure 3:

From the above diagram, we can broadly classify the main steps involved in the analytics workflow as follows:

- API access
- Data access
- Data processing and normalization
- Data analysis
- Insights

We will now briefly expand upon each of these five processes because the author will be using them extensively in upcoming sections.

- **API Access:** API stands for an application programming interface. It can be supportive to think of the API as a way for different applications to talk to one another. For many users, the main communication with the API will be done by API keys, which allow other apps to access your account without you giving out your password.
- **Data Access:** For access to social media data, you can generally do it using typical data retrieval methods in two ways. The first method is to use official APIs provided by the social media platform or society itself. The second method is to use unauthorized mechanisms like web crawling and scraping. A significant point to recall is that crawling and scraping social media websites and using that data for commercial purposes, like selling the data to other organizations, is usually against their terms of service. The author will therefore not be using such approaches in this paper. Above and beyond this, the author will be following the required politeness strategies while accessing social media data using their APIs, so that we do not overload the server with too many requests. Obtained data from social media is in the raw data form which can be further processed and normalized as needed.

- **Data Processing and Normalization:** The data obtained from data retrieval using social media APIs may not be structured and clean or it can be a combination of structured and unstructured data. In fact, data gained from social media is noisy, unstructured and often holds unnecessary tokens such as HTML tags and other metadata. Usually, data streams from social media APIs have JavaScript Object Notation (JSON) response objects, which consist of key-value pairs just like the example shown in figure 4:

Figure 4. JSON code

```
{
"user": {
"profile_sidebar_fill_color": "DBBCCD",
"profile_sidebar_border_color": "AABBCC",
"profile_background_tile": false,
"name": "Arvind panwar",
"profile_image_url": "http://arvind.com/img/arvind.
jpg",
"created_at": "Tue sep 07 19:05:07 +0000 2017",
"location": "Delhi, India",
},
"followers_count": 245,
"statuses_count": 711,
"friends_count": 327
}
```

The previous JSON object contains a typical response from the Twitter API showing details of a user profile. Few APIs may return data in different formats, such as Extensible Markup Language (XML), or Comma Separated Values (CSV) and each format require to be handled appropriately. Frequently social media data contains unstructured textual data that needs additional text pre-processing and normalization before it can be nourished into any standard data mining or machine learning algorithm. Text normalization is usually done using numerous methods to clean and normalize the text. Some of them are:

- Text tokenization
- Removing special characters and symbols
- Spelling corrections .
- Contraction expansions
- Stemming
- Lemmatization

Data Analysis: This is the center of the complete workflow, where we put on various methods to analyze the data: this could be the raw inherent data itself, or the processed and curated data. Usually, the techniques used in the analysis can be broadly classified into three areas:

- Data mining or analytics
- Machine learning
- Text analytics and NLP

Data mining, Machine learning, and deep learning have numerous overlapping concepts, including the fact that both use statistical techniques and try to find patterns from original data. In Data mining we are finding key patterns or insights from data; whereas machine learning is more about using mathematics, statistics, and even some of these data mining algorithms, to make models to forecast or prediction outcomes. Even though both methods need numeric and structured data to work with them, further complex analyses with unstructured textual data are generally handled in the distinct realm of text analytics by leveraging natural language processing which permits us to use some tools, methods and procedures to analyze free-flowing unstructured text. The author will be using methods, from these three areas to analyze data from social media platforms in this paper.

- **Insights:** In the end outcomes from our workflow are the real perceptions that act as facts or concrete data points to achieve the objective of the analysis. The outcome can be anything from a business intelligence report to visualizations such as charts, bar graphs, histograms, or even word or phrase clouds. Outcomes must be crisp, clear, and actionable so that it can be easy for businesses to take valuable decisions in time by leveraging them.

Opportunities

Based on the benefits of social media, we can originate plentiful opportunities that lie within the space of social media analytics. As the author says in previous section companies can save a lot of costs involved in targeted advertising and promotions by analyzing your social media traffic patterns. companies can watch how users involve with your brand or business using social media, for example, when it is the perfect time to share something new, something interesting, such as a new service, a new product, or even an interesting tale about your company. Even though traffic come from different geographies location, companies can analyze and understand the preferences of users from different parts of the globe. Companies can publish promotions in their language because Users love it if you publish promotions in their local language, and businesses are already leveraging such capabilities from social media platforms, to target consumers in specific cities from different countries depends upon localized content.

The social media analytics landscape is young and developing technology and has a lot of untouched potentials. Let us recognize the potential of social media analytics better by taking a real-world example. Suppose a person is running a money-making business with dynamic engagement on various social media networks. How can that person use the data produced from social media to know how that person is doing and how his competitors are doing? Real data streams from Twitter could be uninterruptedly analyzed to get the real-time sentiment, mood, opinion, emotion, and reactions of the public to his products and services. That person could even analyze the same for his competitors to see when they are launching their merchandise and how users are reacting to them. With the help of Facebook, you can do the similar and smoothly push localized promotions and advertisements to see if they help in producing better revenue. News websites would give us live feeds of trending news articles and insights into the present state of the economy and existing events and help you choose if these are promising times for a thriving business or should you be preparing for some tough times. Concept mining, Sentiment analysis, opinion, topic models, clustering, and inference are just a few examples of using analytics on social media. The opportunities are massive—you just need to have a clean and clear objective in mind so that you can use analytics efficiently to solve that objective.

Challenges

Before we investigate the challenges linked with social media analytics let us look at the following interesting facts:

- Facebook has over 2 billion active users
- There are over 300 million active Twitter users
- Facebook produces 800-900+ terabytes of data day-to-day (and it could be more now)
- Twitter generates 20-25+ terabytes of data every day
- Facebook generates over 4 to 5 million posts per minute
- Instagram generates over millions of likes in fractions of a minute

Above fact and figures give you a rough idea about the massive scale of data being produced and used up in these social media platforms. This leads to some challenges:

- Big data: Due to the massive volume of data produced by social media websites and apps, it is sometimes very difficult to analyze the complete dataset using outdated analytical methods because the whole data would never fit in memory. Other tactics and tools, such as Hadoop and Spark, need to be used.
- Accessibility issues: Social media websites and apps produce huge data but getting access to them directly is not always easy. There are amount limits for their official APIs and it's rare to be able to access and supply complete datasets. Above and beyond this, each social media platform has its own terms and conditions, which should be followed when accessing their data.
- Unstructured and noisy data: Maximum of the data which is produced by social media APIs is unstructured, noisy, and have a lot of junk in them. Dealing with data cleaning and processing becomes bulky and every so often analysts and data scientists end up spending 70% of their time and effort in trying to clean and preprocess the data for analysis.

These are possibly the maximum prevalent challenges when analyzing social media data, among many other challenges, that you might face in your social media analytics journey.

SENTIMENT ANALYSIS

Sentiment analysis is the arena of learning that analyzes the public's emotions, attitudes, opinions, evaluations, and assessments to objects such as facilities, persons, products, happenings, movies, organizations, issues, themes, and their characteristics. It denotes a big problematic space. There are also numerous names and to some extent, diverse jobs, e.g., belief mining, sentiment analysis, sentimentality mining, opinion extraction, emotion analysis, review mining, affect analysis, etc. although, all are under one roof of opinion mining or sentiment analysis. Even though in industry, the term sentiment analysis is frequently used, in academic world opinion mining is normally active. Regardless, they basically denote the same field of learning. In (Morinaga, Yamanishi, Tateishi, & Fukushima, 2002), the research on opinions and sentiments give the idea earlier by (Drews, 2011; Hatzivassiloglou & McKeown, 1997; Hearst, 1992; M. Rababah, K. Hwaitat, Al Qudah, & Halaseh, 2016; Turney, 2006; J. M. Wiebe, 1982). In this paper, the author uses the keywords opinion mining and sentiment analysis exchangeable. To streamline the arrangement, during this paper the author will use the term opinion or sentiment to indicate belief, emotion, valuation, assessment, approach, and sentiment. Although, these thoughts are not equal. The author will differentiate them whenever required. The meaning of belief itself is still very wide-ranging. Opinion mining and Sentiment analysis primarily focus on sentiments that express or hint at negative or positive opinions.

Even though dialectology and NLP have a lengthy past, slight research had been carried out about the public's sentiments and opinions beforehand in early 2000. After then, the topic sentiment analysis has developed a precise dynamic research area. Numerous of motives behind this. First, it has a wider range of applications area, nearly in every field. The business who uses opinion investigation has also succeeded due to the spread of moneymaking applications. This delivers a solid inspiration for research. Secondly, it suggests many thought-provoking research complications, which had not ever been deliberate previously. Third, for the first time in the history of human or computer, we now have a giant volume of opinionated data in the social media on the Web. Lacking this data, a lot of research would not have been imaginable. Even though, research in the area of sentiment analysis primarily underway from 1999, there was some previous work on understanding of subjectivity, metaphors, viewpoints, sentiment adjectives and affects (M., Janyce Wiebet, Rebecca, 1998; Waters & Cruces, 1994; J. Wiebe, Bruce, Martin, Wilson, & Bell, 2004; J. Wiebe, Wilson, & Cardie, 2005; J. M. Wiebe, 1990; J. Wiebe & Mihalcea, 2006; J. Wiebe & Riloff, 2005; Yi, Nasukawa, Bunescu, & Niblack, 2003).

Experimental Work

This section presents experimental work on the game review dataset. To carry out this work author use the Hadoop ecosystem to store data in HDFS (Hadoop File Distributed System). To clean, processing and analyze this data a wide range of Hadoop tools is used such as HIVE, Pig, Mahout etc. Figure 5 shows the framework used to carry this work.

Figure 5. Framework used to carry experimental work

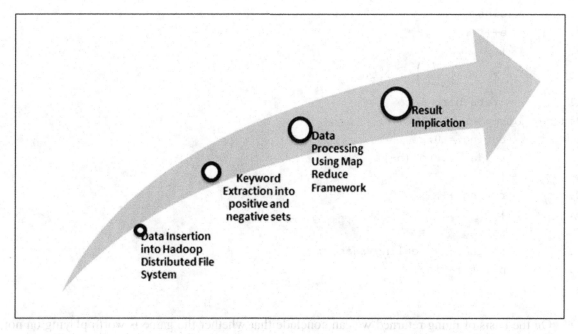

Mapper and Reducer Programming Framework

Map Reduce is a program writing model that can run parallel processing jobs on nodes in a cluster concurrently and is able to both processes and generate large data sets with ease. It takes data input and provides the output in the form of key-value pairs.

Algorithm

```
Input: Game Data Set
Output: Rating on the scale of 1 to 5
P: Positive Analysis Keywords
N: Negative Analysis Keyword
t = total critics
C[t] = experience level of critic's store in an array
where C[i] = experience level of i^th   critic, 0 <= c[i] <=1
A [] [t]: critic's review
Where A[] [t] is an array of review given by an i^th          critic
r= game rating
Mapper (critics index, game rating)
1.       d = 0, e = 0, r = 0;
2.       n= size of A[][t]
3.       for m = 0 to (n-1)
4.       if(R[m][i]  ∈ P)
5.       {
```

```
6.          d++
7.          else
8.          e++
9.          }
```

10. $\quad r = \left(\dfrac{d}{d+e}\right) \cdot C[t]$

```
11.         return r;
Reducer (game, game rating):
1.          rating = 0;
2.          for a = 0 to (b-1)
3.          {
4.          rating ++;
5.          }
6.          rating / = t
7.          rating * = scaling factor;
8.          print rating;
```

1) On the basis of rating returned we can conclude that whether the game is worth playing on not, using the following rating table.

Table 1. Rating table

Rating	Description
1-1.9	Time waste
2-2.9	Average
3-3.9	Good
4-4.4	Excellent!
4.5-5	Must Play

Formulas Used: $\dfrac{\sum_{a=0}^{b-1}\left(\dfrac{D_a}{D_a + E_a}.F[c]\right)}{b}$ * Scaling Factor

```
D  = review count in A [] [t]∃ A[c] [t] ∈ P∀ 0 < =  c  < size of A[] [t]
 a
E  = review count in A[][t] ∃ A[c] [t] ∈ N ∀ 0 < =  c  < = size of A[] [t]
 a
```

2) Type of game liked by different age groups

```
Input: game dataset.
Output:  games likes by different age group
```

```
Pig Script:
X = Filter movie by rating greater than 3 and rating less than 5.0  and view-
ers age;
Y= Group X by game type;
Z = create SUM (count by type);
Store Data;
```

Table 2. Different game type

Game Type
Tremendously Multiplayer Online
Recreations
Real-Time Tactic
Adventure
Brainteaser
Action
First Person Shooter
Stealth Shooter
Battle
Educational
Sporting
Role-Playing

Table 3. Different age group is categorized on the basis of the following

Age Gap	Description
Age less than 18	Childhood
Age between 18 to 35	Youth
Age between 35 to 45	Young adulthood
Age between 45 to 55	Middle adulthood
Age greater than 55	senior hood

The game can be reviewed on the basis of a number of characteristics and by the rating given by critics. Figure 6 shows Outline the types of games liked by different age group, Multiplayer games are mostly liked by the young adulthood while least liked by the senior hood. A simulation game attracts young adulthood much in comparison to senior hood. Puzzle, Combat, stealth shooter games, real-time strategy games and educational games are fairly liked by each group. From our analysis, it could be interpreted that action games and adventure games attract youth age the most. Childhood likes the first-person shooter games the most while role-playing games the least.

Figure 6. Result

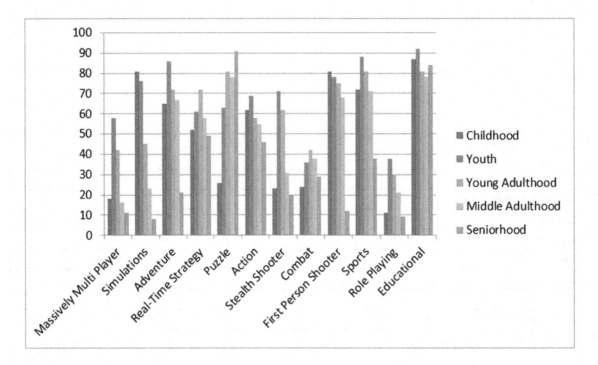

CONCLUSION

The Internet, and more unambiguously the creation of WWW at the starting of the 1990s, facilitated folks to form an organized worldwide stage where data and information can be kept, consumed and shared by everybody with an electric gadget which has the ability to connect to the Web. An interactive platform was born, to share ideas, to post content, to share messages and opinions under one roof, and the platform is known as social media. Social media has acquired massive popularity and importance that why today almost everyone can't stay away from it. Social media is not only a medium for people to express their thoughts, moreover, but it is also a very influential tool that can be used by businesses to focus on new and existing clients and increase profit with the help of social media analytics. It can be well-defined as the process of gathering data from social media platforms and analyzing the data. One major challenge is sentiment analysis in social media analytics. This paper presented a complete overview of social media and social media analytics. Paper says sentiment analysis is a big problem in social media analytics which can help to improve business by-product review, opinion mining. This paper shows the importance of sentiment analysis for business with the help of the experiment.

REFERENCES

Asur, S., & Huberman, B. A. (2010). Predicting the future with social media. *Proceedings - 2010 IEEE/WIC/ACM International Conference on Web Intelligence, WI 2010, 1*, 492–499. 10.1109/WI-IAT.2010.63

Bar-Haim, R., Dinur, E., Feldman, R., Fresko, M., & Goldstein, G. (2011). Identifying and following expert investors in stock microblogs. *EMNLP 2011 - Conference on Empirical Methods in Natural Language Processing, Proceedings of the Conference*, 1310–1319.

Bollen, J., Mao, H., & Zeng, X. (2011). Twitter mood predicts the stock market. *Journal of Computational Science*, *2*(1), 1–8. doi:10.1016/j.jocs.2010.12.007

Brown, J., Broderick, A. J., & Lee, N. (2007). Word Of Mouth Communication Within Online Communities. *Journal of Interactive Marketing*, *21*(3), 2–21. doi:10.1002/dir.20082

Castellanos, M., Dayal, U., Hsu, M., Ghosh, R., Dekhil, M., & Lu, Y., … Schreiman, M. (2011). LCI: A social channel analysis platform for live customer intelligence. *Proceedings of the ACM SIGMOD International Conference on Management of Data*, 1049–1057. 10.1145/1989323.1989436

Cerezo, M. (2004). Las nociones de Sachverhalt, Tatsache y Sachlage en el Tractatus de Wittgenstein. *Anuario Filosofico*, *37*(2), 455–479.

Chen, B., Zhu, L., Kifer, D., & Lee, D. (2010). What is an opinion about? Exploring political standpoints using opinion scoring model. *Proceedings of the National Conference on Artificial Intelligence*, *2*, 1007–1012.

Chen, Y., & Xie, J. (2008). Online consumer review: Word-of-mouth as a new element of marketing communication mix. *Management Science*, *54*(3), 477–491. doi:10.1287/mnsc.1070.0810

Das, S. R., & Chen, M. Y. (2007). Yahoo! for amazon: Sentiment extraction from small talk on the Web. *Management Science*, *53*(9), 1375–1388. doi:10.1287/mnsc.1070.0704

Drews, F. (2011). Réception existentielle. Die augustinus-leserin sophie scholl im spiegel ihrer tagebuchaufzeichnungen und briefe. *Antike Und Abendland*, *57*(July), 151–168. doi:10.1515/9783110239171.151

Ghose, A., & Ipeirotis, P. G. (2007). Designing novel review ranking systems: Predicting the usefulness and impact of reviews. *ACM International Conference Proceeding Series*, *258*, 303–310. 10.1145/1282100.1282158

Groh, G., & Hauffa, J. (2011). Characterizing Social Relations Via NLP-based Sentiment Analysis. *Proceedings of the Fifth International AAAI Conference on Weblogs and Social Media*, 502–505.

Hatzivassiloglou, V., & McKeown, K. R. (1997). *Predicting the semantic orientation of adjectives*. 174–181. doi:10.3115/979617.979640

Hearst, M. A. (1992). Direction-Based Text Interpretation as an Information Access Refinement. *Text-Based Intelligent Systems*, 257–274.

Hong, Y., & Skiena, S. (2010). The wisdom of bookies? Sentiment analysis versus the NFL point spread. *ICWSM 2010 - Proceedings of the 4th International AAAI Conference on Weblogs and Social Media*, 251–254.

Hu, M., & Liu, B. (2004). Mining and summarizing customer reviews. *KDD-2004 - Proceedings of the Tenth ACM SIGKDD International Conference on Knowledge Discovery and Data Mining*, 168–177.

Hu, N., & Pavlou, P. A. (2006). *Can Online Word-of-Mouth Communication Reveal True Product Quality ? Experimental Insights, Econometric Results, and Analytical Modeling Jennifer Zhang University of Toledo Can Online Word-of-Mouth Communication Reveal True Product Quality ? Experimenta.* (April).

Joshi, M., Das, D., Gimpel, K., & Smith, N. A. (2010). Movie reviews and revenues: An experiment in text regression. *NAACL HLT 2010 - Human Language Technologies: The 2010 Annual Conference of the North American Chapter of the Association for Computational Linguistics, Proceedings of the Main Conference,* 293–296.

Koellner, G., & Müller, U. (1989). Verfeinerung der struktur von (SiCH3)8O12. *Acta Crystallographica. Section C, Crystal Structure Communications, 45*(7), 1106–1107. doi:10.1107/S0108270189000326

Le Caillec, J. M., Itani, A., Guriot, D., & Rakotondratsimba, Y. (2017). Stock Picking by Probability-Possibility Approaches. *IEEE Transactions on Fuzzy Systems, 25*(2), 333–349. doi:10.1109/TFUZZ.2016.2574921

Liu, J., Cao, Y., Lin, C. Y., Huang, Y., & Zhou, M. (2007). Low-quality product review detection in opinion summarization. *EMNLP-CoNLL 2007 - Proceedings of the 2007 Joint Conference on Empirical Methods in Natural Language Processing and Computational Natural Language Learning,* (June), 334–342.

M., Janyce Wiebet, Rebecca, T. (1998). *P99-1032.pdf.* 246.

Marvell Solutions. (n.d.). *88E111 Datasheet.*

McGlohon, M., Glance, N., & Reiter, Z. (2010). Star quality: Aggregating reviews to rank products and merchants. *ICWSM 2010 - Proceedings of the 4th International AAAI Conference on Weblogs and Social Media,* 114–121.

Miller, M., Sathi, C., Wiesenthal, D., Leskovec, J., & Potts, C. (2011). Sentiment Flow Through Hyperlink Networks. *Fifth International AAAI Conference on Weblogs and Social Media,* 550–553. Retrieved from http://www.aaai.org/ocs/index.php/ICWSM/ICWSM11/paper/viewPDFInterstitial/2883%7D/3227%5C nhttp://www.aaai.org/ocs/index.php/ICWSM/ICWSM11/paper/viewFile/2883%7D/3227

Mohammad, S. M. (2012). From once upon a time to happily ever after: Tracking emotions in mail and books. *Decision Support Systems, 53*(4), 730–741. doi:10.1016/j.dss.2012.05.030

Mohammad, S. M. Tony, & Yang. (2013). *Tracking Sentiment in Mail: How Genders Differ on Emotional Axes.* 70–79. Retrieved from https://arxiv.org/abs/1309.6347

Morinaga, S., Yamanishi, K., Tateishi, K., & Fukushima, T. (2002). Mining product reputations on the web. *Proceedings of the ACM SIGKDD International Conference on Knowledge Discovery and Data Mining,* 341–349.

Nikolay, A., Anindya, G., & Panagiotis, G. I. (2011). Deriving the pricing power of product features by mining consumer reviews. *Management Science, 57*(8), 1485–1509. doi:10.1287/mnsc.1110.1370

Park, D. H., Lee, J., & Han, I. (2007). The effect of on-line consumer reviews on consumer purchasing intention: The moderating role of involvement. *International Journal of Electronic Commerce, 11*(4), 125–148. doi:10.2753/JEC1086-4415110405

Rababah, M., O., K. Hwaitat, A., Al Qudah, D. A., & Halaseh, R. (. (2016). Hybrid Algorithm to Evaluate E-Business Website Comments. *Communications and Network*, *08*(03), 137–143. doi:10.4236/cn.2016.83014

Sadikov, E., Parameswaran, A., & Venetis, P. (2009). Blogs as predictors of movie success. *Third International AAAI Conference on Weblogs and Social Media*, 304–307. Retrieved from http://www.aaai.org/ocs/index.php/ICWSM/09/paper/viewPDFInterstitial/165/489

Sakunkoo, P., & Sakunkoo, N. (2009). Analysis of Social Influence in Online Book Reviews. *AAAI's ICWSM 2009*, 1968–1970. Retrieved from https://pdfs.semanticscholar.org/2623/6f6873c2d79806cc8 7404fcc2796cac61423.pdf%0Ahttp://citeseerx.ist.psu.edu/viewdoc/download?doi=10.1.1.558.9792& rep=rep1&type=pdf

Turney, P. D. (2006). *Turney-Acl02-Final*. 8. Retrieved from file://localhost/Volumes/alexvanvenrooij 1/Elektronische Artikelen/Papers/Unknown/2006-54.pdf

Waters, M., & Cruces, L. (1994). Tracking Point of View in Narrative. *Computational Linguistics*, *20*(2), 233.

Wiebe, J., Bruce, R., Martin, M., Wilson, T., & Bell, M. (2004). Learning a subjective language. In Computational Linguistics (Vol. 30). doi:10.1162/0891201041850885

Wiebe, J., & Mihalcea, R. (2006). Word sense and subjectivity. *COLING/ACL 2006 - 21st International Conference on Computational Linguistics and 44th Annual Meeting of the Association for Computational Linguistics, Proceedings of the Conference*, *1*, 1065–1072.

Wiebe, J., & Riloff, E. (2005). Creating subjective and objective sentence classifiers from unannotated texts. *Lecture Notes in Computer Science*, *3406*, 486–497. doi:10.1007/978-3-540-30586-6_53

Wiebe, J., Wilson, T., & Cardie, C. (2005). Annotating expressions of opinions and emotions in language. *Language Resources and Evaluation*, *39*(2–3), 165–210. doi:10.100710579-005-7880-9

Wiebe, J. M. (1982). *AAAI00-113.pdf*. (1).

Wiebe, J. M. (1990). *Identifying subjective characters in the narrative*. (Uspensky 1973), 401–406. doi:10.3115/997939.998008

Yano, T., & Smith, N. A. (2010). What's worthy of comment? Content and comment volume in political blogs. *ICWSM 2010 - Proceedings of the 4th International AAAI Conference on Weblogs and Social Media, i*, 359–362.

Yi, J., Nasukawa, T., Bunescu, R., & Niblack, W. (2003). Sentiment analyzer: Extracting sentiments about a given topic using natural language processing techniques. *Proceedings - IEEE International Conference on Data Mining, ICDM*, 427–434.

Zhang, W., & Skiena, S. (2010). Trading strategies to exploit blog and news sentiment. *ICWSM 2010 - Proceedings of the 4th International AAAI Conference on Weblogs and Social Media, d*, 375–378.

Chapter 27
Time Series for Forecasting Stock Market Prices Based on Sentiment Analysis of Social Media

Babu Aravind Sivamani
SSN College of Engineering, Chennai, India

Dakshinamoorthy Karthikeyan
SSN College of Engineering, Chennai, India

Chamundeswari Arumugam
SSN College of Engineering, Chennai, India

Pavan Kalyan
SSN College of Engineering, Chennai, India

ABSTRACT

This paper attempts to find a relation between the public perception of a company and its stock value price. Since social media is a very powerful tool used by a lot of people to voice their opinions on the performance of a company, it is a good source of information about the public sentiment. Previous studies have shown that the overall public sentiment collected from sites like Twitter do have a relation to the market price of a company over a period of time. The goal is to build on their research to improve the accuracy of predictions and determine if the public perception surrounding a company is a driving factor of its stock growth.

DOI: 10.4018/978-1-6684-6303-1.ch027

1. INTRODUCTION

Previous studies(Mankar et al., 2018) on the effect of social media on the stock market have shown that the aggregate public mood towards a company over a short time span has a relation to the closing price of that company at the end of the time span. Studies have been able to utilize data collected from any one reputed social media site (Ex: Twitter, Stocktwits, Weibo, etc.) to produce a model that predicts stock market prices with ~70% accuracy(Acosta et al., 2017). This paper attempts to more accurately gauge the public sentiment of a company from social media websites such as Twitter by implementing time series analysis at minute intervals to find correlations that will likely produce a better stock estimate.

Stock price of a company is determined by a large number of independent traders all over the world. Previous studies have not taken into account the reasons why an individual trader makes the decision to buy or sell. As social media has been shown to offer an insight into the mindset of people, it was realized that the posts online may be an indication of how the market at large is inclined towards a company. The main objective of this paper is to find whether the public sentiment surrounding a company is able to determine the growth of its stock price. Here in this paper, the company Apple (NASDAQ: AAPL) was selected because it is prominent in the public spotlight and hence ideally suited for an analysis of this kind.

First the selected social media platform is queried for posts in the time period containing any of the keywords in our search term. The search term must be carefully selected to ensure that the number of off-topic posts is limited, while not missing out on any messages with important content. Then any irrelevant posts which passed through the search query are found and filtered out. Data pre-processing procedures such as the removal of non-English characters, stop words, hashtags and user mentions is carried out. Sentiment analysis is performed on the pre-processed text data and each post is classified as positive, negative or neutral corresponding to whether the market for Apple is bullish, bearish or not having any effect. Finally, the aggregate sentiment values from all collected websites will be fed into the model which would use a machine learning algorithm to produce a correlation between the media posts and the stock market price which can then be used to predict the closing market value, given the opening price and overall public sentiment.

The organization of this paper proceeds as follows. Section 2 discusses the literature survey, while Section 3 elaborates on the proposed methodology. Section 4 details with the result and discussion, and Section 5 details the conclusion and future work.

2. LITERATURE SURVEY

Venkata et al.(2016) used Word2vec and N-gram representation of text to train a classifier model to predict the stock market movements and picked Word2vec representation due to its high accuracy in large datasets. Rakhi et al.(2018) collected the sentiment data, and the stock price data to predict stock market price using a support-vector machine (SVM) classifier and observed that if the data size increases the accuracy obtained will also increase. Scott et al.(2017) used smart user classification to filter the tweets by computing scoring weights based on number of likes, number of followers count and how often the user is correct. Further, they used Tf-Idf vectorizer for textual representation and linear regression classifier for the sentiment prediction. Zhaoxia et al.(n.d.) used the sentiments of the news data to predict the stock market price using neural networks.

Sreelekshmy et. al.(2017) applied Recurrent Neural Networks(RNN), Long short-term memory(LSTM) and Convolutional Neural Networks(CNN) - sliding window architecture for stock price prediction of Infosys, TCS and Cipla and concluded that CNN outperforms the other two models in the stock market analysis due to the irregular changes that happen in the stock market. Few works have used the previous stock market data to predict the movements of the stock market while another few used the sentiments from social media to predict the same using SVM, random forest and other machine learning algorithms. Also it is clear that Word2Vec representation of text will be ideal for data that is fed into the neural network layers for building the classifier that predicts the trends of the stock market.

Stock market predictions have become an interesting research area, Correlation of social sentiment data about a company and it's stock values there exists research papers that provide solid efficacy to perform a time series analysis on prediction of stock prices and ensemble models that increases the accuracy of the prediction by performing a sentiment analysis on the co-related socio-economic data of that particular company, though it's limitation was performed on a 24-hour interval; This research paper extends this notion by performing minute-wise stock price sentiment analysis that gives you a more through window for predicting stock rise and stock fall.

3. PROPOSED METHODOLOGY

Twitter was considered to be the source for the dataset because many companies practice public relations via tweets and also it provided a concrete API with filtering that would prove imperative to the selection criteria for a specified category of text data. The collected twitter dataset will be pre-processed for any missing inconsistencies, and cleaned using our custom data-cleaning libraries. After preprocessing, a subset of that dataset is manually labeled with a sentiment-value. A Random Forest Classifier is used to classify the rest of the sentiment based on the labeled dataset. For stock price prediction, the stock market data was downloaded from Finam and after it undergoes pre-processing, the processed prices dataset along with the labeled sentiment dataset is run through a LSTM model. A graphical overview of the system structure is shown in Figure 1.

Figure 1. Proposed system structure

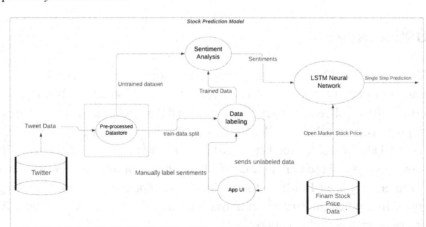

3.1. Data Collection

Data collection is defined as "the process of acquiring raw, unprocessed data and storing in a mutable format". The data collection period was a little over three months, and approximately two million tweets were scraped for the last quarter of 2018. For collection of tweets from Twitter, A python module: 'TwitterScraper' was used, it supports querying of the Twitter database with advanced search parameters and operators (Available parameters include followers_count, friends_count, and also the logical operators AND, OR and NOT)(Standard search operators available in the Twitter search query field, n.d.) that limits results to tweets that match our query, as well as additional metadata such as ensuring that the time of the tweet fits inside our selected time period. The exact search query given to the module is 'apple OR ((bullish OR bearish) AND (AAPL OR apple))'. This query has proven effective in filtering out the majority of completely unrelated tweets from the result set.

The result object returned by this module is a JSON array of tweet objects, where each tweet is a JSON Object with the following fields: username, user id, html, text, likes, retweets, comments, timestamp, profile-picture, profile display-name, etc. An Example of the raw Tweet data is represented in Figure 2.

Figure 2. Raw Tweet Data

```
{
        "fullname": "BofM_Jeremy",
        "html": "<p class=\"TweetTextSize js-tweet-text tweet-text\" data-aria-label-part=\"0\"
lang=\"en\">Considering moving from non-smart watch to an <strong>Apple</strong> Watch - Series 3
with no cellular in order to save a few bucks.  Am I forgoing anything critical by not getting
4+cellular?</p>",
        "is_retweet": 0,
        "likes": 1,
        "replies": 9,
        "retweet_id": "",
        "retweeter_userid": "",
        "retweeter_username": "",
        "retweets": 0,
        "text": "Considering moving from non-smart watch to an Apple Watch - Series 3 with no
cellular in order to save a few bucks.  Am I forgoing anything critical by not getting
4+cellular?",
        "timestamp": "2018-11-18T23:59:35",
        "timestamp_epochs": 1542585575,
        "tweet_id": "1064307161742934017",
        "tweet_url": "/BofM_Jeremy/status/1064307161742934017",
        "user_id": "4645206635",
        "username": "BofM_Jeremy"
},
```

The fields user_id, text, and timestamp are extracted from the tweets and other unwanted fields are deleted.

There are several services that provide access to historical intraday stock prices for NASDAQ listed companies like Apple (Publicly Available sources of Intra-day stock market data for listed companies, n.d.). Finam(Finam.ru, n.d.) is a Russian website that provides data for the stock, futures, ETF and Forex markets for research and analysis purposes. The data is available for only very highlight capitalized securities, however for these one can avail several months worth of tick data. A representation of the finam stock dataset is shown in Figure 3.

Figure 3. Raw Finam stock dataset

	A	B	C	D	E	F	G
1	<DATE>	<TIME>	<OPEN>	<HIGH>	<LOW>	<CLOSE>	<VOL>
2	20180926	100100	161.26	161.3	160.74	160.88	267350
3	20180926	100200	160.91	160.98	160.52	160.76	163520
4	20180926	100300	160.67	160.86	160.65	160.84	40670
5	20180926	100400	160.75	160.88	160.72	160.87	34280
6	20180926	100500	160.84	160.86	160.64	160.7	61070
7	20180926	100600	160.65	160.78	160.64	160.67	51490
8	20180926	100700	160.65	160.68	160.49	160.49	69370
9	20180926	100800	160.53	160.54	160.37	160.37	48950
10	20180926	100900	160.48	160.48	160.15	160.15	113360
11	20180926	101000	160.15	160.45	160.15	160.45	103510

3.2. Data Pre-Processing

Data preprocessing is a technique which is used to transform the raw data in a useful and efficient format. In this section unnecessary data or noise is removed from the raw text twitter data. Firstly, the raw text data is converted to lower-case. Secondly, text data which contain words that begin with #(hashtags), @ (user mentions) are simply replaced with the actual word content of the hashtag and username. Thirdly, long URLs are replaced with just the domain name of the URL. For example, https://techcrunch. com/2019/10/19/the-new-iphone-is-ugly/ is replaced with techcrunch. The identification of these words is implemented through regex matching. Then the special symbols like non-english characters are removed.

The final step in pre-processing of text is stop-word removal, which is the removal of words in the text that do not contribute to the overall meaning of the post. Examples of such words include a, an, the, I, for, etc. The text of each post is tokenized and compared with any publicly available curated list of stop words(Curated list of English stop-words extracted from Python's NLTK library, n.d.). The above preprocessing steps were repeated for the remaining two million raw text data. The data preprocessing outcome of an instance is displayed in Table 1.

Table 1. An instance of data pre-processing outcome

Before data pre-processing	#Apple could have made all their products' current design years ago, now their products are now left behind by @Samsung and others http://gizmo.do/Twg8I8i
After data pre-processing	apple could made products current design years ago products left behind samsung others gizmodo

3.3. Sentiment Analysis Module

After collecting a large twitter dataset, sentiment analysis is performed on the text. For this purpose, the library Word2vec(Mikolov, 2013) is used, which is an advanced Natural Language Processing (NLP) technique for mapping words to a vector representation of any dimension. A 200-dimension vector is used for generation in this case. When run on the dataset of text, Word2vec will generate a unique vector for every word in the dataset which will exactly preserve the context of the words and the relation between similar meaning words in vector space. Then the word2vec representations along with around 15000 messages manually labelled as positive(1), neutral(0) or negative(2). An android app was developed with google's firebase backend systems. The app was distributed to a group of trained people for labeling the tweets. The app contains three buttons for inputting the sentiments below the text data. An instance of the tweet in the app is shown in Figure 4.

Figure 4. An instance of app tweet data with sentiment labels

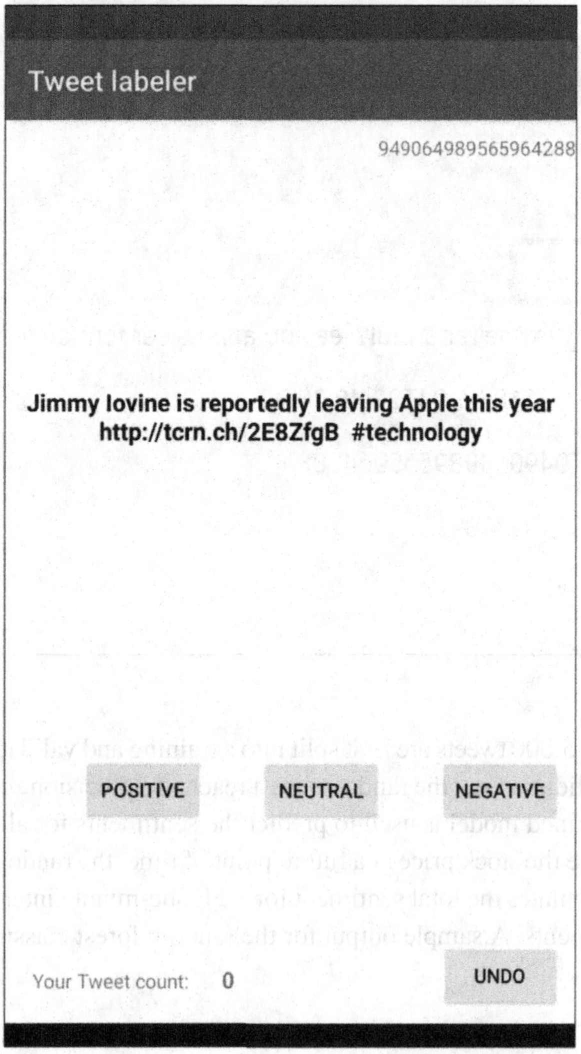

The output of the app tweet data is then stored within a firebase datastore along with the labeled sentiment. This is highlighted in Figure 5.

Figure 5. An instance of labeled tweet data

The manually labeled 15,000 tweets are first split into a training and validation set to train the random forest classifier. On the validation set, the random forest reached a precision score of 90%, Recall of 88% and F1 score 90%. The trained model is used to predict the sentiments for all the two million tweets in the datastore. To determine the stock price at a future point of time, the random forest classifier predicts social sentiments, and calculates the total sentiment for each one-minute interval as the number of positive minus negative sentiments. A sample output for the random forest classifier is shown in Figure 6.

Figure 6. Five samples of random forest classifier output

	text	timestamp	sentiment
0	liveblog news apple making brooklyn event bit ...	2018-10-27 14:55:00	1
1	spotify apple music	2018-11-16 19:56:08	0
2	ready upgrade tv room ultimate home theater en...	2018-11-08 21:22:05	0
3	technews trending apple launches portal users ...	2018-10-17 18:14:20	1
4	depends type apple watch want come different s...	2018-12-25 20:40:32	1

4. RESULTS AND DISCUSSION

A time series forecasting method using LSTM is used here as both the social media posts as well as the financial stock price dataset has a time component. LSTM was trained using Google's open source TensorFlow libraries which comes with an implementation of LSTM. As the dataset contains two distinct features namely the sentiment and the stock price, a multivariate version of the dataset was created for training. In this process, overlapping sliding windows of length 720 minutes (12 hours) are applied on the dataset. To get a single step dataset, the starting point of the window is set to the point immediately after the start of the previous window, i.e. a new window begins every minute. Finally the dataset contains 35634 minutes of data, which is divided into a testing and validation set (80-20% ratio).

Figure 7. First sample prediction of LSTM

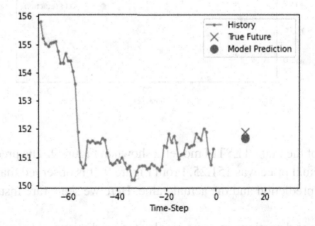

The first prediction of the trained LSTM model at a future time from the validation set is shown in Figure 7. The blue line shows a subset of the stock price history passed as input to the LSTM. The green circle represents the price predicted by the model (151.79), whereas the red cross shows the actual value that came to pass at that point of time (151.93). From Figure 7, it is observed that the model is accurately predicting the sentiment of the tweet.

Figure 8. Second sample prediction of LSTM

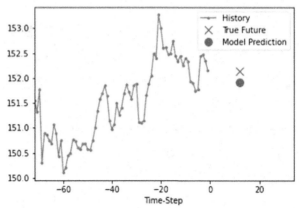

The second prediction of the trained LSTM model at a future time from the validation set is shown in Figure 8. The predicted price was 152.81 whereas the observed actual price was 152.15. From Figure 8, it is observed that the model is accurately predicting the sentiment of the tweet.

Figure 9. Third sample prediction of LSTM

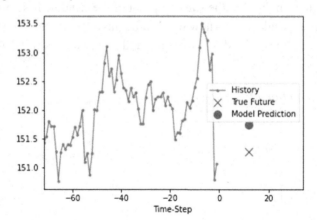

The third prediction of the trained LSTM model is shown in Figure 9. The predicted price was 151.75 whereas the observed actual price was 151.25. From Figure 9, it is observed that there is a small deviation between the model prediction and the actual value. Here we see a rare instance of inconsistencies with the prediction.

Though there are minor deviations in some single step predictions, this process usually consists of a large sample of 60 single step predictions which allows the algorithm to make an accurate prediction overall, marginally on the error of 0.5.

It is observed from Figure 10 that as the step size and history size decreases, the Mean Squared Error(MSE) also reduces, indicating an improvement in the accuracy rate (Table 2).

Figure 10. Variation of MSE with different History and Step size

History size	Step Size	MSE
720	50	38.47090527
720	80	28.47415585
360	50	36.9319954
60	20	35.79312783
30	10	32.89082675
15	5	5.930060326
15	10	5.187107316

The above data is taken from a random portion of the validation set. It is observed that the LSTM is able to learn and accurately predict with errors less than 1 in the vast majority of cases at each minute interval. The system is well trained over various curves, rises, falls over the last quarter of 2018.

Though there are a multitude of factors which could determine the exact values of stock prices, based on the outcome of the system. The public image of the company seems to be one of the driving forces. The LSTM Neural Network was accurate enough to forecast the stock values, which indicates the existence of a correlation between the sentiments and stock prices. This suggests that the public image of a company has a bearing on the market performance of a company. The visualisation found between the stock prices and sentiments are shown in the Figure 11. The y-axis for the blue line shows the market price and the total sentiment is shown in the orange graph. The x-axis represents the time component, i.e the number of minutes since the start of Q4 2018.

Table 2. Stock prediction and error

Date	Time	Actual Price	Predicted	Error
20181218	155200	151.42	151.68074	-0.26074
20181218	155300	151.27	151.69843	-0.42843
20181218	155400	151.44	151.9058	-0.4658
20181218	155500	151.49	151.82811	-0.33811
20181218	155600	151.27	151.72792	-0.45792
20181218	155700	151.33	151.73984	-0.40894
20181218	155800	151.35	151.96754	-0.61754
20181218	155900	151.34	151.75021	-0.41021
20181218	160000	151.36	151.98468	-0.62468
20181218	160100	151.35	151.85138	-0.50138
20181218	160200	151.35	151.78558	-0.43558
20181218	160300	151.46	151.78085	-0.32085
20181218	160400	151.55	151.88606	-0.33606
20181218	160500	151.61	151.85497	-0.24497

Figure 11. Visualization of processed training dataset

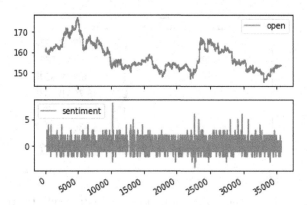

5. CONCLUSION AND FUTURE WORK

In this paper, the rise and fall of stock prices were predicted at every minute interval. Intraday (1 minute intervals) stock market data on Apple Inc. (NASDAQ: AAPL) was collected for Q4, 2018. Twitter was scraped to find all tweets related to Apple over the same time period. Total sentiment in each one-minute interval was calculated and combined with market price histories to forecast the future prices.

The accuracy of the sentiment analysis model could be improved by performing more manual labelling of tweets to improve the quality of training dataset for sentiment analysis and by exploring other ML models for classification of tweets. The usage of streaming APIs could result in a narrower time frame for the time series analysis, possibly for each continuous second.

REFERENCES

Acosta, Lamaute, Luo, Finkelstein, & Cotoranu. (2017). Sentiment Analysis of Twitter Messages using Word2Vec. In *Proceedings of Student-Faculty Research Day, CSIS*. Pace University.

Curated list of English stop-words extracted from Python's NLTK library. (n.d.). https://gist.github.com/sebleier/554280/raw/7e0e4a1ce04c2bb7bd41089c9821dbcf6d0c786c/NLTK's%2520list%2520of%2520english%2520stopwords

Finam.ru - A website that provides several months of tick data for highly capitalized securities. (n.d.). https://www.finam.ru/profile/moex-akcii/gazprom/export/

Mankar, T., Hotchandani, T., Madhwani, M., Chidrawar, A., & Lifna, C. S. (2018). Stock Market Prediction based on Social Sentiments using. *Machine Learning*, 1–3. Advance online publication. doi:10.1109/ICSCET.2018.8537242

Mikolov, T. (2013). Efficient Estimation of Word Representations in Vector Space. Academic Press.

Publicly Available sources of Intra-day stock market data for listed companies. (n.d.). https://www.quantshare.com/sa-636-6-new-ways-to-download-free-intraday-data-for-the-us-stock-market

Rakhi, B., & Sher, M. D. (2018). Integrating StockTwits with Sentiment Analysis for better Prediction of Stock Price Movement. *IEEE International Conference on Computing, Mathematics and Engineering Technologies – iCoMET*.

Scott, C., & Preveen, M. (2017). Forecasting Stock Prices using Social Media Analysis. *IEEE 15th Intl Conf on Dependable, Autonomic and Secure Computing, 15th Intl Conf on Pervasive Intelligence and Computing, 3rd Intl Conf on Big Data Intelligence and Computing and Cyber Science and Technology Congress*, 1031-1038.

Selvin, Vinayakumar, Gopalakrishnan, Menon, & Kp. (2017). *Stock price prediction using LSTM, RNN and CNN-sliding window model*. doi:10.1109/ICACCI.2017.8126078

Standard search operators available in the Twitter search query field. (n.d.). https://developer.twitter.com/en/docs/tweets/rules-and-filtering/overview/standard-operators

Venkata, S. P., Kamal, N. C., Ganapati, P., & Babita, M. (2016). Sentiment Analysis of Twitter Data for Predicting Stock Market Movements. *International conference on Signal Processing, Communication, Power and Embedded System*, 1345 – 1350.

Wang, Z., Seng-Beng, Ho., & Lin, Z. (n.d.). *Stock market prediction by incorporating social media news as sentiment*. https://ieeexplore.ieee.org/document/8637365

This research was previously published in the International Journal of Business Strategy and Automation (IJBSA), 2(2); pages 16-25, copyright year 2021 by IGI Publishing (an imprint of IGI Global).

Chapter 28
Feature Optimization in Sentiment Analysis by Term Co–occurrence Fitness Evolution (TCFE)

Sudarshan S. Sonawane

Department of Computer Engineering, Shri Gulabrao Deokar College of Engineering, Jalgaon, India

Satish R. Kolhe

School of Computer Sciences, Kavayitri Bahinabai Chaudhari North Maharashtra University, Jalgaon, India

ABSTRACT

The opinion of a target audience is a major objective for the assessing state of efficacy pertaining to reviews, business decisions surveys, and such factors that require decision making. Feature selection turns out to be a critical task for developing robust and high levels of classification while decreasing training time. Models are required for stating the scope for depicting optimal feature selection for escalating feature selection strategies to escalate maximal accuracy in opinion mining. Considering the scope for improvement, an n-gram feature selection approach is proposed where optimal features based on term co-occurrence fitness is proposed in this article. Genetic algorithms focus on determining the evolution and solution to attain deterministic and maximal accuracy having a minimal level of computational process for reflecting on the sentiment scope for sentiment. Evaluations reflect that the proposed solution is capable, which outperforms the separate filter-oriented feature selection models of sentiment classification.

DOI: 10.4018/978-1-6684-6303-1.ch028

INTRODUCTION

User-generated content analysis has become very vital in terms of analyzing the data insights that are generated by the organization. Sentiment analysis as a subject has gained momentum and globally there are many companies that are focusing on using the user-centric data to analyze the issues and identify the insights that they could use for enhancing the user experience.

Analyzing user opinions are very critical in the decision making and globally many companies have reaped potential benefits of same. Profoundly, the sentiment analysis enables users to have an opinion and the consumer behavior patterns. Opinion of one single individual might be ignorable but considering the viewpoints of the macro set of consumers is very essential to evaluate and adjudge the brand perception among the customers, as divergent views of customers can be envisaged from such process (Hu & Liu, 2004).

In NLP (Natural Language Processing) opinion mining and the process of sentiment analysis has gained profound importance (Liu, 2012) and profoundly in the case of web mining, analytics of social media messages data mining has become an important part.

The study (Cambria, Das, Bandyopadhyay, & Feraco, 2017) emphasizes the importance of opinion mining as:

- Entity (E) (Deng & Wiebe, 2015), the ones that focus on the entity, event, a service or an individual task
- Entity Aspects (A) are the ones related to a product, an organization, resulting outcome of an event or service.
- Opinion Articulated Time (T) which reflects the event of time wherein the opinion is expressed.
- The sentiment (S) like the positive, or opinion oriented like negative or neutral or the ones that relate to aspect of entity.

It is imperative from the aforesaid objectives that the sentiment analysis are being resourceful in various dimensions that are stated above, that focus on the overall opinion of target set representatives. Majority of the sentiment analysis solutions contributed are machine-learning solutions that focus on the opinion aspects.

The process of feature representation usually impacts the efficacy of machine learning approaches (LeCun, Bengio & Hinton, 2015) and there is need for focused attempt in terms of using the feature selection strategies that can deliver better outcome (Mohammad, Kiritchenko & Zhu, 2013). Learning mechanisms are very effective in terms of choosing the discriminative features (Bengio, Courville & Vincent, 2013), learners ensemble (LeCun, Bengio & Hinton, 2015) which leads to more opportunities for learning from the chosen data at distinct levels and can it can lead to deep learning conditions. However, the majority of contemporary contributions related to opinion mining are portraying the optimal features from individual elements such as terms (subject, predicates, or sentiment lexicons) of the learning data selection.

In this paper, an improved n-gram feature selection approach and optimal features based on term co-occurrence fitness evolution are proposed. The proposed model is compared with genetic rank aggregation model. Performance analysis shows that the proposed model is outstanding and robust with high classification accuracy as compared with genetic rank aggregation model.

RELATED WORK

The Authors of (Turney, 2002; Taboada, Brooke, Tofiloski, Voll & Stede, 2011) have focused on sentimental words repository that consists intensification, sentiment polarity and negation incorporation towards computation of sentiment polarity in every sentence. Author of (Turney, 2002) adapted the process of representative lexicon-oriented method, wherein the extraction phase is carried out in the first stage, wherein the postages affirm patterns that are based on pre-defined conditions. In the second stage, PMI (point-wise mutual information) comprising measured degree of dependency between two terms were targeted. In the final stage, average of polarity for all the stages of review are considered and addressed as sentiment polarity.

In the other study authors of (Ding, Liu & Yu, 2008) focused on negation words for improving performance of lexicon-based methods. The Authors of (Taboada, Brooke, Tofiloski, Voll & Stede, 2011) focused on integration and intensification of negation words for sentiment lexicons, by annotating them based on strength and polarity. The authors of (Thelwall, Buckley, & Paltoglou, 2012) developed Senti strength based on lexicons that relate to lexicons and certain language rules which denote the strength of sentiments in tweets.

The authors of (Reckman et al., 2013) discuss rule-based system for addressing sentiment analysis challenges of Twitter was considered wherein in the system adapts some basic rules wherein the appropriate words or sequence of set are considered. Lexicon based approaches and sentiment orientation towards a target is computed based on sentiment aggregation function that depends on distances of sentiment expression and the opinion target in sentence, towards identifying application scope for every sentiment expression.

In the other dimension, lexicon of sentiment expressions constituting sentiment words, idioms, phrases, composition instructions and other such elements are used as set of rules for addressing distinct set of nguage constructs and numerous sentences (Chaturvedi, Cambria, Welsch, & Herrera, 2018). Also, sentiment aggregation function and the associated relationship among them leads to parse tree for tracing sentiment orientation to every target (Ding, Liu & Yu, 2008; Liu, 2012).

Many of the NLP systems that are developed in the recent past has the pre-trained vectors which are very vital (Collobert et al., 2011). Such representations focused by using the modeling word co-occurrence for improving the data efficiency and generalization scope of NLP systems (Chen & Manning, 2014). Topic modeling can also comprise a corpus of text wherein the alignment is much easier to interpretable concepts (Blei, Ng, & Jordan, 2003).

A study in (Fahrni & Klenner, 2008) model of co-occurrence patterns and the seed opinion of words were proposed, which relies on the statistical techniques. LSA is used for semantic characteristics in (Cao, Duan & Gan, 2011) wherein the characteristics are reviewed from texts to inspect the impact of distinct set of features. Using the data of CNET, wherein in the users have provided their feedback or opinion, it signifies semantic characteristics that affect resourcefulness of the vote reviews.

The authors of (Xu, Peng & Cheng, 2012) targeted a novel method that has HAL as the base system and proposed S-HAL. The outcome of the proposed model signifies certain weighted features based on the surrounding words, which were tested on certain Chinese data set. Results from the process signify that there are certain developments that outperformed the SO-PMI and it depicts benefits of modeling semantic orientation rather than the actual HAL model.

The authors of (Pai, Chu, Wang & Chen, 2013) focused on the semantic approach to developing varied application based on lexicon model to detail verbs, nouns, and adjectives which are usually used in the case of sentiment analysis. The model combined with subjectivity relations amidst the actors for a sentence detailing of the actors.

The semantics of eWOM content (Pai, Chu, Wang & Chen, 2013) is proposed to evaluate e WOM content. It can be very useful for the organization to gain analysis into product or the service related appraisals. Similar kind of solution was proposed in (Zhang, Xu, & Wan, 2012) too, wherein the experimental results depict that weak response to a product can be very well envisaged in the process.

Such models profoundly rely on the filter-based approaches for selecting optimal features. Constraints are much similar to the ones that are identified in many of the contemporary models and the inconsistency for predictive accuracy impacts because of certain unstable features is chosen using the filtering techniques. Stable feature selection might not be consistent in the case of text data.

Certain studies also had the contrary view point that the filter technique of an individual may not be as significant when compared to distinct set of text corpuses chosen for opinion mining. Feature selection technique that leads to optimal levels of predictive analysis of sentiment using the significant feature selection usually fails for another corpus, but the other techniques might be effective in choosing optimal features.

Considering the limitations of the study, few of the models have focused on ensemble approach of feature selection, wherein more than one filter technique is used for reducing the feature space. Some of the contemporary models in the segment are explored in following description.

The study in (Jong, Mary, Cornuejols, Marchiori & Sebag, 2004), has discussed ensemble feature ranking method that couples feature rankings attained from distinct runs of evolutionary feature selection approach which is denoted as ROGER. The algorithm leads to linear combination of features that are based on the ROC curve.

In (Prati, 2012), performance of certain rank aggregation methods was carried out. Borda, Condorcet, Schulze, Markov Chain model of rank aggregation methods were used. For attaining the feature rankings, symmetric uncertainty, gain ratio, information gain, Chi-Square, OneR and Relief feature selection methods were considered. Results from the study signify that Schulze rank aggregation method can deliver better performance.

The authors of (Dittman, Khoshgoftaar, Wald & Napolitano, 2013) evaluated performance of distinct set of rank aggregation methods to ensemble the gene selection. Feature ranking methods like the ROC curve, F-Measure, deviance, geometric mean and Gini Index was utilized. To understand the efficacy of distinct set of rank aggregation methods, majorly, nine rank aggregation methods were implemented. Based on the experimental valuations, it is imperative that rank aggregation methods profoundly deliver high-quality performance whereas the differences among the distinct rank aggregation methods are not significant statistically.

The authors of (Bouaguel, Brahim & Limam, 2013) have presented ensemble feature selection method that couples relief algorithm, and the correlation-based feature selection and information gain measure models. For attaining consensus ranked list from the ranked list of individual feature selection models, a genetic algorithm usage was proposed. The authors of (Wald, Khoshgoftaar, & Dittman, 2013) examined ensemble methods that can lead to improvement in performance of individual set of feature selection models in a gene selection. Individual feature selection methods with ROC curve, fold change ratio, information gain, signal-to-noise ratio, probability ration was selected. To combine such individual methods, mean rank aggregation models were chosen. Results of the experimental study denote that performance of information gain and fold change ratio can be improved with inclusion of mean rank aggregation.

The authors of (Bouaguel, Mufti & Limam, 2013) proposed a rank aggregation related feature selection method to understand the credit scoring. Relief, Pearson correlation coefficient and other such information methods were used for individual feature selection methods. Such methods, when combined using two distinct set of aggregation techniques denote effective outcome from the process. Results of the experiments signify that aggregation techniques usually lead to better performance in terms of credit scoring domain.

The authors of (Sarkar, Cooley & Srivastava, 2014) have focused on feature selection method that targets information gain, chi-square and other symmetrical uncertainty related feature selection methods comprising Borda set of rank aggregation. The authors of (Onan & Korukoğlu, 2017) discussed the way of combining multiple individual feature selection methods and the factors of determining efficient components that are to be included to feature selection model for ensemble of feature selection strategies. Genetic rank aggregation is the other ensemble feature selection strategy that is proposed, which targets to address constraint stated about existing ensemble approaches.

Empirical analysis by authors reflects that the model genetic rank aggregation model can be stable for predictive analysis accuracy comprising more than 90% in divergent size of dataset. The critical constraint of the model is based on performance of the model being limited to set of diversity for dataset in terms of quantity. But the experiments are vague as usually the datasets of product reviews, and the size of datasets are sparse and are far from real-time practices.

Productivity gains of ensemble models are not significant to context of process complexity and another such key constrains wherein the models targeted under presumption at least one among the existing filter methods are assured for delivering significance to selecting optimal features.

The contemporary method by (Socher et al., 2013) achieved 85% precision on the similar dataset by utilizing a recurrent "Neural Tensor Network (NTN)". Many of the contemporary studies utilize "microblogging text" or "Twitter specific features" like URLs, emoticons, capitalizations, hashtags, elongations, and @symbols to augment sentiment analysis for tweets. To achieve word implanting to the words which are frequently utilized in tweets by using a "neural network" by (Tang et al., 2014a) and (Dos Santos & Gatti, 2014) engaged a profound CNN aimed at sentiment identification in petite texts. Contemporary methods also concentrate on evolving word implanting's based on the sentiment corpora by (Tang et al. 2014b). Aforesaid word vectors comprise many sentimental clues than usual word vectors & generate best results for the tasks like aspect extraction, sarcasm detection and emoticon recognition (Cambria, Poria, Gelbukh, & Thelwall, 2017).

However, in reality presentation of some of the feature selection methods are very vital in attributing the frequency related to 1-gram, bi-gram, n-gram and another set of features. So based on the feature selection accuracy among the filter techniques is effective reliable on the dimensionality of features that are spread based on the chosen corpus.

The other key observation imperative from the afore-discussed models are that the filter techniques either in the form of sentiment lexicons, or the general terms that are used for reviews or the ones that treat the entire bag of words as term set targets the fact of general text mining process.

PROBLEM STATEMENT AND OBJECTIVE

Many of the earlier contributions published in the domain of sentiment analysis have explored varied new techniques. From the review of literature, it is imperative that part of the earlier works have focused on identifying the sentiment orientation of text. These models are considering 1-gram, bi-gram, tri-gram or n-gram term co-occurrence strategy that applied on either sentiment lexicons or bag of words as features. Hence the models limiting their performance to predict the sentiment represented in the form of sarcasm and the diplomatic opinions those reflects the both positive and negative polarity of the sentiment.

Related to constraints that were earlier reported, it is evident that feature selection techniques have to perform irrespective of the attribute frequency conditions. Hence, a contemporary model that takes in to account the attribute and sentiment lexicons association as the key fitness objective is proposed. Implication scope of such attribute for both the positive and negative sentiment lexicons were considered pertaining to optimal feature selection that strengthens predictive accuracy at boundary levels and towards positive and negative sentiment scope.

METHODS AND MATERIALS

The overall process of the proposed model incorporates the following:

1. Pre-processing is carried out and denoting of every review as a word vector
2. Identify 2-grams from every review that are denoted by respective word vector that belongs to training set
3. Identify N-grams by adapting DE evaluation technique
   - No Crossovers essential
   - Fitness of n-gram is denoted using the correlation and sentiment lexicons
   - N-gram term-sets are discovered based on positive and negative lexicons, thus finding n-grams for both the negative and positive sentiment.
4. n-grams that are exclusive for positive sentiment and the ones that are optimal for use to discover positive sentiment scope of test data.
5. n-grams that are categorical to negative sentiment and optimal to use for discovering negative sentiments amidst the scope of test data.
6. Usage of N-grams that are essential for discovering both positive and negative sentiment scope for carrying out predictive analysis.

The methods and materials adapted in order to perform the steps included in proposed model are explored in following sections.

Preprocessing

Segmenting or Tokenizing

During the phase of pre-processing, tokenization carried out by splitting documents in to list of words. Tokens comprising of words and numbers extracted by scanning the reviews and accordingly the documents are used for further processing.

Eliminating Stop Words

Performance of the feature selection algorithms can be improved upon eliminating spaces, Stop words and high-frequency words by filtering them from the document. Process of removing the stop words reduces the dimensionality of datasets, and also traces the keywords in review corpus using automatic feature extraction techniques. Certain functional words like "about", "me", "is", "the" which do not carry any kind of sentiment information. In the proposed model, the stop words are removed using file index size which does not affect accuracy levels.

Stemming

In feature extraction models, stemming is profoundly used in pre-processing phase. Stemming transforms words from a text in to stem or to a root form. Stemming as a process is much simple and is faster in extraction process. Porter's stemmer model is widely engaged in stemming process of English language text.

Differential Evolution Algorithm

Among the many of evolutionary techniques related to optimization process, the differential evolution approach (Storn & Price, 1997) is one that notified as robust for global optimization. The context of the DE is approximately similar to GA (Mitchell, Forrest & Holland, 1992). However, t differs with GA in regard to considering the new genotypes (new population). The parent and child chromosomes always being compared in regard to their fitness context, if child chromosomes are fittest, then survives and parents will be discarded, if not parent chromosomes only survive. In a gist, the fittest child chromosome only replaces the parent chromosome.

The diversified fitness functions and different crossover strategies used by DE reflects the difference between different differential evolution approaches depicted in contemporary literature (Islam, Das, Ghosh, Roy, Suganthan, 2012). Such novel DE strategies explored in contemporary survey (Das & Suganthan, 2011).

Differential Evolution can be very resourceful for accomplishing task of identifying n-gram termsets like optimal features. 2-gram sets are the initial input set of evolution process in DE that represents word vectors formed from the pre-processing levels. The key criteria for selection of the proposal for evaluating the survival of fittest, wherein n-gram term sets that are formed by union of two sets like the mutation operation. The Evolutions count of GA are profoundly probabilistic and evolutions terminate after the randomly selected number of iterations, wherein in the adapted DE model, evolution count turns out to be deterministic, that terminates if any new candidate solution comprising higher fitness than the earlier ones.

T-Test for Variance Estimation

N-gram term sets like the feature obtained in the second stage of the proposed model that are further filtered for attaining optimal features. Selection of optimal features on the basis of covariance amidst the co-occurrence frequency for positive and negative sentiment lexicons towards addressing every feature.

For estimating variance of every feature, co-occurrence frequency pertaining to positive and negative sentiment representative lexicons, in the proposed solution focus is on t-test. Inspired from (Budak

& Taşabat, 2016), the variance assessment strategy called t-test is considered for the proposed model, which is adapted to select optimal features respective to each positive and negative words of the sentiment representative lexicons. The t-test is embraced for choosing optimal features related to both positive and negative sentiment records projected in training set.

The diversity of the values in two different vectors can be represented by t-score, which is estimated as follows:

$$t-score = \frac{(M_{v1} - M_{v2})}{\sqrt{\frac{\sum_{i=1}^{|v1|}(x_i - M_{v1})^2}{|v1|-1} + \frac{\sum_{j=1}^{|v2|}(x_j - M_{v2})^2}{|v2|-1}}} \tag{1}$$

Here in the above equation

- M_{v1}, M_{v2} represents the mean of the values observed in respective vectors $v1$, $v2$
- The notations x_i, x_j represents each element of respective vectors $v1$, $v2$ of corresponding sizes $|v1|$, $|v2|$

The t-score is the ratio between the mean differences of respective vectors and the square root of sum of mean square distances of the respective vectors.

Then find the degree of probability (p-value) (Sahoo & Riedel, 1998) in t-table (http://www.sjsu.edu/faculty/gerstman/StatPrimer/t-table.pdf) for the t-score obtained. The p-value that is less than the probability threshold $\tau(0 \leq \tau \leq 0.05)$ indicates both vectors are distinct; hence, the feature representing respective vectors is optimal feature.

The Classifier

Classifying the identified datasets into appropriate categories and focusing on right mapping for the emerging observation is a critical process in terms of machine learning modeling. Success in terms of appropriate identification is based on data training set that comprises relevant observations for category membership in a trained dataset. The gamut of machine learning and supervised learning is termed for classification, whereas the clustering is the defined term of supervised learning process. For the process of clustering, grouping of data takes place by the set of few measures in terms of similarities that are identified.

AdaBoost (An & Kim, 2010) is the resourceful solution for enhancing the deliverable outcome of decision trees when compared to the other binary classification related issues. It is also vividly used in improving the outcome of varied algorithms related to machine learning, categorically the weak learner kind of algorithms. Decision trees of a specific level and the ones that are more suited for implementation with AdaBoost. Trees are usually considered as decision stumps, as they are short and usually have only one decision for classification.

Recurrent usage of a week classifier on given corpus is the objective of the AdaBoost algorithm. In regard to the method proposed here in this manuscript, the week classifier is used to signify the n-gram feature towards binary classification. The classification process is recurrent and on each iteration of the week classifier, the part of the corpus that failed to be classified correctly will be the probable of the next iteration of the classifier, which is termed often as boosting. The weak classifier that used on each iteration will be denoted by their classification weight. Upon completion of the iterative calls of the weak classifier, correctly classified records from all of these week classifiers will be rationalized. In regard to the proposed model, each of the weak classifiers used by AdaBoost algorithm signifies the certain n-gram towards classification accuracy. Further the classification results of these weak classifiers will be rationalized to identify the polarity of the given records.

TERM CO-OCCURRENCE FITNESS EVOLUTION

This section explores the formulation of the proposed model in detail about the implementation of the methods and materials used.

The Data

Let the corpus $C=\{r_1, r_2, \ldots, r_{|C|}\}$ of size $|C|$ comprise the set of reviews which are termed either positive or negative denotation of the opinion. Firstly, the corpus undergoes preprocessing phase which readies the dataset $\overline{C} = \{bw_1, bw_2, \ldots, bw_{|C|}\}$ constituting transactions of size $|C|$. Every transaction bw_i is a bag of words gathered from individual review of the corpus C. The preprocessing comprises the process of tokenization, stop-word removal, and stemming resulting in the corresponding bag of words bw_i from individual review r_i of the corpus C. Every transaction bw_i of the dataset $\overline{C}$ involves the corresponding label of the particular review r_i. Further, classify the resultant dataset $\overline{C}$ as two sets C_P, C_N comprising positive and negative transactions correspondingly.

Later, from each set C_P, C_N, focus on the unique set of sentiment lexicons $C_P(l), C_N(l)$, comprising sentiment lexicons detailed for all of the records in corresponding datasets C_P, C_N. The representation of the sentiment lexicons from the dealings of the corresponding datasets are performed with support of the sentiment lexicon corpus (http://www.cs.uic.edu/~liub/FBS/opinion-lexicon-English.rar).

Depiction of n-grams

Term and sentiment lexicon association is very complex and is adapted for the proposed solution. Overall terms that are not appearing as sentiment lexicons will be considered as set of 1-grams G_1.

The process of modeling defines set of n-grams from depicted 1-grams, wherein n can be depicted as number starts at 1 for a total number of 1-grams. Considering such factors, the model adapts differential evolution algorithm with objective of fittest n-grams having max size survives, with example of 2-gram term set $[g_i, g_j]$ comprising fitness $f([g_i, g_j])$ higher than or equal to the fitness $f(g_i), f(g_j)$ of individual 1-grams g_i, g_j, rather than 2-gram $[g_i, g_j]$ endures and the 1-grams g_i, g_j will be discarded.

Support of n-grams associability comprising sentiment lexicons for the respective set of records considered as fitness.

Let and n-gram g identified to be associated using the sentiment lexicons $\{l_1, l_2, l_3\}$. Then the fitness $f(g)$ of the n-gram g are evaluate as basis

$$f(g) = \frac{rc_{[g,\{l_1,l_2,l_3\}]}}{rc_{\{l_1,l_2,l_3\}}} \tag{2}$$

In the notion, $rc_{[g,\{l_1,l_2,l_3\}]}$ denotes cumulative number of records comprising having n-gram g and any other set of lexicons based on set $\{l_1,l_2,l_3\}$, and the notation $rc_{\{l_1,l_2,l_3\}}$ is cumulative set of records comprising any of the lexicon from set $\{l_1,l_2,l_3\}$.

Process of best fit n-gram selection is identical to both transaction sets C_P, C_N and detailed exploration for the process

$k=1$

$evs = true$

step 1: *while(evs)* Begin

step 2: $G_{k+1}=\{\}$ // is an empty set holds the $(k+1)$–gram term sets if any...

step 3: $\underset{i=1}{\overset{|G_k|}{\forall}} \{g_i \exists g_i \in G_k\}$ Begin

step 4: $\underset{j=i+1}{\overset{|G_k|}{\forall}} \{g_j \exists g_j \in G_k\}$ begin

step 5: $g_{\{i,j\}} = g_i \bigcup g_j$ // mutation operation of the DE that mutates two populations using union operation

step 6: $\underset{x=1}{\overset{|C(l)|}{\forall}} \{l_x \exists l_x \in C(l)\}$ begin // for each sentiment lexicon of the corresponding records set

step 7: if $(d[l_x, g_{i,j}] \geq 1)$ begin // finding that the count of transactions $a[l_x, g_{i,j}]$ those contain both lexicon l_x and n-gram $g_{i,j}$ is at least 1

step 8: $g_{i,j}^l \leftarrow l_x$ // collect all lexicons those meeting the condition in step 7 as a set $g_{i,j}^l$

step 9: End //of step 7

step 10:   End of step 6

step 11: $f(g_{i,j}) = \dfrac{rc_{[g_{i,j},\{g_{i,j}^l\}]}}{rc_{\{g_{i,j}^l\}}}$ // find the fitness of the depicted n-gram, which the ratio of number of records $rc_{[g_{i,j},\{g_{i,j}^l\}]}$ contain the depicted $(k+1)$-gram $g_{i,j}$ and the any of the lexicon from set $g_{i,j}^l$ and the number of records $rc_{\{g_{i,j}^l\}}$ those contains any of the lexicon from the set $g_{i,j}^l$

step 12:   if $\left(f(g_{i,j}) \leq \left[f(g_i) \wedge f(g_j) \right] \right)$ begin

step 13: $G_{k+1} \leftarrow \{g_i, g_j\}$ // move both inputs $\{g_i, g_j\}$ of the mutation operation f step 5 to $(k+1)$–gram set.

step 14:   End //of step 12

step 15:   Else begin

step 16: $G_{k+1} \leftarrow g_{i,j}$ // move the result $g_{i,j}$ of the mutation operation f step 5 to $(k+1)$–gram set.

step 17:   End of step 15

step 18:   End //of step 4

step 19:   End // of step 3
step 20:   if $(G_k \neq G_{k+1})$ begin // if the entries of the sets G_k, G_{k+1} are not identical
step 21: $k+k+1$
step 22:   End // of step 20
step 23:   Else // if the entries of both sets G_k, G_{k+1} identical, which indicates no new term sets depicted, hence the further evolutions not required
step 24:   *evs=false*
step 25:   End //of step 1

In this section, the process model of n-grams depiction, that is similar to both transaction sets C_P and C_N. Resultant n-grams from DE evolutions are applied for both transaction sets C_P and C_N which can refer as n-gram sets G_P and G_N.

The key factor to be identified is that the n-grams for both the positive and negative transactions shall have n value with range beginning at 1 and terminating at a number of unique terms that are observed for corresponding set of transactions.

At the end of the DE process, for all the transactions sets C_P and C_N the following steps are adapted.

$C_P(l)$ and $C_N(l)$// the sets of positive and negative sentiment lexicons depicted in corresponding positive and negative transaction sets C_P and C_N

G_P and G_N// the sets of n-grams depicted from DE evolutions that applied on corresponding positive and negative transaction sets C_P and C_N

Optimal Feature Selection

In this set of study, biface variance estimation process is used for evaluating optimal features related to positive and negative transactions that are set of n-grams gathered from respective set of G_P and G_N.

The first step of the process is to develop matrices M_P and M_N and the ones that comprise association ratio for every n-gram pertaining to every sentiment lexicon for respective order of related sets G_P and G_N. The matrix formation of each of the sets G_P and G_N is follows:

step 1: Let matrix $M_P=\{ \{\},\{\} \}$ be empty and retains the association support of each n-gram in respective to each positive sentiment lexicon

step 2: $\bigvee_{i=1}^{|G_P|} \{g_i \exists g_i \in G_P\}$ Begin // for each n-gram related to the positive sentiment transactions

step 3: $R_i \leftarrow \{\}$ // an empty vector representing the ith row of the matrix M_P

step 4: $\bigvee_{j=1}^{|C_P(l)|} \{l_j \exists l_j \in C_P(l)\}$ Begin // for each positive sentiment lexicon

step 5: $rc_{\{l_j\}} = 0$

step 6: $rc_{\{g_i,l_j\}} = 0$

step 7: $\bigvee_{k=1}^{|C_P|} \{r_k \exists r_k \in C_P\}$ Begin // for each transaction of the positive sentiment corpus

step 8: if $\left(l_j \subseteq r_k\right)$ Begin

step 9: $rc_{\{l_j\}} + = 1$

step 10:   End // of step 8

step 11:   if $\left(\{g_i, l_j\} \subseteq r_k\right)$ Begin

step 12: $rc_{\{g_i, l_j\}} += 1$

step 13:   End //of step 11

step 14:   End//of step 7

step 15: $R_i \leftarrow \dfrac{rc_{\{g_i, l_j\}}}{rc_{\{l_j\}}}$ //finding the association ratio of given n-gram g_i and sentiment lexicon l_j

and moving it row R_i of the matrix M_p

step 16:   End //of step 4

step 17: $M_p \leftarrow R_i$ // moving row R_i to the matrix M_p

step 18:   End //of step 2

step 19:   End// of the matrix formation process

A similar set is performed to develop matrix M_N from n-grams and sentiment lexicons $G_N, C_N(l)$ chosen for negative transaction set C_N.

Further, the optimal n-grams selection process is considered as features for respective positive and negative polarity sentiment transactions chosen for training. For doing it, the biface composite variance estimation process for every row indicating sentiment lexicon association ration of n-gram comprising both matrices are considered M_P, M_N.

Such process results in t-score and degree of probability amidst two rows respective to an n-gram chosen from matrices M_P, M_N as vectors v_1, v_2. Based on the degree of probability is much lower than the threshold chosen as 0.1, 0.5 and 0.01, and also depicted t-score is being positive, wherein the n-gram depicting both vectors v_1, v_2 are considered as optimal feature towards sentiment polarity that is positive, else the equivalent n-gram is treated as optimal feature for sentiment polarity having negativity. If the degree of probability that showed is not less than the given threshold then the respective n-gram which is discarded as it is not the optimal. The method of optimal feature depiction follows:

step 1: $G_{PN} \leftarrow G_P \cap G_N$ // collect the n-grams that common for both sets G_P, G_N as a set G_{PN}

step 2: $OG_P \leftarrow \{G_P \backslash G_{PN}\}$ // The n-grams that exists in G_P and does not exists in G_N are considered as default optimal features of positive sentiment polarity

step 3: $OG_N \leftarrow \{G_N \backslash G_{PN}\}$ // The n-grams that exists in G_N and does not exists in G_P are considered as default optimal features of negative sentiment polarity

step 4: $\bigvee\limits_{i=1}^{|G_{PN}|} \{g_i \exists g_i \in G_{PN}\}$ Begin // for each n-gram related to the positive sentiment transactions

step 5: $v_1 \leftarrow R_{M_P}(g_i)$ // consider the values depicted in row $R_{M_P}(g_i)$ that representing the n-gram g_i in matrix M_P as vector v_1

step 6: $v_2 \leftarrow R_{M_N}(g_i)$ // consider the values depicted in row $R_{M_N}(g_i)$ that representing the n-gram g_i in matrix M_N as vector v_2

step 7: $bcve(g_i) = \dfrac{\left(\langle v_1 \rangle - \langle v_2 \rangle\right)}{\sqrt{stdv(v_1) + stdv(v_2)}}$ // finding he biface composite variance between the given vectors v_1, v_2 (see sec 3.3 for detailed description) step 8: $p_{bcve(g_i)} = p - value(bcve(g_i))$ // finding the degree of probability $p_{bcve(g_i)}$ from t-table (http://www.sjsu.edu/faculty/gerstman/StatPrimer/t-table.pdf)

step 9: if $\left(p_{bcve(g_i)} \leq \tau \right)$ Begin // if the degree of probability $p_{bcve(g_i)}$ is less than the threshold τ

step 10:   if $(bcve(g_i)>0)$ Begin // if biface composite variance is greater than 0

step 11: $OG_P \leftarrow g_i$

step 12:   End //of step 10

step 13:   Else begin // if condition given in step 10 is not meeting the criteria

step 14: $OG_N \leftarrow g_i$

step 15:   End //of step 13

step 16:   End // of step 4

In the end process, optimal n-grams comprising features for positive and negative sentiment polarities comprises respective sets as OG_P, OG_N. By completing optimal n-grams chosen for both positive and negative sentiment level of polarity for chosen training set, the chosen classifier shall is trained wherein the classifier focus on label of the chosen set of transactions. Experimental study and the performance analysis of the model is discussed in the following section.

EXPERIMENTAL STUDY

An experimental study conducted on three divergent datasets of target audience opinion over the movies, twitter trends and products. The key criteria for selection of datasets are the quantity, diversity and review presentation. Dataset statics pertaining to input corpus and the training set are explored in section datasets and statistics. Performance analysis based on experimental results is identified with classification process adapted for selective test based on Adaboost classifier in section performance analysis.

Datasets and Statistics

Table 1. Data statistics for each dataset

Dataset Statistics					
Dataset	**Total # of records**	**Positive Records**	**Negative Records**	**Records used for training**	**Records used for testing**
Twitter Trends	29700	17820	11880	19800	9900
Movie Reviews	21933	13160	8773	14622	7311
Product Reviews	28310	16986	11324	18873	9437

Product review datasets (http://jmcauley.ucsd.edu/data/amazon/), Twitter dataset sentiment analysis (http://thinknook.com/wp-content/uploads/2012/09/Sentiment-Analysis-Dataset.zip), movie reviews dataset (http://www.cs.cornell.edu/people/pabo/movie-review-data/) are the major sets chosen for analysis. 27886 records are part of movie dataset wherein 21993 are considered for experiments and the rest discarded for complexity noticed for pre-processing step. Original twitter dataset (http://thinknook.com/

wp-content/uploads/2012/09/Sentiment-Analysis-Dataset.zip) with tweets marked as positive and negative. Various records wherein 29700 records were retained post the pre-processing stage. Other dataset product reviews of Amazon Instant video from the Amazon product that is constructed in the form of USCD (http://jmcauley.ucsd.edu/data/amazon/), which are considered for experiments. 28310 reviews were chosen for pre-processing. Majority of the datasets were pre-processed and numerous instances that were available were depicted in Table 1. Data sets of Movie Reviews and Product Review contain uniform distribution, whereas Twitter datasets are skewed. Figures 1 and 2 showcase the statistics of the respective transactions depicted in the datasets.

For every dataset, overall positive and negative labeled records are classified as 3:3 ratio for training and the testing process categorically. Statistics pertaining to training set are detailed in Table 2 Wherein the positive and negative records are adapted from every dataset and are depicted with sentiment lexicons for each of the corresponding datasets.

Performance Analysis

In this section, the results attained from the classification process based on Adaboost classifier, wherein the optimal features chosen from proposed feature selection strategy TCFE and results attained from classification process based on same classifier which trains the optimal features chosen from the novel model of genetic rank aggregation set. But the optimal feature selection on the basis of both models that carry divergent datasets used in section datasets and statistics using the same statistics. Critical argument of the paper related to contemporary models and the solution for assessing the performance analysis section.

Precision, sensitivity, accuracy are some of the metrics of statistical assessment (Powers, 2011), which are assessed for results for both proposed and the contemporary feature selection models. Diversity and robustness for the intrinsic elements considered for predictive accuracy when compared to contemporary model.

Test statistics and the values attained for performance metrics are discussed in Table 3 (Figure 3) and Table 4 for the TCFE. Label prediction stats that are attained for TCFE and genetic rank aggregation are seen in Figure 4 and Figure 5 respectively.

It is imperative that the statistics discussed in Table 3 and Table 4 for the proposed model reflects that outperformed the contemporary model for predictive accuracy. Such metric used in the form of sensitivity reflects the ability in terms of predicting the sentiments that are positive, which are envisaged for 90% from the optimal features chosen for TCFE. However, the sensitivity observed for the novel model is around 82% which is comparatively lower than the model proposed (results represented in Figure 6). In the situation of negative sentiment prediction the presentation of models were 90% and 81% respectively for the proposed and the benchmark model.

Average predictive accuracy observed is TCFE and another contemporary model level genetic rank aggregation, wherein the three input corpses are discussed in Table 5 and the figurative representation is depicted in Figure 7. Pertaining to the experiments that are carried out iteratively for the all the chosen datasets, the first set performed 10% of the transactions based on every dataset and is incremented based on 10% as the iteration is carried out in further.

Predictive accuracy attained from the TCFE over the corpus tuples reflect that TCFE is sturdy and retains the stability in terms of predictive accuracy, irrespective of dataset size. In contrast, even the predictive accuracy targeted for the contemporary model focus on genetic rank aggregation using the same experimental conditions that are not stable and is inversely proportionate for the size of the corpus size. A statistical model of t-test that is applied reflect that the predictive accuracy observed in TCFE is much stable and distinct when compared to the other compared models. Results of t-test reflect that there is more accuracy by t-value being 4.27245, that has positive outcome. Hence, it can be stated that TCFE is much accurate with degree of probability as 0.000458.

Figure 1. The statistics of the transactions depicted in datasets

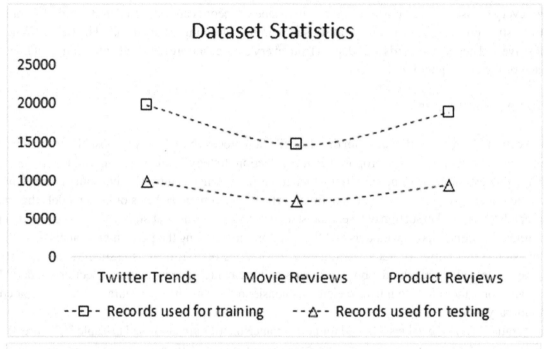

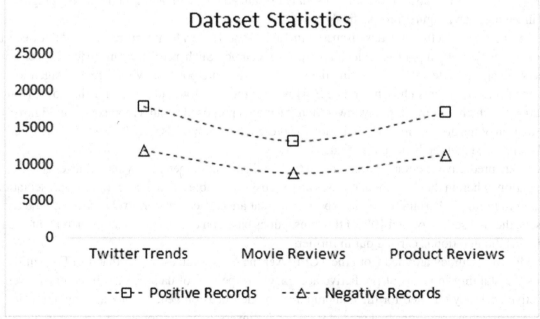

Table 2. Training set statistics

	Records with Positive Sentiment Labels	Records with Negative Sentiment Labels	Positive Sentiment Lexicons	Negative Sentiment Lexicons
Twitter Trends	10692	7128	23	16
Movie Reviews	7896	5264	22	15
Product Reviews	10192	6794	13	8

Figure 2. The statistics of the transactions depicted in training set

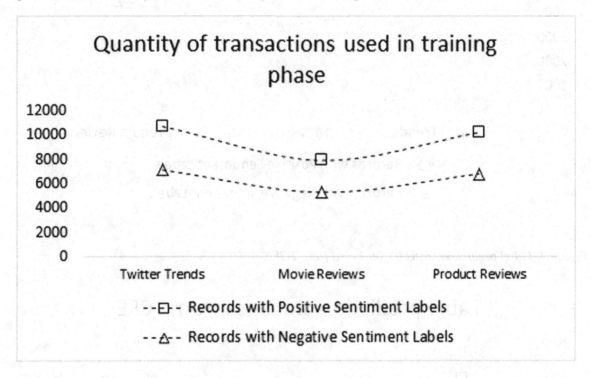

Table 3. Test set and performance statistics of TCFE

	Records with Positive Sentiment Labels	Records with Negative Sentiment Labels	True Posi-tives	False Posit-ives	True Negati-ves	False Negati-ves	Precision	Specificity	Sensitivity	Accuracy
Twitter Trends	7128	4752	6658	456	4296	470	0.935901	0.90404	0.934063	0.922054
Movie Reviews	5264	3509	4950	315	3194	314	0.940171	0.910231	0.94035	0.928303
Product Reviews	6794	4530	6366	426	4104	428	0.937279	0.90596	0.937003	0.924585

Figure 3. Statistics of test sets used in experiments

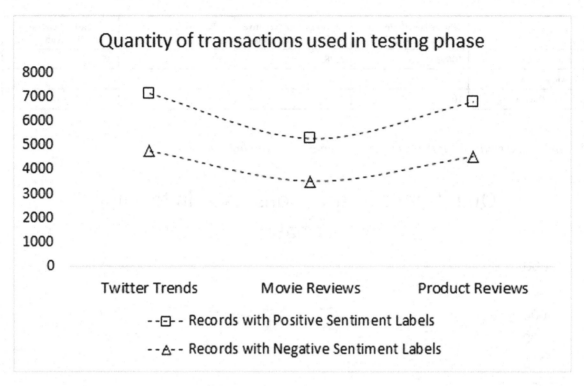

Figure 4. Label prediction statistics observed from TCFE

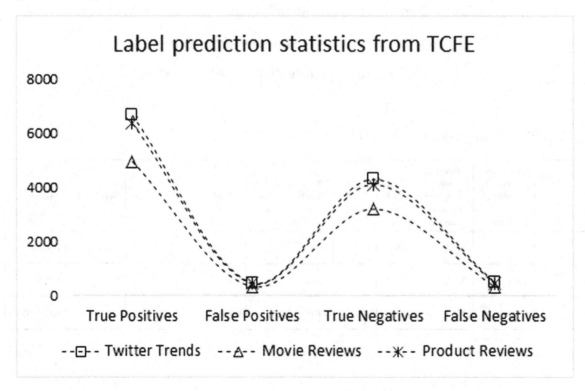

Table 4. Test set and performance statistics of genetic rank aggregation model

	Records with Positive Sentiment Labels	Records with Negative Sentiment Labels	True Posit-ives	False Posit-ives	True Negat-ives	False Negat-ives	Precision	Specificity	Sensitivity	Accuracy
Twitter Trends	7128	4752	6016	931	3821	1112	0.865985	0.804082	0.843996	0.82803
Movie Reviews	5264	3509	4266	631	2878	998	0.871146	0.820177	0.81041	0.814317
Product Reviews	6794	4530	5530	879	3651	1264	0.862849	0.80596	0.813953	0.810756

Figure 5. Label prediction statistics observed from genetic rank aggregation

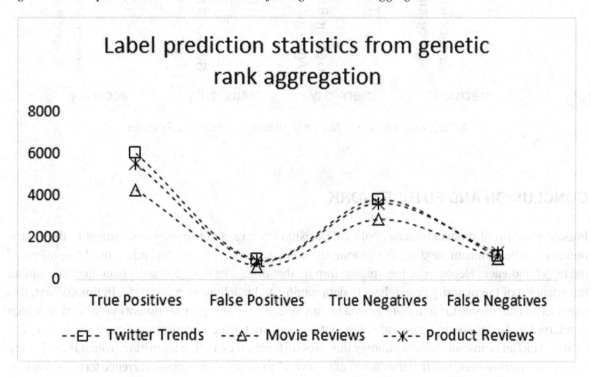

Table 5. Average Predictive accuracy at divergent sizes of the input datasets

	10%	20%	30%	40%	50%	60%	70%	80%	90%	100%
TCFE	0.929	0.929	0.928	0.928	0.927	0.926	0.926	0.926	0.926	0.925
Genetic Rank Aggregation	0.918	0.918	0.918	0.917	0.827	0.826	0.825	0.825	0.824	0.818

Figure 6. The results obtained for performance metrics from both TCFE and Genetic Rank Aggregation

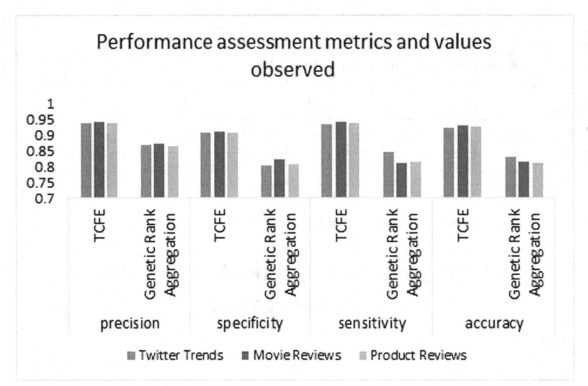

CONCLUSION AND FUTURE WORK

Present scenario of product updates, political decision making, and response assessment to the contributions in entertainment field are few among the many sectors critically depending on the opinions of the target audience. Henceforth, the opinion mining that often mentioned as sentiment analysis gaining the attention of the majority researchers in data mining and machine learning field. In this context, this manuscript endeavored to contribute a novel feature selection strategy for sentiment classification, which is referred as feature optimization in sentiment analysis by term co-occurrence fitness evolution. The depicted model is an evolutionary strategy that uses differential evolution algorithm, which is evaluating the input chromosomes such that the "fittest can survive" to select n-gram co-occurrence terms as features from the opinions with both positive and negative sentiment polarity. Upon depiction of the n-gram co-occurrence terms features corresponding to the opinions with positive and negative sentiment polarity respectively, biface composite variance estimation is using to depict the optimal features associated to both the positive and negative opinions. The context of defining an n-gram term as optimal feature is that the corresponding feature is uniquely associated to the sentiment lexicons either of positive or of negative polarity. In accordance to this, the features shown significance of the association with positive sentiment lexicons and the same is poorly bonded with negative sentiment lexicons are depicted as optimal features of the positive opinions, vice versa, the features shown significance of the association with negative sentiment lexicons and the same is poorly bonded with positive sentiment lexicons are depicted as optimal features of the negative opinions. Further, the renowned classifier called AdaBoost is used to classify the given test corpus, which is trained using the selected optimal features corresponding to both the opinions with positive and negative sentiment polarity respectively. The experimental study conducted on divergent benchmark datasets and the depicted results from the proposed model are compared to the results obtained from the other contemporary model called genetic rank aggregation model. The performance analysis evincing that the proposed model is significant and robust with high classification accuracy that compared to the genetic rank aggregation model.

The observations learned from the model depicted motivating the future research to incorporate other contemporary evolution strategies to optimize the feature selection and improved classification accuracy. The other dimension of future research can be the ensemble classification technique to define to defend the diversity of the features in large volume of training data.

Figure 7. Average predictive Accuracy observed against divergent count of transactions from the given input corpuses

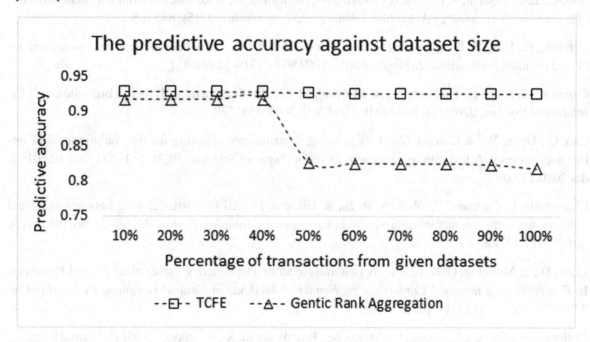

ACKNOWLEDGEMENT

The authors are thankful to the University Grants Commission, New Delhi for supporting this research at School of Computer Sciences, Kavayitri Bahinabai Chaudhari North Maharashtra University, Jalgaon under the Special Assistance Programme (SAP) at the level of DRS-II

REFERENCES

An, T.-K., & Kim, M.-H. (2010). A New Diverse AdaBoost Classifier. In *Proceedings of International Conference on Artificial Intelligence and Computational Intelligence (AICI)* (pp. 359-363), Sanya, China.

Bengio, Y., Courgville, A., & Vincent, P. (2013). Representation learning: A review and new perspectives. *IEEE Transactions on Pattern Analysis and Machine Intelligence*, *35*(8), 1798–1828. doi:10.1109/TPAMI.2013.50 PMID:23787338

Blei, D. M., Ng, A. Y., & Jordan, M. I. (2003). Latent dirichlet allocation. *Journal of Machine Learning Research*, *3*, 993–1022.

Bouaguel, W., Brahim, B. B., & Limam, M. (2013). Feature selection by rank aggregation and genetic algorithms. In *Proceedings of the international conference on knowledge discovery and information retrieval and the international conference on knowledge management and information sharing* (pp. 74-81).

Bouaguel, W., Mufti, G. B., & Limam, M. (2013). Rank aggregation for filter feature selection in credit scoring. In Mining Intelligence and Knowledge Exploration (pp. 7–15). doi:10.1007/978-3-319-03844-5_2

Budak, H., & Taşabat, S. (2016). A modified t-score for feature selection. *Anadolu University Journal of Sciences and Technology A-Applied Sciences and Engineering*, *17*(5), 845–852.

Cambria, E., Das, D., Bandyopadhyay, S., & Feraco, A. (2017). *A practical guide to sentiment analysis* (Vol. 5). Cham, Switzerland: Springer. doi:10.1007/978-3-319-55394-8_1

Cambria, E., Poria, S., Gelbukh, A., & Thelwall, M. (2017). Sentiment analysis is a big suitcase. *IEEE Intelligent Systems*, *32*(6), 74–80. doi:10.1109/MIS.2017.4531228

Cao, Q., Duan, W., & Gan, Q. (2011). Exploring determinants of voting for the "helpfulness" of online user reviews: A text mining approach. *Decision Support Systems*, *50*(2), 511–521. doi:10.1016/j.dss.2010.11.009

Chaturvedi, I., Cambria, E., Welsch, R. E., & Herrera, F. (2018). Distinguishing between facts and opinions for sentiment analysis: Survey and challenges. *Information Fusion*, *44*, 65–77. doi:10.1016/j.inffus.2017.12.006

Chen, D., & Manning, C. D. (2014). A Fast and Accurate Dependency Parser using Neural Networks. In *Proceedings of the 2014 Conference on Empirical Methods in Natural Language Processing* (pp. 740-750). 10.3115/v1/D14-1082

Collobert, R., Weston, J., Bottou, L., Karlen, M., Kavukcuoglu, K., & Kuksa, P. (2011). Natural language processing (almost) from scratch. *Journal of Machine Learning Research*, *12*, 2493–2537.

Das, S., & Suganthan, P. N. (2011). Differential evolution: A survey of the state-of-the-art. *IEEE Transactions on Evolutionary Computation*, *15*(1), 4–31. doi:10.1109/TEVC.2010.2059031

Deng, L., & Wiebe, J. (2015). *MPQA 3.0: An Entity/Event-Level Sentiment Corpus* (pp. 1323–1328). Denver, CO: HLT-NAACL.

Ding, X., Liu, B., & Yu, P. (2008). A holistic lexicon-based approach to opinion mining. In *Proceedings of the 2008 international conference on web search and data mining* (pp. 231-240). 10.1145/1341531.1341561

Dittman, D. J., Khoshgoftaar, T. M., Wald, R., & Napolitano, A. (2013). Classification performance of rank aggregation techniques for ensemble gene selection. In *Proceedings of the twenty-sixth international FLAIRS conference* (pp. 420-425).

Dos Santos, C. N., & Gatti, M. (2014). *Deep convolutional neural networks for sentiment analysis of short texts* (pp. 69–78). COLING.

Fahrni, A., & Klenner, M. (2008). Old wine or warm beer: Target-specific sentiment analysis of adjectives. In *Proceedings of the Symposium on Affective Language in Human and Machine* (pp. 60-63).

Hu, M., & Liu, B. (2004). Mining and summarizing customer reviews. In *Proceedings of the tenth ACM SIGKDD international conference on Knowledge discovery and data mining* (pp. 168-177).

Islam, S. M., Das, S., Ghosh, S., Roy, S., & Suganthan, P. N. (2012). An adaptive differential evolution algorithm with novel mutation and crossover strategies for global numerical optimization. *IEEE Transactions on Systems, Man, and Cybernetics. Part B, Cybernetics, 42*(2), 482–500. doi:10.1109/TSMCB.2011.2167966 PMID:22010153

Jong, K., Mary, J., Cornuejols, A., Marchiori, E., & Sebag, M. (2004). Ensemble feature ranking. *Lecture Notes in Computer Science, 3202*, 267–278. doi:10.1007/978-3-540-30116-5_26

LeCun, Y., Bengio, Y., & Hinton, G. (2015). Deep learning. *Nature, 521*(7553), 436–444. doi:10.1038/nature14539 PMID:26017442

Liu, B. (2012). Sentiment analysis and opinion mining. Morgan & Claypool.

McAuley, J. (n.d.). Amazon product data (dataset). Retrieved from http://jmcauley.ucsd.edu/data/amazon/

Mitchell, M., Forrest, S., & Holland, J. H. (1992). The royal road for genetic algorithms: Fitness landscapes and GA performance. In *Proceedings of the first European conference on artificial life* (pp. 245-254).

Mohammad, S. M., Kiritchenko, S., & Zhu, X. (2013). NRC-Canada: Building the state-of-the-art in sentiment analysis of tweets. In *Second Joint Conference on Lexical and Computational Semantics (*SEM), Seventh International Workshop on Semantic Evaluation (SemEval 2013)* (Vol. 2, 321-327). Atlanta, Georgia.

Onan, A., & Korukoğlu, S. (2017). A feature selection model based on genetic rank aggregation for text sentiment classification. *Journal of Information Science, 43*(1), 25–38. doi:10.1177/0165551515613226

Pai, M.-Y., Chu, H.-C., Wang, S.-C., & Chen, Y.-M. (2013). Electronic word of mouth analysis for service experience. *Expert Systems with Applications, 40*(6), 1993–2006. doi:10.1016/j.eswa.2012.10.024

Pang, B. & Lee, L. (n.d.). Movie review data. Retrieved from http://www.cs.cornell.edu/people/pabo/movie-review-data/

Powers, D. M. W. (2011). Evaluation: From precision, recall and F-measure to ROC, informedness, markedness and correlation. *Journal of Machine Learning Technologies, 2*(1), 37–63.

Prati, R. C. (2012). Combining feature ranking algorithms through rank aggregation. In Proceedings of international joint conference on neural networks (pp. 1-8).

Reckman, H., Baird, C., Crawford, J., Crowell, R., Micciulla, L., Sethi, S., & Veress, F. (2013). Teragram: Rule-based detection of sentiment phrases using SAS sentiment analysis. In *Second Joint Conference on Lexical and Computational Semantics (*SEM), Seventh International Workshop on Semantic Evaluation (SemEval 2013)*, Atlanta, GA (*Vol. 2*, pp. 513-519).

Sahoo, P. K., & Riedel, T. (1998). *Mean Value Theorems and Functional Equations*. World Scientific. doi:10.1142/3857

Sarkar, C., Cooley, S., & Srivastava, J. (2014). Robust feature selection technique using rank aggregation. *Applied Artificial Intelligence, 28*(3), 243–257. doi:10.1080/08839514.2014.883903 PMID:24839351

SJSU. (n.d.). t-table. Retrieved from http://www.sjsu.edu/faculty/gerstman/StatPrimer/t-table.pdf

Socher, R., Perelygin, A., Wu, J., Chuang, J., Manning, C. D., Ng, A., & Potts, C. (2013). Recursive deep models for semantic compositionality over a sentiment treebank. In *Proceedings of the 2013 conference on empirical methods in natural language processing* (pp. 1631-1642).

Storn, R., & Price, K. (1997). Differential evolution–a simple and efficient heuristic for global optimization over continuous spaces. *Journal of Global Optimization, 11*(4), 341–359. doi:10.1023/A:1008202821328

Taboada, M., Brooke, J., Tofiloski, M., Voll, K., & Stede, M. (2011). Lexicon-based methods for sentiment analysis. *Computational Linguistics, 37*(2), 267–307. doi:10.1162/COLI_a_00049

Tang, D., Wei, F., Qin, B., Liu, T., & Zhou, M. (2014a). Coooolll: A deep learning system for twitter sentiment classification. In *Proceedings of the 8th International Workshop on Semantic Evaluation* (pp. 208-212). 10.3115/v1/S14-2033

Tang, D., Wei, F., Yang, N., Zhou, M., Liu, T., & Qin, B. (2014b). *Learning sentiment-specific word embedding for twitter sentiment classification* (pp. 1555–1565). ACL. doi:10.3115/v1/P14-1146

Thelwall, M., Buckley, K., & Paltoglou, G. (2012). Sentiment strength detection for the social web. *Journal of the American Society for Information Science and Technology, 63*(1), 163–173. doi:10.1002/asi.21662

Thinknook. (2012). Sentiment analysis dataset. Retrieved from http://thinknook.com/wp-content/uploads/2012/09/Sentiment-Analysis-Dataset.zip

Turney, P. (2002). Thumbs up or thumbs down? Semantic orientation applied to unsupervised classification of reviews. In *Proceedings of the 40th annual meeting on association for computational linguistics* (pp. 417-424).

Wald, R., Khoshgoftaar, T. M., & Dittman, D. J. (2013). Ensemble gene selection versus single gene selection: Which is better? In *Proceedings of the twenty-sixth international FLAIRS conference* (pp. 350–355).

Xu, T., Peng, Q., & Cheng, Y. (2012). Identifying the semantic orientation of terms using S-HAL for sentiment analysis. *Knowledge-Based Systems, 35*, 279-289. doi:10.1016/j.knosys.2012.04.011

Zhang, W., Xu, H., & Wan, W. (2012). Weakness Finder: Find product weakness from Chinese reviews by using aspects based sentiment analysis. *Expert Systems with Applications, 39*(11), 10283–10291. doi:10.1016/j.eswa.2012.02.166

This research was previously published in the International Journal of Information Technology and Web Engineering (IJITWE), 14(3); pages 16-36, copyright year 2019 by IGI Publishing (an imprint of IGI Global).

Chapter 29
Rule–Based Polarity Aggregation Using Rhetorical Structures for Aspect–Based Sentiment Analysis

Nuttapong Sanglerdsinlapachai

Sirindhorn International Institute of Technology, Thammasat University, Pathumthani, Thailand & Japan Advanced Institute of Science and Technology, Ishikawa, Japan

Anon Plangprasopchok

National Electronics and Computer Technology Center, Pathumthani, Thailand

Tu Bao Ho

John von Neumann Institute, Vietnam National University, Ho Chi Minh City, Vietnam & Japan Advanced Institute of Science and Technology, Ishikawa, Japan

Ekawit Nantajeewarawat

Sirindhorn International Institute of Technology, Thammasat University, Pathumthani, Thailand

ABSTRACT

The segments of a document that are relevant to a given aspect can be identified by using discourse relations of the rhetorical structure theory (RST). Different segments may contribute to the overall sentiment differently, and the sentiment of one segment may affect the contribution of another segment. This work exploits the RST structures of relevant segments to infer the sentiment of a given aspect. An input document is first parsed into an RST tree. For each aspect, relevant segments with their relations in the resulting tree are localized and transformed into a set of features. A set of classification rules is subsequently induced and evaluated on data. The proposed framework performs well in several experimental settings, with the accuracy values ranging from 74.0% to 77.1% being achieved. With proper strategies for removing conflicting rules and tuning the confidence threshold, f-measure values for the negative polarity class can be improved.

DOI: 10.4018/978-1-6684-6303-1.ch029

INTRODUCTION

Sentiment analysis or opinion mining is an interesting research topic in recent years (Pang & Lee, 2008). It is widely applied to textual information in various domains, i.e., reviews of products and services by customers (Hu & Liu, 2004; Ding et al., 2008; Jo & Oh, 2011), financial criticism on microblogs (Si et al., 2013), medical records (Denecke & Deng, 2015), and online news (Chen & Li, 2017). Instead of determining the sentiment of the whole text, several research works, e.g., Jo and Oh (2011) and Moghaddam and Ester (2012), addressed sentiments at smaller levels such as parts, components, attributes, or aspects of an entity of interest. This kind of analysis is referred to as aspect-based sentiment analysis. It basically involves two main tasks, i.e., aspect extraction and sentiment classification of extracted aspects (Liu & Zhang, 2012).

For aspect extraction, descriptive statistics and topic modelling techniques have been used; for example, term frequencies and Latent Dirichlet Allocation (LDA) were used in the works of Hu and Liu (2004) and Jo and Oh (2011), respectively. For determining aspect sentiments, two major approaches, machine-learning-based and lexicon-based, have been applied. These two approaches, however, still perform poorly when they are applied to complicated text with rich linguistic structures. Consider, for example, the sentence "The new phone is fine, but its battery still lacks capacity for one-day use", which should be classified as negative with respect to the "power" aspect. Since the terms "fine" and "lacks" indicate positive and negative sentiments, respectively, this sentence may be misclassified as neutral by using a lexicon-based method. For training a machine-learning classification model, when this sentence is used as a negative instance, terms in the first clause "The new phone is fine" may be incorrectly taken as features for the negative class. The use of linguistic structures makes it possible to consider only the second clause "but its battery still lacks capacity for one-day use" to be relevant to the "power" aspect, and the undesired effects of terms occurring in the first clause can be eliminated.

Recently, attempts to utilise linguistic structures to the sentiment analysis have been reported. Polanyi and van den Berg (2011) discussed the application of the Linguistic Discourse Model to sentiment analysis and observed that a discourse structure affects sentiments at the discourse level; however, no experimental result was reported. Zirn, Niepert, Stuckenschmidt, and Strube (2011) applied the Rhetorical Structure Theory (RST) (Mann & Thompson, 1988) to indicate parts of text that are relevant to a sentiment in product reviews, and an overall sentiment score was calculated from the indicated parts, with the sentiment classification accuracy of 69% being achieved. Sanglerdsinlapachai, Plangprasopchok, and Nantajeewarawat (2016) applied RST to identify text portions relevant to specific aspects in a dataset containing mobile phone reviews, and the sentiment classification accuracy of 72.4% was obtained by averaging the polarity scores of the relevant parts.

In this study, the authors step further by investigating the dependence of the overall sentiment of a given group of related text portions and the polarity scores of its main part (nucleus) and complement parts (satellites) and examining the effects of RST relation types on polarity score aggregation. Sentiment classification rules are induced from RST components, i.e., nuclei, satellites, and/or relation types. The induced rules are evaluated at the level of local aspect segments, each of which consists of related text portions with a well-defined boundary and can be easily annotated with a sentiment. Comparisons with methods that do not employ information about RST components are conducted.

The rest of this paper is organized as follows: The second section describes how RST can be potentially useful for sentiment analysis. The third section presents data preparation and rule induction methods. The fourth section describes experiments on rule-based sentiment analysis and their results. The fifth section discusses three possible heuristic approaches for improvement of rule application. The last section concludes this study and findings.

RHETORICAL STRUCTURE THEORY IN SENTIMENT ANALYSIS

The rhetorical structure theory (RST) is a linguistic theory that defines relations between phrases or clauses in a document (Mann & Thompson, 1988). The relation usually connects two parts, each of which is either a nucleus or a satellite. A nucleus is the main part or the core of an entire given text portion, while a satellite is a complement of the nucleus. Most relation types connect a satellite to a nucleus, while some of them connect two nuclei together, e.g., joint and contrast relations. An elementary discourse unit (EDU) is a leaf node of an RST tree; it is the smallest unit in RST, representing a phrase or a clause. An example of an RST is given in Figure 1, which is generated from the sentence "The placement of the headphone jack and speakers on the bottom of the phone also made it easy for me to have headphones plugged in and put my phone in my pocket." Due to its ability to identify important parts of text, RST is applied to analyse the sentiment of a document in several research works, which are summarised in Table 1.

Figure 1. An example of an RST tree

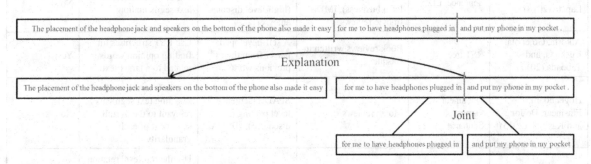

In the previous work on aspect-based sentiment analysis (Sanglerdsinlapachai et al., 2016), rhetorical structures were used to expand parts of content that are related to a key EDU, i.e., an EDU that contains a keyword of an aspect. The expanded group of EDUs is called a local aspect segment. The average polarity score of all EDUs in a local aspect segment often fails to represent the overall polarity of the segment. For example, consider a local aspect segment consisting of the two clauses "On the hardware front I was not sure about 5-inch screen at first," and "but I wanted that special antenna and the stereo speakers," connected by a "contrast" relation, which is relevant to the "sound" aspect. Its nucleus is the EDU containing the second clause, with a positive polarity score of 0.029 (calculated based on Senti-WordNet (Esuli & Sebastiani, 2006)). Its satellite part is the first clause, with a negative polarity score of -0.030. The average value of these polarity scores is negative, whereas the actual polarity concerning the "sound" aspect of this local aspect segment should be positive.

As studied in recent related works, e.g., Hogenboom et al. (2015), Chenlo et al. (2014), Chenlo and Losada (2014), Wachsmuth et al. (2014), and Wang and Wu (2013), in Table 1, RST is influential in identifying parts of content that are relevant to the overall sentiment of a document. Different RST components may differently affect how the polarity scores of the EDUs in a local aspect segment should be aggregated. Considering the local aspect segment illustrated in the previous paragraph, for example, the authors expect that a classification rule such as

$$((\text{relation} = \text{contrast}) \wedge (\text{nucleus} = \text{positive}) \wedge (\text{satellite} = \text{negative})) \Rightarrow (\text{segment} = \text{positive})$$

could be useful for more accurate sentiment classification. The intended meaning of this rule is as follows: If a local aspect segment consists of a "positive" nucleus and a "negative" satellite with the relation between the nucleus and the satellite being "contrast", then the polarity of the local aspect segment is "positive". (The term "segment" on the right-hand side of the rule refers to the "local aspect segment".)

Table 1. Related works with application of RST to sentiment analysis

Author(s)	Granularity	Dataset	RST Parser	RST Usage	Relation Type Usage?
Kraus and Feuerriegel (2019)	Document	Rotten Tomatoes, IMDb (movie reviews), Amazon Fine Foods (food reviews)	DPLP (discourse parsing from linear projection)	Use RST trees as features for Tree-LSTM (long short-term memory) method	Yes
Angelidis and Lapata (2018)	Sentence, EDU	Yelp'13 corpus (customer reviews of local business), IMDb (movie reviews)	A parser developed based on HILDA (high-level discourse analyser)	Use RST structures for text segmentation	No
Alkorta, Gojenola, Iruskieta, and Taboada (2017)	RST tree	Book reviews written in Basque	A self-developed parser from their previous work	Use RST structures for finding opinion words related to a target text	Yes
Hogenboom, Frasincar, De Jong, and Kaymak (2015)	Document, Paragraph, Sentence	Movie reviews	SPADE (sentence-level parsing of discourse), HILDA	Use RST structures for selecting text segments relevant to the overall sentiment of each granularity	No
Chenlo, Hogenboom, and Losada (2014)	Document, Sentence	BLOGS06 (blog posts), MOAT (news articles), FSD (product reviews)	SPADE	Use the top-level relation type of a document for adjusting how the polarity of a satellite part affects the overall sentiment	Yes
Chenlo and Losada (2014)	Sentence	MOAT (news articles), FSD (product reviews), MPQA (news articles)	SPADE	Use relation types as features for machine-learning methods	Yes
Wachsmuth, Trenkmann, Stein, and Engels (2014)	Document	Movie reviews, ArguAna TripAdivor (hotel reviews)	Lightweight lexicon-based discourse relation extractor (self-developed)	Extract sentiment flow patterns and use them as features for a machine-learning method (support vector machine)	Yes
Wang and Wu (2013)	Document	Product reviews written in Chinese with 10 product domains	A self-developed parser from their previous work	Use RST structures for aggregating the polarity score of a document	Yes

DATA PREPARATION AND RULE INDUCTION

Figure 2 shows the data preparation and rule induction framework proposed in this work. Intuitively, a local aspect segment is a text portion considered to be relevant to a given aspect. After local aspect segments for a certain aspect are extracted and the polarity scores of all EDUs are calculated, local aspect segments are transformed to feature vectors representing their top-level structures. These feature vectors are used for training a classification model. Although several classification algorithms are applicable, the authors apply rule-based algorithms, with an expectation that how rhetorical relation types are utilized can be clarified in a human readable manner through the content of the resulting classification rules.

Figure 2. Data preparation and rule induction framework

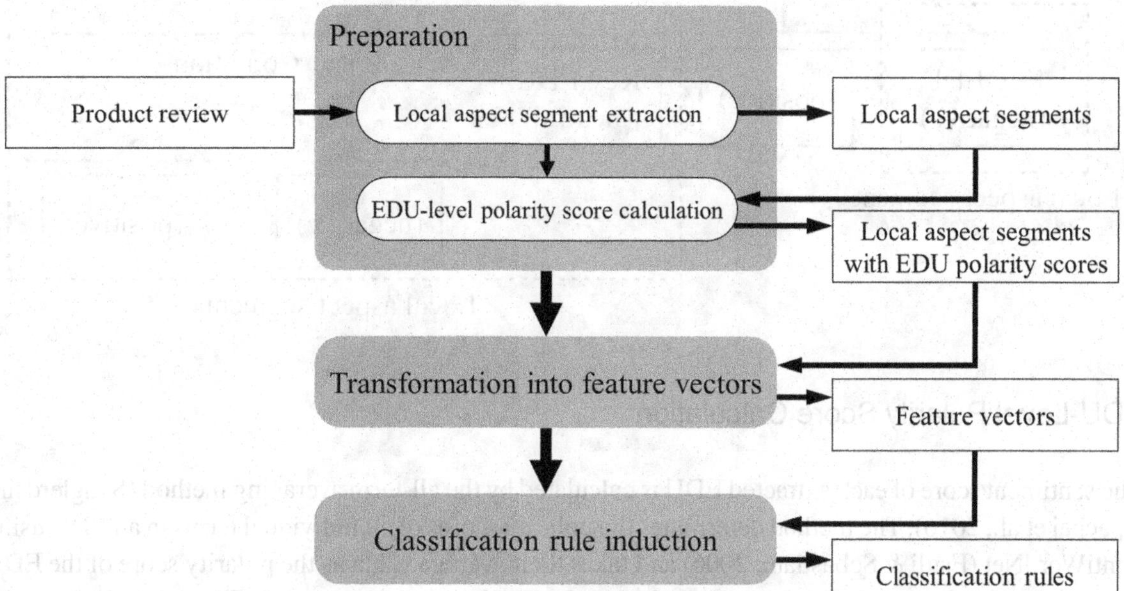

Preparation Steps

Local Aspect Segment Extraction

To extract a local aspect segment from given sentences, an RST parser (Duverle & Prendinger, 2009) is first employed to divide the sentences into EDUs, connected by RST relations. Keywords of a target aspect are prepared in advance. An EDU that contains at least one of the prepared keywords is considered as a key EDU. Starting from a key EDU, a local aspect segment is formed as follows:

- If the key EDU is a satellite node of an RST relation, then the local aspect segment consists of only the key EDU;
- If the key EDU is a nucleus node, then the local aspect segment is the span of text that has the key EDU as its nucleus.

Figure 3 depicts two local aspect segments. One contains only a satellite key EDU, and the other is a span containing a nucleus key EDU with "contrast" being its top-level relation. They appear as the left local aspect segment and the right one, respectively, in the figure.

Figure 3. Examples of local aspect segments expanded from key EDUs

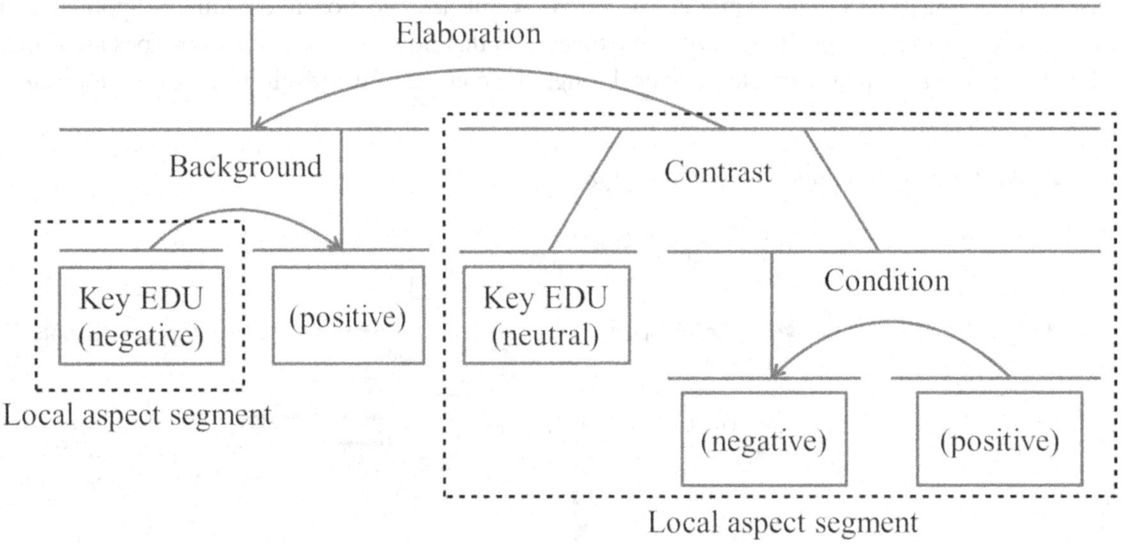

EDU-Level Polarity Score Calculation

The sentiment score of each extracted EDU is calculated by the all-term averaging method (Sanglerdsin-lapachai et al., 2016). The method determines the polarity scores of all individual terms in an EDU using SentiWordNet (Esuli & Sebastiani, 2006) and takes their average value as the polarity score of the EDU as a whole. If at least one negation term exists in the EDU, its polarity score is flipped to the opposite sign (i.e., positive or negative).

Transformation Into Feature Vectors

Before applying a rule induction algorithm to local aspect segments, the authors simplify them by transformation into feature vectors containing only the main relations of their key EDUs. To compare the effect of RST relation types, two types of feature vectors are considered. A vector of the first type is referred to as an NRT vector (a vector "with no relation type"). Given a local aspect segment E, the NRT vector of E is constructed as follows:

1. If E consists only of a key EDU, say K, and its satellite EDU, say S, with no other EDU, then the NRT vector of E is $[P_K, P_S]$, where P_K and P_S are the polarity of K and that of S, respectively;
2. If E consists only of a key EDU, say K, with no other EDU, then the NRT vector of E is [outside, P_K], where P_K is the polarity of K. In this case, K is always a satellite EDU. The term 'outside' is

used to indicate that the nucleus of the RST relation connected with K is outside E and is ignored for sentiment consideration;

3. If E consists of a key EDU, say K, and a subtree, say ST, as the satellite of its top-level RST relation, then the NRT vector of E is $[P_K, P_{ST}]$, where P_K is the polarity of K and P_{ST} represents the average polarity of the EDUs in ST. P_{ST} takes the values 'positiveTree', 'neutralTree', and 'negativeTree' when the average polarity of the EDUs in ST is positive, neutral, and negative, respectively.

A vector of the second type, referred to as a WRT vector (a vector "with a relation type"), extends that of the first type by including the top-level relation type of a local aspect segment as an additional feature. Ten RST relation types are considered. They account for more than 95% of the top-level relations in the datasets used in this work. Table 2 shows these ten relation types, their descriptions, and the percentage of top-level relations having each of these types in the datasets.

Table 2. RST relation types used for generating WRT feature vector

Relation Type	Percentage	Description
attribution	9.4%	The satellite is a clause containing a reporting verb and the nucleus is the content of the reported message.
background	2.8%	The satellite establishes the context with respect to which the nucleus is interpreted.
condition	3.3%	The nucleus is a consequence of the fulfilment of the condition in the satellite.
contrast	8.3%	The situation presented in the nucleus comes in contrast with the situation presented in the satellite.
elaboration	41.2%	The satellite gives additional information about the situation presented in the nucleus.
enablement	2.2%	The action presented in the satellite increases the chances of the situation in the nucleus being realized.
evaluation	2.6%	The satellite assesses the situation presented in the nucleus on a scale of good to bad.
explanation	2.8%	The satellite provides an explanation for the situation presented in the nucleus.
joint	15.2%	The nucleus and the satellite can be listed as alternatives.
same-unit	8.4%	The nucleus and the satellite are really a single EDU.

To illustrate feature vectors, assume that:

- E_1 is a local aspect segment that consists of two EDUs, which are a nucleus (key) EDU with positive polarity and a satellite EDU with negative polarity, connected by an "elaboration" relation;
- E_2 is the left local aspect segment in Figure 3, consisting solely of a key EDU with negative polarity, which is a satellite EDU of a "background" relation; and
- E_3 is the right local aspect segment in Figure 3, containing a nucleus (key) EDU with neutral polarity and a satellite subtree of a "condition" relation with the average polarity score being positive.

The NRT feature vectors and the WRT feature vectors obtained from E_1, E_2, and E_3 are shown in Table 3.

Table 3. Examples of feature vectors

Example	Feature Vector	
	NRT	**WRT**
E_1	[positive, negative]	[elaboration, positive, negative]
E_2	[outside, negative]	[background, outside, negative]
E_3	[neutral, positiveTree]	[contrast, neutral, positiveTree]

Classification Rule Induction

Two rule induction methods, PRISM and PART, are used in this study. They represent two major rule generation paradigms, i.e., rule generation based on sequential covering and that based on a decision tree. WEKA API (Hall et al., 2009) is used for implementation of rule induction methods.

PRISM

PRISM employs a sequential covering technique (Cendrowska, 1987). It produces rules to cover all training instances of each classification class (e.g., positive polarity or negative polarity) separately, one by one. When dealing with a class, PRISM starts by considering rules with only one attribute-value pair in their conditions, e.g., (relation = elaboration) or (nucleus = positive). The rule with the highest confidence is first considered. If its confidence value is equal to 1.0, the rule is included in the resulting rule set. If its confidence value is less than 1.0, a set of new rule candidates is generated by adding another attribute-value pair into the condition part. A new rule candidate is selected and proceeded by the same criteria, but only the group of instances that satisfy the previous condition are considered for determining the confidence value. After the selected rule candidate is added to the rule set, all instances that satisfy the candidate rule are removed. The process is repeated to produce another new rule until all instances of the class being considered are covered. The training set is then restored, and the process is repeated for another class.

PART

PART constructs a decision tree from training data and uses the resulting tree to generate classification rules (Frank & Witten, 1998). The main difference between PART and other rule induction methods based on decision trees, e.g., C4.5 (Quinlan, 1992) and RIPPER (Cohen, 1995), is that PART creates a "partial" tree and generates only one rule at a time. After a rule has been generated, the instances covered by the rule are removed from the training set, and the generation process is continued to produce another rule. To avoid a situation in which some significant rules with low coverage are swallowed by rules with higher coverage during a rule pruning process, PART does not perform global optimization on a rule set.

RULE-BASED CLASSIFICATION: PRELIMINARY EXPERIMENTS

Datasets

In this study, experiments are conducted on two datasets of customers' product reviews, which are described below.

CNET Mobile Phone Reviews

The first dataset, referred to as D1, consists of 139 reviews concerning mobile phone models from CNET. com (http://www.cnet.com). 664 local aspect segments were extracted and manually annotated with positive or negative labels, resulting in 492 positive and 172 negative local aspect segments.

Liu Bing's Dataset

The second dataset, referred to as D2, contains 640 product reviews from Amazon.com (http://www. amazon.com) and CNET.com. It was collected by Liu Bing's research group and was used in Hu and Liu (2004), Ding et al. (2008), and Liu, Gao, Liu, and Zhang (2005). The product reviews in D2 belong to six domains, i.e., cameras, media players, mobile phones, networking devices, software and miscellanea. Sentences in these reviews were originally annotated with aspect keywords and their polarity scores. To analyse them at the level of local aspect segments, the authors manually grouped all annotated keywords into aspects and formed local aspect segments for these aspects using rhetorical structures. 2,638 local aspect segments were obtained, 1,807 and 831 of which are positive and negative, respectively.

Experimental Settings

Table 4 outlines experimental settings, which are detailed below.

Usage of Relation Types

All experiments are conducted separately for each feature vector type (i.e., NRT and WRT) to study the influence of RST relation types on classification rule induction. The NRT type represents the setting in which the information about RST relation types is not used. The WRT type takes RST relation types into the consideration.

Evaluation Schemes

Two evaluation schemes are used in experiments:

- **10-fold Cross Validation:** This scheme applies 10-fold cross validation on each dataset. When the cross validation is applied to the D1 and D2 datasets, the scheme is referred to as D1-CV and D2-CV, respectively. The 10-fold cross validation is also applied on the mixture of the D1 and D2 datasets and is referred as D3-CV;

- **Cross-dataset Rule Application:** In this scheme, one dataset is used to generate a set of rules and the other dataset is then used to test the obtained rules. The scheme that applies the rules learned from D2 to D1 is referred to as D1-XR. On the other hand, when the rules learned from D1 are applied to D2, the scheme is referred to as D2-XR.

Table 4. Experimental settings and their options

Experimental Setting	Option	Description
Usage of relation types	NRT	Use a feature vector with no RST relation type
	WRT	Use a feature vector with an RST relation type
Evaluation scheme	D1-CV	Use 10-fold cross validation on D1
	D2-CV	Use 10-fold cross validation on D2
	D3-CV	Use 10-fold cross validation on the mixture of D1 and D2
	D1-XR	Apply the rules learned from D2 to D1
	D2-XR	Apply the rules learned from D1 to D2
Rule ordering (only for PRISM)	default	Use the rule ordering sequence produced by PRISM
	confidence-based	Use confidence values for rule ordering
	coverage-based	Use coverage values for rule ordering

Rule Ordering

The PRISM method produces rules based on a predetermined class ordering. When applied to the datasets, it produces rules for the positive polarity class before producing those for the negative one. The resulting rules are applied in the same ordering. Consequently, when two applicable rules are in conflict, a data instance will be classified depending on the class ordering; for example, when two rules with the same condition but different polarity predictions are both applicable to a local aspect segment, the segment will be classified as positive. To prevent unfair class polarity setting, two measurements, confidence and coverage, are used for rule ordering in this study. The first measurement indicates the precision of a rule on training instances. The second one indicates the proportion of training instances covered by a rule to those belonging to the class predicted by the rule. Let r be a rule ($P \Rightarrow Q$). The confidence of r and the coverage of r, denoted by $conf(r)$ and $cov(r)$, respectively, are defined by:

$$conf(r) = n(P \wedge Q) \,/\, n(P); \text{ and}$$

$$cov(r) = n(P \wedge Q) \,/\, n(Q)$$

where for any given condition C, $n(C)$ denotes the number of training instances that satisfy C.

Baseline Methods

The following two score aggregation methods for local aspect segments are used as baselines in this study:

Baseline-I: Only the polarity score of a key EDU is used to determine the polarity of a local aspect segment.

Baseline-II: The average value of the polarity scores of all EDUs in a local aspect segment is used to determine the polarity of the segment.

These two methods were employed for score aggregation in Sanglerdsinlapachai et al. (2016). Neither of them employs RST relation information.

RESULTS

Table 5 shows the resulting f-measure for the positive and negative polarity classes (f_{pos} and f_{neg}) and the accuracy obtained from each experimental setting, where the datasets and evaluation schemes are shown as columns and the classification methods are divided into three groups by rows. The first group shows the performance of the two baseline methods, Baseline-I and Baseline-II. The second and the third groups show the performance of the rule-based classification methods when NRT and WRT feature vectors, respectively, are used. Each of them consists of the results obtained using PRISM and PART. The results obtained from PRISM are divided into three rows, with different rule ordering schemes, where "default" denotes the original rule ordering sequence produced by PRISM (starting with the rules for the positive class, followed by those for the negative class), and "confidence-based" and "coverage-based" denote the descending sequences of rules ordered by confidence values and coverage values, respectively.

Table 5. Accuracy (acc) and f-measure for the positive and negative polarity classes (f_{pos} and f_{neg})

Feature Vector Type	Method	D1-CV			D2-CV			D3-CV			D1-XR			D2-XR		
		f_{pos}	f_{neg}	acc	f_{pos}	f_{neg}	acc	f_{pos}	f_{neg}	acc	f_{pos}	f_{neg}	acc	f_{pos}	f_{neg}	Acc
	Baseline-I	.807	.517	.714	.772	.544	.664	.779	.539	.674	.807	.517	.714	.772	.544	.664
	Baseline-II	.811	.463	.717	.775	.502	.669	.783	.495	.678	.811	.463	.717	.775	.502	.669
NRT	PRISM															
	default	.849	n/a	.738	.813	n/a	.685	.821	n/a	.696	.851	n/a	.741	.813	n/a	.685
	confidence-based	.837	.358	.739	.813	.525	.732	.820	.488	.733	.836	.500	.753	.825	.491	.740
	coverage-based	.789	.478	.699	.795	.560	.721	.802	.550	.725	.821	.499	.736	.793	.534	.713
	PART	.847	.446	.761	.823	.504	.740	.829	.493	.744	.851	.467	.767	.824	.510	.741
WRT	PRISM															
	default	.834	.042	.708	.811	.066	.683	.819	.037	.694	.849	.065	.739	.802	.102	.667
	confidence-based	.818	.342	.706	.810	.480	.719	.812	.451	.718	.841	.451	.753	.795	.324	.676
	coverage-based	.769	.512	.678	.761	.534	.682	.758	.527	.678	.798	.520	.715	.720	.515	.636
	PART	.825	.386	.727	.814	.507	.730	.826	.489	.741	.855	.457	.771	.794	.291	.680

In terms of accuracy, when NRT vectors are used, both PRISM and PART improve the classification performance, compared to the two baseline methods, on all evaluation schemes, except for the case when PRISM is applied on D1-CV with the coverage-based rule ordering. Using WRT vectors, both of them also improve the classification performance on most schemes, except for the application of PRISM to D1-CV. PART yields slightly higher accuracy compared to PRISM with its best setting, i.e., PRISM with the confidence-based rule ordering. Compared to Baseline-II, PART improves the accuracy from 71.7% to 76.7% on D1-XR and improves approximately 4–7% of accuracy on the other schemes. The accuracy values are not improved when WRT feature vectors are used instead of NRT feature vectors. The top three rules, ranked by confidence and then by coverage, produced by PRISM and PART on D1-XR are shown in Table 6.

Table 6. Top three rules, ranked by confidence and then by coverage, obtained from D1-XR using PRISM and PART

Feature Vector Type	Rule Induction	Example Rule	Confidence	Cove-rage
NRT	PRISM	$((nucleus = neutral) \wedge (satellite = negativeTree)) \Rightarrow (segment = positive)$	1.000	0.008
		$((nucleus = neutral) \wedge (satellite = neutralTree)) \Rightarrow (segment = positive)$	1.000	0.008
		$((nucleus = neutral) \wedge (satellite = neutral)) \Rightarrow (segment = positive)$	1.000	0.006
	PART	$(nucleus = positive) \Rightarrow (segment = positive)$	0.831	0.549
		$(satellite = positive) \Rightarrow (segment = positive)$	0.803	0.514
		$(nucleus = negative) \Rightarrow (segment = negative)$	0.518	0.337
WRT	PRISM	$((relation = evaluation) \wedge (nucleus = positive) \wedge (satellite = positive)) \Rightarrow (segment = negative)$	1.000	0.023
		$((relation = attribution) \wedge (nucleus = positive) \wedge (satellite = positive)) \Rightarrow (segment = positive)$	1.000	0.018
		$((relation = enablement) \wedge (satellite = neutral)) \Rightarrow (segment = negative)$	1.000	0.017
	PART	$((relation = elaboration) \wedge (nucleus = positive)) \Rightarrow (segment = positive)$	0.908	0.219
		$((relation = joint) \wedge (nucleus = positive)) \Rightarrow (segment = positive)$	0.917	0.134
		$((relation = elaboration) \wedge (satellite = positive)) \Rightarrow (segment = positive)$	0.871	0.248

A closer examination on each polarity class reveals that the rule-based classification methods improve the f-measure for the positive polarity class; however, they worsen the f-measure for the negative polarity class. PRISM with the coverage-based rule ordering is the only method with the resulting f-measure for the negative polarity class being comparable to that obtained from the baseline methods. However, its accuracy is lower than PART and PRISM with other schemes. To address the issue of the negative polarity class, recall and precision values for the class are examined. Compared to the baseline methods, the recall values for the negative class are obviously decreased on each rule-based scheme, except for PRISM with the coverage-based rule ordering. Some attempts to remedy the situation are made, i.e., a combination with a baseline method, setting a confidence threshold, or removal of conflicting rules. They are detailed in the next section.

CLASSIFICATION RULES WITH HEURISTICS

A Combination With a Baseline Method

Unlike PART, PRISM does not produce a complement rule to classify a local aspect segment when no rule is applicable to it. To complement the PRISM rule-based classifier, the Baseline-I method is applied when there is no applicable rule. The authors refer to this combination as PRISM+BL. The obtained results are shown in Table 7. PRISM+BL yields better accuracy compared to PRISM with WRT feature vectors (cf. Table 5). When NRT feature vectors are used, both PRISM and PRISM+BL yield the same results.

Setting Rule Confidence Thresholds

The confidence value of a rule indicates its precision on training instances. Rules with low confidence values tend to yield low classification accuracy on test sets. One possible strategy to improve classification performance is to set a confidence threshold for discarding such rules.

The authors first conduct experiments by varying confidence threshold values in the range of 0.0–1.0 and applied them to the rules obtained from PRISM. Assuming that a threshold value t is used, a local aspect segment E is classified if and only if some rule with the confidence value greater than t is applicable to E. Figure 4 shows the average percentage of classified local aspect segments, calculated from all evaluation schemes, at each threshold value. Each bar in the figure is divided into two parts representing the proportion of correctly (TRUE) classified segments to incorrectly (FALSE) classified segments. As the confidence threshold value increases, the proportion of correctly classified segments tends to increase, however, the percentage of classified segments continuously decreases due to the reduction of the overall rule coverage.

Table 7. The classification performance obtained from PRISM+BL

Feature Vector Type	Method	D1-CV			D2-CV			D3-CV			D1-XR			D2-XR		
		f_{pos}	f_{neg}	acc	f_{pos}	f_{neg}	acc	f_{pos}	f_{neg}	acc	f_{pos}	f_{neg}	acc	f_{pos}	f_{neg}	acc
NRT	PRISM+BL															
	default	.849	n/a	.738	.813	n/a	.685	.821	n/a	.696	.851	n/a	.741	.813	n/a	.685
	confidence-based	.837	.358	.739	.813	.525	.732	.820	.488	.733	.836	.500	.753	.825	.491	.740
	coverage-based	.789	.478	.699	.795	.560	.721	.802	.550	.725	.821	.499	.736	.793	.534	.713
WRT	PRISM+BL															
	default	.837	.090	.723	.811	.074	.686	.821	.046	.697	.850	.065	.741	.806	.147	.682
	confidence-based	.822	.368	.721	.811	.483	.723	.814	.455	.721	.842	.451	.755	.799	.353	.691
	coverage-based	.773	.527	.693	.762	.536	.685	.760	.530	.681	.799	.520	.717	.725	.531	.651

Figure 4. Classification results obtained from PRISM using the confidence-based rule ordering at confidence threshold values between 0.0–1.0

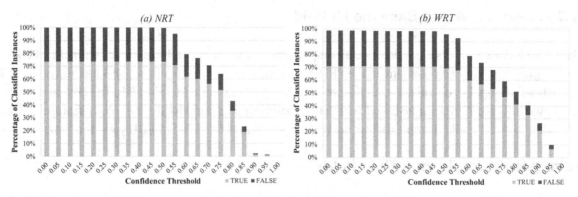

To address the rule coverage issue, the authors next use PRISM+BL, instead of PRISM, in the same experiment setting. Figure 5 shows the obtained results. PRISM+BL with confidence threshold setting slightly improves the accuracy and decreases the incorrect-classification rate, compared to that without threshold setting (which can be seen from the bars at the threshold value zero). For WRT feature vectors, the highest accuracy of 72.0% is obtained at the threshold value 0.6, and the incorrect-classification rate is 26.9% at this threshold value. (At the threshold value zero with WRT vectors, the accuracy is 71.6% and the incorrect-classification rate is 28.1%.) For NRT feature vectors, when the threshold value is higher than 0.6, the accuracy slightly decreases, compared to that without threshold setting.

The authors extend PRISM+BL by setting a threshold value based on the Baseline-I method. More precisely, the threshold value is set to be the minimum confidence value on training instances of the four rules in Figure 6, the application of which corresponds to the application of the Baseline-I method. The method obtained by this extension is referred to as PRISM+BL+TH$_{BL}$. PART is also extended in the same way into PART+BL+TH$_{BL}$. Table 8 shows the results obtained from these extended methods. Compared to PRISM+BL (cf. Table 7), PRISM+BL+TH$_{BL}$ improves the classification performance, especially the f-measure values for the negative class on all evaluation schemes. PART+BL+TH$_{BL}$, however, does not improve the performance of PART (cf. Table 5).

Figure 5. Classification results obtained from PRISM+BL using the confidence-based rule ordering at confidence threshold values between 0.0–1.0

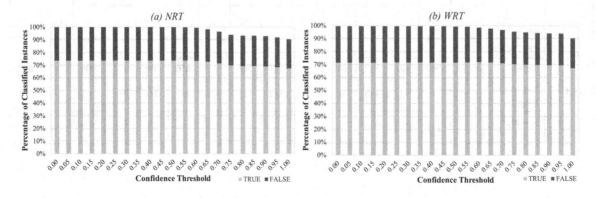

Figure 6. Rules corresponding to the Baseline-I method

$$(nucleus = positive) \Rightarrow (segment = positive)$$
$$((nucleus = outside) \wedge (satellite = positive)) \Rightarrow (segment = positive)$$
$$(nucleus = negative) \Rightarrow (segment = negative)$$
$$((nucleus = outside) \wedge (satellite = negative)) \Rightarrow (segment = negative)$$

Handling Conflicting Rules

Conflicting rules are rules that have the same condition part but different polarity predictions. Basic conflict resolution by rule ordering tends to improve the classification performance, e.g., the results obtained using the confidence-based rule ordering tend to be better than those obtained using the default rule ordering (cf. Table 5). To further analyse the effect of rule conflicts, PRISM+BL and PRISM+BL+TH$_{BL}$ are extended by removing all conflicting rules before a rule application process. The two resulting methods are referred to as PRISM+BL+RM$_{all}$ and PRISM+BL+TH$_{BL}$+RM$_{all}$, respectively. Their performance is shown by the first six rows for each feature vector type in Table 9. On most evaluation schemes, these methods yield higher accuracy compared to the baseline methods (cf. the first two rows of Table 5), while their obtained f-measure values for the negative class are comparable. Compared to PRISM+BL and PRISM+BL+TH$_{BL}$ (cf. Tables 7 and 8, respectively), although the overall resulting accuracy is higher only on a few evaluation schemes, PRISM+BL+RM$_{all}$ and PRISM+BL+TH$_{BL}$+RM$_{all}$ yield higher f-measure values for the negative class on most schemes. When all conflicting rules are removed, the methods with WRT vectors yield higher accuracy compared to those with NRT vectors on all evaluation schemes, except for D1-CV.

Table 8. The classification performance obtained from PRISM+BL+TH$_{BL}$ and PART+BL+TH$_{BL}$

Feature Vector Type	Method	D1-CV			D2-CV			D3-CV			D1-XR			D2-XR		
		f_{pos}	f_{neg}	acc	f_{pos}	f_{neg}	acc	f_{pos}	f_{neg}	acc	f_{pos}	f_{neg}	acc	f_{pos}	f_{neg}	acc
NRT	PRISM+BL+TH$_{BL}$															
	Default	.842	.432	.753	.813	.544	.732	.816	.534	.734	.834	.517	.752	.825	.491	.740
	confidence-based	.842	.432	.753	.813	.550	.735	.816	.534	.735	.834	.513	.752	.825	.491	.740
	coverage-based	.830	.518	.747	.795	.545	.702	.802	.539	.710	.821	.517	.735	.814	.544	.735
	PART+BL+ TH$_{BL}$	.847	.451	.761	.823	.497	.737	.829	.488	.742	.851	.471	.767	.824	.503	.738
WRT	PRISM+BL+TH$_{BL}$															
	default	.830	.365	.732	.804	.518	.713	.810	.504	.720	.833	.471	.744	.815	.352	.709
	confidence-based	.820	.404	.723	.804	.516	.716	.809	.503	.720	.833	.466	.744	.805	.360	.699
	coverage-based	.821	.528	.738	.791	.532	.697	.801	.530	.710	.822	.511	.735	.784	.520	.688
	PART+BL+ TH$_{BL}$	.825	.365	.726	.816	.504	.730	.826	.491	.740	.855	.457	.771	.800	.271	.687

Table 9. The classification performance obtained from additional experimental settings for eliminating conflicting rules

Feature Vector Type	Method	D1-CV			D2-CV			D3-CV			D1-XR			D2-XR		
		f_{pos}	f_{neg}	acc	f_{pos}	f_{neg}	acc	f_{pos}	f_{neg}	acc	f_{pos}	f_{neg}	acc	f_{pos}	f_{neg}	acc
NRT	PRISM+BL+RM$_{all}$															
	default	.818	.524	.733	.772	.544	.664	.779	.539	.674	.807	.517	.714	.791	.544	.696
	confidence-based	.818	.524	.733	.772	.544	.664	.779	.539	.674	.807	.517	.714	.791	.544	.696
	coverage-based	.818	.524	.733	.772	.544	.664	.779	.539	.674	.807	.517	.714	.791	.544	.696
	PRISM+BL+TH$_{BL}$+RM$_{all}$															
	default	.819	.518	.733	.772	.544	.664	.779	.539	.674	.807	.517	.714	.791	.544	.696
	confidence-based	.819	.518	.733	.772	.544	.664	.779	.539	.674	.807	.517	.714	.791	.544	.696
	coverage-based	.819	.518	.733	.772	.544	.664	.779	.539	.674	.807	.517	.714	.791	.544	.696
	PRISM+BL+RM															
	default	.850	.086	.742	.812	.005	.684	.820	.006	.695	.851	n/a	.741	.813	n/a	.685
	confidence-based	.837	.399	.744	.812	.525	.731	.818	.489	.732	.836	.500	.753	.825	.491	.740
	coverage-based	.789	.478	.699	.795	.560	.721	.802	.550	.725	.821	.499	.736	.793	.534	.713
	PRISM+BL+TH$_{BL}$+RM															
	default	.842	.432	.753	.813	.544	.732	.816	.534	.734	.834	.517	.752	.825	.491	.740
	confidence-based	.842	.432	.753	.813	.550	.735	.816	.534	.735	.834	.513	.752	.825	.491	.740
	coverage-based	.830	.518	.747	.795	.545	.702	.802	.539	.710	.821	.517	.735	.814	.544	.735
WRT	PRISM+BL+RM$_{all}$															
	default	.811	.449	.718	.780	.536	.682	.780	.527	.682	.816	.524	.730	.791	.509	.704
	confidence-based	.812	.475	.723	.779	.535	.680	.779	.527	.681	.816	.524	.730	.788	.515	.702
	coverage-based	.811	.487	.723	.779	.536	.681	.779	.527	.681	.816	.524	.730	.777	.520	.693
	PRISM+BL+TH$_{BL}$+RM$_{all}$															
	default	.831	.481	.744	.782	.539	.682	.786	.532	.686	.818	.515	.730	.811	.524	.727
	confidence-based	.831	.500	.747	.781	.538	.681	.786	.532	.686	.818	.515	.730	.808	.522	.724
	coverage-based	.830	.520	.747	.782	.538	.682	.785	.533	.685	.818	.515	.730	.798	.521	.704
	PRISM+BL+RM															
	default	.829	.138	.714	.809	.104	.684	.821	.099	.700	.843	.129	.733	.806	.170	.683
	confidence-based	.814	.387	.714	.809	.493	.721	.815	.477	.725	.835	.471	.747	.799	.364	.692
	coverage-based	.786	.536	.706	.764	.536	.685	.761	.530	.682	.801	.518	.717	.738	.531	.662
	PRISM+BL+TH$_{BL}$+RM															
	default	.829	.364	.730	.804	.518	.713	.810	.503	.720	.833	.471	.744	.815	.352	.709
	confidence-based	.819	.403	.721	.804	.516	.716	.809	.503	.720	.833	.466	.744	.805	.360	.699
	coverage-based	.823	.528	.741	.791	.533	.698	.802	.531	.711	.822	.507	.735	.784	.520	.688

A detailed investigation shows that many rules that are in conflict have different confidence values. The conflicts created by such rules can be resolved by the confidence-based rule ordering. This rule ordering, however, does not resolve conflicts between a pair of rules having the same confidence value. The authors consider another extension of PRISM+BL and PRISM+BL+TH$_{BL}$ by removing every pair of conflicting rules that have the same confidence value. These two methods are referred to as PRISM+BL+RM and

PRISM+BL+TH$_{BL}$+RM, respectively. Their performance is shown by the third and fourth row groups (rows 7–12) for each feature vector type in Table 9. These methods slightly improve f-measure values for the negative class compared to PRISM+BL and PRISM+BL+TH$_{BL}$, while their accuracy values are quite similar. Compared to their corresponding methods in which all conflicting rules are removed, PRISM+BL+RM and PRISM+BL+TH$_{BL}$+RM yield higher accuracy on most evaluation schemes.

CONCLUSION

By using rules induced from feature vectors representing RST structures, the accuracy of aspect-based sentiment classification has been shown to be improved by approximately 4–7% on the datasets, compared to a simpler classification method that relies solely on the average polarity score of relevant EDUs. Although the overall accuracy values are improved by using rules induced by the PRISM and PART algorithms, the f-measure values for the negative polarity class are decreased. To address this issue, three heuristic approaches, i.e., a combination with a baseline method, confidence threshold setting, and removal of conflicting rules, are applied. The combination of these three heuristic approaches yields satisfactory classification results, without sacrificing the f-measure values for the negative class. More precisely, compared to PRISM, the method PRISM+BL+TH$_{BL}$+RM gives higher accuracy and f-measure values for the negative class on most experimental settings. To improve PRISM+BL+TH$_{BL}$+RM further, additional techniques for handling conflicting rules may be applied. For example, instead of simply eliminating conflicting rules with the same confidence value, one of them may be selected by using some heuristics. Further work also includes an extension of the representation of local aspect segments, e.g., by incorporation of information about deeper levels of RST relations into feature vectors. In order to sufficiently cover EDUs relevant to an aspect, an appropriate depth of an RST tree should be investigated.

ACKNOWLEDGMENT

This work was partially supported the Intelligent Informatics and Service Innovation (IISI) Center, Sirindhorn International Institute of Technology (SIIT), Thammasat University; and the Centre of Excellence in Intelligent Informatics, Speech and Language Technology and Service Innovation (CILS), Thammasat University.

REFERENCES

Alkorta, J., Gojenola, K., Iruskieta, M., & Taboada, M. (2017, September). Using lexical level information in discourse structures for Basque sentiment analysis. *Proceedings of the 6th Workshop on Recent Advances in RST and Related Formalisms* (pp. 39-47). Association for Computational Linguistics. 10.18653/v1/W17-3606

Angelidis, S., & Lapata, M. (2018). Multiple instance learning networks for fine-grained sentiment analysis. *Transactions of the Association for Computational Linguistics*, 6, 17–31. doi:10.1162/tacl_a_00002

Cendrowska, J. (1987). PRISM: An algorithm for inducing modular rules. *International Journal of Man-Machine Studies*, *27*(4), 349–370. doi:10.1016/S0020-7373(87)80003-2

Chen, Z. Y., & Li, W. T. (2017). Topic-independent Chinese sentiment identification from online news. *International Journal of Knowledge and Systems Science*, *8*(3), 34–44. doi:10.4018/IJKSS.2017070103

Chenlo, J. M., Hogenboom, A., & Losada, D. E. (2014). Rhetorical structure theory for polarity estimation: An experimental study. *Data & Knowledge Engineering*, *94*, 135–147. doi:10.1016/j.datak.2014.07.009

Chenlo, J. M., & Losada, D. E. (2014). An empirical study of sentence features for subjectivity and polarity classification. *Information Sciences*, *280*, 275–288. doi:10.1016/j.ins.2014.05.009

Cohen, W. W. (1995). Fast effective rule induction. In *Machine Learning Proceedings 1995* (pp. 115–123). Morgan Kaufmann. doi:10.1016/B978-1-55860-377-6.50023-2

Denecke, K., & Deng, Y. (2015). Sentiment analysis in medical settings: New opportunities and challenges. *Artificial Intelligence in Medicine*, *64*(1), 17–27. doi:10.1016/j.artmed.2015.03.006 PMID:25982909

Ding, X., Liu, B., & Yu, P. S. (2008, February). A holistic lexicon-based approach to opinion mining. *Proceedings of the 2008 International Conference on Web Search and Data Mining* (pp. 231–240). ACM. 10.1145/1341531.1341561

Duverle, D. A., & Prendinger, H. (2009, August). A novel discourse parser based on support vector machine classification. *Proceedings of the Joint Conference of the 47th Annual Meeting of the ACL and the 4th International Joint Conference on Natural Language Processing of the AFNLP: Volume 2-Volume 2* (pp. 665–673). Association for Computational Linguistics. 10.3115/1690219.1690239

Esuli, A., & Sebastiani, F. (2006, May). Sentiwordnet: A publicly available lexical resource for opinion mining. *Proceedings of the 5th Conference on Language Resources and Evaluation* (Vol. 6, pp. 417–422). European Language Resources Association.

Frank, E., & Witten, I. H. (1998, July). Generating accurate rule sets without global optimization. *Proceedings of the 15th International Conference on Machine Learning* (pp. 144–151). Morgan Kaufmann.

Hall, M., Frank, E., Holmes, G., Pfahringer, B., Reutemann, P., & Witten, I. H. (2009). The WEKA data mining software: An update. *ACM SIGKDD Explorations Newsletter*, *11*(1), 10–18. doi:10.1145/1656274.1656278

Hogenboom, A., Frasincar, F., De Jong, F., & Kaymak, U. (2015). Using rhetorical structure in sentiment analysis. *Communications of the ACM*, *58*(7), 69–77. doi:10.1145/2699418

Hu, M., & Liu, B. (2004, August). Mining and summarizing customer reviews. *Proceedings of the 10th ACM SIGKDD International Conference on Knowledge Discovery and Data Mining* (pp. 168–177). ACM.

Jo, Y., & Oh, A. H. (2011, February). Aspect and sentiment unification model for online review analysis. *Proceedings of the 4th ACM International Conference on Web Search and Data Mining* (pp. 815–824). ACM. 10.1145/1935826.1935932

Kraus, M., & Feuerriegel, S. (2019). Sentiment analysis based on rhetorical structure theory: Learning deep neural networks from discourse trees. *Expert Systems with Applications*, *118*, 65–79. doi:10.1016/j.eswa.2018.10.002

Liu, B., & Zhang, L. (2012). A survey of opinion mining and sentiment analysis. In *Mining text data* (pp. 415–463). Boston, MA: Springer. doi:10.1007/978-1-4614-3223-4_13

Liu, Q., Gao, Z., Liu, B., & Zhang, Y. (2015, June). Automated rule selection for aspect extraction in opinion mining. *Proceedings of the 24th International Joint Conference on Artificial Intelligence* (pp. 1291–1297). AAAI Press.

Mann, W. C., & Thompson, S. A. (1988). Rhetorical structure theory: Toward a functional theory of text organization. *Text-Interdisciplinary Journal for the Study of Discourse*, *8*(3), 243–281. doi:10.1515/text.1.1988.8.3.243

Moghaddam, S., & Ester, M. (2012, October). On the design of LDA models for aspect-based opinion mining. *Proceedings of the 21st ACM International Conference on Information and Knowledge Management* (pp. 803–812). ACM.

Pang, B., & Lee, L. (2008). Opinion mining and sentiment analysis. *Foundations and Trends in Information Retrieval*, *2*(1–2), 1–135. doi:10.1561/1500000011

Polanyi, L., & van den Berg, M. (2011, December). Discourse structure and sentiment. *Proceedings of the 2011 IEEE 11th International Conference on Data Mining Workshops* (pp. 97–102). IEEE. 10.1109/ICDMW.2011.67

Quinlan, J. R. (1992). *C4.5 Programs for Machine Learning*. San Mateo, CA: Morgan Kaufmann.

Sanglerdsinlapachai, N., Plangprasopchok, A., & Nantajeewarawat, E. (2016). Exploring linguistic structure for aspect-based sentiment analysis. *Maejo International Journal of Science and Technology*, *10*(2), 142.

Si, J., Mukherjee, A., Liu, B., Li, Q., Li, H., & Deng, X. (2013). Exploiting topic based twitter sentiment for stock prediction. *Proceedings of the 51st Annual Meeting of the Association for Computational Linguistics* (Vol. 2, pp. 24–29). Association for Computational Linguistics.

Wachsmuth, H., Trenkmann, M., Stein, B., & Engels, G. (2014). Modeling review argumentation for robust sentiment analysis. *Proceedings of the 25th International Conference on Computational Linguistics: Technical Papers* (pp. 553–564). Association for Computational Linguistics.

Wang, F., & Wu, Y. (2013, August). Exploiting hierarchical discourse structure for review sentiment analysis. *Proceedings of the 2013 International Conference on Asian Language Processing* (pp. 121–124). IEEE. 10.1109/IALP.2013.42

Zirn, C., Niepert, M., Stuckenschmidt, H., & Strube, M. (2011, November). Fine-grained sentiment analysis with structural features. *Proceedings of 5th International Joint Conference on Natural Language Processing* (pp. 336-344). Asian Federation of Natural Language Processing.

This research was previously published in the International Journal of Knowledge and Systems Science (IJKSS), 10(3); pages 44-60, copyright year 2019 by IGI Publishing (an imprint of IGI Global).

Chapter 30
Sentiment Analysis of Tweets Using Naïve Bayes, KNN, and Decision Tree

Kadda Zerrouki
Higher School of Computer Science May 8, 1945, ESI Sidi Bel Abbes, Algeria

Reda Mohamed Hamou
https://orcid.org/0000-0002-0388-1275
GeCoDe Labs, University of Saida Dr Moulay Tahar, Algeria

Abdellatif Rahmoun
Higher School of Computer Science May 8, 1945, ESI Sidi Bel Abbes, Algeria

ABSTRACT

Making use of social media for analyzing the perceptions of the masses over a product, event, or a person has gained momentum in recent times. Out of a wide array of social networks, the authors chose Twitter for their analysis as the opinions expressed there are concise and bear a distinctive polarity. Sentiment analysis is an approach to analyze data and retrieve sentiment that it embodies. The paper elaborately discusses three supervised machine learning algorithms—naïve bayes, k-nearest neighbor (KNN), and decision tree—and compares their overall accuracy, precision, as well as recall values, f-measure, number of tweets correctly classified, number of tweets incorrectly classified, and execution time.

DOI: 10.4018/978-1-6684-6303-1.ch030

INTRODUCTION

Twitter is a popular micro blogging service where users create status messages (called "tweets"). These tweets sometimes express opinions about different topics. We propose a method to automatically extract sentiment (positive or negative) from a tweet.

Sentiment Analysis is the process of finding the opinion of user about some topic or the text in consideration. It is also known as opinion mining. In other words, it determines whether a piece of writing is positive or negative.

Sentiment analysis is a process where the dataset consists of emotions, attitudes or assessment which takes into account the way a human thinks, as noted by Feldman Ronen (Feldman, 2013). In a sentence, trying to understand the positive and the negative aspect is a very difficult task. The features used to classify the sentences should have a very strong adjective in order to summarize the review. These contents are even written in different approaches which are not easily deduced by the users or the firms making it difficult to classify them.

This task has received a lot of interest from the research community in the past years. The work is regarded the manner in which sentiment can be classified from texts pertaining to different genres and distinct languages, in the context of various applications, using knowledge-based, semi-supervised and supervised methods, as noted by Liu Bing (Liu, 2011). The result of the analyses performed have shown that the different types of text require specialized methods for sentiment analysis, as, for example, the sentiments are not conveyed in the same manner in newspaper articles and in blogs, reviews, forums or other types of user-generated contents, as noted by Balahur Alexandra and al (Balahur, Steinberger, Kabadjov, Zavarella, Van Der Goot, Halkia & Belyaeva, J. 2013).

The Sentiment found within comments, feedback or critiques provide useful indicators for many different purposes and can be categorized by polarity, as noted by Kalaivani and Shunmuganathan (Kalaivani & Shunmuganathan, 2013). By polarity we tend to find out if a review is overall a positive one or a negative one. For example:

- **Positive Sentiment in Subjective Sentence:** "I loved the movie Mary Kom": This sentence is expressed positive sentiment about the movie Mary Kom and we can decide that from the sentiment threshold value of word "loved". So, the threshold value of the word 'loved' has positive numerical threshold value;
- **Negative Sentiment in Subjective Sentences:** "Phata poster nikla hero is a flop movie" defined sentence is expressed negative sentiment about the movie named: "Phata poster nikla hero" and we can decide that from the sentiment threshold value of a word: "flop". So, the threshold value of a word: "flop" has negative numerical threshold value;
- **Sentiment Analysis is of Three Different Types:** Document level, Sentence level and Entity level (Kiritchenko, Zhu, & Mohammad, 2014).

The difficulties in Sentiment Analysis are an opinion word which is treated as positive side may be considered as negative in another situation. Also the degree of positivity or negativity also has a great impact on the opinions. For example: "good" and "very good" cannot be treated same. Although the traditional text processing says that a small change in two pieces of text does not change the meaning of the sentences (Kalaivani & Shunmuganathan, 2013). However the latest text mining gives room for advanced analysis, measuring the intensity of the word. Here is the point where we can scale the accuracy and efficiency of different algorithms (Fan, Wallace, Rich, & Zhang, 2006).

In this paper for Sentiment Analysis we are using three Supervised Machine Learning algorithms: Naïve Bayes, K-Nearest Neighbor (KNN) and Decision Tree to calculate the accuracy, precisions (of positive and negative corpuses) and recall values (of positive and negative corpuses), F-Measure, Number of tweets correctly classified, Number of tweets incorrectly classified and Execution Time.

The rest of the paper is organized as follows: Section 2 deals with the related works of our study, Section 3 presents the techniques used for Sentiment Analysis (SA), Section 4 presents our proposed work (Data sets used in our study along with the models and methodology used), Section 5 presents all our experimental results, Section 6 presents the conclusion and future works.

RELATED WORKS

Go Alec, Richa Bhayani, and Lei Huang used the first studies on the classification of polarity in tweets was (Go, Bhayani, & Huang, 2009). The authors conducted a supervised classification study on tweets in English, using the emoticons (e.g. ":)", ":(", etc.) as markers of positive and negative tweets. If anything characterizes Twitter it is the vast amount of information published and the wide variety of topics on which users write. This makes very difficult and expensive the construction and manual tagging of a corpus for the supervised classification of polarity. Thus the authors use the emoticons that usually appear in tweets to differentiate between positive and negative tweets. The validity of this technique was demonstrated in Read Jonathon (Read, 2005).Through Twitter Search APIs, the authors generated a corpus of positive tweets, with positive emoticons ":)", and negative tweets with negative emoticons ":(". The corpus is used to study which features and which classification algorithm is best for the classification of polarity in Twitter.

Read Jonathon (Read, 2005) employed this method to generate a corpus of positive tweets, with positive emoticons ":)", and negative tweets with negative emoticons ":(". Subsequently, they employ different supervised approaches (SVM, Naïve Bayes and Maximum Entropy) and various sets of features and conclude that the simple use of anagrams leads to good results, but it can be slightly improved by the combination of unigrams and bigrams.

In the same line of thinking, Pak Alexander and Patrick Paroubek (Pak, & Paroubek, 2010) also generated a corpus of tweets for sentiment analysis, by selecting positive and negative tweets based on the presence of specific emoticons.

Subsequently, they compare different supervised approaches with n-gram features and obtain the best results using Naïve Bayes with anagrams and part-of- speech tags.

Another approach on sentiment analysis in the tweet is that of (Ley Zhang, Riddhiman Ghosh, Mohamed Dekhil, Meichun Hsu and Bing Liu) (Zhang, Ghosh, Dekhil, Hsu, & Liu, 2011). Here, the authors employ a hybrid approach, combining supervised learning with the knowledge on sentiment-bearing words, which they extract from the DAL sentiment dictionary, used by Whissell Cynthia (Whissell, 2009). Their pre-processing stage includes the removal of retweets, translation of abbreviations into original terms and deleting of links, a tokenization process, and part-of-speech tagging.

They employ various supervised learning algorithms to classify tweets into positive and negative, using n-gram features with SVM and syntactic features with Partial Tree Kernels, combined with the knowledge on the polarity of the words appearing in the tweets. The authors conclude that the most important features are those corresponding to sentiment bearing words. Finally, (Vo Duy-Tin and Yue Zhang) (Vo & Zhang, 2015) classify sentiment expressed on previously-given "targets" in tweets. They add information on the context of the tweet to its text (e.g. The event that it is related to). Subsequently, they employ SVM and General Inquirer and perform a three-way classification (positive, negative and neutral).

TECHNIQUES USED FOR SENTIMENT ANALYSIS

A lot of work has been done in the field of sentiment analysis for well over a decade now. Different techniques are used for sentiment analysis.

Rambocas Meena and João Gama (Rambocas & Gama, 2013) used the keyword based approach to classify sentiment. He worked on identifying keywords basically an adjective which indicates the sentiment. Such indicators can be prepared manually or derived from Wordnet.

Fan Weiguo and al (Fan, Wallace, Rich, & Zhang, Z. 2006) used a different machine learning algorithms such as Naïve Bayes, Support vector machine and maximum entropy.

Vanitha, Sumathi and Soundariya (Vanitha, Sumathi, & Soundariya, 2018) performed document and sentence level classification. He fetched review data from different product destinations such as automobiles, banks, movies and travel. He classified the words into positive and negative categories. He then calculated the overall positive or negative score for the text. If the number of positive words is more than negative, then the document is considered positive, otherwise negative.

Jalaj S. Modha, Gayatri S. Pandi and Sandip J. Modha (Modha, Pandi, & Modha, 2013) worked on techniques of handling both subjective as well as objective unstructured data.

Theresa Wilson, Janyce Wiebe and Paul Hoffman (Wilson, Wiebe, & Hoffmann, 2009) worked on a new approach on sentiment analysis by first determining whether an expression is neutral or polar and then disambiguates the polarity of the polar expression. With this approach the system is able to automatically identify the contextual polarity for a large subset of sentiment expressions, hence achieving results which are better than baseline.

In (Ayetiran, & Adeyemo, 2012) Eniafe Festus Ayetiran and Adesesan Barnabas Adeyemo designed a predictive response model to identify the customers who are more likely to respond to new product offers. The Naïve Bayes algorithm is applied in constructing the classifier system. Both filter and wrapper feature selection techniques are used in determining inputs to the model.

Additionally, sentiment analysis research can use fuzzy logic and AI-based methods to make better nand more accurate analysis (Karyotis, Doctor, Iqbal, James, & Chang, 2018) which can be further assisted with cloud computing approach.

METHODOLOGY

The methodology used in our proposed system is shown in Figure 1. Figure 1 shows the steps of block diagram of the proposed system. First, preprocessing tasks are used to eliminate the incomplete noisy and inconsistent data. Then, we apply three Supervised Machine Learning algorithms: Naïve Bayes, K-Nearest Neighbor (KNN) and Decision Tree, are used to classify sentiments into positive and negative classes. Finally, presentation of results.

Figure 1. Block diagram of the proposed system

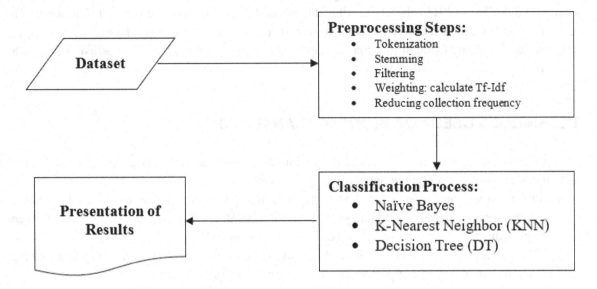

Dataset

This is the sentiment140 dataset. It contains 1.059.218 tweets extracted using the twitter API. The tweets have been annotated (0 = Negative, 1 = Positive) and they can be used to detect sentiment.

Preprocessing Text

In text classification, text data will be represented in the vector space model (Garnes Øystein Løhre) (Garnes, 2009). The steps in preprocessing text are as follows:

- **Tokenizing:** Change sentence into a collection of a single word;
- **Stemming:** Returns a word in basic form (root word) by eliminating existing additive. Stemming algorithm used is Porter Stemmer for English language and Nazief-Andriani for Indonesian language (Nazief Bobby and Mirna Adriani) (Nazief & Adriani, 1996);
- **Filtering:** Eliminating stop words. Stop word is a common word that has little or no meaning, but required in the structure of grammatical language;
- **Weighting:** Calculate TF-IDF for each word, is defined by Equation (1):

$$TF - IDF_t = f_{t,d} * \log \frac{N}{df_t} \qquad (1)$$

$TF - IDF_t$ = weight of term t

$f_{t,d}$ = occurrences term t in document d

N = total document

df_t = number document contains term t

Reducing the collection frequency or total number instances in a dataset.

Classification Process

For the purpose of classification of tweets, three (3) classifiers or algorithms (Naïve Bayes, K-Nearest Neighbor [KNN], and Decision Tree [DT]) used here for classification are described below.

Naïve Bayes Classifier

Bayesian network classifiers are a popular supervised classification paradigm. A well-known Bayesian network classifier is the Naïve Bayes classifier is a probabilistic classifier based on the Bayes theorem, considering Naïve (Strong) independence assumption.

Naïve Bayes is a classification algorithm based on the application of Bayes theorem (Melucci, 2015) (Pratama, & Sarno, 2015). For the purpose of classification of tweets, we make use of Naïve Bayes classifier. Naïve Bayes is a probabilistic classifier based on Bayes" theorem. It classifies the tweets based on the probability that a given tweet belongs to a particular class. We consider two classes namely, positive and negative. We assign class **C*** to tweet **d** where, is defined by Equation (2):

$$C^* = \arg mac_c P_{NB}(c \mid d) \qquad (2)$$

The probability of each of its attributes occurring in a given class is independent, is defined by Equation (3), we can estimate the probability as follows:

$$P_{NB}(c \mid d) = \frac{\left(P(c) * \sum_{i=1}^{m} P(f \mid c)^{n_i(d)}\right)}{P(d)} \qquad (3)$$

f = represents a feature

$n_i(d)$ = represents the count of feature f_i found in tweet d

m = represents the total of feature

$P(c)$ and $P(f|c)$

are obtained through maximum likelihood estimates, and **add-1** smoothing is utilized for unseen features.

K-Nearest Neighbor Classifier (KNN)

K-Nearest Neighbors (KNN) is a classification algorithm that uses a distance function between the train data to test data and the number of nearest neighbors to determine the classification results. Distance function used in this experiment is the cosine similarity. Cosine similarity is one of the functions that are widely used in the document classification to find similarity between some documents (Pratama, & Sarno, 2015). Scoring function of KNN shown in Equation (4). Determining document class is done by voting on a K nearest neighbor. The nearest neighbor is the K-document with the highest similarity value. KNN as a vector in **document-i/VD_i**:

$$Score(C, D_1) = \sum_{D_2 \in S_k D_1} I_C(D_2) \cos(VD_1, VD_2) \tag{4}$$

Score(C, D_1) = scores of test document

D_1 = test document

D_2 = train document

VD_1 = vector test document

VD_2 = vector train document

I_C = 1 if D_2 is in class C; 0 otherwise

$S_k D_1$ = set of K nearest in test document

   K-NN is a type of instance-based learning, or lazy learning where the function is only approximated locally and all computation is deferred until classification. It is a non parametric method used for classification or regression. In case of classification the output is classed membership (the most prevalent cluster may be returned), the object is classified by a majority vote of its Neighbors, with the object being assigned to the class most common among its K-Nearest Neighbors. This rule simply retains the entire training set during learning and assigns to each query a class represented by the majority label of its k-Nearest Neighbors in the training set. The KNN classifier is given in Figure 2 (see Figure 2).

Decision Tree Classifier (DT)

The decision trees are used as an embedded method of feature selection. In the proposed decision tree based feature ranking, a Decision Tree induction selects relevant features and ranks the features. Decision Tree induction is decision tree classifiers learning, constructing a tree structure with internal nodes (non-leaf node) denoting an attribute test. Each branch represents a test outcome and external node (leaf node) denotes class prediction (Jotheeswaran & Koteeswaran, 2015), (Suresh & Bharathi, 2016).

Figure 2. KNN classifier

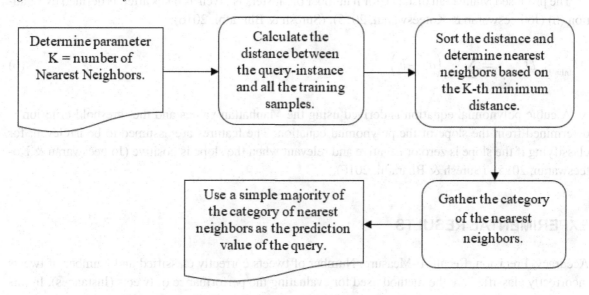

The algorithm at each node chooses best attribute to partition data into individual classes. Information gain measure is used to choose the best partitioning attribute by attribute selection. Attribute with highest information gain splits the attribute, is defined by Equation (5). The attribute's information gain is found by (Jotheeswaran & Koteeswaran, (2015), (Suresh & Bharathi, 2016):

$$info\big(D\big) = -\sum_{i=1}^{m} P_i * \log_2 * P \tag{5}$$

where P_i is the probability that an arbitrary vector in D belongs to a class c_i. A **log** function to base **2** is resorted to as information is encoded in bits. infor(D) is the average information needed to identify the vector D class name. Before constructing trees, base cases are considered with the following points:

- A leaf node is created if all samples belong to a same class;
- When no features provide information gain, it creates a decision node higher up the tree using the expected class value.

The decision tree induction algorithm in general checks for base cases and/or each attribute (a), locates information gain of each attribute for splitting. Let a-best be attributed with highest information gain. Create decision node that splits a-best. Return with sub lists obtained by splitting a-best, adding nodes as children for tree.

The proposed method defines a threshold measure to choose relevant features. The threshold measure is based on the information gained value and the proposed Manhattan distance for selecting of the features.

The proposed decision tree method searches heuristically for relevant features. The features are ranked by computing the distance between the hierarchical clusters.

The proposed Manhattan distance for **n** number of clusters is given as takes after, is defined by Equation (6) (Jotheeswaran & Koteeswaran, 2015), (Suresh & Bharathi, 2016):

$$M_{\text{anhattan}} D_{\text{istance}} = \sum_{i=1}^{n} \left(a_i - b_i \right) \tag{6}$$

A cubic polynomial equation is derived using the Manhattan values and the threshold criterion is determined from the slope of the polynomial equation. The features are assumed to be irrelevant for classifying if the slope is zero or negative and relevant when the slope is positive (Jotheeswaran & Koteeswaran, 2015), (Suresh & Bharathi, 2016).

EXPERIMENTAL RESULTS

Accuracy, Precision, Recall, F-Measure, Number of tweets correctly classified and Number of tweets incorrectly classified are the method used for evaluating the performance of tweets (Instances). In this section, based on the result of Naïve Bayes, KNN (K=1; K=3; K=5; K=7 and K=9) and Decision Tree. Here we give the Accuracy, Precision, Recall, F-Measure, Number of tweets correctly classified and Number of tweets incorrectly classified of Naïve Bayes, different versions of KNN and Decision Tree on 1059218 tweets (Instances). All the experimental results (accuracy, Precision, recall, number of correct classifications, number of incorrect classifications and execution time in seconds) are measured according to the Table 1 (see Table 1) with similar approaches as in (Chang, & Ramachandran, 2016). The performance of Naïve Bayes is compared with different versions of KNN (K=1; K=3; K=5; K=7 and K=9) and Decision Tree are used for the classification of positive and negative tweets. The formula of Accuracy is given by Equation 7, Precision is defined with Equation 8, Recall is defined by Equation 9 and F-Measure is defined by Equation 10 (Prabowo, & Thelwall, 2009):

$$Accuracy = \frac{Number\ of\ tweets\ correctly\ classified}{Total\ Number\ of\ tweets} \tag{7}$$

$$Precision = \frac{True\ Positive}{True\ Positive + False\ Positive} \tag{8}$$

$$Recall = \frac{True\ Positive}{True\ Positive + False\ Negative} \tag{9}$$

$$F - Measure = (2 * Precision * Recall) / (Precision + Recall) \tag{10}$$

Figure 3 shows the comparison of accuracy of Naïve Bayes, KNN(K=1), KNN(K=3), KNN(K=5), KNN(K=7), KNN(K=9) and Decision Tree.

Table 1. Results of accuracy, precision, recall, f-measure, number of tweets correctly classified and number of tweets incorrectly classified

Algorithm	Accuracy	Precision	Recall	F-Measure	Number of Tweets Correctly Classified	Number of Tweets Incorrectly Classified	Total Number of Tweets
Naïve Bayes	0.550	0.562	0.67	0.61	582824 (55.024%)	476394 (44.976 %)	
KNN (K=1)	0.557	0.623	0.41	0.49	590443 (55.7433%)	468775 (44.2567%)	
KNN (K=3)	0.577	0.619	0.51	0.56	611708 (57.7509%)	447510 (42.2491%)	
KNN (K=5)	0.585	0.616	0.57	0.59	620524 (58.5832%)	438694 (41.4168%)	1059218
KNN (K=7)	0.590	0.614	0.60	0.61	625422 (59.0456%)	433796 (40.9544%)	
KNN (K=9)	0.593	0.613	0.62	0.62	628666 (59.3519%)	430552 (40.6481%)	
Decision Tree	0.528	0.528	1.0	0.69	559826 (52.8528%)	499392 (47.1472%)	

From Figure 3, we see that the accuracy of different versions of KNN is always higher than the accuracy of Naïve Bayes and of Decision Tree. From the accuracy, we see that KNN performs better than of Naïve Bayes and better than of Decision Tree for the dataset.

Figure 4 shows the comparison of Precision of Naïve Bayes, KNN(K=1), KNN(K=3), KNN(K=5), KNN(K=7), KNN(K=9) and Decision Tree.

Figure 3. Comparison of accuracy of Naïve Bayes, KNN(K=1), KNN(K=3), KNN(K=5), KNN(K=7), KNN(K=9) and Decision Tree

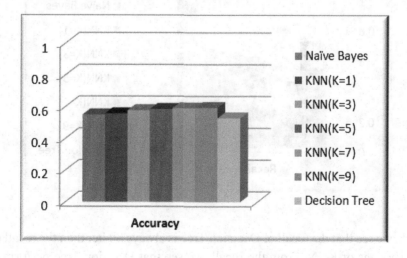

Figure 4. Comparison of precision of Naïve Bayes, KNN(K=1), KNN(K=3), KNN(K=5), KNN(K=7), KNN(K=9) and Decision Tree

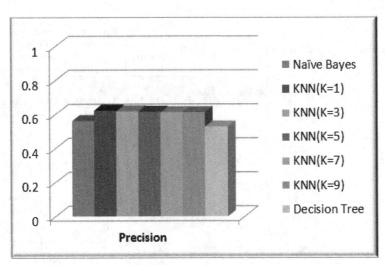

As the precision of different versions of KNN is higher of Naïve Bayes and is higher of Decision Tree (from Figure 4), we can conclude that based on precision, KNN performs better than Naïve Bayes and better than Decision Tree.

Figure 5 shows the comparison of Recall of Naïve Bayes, KNN(K=1), KNN(K=3), KNN(K=5), KNN(K=7), KNN(K=9) and Decision Tree.

Figure 5. Comparison of recall of Naïve Bayes, KNN(K=1), KNN(K=3), KNN(K=5), KNN(K=7), KNN(K=9) and Decision Tree

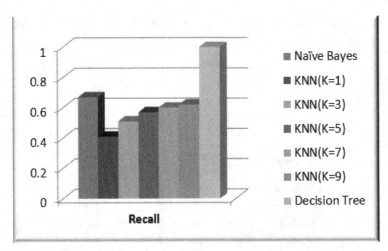

From Figure 5, we see that the recall of Decision Tree is always higher than the recall of Naïve Bayes and of different versions of KNN. From the recall, we see that Decision Tree performs better than of Naïve Bayes and performs better than of different versions of KNN.

Figure 6 shows the comparison of F-Measure of Naïve Bayes, KNN(K=1), KNN(K=3), KNN(K=5), KNN(K=7), KNN(K=9) and Decision Tree.

Figure 6. Comparison of F-Measure of Naïve Bayes, KNN(K=1), KNN(K=3), KNN(K=5), KNN(K=7), KNN(K=9) and Decision Tree

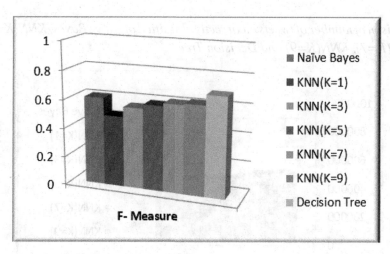

As the F-Measure of Decision Tree is higher of Naïve Bayes and is higher of different versions of KNN (Figure 6), we can conclude that based on F-Measure, Decision Tree performs better than Naïve Bayes and performs better than of different versions of KNN.

Figure 7 shows the comparison of Number of tweets correctly classified of Naïve Bayes, KNN(K=1), KNN(K=3), KNN(K=5), KNN(K=7), KNN(K=9) and Decision Tree.

Figure 7. Comparison of number of tweets correctly classified of Naïve Bayes, KNN(K=1), KNN(K=3), KNN(K=5), KNN(K=7), KNN(K=9) and Decision Tree

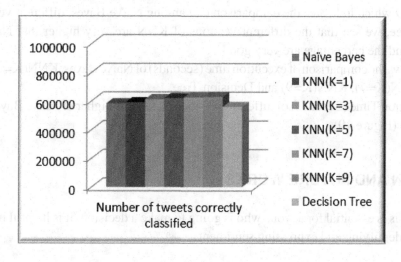

From Figure 7, we see that the Number of tweets correctly classified of different versions of KNN is always higher than the accuracy of Naïve Bayes and of Decision Tree. From the Number of tweets correctly classified, we see that KNN performs better than of Naïve Bayes and better than of Decision Tree.

Figure 8 shows the comparison of Number of tweets incorrectly classified of Naïve Bayes, KNN(K=1), KNN(K=3), KNN(K=5), KNN(K=7), KNN(K=9) and Decision Tree.

Figure 8. Comparison of number of tweets incorrectly classified of Naïve Bayes, KNN(K=1), KNN(K=3), KNN(K=5), KNN(K=7), KNN(K=9) and Decision Tree

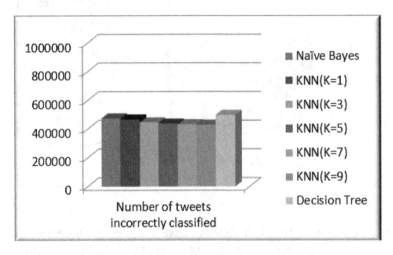

As the Number of tweets incorrectly classified of Decision Tree is higher of Naïve Bayes and is higher of different versions of KNN (Figure 8), we can conclude that based on Number of tweets incorrectly classified, the different versions of KNN and Naïve Bayes performs better than Decision Tree.

Figure 9 shows the comparison of number of tweets correctly classified (%) and number of tweets incorrectly classified (%) of Naïve Bayes, KNN(K=1), KNN(K=3), KNN(K=5), KNN(K=7), KNN(K=9) and Decision Tree.

From Figure 9 which indicates the comparison (%) among Naïve Bayes, different versions of KNN and Decision Tree, we see that the different versions of KNN are very higher that Naïve Bayes and Decision Tree, and the percentage are very good.

Figure 10 shows the comparison of execution time (seconds) of Naïve Bayes, KNN(K=1), KNN(K=3), KNN(K=5), KNN(K=7), KNN(K=9) and Decision Tree.

As the Execution Time (Seconds) of different versions of KNN is higher of Naïve Bayes and is higher of Decision Tree (Figure 10).

CONCLUSION AND FUTURE WORKS

Sentiment analysis is essential for anyone who is going to make a decision. It is helpful in different field for calculating, identifying and expressing sentiment.

Figure 9. Comparison of number of tweets correctly classified (%) and number of tweets incorrectly classified (%) of Naïve Bayes, KNN(K=1), KNN(K=3), KNN(K=5), KNN(K=7), KNN(K=9) and Decision Tree

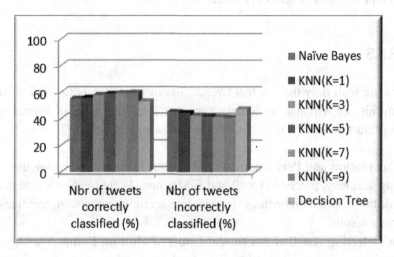

Figure 10. Comparison of execution time (seconds) of Naïve Bayes, KNN(K=1), KNN(K=3), KNN(K=5), KNN(K=7), KNN(K=9) and Decision Tree

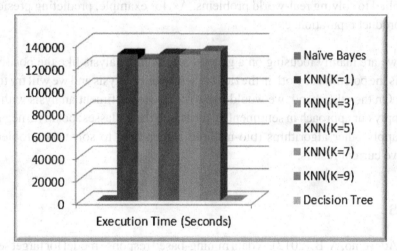

Sentiment analysis based on micro-blogging is still in the developing stage and far from complete. As an example a positive sentiment is "It is a nice Day!" and a negative sentiment is "it is a horrible day!". In this paper, we will try to find out the positive and negative sentiment on Twitter data.

In this paper, we compared three algorithms Naïve Bayes, different versions of KNN (K=1, K=3, K=5, K=7 and K=9) and Decision Tree on 1059218 tweets. The experimental results show that the Decision Tree approach, giving above 90% accuracy and recall than the Naïve Bayes approach and the different versions of KNN approach.

And show that the different versions of KNN approach, giving above 80% precision and Number of tweets correctly classified than the Naïve Bayes approach and Decision Tree approach.

And finally show that the Decision Tree approach, giving above 85% F-Measure than the Naïve Bayes approach and different versions of KNN approach.

FUTURE WORKS

In this paper, we work with only the English tweets. So our next plan is to work with other language tweets. Apart from this, we will also try to detect another sentiment label of human being. From this, we can say that our future works list may contain the following actions:

- **Accuracy Calculation and Performance Evaluation:** In current work, we use confusion matrix for calculating accuracy, precision recall and F-Measure. In future Apply others algorithms (metaheuristics or bio-inspired algorithms) to calculate accuracy, precision, recall and F-Measure, to improve current results;
- **Focusing on Detecting Another Sentiment Label of Human Being:** We only work with positive and negative sentiment label. We will extend our work to consider other sentiment labels (Neutral);
- **Working With Real World Problems:** Given an efficient sentiment label, we will try to see how it can be applied to solving real-world problems. As, for example, predicting presidential election, estimating product reputation, etc.

In this paper, we are mainly focusing on a general sentiment analysis like the positive and negative sentiment. There is the potential of work in the field of sentiment analysis and we will try to use our knowledge in this field. On the other hand, we would like to compare sentiment analysis with other domains.

In the future apply our approach in sentiment analysis into three classes: positive, negative and neural.

And Finally, apply other algorithms (bio-inspired algorithms) to solve the problem of sentiment analysis to improve current results.

REFERENCES

Ayetiran, E. F., & Adeyemo, A. B. (2012). A data mining-based response model for target selection in direct marketing. *IJ Information Technology and Computer Science*, *1*(1), 9–18. doi:10.5815/ijitcs.2012.01.02

Balahur, A., Steinberger, R., Kabadjov, M., Zavarella, V., Van Der Goot, E., Halkia, M., . . . Belyaeva, J. (2013). *Sentiment analysis in the news*. arXiv preprint arXiv:1309.6202.

Chang, V., & Ramachandran, M. (2016). Towards achieving data security with the cloud computing adoption framework. *IEEE Transactions on Services Computing*, *9*(1), 138–151. doi:10.1109/TSC.2015.2491281

Fan, W., Wallace, L., Rich, S., & Zhang, Z. (2006). Tapping the power of text mining. *Communications of the ACM*, *49*(9), 76–82. doi:10.1145/1151030.1151032

Feldman, R. (2013). Techniques and applications for sentiment analysis. *Communications of the ACM*, *56*(4), 82–89. doi:10.1145/2436256.2436274

Garnes, Ø. L. (2009). *Feature selection for text categorization* (Master's thesis). Institutt for datateknikk og informasjonsvitenskap.

Go, A., Bhayani, R., & Huang, L. (2009). Twitter sentiment classification using distant supervision. CS224N project report, Stanford, 1(12), 2009.

Jotheeswaran, J., & Koteeswaran, S. (2015). Decision tree based feature selection and multilayer perceptron for sentiment analysis. *Journal of Engineering and Applied Sciences (Asian Research Publishing Network)*, *10*(14), 5883–5894.

Kalaivani, P., & Shunmuganathan, K. L. (2013). Sentiment classification of movie reviews by supervised machine learning approaches. *Indian Journal of Computer Science and Engineering*, *4*(4), 285–292.

Karyotis, C., Doctor, F., Iqbal, R., James, A., & Chang, V. (2018). A fuzzy computational model of emotion for cloud based sentiment analysis. *Information Sciences*, *433*, 448–463. doi:10.1016/j.ins.2017.02.004

Kiritchenko, S., Zhu, X., & Mohammad, S. M. (2014). Sentiment analysis of short informal texts. *Journal of Artificial Intelligence Research*, *50*, 723–762. doi:10.1613/jair.4272

Liu, B. (2011). Opinion mining and sentiment analysis. In *Web Data Mining* (pp. 459–526). Springer. doi:10.1007/978-3-642-19460-3_11

Melucci, M. (2015). *Introduction to information retrieval and quantum mechanics*. Springer Berlin Heidelberg. doi:10.1007/978-3-662-48313-8

Modha, J. S., Pandi, G. S., & Modha, S. J. (2013). Automatic sentiment analysis for unstructured data. *International Journal of Advanced Research in Computer Science and Software Engineering*, *3*(12), 91–97.

Nazief, B., & Adriani, M. (1996). *Confix Stripping: Approach to Stemming Algorithm for Bahasa Indonesia. Internal publication.* Faculty of Computer Science, University of Indonesia.

Pak, A., & Paroubek, P. (2010). Twitter as a corpus for sentiment analysis and opinion mining. In *LREc* (Vol. 10, pp. 1320–1326). No. May.

Prabowo, R., & Thelwall, M. (2009). Sentiment analysis: A combined approach. *Journal of Informetrics*, *3*(2), 143–157. doi:10.1016/j.joi.2009.01.003

Pratama, B. Y., & Sarno, R. (2015). Personality classification based on Twitter text using Naive Bayes, KNN and SVM. In *2015 International Conference on Data and Software Engineering (ICoDSE)* (pp. 170-174). IEEE. 10.1109/ICODSE.2015.7436992

Rambocas, M., & Gama, J. (2013). *Marketing research: The role of sentiment analysis* (No. 489). Universidade do Porto, Faculdade de Economia do Porto.

Read, J. (2005, June). Using emoticons to reduce dependency in machine learning techniques for sentiment classification. In *Proceedings of the ACL student research workshop* (pp. 43-48). 10.3115/1628960.1628969

Suresh, A., & Bharathi, C. R. (2016). Sentiment classification using decision tree based feature selection. *IJCTA*, *9*(36), 419–425.

Vanitha, V., Sumathi, V. P., & Soundariya, V. (2018). An Exploratory Data Analysis of Movie Review Dataset. *International Journal of Recent Technology and Engineering*, *7*(4S), 380–384.

Vo, D. T., & Zhang, Y. (2015). Target-dependent twitter sentiment classification with rich automatic features. *Twenty-Fourth International Joint Conference on Artificial Intelligence*.

Whissell, C. (2009). Using the revised dictionary of affect in language to quantify the emotional undertones of samples of natural language. *Psychological Reports*, *105*(2), 509–521. doi:10.2466/PR0.105.2.509-521 PMID:19928612

Wilson, T., Wiebe, J., & Hoffmann, P. (2009). Recognizing contextual polarity: An exploration of features for phrase-level sentiment analysis. *Computational Linguistics*, *35*(3), 399–433. doi:10.1162/coli.08-012-R1-06-90

Zhang, L., Ghosh, R., Dekhil, M., Hsu, M., & Liu, B. (2011). *Combining lexicon-based and learning-based methods for Twitter sentiment analysis*. HP Laboratories. *Technical Report HPL, 2011*, 89.

This research was previously published in the International Journal of Organizational and Collective Intelligence (IJOCI), 10(4); pages 35-49, copyright year 2020 by IGI Publishing (an imprint of IGI Global).

Chapter 31
Method to Rank Academic Institutes by the Sentiment Analysis of Their Online Reviews

Simran Sidhu
Central University of Punjab, India

Surinder Singh Khurana
Central University of Punjab, India

ABSTRACT

A large number of reviews are expressed on academic institutes using the online review portals and other social media platforms. Such reviews are a good potential source for evaluating the Indian academic institutes. This chapter aimed to collect and analyze the sentiments of the online reviews of the academic institutes and ranked the institutes on the basis of their garnered online reviews. Lexical-based sentiment analysis of their online reviews is used to rank academic institutes. Then these rankings were compared with the NIRF PR Overall University Rankings List 2017. The outcome of this work can efficiently support the overall university rankings of the NIRF ranking list to enhance NIRF's public perception parameter (PRPUB). The results showed that Panjab University achieved the highest sentiment score, which was followed by BITS-Pilani. The results highlighted that there is a significant gap between NIRF's perception rankings and the perception of the public in general regarding an academic institute as expressed in online reviews.

INTRODUCTION

A sentiment (Kaur and Solanki, 2018) in generic terms refers to a feeling, an attitude, an opinion or an emotion expressed by a person. Sentiments cannot be termed as facts as they may vary from person to person. Hence, sentiments can be labeled as subjective impressions. Having given a text written by a

DOI: 10.4018/978-1-6684-6303-1.ch031

person we need to understand the sentiment that it conveys. This comprises of sentiment analysis. Sentiment analysis is also referred to as opinion mining. Sentiment analysis being an interdisciplinary field of study covers various fields like artificial intelligence, text mining and natural language processing.

In today's digital age, online reviews, comments and critiques about various entities like consumer product reviews, movie reviews, tweets, university reviews and college reviews are found on numerous web portals. Sentiment analysis is the process of extracting sentiment from the text. The text can be in the form of online customer reviews, Tweets, blogs, news clips or any piece of text that people write to express their opinions about varied things or even about populist events. These reviews that are written by the public express opinions about the aforementioned articles and hence they help in swaying the mind of a new user in buying or rejecting a product. Sentiment analysis deals with understanding the sentiments behind those reviews..

Given the wide range of review websites available online, we needed a method to make sense of these vast available online review data of the Indian academic institutes. This required a method that could automatically analyze the sentiments of the reviews and thus help the students in making a conscious decision about the choice of institute they should join for further study. This method can efficiently augment the rankings as ranked by the NIRF and help it in adding to it the real sentiments of the people regarding an academic institute over a longer period of time. This research aimed to analyze and perceive the online reviews of the various different Indian academic institutes collected from a wide range of online review portals of universities and colleges. The data was analyzed by text categorization tools, natural language processing tools and the sentiment analysis approaches to determine the sentiment of people towards a particular academic institute of India. The results of which were used to rank the academic institutes. Furthermore, these ranks shall be compared with the yearly standardized rankings of the institutes that are issued annually NIRF namely, the NIRF Rankings 2017.

According to a review of research on Sentiment analysis as of 2017 (Mäntylä, et. al., 2018), Sentiment analysis is a field of research that is one of the fastest growing fields in computer science.

But, most of the work done in the field of sentiment analysis has been in context with social media like Twitter, Facebook and other domains of micro blogging which express movie and product reviews. Little has been done in the application of sentiment analysis to the reviews posted about the academic institutes like universities and colleges of India. This online data comprising of university and college reviews that is available on multiple websites needs to be harnessed to its full potential so that the public opinion and perception about these academic institutes of India comes to the fore.

SENTIMENT ANALYSIS USING SEMANTIC ANALYSIS APPROACH

In this approach a predefined lexicon/dictionary is used. This lexicon is full of words that have already been assigned a polarity value i.e. some words have been assigned negative polarity values while the others have been assigned positive polarity values. Firstly, pre-processing tools are applied on the text that we want to analyze and these tools segregate the full text into words/tokens after the initial pre-processing steps. These pre-processing steps comprise of normalization of the text with lemmatization and stemming of the text. After the whole of the text has been converted into words/tokens these are matched with the entries of the lexicon. If a match is found of that word in the lexicon, then the polarity values are assigned to each of these words. Then the aggregate polarity of the whole text is ascertained by adding up the polarity values of the words that comprise the text.

Figure 1. showing the popularity of sentiment analysis based upon worldwide searches on Google from 2004 to 2017

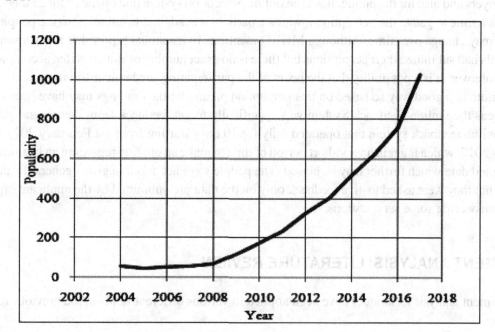

INDIAN INSTITUTE RANKINGS FRAMEWORK

National Institutional Ranking Framework (NIRF) is an MHRD ranking framework that ranks the all the major Indian educational institutes annually based on five major parameters. It was first launched by MHRD in September 2015 and the first ranking list was released in April 2016. The second rankings list was released for 2017 which included the same five major parameters but there were some changes made regarding the sub parameters.

Parameters Used for NIRF Ranking:

The five major parameters and their subsequent underlying parameters that the NIRF ranking system used to assign a rank to the Institute were the following:

1. Teaching, Learning and Resources
2. Research and Professional Practice
3. Graduation Outcomes
4. Outreach and Inclusivity
5. Perception: Peer Perception: Employers and Research Investors (PREMP), Peer Perception: Academics (PRACD),
6. Public Perception (PRPUB), Competitiveness (PRCMP)

Focusing mainly on the fifth parameter 'Perception' involved in the NIRF ranking framework we see that the data collected by MHRD in this field was mainly done by the following two methods: online perception system and the online feedback system. The Online Perception System was open for the peers, the employers and also for the public. It was an online perception system that operated for 23 days, which is too less a time to gauge the perception towards a particular academic institute. Also the people's perceptions may change over time. Although MHRD mentions in its annual report that a large number of individuals had submitted their perceptions but there is no exact number or statistics that accompany this claim. Moreover, it is a possibility that the peers of the participating academic institutes perceived their own institute in a good way so based on this perception parameter the rankings may have been biased.

Whereas the Online Feedback System was specifically to get feedback from the general public; it was an online feedback system that operated only for 10 days starting from 1st February 2017 to 12th February 2017, which is again a very short period of time to make an opinion regarding an institute based upon limited data which further may be biased. The people were not asked to give a general feedback or a review but they were asked to give feedback only on the data pre-submitted by the applicant organizations by answering some set questions.

SENTIMENT ANALYSIS: LITERATURE REVIEW

The sentiment analysis techniques have been applied in various different fields in the previous research works:

All the known word net methods and approaches that were used to develop them were formulated in 1990, under a study (Miller et.al, 1990). It included word nets in various languages from around the world. It summarized the word net methods.

A comparison of the different sentiment analysis techniques was presented (MD, Sunitha& Ganesh, 2016). It compared and analyzed the Machine learning approach, Rule Based sentiment analysis approach and the Lexical Based sentiment analysis approach. It demonstrated that using each of these approaches of sentiment analysis would yield different results. Comparing the accuracy, performance and efficiency of these three approaches it concluded that the machine learning approach provided the best overall results surpassing the Rule based approach and the Lexical based approach. It further analyzed the various machine learning approaches used in sentiment analysis such as Support Vector Machine (SVM), N-gram Sentiment Analysis, Naïve Bayes (NB) method, Maximum Entropy (ME) Classifier, k-Nearest Neighbors (kNN) Method, Weighted kNN method, Multilingual sentiment analysis, Feature driven sentiment analysis. Upon considering the advantages and disadvantages of these approaches it was concluded that SVM method works best when the training set is vast and the NB approach is efficient only for a small training set. Max Entropy is a computationally complex approach but can handle vast datasets whereas Feature driven SA is not efficient for small datasets. The kNN approach is demonstrated as a computationally efficient approach. Multilingual SA is specifically used when the dataset comprises of different languages and can handle up to 15 different languages.

Sentiment analysis has been extensively used for the micro-blogging website Twitter. One of the earliest popular works in this field was attempted using distant supervision technique (Go, Bhayani &Huang, 2009). The tweets were classified as positive and negative based on the happy or sad emoticons used in the tweets. The research demonstrated that the SVM and NB classifiers were the most efficient and readily beat the MaxEnt classifier.

Using the same technique of distant supervision technique but additionally adding the neutral class for tweets based on the emoticons (Pak & Paroubek, 2010). Hence, a three-way classification of tweets was performed. TreeTagger was used over tweets collected related specifically to news for POS-tagging. The classifier used was SVM, CRF and the multinomial NB classifier. The multinomial NB classifier yielded the best performance. Comparing the unigram approach, bigram approach and the trigram approach they received the highest performance with the bigram approach as the bigrams provided the requisite balance between the unigrams and the trigrams. The unigram approach provided the best requisite coverage whereas the trigram approach provided the best capturing of the sentiment expression, so the bigram approach provided the requisite mix of the two approaches giving the best performance.

Sentiment analysis on movie review data was presented and the classification was done based on SVM, NB and Maximum Entropy Classifier (Pang, Le & Vaithyanathan, 2002) using the movie reviews dataset collected from IMDB. It uses a three-fold cross validation scheme. Feature selection was based on the unigram and the bigram approach. SVM emerged as the best classification algorithm and NB fared the worst. Also the unigram approach performed better than the bigram approach in capturing the sentiment of the reviews.

Sentiment analysis of movie reviews was carried out using labeled movie reviews from IMDB (Sokolov Aleksey, 2015). It specifically aimed at analyzing the quality of the word to vector representation which is used in sentiment analysis. The most accurate results were yielded by using the random forest algorithm in combination with the tf-idf model while using the random forest approach with the bag of words approach was the least accurate. It was concluded that this accuracy primarily depended upon the methods that are used for feature extraction.

Sentiment analysis of movie reviews using the Naïve Bayes model and the n-grams method was carried out. Also a novel optimized version of the Naïve Byes Model was proposed (Uan Sholanbayev, 2016). Using the trigram approach yielded an accuracy of 74% whereas while using the trigram and the bigram approach together, the accuracy levels fluctuated around 78% and could not reach the level of precision that it was expected to reach. Using the basic Naïve Byes Model yielded elevated the accuracy up to 82%. The optimized version of the basic Naïve Bayes model used a filtering operation that filtered out the redundant data keeping only the informative text of the movie reviews passing out its output to the machine learning classifier that worked in the same way as the basic version did. Naïve Bayes's way of assigning the same weights to all the features works against it and hence to have an increased degree of accuracy in NB the weights should be assigned differently to different features.

An in-depth comparison of the three popular machine learning classifiers for the classification of movie review data was presented (Cheng-Tao, Takahashi &Wang, 2017). The three machine learning classifiers used for the study were Maximum Entropy (MaxEnt), Support Vector Machine (SVM) and the Decision Tree (DT). The movie review data used was the same as that used by Pang, Le & Vaithyanathan (2002). Taking the 1000 positive and 1000 negative reviews of movies, POS (Parts-of-Speech) Tagging was applied on it, from which further the features were extracted. The two feature selection algorithms used were: Fisher Score and the Singular Value Decomposition (SVD). The experiments conducted on the data to find the sentiment of the reviews used a combination of the two feature selection methods and the three machine learning classifiers. In all the cases the accuracy of classification of reviews was always higher for positive reviews than the negative ones. Also when fewer features are selected the classification accuracy of the positive reviews improves while at the same time the accuracy levels of the negative reviews degrade. Overall the MaxEnt classifier classification accuracy was 82.6% while the SVM stood at the same accuracy of 82.6% when 28680 features are used. The DTs performed rather poorly with an accuracy of 61.1%.

A novel method that is adaptable and used a fine grained approach was used to generate summary of the Naver movies dataset (Amplayo & Song, 2017). This approach proved that using natural language processing in conjunction with the machine learning procedures yielded better results than using a single-level classifier. It uses a word n-gram SVM classifier and a character n-gram SVM classifier approach for using multilevel sentiment classification. The classifier tool they use outperforms the LingPipe classifier, the Standford Core NLP and also the ASUM classifier. The ASUM classifier fared lowly because it uses short review texts only which are not effective in judging the sentiment analysis of a text. The novel classification method used is an adaptable sentiment extraction algorithm as it can be used over datasets in different languages and across different domains. It uses multiple datasets like the Rotten Tomatoes dataset for English movies, the Amazon movie reviews dataset also for English movies, the Douban dataset for Chinese movies and the Naver dataset for Korean movies. It further ranks the movies based on the reviews collected from the Naver dataset and compares these ranks with the ranks obtained by the same movie in the Blue Dragon Film Awards. It demonstrated that the movies that won awards were also the ones that got a higher score based on aspect sentiment.

Research on sentiment analysis in Hindi has also been carried out successfully (Narayan et. al., 2002) was the first step towards developing a Hindi Senti Word Net. The Indo-word net was though nascent in its approach paved a way for further study in developing a proper Hindi Senti word net. Karthikeyan et al. in their 2010 thesis for IIT Bombay, proposed an efficient way of English-Hindi WordNet Linking.

A Fall-back Strategy for Sentiment Analysis in Hindi was proposed (Joshi et al. in 2010). Taking inspiration from the English SentiWordNet, this research built the first version of H-SWN (Hindi-SentiWordNet). It used two known lexical resources for building the same. The two resources were the existing English SentiWordNet and along with it, it also made use of the English-Hindi WordNet Linking developed (Karthikeyan et al). Making use of this WordNet linking the words in the existing English SentiWordNet were successfully replaced with their equivalent Hindi words. The result was the first Hindi SentiWordNet (H-SWN). This paper paved the way for research in Hindi sentiment analysis. This research work was the first one known for sentiment analysis in Hindi language.

Other English sentiment analysis approaches include, a sentiment topic recognition model called the STR Model was presented to compute the Air Quality Rating (AQR) of three major airline companies namely, AirTran Airways, Frontier and SkyWest Airlines (Adeborna &Siau, 2014). This model was based on the algorithm called Variational Expectation-Maximization (VEM) and also on Correlated Topics Models (CTM). The AQR was calculated per 1000 tweets. Because of the limited number of tweets used the results were of a commendable accuracy.

A paper which focused on analyzing the Twitter data for the sentiment analysis and opinion mining of the tweets about the airlines of the United States of America was presented (Yuan, Zhong, & Uang, 2015). The dataset comprised of 14640 tweets which were split into 80% and 20% for training and testing respectively. For each of the tweets, n-grams of each of the letters were taken and the words of the tweets were used as features. These features were stored in a sparse matrix. Four approaches were further used namely, Lexicon-based Sentiment Classification, Multinomial Naïve Bayes (Multinomial NB), Linear Support Vector Machine (Linear SVM), Convolutional Neural Networks (CNN)(Pandey and Solanki, 2019). The overall accuracy for the sentiment classification task was highest for Linear SVM at 0.796, Convolutional Neural Networks stood at an accuracy level of 0.790. Multinomial Naïve Bayes achieved an accuracy of 0.712 and the Lexicon based approach achieved an accuracy of 0.652. Here, Multinomial Naïve Bayes runs faster than SVM due to its inherent model simplicity.

Sentiment analysis has been applied to the feedback of the airline passengers that has been obtained from the airline forum (Venu, Annie & Mohan, 2016).The machine learning algorithms that are used are Linear Support Vector and Multinomial Naïve Bayes. The dataset used for training the same include 1217 reviews that are positive in nature and 955 reviews that are negative in nature. The testing dataset comprises of 868 reviews. The outcomes of the study are represented in the form of a bar graph. Linear Support Vector model yielded an accuracy of 88.59% and the Multinomial Naïve Bayes model fared slightly lower than the Linear Support Vector model, with an accuracy of 84.56%. The study also presented the runtime analysis of the two models with runtime in seconds. Overall in terms of accuracy levels the Linear Support Vector fared better than Multinomial Naïve Bayes but based on the runtime results it was concluded that Multinomial Naïve Bayes fared better than the Linear Support Vector model.

Twitter data pertaining to the Indian election was analyzed to see the effect the micro blogging website Twitter has on the way the elections in the Indian states and the whole nation turns out (Wani & Alone, 2015). The main election tweets that this model analyzed was the Maharashtra state assembly election. The proposed model makes use of trend and volume analysis in addition to the sentiment analysis of the tweets. Firstly the tweets are cleaned by using the Porter Stemmer algorithm then the tweets are clustered using the K-Means Clustering algorithm then finally the Naive Bayes algorithm is used to do the three way sentiment classification of tweets as negative, positive and neutral tweets. The hash tag based tweet count was also graphically analyzed.

An analysis of the Twitter network pertaining to the 2014 Indian election was carried out (Lu, Shah, & Kulshrestha, 2014). Each of the 15.5 million user accounts that were analyzed were taken as nodes in the network. The followers of these accounts were taken as the edges of the network and these were up to 5000 for each of the nodes under study. The total tweet dataset comprised of 10,595,729 tweets which is approximately 7GB of data. The sentiment analysis of these showed that the NDA, the party that won the 2014 election had very less negative tweets compared to its arch rival UPA. The volume of tweets increased substantially in the months proceeding to the election with April and May having a chunk of the tweets. A new algorithm was devised using the augmented contagion model. Retweet analysis and the Supporter Strength analysis was also carried out to reach the final outcome. The final outcome of NDA against every metric was far above the UPA ones which ultimately led to the win of the NDA against the UPA.

A review paper regarding the various techniques used in predicting the outcome of the elections was presented (Salunkhe, Surnar, &Sonawane, 2017). The various strategies discussed in the outline of the paper were ideological learning via the political tweets, user graph analysis, linguistic behavior, re-tweeting trends etc. Overall this paper gave a bird's eye view of the trends in election prediction via Twitter.

An application of sentiment analysis to classify the users as pessimists or optimists based on their IMDB comments was proposed (Garcia-Cumbreras, Montejo-Raez and Diaz-Galiano, 2013). It advocates for the improvement of the sentiment analysis by looking for similarities between the user's comments and the entire user community in general. This approach is particularly useful for sentiment analysis based recommendation systems. It generates a new corpus from the Internet Movie Database (IMDB) comprising of 80,848 movie opinions based on the user critical comments and ratings and categorizes all the users based on their comments into two classes; as optimists or pessimists and then performs experiments on how these can be used efficiently in collaborative filtering methods by combining them with opinion mining approaches. The approaches used were SVM and kNN. The kNN approach used the Euclidean distance. 10-fold cross validation using stratified sampling technique along with the Root Mean Square Error (RMSE) and the Mean Square Error (MSE) estimators were used for evaluation.

It was demonstrated that SVM approach clearly improves upon the kNN approach. A more accurate result was obtained when only the users were classified as pessimists or optimists and the predication of the sentiment when these user orientations were applied to the whole community in general resulted in lesser accuracy.

A fine grained social analytics fuzzy ontology methodology on the customer reviews was adopted (Lau, Li & Liao, 2014). This methodology used a semi-supervised fuzzy learning approach for the fine grained extraction instead of the coarse-grained extraction used previously. The approach used for sentiment analysis is context sensitive and it does not presume that the polarity of a text can only be two fold or it can be same for all different product domains. A seven step LDA based aspect oriented sentiment analysis methodology was applied to the customer's product reviews to gauge the product ontology automatically. It also provided an extension of the LingPipe to make way for a novel Gibbs approach that was used as a sampling algorithm using a WD (Word Divergence) measure to measure the strength of polarity of the words occurring in the customer reviews. ProdOntLearn was the novel algorithm developed that computationally facilitated the learning of the product ontology automatically based on the customer review corpus in this proposed OBPRM system.

Sentiment analysis for evaluating the German Universities using Twitter was presented (Tummel, &Richert, 2015). 16488 tweets pertaining to nine German Universities were collected for the duration of one semester via the Twitter API. Out of these 5000 randomly chosen tweets were then segregated into positive and not positive tweets and were fed into the NB classifier which gave an accuracy of 73.6%. A Python script using the NLTK library was used to create a tool to rank the nine Institutes based on the percentage of positive and not positive Twitter reviews. The word frequency analysis was also carried out which showed the most frequently used words in the university tweets.

INSTITUTION RANKING: AN APPLICATION OF SENTIMENT ANALYSIS

Sentiment analysis was applied to know the tone of the online reviews. The steps of the methodology that were used to perform the sentiment analysis on the online reviews of the selected academic institutes of India were as follows:

1. Designed a dataset comprising of the Institute review corpus of fifteen academic institutes of India.
2. Preprocessed the reviews.
3. Performed the sentiment analysis of the initially processed reviews.
4. Ranked the institutes according to the sentiment score of their garnered reviews.
5. Compared and analyzed the rankings as obtained by the method with the rankings of the Institutes as per NIRF rankings of 2017.

Phases of Methodology

The technique used for performing the sentiment analysis of the academic institutes was the lexicon based sentiment analysis. The Lexical based technique of sentiment analysis was chosen over the machine based technique because the review dataset was not a balanced one i.e. it contained more of positive reviews than the negative ones.

Phase 1: Data Collection: In phase 1, the datasets comprising of the reviews of the academic institutes were created. The academic institutes chosen for the research were the ones that featured in the top 100 overall ranking list of NIRF 2017. Firstly, the institute whose ranks were a multiple of three was picked. Their reviews were searched online. If sufficient number of their reviews were available then that institute was chosen, if not so, then the next one in the list was chosen. Hence, the institutes with their ranks that were chosen for the study were, IISc Bangalore (Rank 1), IIT-Bombay (Rank 3), JNU Delhi (Rank 6), IIT-Roorkee (Rank 9), Jadavpur University (Rank 12) was skipped along with ranks 13, Anna University and rank 14, University of Hyderabad as not a wide variety of their reviews were available online, so University of Delhi (Rank 15) was the next to be picked. Rank 18, Savitribai Phule Pune University again didn't have many reviews online, so it was skipped and rank 19, Aligarh Muslim University was chosen. Rank 21, BITS-Pilani was chosen next. The other universities that were randomly chosen pertained to the availability of many reviews regarding them online as in, IIM-Ahmedabad (Rank 17), Vellore Institute of Technology (Rank 22), IIM-Bangalore (Rank 25), Osmania University (Rank 38), Panjab University (Rank 54), ISM-Dhanbad (Rank 53), Thapar University (Rank 75), NIT-Warangal (Rank 82). All these ranking were from the Overall Rankings list of NIRF 2017.Approximately three hundred reviews per institute were collected for seven universities and for the rest of the eight institutes approximately two hundred reviews per institute were collected. Total reviews collected were 3695 reviews.

Phase 2: Data Analysis of the Collected Data Sets: Data analysis was performed on the collected reviews to know the length of the reviews for each institute. Maximum, minimum and average length of the reviews of each institute was calculated depending on the number of words contained in each of those reviews. The average and the maximum length of the reviews were gathered in a tabular form.

Phase 3: Manual Annotation of the Reviews: Each of the 3695 collected reviews were read and analyzed and tagged (annotated) manually as ''Pos'' or ''Neg'' considering whether they were positive or negative reviews. This manual annotation was done so that the annotation done by the method can be compared with the manual annotation and checked for its accuracy.

Phase 4: Initial Pre-processing of the Review Data: Phase 3 involved writing a script in Python langauge that performs the initial preprocessing of the collected reviews. The script performed all the three initial preprocessing steps on each of the reviews..

Phase 5: NLTK Processing of the Reviews: After all the reviews had been initial pre-processed, the next step involved using the Natural Language Tool Kit (NLTK) of Python for the pre-processing of the reviews. All the three of the most popular NLTK pre-processing steps were carried out in this *work*, namely:

  ◦ Tokenization of the Reviews
  ◦ Lemmatization
  ◦ Parts-of-Speech (POS) tagging of the words contained in the Reviews

Phase 6: Tagging and Calculating the Sentiment Score of the Reviews: The same NLTK script also comprised of the code to get the Sentiment Score for each of the Reviews and for the tagging of the reviews. The reviews were tagged by the Python script as 'Pos' (Positive) or 'Neg' (Negative Review) depending upon their Sentiment Scores. The sentiment scores were calculated based on the synsets of the words contained in the review. After the sentiment score of the review was computed by the method, further the tagging of the reviews was done based on the total sentiment score that the review has gained. The reviews were annotated with a Positive tag or a Negative tag depending on the sentiment score of the review.

The lexical resource used for the sentiment analysis was SentiWordNet 3.0 (Baccianella et. al. 2010) which has automatically annotated all the possible WordNet synsets in three categories namely, their degree of neutrality, positivity and their degree of negativity.

Phase 7: Ranking the Academic Institutes: The sentiment scores of all the reviews of any particular institute were added to get their cumulative effect. Then the total sentiment score was divided by the total number of reviews of that particular institute to get the sentiment score per review. The academic institutes were then ranked based on the sentiment scores per review.

Phase 8: Comparing the Ranks of the Institutes with NIRF Ranks: The ranks of the academic institutes based on their sentiment scores were compared to the ranks garnered by the academic institutes in the NIRF overall university rankings list 2017.

Phase 9: Analyzing the results: The ranks of the academic institutes based on their sentiment scores were compared to the average length of the reviews and also only the sentiment scores of the uniform Google reviews were compared.

Phase 10: Documenting the Results: Each and every result pertaining to each phase of the *work* was documented accordingly.

PARAMETERS RECORDED

The parameters that were recorded were:

1. Total Number of Positively Tagged Reviews by the method
2. Total Number of Negatively Tagged Reviews by the method
3. Sentiment Scores of each of the reviews as computed by the method
4. Total Sentiment Score of the Academic Institute, which was the additive effect of all the sentiment scores of all the reviews pertaining to an academic institute.
5. Total correctly annotated reviews by the Method: The annotated reviews by the method were compared to the manually annotated reviews to check the total number of correctly annotated reviews by the method
6. Total number of incorrectly annotated reviews by the Method: The annotated reviews by the method were compared to the manually annotated reviews to check the total number of incorrectly annotated reviews by the method
7. Finally the accuracy of the sentiment analysis method was computed as per the formula: Accuracy of the Sentiment Analysis method for each institute = (Correctly Annotated Reviews / Total Number of Reviews of that academic institute) * 100

SOFTWARE TOOLS USED

- Python software: Python Version 3.5.4 Release Date: 2017-08-08 (Freeware)
- Natural language toolkit: NLTK Version 3.2.5 (Freeware)
- SentiWordNet Version 3.0 (Freeware)
- MS Office (Pre-packaged in the Windows OS)

RESULTS

Online reviews pertaining to fifteen academic institutes were collected. These fifteen academic universities were the ones that featured in the Overall Rankings top 100 list of NIRF 2017. Out of those 100 academic institutes, only those institutes were chosen whose reviews were readily available online. Approximately 300 reviews per institute were collected for seven academic institutes and approximately 200 reviews per institute were collected for the other eight institutes as in Table 1. The reviews collected were stored in excel spreadsheets.

Table 1. Number of reviews collected of each academic institute

Sr. No.	Academic Institute	Total Number of Reviews Collected
1	IIT-Bombay	300
2	IISc Bangalore	300
3	IIM-Ahmedabad	299
4	BITS-Pilani	300
5	JNU Delhi	300
6	IIM-Bangalore	199
7	Vellore Institue of Technology (VIT)	200
8	IIT-Roorkee	299
9	Delhi University	300
10	Panjab University	200
11	Aligarh Muslim University	200
12	Thapar University	200
13	Osmania University	200
14	ISM Dhanbad	200
15	NIT-Warangal	198
	Total Reviews	**3695**

The review data for the *work* was collected manually from varied online review portals as in Table 2. The 3695 reviews that were collected were primarily Google Reviews The total number of reviews that were collected was 3695 reviews, which comprised of 2674 Google Reviews i.e. approximately 72% of the reviews used in this study were Google Reviews. Google reviews were shorter in length as compared to the reviews from other online review portals like Glassdoor and Careers 360. The reviews were collected from twelve online review portals Table 2.

In, Table 3, the number of reviews collected from each of the different websites pertaining to each of the different academic institutes is tabulated. As can be seen in Table 3, in case of each of the academic institutes, the most number of reviews collected were from Google, namely they were the Google Reviews. The other two online review websites that significantly added up to the review collection were Glassdoor and Careers 360. Google Reviews were relatively shorter in length as compared to the other review portals.

Table 2. Sources of the collected reviews

Sr. No.	Source	Review Count
1	Google	2674
2	Glassdoor	551
3	Careers 360	153
4	Shiksha	101
5	MouthShut	79
6	Indeed	45
7	CollegeBol	26
8	GetMyUni	23
9	CollegeDunia	23
10	Youtube	16
11	Quora	3
12	CollegeSearch	1
	Total Reviews	**3695**

Table 3. Table showing the sources of the reviews of every academic institute

Source of Review / Academic Institute	Google	Glassdoor	Careers 360	Indeed	Youtube	Shiksha	Get My Uni	Mouth Shut	College Dunia	College Search	College Bol	Quora	Total Number of Reviews
Panjab University	200	0	0	0	0	0	0	0	0	0	0	0	200
BITS-Pilani	204	30	0	0	0	66	0	0	0	0	0	0	300
NIT Warangal	118	0	54	0	0	0	0	0	0	1	26	0	198
IIM- Bangalore	199	0	0	0	0	0	0	0	0	0	0	0	199
IIT-Roorkee	218	39	23	0	0	19	0	0	0	0	0	0	299
Thapar University	136	33	22	0	0	0	0	9	0	0	0	0	200
ISM Dhanbad	200	0	0	0	0	0	0	0	0	0	0	0	200
Aligarh Muslim University	200	0	0	0	0	0	0	0	0	0	0	0	200
IIM- Ahmedabad	169	29	34	0	16	13	17	12	9	0	0	0	299
Vellore Institute of Technology	200	0	0	0	0	0	0	0	0	0	0	0	200
JNU Delhi	219	8	17	0	0	3	6	30	14	0	0	3	300
Osmania University	200	0	0	0	0	0	0	0	0	0	0	0	200
Delhi University	182	54	0	36	0	0	0	28	0	0	0	0	300
IIT-Bombay	108	192	0	0	0	0	0	0	0	0	0	0	300
IISc Bangalore	122	166	3	9	0	0	0	0	0	0	0	0	300
Total	**2674**	**551**	**153**	**45**	**16**	**101**	**23**	**79**	**23**	**1**	**26**	**3**	**3695**

Table 4. Maximum, minimum and average length of the reviews of each academic institute

Academic Institute	Minimum length of Review [Number of Words]	Maximum length of Review [Number of Words]	Average Length of Reviews
BITS Pilani	1	732	68.4466667
NIT Warangal	1	561	56.57575758
IIM-Ahmedabad	1	1161	55.95986622
IIT Roorkee	1	781	46.69899666
JNU Delhi	1	600	43.75
Delhi University	1	436	42.1566667
IISc Bangalore	1	191	38.4766667
IIT Bombay	3	154	35.6066667
Vellore Institute of Technology	1	660	32.385
Thapar University	1	203	30.985
Osmania University	1	410	26.46
Aligarh Muslim University	1	517	24.345
ISM Dhanbad	1	416	19.01
Panjab University	1	200	17.5
IIM-Bangalore	1	128	12.70854271

The collected reviews were analyzed to find the minimum, maximum and the average length of the collected reviews. The lengths of the reviews were based on the number of words in the reviews. The minimum length of most of the academic institute reviews was one word. BITS Pilani had the highest average length of the review at 68.44 words per review and IIM-Bangalore had the lowest average at 12.655. The length of the longest review was of IIM-Ahmedabad which comprised of 1161 words. The academic institutes are ranked based on their average length of their reviews in Table 4.

The graphical plots comparing the maximum and the average lengths of the reviews of each of the academic institutes are shown in Figure 2 and Figure 3.

Sentiment Analysis of the Reviews

The sentiment analysis was carried out fifteen academic institutes that featured in the top 100 list of NIRF 2017 and the reviews were given sentiment scores and were tagged as 'Pos' or 'Neg' reviews. Total Number of Positive Reviews (As annotated by the Method) and the Total Number of Negative Reviews (As annotated by the Method) for each of the academic institute is provided in Table 5.

Out of the total 3695 reviews, according to the annotation done by the method, 3464 were positive reviews and 231 were negative reviews. It is concluded that according to the method, 93.74% of the total collected reviews were positive reviews and 6.25% of them were of a negative nature. As can be seen in Table 6, the highest by the percentage of positively tagged reviews method belonged to IIT-Bombay whose 96.67% of the total 300 reviews were annotated a 'Pos' tag. NIT-Warangal followed a close second with the percentage of positively tagged reviews method being 96.46%. The academic institute with the lowest percentage of positive reviews belonged to Vellore Institute of Technology with 90% positive reviews and 10% negative reviews.

Figure 2. Plot comparing the maximum length of the reviews of the academic institutes

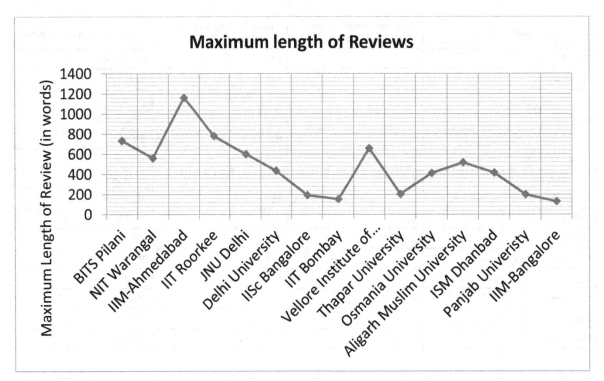

Figure 3. Plot comparing the average length of the reviews of the academic institutes

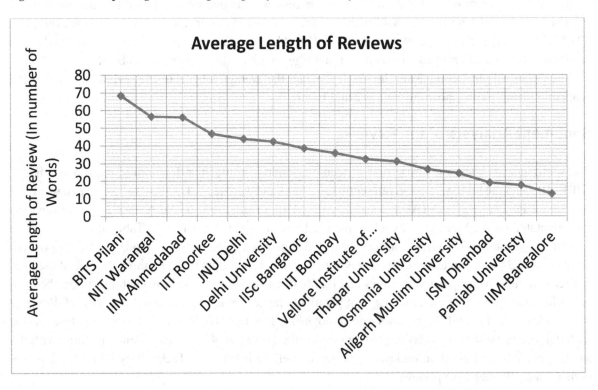

Table 5. Total number of positive and negative reviews of each academic institute (as annotated by the method)

Academic Institute	Total Number of Positive Reviews (As annotated by the Method)	Total Number of Negative Reviews (As annotated by the Method)	Total Number of Reviews
NIT-Warangal	191	7	198
BITS-Pilani	287	13	300
IIT-Roorkee	281	18	299
Thapar University	190	10	200
IIM-Ahmedabad	284	15	299
Panjab University	188	12	200
IIM-Bangalore	183	16	199
IIT-Bombay	290	10	300
ISM Dhanbad	187	13	200
Aligarh Muslim University	185	15	200
JNU Delhi	279	21	300
Delhi University	270	30	300
Vellore Institute of Technology	180	20	200
IISc Bangalore	280	20	300
Osmania University	189	11	200
Total	**3464**	**231**	**3695**

Table 6. Percentage of positive and negative reviews of each academic institute

Academic Institute	% of Positive Reviews	% of Negative Reviews
IIT-Bombay	96.67	3.33
NIT-Warangal	96.46	3.54
BITS-Pilani	95.67	4.33
Thapar University	95.00	5.00
IIM-Ahmedabad	94.98	5.02
Osmania University	94.50	5.50
Panjab University	94.00	6.00
IIT-Roorkee	93.98	6.02
ISM Dhanbad	93.50	6.50
IISc Bangalore	93.33	6.67
JNU Delhi	93.00	7.00
Aligarh Muslim University	92.50	7.50
IIM-Bangalore	91.96	8.04
Delhi University	90.00	10.00
Vellore Institute of Technology	90.00	10.00

Accuracy of the Sentiment Analysis Method

Figure 4 shows the graphical form of the percentage of Positive and Negative Reviews of each Academic Institute as Annotated by the Method. The tags annotated by the method were then compared with the tags annotated manually to each of the reviews and the total number of correctly annotated reviews by the method [TC] and the total number of incorrectly annotated reviews by the method [TI] were computed as shown in Table 7. The accuracy of the sentiment analysis method was computed for each of the academic institutes based on the following formula:Accuracy of the Sentiment Analysis method for each institute = (Correctly Annotated Reviews / Total Number of Reviews of that academic institute) * 100. In this research, the accuracy of the method in tagging the reviews correctly was computed using the formula, [(TC/N)*100] where TC was the total number of correctly annotated reviews and N was the total number of reviews under consideration of that particular academic institute.

Delhi University reviews managed to gain the top slot here with an accuracy of 99% by the method correctly annotating 297 out of the total 300 reviews while IIM-Bangalore's reviews were the ones that fared the lowest with an accuracy of 92.46%, so the accuracy of the method in annotating the reviews correctly as 'Pos' or 'Neg' was 96.238%. As shown in Table 7, where the results of the academic institutes are stored based on the sentiment analysis method's accuracies for the tagging of their reviews, it can be seen that out of the total 3695 reviews that were collected for fifteen academic institutes, 3556 were correctly annotated by the method and 139 reviews were incorrectly annotated, which makes the overall accuracy of the method as 96.23%. The graph showing the percentage of correctly and incorrectly annotated reviews by the method is shown in Figure 5.

Figure 4. Showing the percentage of positive and negative reviews of each academic institute as annotated by the method

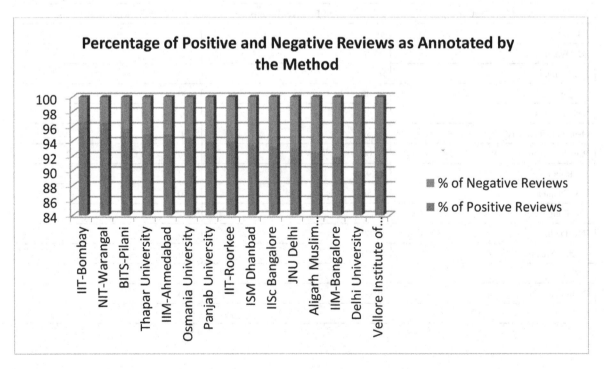

Table 7. Total number of correctly and incorrectly annotated reviews by the method and the Accuracy of the method for each academic institute

Academic Institute	Total Number of Reviews [N]	Total corrected annotated reviews by the method [TC]	Total incorrectly annotated reviews by the method [TI]	Accuracy of the Method [(TC/N)*100]
NIT-Warangal	198	193	5	97.47%
BITS-Pilani	300	287	13	95.67%
IIT-Roorkee	299	288	11	96.32%
Thapar University	200	197	3	98.50%
IIM-Ahmedabad	299	289	10	96.65%
Panjab University	200	195	5	97.50%
IIM-Bangalore	199	184	15	92.46%
IIT-Bombay	300	294	6	98.00%
ISM Dhanbad	200	194	6	97.00%
Aligarh Muslim University	200	186	14	93.00%
JNU Delhi	300	291	9	97.00%
Delhi University	300	297	3	99.00%
Vellore Institute of Technology	200	185	15	92.50%
IISc Bangalore	300	285	15	95.00%
Osmania University	200	191	9	95.50%
Total	**3695**	**3556**	**139**	**Overall Accuracy 96.23%**

Sentiment Analysis of all the Reviews

Along with the tags of 'Pos' and 'Neg' that were annotated by the method to each of the collected reviews, the sentiment score of the reviews was also computed. For each of the fifteen academic institutes, each of its reviews' sentiment scores was added and the summation of the sentiment scores of all the reviews of a particular academic institute was calculated. This was termed as the Total Sentiment Score (TSS). To compare the TSS values of all the institutes, the TSS score was multiplied by 100 and then divided by the total number of reviews for which the TSS was calculated as shown in Table 8. The outcome was the sentiment score per review (SSR). Panjab University topped the list by scoring 13.44 as the Sentiment Score per Review, which was followed by BITS-Pilani with a sentiment score per review of 13.21.

Surprisingly, the institute that topped the NIRF 2017 overall list based on the public perception factor fared the worst in the research by gaining a sentiment score per review of 6.57. The graph showing the SSRs of the fifteen academic institutes is presented in Figure 6.

Figure 5. Percentage of Correctly and Incorrectly annotated reviews by the method

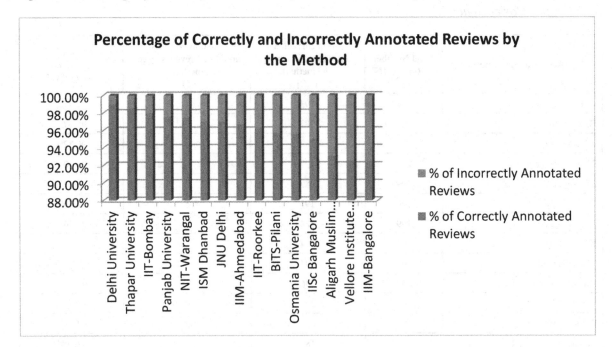

Table 8. Total Sentiment Scores and Sentiment Score per Review of each academic institute

Ranks based on Sentiment Score per Review	Academic Institute	Total Sentiment Score (TSS)	Total Number of Reviews Used (N)	Sentiment Score per Review (SSR) [(TSS*100)/N]
1	Panjab University	26.8949496	200	13.4474748
2	BITS-Pilani	39.6310579	300	13.2103526
3	NIT Warangal	25.9704581	198	13.116393
4	IIM- Bangalore	24.9942405	199	12.5599198
5	IIT-Roorkee	36.5325477	299	12.2182434
6	Thapar University	24.3426583	200	12.1713291
7	ISM Dhanbad	22.6407291	200	11.3203646
8	Aligarh Muslim University	22.5779751	200	11.2889876
9	IIM- Ahmedabad	31.077702	299	10.3938803
10	Vellore Institute of Technology	18.688773	200	9.34438648
11	JNU Delhi	26.7892957	300	8.92976523
12	Osmania University	16.6372043	200	8.31860217
13	Delhi University	23.498462	300	7.83282067
14	IIT-Bombay	21.5477502	300	7.18258338
15	IISc Bangalore	19.7376616	300	6.57922053

Figure 6. Sentiment Score per Review (SSR) of each academic institute

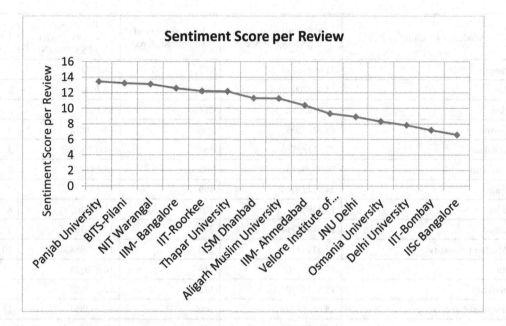

Results of the Sentiment Analysis of the Google Reviews

To check if the varied nature and lengths of the reviews that were collected from twelve varied online portals had any effect on the results of sentiment analysis. The sentiment analysis method was carried out only on the Google Reviews so that the reviews are uniform. The results of the same are tabulated in Table 9.The results showed that NIT-Warangal secured the highest Sentiment Score per Review (SSR) at 18.46. BITS-Pilani managed to retain its second position that it had secured when the reviews from all platforms were taken into consideration. The NIRF 2017 PR second ranker IISc-Bangalore still fared lowly managing a rank of 14 out of the 15 academic institutes under study. The graph portraying the SSRs of the academic institutes is shown in Figure 7.

Effect of Average Length of the Reviews on the Sentiment Scores

Now, considering the SSRs computed for all the reviews irrespective of the source of the reviews, the academic institutes were ranked based on the SSRs and their garnered ranks were compared with the average length of their reviews of all the fifteen academic institutes, to see the effect of the lengths of the reviews on the relative ranks of the institutes. The results are given in Table 10. It can be seen from the table while comparing the average length of the reviews with the ranks accorded to the institute based on the sentiment score per review (SSR) that the average length of the reviews does not depend significantly on the sentiment score per review of the institute, as the rank 1 institute, Panjab University has an average length of 17.5 words per review while the rank 2 institute BITS, Pilani has an average length of 68.44 words per review, which is also the highest amongst all the institutes. Similarly the ranks and the average lengths of the reviews do not seem to follow any set pattern.

Table 9. Sentiment Score per Review of each institute based on Google Reviews

Academic Institute	Total Sentiment Score [Only Google Reviews]	Total Number of Google Reviews	Sentiment Score per Review [SSR] [(TSS*100)/N]	Ranks based on SSR
NIT-Warangal	21.60332494	117	18.46438	1
BITS-Pilani	35.42220079	204	17.363824	2
IIT-Roorkee	33.0495258	218	15.160333	3
Thapar University	19.8983206	136	14.631118	4
IIM-Ahmedabad	23.81189526	169	14.089879	5
Panjab University	26.89494957	200	13.447475	6
IIM-Bangalore	24.99424046	199	12.55992	7
IIT-Bombay	12.549821	108	11.620205	8
ISM Dhanbad	22.64072914	200	11.320365	9
Aligarh Muslim University	22.57797512	200	11.288988	10
JNU Delhi	23.25851768	219	10.620328	11
Delhi University	17.58187207	182	9.6603693	12
Vellore Institute of Technology	18.68877297	200	9.3443865	13
IISc Bangalore	10.99237998	122	9.0101475	14
Osmania University	16.63720433	200	8.3186022	15

Figure 7. Sentiment score per review of Google reviews of each institute

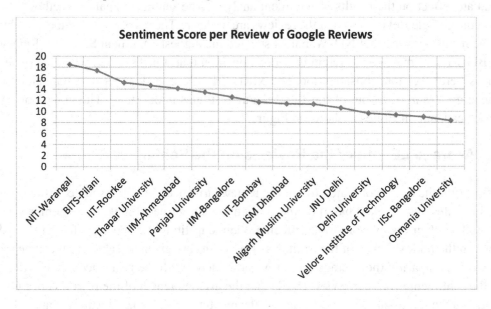

574

Table 10. Comparing the average length of the reviews with the ranks garnered

Academic Institute	Average Length of Reviews	Ranks According to Sentiment Score per Review
BITS Pilani	68.4466667	2
NIT Warangal	56.57575758	3
IIM-Ahmedabad	55.95986622	9
IIT Roorkee	46.69899666	5
JNU Delhi	43.75	11
Delhi University	42.1566667	13
IISc Bangalore	38.4766667	15
IIT Bombay	35.6066667	14
Vellore Institute of Technology	32.385	10
Thapar University	30.985	6
Osmania University	26.46	12
Aligarh Muslim University	24.345	8
ISM Dhanbad	19.01	7
Panjab Univeristy	17.5	1
IIM-Bangalore	12.70854271	4

Comparison of the NIRF ranks with the ranks based on Sentiment Analysis

The actual NIRF PR in the Overall rankings list of NIRF 2017 is tabulated in Table 11. The NIRF PR ranks of 2017 are taken from this list for the fifteen academic instates under study and their relative ranks are computed with IIT-Bombay topping the rank list and NIT-Warangal at the fifteenth spot. These NIRF PR 2017 ranks were compared with the ranks garnered by the institutes based on their sentiment scores per review (SSR) of all their reviews as in Table 4.11. Panjab University topped the list whereas it had a relative NIRF 2017 rank of being at the 10th place amongst the fifteen academic institutes under study. IIT-Bombay with NIRF 2017 rank 1 stood at the fourteenth place and IISc Bangalore with NIRF 2017 rank 2 stood at the fifteenth place. The results clearly showed that the public perception parameter system adopted by the NIRF rakings does not reflect the public perception as reflected in the reviews about the academic institute posted online by the people.

The reason for the difference between the ranking based on this analysis and NIRF ranking may be due to time lags, change in the public perception. The other reason for the differences may be due to the interpretation of the reviews. The difference between the weightage assigned to different types of sentiments may also be reason for the same.

The results obtained by the sentiment analysis method and the ranking done based on the sentiment score per review of each institute are not consistent with the NIRF rankings 2017. The reason for the same can be understood by the way the 'Perception' parameter works of the NIRF ranking framework. If we tend to focus on the fifth parameter that aimed to perceive the institute involved we can clearly see that the data for perceiving the institute was collected by MHRD by the two methods namely, the online perception system and the online feedback system.

Table 11. Ranks based on NIRF 2017 versus the sentiment analysis ranks based on the method

Academic Institute	NIRF PR Rank 2017 [From NIRF Overall Ranking 2017]	Relative NIRF PR Ranks 2017	Ranks According to Sentiment Analysis score per Review (SSR)
IIT-Bombay	1	1	14
IISc Bangalore	2	2	15
IIM-Ahmedabad	7	3	9
BITS-Pilani	8	4	2
JNU Delhi	9	5	11
IIM-Bangalore	12	6	4
Vellore Institute of Technology	14	7	10
IIT-Roorkee	15	8	5
Delhi University	16	9	13
Panjab University	36	10	1
Aligarh Muslim University	41	11	8
Thapar University	55	12	6
Osmania University	63	13	12
ISM Dhanbad	97	14	7
NIT-Warangal	106	15	3

Here we compared the sentiment analysis approach that was used in this research with the approach used by NIRF to get the public perception.

Firstly, the NIRF's Online Perception System was open only for the employers, the peers, and also for the public in general. It was an online perception system that operated for only 23 days, which was too less a time to gauge the actual perception towards any particular academic institute under study. Also the people's perceptions may change over time. In comparison, in this research the reviews that were used ranged several years.

Secondly, although MHRD mentioned in its 2017 annual NIRF ranking report that a large number of individuals had submitted their perceptions online on its online perception system, but it didn't specify the exact number people who participated in that. In this research we collected a total of 3695 reviews.

Thirdly, it is a big possibility that on the online perception system of NIRF the peers of the participating academic institutes could have perceived their own academic institute in a good way so based on this perception parameter the rankings may have been biased or tilted towards a particular institute. Whereas in this research we collected the raw reviews that were posted by the wider range of online users who may or may not have been a part of that institute but who have experienced the good and bad features of the institute. With this we perceived the academic institutes the way the general public perceives them.

Apart from the Online Perception System used by NIRF, another system called the Online Feedback System was used to specifically to get online feedback from the general public. It again had some flaws in it. Firstly, it operated only for ten days starting from 1st February 2017 to 12th February 2017, which is a really short period of time to make a long lasting opinion regarding any academic institute. This research on the other hand collected reviews that ranged over years. Secondly in the Online Perception System used by NIRF, the people were not asked to post a general feedback or a review that was natural but they were asked to give a specified feedback only on the data that was initially pre-submitted by the applicant organizations under study by answering some set questions. Answering some set questions to get the feedback was not as good as looking for feedback pertaining to any or all aspects of the institute, as found in the online reviews that naturally reflect the public opinion that was explored in this *work*, but given the wide range of review websites available online, we needed a method to make sense of these vast available online review data of the Indian academic institutes. This required a method that could automatically analyze the sentiments expressed in those online reviews and thus help the students in making a conscious decision about the choice of institute they should join for further study. This method can efficiently augment and enhance the NIRF rankings and help it in adding to it the real sentiments of the people regarding an academic institute over a longer period of time.

ISSUES AND FUTURE DIRECTIONS

According to an April 2018 poll conducted by Education Times, 73% of the students agreed that the NIRF Rankings would help them choose a particular college or course. Given that the NIRF rankings can sway the public opinion towards a particular academic institute, it must ensure that it strives to take into account all the factors while ranking a particular academic institute. The public perception factor of NIRF was the one that was the most neglected while it was also the most important one. In this chapter an application of sentiment analysis on the online reviews was presented.Aspect based feature extraction can be used for the sentiment classification of reviews and to summarize them based on features like placement, hostel life, academics, extracurricular activities and so on. Some reviews are written on the university review portals in Romanized Hindi. In the future, such reviews can be specifically collected to perform Romanization Transliteration on them and then they can be analyzed to extract their sentiments. This research can be improved upon by inculcating emoticons present in the reviews and the sentiments they express. Further this research also open directions for social science researchers to study the reasons behind differences among the online available public reviews and public perception received for the purposes of NIRF ranking.

CONCLUSION

In this chapter, we discussed various Sentiment Analysis approaches and then applied the same to perform the sentiment analysis of online reviews. This work collected 3695 reviews from online review portals, pertaining to 15 NIRF top 100 ranked academic institutes and performed the sentiment analysis of the reviews using the lexical approach. The method used for the research initially preprocessed the raw reviews by conversion of the review data to lowercase, removing the digits from the data and stripping the punctuation from the reviews. The initial pre-processing of the reviews was followed by the NLTK Pre-processing which included three steps: Tokenization, POS Tagging and Lemmatization of the reviews. After that for performing the sentiment analysis of the reviews, SentiWordNet 3.0 was used as the lexical resource for the research, based upon which the reviews were tagged as 'Pos' or 'Neg' by the method and along with the tagging the sentiment scores of each of the reviews was also computed by the method. These scores were analyzed to get the sentiment score per review of each of the institutes under study. The reviews had also been manually annotated and compared with the ones annotated by the method to check their accuracy- 96.23%. The academic institutes were ranked based on these scores and their ranks were compared with their NIRF ranks. The results showed that the forerunner was Panjab University, followed by BITS-Pilani and NIT-Warangal.

REFERENCES

A Complete Guide to k-Nearest Neighbors with applications in Python and R. (2017). Retrieved from http://www.kevinzakka.github.io/2016/07/13/k-nearest-neighbor/

Adeborna, E., & Siau, K. (2014, July). *An Approach to Sentiment Analysis-the Case of Airline Quality Rating*. PACIS.

Amplayo, R. K., & Song, M. (2017). An adaptable fine-grained sentiment analysis for summarization of multiple short online reviews. *Data & Knowledge Engineering*, *110*, 54–67. doi:10.1016/j.datak.2017.03.009

Baccianella, S., Esuli, A., & Sebastiani, F. (2010, May). Sentiwordnet 3.0: an enhanced lexical resource for sentiment analysis and opinion mining. In Lrec (Vol. 10, No. 2010, pp. 2200-2204). Academic Press.

García-Cumbreras, M. Á., Montejo-Ráez, A., & Díaz-Galiano, M. C. (2013). Pessimists and optimists: Improving collaborative filtering through sentiment analysis. *Expert Systems with Applications*, *40*(17), 6758–6765. doi:10.1016/j.eswa.2013.06.049

Go, A., Bhayani, R., & Huang, L. (2009). Twitter sentiment classification using distant supervision. CS224N Project Report, 1(12).

Google Trends. (2017, September 20). Retrieved from https://trends.google.com/trends/

Google Trends. (2017, September 27). Retrieved from https://en.wikipedia.org/wiki/Google_Trends

Indeed Reviews. (2017, September). *Reviews from Indeed*. Retrieved from https://www.indeed.co.in/

Introduction to Support Vector Machines. (2017, August 29). Retrieved from http:// www.svms.org/introduction.html

K-nearest neighbors (k-nn) classification – Intro. (2017, August 29). Retrieved from https:// www.solver.com/k-nearest-neighbors-k-nn-classification-intro

Kaur, N., & Solanki, N. (2018). Sentiment Knowledge Discovery in Twitter Using CoreNLP Library. *8th International Conference on Cloud Computing, Data Science & Engineering (Confluence)*. 10.1109/CONFLUENCE.2018.8442439

Lau, R. Y., Li, C., & Liao, S. S. (2014). Social analytics: Learning fuzzy product ontologies for aspect-oriented sentiment analysis. *Decision Support Systems*, *65*, 80–94. doi:10.1016/j.dss.2014.05.005

Mäntylä, M. V., Graziotin, D., & Kuutila, M. (2018). The evolution of sentiment analysis—A review of research topics, venues, and top cited papers. *Computer Science Review*, *27*, 16–32. doi:10.1016/j.cosrev.2017.10.002

Miller, G. A., Beckwith, R., Fellbaum, C., Gross, D., & Miller, K. J. (1990). Introduction to WordNet: An on-line lexical database. *International Journal of Lexicography, 3*(4), 235-244.

Multinominal, N. B. (2017, October 20). Retrieved fromhttp://scikitlearn.org/stable/modules/generated/sklearn.naive_bayes.MultinomialNB.html

Naïve Byes. (2017, August 29). Retrieved from http://www.python-course.eu/naive_byes_classifier_introduction.php

Narayan, D., Chakrabarti, D., Pande, P., & Bhattacharyya, P. (2002, January). *An experience in building the indo wordnet-a wordnet for Hindi*. In *First International Conference on Global WordNet*, Mysore, India.

NIRF Ranking 2018. (2018, April 22). Retrieved from https://www.nirfindia.org/2018/Ranking2018.html

Pak, A., & Paroubek, P. (2010, May). Twitter as a corpus for sentiment analysis and opinion mining. In LREc (Vol. 10, No. 2010, pp. 1320-1326). Academic Press.

Pandey, S., & Solanki, A. (2019). Music Instrument Recognition using Deep Convolutional Neural Networks. International Journal of Information Technology. doi:10.1007/s41870-019-00285-y

Pang, B., Lee, L., & Vaithyanathan, S. (2002, July). Thumbs up?: sentiment classification using machine learning techniques. In *Proceedings of the ACL-02 conference on Empirical methods in natural language processing-Volume 10* (pp. 79-86). Association for Computational Linguistics. 10.3115/1118693.1118704

Parameters. (2017, August 31). Retrieved from https://www.nirfindia.org/Parameter

Reviews from Careers 360. (2017, September). Retrieved from https://www.careers360.com/

Reviews from College Bol. (2017, September). Retrieved from https://www.collegebol.com

Reviews from College Dunia. (2017, September). Retrieved from https://collegeDunia.com/

Reviews from College Search. (2017, September). Retrieved from https://www.collegesearch.in/

Reviews from Get My Uni. (2017, September). Retrieved from https://www.getmyuni.com

Reviews from Glassdoor. (2017, September). Retrieved from https://www.glassdoor.co.in/index.htm

Reviews from Google Reviews. (2017, September). Retrieved from https://www.google.co.in/

Reviews from Mouth Shut. (2017, September). Retrieved from https://www.mouthshut.com

Reviews from Quora. (2017, September). Retrieved from https://www.quora.com

Reviews from Shiksha. (2017, September). Retrieved from https://www.shiksha.com/

Reviews from Youtube. (2017, September). Retrieved from https://www.youtube.com

Salunkhe, P., Surnar, A., & Sonawane, S. (2017). *A Review: Prediction of Election Using Twitter Sentiment Analysis*. Academic Press.

SENTIWORDNET. (2006). *A publicly available lexical resource for opinion mining*. Andrea Esuli and Fabrizio Sebastiani.

Sokolov Aleksey. (2015). *Movie Reviews Sentiment Analysis*. Author.

Tummel, A. A. D. J. C., & Richert, S. J. A. (2015, December). Sentiment Analysis of Social Media for Evaluating Universities. In *The Second International Conference on Digital Information Processing, Data Mining, and Wireless Communications (DIPDMWC2015)* (p. 49). Academic Press.

Uan Sholanbayev. (2016). *Sentiment Analysis on Movie Reviews*. Author.

Venu, S.H., Annie, A.X., & Mohan, V. (2016). *Sentiment Analysis Applied to Airline Feedback to Boost Customer's Endearment*. Academic Press.

Wani, G. P., & Alone, N. V. (2015). Analysis of Indian Election using Twitter. *International Journal of Computer Applications, 121*(22).

Will the NIRF ranking help students choice of courses & colleges? (2018 May 1). Retrieved from http://www.educationtimes.com/article/93/201804112018041112285278ld9010d4f/Will the-NIRF-ranking-help-students-choice-of-coursescollege.html

Yuan, P., Zhong, Y., & Huang, J. (2015). *Sentiment Classification and Opinion Mining on Airline Reviews*. Academic Press.

This research was previously published in the Handbook of Research on Emerging Trends and Applications of Machine Learning; pages 1-26, copyright year 2020 by Engineering Science Reference (an imprint of IGI Global).

Chapter 32
Sentiment Analysis Using Machine Learning Algorithms and Text Mining to Detect Symptoms of Mental Difficulties Over Social Media

Hadj Ahmed Bouarara

iD https://orcid.org/0000-0002-4973-4385

GeCoDe Laboratory, Algeria

ABSTRACT

A recent British study of people between the ages of 14 and 35 has shown that social media has a negative impact on mental health. The purpose of the paper is to detect people with mental disorders' behavior in social media in order to help Twitter users in overcoming their mental health problems such as anxiety, phobia, depression, paranoia, etc. For this, the author used text mining and machine learning algorithms (naïve Bayes, k-nearest neighbours) to analyse tweets. The obtained results were validated using different evaluation measures such as f-measure, recall, precision, entropy, etc.

INTRODUCTION AND PROBLEMATIC

Instagram, Twitter, Facebook and Snapchat: these platforms attract the attention of 91% of 16–24-year-olds. Between narcissism and harassment, creativity and self-expression, social networks are at the origin of a social revolution, especially among "millennials" (born between 95 and the early 2000s). Unfortunately, the conclusion of StatusOfMind is that: social networks are, for the most part, bad for the morale of its young users. Thus, twitter is considered to be the most harmful followed closely by Snapchat, then Facebook and finally Instagram (Koenig & McLaughlin, 2018).

DOI: 10.4018/978-1-6684-6303-1.ch032

According to a study by the public health foundation (Mental Health Foundation, 2015), the rate of anxiety and depression has jumped 70% among young people in the last 25 years when it correlated these figures with the increased use of social media. The study established a list of the negative consequences of social networks: cyber-harassment, Addiction (or the feeling of anxiety about missing something), Anxiety, depression, the feeling of loneliness, lack of sleep, physical ill-being. more than one in two (55%) say they have been embarrassed in their daily life by "symptoms of mental difficulty" (anxiety, phobia, depression, paranoia). Even more worrying: one in five young people (22%) say they have felt this discomfort significantly (Barr et al., 2015).

In recent years, we are in a digital world where information is available in large quantities and in various forms. 80% of this mass of information was in textual form. For this reason, we need specific tools to access sentiments and meanings hidden in these data, in order to reduce human intervention. Opinion Mining groups methods and techniques for identifying opinions in textual data.

In this paper we are interested in a subdomain of opinion mining which is the contextual analysis of social networks which attracted many researchers, which gave birth to many works. In our work we are based on a corpus (Corpus-based Approach) principle of assigning data to a classifier for learning in a supervised way, which generates a model that is used for the test part. We used twitter as a social network which is a networking site allows users to write short articles, called "tweets". The content of this paper discusses the different steps of our proposed approach to solve the problem of detecting depressed people through a decision analysis of tweets. Then we will define the tools used for the realization of the practical part of our work with a general presentation of the results obtained by discussing the different comparisons applied between the different techniques used and proposed during our work.

The general structure of the paper will be as follows: we start with a state of the art for presenting the essential works in this topic, after we go on with a section detailing our approach and proposed components then an experimental and comparative study will be carried out for presenting the best results obtained. Finally, we will finish with a conclusion and describing some lines of thought that remain open and that we want to share them with you.

LITERATURE REVIEW (RELATED WORK)

The work of Hatzivassiloglou and McKeown in 1997 (1997) consists in using the coordinating conjunctions present between a word already classified and an unclassified word, followed by the contributions of researcher Nasukawa and his team in 2003 (2003) who proposed a new method for extracting associated concepts from segments and summing the orientations of the opinion vocabulary present in the same segment.

In the same year, researchers Yu and Hatzivassiloglou (2003) used the probability of ranking a word to measure the strength of the orientation of the named entities. In 2006, researchers Kanayama and Nasukawa (2006) as well as Ding and Liu (2008) in 2008 proposed, for their part, a learning-based approach that uses the coordination conjunctions present between a word already classified and a word unclassified.

The approaches of Pang et al introduced in 2002 (2002), and that of Charton and Acuna-Agost published in 2007 (2007) consist of classifying the texts according to a global polarity (positive, negative and neutral). These methods were optimized by Wilson and his research team in 2005 (2005). However, the difficulty lies in the constitution of these corpora of learning, which is a manual process to perform for each area studied. Finally, Vernier and his team (2009), have relied on a method of detection and categorization of the evaluations locally expressed in a corpus of multi-domain blogs. The second Dictionary-based Approach has had a lot of work. In 2015, Rosenthal and his team (2015) built General Inquiry which contains 3596 words labeled positive or negative. In Nakov and al work published in 2016 (2016), they use only adjectives for the detection of opinions. They manually build a list of adjectives they use to predict sentence direction and use WordNet to populate the list with synonyms and antonyms of polarity-known adjectives.

THE PROPOSED APPROACH

Our approach consists of 3 main modules as shown in Figure 1:

Figure 1. general architecture of our approach

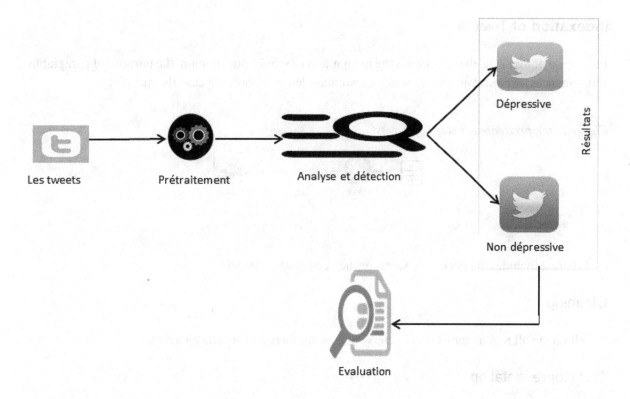

Tweets2011 Corpus (Tweets):

In our experiments we used the Tweets2011 corpus that was used in information retrieval famous competition called TREC 201. This specialized body built to keywords. The authors of this corpus have used the API to retrieve Twitter4J 649 tweets where they used keywords (politics, cinema, sport, music, war, science). After TREC in 2012 these tweets were classified in two class (depressive tweet, tweet not depressed). (McCreadie et al., 2012) Table 1 summarizes the classification of tweets.

Table 1. General Statistical Dataset Tweets2011

Category	Depressed	not depressed
Cinema	85	62
Policy	49	33
War	64	13
Sport	33	58
Music	119	56
Science	19	58
Total	369	280

Indexation of Tweets

In the case of text data, the first step is the recognition of words, punctuation, the purpose of paragraphs and sentences. We must also unify writing lowercase letters in order to ease the mapping.

Figure 2. the pretreatment steps of tweets

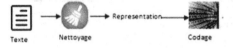

Figure 2 includes the necessary steps for the vectorization tweets.

Cleaning

We eliminate all non-alphabetic characters such as numbers and special characters.

Text Representation

This step ensures the transformation of tweets into a list of terms. We have implemented different representation techniques such as Bag words, N-gram characters and Stemming.

Coding

This step calculates the importance of each term in each tweets using different weighting methods such as:

- Term frequency (TF): TF can calculate the number of occurrences of each term in each tweets.
- The Term frequency (tf)* inversed document frequency (IDF): (TF*IDF) calculates the weight of each term by multiplying the importance of the term T in the tweet with the importance of this term throughout the data set.

$$\text{The inverted frequency documents}\left(T\right) = \log\frac{|D|}{DF\left(T\right)}. \tag{1}$$

- DF (T) represents the number of tweets that include the word T.
- D: The number of tweets in the dataset.

Analysis of the Tweet

For this step we tested three classical algorithms that will be overseen detail later:

Algorithm K Nearest Neighbor (KNN)

The KNN called English K nearest neighbor (KNN) is a simple and naive supervised classification algorithm. The goal is to classified each new example (from the base of tests) on the basis of their distance from the examples of the learning base. It requires the presence of parameters such as: learning basis, the value of the K and A distance measurement.

To predict the class of a new example "X" the algorithm calculates the distance of X with each example of the learning base to find the "K" closest neighbor X. Finally the majority among the K classes will be assigned to X.

```
Pseudo code algorithm K nearest neighbors
i: the example number of the learning base.
C: class Example number i of the learning base.
Input: -Choosing a distance measurement
-        The value of the parameter K.
-        learning base D.
-        X: the new example that we want to know her class.
beginning
        for each ((I, c) ∈ D) to
        Calculate the distance dist (x, i)
        end
        for each {i ∈ kplus close neighbors (x)} to
                count the number of occurrences of each class.
        end
                Attributed to x the most frequent class (majority class).
end
```

Naive Bayes (NB) Algorithm

Naive Bayes is one of supervised classification methods can be used to perform a text classification. The NB classifier is based on Bayes' theorem with the assumptions of independence between the predictors. It is easy to build, without complicated parameters, which makes it particularly useful for very large data sets (Bickel & Levina, 2004). Bayes' theorem provides a way to calculate the posterior probability P (c | x) from P (c), P (x) and P (x | c).

$$P(C \mid X)\frac{P(X \mid C)P(C)}{P(X)} \tag{2}$$

$$P (C \mid x) = P (x1 \mid c) * P (x2 \mid c) \dots\dots\dots P (Xn \mid c) \, p (c). \tag{3}$$

- P (c | x) is the posterior probability of class (target) with given predictor (attribute).
- P (c) is the a priori probability of the class.
- P (x | c) is the probability of the attribute x relative to the probability of the given class c attribute.
- P (x) is the prior probability of the predictor.

Decision Tree Algorithm

The decision tree is a supervised learning algorithm where from a training set, it constructs the tree (predictive model), each path from the root to a leaf corresponding to a classification rule. (Bickel & Levina, 2004)

The principle of building a decision tree is to divide the examples of the learning base recursively based on the idea of Top-Down Induction. We start by building the tree root continuing using the shanon entropy until the subset of learning examples are from the same class. Recursively at each iteration we compute the entropy E (S) (gain ratio) of each attribute of the learning basis. The attribute with the highest gain ratio will be chosen as the root. The algorithm continues for each sub set of attributes. When all the elements in a subset belongs to the same class, this subset will not be covered and this node in the decision tree becomes a leaf node labeled with a label of the same class as the class in which all its elements belong.

- **Entropy:** the algorithm uses entropy to calculate the homogeneity of tweets:

$$E (X) = P (xi) \log P (xi) \tag{4}$$

- P (xi): probability of the attribute xi.
- **Gain of information:** It is based on the entropy value.

$$\text{Gain (T, X)} = \text{Entropy (T)} - \text{Entropy (T, X)} \tag{5}$$

- **Entropy (T):** the entropy of the class.

- **Entropy (T, X):** The entropy for the attribute x relative to the class T.
- **Gain ratio:** The algorithm use the gain ratio to choose the root attribute

$$\text{Gain ratio (T, X)} = \frac{\text{Gain}\left(T, X\right)}{\text{Split info}\left(x\right)} \tag{6}$$

$$\text{Split info (x)} = -\sum_{V \in X} P\left(V\right) \log_2 P\left(V\right) \tag{7}$$

- **V:** value of the attribut x.

Evaluation

The evaluation measures used to evaluate our algorithms are different and each measure has an objective as shown in the following parts.

Confusion Matrix (Table 2)

Table 2. Confusion matrix

Confusion Matrix		Expert judgment	
		Depressive	**Not Depressive**
Judgment of the algorithm	Depressive	TP_i	FP_i
	Not Depressive	FN_i	TN_i
True positive (TP):	The number of instances correctly assigned to the class depressive.		
True Negative (TN):	The number of instances correctly assigned to the class not depressive.		
False Positive (FP)	The number of not-depressive instances that have been classified as depressive.		
false negative (FN):	The number of instances really depressive which are assigned as not depressive.		

Static Kappa (K)

Cohen's kappa coefficient (κ) is a statistic that is used to measure inter-rater reliability (and also Intra-rater reliability) for qualitative (categorical) items. The value of K is always between -1 and 1.

- K = 1 if the algorithms and expert judgment are the same.
- K = -1 if the algorithms and expert judgment are completely different.

$$K = \frac{P_0 - P_C}{1 - P_C} \tag{8}$$

- P_0: Number of people rank well

$$P_C = \frac{\sum_i A_i * R_i}{total^2} \tag{9}$$

- Total: total number of instances in the dataset.
- A_i: Sum of the line items i confusion matrix.
- R_i: Sum of columns in row i of the confusion matrix.

Precision (P)

The ability of an algorithm to return only those correctly depressive instances. It represents the ratio between the number of individuals correctly classified by the algorithm in the depressive class relative to the total number of people classified by the algorithm in the depressive class.

$$P = \frac{TP_i}{TP_i + FP_i} \tag{10}$$

Recall (R)

It represents the ratio between the number of instances correctly classified by our system in depressive class relative to the total number of instances really depressive.

$$R = \frac{VP_i}{VP_i + FN_i} \tag{11}$$

f-Measure

Used to group the performance of the algorithm using the results of the recall and precision.

$$F = \frac{2 * R * P}{R + P} \tag{12}$$

RESULTS AND DISCUSSION

In this part we will every time testing different technical performances to set the ideal parameters for the tweets analysis problem. We will divide this section into three parts:

- comparison in terms of representation (bag of words, stemming, n-gram characters).
- Comparing algorithms (Naive Bayes, C4.5 decision tree and KNN).
- Comparison with bio-inspired algorithms (integrated in the tool of the Ebiri).

The following tables give the best results after testing different colored squares in blue signify the best results and the colored squares in red signified the poor results for each algorithm with the change in representation techniques and coding tf * idf.

1- The Table 3 and Figures 3 and 4 group the best results obtained by the KNN algorithm (K = 1 and cosine distance) by varying the representation techniques and using the coding tf * idf.

Table 3. the results of K nearest neighbors with variation in representation techniques (K = 1 and distance cosine)

		Evaluation Measures							
		Precision	Recall	f-measure	accuracy (%)	ERROR(%)	static kappa	Confusion matrix	
representation techniques	Bag of words	0. 724	0. 699	0.7	67.79%	32.21%	0354	258	98
								111	182
	stemming	0. 786	0617	0.6913	68.72%	31.28%	0386	228	62
								141	218
	2-gram characters	0.819	0.7235	0.769	75.19%	24.81%	0.5038	267	59
								102	221
	3-gram characters	0.86	0.764	0811	79.81	20.19	0.596	282	44
								87	236
	4-gram characters	0918	0791	0854	84.12%	15.86%	0688	292	26
								77	254
	5-gram characters	0844	0.764	0802	78.58	21.42	0.56	282	52
								87	228

Figure 3. Number of depressive and not-depressive tweets obtained by the K nearest neighbors' algorithm (K = 1 and cosine distance)

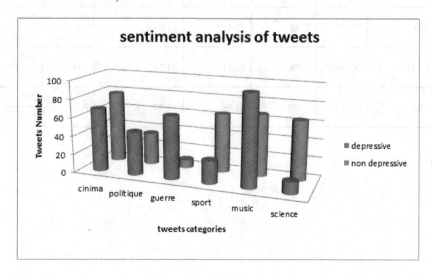

Figure 4. Comparison of tweets representation techniques using the algorithm K nearest neighbors (K = 1 and cosine distance)

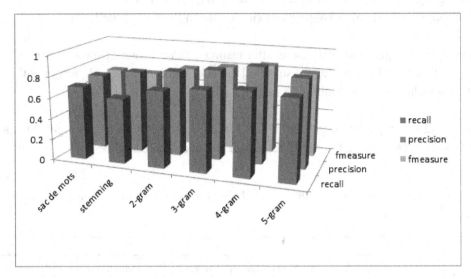

2- Table 4 and Figures 5 and 6 group the best results obtained by the naive Bayes algorithm with the change in representation techniques and the tf*idf as coding technique.

Table 4. The results of the naive Bayes algorithm by varying the representation techniques

Evaluation Measures								
Bag of words	**0.74 Precision**	**0.59 Recall**	**0654 f-measure**	**65.48% accuracy (%)**	**34.52% ERROR(%)**	**0313 static kappa**	**221 Confusion matrix**	**76 204**
Stemming	0.64	0.56	0.6	57.62%	42.37%	0156	207	113
							162	167
2-gram character	0.7222	0577	0645	63.32%	36.67%	0274	213	82
							156	198
3-gram character	0.781	0715	0745	72.41%	27.59%	0.45	264	74
							105	206
4 gram characters	0.7217	0674	0699	66.71	33.29	0347	249	96
							120	184
5-gram characters	0708	0672	0.689	65.63	34.37	0.32	248	102
							121	178

Figure 5. Number of depressive and not depressive tweets obtained by the naive Bayes algorithm

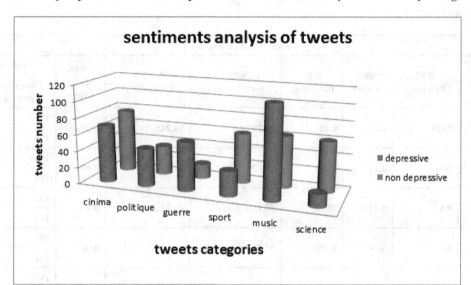

Figure 6. Comparison of representation techniques using the naive Bayes algorithm in terms of recall, precision and F-measure

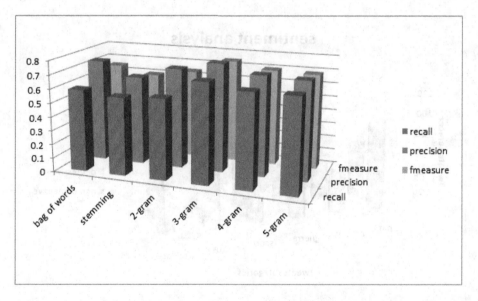

3- Table 5 and Figures 7 and 8 group the best results obtained by the Decision tree algorithm with the variation in representation techniques.

Table 5. The results of sentiments analysis using the decision tree algorithm by varying the representation techniques

Bag of words	Evaluation Measures							
	0.52 Precision	0509 Recall	0.51 f-measure	46.22% accuracy (%)	53.78% ERROR(%)	- 0.05 static kappa	188 Confusion matrix	168 112
stemming	0526	0463	0.49	45.76%	54.24%	-0.06	171	154
							198	126
2-gram characters	0608	0.51	0558	53.62%	46.48%	0.09	190	122
							179	158
3-gram characters	0.6	0.5257	0557	53.15%	47.85%	0083	194	129
							175	151
4-gram characters	0.6	0536	0.569	53.31%	47.69%	0.06	198	132
							171	148
5-gram characters	0613	0533	0.57	54.39%	45.61%	0098	197	124
							172	156

Figure 7. Number of depressive and not depressive tweets obtained by the decision tree algorithm

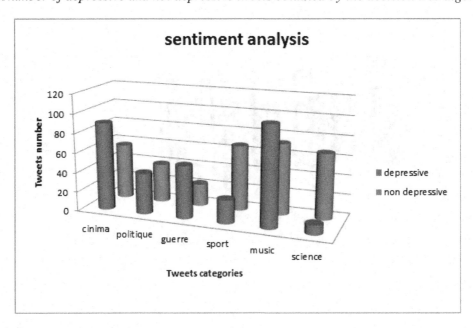

Figure 8. Comparison of representation techniques using the decision tree algorithm in terms of recall, precision and F-measure

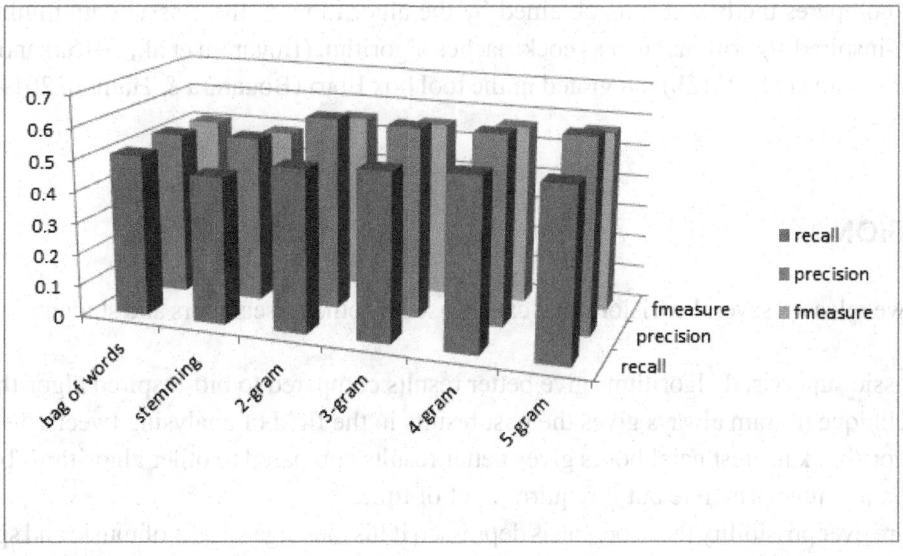

DISCUSSION OF RESULTS

- In terms of representation: The above results clearly show that the technique n-gram characters give the best results from the technical (stemming, word bag) because users of twitter can write their tweets using different language which cause difficulties in technical bag word stemming and has represented these tweets.
- In terms of the analysis algorithm: K nearest neighbors gives best results with 4-gram character representation and coding tf * idf.

Table 6. Comparing conventional supervised learning algorithms and bio-inspired algorithms

		Evaluation Measures							
Algorithms	Naive bayes	0.781 Precision	0715 Recall	0745 f-measure	72.41% accuracy (%)	27.59% ERROR(%)	0.45 static kappa	264	74
								Confusion matrix	206
	Decision tree	0608	0.51	0558	53.62%	46.48%	0.09	190	122
								179	158
	KNN	0918	0791	0854	84.12%	15.86%	0688	292	26
								77	254
	Algorithm cockroaches	0.92	0.74	0.82	82.43	17.57	0.65	276	21
								93	259
	Heart lung machine	0.88	0.82	0848	84.28	15.72	0.68	306	39
								63	241

COMPARATIVE STUDY

This section compares the best results obtained by the algorithms of the classic data mining with the results of bio-inspired algorithms such as cockroaches algorithm (Bouarara et al., 2015a) and heart lung machines (Bouarara et al., 2015b) integrated in the tool box Ebiri (Bouarara & Hamou, 2017) as shown in Table 6.

CONCLUSION

In our work we released several decisions that can be used by other researchers and students in the future:

1. The classic supervised algorithms give better results compared to bio-inspired algorithms.
2. The technique n-gram always gives the best results in the field of analysing tweets.
3. The algorithm k nearest neighbours gives better results compared to other algorithms because it is based on a simple principle but it requires a lot of time.
4. There are over possibility that a person is depressed if his message speaks of music and sport against it there's less chance that a person is not depressed if his message speaks of science and cinema.

REFERENCES

Barr, B., Kinderman, P., & Whitehead, M. (2015). Trends in mental health inequalities in England during a period of recession, austerity and welfare reform 2004 to 2013. *Social Science & Medicine, 147,* 324–331. doi:10.1016/j.socscimed.2015.11.009 PMID:26623942

Bickel, P. J., & Levina, E. (2004). Some theory for Fisher's linear discriminant function, naive Bayes' and Some alternatives When there are many more variables than observations. *Bernoulli, 10*(6), 989–1010. doi:10.3150/bj/1106314847

Bouarara, H.A., & Hamou, R.M. (2017). *Bio-Inspired Environment for Information Retrieval (Ebiri): innovations from nature*. European Academic Editions.

Bouarara, H. A., Hamou, R. M., & Amin, A. (2015a). Novel Bio-Inspired Technology of Artificial Social Cockroaches (CSA). *International Journal of Organizational and Collective Intelligence, 5*(2), 47–79. doi:10.4018/IJOCI.2015040103

Bouarara, H. A., Hamou, R. M., & Amin, A. (2015b). A Novel Bio-Inspired Approach for Multilingual Spam Filtering. *International Journal of Intelligent Information Technologies, 11*(3), 45–87. doi:10.4018/IJIIT.2015070104

Charton, E., & Acuna-Agost, R. (2007). Quel modèle pour détecter une opinion? Trois propositions pour généraliser l'extraction d'une idée dans un corpus. *Actes du troisième DÉfi Fouille de Textes, 35.*

Ding, Y., Liu, X., Zheng, Z. R., & Gu, P. F. (2008). Freeform LED lens for uniform illumination. *Optics Express, 16*(17), 12958–12966. doi:10.1364/OE.16.012958 PMID:18711534

Hatzivassiloglou, V., & McKeown, K. R. (1997, July). Predicting the semantic orientation of adjectives. In *Proceedings of the 35th annual meeting of the association for computational linguistics and eighth conference of the european chapter of the association for computational linguistics* (pp. 174-181). Association for Computational Linguistics.

Kanayama, H., & Nasukawa, T. (2006, July). Fully automatic lexicon expansion for domain-oriented sentiment analysis. In *Proceedings of the 2006 conference on empirical methods in natural language processing* (pp. 355-363). Association for Computational Linguistics. 10.3115/1610075.1610125

Koenig, A., & McLaughlin, B. (2018). Change is an emotional state of mind: Behavioral responses to online petitions. *New Media & Society*, 20(4), 1658–1675. doi:10.1177/1461444817689951

McCreadie, R., Soboroff, I., Lin, J., Macdonald, C., Ounis, I., & McCullough, D. (2012, August). One building has reusable Twitter corpus. In *Proceedings of the 35th International ACM SIGIR conference on Research and development in information retrieval* (pp. 1113-1114). ACM.

Nakov, P., Ritter, A., Rosenthal, S., Sebastiani, F., & Stoyanov, V. (2016). SemEval-2016 task 4: Sentiment analysis in Twitter. In *Proceedings of the 10th international workshop on semantic evaluation (semeval-2016)* (pp. 1-18). Academic Press.

Nasukawa, T., & Yi, J. (2003, October). Sentiment analysis: Capturing favorability using natural language processing. In *Proceedings of the 2nd international conference on Knowledge capture* (pp. 70-77). ACM. 10.1145/945645.945658

Pang, B., Lee, L., & Vaithyanathan, S. (2002, July). Thumbs up? Sentiment classification using machine learning techniques. In *Proceedings of the ACL-02 conference on Empirical methods in natural language processing-Volume 10* (pp. 79-86). Association for Computational Linguistics. 10.3115/1118693.1118704

Pilgrim, D. (2019). *Key concepts in mental health*. SAGE Publications Limited.

Rosenthal, S., Nakov, P., Kiritchenko, S., Mohammad, S., Ritter, A., & Stoyanov, V. (2015). Semeval-2015 task 10: Sentiment analysis in twitter. In *Proceedings of the 9th international workshop on semantic evaluation (SemEval 2015)* (pp. 451-463). 10.18653/v1/S15-2078

Vernier, M., Monceaux, L., Daille, B., & Dubreil, E. (2009). Catégorisation des évaluations dans un corpus de blogs multi-domaine. *Revue des nouvelles technologies de l'information*, 45-70.

Wilson, T., Wiebe, J., & Hoffmann, P. (2005, October). Recognizing contextual polarity in phrase-level sentiment analysis. In *Proceedings of the conference on human language technology and empirical methods in natural language processing* (pp. 347-354). Association for Computational Linguistics. 10.3115/1220575.1220619

Yu, H., & Hatzivassiloglou, V. (2003, July). Towards answering opinion questions: Separating facts from opinions and identifying the polarity of opinion sentences. In *Proceedings of the 2003 conference on Empirical methods in natural language processing* (pp. 129-136). Association for Computational Linguistics. 10.3115/1119355.1119372

This research was previously published in the International Journal of Information Systems and Social Change (IJISSC), 12(2); pages 1-15, copyright year 2021 by IGI Publishing (an imprint of IGI Global).

Chapter 33
Classification of Code–Mixed Bilingual Phonetic Text Using Sentiment Analysis

Shailendra Kumar Singh

ⓘD https://orcid.org/0000-0001-9658-1441

Computer Science and Engineering, Sant Longowal Institute of Engineering and Technology, India

Manoj Kumar Sachan

Computer Science and Engineering, Sant Longowal Institute of Engineering and Technology, India

ABSTRACT

The rapid growth of internet facilities has increased the comments, posts, blogs, feedback, etc., on a large scale on social networking sites. These social media data are available in an unstructured form, which includes images, text, and videos. The processing of these data is difficult, but some sentiment analysis, information retrieval, and recommender systems are used to process these unstructured data. To extract the opinion and sentiment of internet users from their written social media text, a sentiment analysis system is required to develop, which can work on both monolingual and bilingual phonetic text. Therefore, a sentiment analysis (SA) system is developed, which performs well on different domain datasets. The system performance is tested on four different datasets and achieved better accuracy of 3% on social media datasets, 1.5% on movie reviews, 1.35% on Amazon product reviews, and 4.56% on large Amazon product reviews than the state-of-art techniques. Also, the stemmer (StemVerb) for verbs of the English language is proposed, which improves the SA system's performance.

1. INTRODUCTION

With the enhancement of internet services and facilities, social networking sites such as YouTube, Google Plus, LinkedIn, Twitter, and Facebook have increased rapidly (Press Trust of India, 2013). These social networking sites provide facilities to share the users' feelings, emotions, comments, feedbacks, and reviews over the internet. Thus, the size of such content over social media (SM) increases exponentially day

DOI: 10.4018/978-1-6684-6303-1.ch033

by day. Most of the SM text contents are written using more than one language and called code-mixed language. The text of languages other than English is written using Roman script's alphabets called phonetic text. The phonetic text mixed with English language text, but there is no fixed format for these SM texts (Dutta et al., 2015). These contents are used as input text to extract information, opinion, text summarization, etc., using various linguistic computations, natural language processing, text mining, and information retrieval systems (S. K. Singh & Sachan, 2019b).

Opinion mining or sentiment analysis (SA) is a sub-field of text mining and is one of the most recent research topics of interest (Pang & Lee, 2008). The SA is related to predicting and analyzing hidden information, emotion, and feelings from the written text. The SA is widely used to analyze feedbacks on government regulation and policy proposed, to analyze the customers' likes/dislikes, to know the product demand, brand reputation, real-world event monitoring and analyzing of political party demand, competitors products' merit or demerit analyzes, and subtask component of recommender system (Bonadiman et al., 2017; D'Andrea et al., 2015). In April 2013, 90% of consumers decided to purchase things or services based on online reviews (Peng et al., 2014).

The user-written texts are classified using SA into two or three classes based on different formats such as positive/negative/neutral, like/dislike, and good/bad (Hopken et al., 2017; S. K. Singh & Sachan, 2019b). Mostly two approaches are used to classify the text using SA, such as (i) feature-based and (ii) bag-of-words. Machine learning techniques are based on features, while lexicon-based techniques use bag-of-words approaches. In SA of products and services, machine learning is widely used, but the bag-of-words are used for social issues (Karamibekr & Ghorbani, 2012). Machine learning systems are trained on the labeled dataset(s) and classify the testing dataset(s) based on the trained system. The lexicon-based techniques are categorized as two approaches such as corpus-based and dictionary-based (S. K. Singh & Sachan, 2019b). The text classification using the dictionary-based approach depends upon the opinion word's sentiment score. This dictionary consists of opinion words and their sentiment scores (Alharbi & Alhalabi, 2020). The opinion words are nouns, verbs, adverbs, and adjectives, which act as features in dictionary-based approach as discussed in the articles (Hopken et al., 2017; Shamsudin et al., 2016; P. K. Singh et al., 2015; R. K. Singh et al., 2020; S. K. Singh & Sachan, 2019b). These opinion words are used to develop opinion dictionaries such as SentiWordNet 3.0 (Baccianella et al., 2010), the latest SenticNet 4 (Cambria et al., 2016), etc.

The SM text is available in monolingual, bilingual, and multilingual. The processing of multilingual texts is a difficult task as compared to bilingual and monolingual text. Monolingual text can be easily processed, but bilingual text up to some extent. Taboada et al. (2011) developed "Semantic Orientation CALculator (SO-CAL)" using a dictionary, which includes opinion words (nouns, adverb, verbs, and adjectives) along with their polarity and strength value (Taboada et al., 2011) and achieved the best performance in term of the accuracy 70.10% on movie dataset among other datasets. In 2012, Karamibekr & Ghorbani developed a sentiment classification system in which verbs are considered the core element of the system and created an opinion verb dictionary of 440 verbs and 1726 terms for the term opinion dictionary. The value of polarity is assigned to each word in the dictionary ranging from +2 to -2, and their system was tested on a dataset related to social issues with an accuracy of 65% (Karamibekr & Ghorbani, 2012). P. K. Singh et al., (2015) used negation handling rules and a dictionary-based approach to classify the social issues related dataset into positive or negative class and achieved an accuracy of 79.16% for negative sentences. Iqbal et al., (2015) proposed a Bias-aware thresholding (BAT) method with the combination of AFINN and SentiStrength to reduce the bias in the lexicon-based method for SA and obtained 69% of accuracy using Naïve Bayes classifier.

In 2016, Bhargava et al. developed a system of SA for code-mixed sentences of the English language with four Indian languages (Hindi, Telugu, Bengali, and Tamil) using the count-based approach and language-specific SentiWordNets to determine the word's polarity value. Their system classified sentences based on the number of negative and positive words present within the sentence and obtained 54.4% of F score on English_Hindi mixed dataset. In the same year, a lexical-based method was proposed by (Shamsudin et al., 2016) to classify the Facebook comments written in Malay language using the verb, adverb, and negation. The Verb + Negation combination achieved the highest accuracy of 52.12%.

In 2017, a SA system for a specific domain text was proposed by (Cruz et al., 2017), using a dictionary-based approach. The system was tested on different datasets such as kitchen, book, movie reviews, and agriculture; and achieved the best performance on movie reviews (F score of 66%). A multi-task tri-training model based on deep learning was proposed by (Ruder & Plank, 2018). They have trained their model with three model-specific outputs jointly and achieved 79.15% accuracy on Amazon product reviews. Later, in 2018 Han et al. proposed a method to reduce the bias in the lexicon-based approach. They used SentiWordNet and tried to improve accuracy but achieved 69.52% accuracy and 69.65% F score (Han et al., 2018). Baoxin Wang (2018) proposed a deep learning-based Disconnected Recurrent Neural Networks model, and Yu & Liu (2018) proposed Sliced Recurrent Neural Networks model. They have tested their models on large Amazon product reviews, but their system achieved less than 65.00% accuracy.

SentiVerb system was developed by (S. K. Singh & Sachan, 2019b) and tested on GST dataset and movie reviews. The system considered verb as a feature, and obtained 82.50% accuracy on the GST dataset and 71.30% accuracy on movie reviews even with small dataset availability. In 2020, an event named SemEval-2020 Task 9 was conducted on SA of code-mixed tweets, and the highest performance was reported as 75.00% F score by one participant on bilingual (English_Hindi) text using XLM-R method (Patwa et al., 2020). In 2020, a method to automatically label the document with polarity or sentiment class was proposed and reduce human intervention, process time, and cost (Kansal et al., 2020). Their polarity detection task, along with the sentiment classification system, achieved 81.98% accuracy on Amazon product reviews using a logistic regression approach.

It is observed that most of the research work has been conducted on SA/opinion mining for monolingual language text instead of bilingual and multilingual text for resource-scarce languages (Lo et al., 2017) as per Table 1 and recent survey articles (Drus & Khalid, 2019; Guellil & Boukhalfa, 2015; Hussein, 2018; Medhat et al., 2014; Ravi & Ravi, 2015; Serrano-Guerrero et al., 2015; R. K. Singh et al., 2020; Yue et al., 2019). The highest accuracy on SM dataset is 82.5%; 71.3% on movie reviews (S. K. Singh & Sachan, 2019b); 81.98% on Amazon product reviews (Kansal et al., 2020) and 64.43% on large Amazon product reviews. Most of the studies other than English language are in Chinese, Japanese, German, Spanish, French, Italian, Swedish, Arabic, and Romanian (Lo et al., 2017). Therefore, a smaller number of studies and experiments have been conducted for bilingual and multilingual text and have not shown adequate system performance. There is no work found related to the sentiment classification of code-mixed bilingual (English and Punjabi) phonetic text. The machine learning techniques require a large amount of labeled dataset(s) for training purposes, and code-mixed phonetic text dataset(s) is not available sufficiently. Hence, there is a need to design and develop a SA system, which can give better performance for both monolingual and bilingual code-mixed phonetic text. With this perspective, a system is designed and developed for SA of bilingual (English and Punjabi) code-mixed phonetic text using a rule-based classifier and dictionary-based approach. The first time the verb opinion dictionary

(VOD) for Punjabi words is developed with the motivation of the opinion verb dictionary (OVD) of the English language (S. K. Singh & Sachan, 2019b).

Table 1. Analysis of existing works related to SA

Authors	Method	Accuracy (%)	F Score (%)	Limitations
(Taboada et al., 2011)	Lexicon-based	70.10		● Small data size (5100) ● Only for English language text
(Karamibekr & Ghorbani, 2012)	Dictionary-based	65.00		● Small data size (1016) ● Only tested on social issue dataset ● Only for English language text
(Iqbal et al., 2015)	BAT with Lexicon-based	69.00		● System designed only for English language text
(P. K. Singh et al., 2015)	Dictionary-based	79.00		● Very Small data size (48) ● Considered only negative comments for testing. ● Only for English language text
(Shamsudin et al., 2016)	Dictionary-based	52.12		● Very Small data size (450 Facebook comments) ● Limited to Malay language text ● Not sufficient accuracy
(Bhargava et al., 2016)	Sentiwordnet		54.40	● Small dataset (637) ● Not considered Punjabi and English code-mixed text ● Performance not sufficient
(Cruz et al., 2017)	Dictionary-based		66.00	● Small dataset (4183) ● Only for English language text
(Ruder & Plank, 2018)	Multi-task tri-training	79.15		● Only for English language text
(Han et al., 2018)	Dictionary-based	69.52	69.60	● Small dataset (2000) ● Only for English language text ● Only Amazon product reviews
(Baoxin Wang, 2018)	Disconnected Recurrent Neural Networks	64.43		● Only for English language text ● Not sufficient accuracy
(Yu & Liu, 2018)	Sliced Recurrent Neural Networks	61.65		● Only for English language text ● Not sufficient accuracy
(S. K. Singh & Sachan, 2019b)	Dictionary-based	82.50	87.04	● Small dataset (400) ● Only for English language text
(S. K. Singh & Sachan, 2019b)	Dictionary-based	71.30	71.39	● Small dataset (2000) ● Only for English language text
(Patwa et al., 2020)	XLM-R		75.00	● Considered only Hindi and English code-mixed text
(Kansal et al., 2020)	Logistic regression	81.98		● Small dataset (8000) ● Only for English language text

The significant contributions are: First time bilingual (English & Punjabi) code-mixed phonetic texts are considered for SA. In this article, a sentiment analysis system is proposed to classify code-mixed bilingual (English_Punjabi) phonetic text using handcrafted rules, rule-based classifiers, and dictionaries. The bilingual code-mixed testing datasets (86,400 reviews) are generated from monolingual text. The spell checker, VOD, negation words, positive words, negative prefixes, negation handling rules, stop words, and StemVerb system is developed and used to extract the writer's sentiment from their written text. The VOD of the Punjabi and English language is developed, which includes 653 words of Punjabi and 677 English words. The root verb list of 3582 words and an irregular verb list of 222 words is developed. The StemVerb system (Sub-system of SA system) is proposed to extract the root verb from the inflected form of the English language verb and obtain 22.83% better accuracy than the existing snowball stemmer system. The proposed SA system achieved better performance than state-of-art approaches on all four benchmark datasets, for monolingual text (better accuracy of 3% on SM dataset, 1.5% on movie reviews, 1.35% on Amazon product reviews, and 4.56% on large Amazon product reviews).

This article is organized as follows: Section 1 describes the introduction of SA and the idea about previous research works on SA. Section 2 provides detailed information about the proposed framework of the system and an explanation of the different phases for the implementation of the system. Section 3 is related to the performance evaluation of the proposed system on the different dataset(s) and result analysis along with the comparison of performance with state-of-the-art techniques. Finally, a brief detailed conclusion of this article is provided along with the future scope in the last section.

2. PROPOSED SYSTEM FRAMEWORK AND IMPLEMENTATION

The proposed system classifies the code-mixed phonetic text into positive or negative using a dictionary-based approach. This system considered verb words as a feature. This system has been designed which can handle bilingual phonetic text and constituted by (a) lower case conversion (b) tokenization (c) spell checker (d) part-of-speech (POS) tagging (e) stop words elimination (f) stemming(g) sentiment calculation (h) document classification as shown in Figure 1.

Figure 1. Proposed system framework for code-mixed bilingual phonetic text

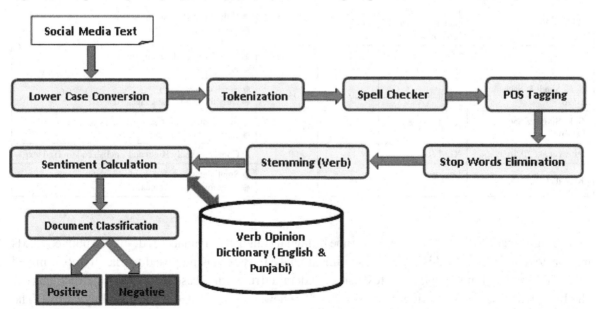

2.1. Testing Datasets Generation

The existing four datasets in the English language are used to generate bilingual (English_Punjabi) code-mixed phonetic text datasets (shown in Table 2) with the help of a bilingual dictionary of English and Punjabi words. The Punjabi words are written in phonetic using Roman script letters. The transliteration of Punjabi words into phonetic words is done using the GRT system (S. K. Singh & Sachan, 2019a). The GST implementation Facebook comments are taken from an article (S. K. Singh & Sachan, 2019b), movie reviews (Pang & Lee, 2004), Amazon product reviews (Book, DVD, Electronics, Kitchen) (Blitzer et al., 2007) and large Amazon product reviews (He & McAuley, 2016). The size of the dataset for testing is 172,800 comments/reviews (86,400 for each English and English_Punjabi language).

Table 2. Testing datasets

Sr. No.	Datasets	Size	Language	
			Existing	Generated
1	GST Implementation	400 comments	English	English and Punjabi
2	Movie Reviews	2000 reviews	English	English and Punjabi
3	Amazon Product Reviews	8000 reviews	English	English and Punjabi
4	Large Amazon Product Reviews	76,000 reviews	English	English and Punjabi

2.2. Conversion in Lower Case and Tokenization

The proposed system uses various dictionaries in which data are stored in lower case, so the testing dataset must be converted into lower case. The comments are split into sentences, and sentences into words because the proposed system works at the word level. The importance of tokenization (splitting) is discussed in the article (P. K. Singh et al., 2015).

2.3. Spell Checker of Bilingual Text

The testing dataset is generated by inserting the Punjabi (Phonetic) words within the English language sentence, and only correct Punjabi words without spelling mistakes are used. So, there is no need to check the spelling of Punjabi words. The misspelled word is detected and corrected using the existing system for English words (S. K. Singh & Sachan, 2019b).

2.4. POS Tagging

Python's NLTK tool is used to tag Part-of-speech (POS) along with each word. The POS tagging makes it easy to identify the verb, adverb, adjective (Turney, 2002) from the sentence.

2.5. Elimination of Stop Words from the Bilingual Text

The stop words are those words that are useless for some natural language processing tasks. The uses of stop words depend upon tasks where these words will be used. The significance of stop words removal and various methods to eliminate such words are explained in the article (Saif et al., 2014). After removing these words, the remaining words are further processed. There are 217 stop words in the dictionary, which include 134 English stop words from the article (S. K. Singh & Sachan, 2019b) and 83 selected Punjabi stop words from the article (Kaur & Saini, 2016).

2.6. Stemming

Stemming is the process of finding the root word from its inflectional form. During the stemming, generally the suffixes and prefixes are removed from its inflectional form to get the root word (Jivani, 2011). For example- *keeps, kept, keeping* are the inflectional (grammatical) form of the 'keep' word. Here, the root word 'keep' is found using the removal of suffixes from *keeps* and *keeping* words. The size of the database becomes bulky when all forms of a word are stored. Hence, the database stores only root words. Therefore, a verb stemmer system is developed for English language text, as shown in Figures 2 and 3, in algorithms 1 and 2. The stemming is done only for verbs of English language words because VOD contains only opinion verbs. StemVerb algorithm 1 is used to extract the root verb word from a different form of a verb. The POS taggers are attached with each word, and identified all verbs for stemming. There are three sub-stemming functions based on verb forms, such as extraction from (a) 'ing', (b) "ies, es, s" and (c) past and past participle (ied, ed, en, d, n) verb form.

Algorithm 1: *StemVerb*

Input: Word along with POS tag
Output: Word (root/original word)
Step 1:   If POS tag are VBP, VBG, VBZ, VBN and VBD, then word is a verb
Step 2:   **(a)** if word's last letters are 'ing' then call stemming function to find root word from 'ing' verb form (shown in Figure 2)
          (b)   if word's last letters are 'ies', 'es', 's', then call stemming function to find root word from 'ies', 'es', 's' verb form (shown in Figure 3)
          (c)   if word's last letters are 'ied', 'ed', 'en', 'd', 'n' or VBN/VBD POS tag then call stemming function to find root word from past and past participle verb form (algorithm 2)
Step 3:   return word (root word/original word)
Step 4:   Otherwise, word in not verb
Step 5:   Return word.

Figure 2. Extraction of root verb from 'ing' verb form

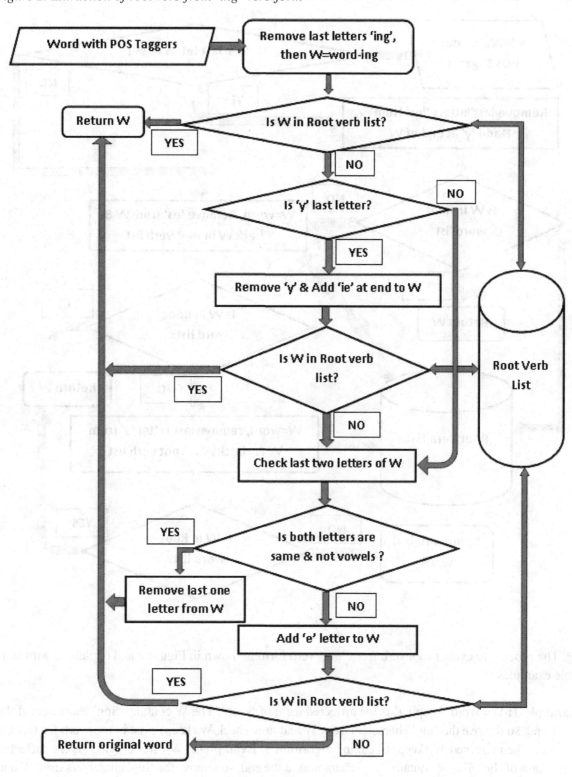

Figure 3. Extraction of root verb from (ies, es, s) verb form

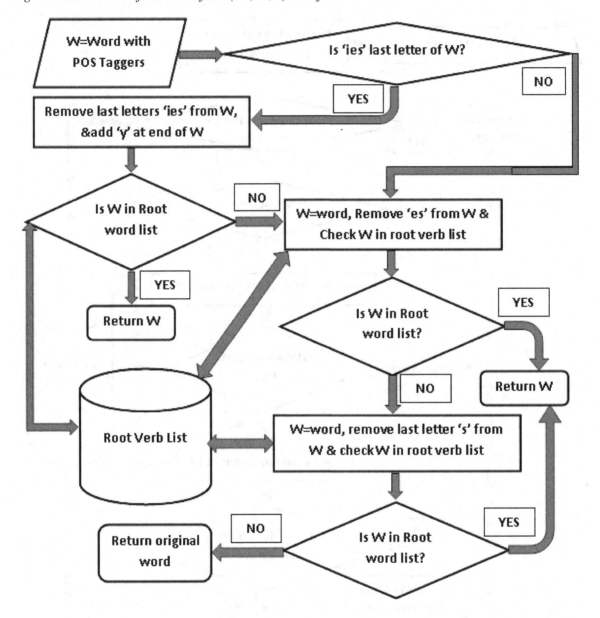

The process to extract root verb from 'ing' verb form is shown in Figure 2 and explained with suitable examples.

Example-1: W=Word 'keeping' is the inflected form of 'keep'. The W contains 'ing' characters at the end, so remove the 'ing' characters from W and now check W (keep) exist in root verb list (RVL), yes then returned W (keep) to calling algorithm 1. **Example-2:** W=Word 'lying' is the inflected form of 'lie'. The W contains 'ing' characters at the end, so remove the 'ing' characters from W and now check W (ly) exist in RVL; no W does not exist in RVL. Then check 'y' is the last character of W (ly), yes so replace 'y' with 'ie', and now W is 'lie', again check in RVL, W exists in RVL. Finally, returned W (lie) to calling algorithm 1.

Example-3: W=Word 'getting' is the inflected form of 'get'. The W contains 'ing' characters at the end, so remove the 'ing' characters from W and now check W (gett) exist in RVL, no W does not exist in RVL. Then check 'y' is the last character of W (gett), no so check last two characters are same and not vowels, yes now remove one last character from W (gett). Finally, W is *'get'* word, which is returned to calling algorithm 1.

Example-4: W=Word 'choosing' is the inflected form of 'choose'. The W contains 'ing' characters at the end, so remove the 'ing' characters from W and now check W (choos) exist in RVL; no W does not exist in RVL. Then check 'y' is the last character of W (choos), no so check last two characters are same and not vowels, no now add 'e' at the end of W (choos). Finally, W is 'choose', check-in RVL, W exists in RVL. Therefore, returned W (choose) to the calling algorithm 1.

Figure 3 shows the process to extract the root verb word from "ies, es, s" verb form and explained with suitable examples.

Example-5: W=word 'applies' is an inflected word of 'apply'. The W contains 'ies' characters at the end. Therefore, 'ies' characters are replaced with 'y', and W (apply) is checked in RVL, yes W exist in RVL, so finally W (apply) is returned to calling algorithm 1.

Example 6: W=word 'bashes' is an inflected word of 'bash'. The W contains 'es' characters at the end. Then remove 'es' from the end of W (bashes) and checked W (bash) in RVL; yes W exist in RVL. Therefore, finally returned W to calling algorithm 1.

Example 7: W=word 'awakes' is an inflected word of 'awake'. The W contains 'es' characters at the end. Then remove 'es' from the end of W (awakes) and checked W (awak) in RVL; no W does not exist in RVL. Now remove 's' from W (awakes) and check W (awake) in RVL; yes W exist in RVL. Finally, W (awake) is returned to calling algorithm 1.

Algorithm 2: *Stemming verb from past and past participle verb form*

Abbreviations Used: W=word, RVL= root verb list, W_T= target word

Input: Word along with POS tagger

Output: Word (Root/Original word)

Step 1:   If word's POS tag (VBN/VBD) and exist in an irregular verb form list, then extract the root verb word from the irregular verb list.

Step 2:   If 'ied' last letter of W, then W_T=W minus 'ied' and add 'y' at end of W_T

(a)   If W_T exist in RVL, then return W_T

(b)   Otherwise return W

Step 3:   If 'ed'/ 'en' last letter of W, then W_T= W minus 'ed'/ 'en' and check W_T in RVL

(a)   If W_T exist in RVL, then return W_T

(b)   If 'd'/ 'n' last letter of W, then W_T= W minus 'd'/ 'n' and check W_T in RVL

(i)   If W_T exist in RVL, then return W_T

(c)   If last two letter of W_T is same, then

(i)	If 'en' is last letter of W, then remove one last letter from W_T
(1)	If W_T exist in RVL, then return W_T
(2)	Otherwise, add 'e' at end of W_T and return W_T
(ii)	Otherwise, remove one last letter from W_T
(1)	If W_T exist in RVL, then return W_T
(2)	Otherwise, return W

Step 4: Otherwise, return W

2.7. Sentiment Calculation

In this section, the sentiment score of each sentence is calculated. Some negation handlings rules are proposed to determine the polarity of sentences or words, whenever negation words, negative prefixes, and positive words occur within the sentence.

2.7.1 Negation Handling

The significance of negation words was first time discussed by (Polanyi & Zaenen, 2006). The six negation handling rules are proposed and are used when the polarity of words changes due to the presence of negation words[1] or negative prefixes in the sentence (P. K. Singh et al., 2015). For example- I do *not* like this movie. Here *'not'* is a negation word due to which the polarity of the sentence changes from positive to negative. Threshold negative (T_n) value is fixed for all negation words, which is equal to -0.25 discussed in the article (S. K. Singh & Sachan, 2019b). The negative prefixes (dis, de, mis, ir, il, in, un) or suffixes are also acting as negation words, so the negation handling rules (shown in Table 5) are used to calculate the sentiment score whenever these negation words and negative prefixes or suffixes occur within a sentence (S. K. Singh & Sachan, 2019b). All 14 negation words, 7 negative prefixes of English language discussed in the article (S. K. Singh & Sachan, 2019b) and 8 negation words (shown in Table 3), 4 negative prefixes (de, ka, da, a) of Punjabi language are used for the implementation of the proposed system.

Table 3. Negation words of Punjabi language

Sr. No.	Negation Word	Sr. No.	Negation Word
1	naahi	5	bekaar
2	nahiin	6	galat
3	viruddh	7	gair
4	bura	8	nakaaraatamak

A sentence's sentiment is expressed by the opinion words (positive words, negation words, and verbs) present within the sentence. The positive words are the opinion words, but they are not opinion verbs. For example- Nice photo. Here 'nice' word is not a verb, but still expresses the sentiment of the sentence. Therefore, these kinds of opinion words are considered as positive words (S. K. Singh & Sachan, 2019b).

There are a total of 35 positive words, out of which 20 words of English are taken from the article (S. K. Singh & Sachan, 2019b) and 15 words of Punjabi language (shown in Table 4). The sentiment score value for these positive words is denoted as threshold positive (T_p), which is equal to 0.125 value as discussed by (S. K. Singh & Sachan, 2019b).

Table 4. Positive words of Punjabi language

Sr. No.	Positive Word	Sr. No.	Positive Word	Sr. No.	Positive Word
1	haan	6	bharosa	11	piaar
2	thiik	7	changa	12	sahaaita
3	dhannavaad	8	shaanadaar	13	kadar
4	khair	9	vadhiia	14	vadhaaiiaan
5	mahaan	10	sahii	15	sakaaraatamak

Table 5. Rules for Negation Handling

S.No.	Opinion verb	Negative Prefixes	Negation Words	Positive Word	Sentiment Score Positive/ negative	Sentiment score calculation
1	Positive	Yes	Yes	No	Positive	$Pos_{score}=Pos_{score}+Word_{score}$
2	Positive	Yes	No	No	Negative	$Neg_{score}=Neg_{score}-1\times Word_{score}$
3	Positive	No	Yes	No	Negative	$Neg_{score}=Neg_{score}-1\times Word_{score}$
4	No	No	Yes	Yes	Negative	$Neg_{score}=Neg_{score}-1\times T_p$
5	Verb out of the dictionary	No	Yes	No	Negative	$Neg_{score}=Neg_{score}-1\times T_n$
6	Negative	No	Yes	No	Positive	$Pos_{score}=Pos_{score}-1\times Word_{score}$

2.7.2 Calculation of Sentiment Score

The VOD consists of opinion verbs of both languages (English and Punjabi) and the sentiment score value. The value of the sentiment score is from -1 to 1. The negation and positive words are not included in this VOD because they may be adverbs, adjectives, determiners, and prepositions. There are 1330 opinion verbs, out of which 677 English words and 553 words of Punjabi language. The sentiment score to these words is assigned manually based on their polarity and with the help of existing English SentiWordNet 3.0 (Baccianella et al., 2010). This VOD is domain-dependent, but it can be further used in other domains only after adding some words from that domain.

The opinion verbs are considered as a feature and are extracted from the subjective sentences; and searched into the VOD, if the word is present in VOD, then extract the value of sentiment score of the opinion verb which is denoted as $Word_{score}$. The value of $Word_{score}$ is positive ($Word_{score}>0$) then the word is positive, otherwise the value of $Word_{score}$ is negative ($Word_{score}<0$), then the word is negative. The positive sentiment score (Pos_{score}) value for all positive opinion words (verb/term) is calculated using Equation (1) and negative sentiment score (Neg_{score}) value for all negative opinion words (verb/term) using Equation

(2) within a sentence. The sentence sentiment score ($Sent_{score}$) is calculated using Equation (3) in which the normalized value of Pos_{score} and Neg_{score} is added. To normalize the Pos_{score} and Neg_{score}, Pos_{score} is divided by the total positive opinion words (p) and Neg_{score} is divided by the total negative opinion words (n) respectively in Equation (3). The document/comment sentiment score is calculated using Equation (4), by taking the summation of the sentiment score value ($Sent_{score}$). of all the sentences, and the total number of sentences is denoted by 's' in Equation (4). The value of each sentence's sentiment score is calculated using the 'calculation of sentiment score' algorithm 3.

$$Pos_{score} = \sum_{i=0}^{p}(Word_{score})_i \text{ if } Word_{score} > 0 \tag{1}$$

$$Neg_{score} = \sum_{j=0}^{n}(Word_{score})_j \text{ if } Word_{score} < 0 \tag{2}$$

$$Sent_{score} = \frac{Pos_{score}}{p} + \frac{Neg_{score}}{n} \tag{3}$$

$$Doc_{score} = \sum_{k=0}^{s}(Sent_{score})_k \tag{4}$$

Algorithm 3: *Calculation of sentiment score*

Notations: W-> Word, VOD -> Verb Opinion Dictionary, NW-> Negation Words, NHR->Negation Handling Rules, NP-> Negative Prefixes, PWL-> Positive Word List

Input: Sentence (text)

Output: Sentence's sentiment score

Step1: Read word (W) by word from the sentence and repeat steps 2 to 5

Step2: If last W of a sentence is a NW, then add T_n to Neg_{score} and add 1 to n, goto step 1

Step3: If W is found in VOD then extract $Word_{score}$ from VOD

    (a)   if NW comes before W, then update Pos_{score} or Neg_{score} using NHR and add 1 to p/n, goto step 1

    (b)   otherwise, update Pos_{score} or Neg_{score} using Equation (1) or (2) and add 1 to p/n, goto step 1

Step4: If W is found in PWL, then

    (a)   if NW comes before W, then update Neg_{score} using NHR and add 1 to n, goto step 1

    (b)   otherwise, update Pos_{score} by adding T_p and add 1 to p, goto step 1

Step5: If W does not find in VOD and PWL, then

    (a)   if NW comes before W, then update Neg_{score} NHR and add 1 to n, goto step 1

(b)   if NP exist in W and root word found in VOD, then extract $Word_{score}$ from VOD

    (i)   if NW comes before W, then update Pos_{score} using NHR and add 1 to p, goto step 1

    (ii)   otherwise, update Neg_{score} using NHR and add 1 to n, goto step 1

Step6: $Sent_{score}$ is updated using Equation (3)

Step7: $Sent_{score}$ is return

2.8. Document Classification

The document is classified into two classes (negative or positive) using binary class classification. The document's sentiment score (Doc_{score}) is calculated using Equation (4), and the document is classified using a rule-based classifier Equation (5). The document is classified as a positive class if its' Doc_{score} value is greater than or equal to zero; otherwise, a negative class using Equation (5). Those documents whose Doc_{score} value is equal to zero is considered positive due to the presence of positive words in most cases in place of an opinion verb (S. K. Singh & Sachan, 2019b).

$$Document = \begin{cases} Positive & if\ Doc_{score} \geq 0 \\ Negative & otherwise \end{cases} \quad (5)$$

3. EXPERIMENTAL RESULTS AND DISCUSSION

The proposed SA system's performance is evaluated for English and English_Punjabi (bilingual) text on four different datasets (discussed in section 2.1). The proposed system used a dictionary-based approach and various dictionaries such as stop words, negative prefixes, negation words, positive words of both English and Punjabi language. The T_n=-0.25 is the threshold negative value and T_p=0.125 is the threshold positive value were used (S. K. Singh & Sachan, 2019b). Also, the performance of the proposed StemVerb system is discussed in this section.

The system performance is measured using performance metrics such as recall, precision, accuracy, and F score (Equation 6 to 9). Its' some related terms are defined as true positive (T_p): positive texts are predicted as positive; false positive (F_p): negative texts are predicted as positive; true negative (T_n): negative texts are predicted as negative and false negative (F_n): positive texts are predicted as negative.

$$Recall = \frac{T_p}{\left(T_p + F_n\right)} \quad (6)$$

$$Precision = \frac{T_p}{\left(T_p + F_p\right)} \quad (7)$$

$$Accuracy = \frac{\left(T_p + T_n\right)}{\left(T_p + F_p + F_n + T_n\right)} \qquad (8)$$

$$F\,score = \frac{2 \times recall \times precision}{recall + precision} \qquad (9)$$

3.1 Performance of System Evaluation on Different Datasets

The performance of the proposed system is discussed in this section on four different dataset(s). All dataset(s) size and its' domain are different. The system's performance is better on the GST implementation dataset than other datasets (shown in Figures 4 and 5). The performance of the proposed system is better in the English than the English_Punjabi language datasets.

The proposed system is designed for code-mixed bilingual phonetic text, but its performance is evaluated on both monolingual (English) and bilingual (English_Punjabi) text. As per Table 6, the system performance is better than the existing state-of-the-art methods on all datasets. The system achieved better performance in terms of accuracy in the range of 3% to 33.38% on social media dataset, 1.5% to 3.8% on movie reviews, 1.35% to 13.81% on Amazon product reviews, 4.56% to 7.34% on large Amazon product reviews for monolingual text. In the bilingual text, system performance is better than other existing methods in terms of F score (13.22% on social media and 17.03% on movie reviews).

Figure 4. Performance of system on the different dataset(s) (English)

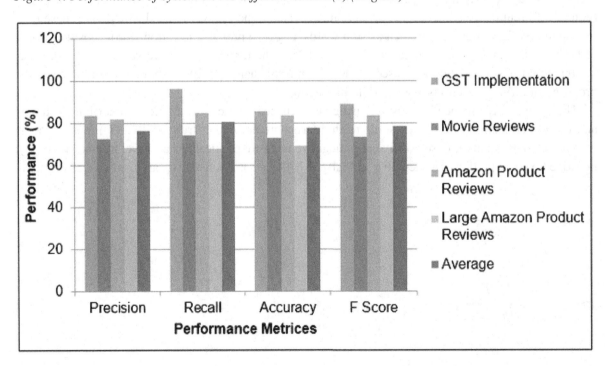

Figure 5. Performance of system on the different datasets (English and Bilingual)

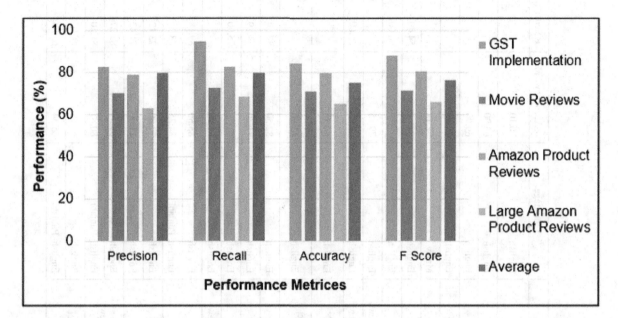

3.2 Performance Evaluation of StemVerb System

A StemVerb system is proposed to extract the root verb from the inflectional form of verbs. The framework and working process of the StemVerb system (discussed in section 2.6). The root verb list of 3582 words and irregular verb forms a list of 222 words is generated with different resources[2,3.]. There are 3992 words used to test the StemVerb system and the existing two algorithms performance, such as Snowball[4] and Lancaster[5]. The StemVerb system is the only proposed for the verb of the English language. The performance of StemVerb is better than Snowball and Lancaster stemmer (shown in Figure 6).

Figure 6. Performance of stemmers (Snowball, Lancaster, and StemVerb)

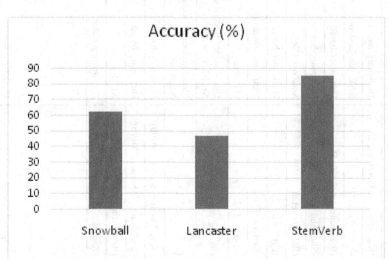

Table 6. Experimental results are compared with state-of-the-art

Authors	Method	POS	Dataset	Language	Accuracy (%)	F Score (%)
(Taboada et al., 2011)	Lexicon-based	Adjective, adverb, verb, noun	Movie reviews	English	70.10	
(Karamibekr & Ghorbani, 2012)	Dictionary-based	Verb, adverb, adjective	Social media	English	65.00	
(Iqbal et al., 2015)	BAT with Lexicon-based		Movie reviews	English	69.00	
(P. K. Singh et al., 2015)	Dictionary-based	Verb	Social media	English	79.00	
(Shamsudin et al., 2016)	Dictionary-based	Verb, adverb, adjective	Social media	Malay	52.12	54.40
(Bhargava et al., 2016)	SentiWordNet		Movie reviews	English_Hindi		66.00
(Cruz et al., 2017)	Dictionary-based	Adjective, noun	Movie reviews	English		
(Ruder & Plank, 2018)	Multi-task tri-training		Amazon product reviews	English	79.15	
(Han et al., 2018)	Dictionary-based		Amazon product reviews	English	69.52	69.60
(Baoxin Wang, 2018)	Disconnected Recurrent Neural Networks		Large Amazon product reviews	English	64.43	
(Yu & Liu, 2018)	Sliced Recurrent Neural Networks		Large Amazon product reviews	English	61.65	
(S. K. Singh & Sachan, 2019b)	Dictionary-based	Verb	Social media	English	82.50	87.04
(S. K. Singh & Sachan, 2019b)	Dictionary-based	Verb	Movie reviews	English	71.30	71.39
(Patwa et al., 2020)	XLM-R		Social media	English_Hindi		75.00
(Kansal et al., 2020)	Logistic regression		Amazon product reviews	English	81.98	
Proposed system	Dictionary-based	Verb	Social media	English	**85.50**	**89.18**
				English_Punjabi	84.25	88.22
			Movie reviews	English	72.80	73.12
				English_Punjabi	71.00	71.43
			Amazon product reviews	English	83.33	83.27
				English_Punjabi	80.87	81.20
			Large Amazon product reviews	English	68.99	68.07
				English_Punjabi	65.34	65.84

The performance of SA system evaluated in terms of accuracy for bilingual text using all three stemmers, but SA system performed better using the StemVerb system than the other two existing stemmers (shown in Figure 7). Also, the accuracy of the proposed SA system has been improved after the stemming of verbs on bilingual datasets (shown in Figure 8). The VOD contains only root verbs along with their sentiment scores. Therefore, the stemming of verb words improves the performance of the proposed SA system.

Figure 7. Sentiment analysis system's accuracy using all three stemmers

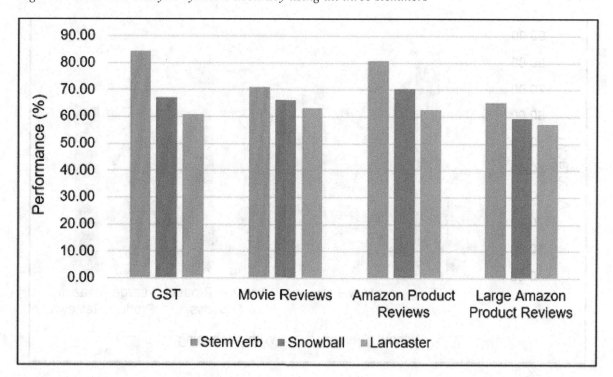

4. CONCLUSION AND FUTURE SCOPE

The sentiment analysis system for bilingual code-mixed phonetic text is developed and tested on four datasets, written in both monolingual and bilingual. The existing monolingual text in English is converted into bilingual (English and Punjabi) code-mixed phonetic text. The spell checker, VOD, negation words, positive words, negative prefixes, negation handling rules, stop words, and StemVerb system is developed and used to extract the writer's sentiment from their written text. The developed VOD for English and Punjabi language, contains 1330 verb opinion words of both English and Punjabi language. The list of irregular verbs of 222 words and root verb list of 3582 words is developed to improve the SA system's performance. The SA system classifies text into negative or positive class using a rule-based classifier and sentiment score value extracted from the VOD. The SA system obtained an accuracy of 85.5% and 84.25% on the GST dataset; 72.8% and 71% on the movie reviews; 83.33% and 80.87% on Amazon product reviews; 68.99% and 65.34% on large Amazon product reviews for monolingual and bilingual text respectively. This system will automatically classify customers' feedback into positive and negative class, and will help customers to decide before purchasing a product; manufacturers can enhance the quality of product and services based on it, and can keep an eye on their competitors; know the mood of the public before election and government policies. The proposed SA system for bilingual text can be further extended to other code-mixed bilingual texts by modifying some components easily. The developed VOD can also be extended for other part-of-speech and to other languages.

Figure 8. Sentiment analysis system's accuracy with and without stemming

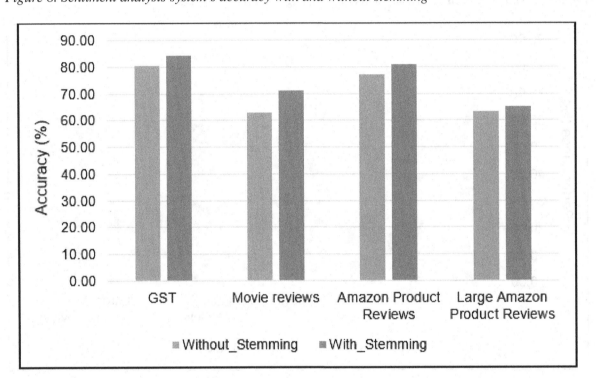

REFERENCES

Alharbi, J. R., & Alhalabi, W. S. (2020). Hybrid Approach for Sentiment Analysis of Twitter Posts Using a Dictionary-based Approach and Fuzzy Logic Methods. *International Journal on Semantic Web and Information Systems*, *16*(1), 116–145. doi:10.4018/IJSWIS.2020010106

Baccianella, S., Esuli, A., & Sebastiani, F. (2010). SENTIWORDNET 3.0: An enhanced lexical resource for sentiment analysis and opinion mining. *7th International Conference on Language Resources and Evaluation*, 2200–2204. http://nmis.isti.cnr.it/sebastiani/Publications/LREC10.pdf

Wang, B. (2018). Disconnected Recurrent Neural Networks for Text Categorization. *56th Annual Meeting of the Association for Computational Linguistics*, 2311–2320. 10.18653/v1/P18-1215

Bhargava, R., Sharma, Y., & Sharma, S. (2016). Sentiment analysis for mixed script Indic sentences. *2016 International Conference on Advances in Computing, Communications and Informatics*, 524–529. 10.1109/ICACCI.2016.7732099

Blitzer, J., Dredze, M., & Pereira, F. (2007). Biographies, bollywood, boom-boxes and blenders: Domain adaptation for sentiment classification. *ACL 2007 - Proceedings of the 45th Annual Meeting of the Association for Computational Linguistics*, 440–447. https://www.aclweb.org/anthology/P07-1056.pdf

Bonadiman, D., Castellucci, G., Favalli, A., Romagnoli, R., & Moschitti, A. (2017). Neural Sentiment Analysis for a Real-World Application. In *Proceedings of the Fourth Italian Conference on Computational Linguistics CLiC-it 2017* (pp. 42–47). Accademia University Press. 10.4000/books.aaccademia.2357

Cambria, E., Poria, S., Bajpai, R., & Schuller, B. (2016). SenticNet 4: A semantic resource for sentiment analysis based on conceptual primitives. *COLING 2016 - 26th International Conference on Computational Linguistics, Proceedings of COLING 2016: Technical Papers*, 2666–2677. https://www.aclweb.org/anthology/C16-1251.pdf

Cruz, L., Ochoa, J., Roche, M., & Poncelet, P. (2017). Dictionary-based sentiment analysis applied to a specific domain. In A.-S. H. Lossio-Ventura J. (Ed.), Communications in Computer and Information Science: Vol. 656 CCIS (pp. 57–68). Springer. doi:10.1007/978-3-319-55209-5_5

D'Andrea, A., Ferri, F., Grifoni, P., & Guzzo, T. (2015). Approaches, Tools and Applications for Sentiment Analysis Implementation. *International Journal of Computers and Applications*, *125*(3), 26–33. doi:10.5120/ijca2015905866

Drus, Z., & Khalid, H. (2019). Sentiment Analysis in Social Media and Its Application: Systematic Literature Review. *Procedia Computer Science*, *161*, 707–714. doi:10.1016/j.procs.2019.11.174

Dutta, S., Saha, T., Banerjee, S., & Naskar, S. K. (2015). Text normalization in code-mixed social media text. *2015 IEEE 2nd International Conference on Recent Trends in Information Systems*, 378–382. 10.1109/ReTIS.2015.7232908

Guellil, I., & Boukhalfa, K. (2015). Social big data mining: A survey focused on opinion mining and sentiments analysis. *2015 12th International Symposium on Programming and Systems*, 1–10. 10.1109/ISPS.2015.7244976

Han, H., Zhang, Y., Zhang, J., Yang, J., & Zou, X. (2018). Improving the performance of lexicon-based review sentiment analysis method by reducing additional introduced sentiment bias. *PLoS One*, *13*(8), e0202523. doi:10.1371/journal.pone.0202523 PMID:30142154

He, R., & McAuley, J. (2016). Ups and Downs: Modeling the Visual Evolution of Fashion Trends with One-Class Collaborative Filtering. *International World Wide Web Conference Committee (IW3C2)*, 507–517. 10.1145/2872427.2883037

Hopken, W., Fuchs, M., Menner, T., & Lexhagen, M. (2017). Sensing the Online Social Sphere Using a Sentiment Analytical Approach. In Z. Xiang & D. R. Fesenmaier (Eds.), *Analytics in Smart Tourism Design Concepts and Methods* (pp. 129–146). Springer. doi:10.1007/978-3-319-44263-1_8

Hussein, D. M. E.-D. M. (2018). A survey on sentiment analysis challenges. *Journal of King Saud University -. Engineering and Science, 30*(4), 330–338. doi:10.1016/j.jksues.2016.04.002

Iqbal, M., Karim, A., & Kamiran, F. (2015). Bias-aware lexicon-based sentiment analysis. *Proceedings of the 30th Annual ACM Symposium on Applied Computing - SAC '15*, 845–850. 10.1145/2695664.2695759

Jivani, A. G. (2011). A Comparative Study of Stemming Algorithms. *International Journal of Computer Technology and Applications, 2*(6), 1930–1938. https://pdfs.semanticscholar.org/1c0c/0fa35d4ff8a2f92 5eb955e48d655494bd167.pdf

Kansal, N., Goel, L., & Gupta, S. (2020). *Cross-domain sentiment classification initiated with Polarity Detection Task.* EAI Endorsed Transactions on Scalable Information Systems., doi:10.4108/eai.26-5-2020.165965

Karamibekr, M., & Ghorbani, A. A. (2012). Verb oriented sentiment classification. *2012 IEEE/WIC/ACM International Conference on Web Intelligence*, 327–331. 10.1109/WI-IAT.2012.122

Kaur, J., & Saini, J. R. (2016). Punjabi Stop Words: A Gurmukhi, Shahmukhi and Roman Scripted Chronicle. *ACM Symposium on Women in Research 2016*, 32–37. 10.1145/2909067.2909073

Lo, S. L., Cambria, E., Chiong, R., & Cornforth, D. (2017). Multilingual sentiment analysis: From formal to informal and scarce resource languages. *Artificial Intelligence Review, 48*(4), 499–527. doi:10.100710462-016-9508-4

Medhat, W., Hassan, A., & Korashy, H. (2014). Sentiment analysis algorithms and applications: A survey. *Ain Shams Engineering Journal, 5*(4), 1093–1113. doi:10.1016/j.asej.2014.04.011

Pang, B., & Lee, L. (2004). A Sentimental Education: Sentiment Analysis Using Subjectivity Summarization Based on Minimum Cuts. *Proceedings of the ACL.* https://arxiv.org/abs/cs/0409058

Pang, B., & Lee, L. (2008). Opinion Mining and Sentiment Analysis. *Foundations and Trends® in Information Retrieval, 2*(1–2), 1–135. doi:10.1561/1500000011

Patwa, P., Aguilar, G., Kar, S., & Pandey, S. (2020). *SemEval-2020 Task 9: Overview of Sentiment Analysis of Code-Mixed Tweets.* https://arxiv.org/abs/2008.04277

Peng, L., Cui, G., Zhuang, M., & Li, C. (2014). What do seller manipulations of online product reviews mean to consumers? In *Digital Commons @ Lingnan University* (HKIBS/WPS/070-1314). https://commons.ln.edu.hk/hkibswp/70

Polanyi, L., & Zaenen, A. (2006). Contextual Valence Shifters. In Computing Attitude and Affect in Text: Theory and Applications (pp. 1–10). Springer-Verlag. doi:10.1007/1-4020-4102-0_1

Press Trust Of India. (2013, July 10). India to have the highest internet traffic growth rate. *Business Standard.* https://www.business-standard.com/article/technology/india-to-have-the-highest-internet-traffic-growth-rate-113071000014_1.html

Ravi, K., & Ravi, V. (2015). A survey on opinion mining and sentiment analysis: Tasks, approaches and applications. *Knowledge-Based Systems, 89*, 14–46. doi:10.1016/j.knosys.2015.06.015

Ruder, S., & Plank, B. (2018). Strong baselines for neural semi-supervised learning under domain shift. *ACL 2018 - 56th Annual Meeting of the Association for Computational Linguistics, Proceedings of the Conference (Long Papers), 1*, 1044–1054. 10.18653/v1/P18-1096

Saif, H., Fernandez, M., He, Y., & Alani, H. (2014). On stopwords, filtering and data sparsity for sentiment analysis of twitter. *9th International Conference on Language Resources and Evaluation*, 810–817. http://oro.open.ac.uk/id/eprint/40666

Serrano-Guerrero, J., Olivas, J. A., Romero, F. P., & Herrera-Viedma, E. (2015). Sentiment analysis: A review and comparative analysis of web services. *Information Sciences, 311*, 18–38. doi:10.1016/j.ins.2015.03.040

Shamsudin, N. F., Basiron, H., & Sa'aya, Z. (2016). Lexical Based Sentiment Analysis – Verb, Adverb & Negation. *Journal of Telecommunication, Electronic and Computer Engineering, 8*(2), 161–166. https://journal.utem.edu.my/index.php/jtec/article/view/976/566

Singh, P. K., Singh, S. K., & Paul, S. (2015). Sentiment classification of social issues using contextual valence shifters. *International Journal of Engineering and Technology, 7*(4), 1443–1452. http://www.enggjournals.com/ijet/docs/IJET15-07-04-335.pdf

Singh, R. K., Sachan, M. K., & Patel, R. B. (2020). 360 degree view of cross-domain opinion classification: A survey. *Artificial Intelligence Review*. Advance online publication. doi:10.100710462-020-09884-9

Singh, S. K., & Sachan, M. K. (2019a). GRT: Gurmukhi to Roman Transliteration System using Character Mapping and Handcrafted Rules. *International Journal of Innovative Technology and Exploring Engineering, 8*(9), 2758–2763. doi:10.35940/ijitee.I8636.078919

Singh, S. K., & Sachan, M. K. (2019b). SentiVerb system: Classification of social media text using sentiment analysis. *Multimedia Tools and Applications, 78*(22), 32109–32136. doi:10.100711042-019-07995-2

Taboada, M., Brooke, J., Tofiloski, M., Voll, K., & Stede, M. (2011). Lexicon-Based Methods for Sentiment Analysis. *Computational Linguistics, 37*(2), 267–307. doi:10.1162/COLI_a_00049

Turney, P. D. (2002). thumbs up or thumbs down? semantic orientation applied to unsupervised classification of reviews. *40th Annual Meeting on Association for Computational Linguistics*, 417–424. 10.3115/1073083.1073153

Yu, Z., & Liu, G. (2018). Sliced Recurrent Neural Networks. *27th International Conference on Computational Linguistics*, 2953–2964. https://www.aclweb.org/anthology/C18-1250

Yue, L., Chen, W., Li, X., Zuo, W., & Yin, M. (2019). A survey of sentiment analysis in social media. *Knowledge and Information Systems, 60*(2), 617–663. doi:10.100710115-018-1236-4

ENDNOTES

[1]   Negation words reverse the polarity of the word or sentence, if these words appear before negative or positive word in the sentence.

[2]   https://www.worldclasslearning.com/english/five-verb-forms.html

[3]   https://www.enchantedlearning.com/wordlist/verbs.shtml

[4]   https://snowballstem.org/demo.html

[5]   https://text-processing.com/demo/stem/

This research was previously published in the International Journal on Semantic Web and Information Systems (IJSWIS), 17(2); pages 59-78, copyright year 2021 by IGI Publishing (an imprint of IGI Global).

Chapter 34
Develop a Neural Model to Score Bigram of Words Using Bag-of-Words Model for Sentiment Analysis

Anumeera Balamurali
St.Joseph's College of Engineering, India

Balamurali Ananthanarayanan
Tamilnadu Agriculture Department, India

ABSTRACT

A Bag-of-Words model is widely used to extract the features from text, which is given as input to machine learning algorithm like MLP, neural network. The dataset considered is movie reviews with both positive and negative comments further converted to Bag-of-Words model. Then the Bag-of-Word model of the dataset is converted into vector representation which corresponds to a number of words in the vocabulary. Each word in the review documents is assigned with a score and the scores are later represented in vector representation which is later fed as input to neural model. In the Kera's deep learning library, the neural models will be simple feedforward network models with fully connected layers called 'Dense'. Bigram language models are developed to classify encoded documents as either positive or negative. At first, reviews are converted to lines of token and then encoded to bag-of-words model. Finally, a neural model is developed to score bigram of words with word scoring modes.

INTRODUCTION: KNOW THE BASIC TERMS?

Natural Language Processing or NLP is generally defined as the automatic understanding of natural language, like speech and text. The study of natural language processing has been popular around for more than fifty years and grew out of the field of linguistics with the evolutions of computers. Current end applications and research includes information extraction, machine translation, summarization,

DOI: 10.4018/978-1-6684-6303-1.ch034

search and human computer interfaces. While complete semantic understanding remains a way still far from distant goal, researchers have studied a divide and conquer approach and identified several subtasks and methods needed for application development and analysis. These ranges varies from the syntactic methods, such as part-of-speech tagging, chunking and parsing, to the semantic method, such as word sense disambiguation, semantic-role labelling, named entity extraction and anaphora resolution. The field of Natural Language Processing (NLP) aims to convert human language into a formal representation which makes easy for computers to manipulate.

As Internet services for movies has increased in popularity, more and more languages are able to make their way online. In such a world, a need exist for the rapid organizing of ever expanding online reviews. A well-trained movie reviews can easily improves the quality of movies provided through online platform: there are so many different reviews other than movies like product review or feedbacks in so many different languages and most of them cannot be parsed immediately with a glance eye. Thus, an automatic language identification system is needed to analyse the reviews so the system is built to take this task. Because of the sheer volume of reviews in online to be handled, the categorization must be efficient, consuming as small storage and little processing time as possible.

N-gram models are the most widely used models for statistical language modelling and sentiment analysis, which is implemented by artificial neural networks (NN). NN is the powerful technique that is widely used in various fields of computer science. Most of the current NLP systems and techniques use words as atomic units which defines that there is no notion of similarity between words, as these are represented as indices in a vocabulary. The observation so far tells that the simple language models trained on huge amounts of data which outperform complex systems trained on less data. An example is the popular N-gram model used for statistical language modelling and text categorization in google, amazon etc...

Text categorization addresses the problem of splitting a given passage of text (or a document) to one or more predefined classes. This is an important area of sentiment analysis research that has been heavily investigated. The goal of text categorization is to classify the given reviews into a fixed number of pre-defined categories which is then listed as result to data analytics companies (Barry, 2016).

Deep learning architectures and algorithms have already created spectacular advances in fields like computer vision and pattern recognition (Brownlee, 2017).

Following this trend, the recent natural language processing is currently more and more specialized in the field of recent deep learning strategies. (Collobert et al., 2011) Deep learning algorithms is found to use the unknown structure for the input distribution to give good representations, usually at multiple levels, with higher-level learned features stated in terms of lower-level features. Deep learning strategies aim at learning feature hierarchies with features from higher levels of the hierarchy with which it is created by the composition of lower level features. Automatic learning features at multiple levels of abstraction permit a system to learn complex functions mapping the input to the output directly from data, while not relying fully on human-crafted features (Youngy et al.,, 2018).

Text Pre-Processing

Tokenization is a way of breaking a text into words or sentences. Tokenization is the method by which huge amount of text is splitted into smaller parts, referred as tokens. Natural language processing is employed for building applications like Text classification, intelligent chatbot, sentimental analysis, language translation, etc. It becomes important to grasp the pattern within the text to attain the above-stated purpose. These tokens are helpful for locating such patterns as well as taken a base step for stemming and lemmatization.

For example, consider the given input string –

Hi, how are you? ◇ the output ◇ ['Hi', 'how', 'are', 'you']

Removal of Stop Words is an initial step: Stop Words are the words that don't contain vital significance to be employed in Search Queries. Usually, these words are filtered out from search queries since the method huge quantity of unnecessary information. Each programming language offers its own list of stop words to use. Most of the stop words are used English language like 'as, the, be, are' etc.

Stemming is the method for removing suffixes from words in English. Removing suffixes is an operation that is very helpful in field of text classification. Stemming and Lemmatization is used in Text Normalization (or generally known as Word Normalization) techniques in the field of natural language processing that are found to prepare text, words, and documents for further process. Stemming and Lemmatization are studied, and algorithms are developed in computer science since the 1960's. Stemming and Lemmatization each generate the base format of the inflected words. The distinction is that stem won't be an actual word whereas; lemma is an actual language word. Stemming follows an algorithm with steps to perform on the words that makes it quicker. Whereas, in lemmatization, researchers used WordNet corpus and a corpus for stop words still provides lemma that makes it slower than stemming.

The architecture is divided into two parts: Training phase and Testing phase. In Training phase, the training data is given into pre-processing stages which includes tokenization. Tokenization is done by using two steps: at first stopwords are removed and then stemming or lemmatization is done. After which feature engineering methods are implemented in pre-processed data that includes: Bag-of-words, TF-IDF and word embedding. The model so far developed is trained and evaluated so that the test data is given as input to test the model. As the result the sentiment analysed predicted output is shown. Figure 1 shows the architecture of the project.

Figure 1. Architecture for the language model
Source: Own

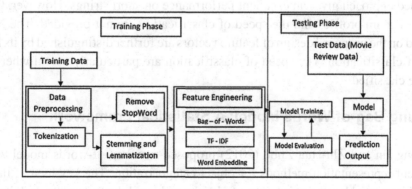

BACKGROUND: SIMILAR TO LITERATURE SURVEY

Comparing Neural Network Approach With NGram Approach For Text Categorization

Suresh Babu and Pavan Kumar(2010) compares Neural network Approach with N-gram approach, for text categorization. And also demonstrates that Neural Network approach is better than the N-gram approach but with less judging time. Both methods demonstrated in this project are aimed at language identification. Feature vectors are calculated from the presence of particular characters, words and the statistical information of word lengths. In an identification experiment the approach is compared with Asian languages where the neural network approach achieved 98% correct classification rate with 600 bytes, but it is six times faster than n-gram based approach.

Figure 2. Schematic diagram of Neural network system
Source: *Comparing Neural Network Approach With NGram Approach For Text Categorization (A. Suresh Babu and P.N.V.S.Pavan Kumar (2010) International Journal on Computer Science and Engineering, Vol.2(1) pg: 80-83)*

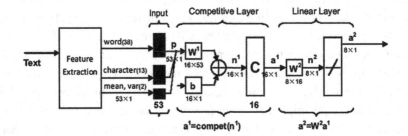

Above figure explains the step by step procedure of neural network approach which starts by text feature extraction to the final linear layer. In this project a method for identifying the 8 Roman alphabet language using Neural networks is proposed. Further the performance of other two N gram-based approaches has been compared to present the better approach. Now a days varies researches showed that the N-gram based approach gives an excellent performance on short strings. However, the information such as size of N-gram profiles and the speed of classification are not provided. The Neural network developed based on the proposed design of feature vectors are further distinguished by its high efficiency and accuracy of classification. The speed of classification are particularly useful when text of longer length has to be classified.

Understanding Bag-of-Words Model: A Statistical Framework

Yin Zhang, Rong Jin and Zhi-Hua Zhou (2012) proposed new bag-of-words model which is one of the most efficient representation methods for object categorization. The key idea of this project is to summarize each extracted key point into one of visual words, and then visualize each image by a histogram of the visual words. For this purpose, a clustering algorithm (e.g., K-means), is used to generate the visual words. Even though a number of studies have shown motivated results of the bag-of-words representation for object categorization. Theoretical studies about the properties of the bag-of-words model is almost unmarked, possibly due to the difficulties of using a heuristic clustering process. In this paper, a statistical framework is presented, which generalizes the bag-of-words representation. Where the visual words are provoked by a statistical process instead of using a clustering algorithm, while the factual performance is competitive to clustering-based method. A theoretical analysis based on statistical consistency is introduced for the proposed framework. Moreover, based on the framework two algorithms are developed which do not rely on clustering.

Statistical framework is presented for key point quantization that concludes the bag-of-words model by statistical expectation. Efficacy and the robustness of the proposed framework are verified by applying it to object recognition. In the future, proposed method can be improvised by introducing a plan to examine the dependence of the proposed algorithms on the threshold ρ [Chih-Fong Tsai. (2012)].

N-Gram Language Modeling Using Recurrent Neural Network Estimation

Ciprian Chelba, Mohammad Norouzi and Samy Bengio [Chelba et al.,, 2017] investigates the effective memory depth of Recurrent Neural Network models by using n-gram language model (LM) for smoothing purpose. LSTM is used in this work which means Long Short Term Memory which is a artificial recurrent neural network. Experiments done on a small corpus (UPenn Treebank, one million words of training data with 10k vocabulary) that have found the LSTM(Long Short Term Memory) cell with a dropout, which is a best model for encoding the n-gram state when compared with both feed-forward and vanilla RNN models. While allowing the dependencies across sentence boundaries, the LSTM with 13-gram language model has almost matched the perplexity of the unlimited history LSTM Language Model.

Developing a LSTM n-gram Language Models may be suitable for some practical situations they are: the state in a n-gram LM can be clearly represented with $(n - 1)* 4$ bytes which is stored in the identity of the words in the context and a set of n-gram contexts are processed in parallel. On the downside, this work concludes that the n-gram context encoding created by the LSTM is removed, that makes the model more expensive than a regular recurrent LSTM Language Model.

Recent Trends in Deep Learning Based Natural Language Processing

Tom Young et al has proposed deep learning methods that uses multiple processing layers to acquire a knowledge on hierarchical representations of data and then produces state-of-the-art results in different domains (Youngy et al., 2018). Now a days, a diversity of model designs and methods have been introduced in the context of natural language processing (NLP). In this work, significant deep learning related models and methods are employed for numerous NLP tasks which provides a overview of their evolution. Finally, various models are summarized, compared and contrast thus put forward a detailed understanding of the past, present and future of deep learning in Natural Language Processing.

To use Noam Chomsky's words, "researchers do not get discoveries in the sciences by just taking huge amounts of data, feeding data into a computer and doing a statistical analysis of data: that's not the way researchers understand things, there is a need of theoretical insights". Depending on machine learning in fact makes a good guess based on past experience, because some of the sub-symbolic methods creates correlation and the decision-making process is more probabilistic.

Figure 3. Schematic diagram of Convolutional Neural Network framework
Source: A unified architecture for natural language processing: Deep neural networks with multitask learning (Collobert and J. Weston in Proceedings of the 25th international conference on Machine learning. ACM, 2008, pp. 160–167)

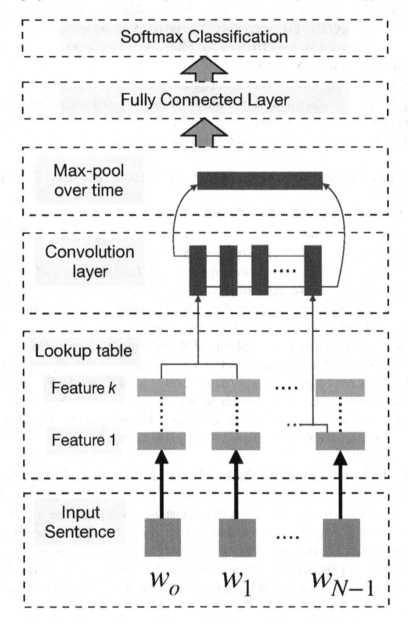

Neural Bag-of-Ngrams

Bofang Li et al introduced a Bag-of-ngrams (BoN) models that are commonly used to represent text (Bofang Li et al., 2017). One of the main disadvantages of traditional BoN models is the ignorance of n-gram's semantics. In this work, the concept of Neural Bag-of-ngrams (Neural-BoN) is proposed, which replaces one single n-gram representation in traditional BoN with different semantic n-gram representations by adding n-grams to word embeddings model. Two different representations are proposed to capture more semantics like topic or sentiment tendencies they are Text guided ngram representation and label guided n-gram representation . Neural-BoN with the former two n-gram representations achieves the results on 4 document level classification datasets and 6 semantic relatedness categories. Compared to traditional BoN models, proposed Neural-BoN is efficient, robust and easy to implement, so further expected it to be a strong baseline method and to be used in more real-world applications.

Neural-BoN model learns a text vector by calculating the belonging neural n-gram vectors along with weights (Bizzoni and Mehdi Ghanimifard, 2018). Compared to the unigram version, bigrams improve the performance of Neural-BoN on most of the datasets, while further trigrams needs larger dataset to improves the performance. As for future research three types of n-gram representations are introduced which shows effectiveness on text classification task and semantic relatedness task: Context Guided N-gram Representation (CGNR), Text Guided N-gram Representation (TGNR) and Label Guided N-gram Representation (LGNR).

THE INFLUENCE OF BIGRAM CONSTRAINTS ON WORD RECOGNITION BY HUMANS: IMPLICATIONS FOR COMPUTER SPEECH RECOGNITION

Ronald A. Cole et al has shown a way to bridge the gap between human and machine performance on speech recognition tasks. Recognition of words in telephone conversations is better than text representation (Cole, Yan and Bailey, 2001). Based on the experience this work summarize that human perception typically delivers much more accurate results than word recognition over the telephone.

One way to address the gap is to study the sources of linguistic information related to the speech signal which is important in word recognition, and then evaluate how well a machine utilize this information relative to humans. As an initial step in this direction, there is a need to measure word recognition performance of listeners presented with vocabulary words from the Switchboard corpus. Stimuli consisted of actual utterances of words that are taken from the Switchboard corpus, which includes high quality recordings of word utterances in Switchboard conversations. Also the recordings of word sequences with zero, medium and high bigram probabilities based on a language model computed from transcriptions of the same datasets. The results show that human listeners are good at understanding the words in the absence of word sequence constraints, but the statistical language models fails to capture much of the high level linguistic information needed to recognize words in a fluent speech.

MAIN FOCUS OF THE CHAPTER: WHATELSE NEEDED TO DO RESEARCH?

The existing Neural networks Language Models (NNLM) have evolved in recent years as an alternative to estimate and store n-gram Language Models. In NNLM, Words are generally represented using a method called embedding vectors. A simple NNLM architecture creates the Markov assumption and gets a input as the concatenated embedding vectors for the vocabulary words represented in the n-gram context to one or more layers each has an affine transform which is followed by a non-linearity function. The output of the last such layer is then given as input to the output layer consisting again an affine transform but this time it is followed by an exponential non-linearity function that is then normalized to get a guaranteed proper probability over the vocabulary words.

The NNLM with affine transform is commonly named as feed-forward architecture for an n-gram LM (FF-NNLM). But the proposed NNLM with recurrent properties uses sigmoid activation function which needs some basic knowledge to understand, so the following topics of main focus concentrates on fundamental terms of the NNLM.

Feature Engineering

The first fundamental term which is needed to be understood in feature engineering, that is usually done after text preprocessing. Nowadays text data offers a wide range of possibilities to generate different types of features. But sometimes, this process ends up with generating lots of different features, to an extent that processing of these features becomes a painful task. Hence there is a need to meticulously analyze the extracted features. Therefore, following methods explained below will help in reducing the dimension of the generated data set. Following subtopic is the list of popular feature engineering methods used now a days:

1. **N-grams:** N-gram is one of the popular feature engineering method which takes words as count from the dataset. In the dataset, one word is known as 1-gram, such as movie, tamil. Similarly, two word in the dataset is called as 2-gram, such as Thank You, Good Movie and then 3-gram etc. The objective behind the above all technique is to explore the chances of using one or two or more words in order to give more information to the neural model.

2. **Feature Hashing:** Feature Hashing method uses the hashing strategy that reduces the dimension of document by achieving lesser column. This method needs only lesser memory because it uses index to access data instead of wasting memory by accessing whole data.

3. **TF - IDF:** TF-IDF is abbreviated as Term Frequency - Inverse Document Frequency. This method proves that a learning algorithm gets more information from the rarely occurring words compared to frequently occurring words. By allocating weight for each terms in vocabulary this method declares importance of each word. While assinging weights for each term, frequently occuring terms are weighted lower and the rarely occurring terms get weighted higher. Term Frequency is calculated as a number of occurences of a term in a document divided by all the terms in the document. Inverse Document Frequency is calculated as a ratio of log for the total documents in the corpus divided by number of documents with the particular terms in the dataset. Finally, TF-IDF is calculated as TF multiplied by IDF.

4. **Jaccard Similarity:** This feature engineering method uses separate distance metric which is used in text analysis. Consider two vector representation created from word vocabulary thus a distance metric can be calculated as ratio of the terms which are found in both vectors divided by the terms which are available in either of the two vectors. In order to create features of the dataset using distance metrics, first create collection of similar documents and then assign a unique label to each document in a new column. So the formula used in this technique is: $(A \cap B)/(A \cup B)$.

5. **Cosine Similarity:** This technique is used to find the similar document from the corpus. Cosine similarity is one of the prevalently used method to calculate the distance metric which is used in text analysis. Distance metric is found by multiplying two vector representation created by using the words from vocabulary.

6. **Levenshtein Distance:** This method is used to create a new feature from the text which is based on the distance between two text. The distance metric is found by analysing long text from which

shorter text is generated and then if another text is given, shorter text is found in both text. If both shorter text is found between the two text, then maximum value 1 is returned.

Bag of Word

BoW or Bag-of-Word model gives different methods to extract the features from the text of dataset, which is further used in modeling like machine learning algorithm, neural network etc.. A BoW approach is used to represent a text from vocabulary that defines the frequency of words within a document in dataset. This includes two important stages they are: First stage creates a vocabulary of a known words and the second stage calculates the frequency of a known words in dataset. A Bag-of-Word approach is a efficient and flexible method that proposes several different way to extract features from the document in dataset.

Bag-of-Word or BoW method is named so because this method ignore any information about the text that includes order or the structure of the text. This model is concerned about the fact that whether the known words are found in the document from the dataset or not in the dataset. In one of the famous natural language processing authors article, the BoW method is defined as a common feature extracting approach which includes both sentence and document from the dataset and also it includes a histogram of the text within the sentence. Thus, this method considers word count as a feature from the document.

Since the frequency of the word is counted from the document it is useful to find whether the documents from the dataset is similar or not. So the goal of Bag-of-word approach is to learn something about the meaning of the content. The complexity of this approach is increased based on the design of creating a vocabulary and also by calculating the presence of the known word from the document. In this work, the movie review document is analysed and the feature is extracted as word count, then finally given as input to the neural model developed.

Word Embedding

Next stage followed by the creation of the vocabulary with the known word is to create a vector representation for the filtered word from the document. By using word embedding method, individual words are considered to create vector representation. Important property for the word embedding method is to generate a similar representation for same words from the sentence or document in dataset. This step is considered as one of the key breakthroughs of deep learning challenge in natural language processing issues.

Each word in the document are represented as real-valued vectors in a predefined vector space [Chih-Fong Tsai, 2012]. Word Embedding is a technique in which individual words are mapped to one vector and that vector values are studied in order to represent those values in a neural network. Thus this technique is often collaborated with deep learning field to achieve good result. Vector representation of a words are displayed in two ways they are: sparse vector representation and dense vector representation. In dense vector representation, each words are mapped to one vector which has one or more dimensions. And in other hand, sparse vector representation uses thousands or millions of vector dimensions for each word that is often used in the hot encoding method.

The hot encoding method uses a individual hot encoded word that is mapped to a single word vector. The developed word vectors are summed up and fed as input into a supervised learning algorithms. But in case of recurrent neural network each word are given as individual input in sequence. Thus a method to learn a embedding layer in a neural network there is a need of lot of training data which makes the above process slow.

In order to learn word embedding process in neural network model, two different models are introduced they are: Continuous Bag-of-Words (CBOW model) and Continuous Skip-Gram model. The former learning model learns the word embedding process by predicting the current text based on the context. And the latter model learns the word embedding process by predicting the surrounding words based on the current word. In both model a configurable parameter is used which is a window of neighbouring words that gives context. This context is used in above both model to learn the word embedding process.

Figure 4. Architecture diagram of Hybrid Model
Source: Weakly Supervised Sentiment Analysis Using Joint Sentiment Topic Detection With Bigrams. Pavitra.R and PCD. Kalaivaani. (2015). IEEE Sponsored Second International Conference On Electronics And Communication Systems.

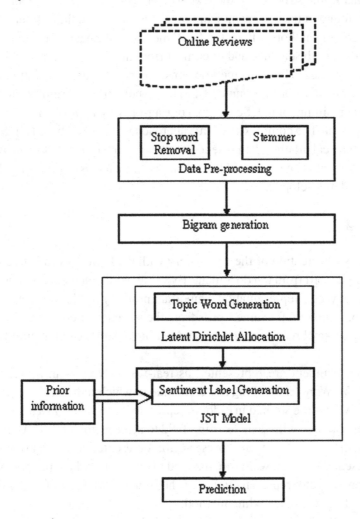

Bigram

Bigram is generated by using N-gram language model in which N=2. Bigram or Digram is a collection of two adjacent words from a string. Main application of bigram model is used for simple statistical analysis of text that is included in cryptography, speech recognition, computational linguistics and so on.

One of the variations from bigram is called as skipping bigram or gappy bigram in which gaps between the words are allowed. This kind of bigram allows some simulation of dependencies and also avoids connecting words. Gappy bigram with explicit dependency relationships are often found in head word bigrams. Bigram helps to calculate the conditional probability of a text given the preceding text.

Thus the conditional probability P() of a word W_n given the preceding word W_{n-1} is equal to the probability of the particular word bigram, other method to find the probability by dividing the co-occurrence of the two words $P(W_{n-1}, W_n)$, by the probability of the preceding word. For example Thank you is a bigram, Indian Great Wall is a trigram and He is my neighbour is a 4-gram. The conditional probability of the bigram are categorized into three parts they are: zero bigram probability, medium bigram probability and high bigram probability.

Text Classification In NLP

Text classification in nlp is similar to that of feature engineering that are more prevalently used in spam detection and sentiment analysis. The features are extracted from the text by using bag-of-word, TF-IDF, cosine similarity and other two different methods. In the text classification, first step is to pre-processing step in which punctuations are removed and all the text are converted into lowercase.

Second stage is to construct the vocabulary with a known word by using a different document from the dataset. After the construction of the vocabulary, vector representation is created for all the individual words in the vocabulary. Then a N-gram language model is constructed for the vector representation of each word that does sentiment analysis.

Most of the text classification methods are based on the document term matrix that are often referred as unigram or bag-of-words. In order to find the sentiment in a document each words from the document are analysed for example, consider a sentence "Good movie must watch it again" which has a sentiment of pleasure. In this sentence word "Good" indicates the happy feeling of the reviewer so a model can easily predict the sentiment of the sentence by analysing each individual words.

SOLUTIONS AND RECOMMENDATION

Movie reviews are categorized in this project by using RNN model which is developed by using keras library in python programming language. Different datasets of movie reviews are collected from online databases which is divided as training set and testing set with bigram words. Anaconda Navigator is used along with neuralnet keras library to implement inbuild RNN(Recurrent Neural Network) model. Most of the online reviews are categorized as very positive, regardless of content. In addition, most of the online movie reviews had almost equal amount likelihood of being in the very negative or very positive category with very positive being more likely most of the time.

Online movie reviews are either very positive or very negative so most of the content from the dataset will fall into one of these categories in the model. So, by adjusting the training data to have equal amounts of reviews for each category will yield better results. The Prediction API for a serious categorization task is implemented, with also a strong enough background in machine learning which tweaks the model before using the Prediction API to analyse and host it. In short, the Prediction API is used as cloud-based access to the existing model that already works with help of libraries. The backward nature of the Prediction API makes it difficult to diagnose and correct any data problems that exists.

. The developed model is trained and tested by giving reviews which produced the following output. The reviews are analysed and the percentage of positivity or negativity is shown to the user inorder to differentiate between positive or negative reviews.

Review: [I would recommend it. Best Movie that I have seen ever!]
Sentiment: POSITIVE (59.25%)
Review: [Waste of time. Bad Movie]
Sentiment: NEGATIVE (70.51%)

Dataset

1. Movie Review Data: http://www.cs.cornell.edu/people/pabo/movie-review-data/
2. Corpora: Online Collection of text and speech which can be used as dataset
3. Movie Review Polarity Dataset:http://www.cs.cornell.edu/people/pabo/movie-review-data/review_polarity.tar.Gz
4. A Sentimental Education: Sentiment Analysis Using Subjectivity Summarization Based on Minimum Cuts, 2004. http://xxx.lanl.gov/abs/cs/0409058

Outputs and Discussions

The dataset is preprocessed by doing different operations like: splitting the tokens on white space, remove the punctuations from words, remove all the words which are not properly comprised of alphabetical characters, remove all the stop words and finally remove all the words that have less than or equal to one characters.

One of the important steps for bag-of-word model is to construct the vocabulary, which is predefined for the datasets. The frequent bigram words from all the datasets are created along with the count and stored in a class. Which is then parsed by a snippet to remove the low occurence bigram words from the vocabulary. Bag-of-word model has a most prevalent job to extract the features from the text which is then given as input to neural model, in this project it is a RNN(Recurrent Neural Network) model.

The vector representation is generated from the words in vocabulary which corresponds to the words in reviews. For example the vocabulary consist of bigram words like good movie, bad movie, not worth, pleasant time etc...Scoring methods are used in this step to provide the score of the words in the vector representation. So at the first stage, reviews are converted into lines of tokens and then reviews are encoded into the bag-of-word model representation. The bigram tokens are filtered from the dataset and lines of tokens are stored into new document. Labels are given to reviews as zero for negative reviews and one for positive reviews.

The encoded reviews are then given as input to the neural model in which the input layer is equal to the number of bigram words in vocabulary. The neural model developed in this project does the sentiment analysis work on the movie reviews. One of the advantages of the RNN model is that the previous output is given as input to the current neuron. The model has the hidden state which stores certain information. Nearly 50 neurons are assigned for hidden layer and the output layer works with stigmoid activation function to yield 0 for negative reviews or 1 for positive reviews.

Scoring methods which exists so far are: binary, count, tfidf and freq. Binary scoring method is used in this project which encounters positive(1) and negative(0) reviews. The aim of the probabilistic language modelling is to evaluate the probability of a sentence of sequence of bigram words:

$$P(w)=P(w_1,w_2,w_3,\dots w_n)$$

and also used to find the probability of the next bigram word in the sequence:

$$P(w_5 \mid w_1,w_2,w_3,w_4)$$

A model that computes either of the operation is called a Language Model. There are different methods used for calculatiing probability and for markov assumption. They are:

Method for calculating probability

- Conditional probability
- Chain rule

Method using markov assumption

- Markov Property
- N-gram model

For the demonstration purpose, IMDB large movie review dataset is used that is made available in online by Stanford. The data in the above dataset contains the ratings given by the reviewer, the polarity and the full comment given by the online movie reviewer. First step is to convert the full comments into the individual sentences with bigram words, then introduce notation for both start and end of sentence and the text is cleaned by removing any punctuation and lowercase of all the bigram words. The unigram model which calculates the probability of words are developed and output is produced for input (has,been), shown in Figure 5.

Figure 5. Unigram probability predicted result
Source: Own

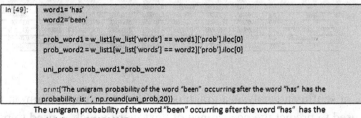

```
In [49]:   word1= 'has'
           word2='been'

           prob_word1 = w_list1[w_list['words'] == word1]['prob'].iloc[0]
           prob_word2 = w_list1[w_list['words'] == word2]['prob'].iloc[0]

           uni_prob = prob_word1*prob_word2

           print('The unigram probability of the word "been" occurring after the word "has" has the
           probability is: ', np.round(uni_prob,20))
```
The unigram probability of the word "been" occurring after the word "has" has the probability is: 0.00006895

Both unigram model and bigram model is developed for comparision purpose. The unigram model developed is not accurate, so the bigram estimation is introduced instead of later model. Applying the bigram model is more complex compared to unigram model, at first calculate the co-occurrences of each words into a word-word matrix fed into new document. The counts of the words are then normalised by the counts of the previous word as shown in the following equation:

$$P(w_i \mid w_{i-1}) \approx$$

Therefore, for example, if the calculation has to be improved for the P(been|has), at first count the occurrences of (has,been) and divide this by the count of occurrences of (t0). count (w_{i-1}). Thus the calculation is improved by using bigram language model which is shown in Figure 6.

Figure 6. Bigram probability predicted result
Source: Own

```
In [49]:   word1=' '+ str ('has') +' '
           word2= str (' been ') +' '

           bigram_prob = len ( re.findall(word1 + word2, word2_list)) / len(re.findall(word2,word2_list))

           print('The bigram probability of the word " been " occurring after the word " has " has the
           probability is: ', np.round(bigram_prob,10))
```

The bigram probability of the word "been" occurring after the word "has" has the probability is: 0.0012500

As studied before, to effectively utilise the bigram language model their is the need to compute the word-word matrix for all bigram word pair occurrences. With this, there is a way to find the most likely word to follow the current word. Even though this also needs an exceptional amount of time if the dataset is large. The output in Figure 7 shows the word to word matrix of the vocabulary which is the first stage of bigram probability model.

Figure 7. Word Matrix generated by the model
Source: Own

```
In [52]:   M_R_Matrix[M_R_Matrix['s']>=0]
Out[52]:
```

	words	<s	best	movie	ever	seen	i	would	recommend	it
0	<s	0.0	0.000569	0.000000	0.000000	0.000561	0.000000	0.002652	0.000000	0.000563
1	best	0.0	0.000000	0.000000	0.000000	0.000000	0.000000	0.000000	0.000000	0.000000
2	movie	0.0	0.000000	0.013256	0.368912	0.000000	0.000000	0.000000	0.000000	0.000000
3	ever	0.0	0.000452	0.000000	0.000000	0.000000	0.000000	0.000000	0.000000	0.365741
4	seen	0.0	0.000000	0.000000	0.134586	0.000000	0.555555	0.000000	0.000000	0.000000
5	i	0.0	0.000388	0.333333	0.000000	0.000000	0.000000	0.168952	0.265893	0.000000
6	would	0.0	0.000000	0.000000	0.000000	0.589423	0.000000	0.000000	0.000000	0.123689
7	recommend	0.0	0.000256	0.000000	0.000000	0.000000	0.000000	0.000000	0.000000	0.000000
8	it	0.0	0.000000	0.000000	0.000000	0.000000	0.000000	0.000000	0.589632	0.000000

As the final stage of sentiment analysis a graph is generated for most common word after a current word. This graph is used to predict the occurrence of next word which is used to predict the sentiment based on the reviews. This model is used in several other businesses like Amazon and Google to predict the users sentiment about particular product. With this, the graph shows some examples of the most likely word to follow the given word (Figure 8).

Figure 8. Graph for Most Common word
Source: Own

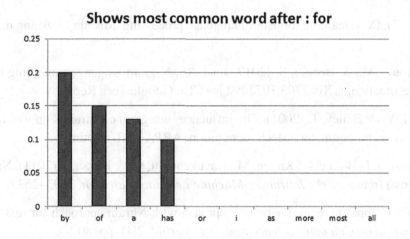

FUTURE RESEARCH AND DIRECTION

The neural network model developed in this work has a important shortcoming that error analysis is not done, this might lead to a interesting future contribution to this project. In future, a better improvement can also be done by implementing systematic analysis of the errors in the developed network model. Extension to this work can be done by elaborating the range of comparing different machine learning algorithms, so that each contribution of the input terms can be found. And the deep learning concept can be improved by included larger datasets with different set of features.

CONCLUSION

In this study, a neural network language model is developed in which bag-of-word approach is used to extract the word count feature for all the individual word from the vocabulary developed at preprocessing step. After extracting the features, bigram of words are maintained to get more accurate prediction as the result. Then the generated vector representation for each known words are given as input to network neural model. This model does the sentiment analysis of the movie reviews and produces the predicted result with the probability. The scoring method uses in binary count method which notes the occurrence of all known words.

REFERENCES

Barry, J. (2016). Sentiment analysis of online reviews using bag-of-words and LSTM approaches. Google Tech Report. A. Suresh Babu and P. N. V. S.

Bizzoni, Y., & Ghanimifard, M. (2018). Bigrams and BiLSTMs Two neural networks for sequential metaphor detection. In *Proceedings of the Workshop on Figurative Language Processing*, pp. 91–101. 10.18653/v1/W18-0911

Brownlee, J. (2017). Deep learning for natural language processing. Machine learning mastery. Edition: v1.1

Chelba, C., Norouzi, M., & Bengio, S. (2017, June 20). N-gram language modelling using recurrent neural network estimation. arXiv:1703.10724v2 [cs.CL]. Google Tech Report

Cole, R. A., Yan, Y., & Bailey, T. (2001). The influence of bigram constraints on word recognition by humans: Implications for computer speech recognition. ARPA HLT meeting.

Collobert, R., Weston, J., Bottou, L., Karlen, M., Kavukcuoglu, K., & Kuksa, P. (2011). Natural language processing (almost) from scratch. *Journal of Machine Learning Research*, 2493–2537.

Kumar, P. (2010). Comparing neural network approach with Ngram approach for text categorization. *International Journal on Computer Science and Engineering, 2*(1). pp. 80-83.

Li, B., Liu, T., & Zhao, Z., Wang, P., & Du, X. (2017). Neural bag-of-Ngrams. In *Proceedings of the Thirty-First AAAI Conference on Artificial Intelligence.* pp. 3067-3074.

Mikolov, T., Chen, K., Corrado, G., & Dean, J. (2013, Sept. 7). Efficient estimation of word representations in vector space. arXiv:1301.3781v3 [cs.CL]. Google Tech Report

Tsai, C.-F. (2012). Bag-of-words representation in image annotation: A review article. *ISRN Artificial Intelligence, 2012*, 1–19. doi:10.5402/2012/376804

Youngy, T., Hazarikaz, D., Poria, S., & Cambria, E. (2018, November). Recent trends in deep learning based natural language processing. arXiv:1708.02709v8 [cs.CL]. Google Tech Report

Zhang, Y., Jin, R., & Zhou, Z.-H. (2012). Understanding bag-of-words model: A statistical framework. In *ECCV Workshop on Statistical Learning in Computer Vision*, Prague, Czech Republic

KEY TERMS AND DEFINITIONS

Bag of Words Model: The bag-of-words model is a method of representing text data while modeling text with machine learning algorithms.

Corpus: Corpus is a original repositories or online dataset which is used in most of the NLP projects.

Deep Learning: This method is also called as hierarchical learning or deep structured learning. It is one of the machine learning method that is based on learning methods like supervised, semi-supervised or unsupervised. The only difference between deep learning and other machine learning algorithm is that deep learning method uses big data as input.

Generalization: Generalization of markov assumption is done by calculating the probability of a word depending on the probability of the n previous words trigrams, 4-grams, etc.

Markov Assumption: Markov assumption calculates the probability of a word depends only on the probability of a limited history.

NLP: Natural Language Processing is prevalently used to analyse the text or speech inorder to make machine understand the words like human.

Sentence: Sentence is a unit of written words which forms a document in a dataset.

Tokens: Token is a total number of words in a sentence from the dataset.

This research was previously published in Neural Networks for Natural Language Processing; pages 122-142, copyright year 2020 by Engineering Science Reference (an imprint of IGI Global).

APPENDIX: N-GRAM ANALYSIS

Natural Language Processing (NLP) is the method used to analyse the written dialect with the help of computer. The real time applications of NLP are sentiment analysis, relationship extraction, language modelling, question answering and much more. In order to understand the N-gram analysis considers a very simple sentence "Worst Experience would never watch this movie again".

First step is to split the sentence into consecutive set of words like (Worst, Experience), (Experience, would), (would, never), ... When splitting the words from sentence n-gram is implemented. Unigram, bigram and trigram are usually practiced in most of the nlp project.

While splitting the words it is important to remove the stop words for example "not a good" is predicted as positive and "good" is also predicted as positive. But the former word is negative, since the model only analyse each word in single manner by seeing "good" in "not a good" sentence it is wrongly predicted as positive. So the solution is to remove the stop word, thus "not a good" is changed into "not good". By considering two words a model can predict accurately the result. This is how the n-gram analysis is done in nlp projects.

Chapter 35
An Opinion Mining Approach for Drug Reviews in Spanish

Karina Castro-Pérez

iD https://orcid.org/0000-0002-1709-0087

Tecnológico Nacional de México, Mexico & IT Orizaba, Mexico

José Luis Sánchez-Cervantes

iD https://orcid.org/0000-0001-5194-1263

CONACYT, Mexico & Instituto Tecnológico de Orizaba, Mexico

María del Pilar Salas-Zárate

Tecnológico Nacional de México, Mexico & ITS Teziutlán, Mexico

Maritza Bustos-López

Tecnológico Nacional de México, Mexico & Instituto Tecnológico de Orizaba, Mexico

Lisbeth Rodríguez-Mazahua

Tecnológico Nacional de México, Mexico & Instituto Tecnológico de Orizaba, Mexico

ABSTRACT

In recent years, the application of opinion mining has increased as a boom and growth of social media and blogs on the web, and these sources generate a large volume of unstructured data; therefore, a manual review is not feasible. For this reason, it has become necessary to apply web scraping and opinion mining techniques, two primary processes that help to obtain and summarize the data. Opinion mining, among its various areas of application, stands out for its essential contribution in the context of healthcare, especially for pharmacovigilance, because it allows finding adverse drug events omitted by the pharmaceutical companies. This chapter proposes a hybrid approach that uses semantics and machine learning for an opinion mining-analysis system by applying natural-language-processing techniques for the detection of drug polarity for chronic-degenerative diseases, available in blogs and specialized websites in the Spanish language.

DOI: 10.4018/978-1-6684-6303-1.ch035

INTRODUCTION

Opinion mining is an area of great importance for the coarse application that has, focuses on analyzing opinions, sentiments, evaluations, assessments, attitudes, and emotions of people towards entities such as products, services, organizations, individuals, problems, and events (Liu, 2012; Jiménez et al., 2018). This technique, emerged thanks to the accelerated growth of resources available on the web, a representative work of the application, in its beginnings, of opinion mining is the study of Das and Chen (2004) in which they found that, in the case of Amazon Inc., there were cumulatively 70,000 messages by the end of 1998 on Yahoo's message board, and this had grown to about 750,000 messages by early 2004. The authors found that many of the messages from Amazon's board offered favorable, pessimistic, confusing, and even spamming opinions, so in their study, they demonstrated the possibility of capturing sentiment by applying statistical language and natural language processing techniques. Thus, sentiment analysis, also known as opinion mining, began to take on relevance. Also, the availability of potential resources for analysis continued to grow exponentially, now through online review sites, shopping sites, and blogs, which increased the challenge of understanding people's opinions, those opinions important to the decision-making process. Pang and Lee (2008) analyzed surveys of American adults, where they found that consumers reported being willing to pay 20% to 99% more for a 5-star item than a 4-star item in an online store, clearly identifying the importance of knowing other people's opinions and feelings about a product.

It is noteworthy that opinion mining is not only applied for analysis in the consumption of goods and services; it has also been applied in the field of politics; generally, it recognized by the full range of applications it has at present. On the other hand, to implement opinion mining, it is necessary to use lexical resources that help to carry out sentiment classification. A widely known resource is SENTIWORDNET 3.0 (Baccianella et al., 2014) created for research purposes, which provides automatic annotation of all WORDNET synsets according to their degrees of positivity, negativity, and neutrality. The process presented by the authors consists of two steps,

1) weak-supervision, semi-supervised learning step;
2) a random-walk step, used to support sentiment classification in opinion mining.

Thus, the industry surrounding sentiment has grown due to the proliferation of analytics for commercial applications, as well as the exponential increase, in recent years, of social networks and video blogs accessed by millions of users, which generate large amounts of unstructured data. Given this fact, manual revision of data is not very feasible, as a consequence of the number of data continuously generated; therefore, it highlights the use and implementation of opinion mining in current systems (Liu, 2012).

Notwithstanding, opinion mining in the area of health care has increased because of the benefits provided for decision-making, one of the analyses that can be performed using this technique is pharmacovigilance, defined as the science and activities related to the detection, assessment, understanding, and prevention of adverse effects or any other drug-related problem (*World Health Organization*, 2015).

In this context, according to the World Health Organization in 2016, diabetes mellitus, hypertension, cardiovascular diseases, cancer, among other diseases, classified as chronic-degenerative, are positioned among the top ten causes of death in Mexico and the world (World Health Organization, 2020). This means that health systems and experts need to analyze important aspects such as eating habits, exercise, and treatments. Therefore, the application of opinion mining is useful because it allows the analysis of patient and health professionals' comments published on the web to identify symptoms and medicines related to the condition. Hence, the main contribution of this work is an approach for an opinion analysis system for drugs in Spanish by applying Web Scraping techniques and Natural Language Processing (NLP) for detection of drugs for chronic-degenerative diseases published in blogs, specialized websites and video blogs in the Spanish language, using a hybrid approach, with the use of supervised machine learning and a Snomed-based medical domain ontology.

The application of Web Scraping techniques and opinion mining is important in our approach because it allows summarizing the information and obtaining accurate knowledge, providing a useful result for health experts. Our system aims, firstly, to provide specialists with the information that helps to speed up the process of identifying and selecting the medicines they prescribe, and also to know the adverse effects that other patients have with the medicines prescribed for their condition, to identify the adverse effects of their patients more quickly, allowing them to spend more time on the physical examination and thus avoid additional complications to the disease, leading to a higher quality of care for patients. The application of Web Scraping and opinion mining techniques are important in our approach because it allows information to be summarized and accurate knowledge to be obtained, providing a useful outcome for health experts. Secondly, to provide patients with information to find out what others think about the medicines they use, and with expert validation, patients can identify comments that do not represent a danger to their health and those that encourage self-medication. The present document is structured as follows: in the background section, a set of recent works related to our proposal is presented, as well as a comparison of the proposals of each revised work. The focus section describes the main proposal and the final architecture and describes the modules that make up the architecture. The Web Scraping section is a fundamental part of our approach, so the use of it is presented. It continues with the Ontology section, which shows and describes the medical domain ontology used in this work. The section on opinion mining describes the tasks performed and shows a brief example. Finally, we present a case study to complement our proposal, showing the proposed approach applied in a functional system. Finally, the conclusions and future work presented.

BACKGROUND

Lee et al. (2017) developed an analysis that describes the difficulty of finding adverse effects in clinical trials conducted by pharmaceutical organizations and the lack of monitoring required in the market to identify side effects of drugs not previously discovered. For this reason, the authors examined a semi-supervised approach because it is a potential resource for detecting ADE in real-time in Twitter publications. In this context, they built models based on Convolutional Neural Network (CNN) using a semi-supervised architecture for the classification of ADE in tweets, making selective use of a variety of untagged data. Experiments conducted from random tweets with:

1) Medical names;
2) Health conditions;
3) Sentences from scientific articles in the medical literature and Wikipedia and,
4) Simulated health-related sentences created from lexicons, and combinations of these data types;

The experiments demonstrate that the ADE classification exceeds the supervised classification models, a +9.9% F1 measurement, and the state-of-the-art supervised models with an accuracy of +14.58%.

An analysis of opinion mining for drug review in which patients express their experiences and opinions about treatments or medications was focused by Cavalcanti and Prudêncio (2017). Besides, they identified that pharmacovigilance benefits drug manufacturers because particular adverse reactions to a drug quickly tracked from publications in social networks or public forums. Therefore, the authors proposed the adoption of a linguistic method and the inclusion of a supervised learning algorithm for the classification of opinion pairs (an aspect term and an opinion term) into one of the four types of aspects: Condition, Adverse Drug Reactions (ADR), Dosage or Effectiveness. Finally, the experiments involved three diseases, Attention Deficit Hyperactivity Disorder (ADHD), AIDS, and anxiety. The results revealed an improvement in performance to extract relevant aspects compared to the reference methods, where the highest F-Measure values appear for all data sets.

A simple and effective method for extracting ADE from Twitter was proposed by (Peng et al., 2016). The authors used a five-step pipeline:

1) Capturing tweets;
2) Data preprocessing;
3) Drug-related classification;
4) Tweet sentiment analysis and,
5) ADE extraction.

The analysis realized by the authors identified that pharmaceutical companies often do not find in the time the secondary effects caused by the drugs, due to the limited size of the clinical trials, which favors withdrawing drugs from the market, resulting in a significant financial loss for pharmaceutical companies. For this reason, it argues the great importance of monitoring and predicting ADEs. However, social media websites, such as Twitter, Facebook, and Google Circle, provides consumers with a way to share experiences with drugs that they do not report to health care providers or the Food and Drug Administration (FDA). The tests performed provided positive information, because the proposed method successfully extracted 1,239 ADEs via the Twitter social network, including 22% new ADE, for five drugs in four months, which is five times more compared to the results of the reference method.

Pharmacovigilance is an area of great importance because it is related to the detection, evaluation, understanding, and prevention of ADE or any other drug-related problem; also, it evaluates the safety of each medication to enhance the safety profile of the marketed drug. In this context, a system called CSIRO Adverse Drug Event Miner (CADEminer) was presented by Karimi et al. (2015). CADEminer which extracts comments from consumers in drug forums, using search and NLP techniques to extract mentions of side effects and other relevant concepts such as drug names and diseases, to compensate for the shortcomings of passive surveillance, that relies on individual reports of potential adverse drug events from different sources, such as health professionals and manufacturers. On the other hand, using a machine learning-based approach that implements conditional random fields for concept extraction, as well as the rules of association mining method that relies on the support and trust of a potential rule. Similarly, the work incorporated an information retrieval approach to filter out the known information extracted from a drug and thus emphasize the potentially unknown side effects, through the use of ontologies that helped map out the concepts, such as SNOMED CT, AMT, and MedDRA. Finally,

CADEminer is useful for regulatory agencies, pharmaceutical companies, and anyone else interested in exploring information about ADE.

A framework for Semantic Extraction and Sentiment Assessment of Risk Factors (SESARF), which combines and maps relevant concepts, finds adjectives and adverbs that reflect the level of severity was proposed by Sabra et al. (2018). It also incorporates a method for semantic enrichment of Venous Thromboembolism (VTE) risk factors to analyze the clinical narratives of Electronic Health Records (EHR) and predict a VTE diagnosis using the SVM (Support Vector Machine) classifier. Studies show that the death rate associated with Pulmonary Embolism (PE) and the rate of VTE is unacceptably high but is consistent with being listed as the third most common cardiovascular disorder; however preventive efforts begin with lifestyle measures to reduce the risk of VTE. On the other hand, the authors evaluated the framework using an NLP approach to assess accuracy and completeness with the use of Semantic Web technologies and machine learning to identify risk factors that are essential to diagnosis and to distinguish levels of severity using Unified Medical Language System (UMLS) of MetaMap and LOD (Linked Open Data). Besides, three analyses performed on the data:

1)   General;
2)   Gender-based;
3)   Age-based, these analyses showed that the age groups did not contribute to any specific observations.

The work presented demonstrates a strong association between the emergence of VTE and the combination of the following three risk factors: diabetes, obesity, and smoking. Finally, it demonstrates that the prediction is feasible and with accuracy without presenting symptoms of 54.5% and completeness of 85.7%.

An analysis describing facets and potentials of sentiment analysis in the context of medicine and health was developed by Denecke and Deng (2015). The authors also developed an extraction method to quantify parts of speech, determine the frequency of occurrence, and calculate term matches with sentiment lexicons from a dataset obtained from clinical narratives and medical social networks from six different sources. In the analysis conducted by the authors, they found that physicians describe their personal views and observations, what may be a judgment or an evaluation, an affective state that ends up influencing clinical decision making. For this reason, the analysis of medical records is crucial for obtaining a complete vision of the patient's health status to provide automated support for decision making and, with the help of opinion mining, determine the impact of written documents. In conclusion, in work found that clinical analyses written by nurses are more subjective than those of radiology reports, but even more objective than social media data; also, the work identified that the lexicons used have different coverage, but many more sentiment terms exist in the SentiWordNet tool.

A neuronal approach as a hierarchical representation of tweets was proposed by Wu et al. (2019). The initiative of the authors arises because detecting the drug name and detecting adverse reactions mentioned in tweets is very difficult, since tweets are usually very noisy and informal, and there are huge spelling errors and user-created abbreviations for these mentions. Besides, these mentions are usually context-dependent. The approach is to learn from the representations of people's words and then to learn the representations of tweets. The authors used an additive attention mechanism to select informative words in tweets to build more informative representations of tweets. Also, they identified that Twitter's social network provides tweets that can be easily collected in real-time and the number of tweets is enormous. Therefore, detecting tweets that mention drug names and ADEs helps uncover serious or unknown consequences of drug use that are not covered by medical records. To address word representation, the authors made three sub-modules, the first being a character embedding layer, the second a CNN, and the third a word embedding that incorporates rich semantic information from tweets. The representation of the tweet consists of three modules:

1) A Bi-directional Long Short Term Memory (Bi-LSTM);
2) Multi-head self-care network, and
3) An additive care network.

Experimental results in two reference data sets validate the effectively the proposed approach in detecting tweets mentioning drug names and ADRs.

A study on the impact of implementing opinion mining for Online Support Groups (OSGs) on breast cancer related to the drug tamoxifen, as it is of great importance in understanding the emotions and opinions of users, was conducted by Cabling et al. (2018). The analysis included the application for 498 users, with the most active users accounting for 80% and the rest being less active users. The aim of comparing the two groups is to explore the possible reasons why users decided to post a comment and how their feeling plays a role in finding or providing online support compared to those who did not post a comment. The authors identified that the higher the stage of cancer a user had, the less likely that she would have posted, and if she were to post, the post would have focused on her side effects and the anxiety/sadness that tailgates those side effects. The lower the stage of cancer a user had, the more likely that she would have posted, additionally remained active on the forum and encouraged more social support. Finally, analysis of user feelings provides an understanding of how specific interactions that promote support lead to the development of intra-group and out-of-group dynamics, as well as hyper-personal communication within OSGs. However, through the Big Data, sentiment analysis and research exploring the development of group cohesion within Computer Mediated Communication (CMC) revealed a richer narrative of what occurs in OSGs and reflected for facilitators to be aware of the dynamics of sentiment.

A method based on opinion mining to detect the emotional reaction of patients with an asthmatic disease on risk factors, physical activities, among other concepts, were proposed by Luna-Aveiga et al. (2018). The disease of asthma is a serious health problem that affects all age groups. Asthma-related hospitalizations and deaths have decreased in some countries; however, the authors argue that the number of patients with symptoms has increased in recent years. On the other hand, the growth of information on health and disease management in forums, blogs, microblogs, and social networks, specifically Twitter, was identified as a powerful tool to disseminate experiences and encourage conversations on disease self-management. The authors present a method that takes advantage of Semantic Web technologies, specifically ontologies, to represent the asthma domain, as well as the SentiWordNet tool to determine the polarity of asthma concepts contained in Twitter messages. In addition, they designed an ontology called OASM that describes concepts such as risk factors, drugs, symptoms, and other concepts related to asthma care. The proposed method is composed of four elements:

1) Normalization module;
2) Semantic annotation module;
3) The ontology for asthma self-management;
4) A polarity identification of feeling module.

Evaluations of approach through the collected tweets gave encouraging results with 82.95% accuracy, 82.27% recall 82.36% F measure. Furthermore, it proved to help raise asthma awareness, thereby motivating additional help-seeking behavior.

Currently, Web 2.0 allows individuals to share valuable data and opinions about products or services purchased online. Shared data and unstructured opinions include emotions, feelings, characteristics, numbers, dates, and facts, so it represents the focus of most researchers trying to collect and capture popular sentiments. In this context, a review of NLP techniques for opinion extraction was conducted by Solangi et al. (2019). Their study identified the preprocessing stages required to structure texts, which are: feature extraction, segmentation, tokenization, grammatical tagging, and analysis in opinion extraction, where tokenization is an essential strategy for most NLP-related tasks. However, for Chinese and Japanese dialects, among others, words are composed differently. The authors added in the review the tools that address Chinese word segmentation and tokenization, such as

1) Fudan NLP in JAVA language
2) The Language Technology Platform (LTP) in the open-source C++ system for lexical analysis
3) Niu Parser in C++ language which is a semantic analyzer and syntactic toolkit in Chinese
4) Gensim Python
5) Stanford CoreNLP

Further, it is exposed that opinion mining aims to extract sentimental orientation from writings, through opinion mining, divided into three levels: document level, sentence level, and fine grain level. Finally, for the preprocessing of texts the techniques designed to consist of checks to track or classify the data, however, detection is not always adequate, so the authors suggest to make modifications to the techniques of the NLP or other relevant techniques since the user or beneficiary provides and receives adequate information data.

Alayba et al. (2017) presented an Arabic language dataset that discusses health services topics collected from the social network Twitter. While there has been a lot of research on sentiment analysis in English, the number of researches and datasets in the Arabic language is limited, so the authors detail the four main steps taken to obtain the Arabic dataset for opinion mining purposes, such as:

1) Data collection;
2) Data filtering;
3) Preprocessing of Arabic text by removing unwanted data, deleting some words and unrelated text, and standardizing the text; and
4) Applying machine learning to the dataset collected.

For the experiments, implemented algorithms such as Machine Learning (Naïve Bayes, SVM, and Logistic Regression) alongside Deep and Convolutional Neural Networks. The results show accuracy results were roughly between 85% and 91%, and the best classifiers were SVM using Linear Support Vector Classification and Stochastic Gradient Descent. The SVM classifier accuracy is similar to the first annotator's accuracy.

An analysis that discusses in detail opinion mining, how the value of polarity relates to something positive or negative, and how to address blog reviews written in the Roman language was conducted by Rathi et al. (2016). In this context, the analysis of the authors shows the existence of different tasks applied in opinion mining, such as opinion mining, sentiment mining and emotional analysis, however, the vital aspect of the action is to collect the information from the comments found in the blogs or other sites and then discover the behavior of that information. There are many opinions on the web, and some opinions contain context-dependent words which present a polarity classification, therefore, to catalog the feelings correctly, it is necessary to eliminate the ambiguity with the help of the tool called word polarity disambiguation, which refers to the computer identification of the polarity of a word in a given context. Likewise identified that existing works focus on the English language and not the Roman language, for this reason, the authors present the possibility of creating a database to provide the opinion value of Roman words for comparison with the English language, which leads to increasing the performance rating of websites related to any product that includes Roman language reviews.

A method for sentiment analysis that effectively detects aspects of diabetes in tweets, using ontologies to semantically describe relationships between concepts in the specific domain, in the English language was developed by Salas-Zárate et al. (2017). The feeling that determines the aspects gets calculated considering the words around the aspect obtained through the methods of "N-gram". On the other hand, the analysis identified that diabetes is a chronic condition that occurs when the body does not produce or use enough insulin; for that reason, it is one of the most significant health emergencies worldwide. It estimated that more than half a million children under age 14 are living with diabetes, 415 million adults have diabetes, and an additional 318 million adults are estimated to have impaired glucose tolerance, putting them at high risk for developing the disease in the future. Thus, social networks such as Twitter are an excellent resource for patients as they connect with people who have similar conditions and similar experiences. However, opinion seeking is a difficult task, because a simple search on Twitter using "Diabetes" returns thousands of tweets; therefore, opinion summary systems using sentiment analysis or opinion mining technologies are needed. Hence, the proposed approach to the classification of feelings consists of three main components: the preprocessing module for cleaning and correcting text, the semantic annotation module for detecting aspects, and the sentiment rating module that calculates the polarity of each aspect found in the SentiWordNet lexicon. Finally, the set of experiments gave results that showed that the "N-gram around" method obtained the best results with an accuracy of 81.93%, a recovery of 81.13%, and an F measure of 81.24%. Also, the experiments showed that the lexicon of general feeling is not sufficient to capture the meanings in health texts. Furthermore, the proposed method requires an ontology that models the domain to identify aspects of the diabetes domain.

On the other hand, a comparison that reviews the different techniques of opinion mining and emphasizes the need to address the specific challenges of the NLP in collecting and examining words related to opinion mining was developed by Khan et al., (2016). They also stressed the need for standard data sets and assessment methodologies to improve models that capture context and proximity. Also, they identified that machine learning techniques are beneficial for opinion mining; such techniques apply in two ways; 1) Supervised, which require tagged data, and 2) Semi-supervised, which require manual adjustment by domain experts. On the other hand, opinion mining is a diversified field of research that includes machine learning, NLP, language identification, and text summarization, in which review texts come from different languages, and for each one, the evaluative and subjective phrases get recognized. Therefore, it has close relevance to NLP, so opinion mining faces problems such as co-reference resolution, negation management, and disambiguation of word meaning.

Usually, the patients who use drugs often search the Internet for stories of patients like themselves, which they usually find among their friends and family. However, exist a few studies investigating the impact of social networks on patients show that, for some health problems, online community support results in a positive effect. A method of opinion extraction that focuses on predicting the level of satisfaction among other patients who have already experienced the effect of a drug, addressing Neural Networks to understand how the general population perceives the safety, reactions, and efficiency of a drug was proposed by Gopalakrishnan and Ramaswamy (2017). In the particular domain of pharmacies, positive, negative, and neutral reactions are equally important in deciding on drug use. On the other hand, from the results, it was demonstrated that the Neural Network-based approach to opinion creation surpasses the SVM method in terms of accuracy, recovery, and F-score. Also, it found that prediction models based on the Radial Base Function of the Neuronal Network (RBFN) performed well in all aspects, better than the Probabilistic Neuronal Network (PNN), because of the deficiencies that tend to get trapped in unwanted local minima to reach the global minimum of a very complex search space. Thus, the approach shows a better result in terms of various performance measures compared to other drug reviews of existing works collected, as well as being a viable and optimal solution for increasing ranking performance.

A study on existing lexicons was conducted by Ding et al. (2008). One of them, WordNet, in which the authors found that it has important deficiencies since it does not have an effective mechanism to deal with the words of opinion depending on the context, therefore, it probably is not possible to know the semantic orientation of the words. The authors propose a lexically based, holistic approach, which focuses on the opinions expressed by customers about products in reviews. The approach, instead of examining only the actual sentence, exploits the information by a method of aggregating the orientations of such words by considering the distance between each word of the opinion and the characteristic of the product. The proposed approach was implemented in the system called Opinion Observer; the experiments carried out by the authors focused on eight products, two digital cameras, a DVD player, an MP3 player, two cell phones, a router, and antivirus software; however, they found that deciding if a sentence offers an opinion for some confusing cases is difficult, so, for the difficult sentences, they made a consensus between the primary human note-takers (the first author of the paper and two students) and the secondary note-taker (the second author of the paper). On the other hand, the proposed method turned out to be useful and effective because it considers explicit and implicit opinions; this makes the proposed technique more complete.

Similarly, Pak and Paroubek (2010) presented an analysis describing how Microblogging has become a popular communication tool, which is why websites are a rich source of data because of the rapidly growing number of users who post messages about their lives, about various topics, examine current issues or about the products and services they use. This data can be used effectively to perform opinion mining analysis and with the results obtained help in decision making in marketing or social studies, to mention a few. The authors presented a method that extracts opinions from the social network Twitter, the content of which varies from personal thoughts to public statements. With the data obtained, they made a corpus that determines the positive, negative, and neutral feeling. Using the corpus, they constructed a sentiment classifier and performed experiments on a set of microblogging posts to prove that the technique presented is effective and performs better than the methods analyzed. In the study, the authors used the classifier is based on the multinomial Naïve Bayes classifier that uses N-gram and POS-tags as features.

As shown in Table 1, the analyzed works use one of several approaches, such as the application of algorithms for the classification of sentiment and the use of semantic methods, which involve the hybrid approach presented in this chapter. Unlike (Lee et al., 2017; Wu et al., 2019; Cabling et al., 2018; Luna-Aveiga et al., 2018; Salas-Zárate et al., 2017; Gopalakrishnan & Ramaswamy, 2017) our approach gets comments from a variety of sources such as forums, blogs, and video blogs, where there is relevant information to analyze in detail, so the scarcity of comments does not prove to be an obstacle as it is with getting tweets about medication from the social network Twitter.

Table 1. Related work comparative

Author	Domain	Approach	Polarity detection	NLP	Data Source
Lee et al. (2017)	Medical	Semi-supervised Convolutional Neural Network.	✔	X	Twitter
Cavalcanti (2017)	Medical	Linguistic method based on Dependency Paths in the Syntactic Tree.	✔	✔	Drugs.com
Peng et al. (2016)	Medical	Supervised Machine learning.	✔	✔	Twitter
Karimi et al. (2015)	Medical	Semantic and Machine learning.	X	✔	Drugs.com RxList.com MedlinePlus.
Sabra et al. (2018)	Medical	Semantic and Supervised Machine Learning.	✔	✔	Biomedical Documents and Clinical Narratives from PubMed.
Denecke and Deng (2015)	Medical	Review of Sentiment Lexicons and Machine Learning.	✔	X	Clinical Narratives, Social Networks, and Specialized Websites.
Wu et al. (2019)	Medical	Neural approach using Multi-Head Self-Attention.	X	X	Twitter
Cabling et al. (2018)	Medical	------	✔	X	Specialized Website
Luna-Aveiga et al. (2018)	Medical	Semantic	✔	X	Twitter
Solangi et al. (2019)	------	Opinion mining for various levels are analyzed and reviewed	✔	✔	-----
Alayba et al. (2017)	Medical	Machine Learning	✔	X	Twitter
Rathi et al. (2016)	------	Semantic	✔	X	Blogs
Salas-Zárate et al. (2017)	Medical	Semantic	✔	✔	Twitter
Khan et al. (2016)	------	Reviews sentiment analysis techniques and NLP.	✔	✔	------
Gopalakrishnan and Ramaswamy (2017)	Medical	Neural Network.	✔	✔	askapatient.com
Ding et al. (2008)	e-commerce	Opinion mining, NLP	✔	✔	amazon.com.
Pak and Paroubek (2010)	General	Opinion mining, NLP and Machine Learning	✔	✔	Twitter

Our approach makes a review on chronic-degenerative diseases, so a vast amount of comments is obtained through Web Scraping and contain information about sentiments regarding a drug, the dosage of the drug, the price, and even the adverse effects that it has on patients. On the other hand, in Cavalcanti and Prudencio (2017), Peng et al. (2016), Karimi et al. (2015) and Sabra et al. (2018) they propose hybrid approaches using semantic web technologies and sentiment classification algorithms such as supervised machine learning and Syntactic dependency paths as well as linguistic methods through external tools. As mentioned by the authors Pak and Paroubek (2010), the use of a corpus for classification in opinion mining is important because it allows training the algorithm to obtain better results; nevertheless, it makes use of a corpus with general opinions of any topic to classify opinions on Twitter, in contrast, as mentioned by Ding et al. (2008) a corpus must contain opinions according to the context to be analyzed to obtain a better classification, therefore, in our approach, we propose a semantic method through the integration of a corpus with opinions focused on the health area, in the Spanish language, which was labeled with the use of supervised machine learning the resulting corpus was reviewed by a specialist in the health area. Besides, it should be noted that our approach, we propose a semantic method through the integration of a corpus that we label automatically, the use of supervised machine learning. Furthermore, our approach gets first-hand comments from patients, unlike the clinical narratives discussed by Denecke and Deng (2015), which are subject to interpretation by third parties by doctors and nurses, so they are less accurate.

Finally, as mentioned in Solangi et al. (2019), Alayba et al. (2017), Rathi et al. (2016) and Khan et al. (2016), very scarce work has been done in the implementation of opinion mining and NLP for data sets in languages other than English, such as Chinese and Japanese, among others, because it requires a great effort for implementation and analysis, while our approach addresses opinion mining and NLP for comments in the Spanish language, recognized as the second most spoken language in the world.

APPROACH

Our work uses a hybrid approach, through supervised machine learning because we use tags in the opinions with the desired solution to generate a model for training the algorithm that allows the classification of new opinions and the linguistic semantics can refer either to the study of meaning in o far as this is expressed in language or to the study of meaning within linguistics, through the use of a medical domain ontology and the bag of words (Lyons, 1995).

With the following approach implemented in a system, it will allow to summarize the information obtained from forums, blogs and video blog, to obtain accurate knowledge and provide health specialists and patients with information about the opinions that speak about medicines, as well as the adverse effects. The following describes the parts that make up our approach, through an architecture.

Architecture

Figure 1 depicts the Spanish opinion analysis system for chronic-degenerative disease drugs, based on Web Scraping techniques that it is integrated by six main modules and a corpus:

1) Data collection module;
2) Pre-processing module;

3) Domain identification module;
4) Processing module;
5) Opinions repository;
6) Expert Validation Module,
7) Data presentation.

Figure 1. Architecture of system

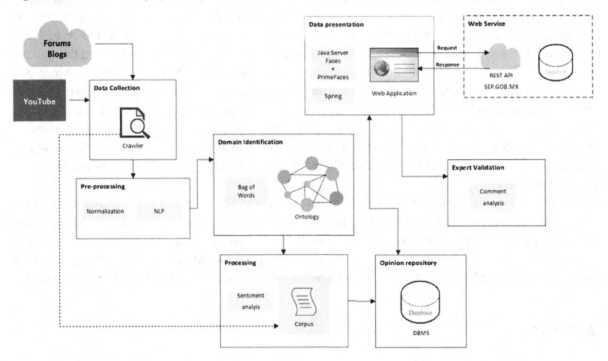

Data Collection Module

In this module, we collected the comments that mention drugs and symptoms of chronic-degenerative diseases published in forums, blogs, specialized websites, and video blogs through a crawler with a series of URLs that it accesses to obtain the comments. This work considers only three types of chronic degenerative diseases: diabetes, hypertension, and hepatitis.

Pre-Processing Module

The preprocessing of data is an important step for the normalization of the text; therefore, we chose to use three phases for the treatment of our data.

1. **Delete unusual characters:** Unique characters that do not provide information removed from the comments.

2. **Delete duplicate comments:** This step is essential because duplicate comments affect the final result of the analysis; therefore, it is crucial to ensure that no duplicate comments exist.
3. **Delete comments that only have URLs:** Comments that only link to other sites do not contribute information to be considered as comments so that no analysis can be applied, for this reason, eliminated.

The application of these tasks on the comments ensures a better analysis of sentiments, but the incorrect use of language is a common scenario, created by the use of abbreviations or spelling errors on behalf of the users, requiring a more considerable effort to carry out opinion mining activities, for that reason, this module also makes use of a spell checker.

Domain Identification Module

The identification of the words is highly relevant within architecture because it allows verifying that the comments collected include the mention of a drug prescribed for diabetes, hypertension, and hepatitis diseases. The result of this module provides a more specific data set with valuable information for the analysis in the next module. In this context, a bag of words was created through a medical domain ontology, based on Snomed an organization nonprofit, which determines standards for a codified language that represents groups of clinical terms, this enables healthcare information to be exchanged globally for the benefit of patients and other stakeholders (NCBO BioPortal, 2019).

The Bag of Words (BoW) is a key element for the approach because it allows corroborating that the comments are of the medical domain, BoW is known to be a model widely used in the domain of NLP because it based on the idea that the frequency of appearance of a word in a text serves as a measure of the meaning that the word (Thanaki, 2017).

Processing Module

Once the data collected are clean of unusual characters and corroborated that they belong to the medical domain, is adopts the supervised machine learning approach which makes use of a semi-automatic labeled corpus, necessary to train the algorithm that performs the sentiment analysis, this permits it to recognize new opinions in the Spanish language and to classify them correctly according to polarity.

Opinions Repository Module

The opinions and polarity of the drugs resulting from the analysis are stored in a database to keep the data available for consultation, as well as the expert's data when validating the comments. The repository adds speed to our system for information retrieval.

Expert Validation Module

The module examines the validation obtained by the expert to verify whether it is a valid comment or a comment that should be attended to by a specialist. This module makes it clear that our system does not encourage self-medication.

Figure 2 depicts in a conceptual way what the expert's validation consists of, i.e., the specialist in the domain can validate the comments shown obtained from Web Scraping. To validate the comments, the expert registers his name, professional license, and comment; these data as validated through a public domain web service provided by the SEP (Secretary of Public Education).

Figure 2. Representation of the expert validation module process

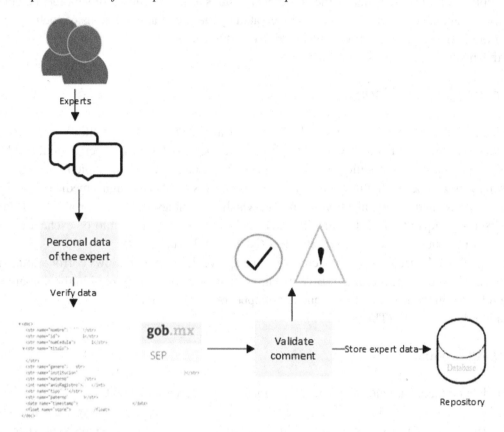

Data Presentation Module

This module refers to the presentation of a web interface that supports the interaction of users with the application to know the comments and the polarity of the drugs prescribed for chronic-degenerative diseases, specifically diabetes mellitus, hepatitis, and hypertension.

3.2 Web Scraping

For carrying out our approach, we use two web scraping techniques, the first, Web Crawling or also known as spider or robots, is characterized by being computer programs to collect web pages automatically has a behavior similar to the navigation performed by users and, first, specifies the set of URLs to which you have to access and then enter each page and download the content, making a repetitive process to complete all the assigned URLs. The second technique used is web information extraction, which allows the identification of structured and semi-structured information that interests users. The main objective is to obtain the text from web pages, images, audios, videos, and other media (Liu,2011; Cho & Garcia-Molina, 2002; Mo et al. 2012).

Figure 3 shows the process that this module performs for the collection of comments. The first step is the sending of a computer agent with a list of URLs from which it extracts the comments, giving, as a result, a set of comments necessary for the analysis of opinions.

Figure 3. Web scraping workflow

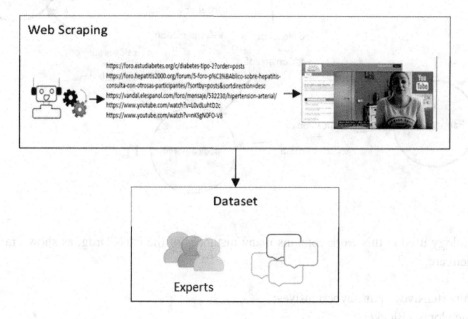

3.3 Ontology

An ontology is an explicit description of a domain that specifies a concept by describing its properties, attributes, and constraints in an organized way to limit complexity (Porras et al., 2018). It is necessary to extract information to populate and improve the ontology, allowing identification and classification using a system with a deeper level of analysis (Abirami et al., 2018).

In this context, the ontology used is important for the creation of the bag of words used for the identification of the medical domain. The ontology is designed in Spanish, and it is populated with drug names, to ensure that the collected comments contain a mention of some drug. The bag of words is widely used in the NLP domain because based on the idea that the frequency of appearance of each word in a text serves as a measure of the word's meaning (Thanaki, 2017). **Figure 4** shows the composition of the ontology used in this work, which contains four main instances called:

1) Medicamento - Drug
2) Efectos adversos - Adverse effects
3) Farmaco - Pharmaco
4) Farmacéutica - Pharmaceutical.

Figure 4. The general structure of the ontology

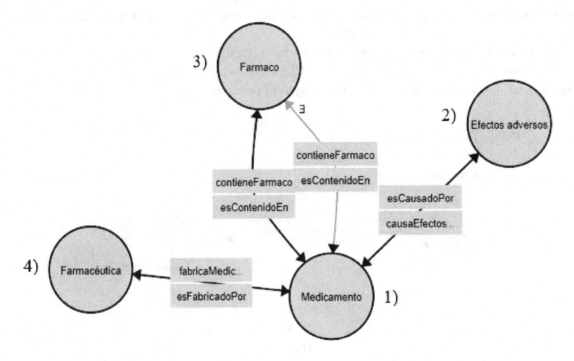

The ontology used in this work contains many instances of the class Drug, as shown in **Figure 5**, some of them are:

1) Antihipertensivos - Anti-hypertensives;
2) Bloqueadores - Blockers;
3) Antidiabéticos - Anti-diabetics;
4) Inhibidores - Inhibitors;
5) Antivirales - Antivirals;
6) Diuréticos - Diuretics;
7) Beta bloqueadores - Beta-blockers;
8) Inmunosupresores - Immunosuppressant.

The Ontology populated with names of drugs used for the treatment of chronic degenerative diseases in the Spanish language, which is listed below:

1) Valsartán - Valsartan
2) Metildopa - Methyldopa
3) Nateglinida - Nateglinide
4) Repaglinida - Repaglinide
5) Telmisartán - Telmisartan
6) Prazosina - Prazosin
7) Metformina - Metformin

8)   Sitagliptina - Sitagliptin
9)   Gliclazide - Gliclazide
10) Vildagliptina - Vildagliptin
11) Saxagliptina - Saxagliptin
12) Tolbutamida - Tolbutamide
13) Linagliptina - Linagliptin
14) Glimepirida - Glimepiride
15) Clorpropamida - Chlorpropamide
16) Glibenclamida – Glibenclamide
to name a few.

Figure 5. Attributes of the Drug instance

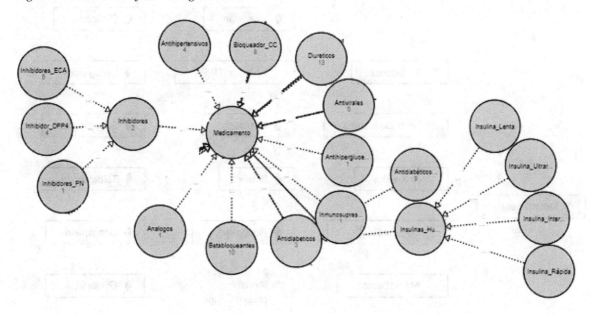

Opinion Mining

Opinion mining, or also called sentiment analysis, is the process of extracting subjective information from user-generated content, also, using NLP and computational intelligence. This field of study analyzes user's opinions, feelings, assessments, emotions, and attitudes towards entities such as products, services, organizations, individuals, events, topics, and their attributes. Some names and tasks are differentiated as sentiment analysis, opinion extraction, sentiment extraction, subjectivity analysis, damages analysis, emotion analysis, mining analysis, among others. Sentiment analysis is a highly restricted NLP problem because the system does not need to understand the semantics of each sentence or document fully but only needs to understand some aspects of it, i.e., positive or negative sentiments and their target entities or topics. In this context, the application of opinion mining involved three key tasks, which are described below:

Task 1 (entity extraction and categorization): Extract all entity expressions and categorize or group entity.

Task 2 (opinion holder extraction and categorization): Extract opinion holders for opinions from text or structured data and categorize them.

Task 3 (aspect sentiment classification): Determine whether an opinion on an aspect is positive, negative or neutral, or assign a numeric sentiment rating to the aspect (Kishore & Kumar, 2016; Liu, 2012).

Figure 6. Populated Ontology

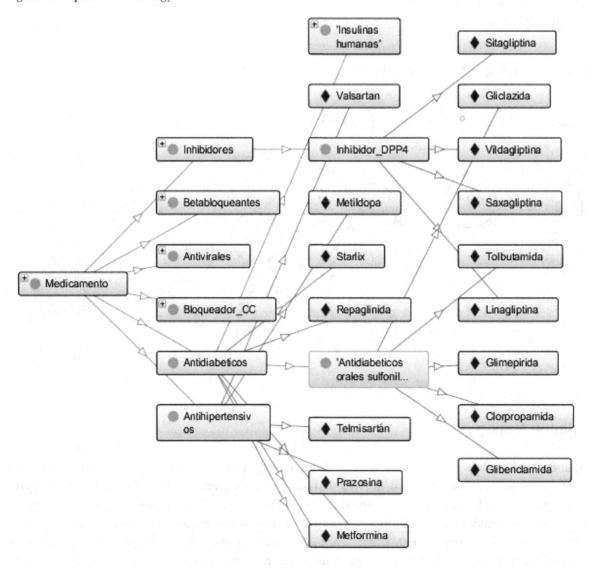

It is important to note that neutral comments are discarded in our work because they do not contain relevant information, i.e., it means that the user does not have an opinion on the subject matter.

Figure 7. Comment analysis

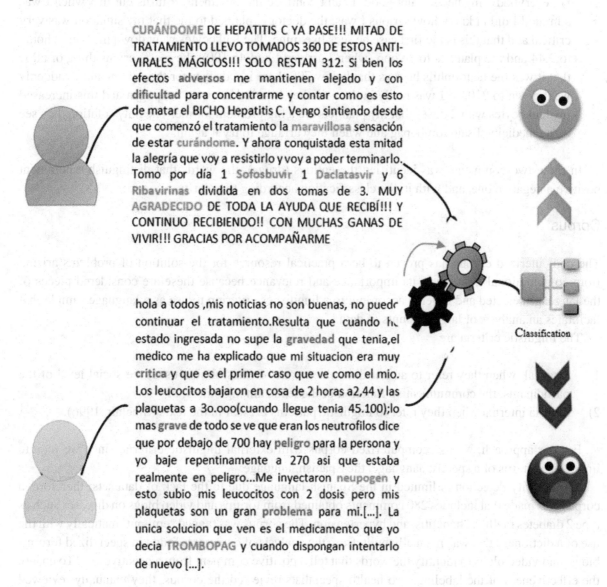

Figure 7 shows two of the comments collected, which read as follows:

1) Curing me of hepatitis c is over!! halfway through my treatment, I've been on 360 of these magic antivirals! Only 312 remains. Although the adverse effects keep me away and I have difficulty concentrating and counting as it is to kill the hepatitis c bug. I have been feeling the amazing sensation of being cured ever since the treatment began. And now that I have conquered this half of the alienation, I will be able to resist it and finish it. I take a day 1 sofosbuvir 1 daclatasvir and 6 ribavirins divided into two takes of 3, and I continue to receive it! With a lot of will to live!!! Thank you for joining me.

2) Hi, everybody, my news is not good. I can't continue the treatment. It turns out that when I was admitted I didn't know how serious I was, the doctor explained to me that my situation was very critical and that this is the first case he sees like mine. The leukocytes went down in about 2 hours to 2.44 and the platelets to 3o.ooo (when I arrived I had 45,100); the most serious thing of all is that it was the neutrophils he says that below 700 there is a danger for the person and I suddenly went down to 270, so I was really in danger...they injected me with neupogen and this increased my leukocytes with 2 doses, but my platelets are a big problem for me. The only solution they see is the medicine I said tombopag and when they arrange to try it again.

In these two comments was identified the entities (drugs), the words that distinguish a comment positive a negative one, and with it, the classification according to polarity.

Corpus

The computerized corpus has proven to be a practical resource for the solution of problems arising from computational linguistics, its importance and relevance because these are considered pieces of the language selected and ordered according to a linguistics criterion to use as a language sample that facilitates an analysis of large amounts of data.

The linguistic criteria are

1) external, when they refer to author data, the means of transmission used, the social level of the participants, the communicative function of the texts, among others; or
2) criteria internal when they refer to linguistic patterns present in the texts (Sinclair, 1996).

For our approach, we use computerized corpus with external linguistic criteria, since we require linguistic patterns of a specific language, the Spanish language.

The polarity detection is limited in the Spanish language due to the lack of data sets; therefore, a corpus was made that includes 280 comments obtained from forums and video blogs on diseases such as type 2 diabetes mellitus, hepatitis, and hypertension. The corpus was tagged semi-automatically with the use of a dictionary that was manually built, from the analysis of comments found in specialized forums, blogs, and video blogs to identify the words that tell a positive comment from a negative one. To ensure the effectiveness of the labeling, two health specialists reviewed the corpus; they manually reviewed each comment to corroborate that both the positive and negative comments presented the corresponding tag. An example of comments included within-corpus is depicted in **Figure 8**, highlighting the words that are of interest to this work, the comments read as follows:

1) POSITIVE: Hello, everyone, and I'm starting off with a lot of courage and strength. I'm 37 years old and I found out about hepatitis C B1 when I had the special tests because I got pregnant, this is already 3.5 years ago. Well, my little girl was born phenomenal (3,500 kg) without infection, at first if it had, but it was negative, I was told that was normal because it was very difficult to transmit to the fetus, especially in hepatitis c [...]; treatment has been phenomenal, no symptoms (no hair loss, no fever, no weight loss, nothing at all) the doctor told me it was a weirdo, I broke statistics, according to them. I took 5 pills a day and the injection (150mcg) once a week. Some days I was more tired, but I took eferalgan 1g or espidifen and it went away, in the end, you get used to that

kind of tiredness [...] Now I can't start the treatment again, not because I want to, I'm very excited but because I have to rest. I'm very happy because my hepatitis is supposed to be the worst, well it's the most difficult to cure, and so far it's effective [...];

2) NEGATIVE: Greetings again, on December 15 I have the exam again to see my state, the truth because of the work I have felt stressed and every time I pass it hurts my right side, the liver, I doubt because I felt a little itch in my body again, could I again present the picture that I present at the beginning of jaundice, and fall back to those levels? How difficult this is.

Figure 8. Sample of the tagged corpus

Tagged comments

1) POSITIVO Hola a todos y empiezo también con mucho ánimo y fuerza. Tengo 37 años y me enteré de que la hepatitis C B1 cuando me hicieron los análisis especiales porque me quedé embarazada, de esto ya hace 3.5 años. Bueno, mi nenita nació fenomenal (3.500 kg) sin contagio, al principio si lo tenía, pero se negativizo, me dijeron que era lo normal porque era muy difícil el contagio al feto, sobretodo en la hepatitis c [...]; el tratamiento me ha ido fenomenal, ningún síntoma (ni caída de pelo, ni fiebre, ni perdida de peso, nada de nada) el médico me decía que era un bicho raro, he roto estadísticas, según ellos. Tomaba 5 pastillas diarias y la inyección (150mcg) una vez a la semana. Algunos días estaba más cansada, pero tomaba eferalgan 1g o espidifen y se me pasaba, al final te acostumbras a esa especie de cansancio [...] Ahora no puedo empezar otra vez el tratamiento, no por ganas porque estoy muy animada sino porque tengo que descansar. Estoy muy contenta porque se supone que mi hepatitis es la peor, bueno es la más difícil de curar y hasta ahora me va funcionando [...]

2) NEGATIVO Saludos de nuevo, en diciembre 15 me toca de nuevo el examen para ver mi estado, la verdad a raíz del trabajo me he sentido estresado y cada vez que me pasa me duele la parte derecha, el hígado, tengo una duda porque volvi a sentí un poco la comezón en mi cuerpo, podría de nuevo volver a presentar el cuadro que presente al inicio de ictericia, y caer de nuevo a esos niveles? Que difícil esto.

Case Study

Polarity analysis in comments published in blogs, forums and video blogs in the Spanish language about prescription drugs for chronic - degenerative diseases

The medical community has detected a lack of records of patients describing symptoms ADE's, even those not previously identified by the pharmaceutical companies. This fact represents misinformation by the health specialists, as well as the patients themselves, for not letting the doctor know in consultations about symptoms added to their condition.

On the other hand, chronic-degenerative diseases are among the top 10 causes of death in Mexico, which represents a large number of people who go to their doctor for routine consultations and examinations. However, because of this requirement, health specialists have little time to check on patients in consultations, and consequently, physical examinations are not very useful as they require additional time. Given this fact, health specialists omit new symptoms independent of the initial condition, that derive from drugs or some other disease, ending up by not being adequately treated as a consequence of the absence of detection.

Similarly, it was found that it is important for patients to investigate, read, ask questions and give feedback to others who publish on the web about the drugs prescribed to their condition, the reasons are:

1) Know the adverse effects,
2) Learn about other treatments,
3) Ask about the adverse effects they suffer and
4) Comment on the percentage of progress they have with treatment, to mention but a few.

Therefore, we present the system called, SentiScrap, it allows the user to analyze the forums that are on the Web and video blogs about medicines for chronic diseases, specifically for diseases: Diabetes, Hypertension, and Hepatitis. The system is capable of performing the necessary extraction of these sources to obtain the opinions of patients and health specialists, resulting in a very valuable set of information to be analyzed through domain recognition and polarity detection.

For this case study, suppose a health specialist needs to know the opinions of patients receiving treatment for diabetes:

- How will the specialist be able to identify the medications that patients talk about for the treatment of diabetes?
- How will the specialist know the comments of patients who publish in forums and video blogs in the Spanish language?
- How will the specialist know the positive and negative impact on the comments?
- How will the specialist be able to validate under his/her medical experience the comments that patients share?
- How will it impact the specialist to know the comments made by patients?
- How will the health specialist be able to contribute to increasing the knowledge of our system?

The healthcare specialist has access to the information provided by patients through a web system, which we call SentiScrap. The system offers a menu of five options which are listed in order of appearance:

1) Diabetes
2) Hepatitis
3) Hypertension
4) Add Sources

5)   Statistics

Figure 9 depicts the content of the main screen.

Figure 9. SentiScrap home page

Suppose a healthcare specialist wants to know about medications that are prescribed for the treatment of diabetes, specifically those medications that patients discuss on forums, blogs, and video blogs. In this case, the specialist selects the disease diabetes a menu; consequently, the system generates a query to a repository to show the medicines, as well as the positive and negative polarity (through an iconography that represents the polarity) of medicines, as shown in **Figure 10**.

The specialist may need to read the collected feedback to identify, evaluate, and prevent adverse effects caused by the medications their patients take to reduce health and quality of life risks. In other words, the specialist obtains concise feedback for a specific disease, which helps to improve the care of their patients. To consult the feedback repository, click on the "+" button.

The SentiScrap system displays all comments with their corresponding classification, positive or negative, as shown in **Figure 11**. Also, each comment contains a button called Expert Validations to find out the data of the specialists who have validated the comment. Likewise, at the bottom, the Validate button to validate the comment according to the health professional's experience.

Figure 10. Diabetes options of the SentiScrap system

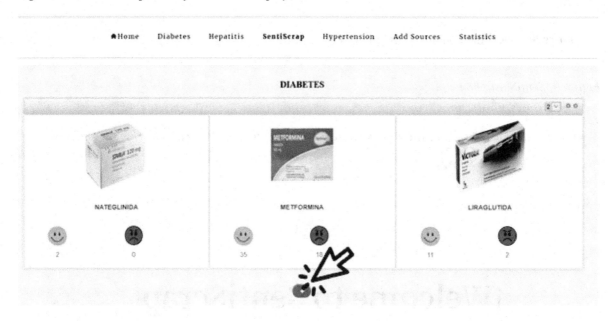

Figure 11. Comments collected about diabetes

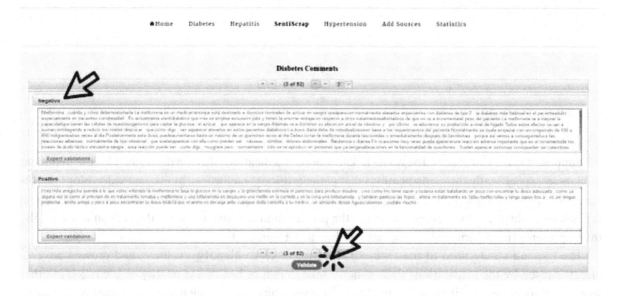

When the health specialist reads the collected comments, he may find malicious comments encouraging self-medication, which can have serious consequences such as adverse effects, which are harmful to health. Due to the situation previously explained, expert validation considered in this work.

The specialist has the possibility of validating the comments shown in SentiScrap, under his medical experience, as shown in **Figure 12**.

Figure 12. Expert validation form, professional card fields, name and surname

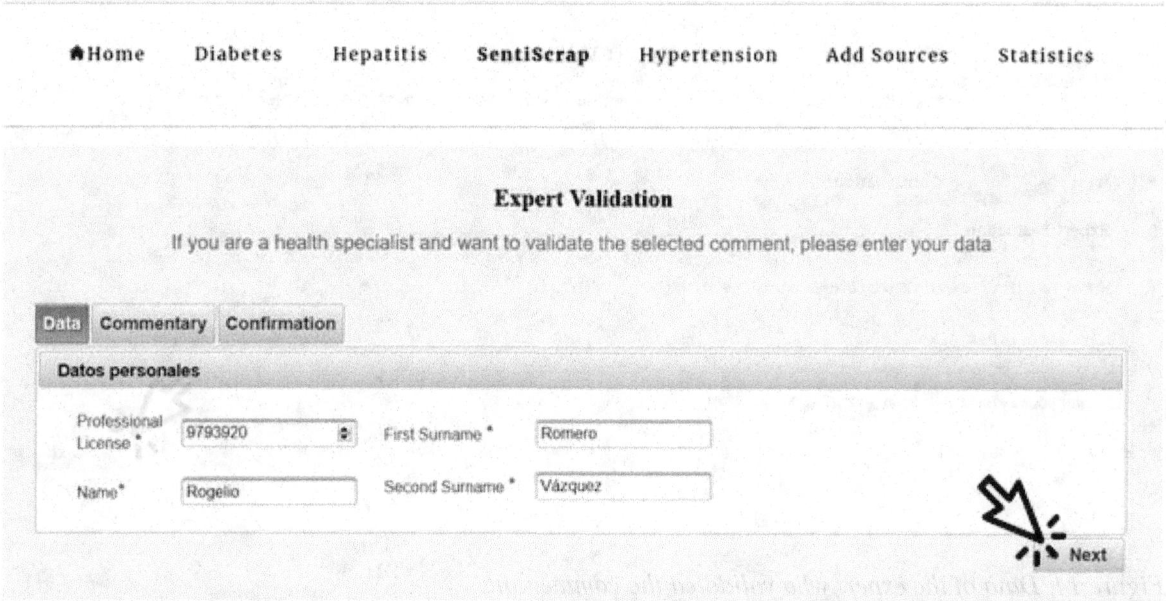

When selecting a comment and clicking on the Validate button, the system displays the following interface, which corresponds to a personal data form with the following information: professional license, name, and surname, to verify his identity. To perform the expert validation, surgeon Rogelio Romero Vázquez made use of our system and validated some of the comments collected.

The system driver receives the full name of the expert and calls the Restful service to find out if it exists; if so, then it temporarily saves the response of the invocation and then iterates until it finds the record that matches the professional card and the name of the expert. Once the response of the method is true, it allows to continue with the form, shown in **Figure 13**, in which you select an option regarding your opinion on the comment you want to validate; also, the expert must enter an email. Finally, the system shows the data entered so that the specialist can review them one last time and confirm the sending of the data to the repository.

When the experts validate the collected comments, the system adds a representation iconography according to the received validations, to show at a glance the comments with which caution should take and the comments that do not represent health risks for the reader, as shown in **Figure 14**.

Also, in the case of non-expert users who need to verify the veracity of the data, we added a button called professional license to go to the official website of the Secretary of Public Education (SEP), in which the user can enter the full name of the health specialist in the record search form, as shown in **Figure 15**.

Besides, SentiScrap provides a form for the healthcare specialist and even patients to add feeds from a file or a single URL for forums and video blogs.

Once the file or URL is sent to the system, the driver takes the URLs and sends them to the class with the method that extracts the information, and then the resulting set goes through the preprocessing method to remove the unusual characters and emoticons. The preprocessed data is then temporarily stored in a file.

Figure 13. Continuation of the expert validation form

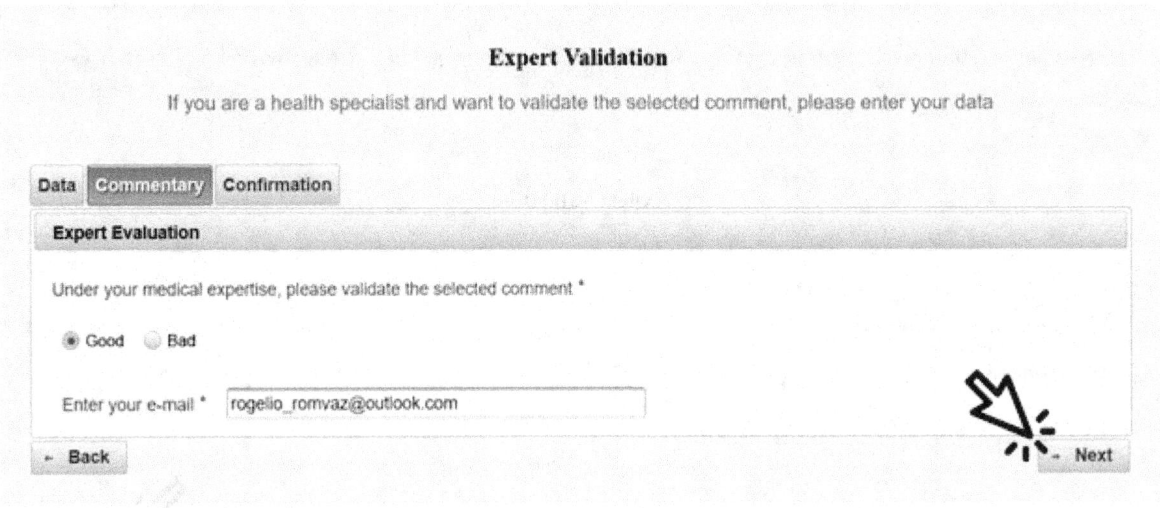

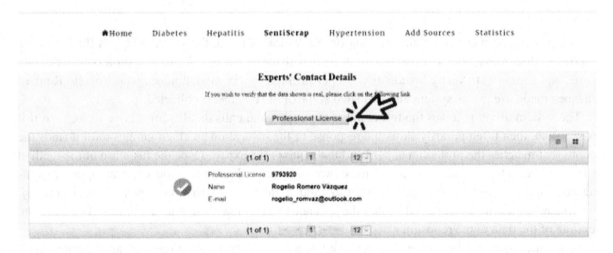

Figure 14. Data of the expert who validated the commentary

Then, the data goes through the class in charge of classifying the data, in this class, the instance is made to the Bang of Word class to invoke the method that makes the bag of words with the names of the medicines contained in the corpus, the system continues the process with the domain identification method that is in charge of checking that the data resulting from the extraction is of medical domain since it has a mention of at least one medicine, if it is so, then it goes to the resulting set that is analyzed later with the classification method, and that is when it is determined if the comment has a positive or negative polarity. When the process is successful, a message is displayed, as shown in **Figure 16**.

Figure 15. Official website of professional licenses
Source: SEP,2020

Finally, when the specialist needs to compare the polarity between the comments of the diseases, he can visualize able it in Statistics, as shown in **Figure 17**. In this view, we present charts on the number of the polarity of the comments, positive and negative ones, besides, the polarity corresponding to each disease, and the chart with the mentions of the drugs referred to for each disease. Also, a pie chart is shown with the ten most mentioned drugs.

Our work aims to show that the information contained in the forums and blogs is of high relevance to health specialists. Because by accessing the comments of patients, the doctor can know the experience and symptoms of each patient, for consulting first-hand data, which are useful for decision making and for improving medical care in clinics and hospitals.

Figure 16. Interface to add new URLs for forums, specialized websites and video blogs

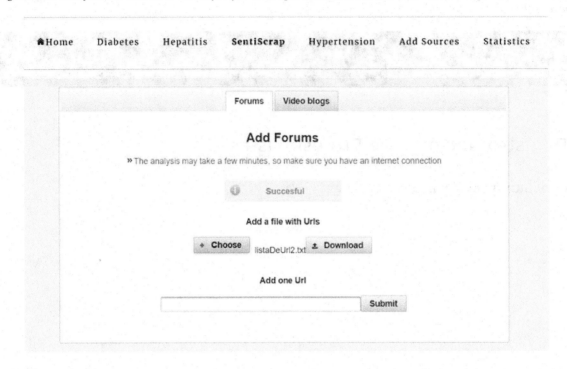

Figure 17. Chart board with statistics of the analyzed information

FUTURE RESEARCH DIRECTIONS

As future work, we have contemplated including more aspects to be analyzed, such as the analysis of adverse effects, identifying the treatment time taken by patients who comment on chronic-degenerative diseases, and identifying prices. Likewise, we would like to incorporate this information into the web application through different types of graphs that allow better visualization and understanding of the information, to provide a concise and summarized analysis for health specialists, which helps to improve the decision making in the hospitals and clinics.

CONCLUSION

The analysis of the related work shows a lack of application of studies that implement opinion mining in the Spanish language. Besides, a large part of the current studies focusses on extracting data from social networks, which, while it is true that it is a rich source of resources, we should not forget that there are other resources with multiple data, such as those addressed in this work. Our approach obtains comments from blogs, specialized websites and video blogs, which focus on the health care context, specifically for hypertension, diabetes and hepatitis diseases, to classify them according to polarity, positive or negative, making use of a tagged corpus to train the model and a medical domain ontology to contrast and obtain those comments that talk about the drugs prescribed for the mentioned diseases. The proposed approach was implemented in a system called SentiScrap, which aims to help health specialists with pharmaco-vigilance since it allows to know first-hand the comments of patients, which mention the symptoms of the conditions, and ADE that are unknown to the patients themselves, and that attribute these symptoms to other conditions and with expert validation help to prevent and reduce the risks to the patient's health. On the other hand, there are a lot of people who self-medicate which is a mistake that affects the quality of life and compromises health; therefore, SentiScrap, provides information to patients or about the medications prescribed for their condition, and also the comments collected identify what other people think, including expert validations that they can contact if they have any questions.

In conclusion, with the presented case study, a result of the interaction that the health specialist had with SentiScrap, we verified the functionality of each module presented in the architecture; also, the correct functioning of the proposed hybrid approach, with which we classified the opinions of the blogs and video blogs entered through a URL to be analyzed, also, we obtained the polarity of the drugs for chronic-degenerative diseases, specifically for diabetes, hypertension, and hepatitis.

ACKNOWLEDGMENT

This research work was sponsored by the National Council for Science and Technology (CONACYT) and the Secretary of Public Education (SEP). The authors are grateful to Tecnológico Nacional de México (TNM) for supporting this work.

REFERENCES

Abirami, A. M., Askarunisa, A., Shiva, R. A., & Revathy, R. (2018). Ontology Based Feature Extraction from Text Documents. In M. Thangavel & P. Karthikeyan (Eds.), Applications of Security, Mobile, Analytic, and Cloud (SMAC) Technologies for Effective Information Processing and Management (p. 175). IGI Global. doi:10.4018/978-1-5225-4044-1.ch009

Alayba, A. M., Palade, V., England, M., & Iqbal, R. (2017). Arabic Language Sentiment Analysis on Health Services. In *2017 1st International Workshop on Arabic Script Analysis and Recognition (ASAR)* (pp.114–118). 10.1109/ASAR.2017.8067771

Baccianella, S., Esuli, A., & Sebastiani, F. (2014). *SentiWordNet 3 . 0 : An Enhanced Lexical Resource for Sentiment Analysis and Opinion Mining*. Academic Press.

Cabling, M. L., Turner, J. W., Hurtado-de-Mendoza, A., Zhang, Y., Jiang, X., Drago, F., & Sheppard, V. B. (2018). Sentiment Analysis of an Online Breast Cancer Support Group: Communicating about Tamoxifen. *Health Communication*, *33*(9), 1158–1165. doi:10.1080/10410236.2017.1339370 PMID:28678549

Cavalcanti, D. & Prudêncio. (2017). Aspect-Based opinion mining in drug reviews. In *Progress in Artificial Intelligence* (Vol 10423, pp.815–827). doi:10.1007/978-3-319-65340-2

Cho, J., & Garcia-Molina, H. (2002). Parallel Crawlers. In *Proceedings of the 11th International Conference on World Wide Web* (pp.124–135). doi:10.1145/511446.511464

Das, S. R., & Chen, M. Y. (2004). Yahoo! for Amazon : Sentiment Extraction from Small Talk on the Web. *Management Science*, *53*(9), 1–16.

Denecke, K., & Deng, Y. (2015). Sentiment analysis in medical settings: New opportunities and challenges. *Artificial Intelligence in Medicine*, *64*(1), 17–27. doi:10.1016/j.artmed.2015.03.006 PMID:25982909

Ding, X., Liu, B., & Yu, P. (2008). A holistic lexicon-based approach to opinion mining. *WSDM'08 - Proceedings of the 2008 International Conference on Web Search and Data Mining*. 10.1145/1341531.1341561

Gopalakrishnan, V., & Ramaswamy, C. (2017). Patient opinion mining to analyze drugs satisfaction using supervised learning. *Journal of Applied Research and Technology*, *15*(4), 311–319. doi:10.1016/j.jart.2017.02.005

Jiménez, R., García, V., Florencia-Juárez, R., Rivera, G., & López-Orozco, F. (2018). Minería de opiniones aplicada a la evaluación docente de la Universidad Autónoma de Ciudad Juárez. *Research in Computing Science*, *147*(6), 167–177. doi:10.13053/rcs-147-6-13

Karimi, S., Metke-Jimenez, A., & Nguyen, A. (2015). CADEminer: A System for Mining Consumer Reports on Adverse Drug Side Effects. *Proceedings of the Eighth Workshop on Exploiting Semantic Annotations in Information Retrieval - ESAIR '15*, 47–50. 10.1145/2810133.2810143

Khan, M. T., Durrani, M., Ali, A., Inayat, I., Khalid, S., & Khan, K. H. (2016). Sentiment analysis and the complex natural language. *Complex Adaptive Systems Modeling*, *4*(1), 2. Advance online publication. doi:10.118640294-016-0016-9

Kishore, B., & Kumar, A. (2016). Evaluation of Faculty Performance in Education System Using Classification Technique in Opinion Mining Based on GPU. In H. S. Behera & D. P. Mohapatra (Eds.), *Computational Intelligence in Data Mining—Volume 2* (pp. 109–111). Springer India. doi:10.1007/978-81-322-2731-1

Lee, K., Qadir, A., Hasan, S. A., Datla, V., Prakash, A., Liu, J., & Farri, O. (2017). Adverse drug event detection in tweets with semi-supervised convolutional neural networks. In *Proceedings of the 26th International World Wide Web Conference, WWW 2017*, (pp.705–714). 10.1145/3038912.3052671

Liu, B. (2011). *Web Data Mining: Exploring Hyperlinks, Contents, and Usage Data*. Springer Berlin Heidelberg. doi:10.1007/978-3-642-19460-3

Liu, B. (2012). Sentiment Analysis: A Fascinating Problem. In Sentiment Analysis and Opinion Mining (p. 7). Morgan & Claypool Publishers.

Luna-Aveiga, H., Medina-Moreira, J., Lagos-Ortiz, K., Apolinario, O., Paredes-Valverde, M. A., Salas-Zárate, M., & Valencia-García, R. (2018). Sentiment Polarity Detection in Social Networks: An Approach for Asthma Disease Management. In N.-T. Le, T. van Do, N. T. Nguyen, & H. A. Le Thi (Eds.), *Advanced Computational Methods for Knowledge Engineering* (pp. 141–152). Springer International Publishing. doi:10.1007/978-3-319-61911-8_13

Lyons, J. (1995). Metalinguistic preliminaries. In *Linguistic Semantics: An Introduction* (p. 2). Cambridge University. Retrieved from https://books.google.com.mx/ books?id=Na2g1ltaKuAC&printsec= frontco ver&dq=semantics+linguistic&hl= es-419&sa=X&ved=0ahUKEwiohJ_27NLmAhUQ2qwKHWyZD ocQ6AEIKTAA#v=onepage &q=semanticslinguistic&f=false

Mo, Q., & Chen, Y. (2012). Ontology-Based Web Information Extraction. In M. Zhao & J. Sha (Eds.), *Communications and Information Processing* (Vol. 288, pp. 118–119). Springer Berlin Heidelberg. doi:10.1007/978-3-642-31965-5_14

NCBO BioPortal. (2019). *BioPortal*. Retreived from https://bioportal.bioontology.org/ontologies

Pak, A., & Paroubek, P. (2010). Twitter as a Corpus for Sentiment Analysis and Opinion Mining. In LREc (pp.1320–1326). Academic Press.

Pang, B., & Lee, L. (2008). Opinion mining and sentiment analysis. *Foundations and Trends in Information Retrieval, 2*(1), 94.

Peng, Y., Moh, M., & Moh, T. S. (2016). Efficient adverse drug event extraction using Twitter sentiment analysis. In *Proceedings of the 2016 IEEE/ACM International Conference on Advances in Social Networks Analysis and Mining, ASONAM 2016*, (pp. 1011–1018). 10.1109/ASONAM.2016.7752365

Porras, J., Florencia-Juárez, R., Rivera, G., & García, V. (2018). Interfaz de lenguaje natural para consultar cubos multidimensionales utilizando procesamiento analítico en línea. *Research in Computing Science, 147*(6), 153–165. doi:10.13053/rcs-147-6-12

Rathi, S., Shekhar, S., & Sharma, D. K. (2016). Opinion Mining Classification Based on Extension of Opinion Mining Phrases. In S. C. Satapathy, A. Joshi, N. Modi, & N. Pathak (Eds.), *Proceedings of international conference on ICT for sustainable development* (pp. 717–724). Springer Singapore. 10.1007/978-981-10-0129-1_74

Sabra, S., Mahmood Malik, K., & Alobaidi, M. (2018). Prediction of venous thromboembolism using semantic and sentiment analyses of clinical narratives. *Computers in Biology and Medicine, 94*, 1–10. doi:10.1016/j.compbiomed.2017.12.026 PMID:29353160

Salas-Zárate, M. D. P., Medina-Moreira, J., Lagos-Ortiz, K., Luna-Aveiga, H., Rodríguez-García, M. Á., & Valencia-García, R. (2017). Sentiment Analysis on Tweets about Diabetes: An Aspect-Level Approach. *Computational and Mathematical Methods in Medicine, 2017*, 1–9. Advance online publication. doi:10.1155/2017/5140631 PMID:28316638

Sinclair, J. (1996). Preliminary Recommendations on Corpus Typology. *EAGLES (Expert Advisory Group on Language Engineering Standards) EAG-TCWG- CTYP/P*, 4–27. Retrieved from http://www.ilc.cnr.it/EAGLES96/corpustyp/node4.html

Solangi, Y. A., Solangi, Z. A., Aarain, S., Abro, A., Mallah, G. A., & Shah, A. (2019). Review on Natural Language Processing (NLP) and Its Toolkits for Opinion Mining and Sentiment Analysis. In *2018 IEEE 5th International Conference on Engineering Technologies and Applied Sciences, ICETAS 2018* (pp. 1–4). doi:10.1109/ICETAS.2018.8629198

Thanaki, J. (2017). Feature Engineering and NLP Algorithms. In Python Natural Language Processing (p. 102). Academic Press.

World Health Organization. (2015). *Pharmacovigilance*. Retrieved from https://www.who.int/medicines/areas/quality_safety/safety_efficacy/pharmvigi/en/

World Health Organization. (2020). *The top 10 causes of death*. Retrieved from www.who.int/newsroom/fact-sheets/detail/the-top-10-causes-of-death

Wu, C., Liu, J., Wu, F., Huang, Y., Yuan, Z., & Xie, X. (2019). MSA: Jointly detecting drug name and adverse drug reaction mentioning tweets with multi-head self-attention.I n *WSDM 2019 - Proceedings of the 12th ACM International Conference on Web Search and Data Mining*, (pp.33–41). doi:10.1145/3289600.3290980

This research was previously published in the Handbook of Research on Natural Language Processing and Smart Service Systems; pages 445-480, copyright year 2021 by Engineering Science Reference (an imprint of IGI Global).

APPENDIX

Listing 1 corresponds to the dataPreprocessing() method receives each collected opinion to remove unusual characters, then with the help of the API used for rating the opinions, we perform the tokenization to remove the commonly used emoticons.

Listing 1. The method dataPreprocessing()

```
1. private String dataPreprocessing(String cadena) {
2.      String cadCaracteres, aux1, aux2, aux3, aux4, frase = "";
3.      cadCaracteres = cadena.replaceAll("[|||'|/|<|>|+||_|@|•|♥|]", "");
4.      Properties props = new Properties();
5.      props.setProperty("annotators", "tokenize,ssplit");
6.      StanfordCoreNLP pipeline = new StanfordCoreNLP(props);
7.      CoreDocument exampleDocument = new CoreDocument(cadCaracteres);
8.      pipeline.annotate(exampleDocument);
9.      //access tokens from a CoreDocument, a token is represented by a CoreLabel
10.     List<CoreLabel> firstSentenceTokens = exampleDocument.tokens();
11.         for (CoreLabel token: firstSentenceTokens) {
12.             if (!token.word().contains("http")) {
13.                 if (!token.word().contains(":-RRB-")) {
14.                     if (!token.word().contains(":D")) {
15.                         if (!token.word().contains(":-LRB-")) {
15.                             if (!token.word().contains(";D")) {
17.                                 frase += token.word() + " ";
18.             } else
19.                 frase += "";
20.         }
21.         aux1 = frase.replace("-LRB- ", "(");
22.         aux2 = aux1.replace(" -RRB-", ")");
23.         aux3 = aux2.replace("-LSB- ", "[");
24.         aux4 = aux3.replace(" -RSB-", "]");
25.         return aux4;
26.     }
```

The next code (Listing 2) corresponds to the method for the creation of the bag of words, which obtains from the ontology the list of the Individuals to obtain the names of the drugs, these drugs can be recognized by another name, in those cases, each individual is gone through, and the sameAsLista is obtained; finally, the drugs are added to the bag of words that is used later.

Listing 2. The method for the creation of the bag of words

```
1. public Bag createBoW() {
2.     //load the ontology model
3.     this.model = ModelFactory.createOntologyModel();
4.     this.model.read(new File(this.file).toURI().toString());
5.     ExtendedIterator<Individual> listaInd = this.model.listIndividuals();
6.     Individual ind = null;
7.     ArrayList medicines = new ArrayList();
8.     Bag drugsBag = model.createBag();
9.     String aux="";
10.         //list of Individuals and each individual their own list SameAs
11.         while (listaInd.hasNext()) {
12.             ind = listaInd.next();
13.             medicines.add(ind.getLocalName());
14.             ExtendedIterator sameAsLista = ind.listSameAs();
15.           while (sameAsLista.hasNext()) {
16.                 Object ind2 = sameAsLista.next();
17.                 int numPosFar = ind2.toString().indexOf("#");
18.                 aux = ind2.toString().substring(numPosFar + 1);
19.                 medicines.add(aux);
20.             }
21.         }
22.
23.         for (int j = 0; j < farmacos.size(); j++) {
24.             drugsBag.add(farmacos.get(j));
25.         }
26.         return drugsBag;
27     }
```

The domainIdentification() method (Listing 3) invokes the BoW class to obtain the bag of words and compare it with each comment to identify the comments that if they talk about any medication, those comments that do not mention medications are discarded. The resulting comments are stored temporarily in a .txt file.

Listing 3. The Method DomainIdentification()

```
1. public void domainIdentification()
2.             throws FileNotFoundException, IOException {
3.     String cadCom;
4.     int intIndex = 0;
5.     //BoW class instance to load the ontology and create the bag of words
6.     BoW l = new BoW(rutOnt);
```

```
7.      l.load();
8.      Bag BagOfW = l.crearBoW();
9.      FileReader f = new FileReader(arcOpiScr);
10.      BufferedReader buffer = new BufferedReader(f);
11.      /*compare each comment with the bag of words for those commentsthat
mention 12.      *a BoW drug */
13.      while ((cadCom = buffer.readLine()) != null) {
14.          StringTokenizer st = new StringTokenizer(cadCom);
15.          while (st.hasMoreTokens()) {
16.              cadCom = st.nextToken("\n");
17.              NodeIterator iter2 = BagOfW.iterator();
18.              while (iter2.hasNext()) {
19.                  String mdicamto = iter2.next().toString().toLowerCase();
20.                  intIndex = cadCom.toLowerCase().indexOf(mdicamto);
21.                  if (intIndex != -1) {
22.                      opinion.add(cadCom);
23.                      break;
24.                  }
25.              }
26.          }
27.      }
28.      buffer.close();
29.      //saves the opinions in a Opiniones.TEST file
30.      BufferedWriter bw = new BufferedWriter(new FileWriter(rutOpiTest));
31.      bw.write("");
32.      for (int i = 0; i < opinion.size(); i++) {
33.          bw.write("\t" + opinion.get(i).toString());
34.          bw.newLine();
35.      }
36.      bw.write("");
37.      bw.close();
38.  }
```

The opinionSorting method (Listing 4) loads three files, the file to be sorted, the corpus tagged and a property file, necessary to perform the sorting, the Stanford CoreNLP API allows the sorting making use of ObjectBank that takes the comment and compares it with the corpus to determine the polarity, the result of this process are the commentaries with their final tag which are stored in a temporary .txt file

Listing 4. The Method opinionSorting()

```
1. public void opinionSorting() throws IOException {
2.     BufferedWriter bw = new BufferedWriter(new OutputStreamWriter(new
3.             FileOutputStream(rutaOpiClasif), "ISO-8859-1"));
```

```
4.    String cadena;
5.    //ColumnDataClassifier to make a context-free (independent)
7.    ColumnDataClassifier cdc = new ColumnDataClassifier(rutArcProp);
8.    //Creation of the classifier from the training data.
10.    Classifier<String, String> cl =
9.          cdc.makeClassifier(cdc.readTrainingExamples(rutArcTrain));
10. // ObjectBanks are taken from the source
11.         for (String line:
12.     ObjectBank.getLineIterator(rutOpiTest, "ISO-8859-1")) {
13.         Datum<String, String> d = cdc.makeDatumFromLine(line);
14.     cadena = cl.classOf(d) + "\t" + line;
15.         bw.write(cadena);
16.         bw.newLine();
17.   }
18.     bw.close();
19. }
```

Chapter 36
Supervised Sentiment Analysis of Science Topics:
Developing a Training Set of Tweets in Spanish

Patricia Sánchez-Holgado

iD https://orcid.org/0000-0002-6253-7087

University of Salamanca, Salamanca, Spain

Carlos Arcila-Calderón

iD https://orcid.org/0000-0002-2636-2849

University of Salamanca, Salamanca, Spain

ABSTRACT

Twitter is one of the largest sources of real-time information on the Internet and is continuously fed by millions of users around the world. Each of these users publishes text messages with their opinions, concerns, information, or simply their daily happenings. It is a challenge to address the analysis of massive data in the network, just as it is an objective to look for ways to understand everything that data can offer today in terms of knowledge of society and the market. The sector of science communication is still discovering everything that the web 2.0 and social networks can offer to reach all audiences. This article develops a classification model of messages launched on Twitter, on science topics, in Spanish, with machine learning techniques. The training of this type of models requires the creation of a specific corpus in Spanish for the subject of science, which is one of the most laborious tasks. The classifier is able to predict the sentiment of the message in real time on Twitter, with a confidence interval greater than 80%. The results of its evaluation are at 72% accuracy.

DOI: 10.4018/978-1-6684-6303-1.ch036

INTRODUCTION

Currently, Twitter is one of the largest sources of real-time information on the Internet, which is continuously fed by millions of users from all over the world, whether real or automatic. Each of these users publishes text messages with their opinions, concerns, information or simply their daily evolution. A large amount of data that are mostly public and that arouse the interest of data researchers. It is a challenge to address the management of mass data in the network, and it is a goal to look for ways to understand everything that data can offer today in terms of knowledge of society and the market.

In this work, we focus on the field of science communication, as an area that is still discovering all that web 2.0 and social networks can offer to reach all audiences. Through the media generated by the user, we can access messages that are disseminated and shared without limits, but our motivation is to find out what we can obtain, how far we can get to know the public through their messages of information or opinion, in a social network that has hardly any control. The data will allow us to experiment with different theories, but the results have to mark the next steps to follow.

In times of post-truth, science gains weight and the mechanisms that affect public opinion have been widely studied. In this context, with a media ecosystem where the producer merges with the receiver and the communication of science adapts to change, the importance of scientific knowledge and its dissemination is vital in the construction of reliable social attitudes and trends. However, the analysis of the polarity of opinions on Twitter is a field that takes off and of which there is little previous research in Spanish.

CONTEXT AND MOTIVATION

There is a growing interest in the study of public opinions using large-scale data produced by social media (Bollen, Mao, & Pepe, 2011; O'Connor, Balasubramanyan, Routledge, & Smith, 2010; Whitman Cobb, 2015). However, most of these studies are based on manual classification or automated content analysis using dictionaries that label words (for example, giving a negative or positive a priori value to each word) (Feldman, 2013) and other approaches such as supervised machine learning or supervised machine learning (Vinodhini & Chandrasekaran, 2012) derived from artificial intelligence are scarce in communication research (Van Zoonen & Van der Meer, Toni, 2016), in the social sciences and in private consultancies in issues of public opinion, political studies and marketing. Additionally, new technological efforts are dedicated to gather the automated analysis of feelings based on machine learning with streaming or live streaming technologies, which are capable of producing a significant amount of data.

Three billion people around the world express their thoughts and opinions on a regular basis through social networks. Twitter is one of the most outstanding, characterized by being a microblogging service, since it brings together features of blog, instant messaging and social network, growing exponentially since its launch in 2006. Twitter users generate content based on short texts of a maximum of 280 characters (up to November 2017, 140 characters were allowed), on any topic and in real time. Most of the messages are public, although it offers the possibility of sending private messages. A message or tweet can reach a very high audience in a few minutes thanks to the fact that users share the messages again in an endless network.

The total number of active monthly users at the beginning of 2018 already reached 330 million. This means a volume of about 500 million tweets per day. In Spain the number of users is close to 5 million.[1]

It is used to share information and to describe any daily activity (Java, Song, Finin, & Tseng, 2007), it allows expressing opinions and interests in real time (García Esparza, O'Mahony, & Smyth, 2012), its influence is observed in that it is present in practically all areas of social, political, economic, educational life and any subject (sports, culture, leisure, science, industry, etc.) (Kwak, Lee, Park, & Moon, 2010).

One of the questions we ask ourselves through this study is:

RQ1: Can we analyze a part of the public data available in the social network Twitter to know attitudes, opinions, and sentiments towards the communication topics of science that are shared and move towards the prediction of future trends?

The decisive role of science in contemporary societies needs an effort of dissemination aimed at increasing the knowledge, on the part of society, of scientific work and research. Researchers must be aware that the opportunity to carry out their work is subject to the financial support of society.

Informing society about science requires the researcher the ability to present their views to a broad public so that they can be understood. It is a skill that can and must be learned (Raes, 2003). It has the function of creating an awareness and at the same time a recognition for science and its relevance to society (Pearson, 2001).

Culture and perception are usually determining factors in the interest of citizens and the more scientific knowledge is valued and its dissemination to build social attitudes, the greater interest can be generated in society and the more importance science will have in the formation of opinions on the social agenda in a time of post-truth.

The way to achieve this is by generating a dialogue on the day-to-day issues that respond to the social needs of each moment, with a comprehensible language adapted to the citizenship without losing quality. Without social communication of science, it is impossible to achieve scientific culture

What makes Twitter a relevant network is its volume of users, the free generation of content and its information in real time. The immediacy is one of the main advantages, but also has as a disadvantage the saturation that suffers. Therefore, as a tool for scientific communication, it has enormous potential and begins to take center stage, but at the same time requires efficient use.

A study by Nature in 2014 showed that 50% of Twitter users who are researchers use it to follow up debates about their area, and 40% that are habitual of this network use it as a means to comment on progress or debate between they (Baker, 2015).

The use of Twitter as a scientific communication strategy is still scarce, but the trend is growing, especially due to the opening of new profiles (Segarra-Saavedra, Tur-Viñes, & Hidalgo-Marí, 2017).

There is a growing presence of specialized and academic journals, of researchers interested in dissemination and especially of science sections belonging to the media. This can give us an idea about the interest that scientific content awakens: Twitter is the most used network by science journalists (Pont-Sorribes, Cortiñas-Rovira, & Di Bonito, 2013), universities and research centers also use it daily, so we understand that scientists seek to win impact (Peters, Dunwoody, Allgaier, Lo, & Brossard, 2014).

Science communicators increasingly turn to digital technology and social networks (Ribas, 2012) and it is also proven that the first data on a scientific or technical scoop are already made public on Twitter (Jarreau, 2015).

On the other hand, a recent study indicates that the opinion shown on Twitter has a direct link with national and international scientific news. This is an important detail to take into account in the study of the opinion in real time in the social network, because it gives an anchor point with which to compare the daily evolution and draw conclusions (Pérez-Rodríguez, González-Pedraz, & Alonso Berrocal, 2018).

Social networks have an important role in scientific communication and the study of the sentiments of the messages and opinions that are issued is interesting to evaluate the interest of the public and detect pulses of the conversation on hot topics.

RESEARCH OBJECTIVES

The objective of this project is to develop and evaluate a classifier for the analysis of sentiment of messages on scientific topics, in Spanish and in real time, on the Twitter social network, using automatic learning techniques. Specifically, it would consist of three secondary objectives:

OS1: Creation of a specific corpus of texts with scientific messages classified by positive or negative sentiment.

OS2: Development of a prototype for the analysis of sentiment of scientific messages on Twitter in real time using machine learning techniques.

OS3: Test the prototype to observe its operation. As we advanced, we will focus on the first phase for the construction of a new specific corpus for the communication of science.

METHOD

There is very little research and scarce application focused on the construction of supervised models of machine learning to classify scientific texts in Spanish language.

The classifier developed in the project, called OPSCIENCE, allows to analyze the tone of scientific tweets in real time using freely available resources such as Python (version 2.7) and the Application Program Interface (API) of Twitter (REST and STREAMING).

For phase 1, a unique tagged corpus of 10,000 tweets has been built with information on scientific topics (5000 positives and 5000 negatives). Based on the NLTK and Sci-Learn libraries for Python, the classifier uses the corpus to train a supervised machine learning predictive model with 6 classification algorithms (Original Naive Bayes, Naive Bayes for multimodal models, Naive Bayes for Bernoulli multivariate models, Logistic regression, Linear Support Vector Classification and linear classifiers with stochastic gradient descent -SGD-). Later, it will connect to the flow of Twitter data in real time (using the API Streaming) and filter tweets written in Spanish about science to predict the sentiment of each tweet and automatically visualize with the Matplot library those with high confidence intervals (> 0.80).

Except for the efforts of García Cumbreras et al. (García Cumbreras, Martínez-Cámara, Villena Román, & García Morera, 2016) and Hurtado, Pla & Buscaldi (Hurtado, Pla, & Buscaldi, 2015), there is very little research focused on the construction of supervised machine learning models to classify scientific texts in the Spanish language.

With this classifier, academic researchers, news agencies or academic journals with an interest in public opinion, may have an opportunity to test the prediction of future trends of scientific subject in

Spanish-speaking countries. In addition, predicting scientific sentiment in real time on Twitter for a long period to perform longitudinal analyzes to detect changes in citizens and to compare these changes with everyday events. The development of this prototype is a result of scientific and technical advances in the field of social sciences in convergence with computer science, artificial intelligence and big data, which are currently being promoted in various studies, progress as evidence in recent impact publications (Arcila-Calderón, Barbosa-Caro, & Cabezuelo-Lorenzo, 2016) and especially in the field of policy (Arcila-Calderón, Ortega-Mohedano, Jiménez-Amores, & Trullenque, 2017).

MACHINE LEARNING

We define data mining as a field of computer science referring to the process that attempts to discover patterns in large volumes of data set. In it converge several areas, such as databases, machine learning and statistics. Machine learning is responsible for extracting patterns from the data, using different approaches for this (Hernández Orallo, Ramírez Quintana, & Ferri Ramínez, 2004). A typical data mining process consists of the following stages: 1. Selection of the data set: It consists in selecting the data set on which the analysis will be carried out. 2. Data preprocessing: As many erroneous and inconsistent data are eliminated as possible. 3. Transformation of the data: Sometimes, the data is transformed into a more suitable format for the subsequent modeling. 4. Modeling: On data collected and prepared, a data mining technique is applied to generate a model from the data. 5. Interpretation and evaluation: Generated models are validated, for example, with a dataset independent of those used to generate them.

Supervised and Unsupervised Machine Learning

Machine learning is a branch of artificial intelligence whose objective is to develop techniques that allow computers to learn. Its objective is to create programs that are capable of generalizing behaviors from unstructured information provided in the form of examples.

Depending on the mechanism you use to learn, it can be of the following types:

1. **Supervised learning:** The algorithm produces a function that establishes a correspondence between the desired inputs and outputs of the system. In this project we will use this type of learning, because the system will try to classify some examples by choosing between two categories or established classes (positive - negative). The knowledge that is given to the system is a base of examples that are already labeled previously;

2. **Unsupervised learning:** The whole modeling process is carried out on a set of examples formed only by inputs to the system. There is no information about the categories of these examples. Therefore, in this case, the system has to be able to recognize patterns in order to label the new entries. In our case, if the examples that are part of the dataset were not labeled, we would have an unsupervised learning problem;

3. **Semi-supervised learning:** This type of algorithm combines the two previous algorithms to be able to classify appropriately. The tagged and untagged data are taken into account;

4. **Reinforcement learning:** The algorithm learns by observing the world around it. Your input information is the feedback or feedback you get from the outside world in response to your actions;

5.   **Translation:** Similar to supervised learning, but does not explicitly construct a function. Try to predict the categories of future examples based on the input examples, their respective categories and new examples to the system;

6.   **Multi-task learning:** Learning methods that use knowledge previously learned by the system in order to face problems similar to those already seen.

Natural Language Processing

Natural Language Processing (NLP) is a field of artificial intelligence that uses algorithms and statistics to understand, learn and reproduce human language. Its main purpose would be to communicate the machines with people to facilitate interaction. Some examples by all known are Siri or Google Assistant, which are already incorporated into our most used devices. Although the audio is already a reality, the NLP is more advanced in the treatment of texts, where there is much more data and are easier to get in electronic format. Basically, there are two general approaches to the problem of linguistic modeling:

Logical models: grammars. Detailed rules of recognition of structural patterns are written, using a specific grammatical formalism. These rules, in combination with the information stored in computer dictionaries, define the patterns that must be recognized to solve the task (search for information, translate, etc.).

Probabilistic models of natural language: based on data. The approach is the opposite of the previous case, since collections of examples (corpus) are collected and from them the frequencies of different linguistic units (letters, words, sentences) and their probability of appearing in a specific context are calculated. By calculating this probability, one can predict what the next unit will be in a given context, without the need to resort to explicit grammatical rules. In this project is the approach followed.

Sentiment Analysis

A key task in natural language processing is the analysis of sentiments. With the large volumes of data that move daily in digital format and through social networks, "big data", tools are developed that are capable of processing them, to obtain interpretable results and to provide information of interest, especially for the decision making Twitter provides a lot of information about the opinions that people publish every day in the network, accompanied by many other data that suppose particular details of each user. In this context, the analysis of Twitter sentiment has an increasing interest for data researchers and for the business sector in general. Sentiment analysis offers the possibility of evaluating opinion streams. It is the computational study of opinions, sentiments and emotions that are expressed through texts (Pang & Lee, 2008).

Performing a sentiment analysis on the social network Twitter means labeling each of the messages posted with a value that indicates the emotional load it transmits. Regarding this classification, we can take into account different variables (Bravo-Marquez, Mendoza, & Poblete, 2014): Polarity: indicates whether the message has a positive or negative sentiment, and can introduce the neutral gender as a third category. Intensity: it is represented with a numerical value that can range from negative to positive. Emotion: add a classification according to a list of emotions, such as joy, sadness or anger.

The biggest difficulty in developing a sentiment analysis applied to large volumes of data is that determining the feeling of a message is not accurate. If a manual labeling is made it can vary depending on who codes it, so it is important to combine automatic and manual tools to make it reliable (Baviera,

2016). In this work, only the biclase polarity of the sentiment of the message will be assessed, as a first approximation to the possibilities it offers.

The main sentiment analysis techniques are divided into two large groups (Medhat, Hassan, & Korashy, 2014): those based on automatic learning (machine learning approach) and those based on dictionaries (lexicon-based approach) (Figure 1).

Figure 1. Typology of sentiment techniques on Twitter

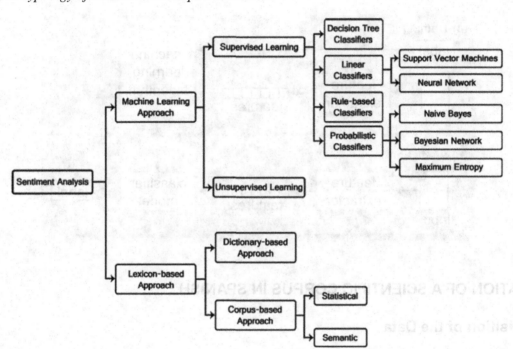

Reference (Medhat et al., 2014)

We will focus on using techniques based on supervised machine learning, using natural language processing, which tries to discover patterns in the language. It consists in that by providing a set of training data (corpus) composed of an instance (message) and a class (positive or negative sentiment), we obtain a model that can be able to predict to which class a new input instance will belong. In this case it is a binary classification model.

The methodology shown in NLTK Natural Language Processing is illustrative of the work process to implement the model that has been followed (Figure 2).

For the development of the complete project three phases have been followed:

Phase 1: The construction of a new corpus of texts with scientific subjects in Spanish language, classified by positive or negative sentiment, for the training of the machine learning models.

Phase 2: Once the corpus has been completed, the model has been trained by dividing the corpus into training and test (70% -30%).

Phase 3: Finally, the prototype classifier of sentiments has been implemented in real time and has been put to the test with data that you have not seen previously.

We can say that a program learns a task if its performance improves with experience. We are therefore going to review the process for the construction of a scientific corpus in Spanish.

Figure 2. Natural language processing methodology. Reference: NLTK (Bird, Klein, & Loper, 2009).

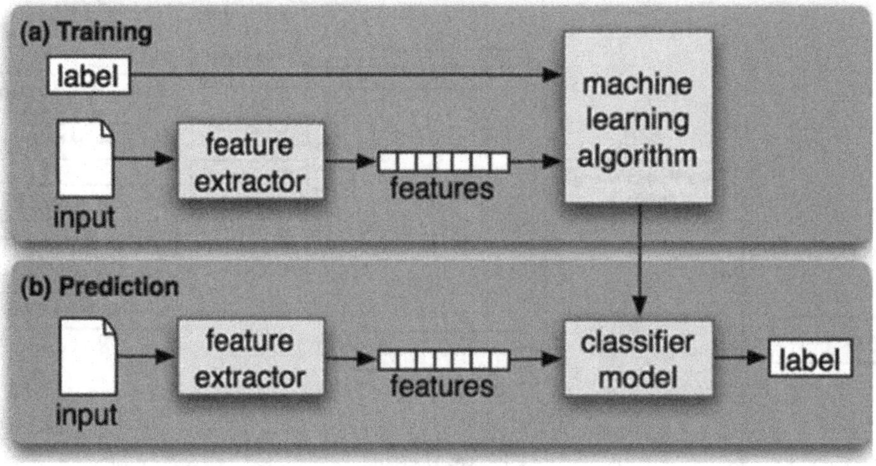

CREATION OF A SCIENTIFIC CORPUS IN SPANISH

Acquisition of the Data

As has been previously advanced, the social network Twitter is used to get the starting data necessary to train machine learning models that allow us to build a classifier of sentiments. Twitter allowed to send short messages of a maximum of 140 characters until November 2017, when it expanded the capacity of its texts up to 280 characters, twice.

Downloading the Data on Twitter

To download the data that we will use to create the text corpus, we will connect to the application that facilitates Twitter to developers: API (Application Programming Interface) Twitter[2].

It is therefore standard protocols for exchange and manipulation of data, which in the case of Twitter are embodied in three APIs. Each of these APIs has specific requirements and limitations for each user, which are described in detail on the page for developers of Twitter[3].

API Search performs a search of the messages, following parameters set by the user. It can be filtered by language and location. In this case, the limitation is 180 requests every 15 minutes.

API Rest (Representational State Transfer): Allows access to the twitter data history. All the operations that can be done via the web can be done from the API, such as viewing the profiles of the users, who are the followers and followed, the tweets that are published, which are the trending topics, etc.

The limitations are variable; it depends on the request that is made. It is measured in requests that can be made during a 15-minute window. The values oscillate between 15 and 900. As an example, requests for tweets from a user account allow 900 queries, being the most permissive, while on the opposite side are the followers or follow-up lists, limited to 15 requests.

API Streaming allows an almost real-time connection to the data flow of the network, which makes it possible to download contents at the same moment they are generated, filtering by one or more keywords, tags or hashtags. It allows establishing very precise filters through the parameters of the Tweet object of Twitter. Since it is a continuous flow, the restriction of the tool is applied to the downloaded volume, which is a maximum of 50 tweets per second.

In this project the Streaming API was used, completed with REST in the information search. To be able to connect to any of the Twitter APIs, you must follow a process that begins with the creation of an app on Twitter, with a user account to link it to and obtain through it a series of access codes that are needed a posteriori to access it.

Creating an App on Twitter

Until July 2018 the creation of an app was allowed freely, through a user account, but after that date Twitter needs an express request because it is making a unification of its tools in the pages for developers. The process developed in this report has been done before that date. Once the space is accessed to register the app, the requested steps are followed. In the Keys and Access Tokens tab, we obtain the relevant data for the subsequent connection: Consumer key, Consumer secret, Access token and Access token secret.

The function of the first two keys is to authenticate the requests we make to Twitter, the next two keys will allow us to make requests to the API on behalf of the account.

To authenticate later in the scripts that we are going to use, we will use these keys through the protocol known as OAuth, which is a standard of secure authorization in an application.

Data Obtained From Twitter

When messages are downloaded from Twitter[4] through a Python script created for this purpose, the data provided by the APIs are in JSON format. The most commonly used objects are the *"User object"* that contains the information of the profile of a user and the *"Tweet object"* that provides the context information of each tweet including the entities (hashtags, mentions to users, URLs and multimedia) and the geo-location . The *"Tweet object"* was used to directly request the data of the messages that were relevant to the project, thus the text ("text") is what interests us most, being completed with the date of the message ("created at") and the username that is displayed ("user", "screen_name") for possible revisions.

The scripts that downloaded information from the Twitter stream, in real time, were connected to the network to download data in different periods of several days from March to June 2018. The content download scripts through REST were used between June and July mainly to complete data. The characteristics of the total Dataset are in the Table 1.

Table 1. Total dataset extract

	Language: Spanish
Tweets downloaded in Streaming:	171.459
Tweets downloaded in Rest:	37.292
Total tweets downloaded:	208.751

Reference: Own elaboration.

Data Preprocessing

The set of data that has been stored after the data acquisition phase, is a list of tweets containing messages, along with the information about the user that issues it and metadata such as those described in the *"Tweet object"* [5]: creation date, identifier, multimedia objects, geolocation, etc.

The dataset is in the rough, so it needs some pre-cleaning before processing. We will pass the data through a preprocessing that consists of several steps, also called a *pipeline*, so that the input of each stage is the output of the previous stage, which will filter the attributes that interest us to conform the corpus of text.

In previous studies, an example of corpus preprocessing has been observed, where the different results obtained according to the phases applied were experimented. As a main observation, there are certain filters that do not bring any improvement, however, when combined with others the result is good. In the case of a study carried out by Dubiau and Ale (Dubiau & Ale, 2013) for the sentiment analysis about a corpus in Spanish, the elements that were used in the best result for processing were: SW + NEG + WL + PUNCT + SC + LC.

Each of them being: SW (Elimination of stopwords), NEG (Negation treatment), WL (Filtering of words of less than 3 characters), LC (Transformation of capitalizations), PUNCT (Elimination of punctuation marks), SC (Transformation of special characters).

Taking into account these results, we have needed to do our own preprocessing, adapted to the needs of the corpus of scientific topics that we are dealing with. The pipeline process of the data is as follows:

- **Store the tweets in text csv:** The download of the data has been stored in .txt files so once we have all the files saved, we pass them together in a csv format to deal with them and then make manual classifications. The process is simply to open all the .txt files in an Excel document and store all the data. The treatment that we are going to carry out only requires the text of the tweets, so when passing the data to csv format we will only be left with the message text element. Deleted the associated metadata and user information. In this way we have completed the total of the data that we are going to discuss;
- **Formats UTF / ANSI:** Review of the total dataset of the formats to make sure that everything is in UTF8 so that we do not have later incidences;
- **Spanish language:** Review of those elements that are not texts written in Spanish directly. There are messages that include the keyword "science" or similar in their text or in their hashtags, but they are written in other languages, especially autonomic or Portuguese languages. We eliminate all those that are not unmistakably Spanish language;
- **Texts in lowercase:** We pass all the text to lowercase so that it is totally unified;

- **Retweets:** Review of messages to suppress if there is a retweet within them. In the main scripts have been filtered, but in the download from REST is not the case and we can still have non-original messages in the data, so we remove them from the dataset;
- **Suppression of possible duplicates with R:** To avoid having possible repeated elements we make a first scan using R and R Studio for speed. In data downloads there are many elements that repeat the same content, mainly because users share them from the media and there are follow-ups or responses. Therefore we will try to eliminate those that are identical through a script;
- **Negations:** Negations in a sentence change the meaning of it. Apparently it is a simple task to look for the deniers (no, but, it is false that, etc.) however, their distribution in the text can be too variable;
- **Other Preprocessing:** Some improvements that may be necessary and effective to improve the performance of the classifier have been: correct grammatical errors, eliminate irrelevant numbers or figures that do not add value to the text in order to classify their sentiment, eliminate certain punctuation, emoticons, special characters, characters repeated several times consecutively, interjections without value for our purpose or dates. This step of general character can be done next to the following one, the manual classification that is already exhaustive;
- **Tokenization:** The process of Tokenizing, or separating the texts in tokens is done within the classifier to unify tasks;
- **Manual classification of the sentiment of the text:** In the last step we must perform a manual process with the dataset, since we are going to classify all the elements according to the sentiment that we identify as positive or negative.

In this same manual review one by one we will also select those messages whose topic is not exclusively from the science sector, since we find elements that even if they have the key words, their objective is clearly political, for example. It is the longest and most laborious step of all, because there is no other way to do it than through a human encoder. We select a volume of 10,000 texts to classify (5,000 positive and 5,000 negative) that will be useful for the training of the model. The rest of the dataset that may have been left over we file for other occasions.

The product of this stage is a list of documents (sentences) called corpus, composed of 10,000 instances, labeled with their kind of positive or negative sentiment.

MODEL TRAINING

In previous studies, we have also observed that in terms of classification algorithms with Naive Bayes, the best results are obtained for small corpora, but their performance decreases slightly for the larger corpus sizes compared to MaxEnt and SVM where the results improve as that the corpus size grows and the maximum performance achieved by the experience is obtained (Dubiau & Ale, 2013).

The data set used to construct the classification model is called the "training set". Each case or sample corresponds to a given class since the training cases are labeled with their class attribute.

The objective we pursue is that our classifier works correctly indicating the positive or negative sentiment of the messages that are downloaded in real time from Twitter, so we will train the data with the corpus of 10,000 elements, composed of 5,000 messages labeled as positive and 5,000 messages labeled as negative. The measurement of the model will give us information to assess the results obtained.

A q% of data is separated to validate the models (q = 30): Training (100 - q) 70% and Validation test (q) 30%. The data is randomly separated to avoid any order or structure underlying the data. The corpus has been divided into a part for training, 70% of the elements, 7,000 texts, and another part for testing, 30% of the elements, 3,000 texts. We use the NLTK (Natural Language Tool Kit) and Scikit-Learn libraries in Python.

This machine learning model uses several algorithms: Naive Bayes original, Naive Bayes for multimodal models, Naive Bayes for multivariate Bernoulli models, Logistic Regression, Linear Support Vector Classification (SVC) and Linear classifiers with stochastic gradient descent -SGD – training.

For this model, we will use a combination of the classification algorithms, which is a common technique, known as interval voting of characteristics since a voting system is created where each algorithm has one vote and the classification that has the most votes is the one chosen. Intervals are constructed for each characteristic [feature] or attribute in the learning phase and the corresponding interval in each characteristic "votes" for each class in the classification phase. As in the Bayesian Naive classifier, each characteristic is treated individually and independently of the rest. A voting system is designed to combine the individual classifications of each attribute separately.

Another interesting element introduced in the model is a confidence interval. It indicates within a scale between 0 and 1 the security of the classification that has been made as positive or negative, serving as control for false positives.

VALIDATION OF THE MODEL AND RESULTS

To perform the test with real new data, we will execute the model by connecting again to the streaming stream of Twitter to download data. From a programmed script it connects to Twitter, downloading messages filtered by a word or keywords, and classifying them with the positive or negative polarity of their feeling according to the classifier model. When evaluating the performance of a model there are several metrics that can be taken into account depending on the classification results obtained.

The main metric is the assessment of the "accuracy" with which the model has classified the instances in the training phase. The Accuracy shows us the percentage of data that the model has correctly classified and the result of each algorithm can be seen in the Table 2.

Table 2. Accuracy of the model for the algorithms used

Algorithms	Accuracy %
Original Naive Bayes Algo	72.64
MNB_classifier	72.24
BernoulliNB_classifier	72.80
LogisticRegression_classifier	71.88
LinearSVC_classifier	70.45
SGDClassifier	71.15

Reference: Own elaboration

It is observed that the best-placed algorithms are Naive Bayes, Original and Bernoulli, which exceed the 70% that is usually the average of this type of models, reaching an optimum figure of 72.80% in the highest case. In the TASS project (García Cumbreras, Villena Román, et al., 2016), similar figures of accuracy are observed, hovering around 72%. Based on the result of the model's accuracy by voting on the algorithms, the following data is obtained: voted_classifier accuracy percent: 72.3107569721:

1. Accuracy measures the accuracy of a classifier. Higher accuracy means less false positives, while lower precision means more false positives. It tells us of the instances that have been recovered in the model, what percentage is relevant, following a formula. The data obtained in the model is 71.35%;
2. The recall measures the sensitivity of a classifier. Improving recall can often decrease accuracy because it is increasingly difficult to be precise as the sample space increases. Recall means that of the relevant instances, what percentage were recovered. The data obtained is 77.2%;
3. F Score is known as a harmonic mean. Accuracy and recall can be combined to produce a single metric known as measure F, which is the weighted harmonic mean of both. The result is 74.13%.

Summing up the data that we have obtained in our calculations, we can see that they are quite approximate to each other in the Table 3.

Table 3. Summary of metrics evaluation of the model created

Metrics	%
Accuracy	72,31%
Precision	71,35%
Recall	77,2%
F-score	74,13%

Reference: Own elaboration

DISSERTATION STATUS

In the public space occupied by the social network Twitter, messages and contents that have different objectives are produced daily, some of which can be analyzed according to the feeling expressed in positive or negative terms. In this first phase of construction of a corpus of scientific texts classified with the label of sentiment, a new element is added to the existing research on the subject until now.

The collection of data for the creation of the corpus has been a process carried out in different temporal stages, and the filtering and cleaning of the texts so that they could build a corpus of training as appropriate as possible is a great added value. According to our knowledge and understanding, this is the first time that the creation of a specific corpus has been addressed to analyze the communication of science on Twitter, so that it can pave the way to continue deepening its study.

The filtering and cleaning processes of the corpus must be adapted to each particular project, since the peculiarities of the language, the jargon, the symbology or the complements of each Twitter message are different depending on the topic in question.

The most difficult thing in the case of a scientific corpus is to find the messages that can contribute negative sentiment, since most of them focus on labor issues, the boom anti-vaccines, homeopathy, skepticism and campaigns against all it. Informative messages that are usually positive or otherwise should be labeled as neutral, are very common in the network, but are constantly repeated, so the process in this case is to delete those texts that are duplicates, even if they have different users and origin.

In dictionary-based models, the lexicon is used to classify the sentiment. Some known examples are: *SentiWordNet* and *Pageranking WordNet*. Learning is not supervised and depends on the lexicon to label the class, but the disadvantage is above all the context, since in the case of sentiment it is often determined by context, not by words. Therefore, corpus-based approaches create patterns from previous training. The biggest advantage of this process is to achieve the adaptation to the topic that interests us, because the corpus is built for it, and will not serve to train any model of other topics.

It has also been able to verify reliably over time that connections have been made to the API Streaming of Twitter, the link that exists between the messages issued and the social news. There are three specific periods that have happened during this time and that have considerably affected the evolution of this work, due to the large volume of messages issued: the Pint of Science scientific festival, held annually in May, the online campaigns against the anti-vaccines movements and the pseudoscience, and finally, and at the same time more complex, the change of government that supposed the creation of a new and non-existent until that moment Ministry of Science, Innovation and Universities, with the minister Pedro Duque, former astronaut head. This last milestone generated an avalanche of thematic messages in the network that mixed science with politics and that most of them have been discarded in the creation of the corpus because they distorted the objective of this project to study the communication of science under normal circumstances.

CURRENT AND EXPECTED CONTRIBUTIONS

The computational methods and services implemented in this project can help other social science researchers study large numbers of scientific tweets in Spanish by running real-time sentiment analysis without the limitations of dictionary-based approaches. The procedure described to monitor streaming scientific tweets could help to focus investments in research or future lines of research, to test traditional and emerging theoretical approaches in public opinion research that require longitudinal data, and could also contribute to Experimental studies that need inputs in real time to create or adapt stimuli.

In this sense, in this phase of the project, the main innovation is the creation of a Corpus of texts of scientific subjects in Spanish, labeled by the polarity of their feeling: positive or negative, for the training of automatic learning models. With this Corpus you can train a classifier of feelings and opinions based on automatic learning oriented to scientific contents in Spanish, transmitted by social networks, which will help to predict the interest, trend or behavior on the main scientific topics treated in Spain and other countries of speaks Spanish.

REFERENCES

Arcila-Calderón, C., Barbosa-Caro, E., & Cabezuelo-Lorenzo, F. (2016). Técnicas Big Data: Análisis de textos a gran escala para la investigación científica y periodística. *El Profesional de la Información, 25*(4), 623–631. doi:10.3145/epi.2016.jul.12

Arcila-Calderón, C., Ortega-Mohedano, F., Jiménez-Amores, J., & Trullenque, S. (2017). Análisis supervisado de sentimientos políticos en español: clasificación en tiempo real de tweets basada en aprendizaje automático, *26*(5), 1699–2407. doi:10.3145/epi.2017.sep.18

Baker, M. (2015). Social media: A network boost. *Nature, 518*(7538), 263–265. doi:10.1038/nj7538-263a PMID:25679032

Baviera, T. (2016). Técnicas para el análisis del sentimiento en Twitter: Aprendizaje Automático Supervisado y SentiStrength [Techniques for sentiment analysis in Twitter : Supervised Learning and SentiStrength].

Bird, S., Klein, E., & Loper, E. (2009). *Natural Language Processing with Python*. O'Reilly. Retrieved from https://pdfs.semanticscholar.org/3673/bccde93025e05431a2bcac4e8ff18c9c273a.pdf

Bollen, J., Mao, H., & Pepe, A. (2011). Modeling Public Mood and Emotion: Twitter Sentiment and Socio-Economic Phenomena. In *Proceedings of the Fifth International AAAI Conference on Weblogs and Social Media*. Association for the Advancement of Artificial Intelligence. Retrieved from https://www.aaai.org/ocs/index.php/ICWSM/ICWSM11/paper/viewPaper/2826

Bravo-Marquez, F., Mendoza, M., & Poblete, B. (2014). Meta-level sentiment models for big social data analysis. *Knowledge-Based Systems, 69*, 86–99. doi:10.1016/j.knosys.2014.05.016

Dubiau, L., & Ale, J. M. (2013). *Análisis de Sentimientos sobre un Corpus en Español: Experimentación con un Caso de Estudio. In Proceedings of the 14th Argentine Symposium on Artificial Intelligence* (pp. 36–47). ASAI. Retrieved from http://42jaiio.sadio.org.ar/proceedings/simposios/Trabajos/ASAI/04.pdf

Feldman, R. (2013). Techniques and applications for sentiment analysis. *Communications of the ACM, 56*(4), 82. doi:10.1145/2436256.2436274

García Cumbreras, M. Á., Martínez-Cámara, E., Villena Román, J., & García Morera, J. (2016). TASS 2015 - The evolution of the Spanish opinion mining systems. *Procesamiento de Lenguaje Natural, 56*, 33–40.

García Cumbreras, M. Á., Villena Román, J., Martínez-Cámara, E., Díaz Galiano, M. C., Martín-Valdivia, M. T., & Ureña-López, L. A. (2016). Resumen de TASS 2016. In *TASS 2016: Workshop on Sentiment Analysis at SEPLN Proceedings* (pp. 13–21). Academic Press. Retrieved from http://ceur-ws.org/Vol-1702/tass2016_proceedings_v24.pdf

García Esparza, S., O'mahony, M. P., & Smyth, B. (2012). Mining the real-time web: A novel approach to product recommendation. *Knowledge-Based Systems, 29*, 3–11. doi:10.1016/j.knosys.2011.07.007

Hernández Orallo, J., Ramírez Quintana, M. J., & Ferri Ramínez, C. (2004). *Introducción a la Minería de Datos*. Pearson Educación.

Hurtado, L.-F., Pla, F., & Buscaldi, D. (2015). ELiRF-UPV en TASS 2015: Análisis de Sentimientos en Twitter. In *Workshop on Sentiment Analysis at SEPLN co-located with 31st SEPLN Conference* (pp. 75–79). Alicante: SEPLN. Retrieved from http://ceur-ws.org/Vol-1397/elirf_upv.pdf

Jarreau, P. B. (2015). *All the Science That Is Fit to Blog: An Analysis of Science Blogging Practices.* Louisiana State University. Retrieved from https://digitalcommons.lsu.edu/gradschool_dissertations/1051

Java, A., Song, X., Finin, T., & Tseng, B. (2007). *Why We Twitter: Understanding Microblogging Usage and Communities. In Proceedings of the 9th WEBKDD and 1st SNA-KDD Workshop.* ACM. doi:10.1145/1348549.1348556

Kwak, H., Lee, C., Park, H., & Moon, S. (2010). What is Twitter, a social network or a news media? In *Proceedings of the 19th international conference on World wide web - WWW '10* (p. 591). ACM Press. 10.1145/1772690.1772751

Medhat, W., Hassan, A., & Korashy, H. (2014). Sentiment analysis algorithms and applications: A survey. *Ain Shams Engineering Journal, 5*(4), 1093–1113. doi:10.1016/j.asej.2014.04.011

O'Connor, B., Balasubramanyan, R., Routledge, B. R., & Smith, N. A. (2010). From Tweets to Polls: Linking Text Sentiment to Public Opinion Time Series. In *Proceedings of the Fourth International AAAI Conference on Weblogs and Social Media* (pp. 122–129). Association for the Advancement of Artificial Intelligence. Retrieved from https://www.aaai.org/ocs/index.php/ICWSM/ICWSM10/paper/viewFile/1536/1842

Pang, B., & Lee, L. (2008). *Opinion mining and sentiment analysis. Foundations and Trends in Information Retrieval* (Vol. 2). Cornell University Press. Retrieved from http://www.cs.cornell.edu/home/llee/omsa/omsa.pdf

Pearson, G. (2001). The participation of scientists in public understanding of science activities: The policy and practice of the UK Research Councils. *Public Understanding of Science (Bristol, England), 10*(1), 121–137. doi:10.3109/A036860

Pérez-Rodríguez, A. V., González-Pedraz, C., & Alonso Berrocal, J. L. (2018). Twitter como herramienta de comunicación científica en España. Principales agentes y redes de comunicación. *Communication Papers, 7*(13), 95–111. Retrieved from https://dialnet.unirioja.es/servlet/articulo?codigo=6442315

Peters, H. P., Dunwoody, S., Allgaier, J., Lo, Y.-Y., & Brossard, D. (2014). Public communication of science 2.0: Is the communication of science via the "new media" online a genuine transformation or old wine in new bottles? *EMBO Reports, 15*(7), 749–753. doi:10.15252/embr.201438979 PMID:24920610

Pont-Sorribes, C., Cortiñas-Rovira, S., & Di Bonito, I. (2013). Challenges and opportunities for science journalists in adopting new technologies: The case of Spain. *SISSA-International School for Advanced Studies. Journal of Science Communication., 12*(3). doi:10.22323/2.12030205

Raes, K. (2003). La responsabilidad social de los científicos. *The IPTS Report, 72.* Retrieved from https://libros-revistas-derecho.vlex.es/vid/responsabilidad-social-cientificos-179708

Ribas, C. (2012). La divulgación y la comunicación de la ciencia, en la encrucijada. *Sociedad Española de Bioquímica y Biología Molecular (SEBBM)*, (173), 10–12. Retrieved from https://www.academia.edu/4630023/La_comunicación_de_la_ciencia_en_la_encrucijada

Segarra-Saavedra, J., Tur-Viñes, V., & Hidalgo-Marí, T. (2017). Uso de Twitter como herramienta de difusión en las revistas científicas españolas de Comunicación. In *Proceedings of the 7ª Conferencia internacional sobre revistas de ciencias sociales y humanidades*. Academic Press. Retrieved from http://thinkepi.net/notas/crecs_2017/J_16_30_Segarra.pdf

Van Zoonen, W., & van der Meer, T. G. L. A. (2016). Social media research: The application of supervised machine learning in organizational communication research. *Computers in Human Behavior*, *63*, 132–141. doi:10.1016/j.chb.2016.05.028

Vinodhini, G., & Chandrasekaran, R. M. (2012). Sentiment Analysis and Opinion Mining: A Survey. *International Journal of Advanced Research in Computer Science and Software Engineering*, *2*(6), 282–292.

Whitman Cobb, W. N. (2015). Trending now: Using big data to examine public opinion of space policy. *Space Policy*, *32*, 11–16. doi:10.1016/j.spacepol.2015.02.008

ENDNOTES

[1]   Reference: https://www.omnicoreagency.com/twitter-statistics/

[2]   Twitter Application Manager: https://apps.twitter.com/

[3]   Twitter Developer Web: https://developer.twitter.com/

[4]   Reference: https://developer.twitter.com/en/docs/tweets/data-dictionary/overview/tweet-object.html

[5]   Tweet Object: https://developer.twitter.com/en/docs/tweets/data-dictionary/overview/tweet-object.html

This research was previously published in the Journal of Information Technology Research (JITR), 13(3); pages 80-94, copyright year 2020 by IGI Publishing (an imprint of IGI Global).

Chapter 37

An Extensive Text Mining Study for the Turkish Language:
Author Recognition, Sentiment Analysis, and Text Classification

Durmuş Özkan Şahin

ⓘ https://orcid.org/0000-0002-0831-7825

Ondokuz Mayıs University, Turkey

Erdal Kılıç

ⓘ https://orcid.org/0000-0003-1585-0991

Ondokuz Mayıs University, Turkey

ABSTRACT

In this study, the authors give both theoretical and experimental information about text mining, which is one of the natural language processing topics. Three different text mining problems such as news classification, sentiment analysis, and author recognition are discussed for Turkish. They aim to reduce the running time and increase the performance of machine learning algorithms. Four different machine learning algorithms and two different feature selection metrics are used to solve these text classification problems. Classification algorithms are random forest (RF), logistic regression (LR), naive bayes (NB), and sequential minimal optimization (SMO). Chi-square and information gain metrics are used as the feature selection method. The highest classification performance achieved in this study is 0.895 according to the F-measure metric. This result is obtained by using the SMO classifier and information gain metric for news classification. This study is important in terms of comparing the performances of classification algorithms and feature selection methods.

DOI: 10.4018/978-1-6684-6303-1.ch037

INTRODUCTION

With the proliferation of the internet, the use of computers, mobile phones and tablets is increasing, and the amount of data is growing day by day. One of the sources of this increasing data type is non-structured textual documents. There is a significant increase in the number of data produced and stored in textual format. For this reason, automatically processing this data via computers and obtaining meaningful information from it will help researchers to develop new products. At the same time, the idea of text mining, a sub-branch of data mining, has appeared. Researchers aim to solve some problems with text mining techniques.

Text categorization can include supervised and unsupervised learning problems (Aggarwal and Zhai, 2012; Kadhim, 2019; Dasgupta and Ng, 2009 and Shafiabady et al., 2016). There is no training stage in unsupervised learning. Clustering algorithms are examples of these approaches. On the other hand, there is a training stage in supervised learning. Classification algorithms create a mathematical formula according to the training model. Classification is then carried out according to that mathematical formula. In a supervised text classification approach texts are divided into two parts, namely training and testing. Then, various rules are learned by classifiers according to the way the classification algorithms work on the training set. Classifiers apply these rules to the text in the test set and classify the text. There are many studies in published literature on text classification (Sebastiani, 2002). Examples include:

- Machine learning-based and text mining-based automatic electronic mail filtering (Clark et al., 2003)
- Classification of webpages (Sun et al., 2002)
- Author recognition (Stamatatos et al., 2000)
- Automatic extraction of text summary (Salton et al., 1997)
- Automatic question–answer system (Soricut and Brill, 2006)
- Sentiment analysis on texts (Dos Santos and Gatti, 2014)
- Document language identification (Artemenko et al., 2006)

In this study, three different Turkish text classification applications were performed. These are news classification, author recognition and sentiment analysis. In order to solve these text classification problems, all operations from the pre-processing step to obtaining the classification performance are explained in detail. In this way, the reader is shown how to make a Turkish text classification application in any programming language. It also explains what methods are used to improve the running time and performance of the classification algorithms. In order to increase classification performance, TF-IDF – a popular term weighting method – and classification algorithms with different working principles were used. Two different feature selection metrics were used to try and reduce the working time of the algorithms. Besides, the keywords extracted from the feature selection methods were compared and interpreted. This study uses many methods on different text classification problems and consequently contribute to existing published literature.

Use of Natural Language Processing and Text Mining in the Business World

Human language is one of the most basic features used by people to communicate and survive. A social person cannot avoid language in their daily life. Apart from speaking, we come across language via texts, signs, menus, emails, SMS, internet pages, advertisements and many other examples that can be found everywhere. In the same way, speech is a language feature in every area of our lives that we use to express ourselves even more easily than writing. Speaking in the mother tongue seems easy, but language acquisition is truly a challenging and time-consuming process. For example, learning a different foreign language is a very difficult process. Besides, language should be considered to be a living organism. Even in colloquial speech, there are many words and statements that change over time. The process of understanding natural language and thinking in natural language has a complex structure inside the brain. It is proposed to process this complex structure using computers by creating the idea of text mining and natural language processing.

Natural language processing and text mining are a broadly and rapidly evolving segment of today's digital technologies. The two concepts are closely interconnected. Text mining studies are data-mining studies that accept text as a data source. In other words, it aims to discover structured data within the text. Natural language processing uses various techniques to understand the complexities of human language. Both techniques benefit from each other. Natural language processing and text mining techniques are used in almost all sectors of the business world. Therefore, the techniques are performed quickly and regularly in the business world. Some areas, where natural language processing techniques and text mining techniques are frequently used in business are as follows:

Banking is one of the areas where natural language processing and text mining techniques are used most frequently (Hassani et al., 2018). The banking process has been very complicated for years. Customers often want to enquire about the bank's policies at the bank counter and since the policies are sometimes confusing, it takes time for customers to understand the policies. A banking assistant is recommended to work with a combination of natural language processing and machine learning techniques (Shah et al., 2017). In this way, chatbots are created where customers can ask about confusing situations.

General-purpose financial statements are shown as examples of increasing data. A business manager usually makes decisions for businesses by looking at these tables. It is not possible to obtain all the necessary information about the business from general purpose financial statements. This situation means the business value is not fully determined and the stakeholders may make the wrong decisions. For this reason, stakeholders turn to other sources. Annual reports, sustainability reports and integrated reports are examples of these resources. However, the analysis of the data contained in these reports becomes a problem for stakeholders, because statistical methods are insufficient in the analysis of these reports – which contain mostly unstructured data. Text mining is an analysis method that solves this problem and has been used frequently in the field of accounting in recent years (Yıldız and Ağdeniz, 2018).

One of the places featuring widespread use of computers is in hospitals. The doctors write reports about the patients they examine. These reports contain words and abbreviations that are difficult to understand. It is difficult for patients and their relatives to understand the report produced. Various machine learning algorithms and natural language processing techniques are used to overcome these difficulties (Leaman et al., 2015). In this way, it aims to let people without medical knowledge understand the reports.

Stock market index forecasting always attracts the attention of researchers due to its difficulty and economic importance. Many studies are using natural language processing and text mining techniques for stock market index prediction (Abdullah et al.; 2013, Khedr and Yaseen, 2017). Abdullah et al. (2013) worked on basic text mining steps by processing news, articles and comments about the stock market. Also, numerical data such as turnover and the volume of companies was used. This information was stored for estimation and analysis after processing. In the last step, the stock index was estimated by taking into account the risk factors based on standard deviation and correlation. In a similar study, data mining and emotion analysis techniques were applied to newspaper news to estimate the stock market index (Khedr and Yaseen, 2017). In addition to stock market index prediction, many financial predictions are made using natural language processing and text mining techniques (Xing et al., 2018).

Motivation

Text data is one of the main sources of increasing data stacks. Extracting meaningful information from these data is a significant problem. Researchers have been trying to make improvements in this field for many years. However, there are still many problems awaiting solutions in this area. One of these problems is the limited studies in the field of Turkish text mining. These problems are our main motivation. This study is primarily a Turkish text mining study. It also investigates three different problems through news classification, author recognition and sentiment analysis.

Contribution

The main contribution of this study is to present a systematic way to deal with Turkish text mining and apply solution methods to different problems. Readers interested in the field of text mining will satisfy most of their needs by acquiring the most basic information when reading this study. This work shows researchers who want to work in the field of text classification the steps they should follow from the very beginning to the end of any text classification application. In this way, readers will be able to develop a textual classification application. There are limited Turkish text mining studies in published literature. Together in this study, three different Turkish text mining applications were considered, and the results were examined thoroughly.

Organization

The study sections are organized as follows:

- Background
- Text Pre-processing and Feature Extraction
- Feature Selection Methods
- Solutions and Recommendations
- Results and Discussions
- Future Research Directions
- Conclusion.

Background: In the first part of the study, a summary of published literature related to author recognition for Turkish documents, sentiment analysis for Turkish sentences and categorization of Turkish texts are given. This part of the study is a brief survey.

Text Pre-processing and Feature Extraction: The second section outlines the basic steps that should be taken in text classification studies to the reader. This will enable readers to adopt basic text classification to any programming language.

Feature Selection Methods: In machine learning studies, feature selection can be considered as keyword selection in text classification. Keyword extraction is a method of information retrieval. How to do this and its mathematical representations will be explained in detail in a separate section.

Solutions and Recommendations: Three different studies will take place in this fourth section. These are author recognition using Turkish documents, sentiment analysis for Turkish sentences and categorization of Turkish texts. This is followed by a detailed explanation of the data sets and machine learning algorithms used in the study. For example, the distribution of the data sets used in the study during the training phase and test phase will be given. Also, the mathematical background of machine learning algorithms used in the study will be explained.

Results and Discussions: There are two different experimental results. The first of these is the Turkish keywords extracted from the three different studies. The second is the classification performance obtained from the machine learning algorithms.

Future Research Directions: In this section, the current unresolved problems in text classification studies are discussed, and the trend techniques frequently used by researchers in this field are highlighted.

Conclusion: The conclusions follow the basic text classification procedures and experimental results.

BACKGROUND

Although the history of computerized text classification applications goes back to the 1960s, it was in the late 1980s and early 1990s that they became more focused. In the early years, the majority of applications were based on the expert systems approach. In the text classification studies performed by expert systems, documents were divided into categories by the rules determined by the developer (Apté et al., 1994). With the increase in the amount of data and the number of categories, this system no longer worked because as the number of data increased, the number of rules increased. These are the disadvantages of rule-based systems.

With the development and reducing costs of electronic hardware parts such as memory and processors, the use of machine learning algorithms has become widespread and has been used on text classification problems. One of the most important of these algorithms is the support vector machine (SVM). The most important application of SVM for text classification is the Joachim (1998)'s study. Apart from this classifier, many machine learning algorithms, such as artificial neural networks (Ruiz and Srinivasan, 1998), Naive Bayes (Kibriya et al., 2004), K-Nearest Neighbor (Yang, 1999) and decision trees (Harrag et al., 2009) have been used extensively on text categorization.

In addition to supervised machine learning algorithms, unsupervised machine learning algorithms are also frequently used in the field of text mining. Unsupervised machine learning algorithms have extensively been studied with respect to textual information. With the use of these algorithms, solutions are created for document organization (Cutting et al., 2017), visualization (Cadez et al., 2003) and categorization (Bekkerman et al., 2001). Unsupervised algorithms used in text classification include hierarchical clustering (Willett, 1998), k-means clustering (Chen et al., 2010), probabilistic latent semantic analysis (Hofmann, 2013) and latent Dirichlet allocation (Blei et al., 2003).

In studies in recent years, data scientists have used graphics processing units (GPU) in machine learning to achieve groundbreaking improvements in a variety of applications, including image classification, video analysis, speech recognition, text classification and natural language learning processing (Deng, 2014). The GPU provides fast and efficient parallel computing. Due to its structure, deep learning is a system whose cost is proportional to its computational complexity. Thanks to the GPU, the usage of deep learning networks, which is more successful than classical machine learning algorithms, has become very popular in text classification in recent years.

In Turkey, there are reported to be 62.07 million internet users, according to January 2020 data (DataReportal, 2020). At the same time, the number of internet users has increased by 2.4 million between 2019 and 2020. More than 80 million people live in Turkey, where there are more than 50 million social media users according to January 2020 data. In addition to these data, 77.39 million mobile connections occurred in January 2020. This increase represents a serious amount of data that has to be processed because there are a limited number of studies on Turkish text mining – especially for author recognition and emotion analysis – this study aimed to contribute to the Turkish text classification area significantly.

There are studies on Turkish texts using different methods for different purposes. Naive Bayes, support vector machines and decision trees have been used in a study to find the author (Amasyalı and Diri, 2006). Also, classifying documents according to the text's genre and identifying the gender of an author are done automatically. The feature vector is generated by using the n-gram technique. The success in determining the author of the text, the genre of the text and gender of the author was found to be 83%, 93% and 96%, respectively. In another study, author recognition was performed on Turkish documents using ridge regression analysis (Kuyumcu et al., 2019). For the solution of the author recognition problem, the features obtained by applying the term frequency-inverse document frequency (TF-IDF) weighting method separately for word 1-3 n-grams and character 2-6 n-grams were combined and represented in vector space. An accuracy of 89.6% was obtained in that study.

The filtering of spam emails in Turkish has been performed by using artificial neural networks (Özgür et al., 2004). Seven hundred and fifty emails were used. Four hundred and ten of them were spam mail and the rest were normal mail. Terms were used as features. Both binary term weighting and probabilistic methods were applied. The mutual information method was implemented as a feature selection. The success in classifying kinds of mail was 90%. In another study on filtering spam emails in Turkish, the performance of Naive Bayes, support vector machines and artificial neural network methods were compared (Tantuğ and Eryiğit, 2006).

By scanning Turkish web pages, a data set of 22000 samples was created to determine the types of these pages (Hüsem and Gülcü, 2017). The n-gram technique was used to construct the feature vector. The information gain technique was used for feature selection. Naive Bayes and SVM were used as classification algorithms. When the number of categories was low, a 92.6% success rate was achieved, and a 79.45% success rate is achieved when the number of categories is high.

More than 20 methods have been tried to measure the similarity of Turkish documents (Keleş and Özel, 2017). The aim of the study was initially considered for the detection of plagiarism. Document similarity was processed in two different ways. In the first, document similarity was measured without a pre-processing step. In the second, document similarity was measured after a pre-processing step. According to the experimental results, it was observed that the pre-processing step increased the similarity detection performance. In all experiments, it was emphasized that the cosine similarity method was more successful than other distance criteria. A similar study was conducted to evaluate the similarities of Turkish words (Aydoğan and Karci, 2019).

A new data set called TTC-3600 was created by Kılınç et al., 2017. This data set consisted of news texts from various newspapers. The dataset consisted of 3600 documents, including 600 news items from six categories. These were the economy, culture–arts, health, politics, sport and technology. Five different classification algorithms were used. These were Naive Bayes, SVM, K-Nearest Neighbor (KNN), J48 and Random Forest. The experimental results showed that the best accuracy criterion value of 91.03% was obtained with the Random Forest classifier. In another study on this data set, the methods of document representation were compared (Yıldırım and Yıldız, 2018). These methods were the traditional bag of words and artificial neural network-based language models. The results indicated that the traditional method was still effective. In the same dataset, classification performance was improved by using a deep learning technique called Convolutional Neural Networks (Çiğdem and Çirak, 2019).

A sentiment analysis study was conducted on the data set containing the film interpretations in IMDB using various feature selection techniques (Kaynar et al., 2017). A data set with 1000 features, including 2000 film interpretations, were used. Seventy-five percent of the data set was reserved for the training phase and the remaining 25% was reserved for the test. Five different feature selection methods were tried and their performances were compared. These methods were chi-square, information gain, gain ratio, Gini coefficient, oneR and reliefF. SVM was used to compare classification performances. The best result was obtained by the Gini coefficient method.

Classification results for different machine learning algorithms were compared for the TREMO data set (Alpkoçak et al., 2019). This data set is constituted from the Turkish sentiment analysis field. Four different machine learning approaches were used. These were artificial neural networks, SVM, Random Forest and KNN algorithms. The first five characters of the words in the texts were used and the features were extracted. A mutual information algorithm was used in the feature selection stage. The most successful classification results were obtained by SVM and artificial neural networks. KNN gave the worst results.

Text data containing 444 opinions from the FATIH project were analyzed (Göker and Tekedere, 2017). TF-IDF weighting was performed on the terms to create the feature vector. Five different machine learning approaches were used. These were artificial neural networks, sequential minimal optimization, KNN, J48 and Naive Bayes algorithms. The highest achieving algorithm for the performance comparison was the sequential minimal optimization algorithm at 88.73%.

Apart from Turkish text classification and natural language processing studies, there are many studies in different languages such as Chinese (Shi et al., 2019), English (Liu et al., 2018), Arabic (Salloum et al., 2018) and Spanish (Cabezudo et al., 2019). Studies in these languages are summarized as follows:

English is the most preferred language worldwide as a foreign language. Therefore, many people use this language even if it is not their native language. Since the language of science is English and people who speak different languages communicate in English, a lot of textual data is produced in English. For these reasons, text classification and natural language processing studies are very often performed in English. Some of the English text mining studies are text summarization (Fattah and Ren, 2008), question answering (Ke and Hagiwara, 2017), sentiment analysis (Tripathi et al., 2015) and author profiling (Estival et al., 2007).

Chinese ranks first among the most spoken languages in the world. A total of 1,300,000,000 people speak Chinese around the world (Babbel Magazine, 2020). Since there are so many people speaking in this language, many researchers continue to study text mining in Chinese. Currently, there are some problems with Chinese text classification problems stemming from the structure of Chinese (Liu et al., 2019). For example, in a Chinese sentence, there is no space between words. For this reason, the tokenization structure becomes very difficult. Generally, the word segmentation approach is used for the solution of this problem. However, it is difficult to get accurate Chinese word segmentation results. To deal with these problems, a convolutional neural network (CNN) and long short-term memory (LSTM) networks based on deep learning are frequently used on Chinese texts (Zhang and Chen, 2016; Li et al.,

2018). With the use of these algorithms, good results are obtained for Chinese texts. In the sentiment analysis study on Chinese texts, the comments of Chinese tourists at hotels in Japan were examined (Carreónet et al., 2019) because there has been a remarkable increase in the number of tourists travelling from China to Japan in recent years. Due to this increase, hotel businesses in Japan needed reliable market research tools. These are considered to be a problem for the hotel industry in Japan. To solve this problem, researchers used text mining techniques (Carreónet et al., 2019). In this study, comments made by Chinese tourists for hotels in Japan were collected and processed. The Stanford Word Segmenter tool was used in the pre-processing of the texts, and the entropy technique based on the theory of information was used in the keyword extraction phase. With the support vector machines algorithm, there was an attempt to try and classify comments as positive or negative. The highest performance achieved was determined to be $F1 = 0.93 \pm 0.05$ and an accuracy $= 0.90 \pm 0.09$. According to the positive comments, the predictions of tourist density were provided to the hotels.

Arabic is among the popular languages of the world. Approximately 315 million people use this language as their first language (Babbel Magazine, 2020), and more than 250 million people use it as their second language. Therefore, Arabic is one of the languages that researchers are interested in for text classification studies. Although Arabic text classification studies are popular, the limited number of data sets is a problem for researchers working in this field. Both single-label and multi-label datasets are very limited to Arabic text classification (Elnagar et al., 2020). For this reason, it is difficult for researchers to try text classification techniques in Arabic. Researchers created both single-label (SANAD) and multi-label (NADIA) data sets (Elnagar et al., 2020). Both data sets were made freely available to the research community looking at Arabic computational linguistics. It was aimed at increasing the classification performance by applying deep learning techniques to the data sets created. While 96.94% success was achieved with the SANAD dataset, 88.68% success was achieved with the NADIA dataset. In another text classification study on Arabic, a linear discriminant analysis (LDA) technique was used (AbuZeina and Al-Anzi, 2018). Arabic is one of the richest languages in the world in terms of the number of words. For this reason, many features appear in Arabic text classification. The high number of features negatively affects classification performance and working time. To eliminate this situation, researchers used the LDA-based dimension reduction technique. When the results obtained in the study were compared to classical machine learning methods, it was emphasized that the LDA technique was promising in the classification of Arabic documents.

Another of the common languages in the world, like Arabic, is Spanish. Spanish is the official language of 20 countries. At the same time, more than 450 million people speak Spanish as their mother tongue (Babbel Magazine, 2020). Since many people speak Spanish, the number of resources produced in this language is quite high. Therefore many researchers want to work on text mining and natural language processing in the Spanish language. In the sentiment analysis study on Spanish texts, Spanish social media messages were examined (Plaza-del-Arco et al., 2019). Researchers proposed a study of different machine learning approaches to automatically recognize emotions in messages written in Spanish on social media. They focused on Spanish texts mainly because it is a major language used in social media. Also, researchers focused on this language because emotional analysis studies on Spanish documents are also limited in published literature. In addition to this study, Molina-González et al. (2015) suggested the integration of domain information for a Spanish polarity classification system, and Martínez-Cámara et al. (2015) carried out a study of different features and machine learning algorithms to classify the polarity of Spanish Twitter posts.

TEXT PRE-PROCESSING AND FEATURE EXTRACTION

Although texts are readable by computers using HTML, PDF, DOC and TXT, they are often not in a format that can be used directly by machine learning algorithms. Texts in these structures are known as non-structured data types. Therefore, before any text classification with any machine learning technique, the texts must be passed through various steps and converted into a type that the computer can understand. Figure 1 shows the pre-processing steps used to construct texts.

Figure 1. The Steps of Text Pre-processing

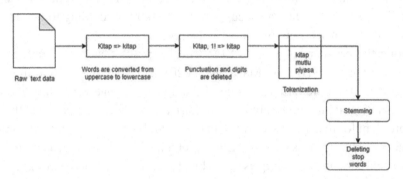

The same words in the text may be written in different forms. These words have the same importance. Therefore, all characters are converted from uppercase to lowercase so that all words in the text are in the same type. There are two important reasons for this transformation. The first is to reduce the total number of words by gathering words of the same structure and meaning into a single form. The second is to prevent the wrong classification result because the number of words will change. For example, the word "**hasta**" can exist in structures such as "**Hasta**" and "**HASTA**". Although they have the same importance, the computer considers these as three different terms. Thereby, they should be transformed into a single structure.

When the sentence "**Yazın en çok tüketilen meyveler karpuz, şeftali, kiraz ve üzümdür.**" is examined, if the comma (,) or dot (.) is not deleted from the sentence, terms such as "**karpuz,**" and "**üzümdür.**" are identified along with the punctuation. Since "**karpuz**" and "**karpuz,**" in another text or document will be different from each other, the frequency of these words will change. For this reason, punctuation, symbols and numbers are removed from the text.

Since words are processed in text classification, all words in the text should be obtained. For example, in the Java programming language, all the words in the text are taken into memory by using the **split()** method. Figure 2 shows how word separation is performed.

Figure 2. The Steps of Tokenization

In most instances, words that have the same meaning can be seen in morphologically different structures within the text. For instance, a plural suffix of the words and time suffix can be given as an example. Hence, in this case the words should be converted to the same structure by the stemming process. For this purpose, stemming libraries for different languages are available. Zemberek for Turkish and Porter Stemmer for English are examples (Zemberek, 2019; Porter Stemmer, 2019). Since this study is an example of Turkish text classification, the Zemberek library is used. This tool is recommended for Turkish. When working on a language other than Turkish, a natural language processing tool developed for that language should be used.

Apart from the Zemberek tool, there are also natural language processing tools developed for Turkish. These tools are (ITU NLP Toolkit, 2020) and (Turkish NLP Toolkit, 2020). ITU NLP Toolkit (2020) provides the Turkish NLP Tools and APIs developed by a Natural Language Processing group at Istanbul Technical University. The details of this work are given in Eryiğit, 2014. The Turkish NLP Toolkit (2020) contains implementations of several natural language processing and machine learning algorithms. Although initial implementations are based on the Turkish language, the system currently contains basic modelling in three languages, English, Turkish and Persian, respectively.

Some words can be seen frequently in each category. These words have no distinguishing features for a particular category. These words are known as stop words. The conjunctions and prepositions in the language can be given as examples. Table 1 gives some stop words for Turkish. Since these words appear in each category, they are eliminated by feature selection methods. However, to avoid the computational cost, a list of stop words should be created and these words should be eliminated directly in the pre-processing phase.

Table 1. Some Stop Words for Turkish

ama	biz	bir	en	bile
her	sey	gibi	değil	böyle
kadar	ancak	var	çok	hiç
ile	bu	ne	veya	göre

The Challenges of Natural Language and Text Processing in Turkish

Speaking and writing in Turkish is difficult. These situations also bring some difficulties in natural language processing and text mining studies of the Turkish language. These difficulties can be summarized as follows:

Turkish is a formal language based on a basic word order of Subject + Object + Verb. It is not possible to make any changes in the creation of words or when forming attachments, nor does it have any rules about the locations of sentence elements. Therefore, syntactic analysis is difficult. Even in official Turkish correspondence, the general structure of the Turkish language (Subject + Object + Verb) is only partially followed. In daily conversations, the subject is usually not used; this process is carried out by the verb. The use of transposed sentences is high and the highlighted parts are used close to the verb. For this reason, a large number of complex algorithms may need to be constructed. Unlike Turkish, attention is paid to the Subject + Verb + Object structure in English. Besides, using transpose sentences is rarely seen in English. As a result, it is relatively easier to process English than Turkish.

Turkish is a root-based language and a suffix one. Being a root-based language increases the intelligibility of the language. The fact that it is also a suffix language creates difficulties in language processing. The large number of suffixes that can be added makes it difficult to analyze the word. Also, the meaning can be completely changed with these additions. The number of synonyms and homophones is high in Turkish. This is why the number of words in Turkish is less than in other languages. A word can have many meanings and multiple words can be used instead of one word. To analyze the sentence properly, it is necessary to correctly determine the meaning of the word. This situation reveals some obstacles in natural language processing. There are also suffixes and prefixes to words in English. However, this is only true for some words. Consequently, again, it is relatively easier to process English than Turkish.

Document Representation

Texts must be converted to a numerical format to use machine learning algorithms on text data. In most text classification studies, a bag of words and the vector space model are preferred to convert text data into a format that computers can understand (Berry, 2004). In the bag of words approach, all the unique words in the training data sets form a vector. In other words, each document is represented by a vector.

$$doc_i = term_{1,i} - term_{2,i} - term_{3,i} - \ldots - term_{i,n} \tag{1}$$

In Equation 1, the document i is represented as a vector. Where n is the total number of words in the training data set. The vector is filled with the weight values of the terms using any term weighting method.

Term Weighting Approach

The most important reason for term weighting in text mining is to reveal the distinctive power of classification algorithms more clearly. For example, if any term appears too few times in some documents and too many times in other documents, this difference must have arisen through the term weighting approach. The most commonly used term weighting methods in text classification are binary term weighting and the TF-IDF methods (Salton and Buckley, 1988).

Binary Term Weighting

This is the most primitive and simple weighting method. If a term is used in the document, it is weighted as 1, otherwise, it is weighted as 0. The advantage of this method is that it is simple to use and has little computational cost. The disadvantage is that it does not make a distinction between terms. For example, a term seen ten times in the same document and a term seen once has the same significance. Another disadvantage is that the number of terms in the documents is ignored. For these reasons, binary term weighting is not as successful as other popular term weighting methods.

Term Frequency: Inverse Document Frequency (TF-IDF)

TF-IDF is one of the most important weighting methods. It was developed by (Jones, 1972; Jones, 2004). It is one of the first examples from information retrieval studies. The method is used for different purposes besides term weighting.

The TF-IDF consists of two factors: term frequency and inverse document frequency. The term frequency is calculated based on the document, while the inverse document frequency is calculated from the whole training set. There are many variations in the calculation of TF (Dogan and Uysal, 2019). The most commonly used TF is the number that specifies how many times a term appears in the document. In Equation 2, the TF-IDF value of any term t is calculated.

$$TF - IDF = TF \times \log \frac{total\ number\ of\ documents}{the\ number\ of\ documents\ containing\ the\ term\ t} \tag{2}$$

TF-IDF is used for different purposes in text classification studies. For example, in (Lan et al., 2008), TF-IDF is used for weighting, while in the (Taşcı and Güngör, 2013) study, it is used for feature selection. TF-IDF is used for weighting in this study.

FEATURE SELECTION METHODS

Machine learning algorithms usually take a long time to run due to their structure. At the same time, the operation of these algorithms is directly related to the size of the data. Document vectors are created by using all the words in the training sets. Therefore, documents are represented by tens of thousands of terms. Most of these terms do not contain important information as they do not positively affect the success of classification. The vector size will be very large, so memory and calculation problems will arise. In the previous subsection, techniques such as stemming words and removing stop words are used to reduce the vector size in the pre-processing stage. Although pre-processing methods and size reduction are used, a feature selection step is needed since it cannot solve the dimension problem completely. Feature selection is the process of finding a subset that best represents all words, rather than using all the terms in the bag of words. Thanks to feature selection:

- Memory wastage can be avoided by reducing the vector size.
- The running time of the text classification process can be reduced.
- Data considered as non-important or considered to be noise may be eliminated.
- Overfitting problems can be solved.

Feature selection methods are generally divided into three main groups (Rong et al., 2019). These are filters, wrappers and embedded methods. In addition to these methods, hybrid methods are also available (Hsu et al., 2019). Filtering is the most preferred method because the computation cost is low and easy to apply compared to the other two methods. Filtering methods are often statistical metrics that are derived from the number of occurrences of terms in their category or opposite categories (Şahin and Kılıç, 2019). Chi-Square (CHI), Information Gain (IG) and DF metrics are examples of filtering methods.

When selecting a feature with filtering methods, the selection is made in two different ways. These are local policies and global policies (Taşçı et al., 2013). In some studies, the local policy is called class-based, and the general policy is called corpus-based (Özgür et al., 2005). Local policies are a better approach to binary classification because the best keywords for each category are found separately (Özgür et al., 2005). As a result, a one-vs-all classification approach and local policy are applied in this study. In the general policy, a single feature vector is obtained by using some optimization techniques among the features obtained for each category. When the number of features is small, the local policy gives good classification achievements (Tasci and Gungor, 2008). When the number of features is too large, a general policy gives good classification achievements (Tasci and Gungor, 2008).

Chi-Square Metric

Chi-Square (CHI) metric is statistics-based and widely used for feature selection. In Equation 3, the CHI value is calculated for each feature value.

$$CHI = N \frac{(ad - bc)^2}{(a+c)(b+d)(a+b)(c+d)} \tag{3}$$

The CHI value of the term t_i in any class c_i is calculated in Equation 3. Where a represents the number of documents that contain the t_i term in c_i, b represents the number of documents that do not contain the t_i term in c_i, c represents the number of documents that contain the t_i term but do not belong to c_i and d represents the number of documents that do not contain the t_i term but do not belong to c_i. N indicates the total amount of documents (i.e. $N=a+b+c+d$). If the CHI value is 0, there is no relationship between the term and the category. As the CHI value increases, the relationship between the term and the category increases.

Information Gain

Information Gain (IG) generates a value. The produced value is the answer to the question of how important it is for the class. In Equation 4, the mathematical representation of information gain is given.

$$IG(t) = -\sum_{i=1}^{M} P(c_i) log P(c_i) + P(t) \sum_{i=1}^{M} P(c_i|t) log P(c_i|t) + P(t') \sum_{i=1}^{M} P(c_i|t') log P(c_i|t') \tag{4}$$

In Equation 4, M is the total number of categories, $P(c_i)$ means the probability that a document belongs to the class c_i in all categories, $P(t)$ means the probability that the term t is included in a document in the corpus, $P(t')$ means the probability that the term t is not included in a document in the corpus, $P(c_i|t)$ is the probability that the term t appears at least once in one of the documents in the class and $P(c_i|t')$ is the probability that the term t does not exist in any of the documents in the c_i class. The terms take values between 0 and 1 according to IG. The terms with the highest value are those that are most relevant to the category.

SOLUTIONS AND RECOMMENDATIONS

In this section, the methods used in the solution of the problems discussed in the study will be given. These are, respectively, the data sets used, the classification algorithms and the performance measures. The steps followed to solve the text classification problems are given in Figure 3.

Figure 3. The General Structure of Text Classification

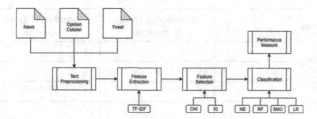

Data Sets Used

In this study, three different data sets were used. The first consisted of documents belonging to news texts received from Turkish newspapers (News Data Set, 2019). This data set normally consists of 13 categories. Six categories of the data set were used in this study. The distribution of the data set is given in Table 2.

Table 2. Distribution of Kemik Natural Language Processing Group News Data Set

Category	Number of Train Documents	Number of Tests Documents	Total Documents
economy	2285	980	3265
magazine	1954	838	2792
health	968	415	1383
politics	1294	555	1849
sport	6697	3300	9997
technology	539	232	771

The second data set was created for sentiment analysis (Çetin and Amasyalı, 2013). The data set was generated from twitter comments about GSM and telecommunication companies. Messages tagged "+" consisted of positive messages for companies and messages tagged "−" consisted of negative messages. Messages were short and often had typos. Therefore, it is a difficult data set to classify. The distribution of the data set is given in Table 3.

The third data set was the author detection data set (Mayda and Amasyalı, 2016). It was composed of the texts of the authors working in some newspapers. It was a balanced and difficult data set to categorize. The writing of six authors and their distributions are given in Table 4.

Table 3. Distribution of Kemik Natural Language Processing Group Tweets Data Set

Category	Number of Train Documents	Number of Tests Documents	Total Documents
+	529	227	756
-	900	387	1287

Table 4. Distribution of Kemik Natural Language Processing Group 500 Opinion Column Data Set

Author's Name	Number of Train Documents	Number of Tests Documents	Total Documents
Cüneyt Özdemir	35	15	50
Ece Temelkuran	35	15	50
İlber Ortaylı	35	15	50
İsmail Küçükkaya	35	15	50
Mustafa Balbay	35	15	50
Uğur Dündar	35	15	50

Classification Algorithms

In this study, four different classification algorithms were used according to the one-vs-all approach. The classification algorithms were Random Forest (RF), Naive Bayes (NB), sequential minimal optimization (SMO) and logistic regression (LR) techniques.

Random Forest

Random Forest is an easy to use, flexible machine learning algorithm. RF can be used for both classification and regression problems. The algorithm forms a random forest. The created forest is a collection of decision trees that are often trained with the bagging method. In other words, the Random Forest creates more than one decision tree. Then, it combines the forests to get an accurate and stable prediction.

Naive Bayes

Naive Bayes is a probability-based classification algorithm based on Bayes theorem. The NB classification aims to determine the class of data given to the system using calculations according to probability principles. Considering a problem with three classes, the algorithm will generate three different probability values to estimate the class of data. The data will be tagged according to the highest probability value. It is an algorithm that can give successful results with little training data. Compared to most classification algorithms, the computational cost is low.

Sequential Minimal Optimization Based Support Vector Machine

SMO is a supervised classification algorithm where a model is created based on training data. According to this model, the test data is included in a certain class. In the support vector machines model, the hyperplane is determined which separates the classes from each other. The determination of this hyperplane is based on maximizing the distance between the support vectors of the classes to process the classification.

Logistic Regression

Logistic Regression solves binary classification problems based on supervised machine learning and statistical models. In regression problems, a continuous variable is generally obtained as the output. In LR, the output is not always continuous. The algorithm can be used in many ways. In this study, results are obtained from the LR algorithm with the one-vs-all approach. Otherwise, the classification process cannot be performed. With this algorithm, the logistic function in mathematics is used to calculate the threshold value. Two classes are defined according to this logistic function. If the value of the logistic function is bigger than 0.5, the result is first class. Otherwise, the result is a second class.

Performance Measure

One of the biggest misconceptions in the studies using classification algorithms is to interpret the accuracy rate as classification success. Especially in imbalanced data sets, accuracy does not give much information about classification performance. In such cases, it would be useful to consider two metrics instead of the accuracy metric. These are recall and precision. Table 5 shows the confusion matrix.

Table 5. Confusion Matrix

ACTUAL			
+ CLASS	**- CLASS**		
True Positive	False Positive	**+ CLASS**	**PREDICTION**
False Negative	True Negative	**- CLASS**	

According to the confusion matrix, the True Positive (TP), False Positive (FP), True Negative (TN) and False Negative (FN) metrics are defined as follows:

TP: This is the case where + labelled instances are estimated as +.
FP: This is the case where − labelled instances are estimated as +.
TN: This is the case where − labelled instances are estimated as −.
FN: This is the case where + labelled instances are estimated as −.

The basic concepts used to evaluate the performance of the model are precision, recall and F-measure. Criteria for precision (π) and recall (ρ) are given in Equations 5 and 6, respectively.

$$\pi = \frac{TP}{TP + FP} \tag{5}$$

$$\rho = \frac{TP}{TP + FN} \tag{6}$$

Precision and recall criteria are not sufficient to give a meaningful comparison by themselves. The F-measure is defined for this purpose. The F-measure is calculated using Equation 5 and Equation 6, as given in Equation 7.

$$F = \frac{2\pi\rho}{\pi + \rho} \tag{7}$$

Since the application works in binary classification, the classification success of each category is calculated separately and an average F-measure is obtained.

RESULTS AND DISCUSSIONS

In this section, the results obtained from the data sets will be given. The results of the study will be presented in two different ways. Firstly, the keywords obtained from feature selection methods will be shown according to categories. Then, the performance of classification algorithms will be given. Classification achievements will be given separately according to feature selection methods.

Comparison of Keywords Extracted by Feature Selection Metrics

Since the working principle of each feature selection metric is different, the extracted keywords by these feature selection metrics are different. Which feature is selected is also an important parameter for the classification algorithms. Table 6 shows the top 10 features obtained from the news data set according to the CHI metric. The English meaning of Turkish words is given in parentheses in Table 6 to Table 11. English meanings for words with the same meaning are not given separately in other tables.

When Table 6 is analyzed, according to the CHI metric, 1 of the 60 words belonging to all categories is a common word. The word **takım** is seen in both the magazine and the sports category. This word, which is very important for the sports category, is misleading for the classification algorithm because it appears in another category. Apart from this word, the CHI metric did not find common words. This result indicated that the CHI metric generates distinguishing keywords.

Table 7 shows the top 10 features obtained from the news data set according to the IG metric. When Table 7 is examined, according to the IG metric, four of the 60 words belonging to all categories are common words. While there are 50 unique words, there are four common words. These words are **takım**, **oyun**, **başkan** and **futbol**. The word **takım** has appeared in the categories for the economy, magazines, sports and technology. The words **oyun**, **başkan** and **futbol** are selected as keywords in two different categories. The word **oyun** is used in the categories for the economy and sports. The word **başkan** is seen in the categories for magazines and politics. Finally, the word **futbol** is seen in the categories for magazines and sports.

Table 6. Kemik Natural Language Processing Group News Data Set - The best-distinguishing terms according to the CHI metric

Category	economy	magazine	health	politics	sport	technology
Top 10 features	milyar (billion)	dizi (series)	hastalık (disease)	parti (political party)	takım (team)	google
	yüzde (percentage)	şarkı (song)	hasta (patient)	başbakan (prime minister)	futbol (football)	bilgisayar (computer)
	şirket (company)	ünlü (famous)	tedavi (treatment)	milletvekil (deputy)	oyna (play)	apple
	sektör (sector)	sanat (art)	sağlık (health)	erdoğan (turkey president's surname)	kulüp (club)	android
	banka (bank)	film (film)	ilaç (drug)	terör (terror)	sezon (season)	iphone
	dolar (dollar)	posta (post)	uzman (expert)	tbmm (grand national assembly of turkey)	oyun (game)	cihaz (device)
	yatırım (investment)	takım (team)	vücut (body)	meclis (parliament)	saha (area)	windows
	piyasa (market)	sahne (scene)	prof (prof)	tayyip (turkey president's name)	transfer (transfer)	telefon (phone)
	lira (turkish lira)	sevgi (love)	besle (feed)	siyasi (political)	galatasaray (the name of football team)	teknoloji (technology)
	fiyat (price)	album (album)	cerrahi (surgical)	millet (nation)	fenerbahçe (the name of football team)	mobil (mobile)

Table 7. Kemik Natural Language Processing Group News Data Set - The best-distinguishing terms according to the IG metric

Category	economy	magazine	health	politics	sport	technology
Top 10 features	yüzde	dizi	hastalık	parti	takım	bilgisayar
	milyar	şarki	hasta	başbakan	futbol	google
	şirket	ünlü	sağlık	milletvekil	kulüp	kullan (use)
	takım	takim	tedavi	erdoğan	oyna	telefon
	sektör	başkan (president)	uzman	terör	sezon	teknoloji
	dolar	kaydet (save)	ilaç	meclis	saha	cihaz
	banka	film	prof	tbmm	fenerbahçe	apple
	yatırım	sanat	vücut	tayyip	galatasaray	takım
	piyasa	posta	hastane (hospital)	başkan (president)	oyun	mobil
	oyun	futbol	besle	siyasi	transfer	facebook

When the keywords obtained from IG and CHI metrics are compared for the news data set, the CHI metric finds more unique words. When the extracted keywords in the economic category are compared, the CHI metric finds the word **fiyat**. This word is directly related to the economy. However, the IG metric cannot find it in the 10 most important words. When the keywords found using IG and CHI methods in the magazine category were compared, seven of the top 10 words were the same. The words **sahne** and **albüm** found by the CHI method can make a remarkable distinction in the magazine category. In the health category, both IG and CHI metrics found nine of the 10 keywords. The CHI metric selects **cerrahi**, and the IG metric selects **hastane**. Both selected words are distinctive in this category. In the politics category, both IG and CHI metrics found nine of the 10 keywords. The CHI metric selects **millet**, and the IG metric selects **başkan**. Both selected words are distinctive for this category. However, since the word **başkan** appeared in other categories, it adversely affected the success of the classification. Both IG and CHI metrics find the same words in the sports category. When the keywords found by IG and CHI metrics in the technology category were compared, seven of the top 10 words were the same. The words **android, iphone** and **windows** were found by CHI. However, the words **kullan, takım** and **facebook** were selected by IG.

Table 8 shows the top 10 features obtained from the Tweets data set according to the CHI metric. When Table 8 is analyzed, according to the CHI metric, three of the 20 words belonging to all categories were common words. These words were **hayat, paylaş** and **mesaj**. Having many keywords in common is a problem. This situation will undermine the performance of the classification algorithm. The prominent words in positive messages were **teşekkür, tesekkurler, ödül** and **fiber**. In negative messages, the words **fatura, para** and **edge** were selected.

Table 9 shows the top 10 features obtained from the Tweets data set according to the IG metric. When Table 9 is examined, according to the IG method, four of the 20 words belonging to all categories were common words. These words were **hayat, paylaş, ödül** and **mesaj**. Selecting a positive word such as **an** in the negative category as a keyword will mislead the classification algorithm. Examples of positive words discovered by the IG metric are the words **teşekkür, tesekkurler, fiber, mutlu** and **memnun**. The words **teşekkür, tesekkurler, mutlu** and **memnun** are very meaningful words for positive messages. These words may positively affect the classification performance. In particular, words **mutlu** and **memnun** are precise positive keywords.

Table 8. Kemik Natural Language Processing Group Tweets Data Set - The best-distinguishing terms according to the CHI metric

Category	positive	negative
Top 10 features	hayat (life)	mesaj
	superonline (company name)	hayat
	teşekkür (thanks)	paylaş
	paylaş (share)	fatura (bill)
	tesekkurler (thanks)	selocan (ad film character)
	mesaj (message)	hala (still)
	manga (group)	para (money)
	turkcellmuzik (turkcell is a gsm operator)	gnctrkcll (youth package belonging to gsm company)
	ödül (prize)	allah (god)
	fiber (fiber)	edge (edge)

Table 9. Kemik Natural Language Processing Group Tweets Data Set - The best-distinguishing terms according to the IG metric

Category	positive	negative
	hayat	mesaj
	superonline	hayat
	mesaj	paylaş
	paylaş	fatura
Top 10 features	teşekkür	selocan
	tesekkurler	hala
	ödül	para
	fiber	gnctrkcll
	mutlu (happy)	allah
	memnun (pleased)	ödül

Table 10 shows the top 10 features obtained from the 500 Opinion Column data set according to the CHI metric. When Table 10 is analyzed, according to the CHI metric, all keywords were selected differently from each other. The absence of common words for each author indicates that effective feature selection has been achieved.

Table 10. Kemik Natural Language Processing Group 500 Opinion Column Data Set - The best-distinguishing terms according to the CHI metric

Category	Cüneyt Özdemir	Ece Temelkuran	İlber Ortaylı	İsmail Küçükkaya	Mustafa Balbay	Uğur Dündar
	gözük (seem)	mühim (important)	imperator (imperial)	kritik (critical)	kasım (november)	okur (reader)
	yayımla (publish)	hala (still)	asır (century)	formül (formula)	vurgula (emphasise)	sevgi (love)
	çıkart (eject)	sebep (reason)	osmanlı (ottoman)	risk (risk)	sandık (chest)	dündar (author's surname)
	film	çünkü (because)	fransa (france)	washington (washington)	yelpaze (range)	yandaş (partisan)
Top 10 features	birkaç (some)	kere (times)	cihan (world)	olağanüstü (splendid)	tablo (table)	uğur (author's name)
	madem (as, since)	neşe (cheer)	vilayet (province)	küresel (global)	seçim (election)	operasyon (operation)
	bakın (look)	mesele (problem)	eski (old)	yönetim (management)	haziran (june)	vatan (motherland)
	bambaşka (disparate)	filan (and so on)	avusturya (austria)	stratejik (strategic)	ilişkin (related)	gözyaş (tear)
	twitter	ziyade (too much)	dahi (genius)	barış (peace)	sapta (determine)	iftira (slander)
	dair (about)	epey (quite)	tanzimat (reorganizations)	bölgesel (regional)	irade (will)	böylece (thus)

Table 11 shows the top 10 features obtained from the 500 Opinion Column data set according to the IG metric. When Table 11 is analyzed, according to the IG metric, all keywords were used differently from each other. The IG metric did not find any common keywords like the CHI metric.

Table 11. Kemik Natural Language Processing Group 500 Opinion Column Data Set - The best-distinguishing terms according to the IG metric

Category	Cüneyt Özdemir	Ece Temelkuran	İlber Ortaylı	İsmail Küçükkaya	Mustafa Balbay	Uğur Dündar
	yayımla	mühim	imparator	risk	kasım	okur
	çıkart	çünkü	asır	kritik	vurgula	sevgi
	gözük	sebep	osmanlı	formül	seçim	dündar
	birkaç	hala	eski	washington	sandık	yandaş
	parti	mesele	fransa	yönetim	tablo	uğur
	film	kere	bazı	küresel	ilişkin	operasyon
Top 10 features	fark (difference)	başkan	avusturya	olağanüstü	haziran	böylece
	bakın	türkiye (turkey)	dahi	barış	parlemento (legislative assembly)	vatan
	madem	öldür (kill)	ordu (military)	stratejik	sapta	gözyaş
	yine (once again)	filan	paşa	ekonomik (economical)	irade	iftira

When the keywords obtained from IG and CHI metrics were compared in the Opinion Column data set, seven keywords related to Cüneyt Özdemir were common to both IG and CHI. Different words found with CHI were **bambaşka**, **twitter** and **dair**. IG selects **parti**, **fark** and **yine**. In both metrics, **birkaç** was selected as a keyword. This word was selected by metrics because it was not included in the stop word list. However, **birkaç** can be considered a stop word. All authors can use this word. There is no distinguishing feature of the word **birkaç**. Similarly, since the words **çünkü**, **kere** and **böylece** are not in the stop words list, they appeared in the keywords table. When the author Ece Temelkuran was examined, both metrics found seven common words. The CHI metric selected **neşe**, **ziyade** and **epey**, while the IG metric selected **başkan**, **türkiye** and **öldür**. Considering these three different words, CHI emphasized words related to the sentence structure used by the author. However, IG extracted keywords about the author's topics. When the features of author İlber Ortaylı were examined, 7 out of 10 words were found by both CHI and IG. İlber Ortaylı writes about Ottoman history. Selected keywords were directly related to history. For this author, the IG metric found the words **cihan**, **vilayet** and **tanzimat**, while the CHI metric found the words **bazı**, **ordu** and **paşa**. Five words – except the word **bazı** – are very meaningful and distinctive keywords for this author. IG and CHI feature selection methods found the same nine keywords for author İsmail Küçükkaya. The different words found were **bölgesel** and **ekonomik**. The word **bölgesel** was selected by CHI and the word **ekonomik** by IG. If the keywords of the author Mustafa Balbay are evaluated, 9 common words were found by CHI and IG. While the word **yelpaze** was selected by CHI, IG selected the word **parlamento**. The words found by IG are more discriminating compared to CHI. All keywords of the author Uğur Dündar were the same. Both CHI and IG cannot find a difference for this author.

Comparison of the Performance of Classification Algorithms

The IG and CHI methods often select different features according to category. Due to these differences, feature vectors also differ. The performance of classification algorithms will change as a result of differences in the feature vector. In this subsection, the results were examined in two different ways. Firstly, classification performances are given according to the features obtained from the metrics. Secondly, the performance of classification algorithms were evaluated in their entirety. All figures given from Figure 4 to Figure 9 were drawn using the plot function of MATLAB (Matlab, 2020; Matlab Plot, 2020).

Figure 4 shows the results of the news data set. The CHI metric was used as a feature selection method in these results. SMO was the most successful classification algorithm when between 60 and 960 features are used. When the number of features was 60, the classification performance was 0.83 according to SMO.

Figure 4. Kemik Natural Language Processing Group News Data Set - Results from CHI metric

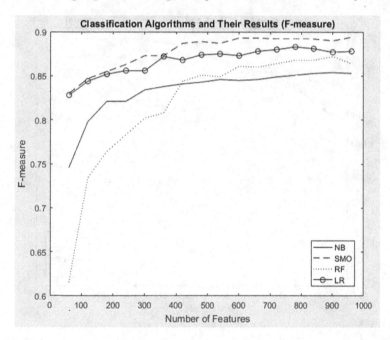

The classification performances obtained from NB, RF and LR algorithms for 60 features were 0.746, 0.616 and 0.828, respectively. The worst classification performance was achieved by the RF algorithm for up to 420 features. The RF algorithm outperformed the NB algorithm when the number of features exceeded 420. The best performance after the SMO algorithm was obtained by the LR algorithm. When the number of features was 780, the LR algorithm returned a value of 0.883. This result was the highest classification performance obtained by the LR algorithm. As the number of features increased, the performance of the algorithms generally increased. The best result obtained with the NB algorithm was 0.854. This result was obtained using 900 features. Similarly, the RF algorithm achieved the best results for 900 features, giving a result of 0.872.

Figure 5 shows the results of the news data set. The IG metric was used as a feature selection method for these results. SMO and LR were the most successful classification algorithms when 60 features were used. When the number of features was 60, the classification performance F-measure was 0.84 according to SMO and LR. The performance of the SMO algorithm outperformed the LR algorithm when using more than 60 features. The classification performances obtained from NB and RF for 60 features was 0.775 and 0.72, respectively. The worst classification performance was achieved by the RF algorithm. The RF algorithm outperformed the NB algorithm once the number of features exceeded 180. The best performance after the SMO algorithm was obtained by the LR algorithm. When the number of features was 840, the LR algorithm returned a value of 0.881. This result was the highest classification performance obtained by the LR algorithm. As the number of features increased, the performance of the algorithms generally increased. The best result obtained with the NB algorithm was 0.85. This result was obtained by using 900 features. The RF algorithm achieved the best results with 960 features with a value of 0.873.

Figure 5. Kemik Natural Language Processing Group News Data Set - Results from IG metric

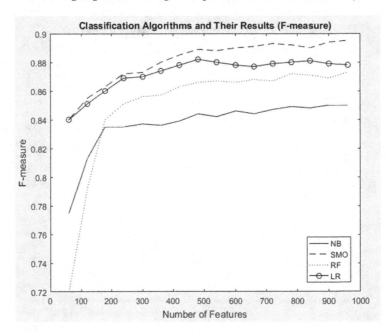

When Figure 4 and Figure 5 are taken into consideration, the IG metric gave better classification results than the CHI metric. This is the case when fewer features were used. Especially for the NB and RF algorithm, the result was more evident. For example, the NB algorithm gave a result of 0.746 in CHI with 60 features, while the NB algorithm using the same number of features returned a value of 0.775 with the IG method. When the RF algorithm was used instead of NB, the results were 0.616 and 0.72, respectively. These results showed that the keywords selected with the IG metric had a positive effect on classification performance. As the number of features increased, this difference in classification performance gradually decreased and the results converged. Considering the results from both metrics, the best results were obtained by the SMO algorithm with the IG metric for 960 features. This result was an F-measure of 0.895.

Figure 6 shows the results for the Tweets data set. The CHI metric was used as a feature selection method for these results. The highest performance was obtained by the RF algorithm. This result was 0.781 when 20 features were used. This result was also the best in Figure 6. The best result after the RF algorithm was obtained by the NB algorithm. Classification performance usually decreased when feature size increased with this dataset. This was because keywords were not distinctive for tweet messages. It also represented a different problem because the message size was short and there were many misspelled words. Since only word-based feature extraction was used, the classification algorithm could not distinguish the tweets messages well.

Figure 6. Kemik Natural Language Processing Group Tweets Data Set - Results from CHI metric

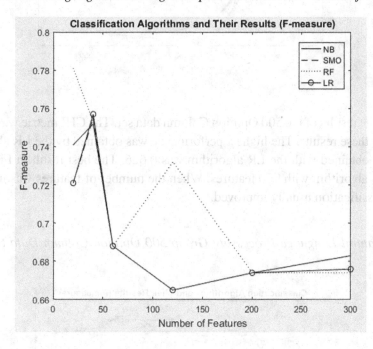

Figure 7 shows the results of the Tweets data set. The IG metric was used as the feature selection method in these results. The highest performance was obtained by the RF algorithm. This result was 0.767 when 20 features were used. This result was also the best in Figure 7. The best results after the RF algorithm were obtained by the NB and SMO algorithms. Classification performance decreased when feature size increased with this dataset.

When Figure 6 and Figure 7 were examined, the CHI gave better classification results than the IG metric. The differences between CHI and IG metrics were not important. For example, the NB algorithm gave a result of 0.741 in CHI with 20 features, while using the same number of features with the NB algorithm returned a value of 0.736 with the IG method. This also applied to the other algorithms.

Figure 7. Kemik Natural Language Processing Group Tweets Data Set - Results from IG metric

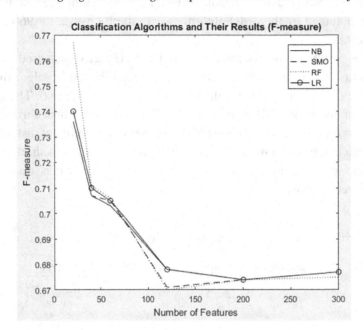

Figure 8 shows the results of the 500 Opinion Column data set. The CHI metric was used as a feature selection method in these results. The highest performance was obtained by the LR algorithm using 60 features. The result obtained with the LR algorithm was 0.626. The best result in Figure 8 was 0.778 obtained by the NB algorithm with 960 features. When the number of features was increased, the performance of the classification usually improved.

Figure 8. Kemik Natural Language Processing Group 500 Opinion Column Data Set - Results from CHI metric

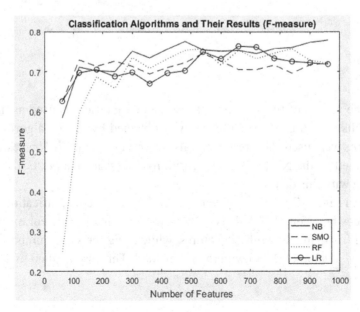

Figure 9 shows the results of the 500 Opinion Column data set. The IG metric was used as a feature selection method in these results. The highest performance was obtained by the SMO and LR algorithms using 60 features. The result obtained with the SMO and LR algorithms was 0.642. The best result in Figure 9 was 0.809 obtained by the NB algorithm using 660 and 720 features. When the number of features increased, the performance of the classification usually improved.

Figure 9. Kemik Natural Language Processing Group 500 Opinion Column Data Set - Results from IG metric

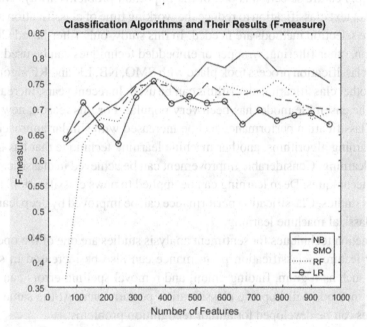

When Figure 8 and Figure 9 were examined, the IG metric gave better classification results than the CHI metric. This was the case when fewer features were used. Especially for the NB and RF algorithms, the result was more evident. For example, the NB algorithm gave a result of 0.584 in CHI with 60 features, while the NB algorithm using the same number of features returned a value of 0.63 with the IG method. When the RF algorithm was used instead of NB, the results were 0.25 and 0.367, respectively. These results showed that the keywords selected with the IG metric had a positive effect on the classification performance when fewer features were selected in comparison to the CHI metric. As the number of features increased, this difference in classification performance gradually decreased and the results converged. When the numbers of features were increased, the performance of the classification algorithms in the CHI metric usually improved. Considering the results from both metrics, the best results were obtained using the NB algorithm with the IG metric for 660 and 720 features. These results gave an F-measure of 0.809.

FUTURE RESEARCH DIRECTIONS

In text classification studies, researchers generally focus on two problems. The first is to increase the classification performance, while the second is to reduce the working time of the classification algorithms. In order to increase the classification performance, only TF-IDF term weighting technique was used in this study. However, there are many term weighting models in published literature. Therefore, classification performances can be improved by using different term weighting approaches. Many researchers also endeavour to develop new term weighting models. Therefore, a new term weighting model may appear in published literature. Feature selection is one of the important problems always waiting for effective solutions in the field of text classification to reduce the working time of classification algorithms. Therefore, effective feature selection methods are needed. In this study, only filter-based CHI and IG metrics were used. In addition, other filtering, wrapper or embedded techniques can be used.

In this study, the classification process took place with SMO, NB, LR and RF algorithms. In addition to these algorithms, other classification algorithms can be used. In recent years, increasing classification performance using the ensemble model has been very popular. For this reason, new ensemble models can be developed. Classification performance can be increased with similar approaches. In addition to classical machine learning algorithms, another machine learning technique that has become popular in recent years is deep learning. Considerable improvement can be achieved in classification achievements using deep learning techniques. Deep learning can be applied to news classification, author recognition and emotion analysis studies. Classification performance can be improved by deep learning, which gives better results than classical machine learning.

New feature extraction techniques for sentiment analysis studies are one of the open problems. With the addition of new features, classification performance can also be increased in sentiment analysis studies. Techniques such as n-gram, finding emoji, and removal spelling errors can be added to emotion analysis. These methods will improve classification performance. At the same time, new feature extraction approaches can be developed for author recognition problems.

CONCLUSION

In this study, a comprehensive Turkish text mining study has been presented. These are the classification of Turkish news, Turkish sentiment analysis and Turkish author recognition studies. It attempted to solve three different problems with classical machine learning techniques. Also, feature selection methods were tried to reduce the execution time of machine learning algorithms to obtain related keywords. In classifying news categories and opinion columns, more than 80% of classification performance was achieved. Nearly 90% success was achieved in separating news categories. In sentiment analysis, the classification performance did not exceed 78.1%. While it is enough to classify the news and authors, it is not enough to use words as a feature in sentiment analysis. The most successful result was generally obtained by the SMO algorithm when considering the keywords selected by both the IG metric and the CHI metric in the classification of news texts. When the feature selection methods were compared, the highest classification performance was found using the IG metric. After the SMO algorithm, the LR algorithm was the most successful algorithm. Compared to the NB algorithm and the RF algorithm, the NB algorithm gave better results when using fewer features. Nevertheless, as the number of features increased, the performance of the RF algorithm was better. Considering the keywords extracted from both the IG metric and the CHI metric in author recognition, the most successful result was usually obtained from the NB algorithm.

When the feature selection methods were compared, the highest classification performance was found using the IG metric. It would not be correct to make a general comparison for the performance of other algorithms other than the NB algorithm because the RF algorithm had the worst performance when the number of attributes was low. However, as the number of attributes increased, the performance of the RF algorithm often exceeded the LR and SMO algorithm.

Considering the keywords extracted from both the IG metric and the CHI metric in the sentiment analysis, the most successful result was generally obtained from the RF algorithm. When the feature selection methods were compared, the highest classification performance was found using the CHI metric. It would not be correct to make a general comparison for the performance of other algorithms other than the RF algorithm because the performance of the algorithms is almost the same. Considering the three different problems discussed in the study, it was seen that the classification performance obtained for sentiment analysis was lower than the others. Therefore, emotion analysis performance needs to be improved.

REFERENCES

Abdullah, S. S., Rahaman, M. S., & Rahman, M. S. (2013). Analysis of stock market using text mining and natural language processing. In *2013 International Conference on Informatics, Electronics and Vision (ICIEV)* (pp. 1-6). IEEE. 10.1109/ICIEV.2013.6572673

AbuZeina, D., & Al-Anzi, F. S. (2018). Employing fisher discriminant analysis for Arabic text classification. *Computers & Electrical Engineering*, *66*, 474–486. doi:10.1016/j.compeleceng.2017.11.002

Aggarwal, C. C., & Zhai, C. (2012). A survey of text classification algorithms. In *Mining text data* (pp. 163–222). Springer. doi:10.1007/978-1-4614-3223-4_6

Alpkoçak, A., Tocoglu, M. A., Çelikten, A., & Aygün, İ. (2019). Türkçe Metinlerde Duygu Analizi için Farklı Makine Öğrenmesi Yöntemlerinin Karşılaştırılması. *Dokuz Eylül Üniversitesi Mühendislik Fakültesi Fen ve Mühendislik Dergisi*, *21*(63), 719–725. doi:10.21205/deufmd.2019216303

Amasyalı, M. F., & Diri, B. (2006). Automatic Turkish text categorization in terms of author, genre and gender. In *International Conference on Application of Natural Language to Information Systems* (pp. 221-226). Springer. 10.1007/11765448_22

Apté, C., Damerau, F., & Weiss, S. M. (1994). Automated learning of decision rules for text categorization. *ACM Transactions on Information Systems*, *12*(3), 233–251. doi:10.1145/183422.183423

Artemenko, O., Mandl, T., Shramko, M., & Womser-Hacker, C. (2006). Evaluation of a language identification system for mono-and multilingual text documents. In *Proceedings of the 2006 ACM symposium on Applied computing* (pp. 859-860). ACM. 10.1145/1141277.1141473

Aydoğan, M., & Karci, A. (2019). Kelime Temsil Yöntemleri ile Kelime Benzerliklerinin İncelenmesi. *Çukurova Üniversitesi Mühendislik-Mimarlık Fakültesi Dergisi*, *34*(2), 181-196.

Babbel Magazine. (2020). *The 10 most spoken languages in the world.* Retrieved from https://www. babbel.com/en/magazine/the-10-most-spoken-languages-in-the-world

Bekkerman, R., El-Yaniv, R., Tishby, N., & Winter, Y. (2001). On feature distributional clustering for text categorization. *Proceedings of the 24th annual international ACM SIGIR conference on Research and development in information retrieval*, 146-153. 10.1145/383952.383976

Berry, M. W. (2004). Survey of text mining. *Computer Review, 45*(9), 548.

Blei, D. M., Ng, A. Y., & Jordan, M. I. (2003). Latent dirichlet allocation. *Journal of Machine Learning Research, 3*(Jan), 993–1022.

Cabezudo, M. A. S., Palomino, N. L. S., & Perez, R. M. (2015). Improving subjectivity detection for Spanish texts using subjectivity word sense disambiguation based on knowledge. In *2015 Latin American Computing Conference (CLEI)* (pp. 1-7). IEEE. 10.1109/CLEI.2015.7360018

Cadez, I., Heckerman, D., Meek, C., Smyth, P., & White, S. (2003). Model-based clustering and visualization of navigation patterns on a web site. *Data Mining and Knowledge Discovery, 7*(4), 399–424. doi:10.1023/A:1024992613384

Carreón, E. C. A., Nonaka, H., & Hiraoka, T. (2019). *Analysis of Chinese Tourists in Japan by Text Mining of a Hotel Portal Site.* arXiv preprint arXiv:1904.13214.

Çetin, M., & Amasyalı, M. F. (2013). Supervised and traditional term weighting methods for sentiment analysis. In *2013 21st Signal Processing and Communications Applications Conference (SIU)* (pp. 1-4). IEEE. 10.1109/SIU.2013.6531173

Chen, Y., Qin, B., Liu, T., Liu, Y., & Li, S. (2010). The Comparison of SOM and K-means for Text Clustering. *Computer and Information Science, 3*(2), 268–274. doi:10.5539/cis.v3n2p268

Çiğdem, A., & Çirak, A. (2019). Türkçe Haber Metinlerinin Konvolüsyonel Sinir Ağları ve Word2Vec Kullanılarak Sınıflandırılması. *Bilişim Teknolojileri Dergisi, 12*(3), 219–228.

Clark, J., Koprinska, I., & Poon, J. (2003). A neural network-based approach to automated e-mail classification. In *Proceedings IEEE/WIC International Conference on Web Intelligence (WI 2003)* (pp. 702-705). IEEE. 10.1109/WI.2003.1241300

Cutting, D. R., Karger, D. R., Pedersen, J. O., & Tukey, J. W. (2017). Scatter/gather: A cluster-based approach to browsing large document collections. In *ACM SIGIR Forum* (Vol. 51, No. 2, pp. 148-159). New York, NY: ACM.

Dasgupta, S., & Ng, V. (2009). Topic-wise, sentiment-wise, or otherwise?: Identifying the hidden dimension for unsupervised text classification. In *Proceedings of the 2009 Conference on Empirical Methods in Natural Language Processing* (vol. 2, pp. 580-589). Association for Computational Linguistics.

DataReportal. (2020). *Digital 2020 report for Turkey.* Retrieved from https://datareportal.com/reports/digital-2020-turkey

Deng, L. (2014). A tutorial survey of architectures, algorithms, and applications for deep learning. *APSIPA Transactions on Signal and Information Processing, 3*, 3. doi:10.1017/atsip.2013.9

Dogan, T., & Uysal, A. K. (2019). On Term Frequency Factor in Supervised Term Weighting Schemes for Text Classification. *Arabian Journal for Science and Engineering, 44*(11), 1–16. doi:10.100713369-019-03920-9

Dos Santos, C., & Gatti, M. (2014). Deep convolutional neural networks for sentiment analysis of short texts. In *Proceedings of COLING 2014, the 25th International Conference on Computational Linguistics: Technical Papers* (pp. 69-78). Academic Press.

Elnagar, A., Al-Debsi, R., & Einea, O. (2020). Arabic text classification using deep learning models. *Information Processing & Management, 57*(1), 102121. doi:10.1016/j.ipm.2019.102121

Eryiğit, G. (2014). ITU Turkish NLP web service. In *Proceedings of the Demonstrations at the 14th Conference of the European Chapter of the Association for Computational Linguistics* (pp. 1-4). Academic Press.

Estival, D., Gaustad, T., Pham, S. B., Radford, W., & Hutchinson, B. (2007). Author profiling for English emails. In *Proceedings of the 10th Conference of the Pacific Association for Computational Linguistics* (pp. 263-272). Academic Press.

Fattah, M. A., & Ren, F. (2008). Automatic text summarization. *World Academy of Science, Engineering and Technology, 37*(2), 192.

Göker, H., & Tekedere, H. (2017). FATİH Projesine Yönelik Görüşlerin Metin Madenciliği Yöntemleri İle Otomatik Değerlendirilmesi. *Bilişim Teknolojileri Dergisi, 10*(3), 291–299. doi:10.17671/gazibtd.331041

Harrag, F., El-Qawasmeh, E., & Pichappan, P. (2009). Improving Arabic text categorization using decision trees. In *2009 First International Conference on Networked Digital Technologies* (pp. 110-115). IEEE. 10.1109/NDT.2009.5272214

Hassani, H., Huang, X., & Silva, E. (2018). Digitalisation and big data mining in banking. *Big Data and Cognitive Computing, 2*(3), 18. doi:10.3390/bdcc2030018

Hofmann, T. (2013). *Probabilistic latent semantic analysis.* arXiv preprint arXiv:1301.6705

Hsu, H. H., Hsieh, C. W., & Lu, M. D. (2011). Hybrid feature selection by combining filters and wrappers. *Expert Systems with Applications, 38*(7), 8144–8150. doi:10.1016/j.eswa.2010.12.156

Hüsem, S. Ş., & Gülcü, A. (2017). Categorizing the Turkish web pages by data mining techniques. *In 2017 International Conference on Computer Science and Engineering (UBMK)* (pp. 255-260). IEEE. 10.1109/UBMK.2017.8093385

ITU NLP Toolkit. (2020). *ITU Turkish Natural Language Processing Pipeline.* Retrieved from http://tools.nlp.itu.edu.tr/index.jsp

Joachims, T. (1998). Text categorization with support vector machines: Learning with many relevant features. In *European conference on machine learning* (pp. 137-142). Springer.

Jones, K. S. (1972). A Statistical Interpretation of Term Specificity and its Retrieval. *The Journal of Documentation, 28*(1), 11–21. doi:10.1108/eb026526

Jones, K. S. (2004). A Statistical Interpretation of Term Specificity and its Retrieval. *The Journal of Documentation, 60*(5), 493–502. doi:10.1108/00220410410560573

Kadhim, A. I. (2019). Survey on supervised machine learning techniques for automatic text classification. *Artificial Intelligence Review, 52*(1), 273–292. doi:10.100710462-018-09677-1

Kaynar, O., Arslan, H., Görmez, Y., & Demirkoparan, F. (2017). Feature selection methods in sentiment analysis. In *2017 International Artificial Intelligence and Data Processing Symposium (IDAP)* (pp. 1-5). IEEE.

Ke, Y., & Hagiwara, M. (2017). An English neural network that learns texts, finds hidden knowledge, and answers questions. *Journal of Artificial Intelligence and Soft Computing Research, 7*(4), 229–242. doi:10.1515/jaiscr-2017-0016

Keleş, M. K., & Özel, S. A. (2017). Similarity detection between Turkish text documents with distance metrics. In *2017 International Conference on Computer Science and Engineering (UBMK)* (pp. 316-321). IEEE. 10.1109/UBMK.2017.8093399

Khedr, A. E., & Yaseen, N. (2017). Predicting stock market behavior using data mining technique and news sentiment analysis. *International Journal of Intelligent Systems and Applications, 9*(7), 22–30. doi:10.5815/ijisa.2017.07.03

Kibriya, A. M., Frank, E., Pfahringer, B., & Holmes, G. (2004). Multinomial naive Bayes for text categorization revisited. In *Australasian Joint Conference on Artificial Intelligence* (pp. 488-499). Springer. 10.1007/978-3-540-30549-1_43

Kılınç, D., Özçift, A., Bozyigit, F., Yıldırım, P., Yücalar, F., & Borandag, E. (2017). TTC-3600: A new benchmark dataset for Turkish text categorization. *Journal of Information Science, 43*(2), 174–185. doi:10.1177/0165551515620551

Kuyumcu, B., Buluz, B., & Kömeçoğlu, Y. (2019). Author Identification in Turkish Documents with Ridge Regression Analysis. In *2019 27th Signal Processing and Communications Applications Conference (SIU)* (pp. 1-4). IEEE.

Lan, M., Tan, C. L., Su, J., & Lu, Y. (2008). Supervised and traditional term weighting methods for automatic text categorization. *IEEE Transactions on Pattern Analysis and Machine Intelligence, 31*(4), 721–735. doi:10.1109/TPAMI.2008.110 PMID:19229086

Leaman, R., Khare, R., & Lu, Z. (2015). Challenges in clinical natural language processing for automated disorder normalization. *Journal of Biomedical Informatics, 57*, 28–37. doi:10.1016/j.jbi.2015.07.010 PMID:26187250

Li, Y., Wang, X., & Xu, P. (2018). Chinese text classification model based on deep learning. *Future Internet, 10*(11), 113. doi:10.3390/fi10110113

Liu, J., Xia, C., Yan, H., Xie, Z., & Sun, J. (2019). Hierarchical Comprehensive Context Modeling for Chinese Text Classification. *IEEE Access: Practical Innovations, Open Solutions, 7*, 154546–154559. doi:10.1109/ACCESS.2019.2949175

Liu, Y., Yi, X., Chen, R., Zhai, Z., & Gu, J. (2018). Feature extraction based on information gain and sequential pattern for English question classification. *IET Software, 12*(6), 520–526. doi:10.1049/iet-sen.2018.0006

Martínez-Cámara, E., Martín-Valdivia, M. T., Ureña-López, L. A., & Mitkov, R. (2015). Polarity classification for Spanish tweets using the COST corpus. *Journal of Information Science, 41*(3), 263–272. doi:10.1177/0165551514566564

Matlab. (2020). *The official home of MATLAB software.* Retrieved from https://www.mathworks.com/products/matlab.html

Matlab Plot. (2020). *2-D line plot - MATLAB plot.* Retrieved from https://www.mathworks.com/help/matlab/ref/plot.html

Mayda, İ., & Amasyalı, M. F. (2016). Cross usage of articles and tweets on author identification. In 2016 Electric Electronics, Computer Science, Biomedical Engineerings' Meeting (EBBT) (pp. 1-4). IEEE. doi:10.1109/EBBT.2016.7483676

Molina-González, M. D., Martínez-Cámara, E., Martín-Valdivia, M. T., & Ureña-López, L. A. (2015). A Spanish semantic orientation approach to domain adaptation for polarity classification. *Information Processing & Management, 51*(4), 520–531. doi:10.1016/j.ipm.2014.10.002

News Data Set. (2019). *Kemik Natural Language Processing Group Tweets Data Set.* Retrieved from www.kemik.yildiz.edu.tr

Özgür, A., Özgür, L., & Güngör, T. (2005). Text categorization with class-based and corpus-based keyword selection. In *International Symposium on Computer and Information Sciences* (pp. 606-615). Springer.

Özgür, L., Güngör, T., & Gürgen, F. (2004). Adaptive anti-spam filtering for agglutinative languages: A special case for Turkish. *Pattern Recognition Letters, 25*(16), 1819–1831. doi:10.1016/j.patrec.2004.07.004

Plaza-del-Arco, F. M., Martín-Valdivia, M. T., Ureña-López, L. A., & Mitkov, R. (2019). Improved emotion recognition in spanish social media through incorporation of lexical knowledge. *Future Generation Computer Systems*.

Porter Stemmer. (2019). *The Porter Stemming Algorithm.* Retrieved from https://tartarus.org/martin/PorterStemmer/

Rong, M., Gong, D., & Gao, X. (2019). Feature Selection and Its Use in Big Data: Challenges, Methods, and Trends. *IEEE Access: Practical Innovations, Open Solutions, 7*, 19709–19725. doi:10.1109/ACCESS.2019.2894366

Ruiz, M. E., & Srinivasan, P. (1998). Automatic text categorization using neural networks. In *Proceedings of the 8th ASIS SIG/CR Workshop on Classification Research* (pp. 59-72). Academic Press.

Şahin, D. Ö., & Kılıç, E. (2019). Two new feature selection metrics for text classification. *Automatika (Zagreb), 60*(2), 162–171. doi:10.1080/00051144.2019.1602293

Salloum, S. A., AlHamad, A. Q., Al-Emran, M., & Shaalan, K. (2018). A survey of Arabic text mining. In *Intelligent Natural Language Processing: Trends and Applications* (pp. 417–431). Springer. doi:10.1007/978-3-319-67056-0_20

Salton, G., & Buckley, C. (1988). Term-weighting approaches in automatic text retrieval. *Information Processing & Management*, 24(5), 513–523. doi:10.1016/0306-4573(88)90021-0

Salton, G., Singhal, A., Mitra, M., & Buckley, C. (1997). Automatic text structuring and summarization. *Information Processing & Management*, 33(2), 193–207. doi:10.1016/S0306-4573(96)00062-3

Sebastiani, F. (2002). Machine learning in automated text categorization. *ACM Computing Surveys*, 34(1), 1–47. doi:10.1145/505282.505283

Shafiabady, N., Lee, L. H., Rajkumar, R., Kallimani, V. P., Akram, N. A., & Isa, D. (2016). Using unsupervised clustering approach to train the Support Vector Machine for text classification. *Neurocomputing*, 211, 4–10. doi:10.1016/j.neucom.2015.10.137

Shah, K. B., Shetty, M. S., Shah, D. P., & Pamnani, R. (2017). Approaches towards building a banking assistant. *International Journal of Computers and Applications*, 166(11), 1–6. doi:10.5120/ijca2017914140

Shi, L., Jianping, C., & Jie, X. (2018). Prospecting information extraction by text mining based on convolutional neural networks–a case study of the Lala copper deposit, China. *IEEE Access: Practical Innovations, Open Solutions*, 6, 52286–52297. doi:10.1109/ACCESS.2018.2870203

Soricut, R., & Brill, E. (2006). Automatic question answering using the web: Beyond the factoid. *Information Retrieval*, 9(2), 191–206. doi:10.100710791-006-7149-y

Stamatatos, E., Fakotakis, N., & Kokkinakis, G. (2000). Automatic text categorization in terms of genre and author. *Computational Linguistics*, 26(4), 471–495. doi:10.1162/089120100750105920

Sun, A., Lim, E. P., & Ng, W. K. (2002). Web classification using support vector machine. In *Proceedings of the 4th international workshop on Web information and data management* (pp. 96-99). ACM.

Tantuğ, A. C., & Eryiğit, G. (2006). Performance Analysis of Naïve Bayes Classification, Support Vector Machines and Neural Networks for Spam Categorization. In *Applied Soft Computing Technologies: The Challenge of Complexity* (pp. 495–504). Springer. doi:10.1007/3-540-31662-0_38

Tasci, S., & Gungor, T. (2008). An evaluation of existing and new feature selection metrics in text categorization. In *2008 23rd International Symposium on Computer and Information Sciences* (pp. 1-6). IEEE.

Taşcı, Ş., & Güngör, T. (2013). Comparison of text feature selection policies and using an adaptive framework. *Expert Systems with Applications*, 40(12), 4871–4886. doi:10.1016/j.eswa.2013.02.019

Tripathi, P., Vishwakarma, S. K., & Lala, A. (2015). Sentiment analysis of english tweets using rapid miner. In *2015 International Conference on Computational Intelligence and Communication Networks (CICN)* (pp. 668-672). IEEE.

Turkish N. L. P. Toolkit. (2020). *Turkish Natural Language Processing Toolkit*. Retrieved from http://haydut.isikun.edu.tr/nlptoolkit.html

Willett, P. (1988). Recent trends in hierarchic document clustering: A critical review. *Information Processing & Management*, 24(5), 577–597. doi:10.1016/0306-4573(88)90027-1

Xing, F. Z., Cambria, E., & Welsch, R. E. (2018). Natural language based financial forecasting: A survey. *Artificial Intelligence Review*, 50(1), 49–73. doi:10.100710462-017-9588-9

Yang, Y. (1999). An evaluation of statistical approaches to text categorization. *Information Retrieval*, 1(1-2), 69–90. doi:10.1023/A:1009982220290

Yıldırım, S., & Yıldız, T. (2018). Türkçe için karşılaştırmalı metin sınıflandırma analizi. *Pamukkale Üniversitesi Mühendislik Bilimleri Dergisi*, 24(5), 879–886.

Yıldız, B., & Ağdeniz, Ş. (2018). Muhasebede Analiz Yöntemi Olarak Metin Madenciliği. *World of Accounting Science*, 20(2), 286–315.

Zemberek. (2019). *Zemberek Natural Language Processing Tool*. Retrieved from https://code.google.com/archive/p/zemberek/

Zhang, L., & Chen, C. (2016). Sentiment classification with convolutional neural networks: An experimental study on a large-scale chinese conversation corpus. In *2016 12th International Conference on Computational Intelligence and Security (CIS)* (pp. 165-169). IEEE.

ADDITIONAL READING

Aggarwal, C. C., & Zhai, C. (Eds.). (2012). *Mining text data*. Springer Science & Business Media. doi:10.1007/978-1-4614-3223-4

Cambria, E., & White, B. (2014). Jumping NLP curves: A review of natural language processing research. *IEEE Computational Intelligence Magazine*, 9(2), 48–57. doi:10.1109/MCI.2014.2307227

Deng, X., Li, Y., Weng, J., & Zhang, J. (2019). Feature selection for text classification: A review. *Multimedia Tools and Applications*, 78(3), 3797–3816. doi:10.100711042-018-6083-5

Forman, G. (2003). An extensive empirical study of feature selection metrics for text classification. *Journal of Machine Learning Research*, 3(Mar), 1289–1305.

Jones, K. S. (2004). A Statistical Interpretation of Term Specificity and its Retrieval. *The Journal of Documentation*, 60(5), 493–502. doi:10.1108/00220410410560573

Lan, M., Tan, C. L., Su, J., & Lu, Y. (2008). Supervised and traditional term weighting methods for automatic text categorization. *IEEE Transactions on Pattern Analysis and Machine Intelligence*, 31(4), 721–735. doi:10.1109/TPAMI.2008.110 PMID:19229086

Otter, D. W., Medina, J. R., & Kalita, J. K. (2020). A Survey of the Usages of Deep Learning for Natural Language Processing. *IEEE Transactions on Neural Networks and Learning Systems*, 1–21. doi:10.1109/TNNLS.2020.2979670 PMID:32324570

Sebastiani, F. (2002). Machine learning in automated text categorization. [CSUR]. *ACM Computing Surveys*, *34*(1), 1–47. doi:10.1145/505282.505283

Zhai, C., & Massung, S. (2016). *Text data management and analysis: a practical introduction to information retrieval and text mining*. Association for Computing Machinery and Morgan & Claypool.

KEY TERMS AND DEFINITIONS

Feature: A structure that characterizes a system, an object, or a class and makes it distinct is called a feature.

Feature Extraction: It is a method frequently used in learning and image processing applications. In the field of text mining, it can be thought of as obtaining the words in the document.

Feature Selection: It is selecting and finding the most useful features in a data set. In other words, instead of using all the features in a data set, a subset of all features is obtained and used. It can also be considered as dimension reduction techniques.

N-Gram: They are words that consist of n-element subsets of a word. If N is equal to 1, 2, and 3, N-gram is called unigram, bigram, and trigram, respectively.

Stop Words: Stop words do not contribute to understanding because they are used very often.

Supervised Learning: It is a machine learning technique. It generates a function to match the inputs to the desired outputs.

Tokenization: Tokenization is defined as dividing a sentence into smaller meaningful units. Tokens are meaningful small units. Words, idioms can be given as examples of tokens.

Unsupervised Learning: It is a machine learning technique. It is used to estimate an unknown structure from unlabeled data.

This research was previously published in Natural Language Processing for Global and Local Business; pages 272-306, copyright year 2021 by Business Science Reference (an imprint of IGI Global).

Section 3
Tools and Technologies

Chapter 38
Tools of Opinion Mining

Neha Gupta

https://orcid.org/0000-0003-0905-5457

Manav Rachna International Institute of Research and Studies, India

Siddharth Verma

Manav Rachna International Institute of Research and Studies, India

ABSTRACT

Today's generation express their views and opinions publicly. For any organization or for individuals, this feedback is very crucial to improve their products and services. This huge volume of reviews can be analyzed by opinion mining (also known as semantic analysis). It is an emerging field for researchers that aims to distinguish the emotions expressed within the reviews, classifying them into positive or negative opinions, and summarizing it into a form that is easily understood by users. The idea of opinion mining and sentiment analysis tool is to process a set of search results for a given item based on the quality and features. Research has been conducted to mine opinions in form of document, sentence, and feature level sentiment analysis. This chapter examines how opinion mining is moving to the sentimental reviews of Twitter data, comments used in Facebook on pictures, videos, or Facebook statuses. Thus, this chapter discusses an overview of opinion mining in detail with the techniques and tools.

INTRODUCTION

Social networks have become part of our digital life and have changed the way we communicate significantly. There are 255 million of websites on the internet and therefore a lot of facts and opinions are available for companies and customers. Everybody is able to publish subjective information about products, brands and companies. The exchange of information and opinions of consumers on the Web 2.0 also means that a greater confidence in the products, brands and services are created, which e.g. in the e-commerce -sector leads to a higher purchase probability. Therefore it is very important that companies are able to find, extract and analyze this user generated content, because these contents contain significant "real" market relevant data. Furthermore it is an easy and cheap way to gain a current market

DOI: 10.4018/978-1-6684-6303-1.ch038

overview to generate new strategic, tactical and operational plans and policies as well as creating relevant brand messages.

Opinion Mining deals with scientific methods in order to find, extract, and systematically analyze product, company or brand related views on the internet. The identification of sentiment orientation (positive, neutral and negative) of consumers' Opinions is an essential part of the opinion mining process.

PROCESS MODEL OF OPINION MINING

The following process model describes steps, methods and tools to find, extract and analyze web data with regard to their sentiment orientation:

1. Selection of relevant data source
2. Selection of relevant method and tool to analyze the data
3. Pre-processing and pre-structuring of the contents on basis of the chosen methods
4. Transformation of the text in standard and further processed structure
5. Analyzing the content in relation to its semantic orientation
6. Evaluation of the methods and tools

Table 1 outlines commonly used methods and tools for each process step.

Table 1. Methods and tools for various steps of opinion mining

Step	Method (examples)	Tools (examples)
Selection of relevant data	1. Information retrieval on Web 2. Relevance Index	1. WebCrawler 2. RSS feeds, 3. APIs for gathering data
Preprocessing	Thesaurus, Ontologies, Tokenizer, Stemmer, Screen scrapper	1. RDF-OWL, 2. Alchemy API 3. GATE 4. UIMA 5. GETESS 6. Openthesaurus.de
Transformation	Part of speech tagger, Sentence splitter, Orthographic co-references	1. Tree Tagger 2. Sentence splitter, 3. Orthographic co-references
Analysis	Classification methods based on document or sentence level	1. Opinion Observer 2. Rapid Miner
Evaluation	Manual classification of sentiment orientation and feedback	

VARIOUS DATA SOURCES AVAILABLE FOR OPINION MINING

There are various data sources available on web, i.e. Blogs, Micro blogs, online posts, News feeds, Forums, review sites etc.

- **Blogs:** Blogs are nothing but the user own space or diary on internet where they can share their views, opinions about topics they want. Example indianbloggers.org, bloggersideas.com, digital-trends.com
- **Online Reviews:** On Internet various review sites are available through that you can check online reviews of any product before purchasing that. Example sitejabber.com, toptenreviews.com, trustedreviews.com, in.pinterest.com
- **Micro Blogging:** Micro blogs allow users to exchange small elements of content such as short sentences, individual images, or video links", which may be the major reason for their popularity. Example twitter.com, jaiku.com, qaiku.com
- **Online Posts:** people share their own ideas, opinions, photos, videos, views, likes, dislikes, comments on specific topics etc. example facebook.com, myspace.com, skype.com, linkedin.com, plus.google.com, whatsapp.com, snapchat.com
- **Forums:** An Internet forum, or message board, is an online discussion site where people can hold conversations in the form of posted messages. Example forums.mysql.com, forums.cnet.com, forum.joomla.org, forums.digitalpoint.com, bookforum.com

VARIOUS TOOLS OF OPINION MINING

A wide variety of tools of opinion mining are available in the market for various purposes like data preprocessing, classification of text, clustering, opinion mining, sentiment analysis etc. List of various tools are:

1. Stanford CoreNLP
2. WEKA
3. NLTK (Python Framework)
4. Apache Open NLP
5. LingPipe
6. Gate
7. Pattern (Python Framework)
8. Opinion Finder

In this book chapter we will be discussing WEKA and NLTK (Python Framework) in detail.

NLTK

NLTK stand for natural language tool kit. It is a leading platform for building Python programs to work with human language data. It provides easy-to-use interfaces to over 50 corpora and lexical resources such as WordNet, along with a suite of text processing libraries for classification, tokenization, stemming, tagging, parsing, and semantic reasoning, wrappers for industrial-strength NLP libraries, and an active discussion forum.

NLTK includes graphical demonstrations and sample data. It is accompanied by a book that explains the underlying concepts behind the language processing tasks supported by the toolkit plus a cookbook. NLTK is intended to support research and teaching in NLP or closely related areas, including empirical linguistics, cognitive science, artificial intelligence, information retrieval, and machine learning. NLTK has been used successfully as a teaching tool, as an individual study tool, and as a platform for prototyping and building research systems. The various steps of NLTK toolkit are:

1. **Tokenization:** A Tokenizer in NLTK follows tokenization approach in natural language understanding by splitting a string into its sub-classes. It provides a lexical scanner that handles all the operators and delimiters.

    Eg: A tokenizer tokenizes sentence into its morphological forms as given: "this is a dog" is tokenized to 'this','is','a','dog' which are the individual tokens generated.

2. **Stemming:** The idea of stemming in natural language processing is a sort of normalizing method. A word can vary and have different variations.

Eg: I was studying at night.
   I studied at night.
   I study.

So verb study has three variations above which can be stemmed to its root or canonical form. Hence studying is brought to its root form study which is shown below in the illustration.

Studying---Study

It can be either prefix stemming or suffix stemming which brings word to its root form. So it is a processing interface that removes suffixes and prefixes from the word and bring it down to its affix form. In NLTK toolkit stem (token) is an interface incorporated in NLTK for stemming

3. **C. Segmentation:** Sentence tokenizer or Sentence disambiguation is also known as sentence breaking or segmentation into its constituent words or tokens.

    Eg: "Hello Sam. How are you." is segmented to two sentences: Hello Sam, How are you.

4. **D. Collocation:** Collocations as defined by (Navgli, 2009) are the words that occur commonly in same context and frequently. For example, the top ten bi-gram collocations in Genesis are listed below, as measured using Point-wise Mutual Information.

Collocation or lexical collocation means two or more words co-occur in a sentence more frequently than by chance. A collocation is an expression that forms a specific meaning. It may be noun phrase like large villa, verbal phrase like go down, idioms, or technical terms. Collocations are defined by constricted compositionality, that is, it is difficult to predict the meaning of collocation from the meaning of its parts. For example,

He is known for his **fair** and **square** dealings and everybody trusts his work.

Here **fair** and **square** means honest but if we take the individual words though the word fair gives somewhat closer meaning as it means just the word square confuses us. So instead of taking individual words one should take the collocation fair and square and find meaning. It shows that collocations play a key role in understanding sentences. Collocations are recursive in nature so they may contain more than two words in a sentence.

5.   **E. Tagging:** Parts of Speech Tagging as discussed by Jose Camacho et al., (2015) means assigning lexical categories to words whether it is a noun phrase, verb phrase or prepositional phrase.

Eg: Cat chases a rat. Here Cat is assigned NN lexical category (noun); Chases is assigned VB lexical category (verb); NN is assigned lexical category (noun).

6.   **E. Parsing:** Parsing as discussed by Huang et al. (2012) or Analyzing the Syntactic Structure of the sentence using Context Free Grammar.

A grammar is said to be recursive in nature only when a lexical category that is present on the left handside of the production rules appear on the right hand side of the production rules.The production Nom -> NP Nom (where Nom is the category of nominals) involves direct recursion on the category Nom, whereas indirect recursion on S arises from the combination of two productions, namely S -> NP DET and DET-> N S.

In this book chapter we will be discussing the NLTK kit using python framework. To work with NLTK kit, first we need to install and configure python as per the NLTK kit. Step by step process with screen shots are explained below:

Step 1: Configuring the Development Environment

Install python 3.5 in windows
Configure python with NLTK kit using the command **pip install nltk** (Figure 1)

Figure 1. Configuring Python

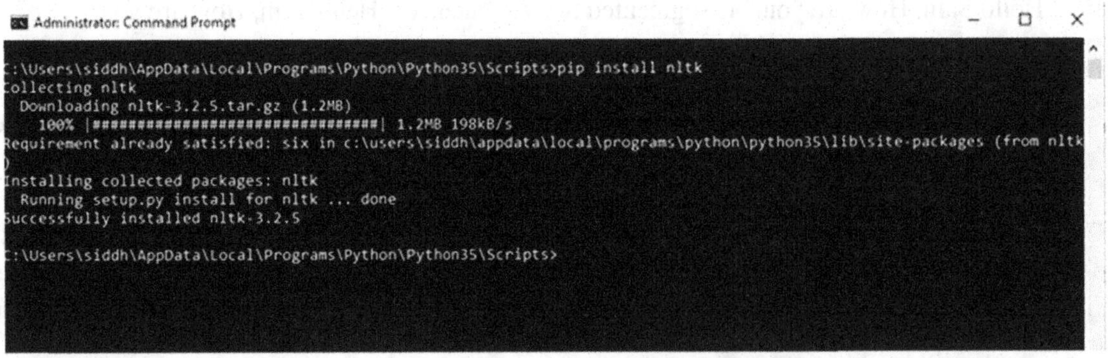

Test nltk (Figure 2)

Figure 2.

```
    Administrator: Command Prompt - python

>>>
>>>
>>> import nltk
>>>
```

Downloading nltk is not enough as nltk will not work without the accompanying datasets.

So datasets needs to be downloaded separately.

The process of downloading and configuring the dataset in NLTK 3.x is simplified, and can be used as GUI utility.

Enter **import nltk** followed by **nltk.download**() in the python prompt.

Just press the download button in the screen below and wait for the data to be downloaded (Figure 3)

Figure 3.

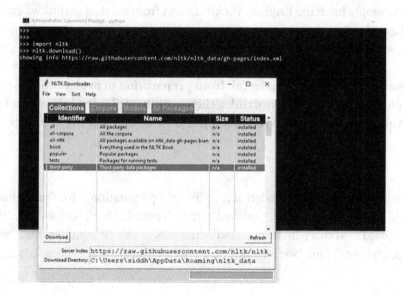

When all the rows turn green and status shows installed in the status column, we are all set to write code. For development Pycharm IDE will be used, the same can also done on any python IDE or even using the basic prompt. (Pycharm makes coding lot easier)

Step 2: Analyzing and Tokenizing a Text Review

In the following program we will analyze any text review and try to convert the review into a numerical score. This is just a simple demonstration program and it needs optimization before using in a practical scenario (Figure 4)

Figure 4.

```
import nltk
class WordExtracter(object):
    def __init__(self):
        self.nltk_splitter = nltk.data.load('tokenizers/punkt/english.pickle')
        self.nltk_tokenizer = nltk.tokenize.TreebankWordTokenizer()

    def split(self, text):
        sentences = self.nltk_splitter.tokenize(text)
        tokenizedData = [self.nltk_tokenizer.tokenize(sent) for sent in sentences]
        return tokenizedData
```

The above class simply loads the **English. Pickle** dataset from the data corpus we earlier downloaded in NLTK. And then tokenizes the review.

So a text review like this

text = """"The food was absolutely wonderful, from preparation to presentation, very pleasing. We especially enjoyed the special bar drinks, the cucumber/cilantro infused vodka martini and the K&P Aquarium was great (even took photos so we could try to replicate at home).""""**

Will become:

[['The', 'food', 'was', 'absolutely', 'wonderful', ',', 'from', 'preparation', 'to', 'presentation', ',', 'very', 'pleasing', '.'], ['We', 'especially', 'enjoyed', 'the', 'special', 'bar', 'drinks', ',', 'the', 'cucumber/cilantro', 'infused', 'vodka', 'martini', 'and', 'the', 'K', '&', 'P', 'Aquarium', 'was', 'great', '(', 'even', 'took', 'photos', 'so', 'we', 'could', 'try', 'to', 'replicate', 'at', 'home', ')', '.']]

Step 3: Tagging the tokens for Parts of Speech

In this step all the tokens will be tagged for parts of speech using pos_tag function in the nltk package.

"The process of classifying words into their parts of speech and labelling them accordingly is known as part-of-speech tagging, POS-tagging, or simply tagging. Parts of speech are also known as word classes or lexical categories. The collection of tags used for a particular task is known as a tagset." (Figure 5)

Ref--http://www.nltk.org/book/ch05.html

Figure 5.

```python
class PartsOfSpeechTagger(object):
    def __init__(self):
        pass

    def pos_tag(self, sentences):
        pos = [nltk.pos_tag(sentence) for sentence in sentences]
        pos = [[(word, word, [postag]) for (word, postag) in sentence] for sentence in pos]
        return pos
```

[[('The', 'The', ['DT']), ('food', 'food', ['NN']), ('was', 'was', ['VBD']), ('absolutely', 'absolutely', ['RB']), ('wonderful', 'wonderful', ['JJ']), (',', ',', [',']), ('from', 'from', ['IN']), ('preparation', 'preparation', ['NN']), ('to', 'to', ['TO']), ('presentation', 'presentation', ['NN']), (',', ',', [',']), ('very', 'very', ['RB']), ('pleasing', 'pleasing', ['VBG']), ('.', '.', ['.'])], [('We', 'We', ['PRP']), ('especially', 'especially', ['RB']), ('enjoyed', 'enjoyed', ['VBD']), ('the', 'the', ['DT']), ('special', 'special', ['JJ']), ('bar', 'bar', ['NN']), ('drinks', 'drinks', ['NNS']), (',', ',', [',']), ('the', 'the', ['DT']), ('cucumber/cilantro', 'cucumber/cilantro', ['NN']), ('infused', 'infused', ['VBD']), ('vodka', 'vodka', ['JJ']), ('martini', 'martini', ['NN']), ('and', 'and', ['CC']), ('the', 'the', ['DT']), ('K', 'K', ['NNP']), ('&', '&', ['CC']), ('P', 'P', ['NNP']), ('Aquarium', 'Aquarium', ['NNP']), ('was', 'was', ['VBD']), ('great', 'great', ['JJ']), ('(', '(', ['(']), ('even', 'even', ['RB']), ('took', 'took', ['VBD']), ('photos', 'photos', ['NNS']), ('so', 'so', ['IN']), ('we', 'we', ['PRP']), ('could', 'could', ['MD']), ('try', 'try', ['VB']), ('to', 'to', ['TO']), ('replicate', 'replicate', ['VB']), ('at', 'at', ['IN']), ('home', 'home', ['NN']), (')', ')', [')']), ('.', '.', ['.'])]]]

The POS tagger class uses pre defined tags and tries to match each and every word with a tag.
The POS Tagger uses Tags. The descriptions of all the tags are provided below. (Figure 6)

733

Figure 6.

Tag	Description
CC	Coordinating conjunction
CD	Cardinal number
DT	Determiner
EX	Existential *there*
FW	Foreign word
IN	Preposition or subordinating conjunction
JJ	Adjective
JJR	Adjective, comparative
JJS	Adjective, superlative
LS	List item marker
MD	Modal
NN	Noun, singular or mass
NNS	Noun, plural
NNP	Proper noun, singular
NNPS	Proper noun, plural
PDT	Predeterminer
POS	Possessive ending
PRP	Personal pronoun
PRP$	Possessive pronoun
RB	Adverb
RBR	Adverb, comparative
RBS	Adverb, superlative
RP	Particle
S	Simple declarative clause, i.e. one that is not introduced by a (possible empty) subordinating conjunction or a wh-word and that does not exhibit subject-verb inversion
SBAR	Clause introduced by a (possibly empty) subordinating conjunction
SBARQ	Direct question introduced by a wh-word or a wh-phrase. Indirect questions and relative clauses should be bracketed as SBAR, not SBARQ
SINV	Inverted declarative sentence, i.e. one in which the subject follows the tensed verb or modal.
SQ	Inverted yes/no question, or main clause of a wh-question, following the wh-phrase in SBARQ.
SYM	Symbol

Step 4: Tag the Words in the Review as Positive and Negative

The next step in the process is to tag the words in the review as positive and negative, for this step we need a pre defined dictionary of negative words for this we will use yaml format. The structure of the file looks like this

ABANDON: [negative]
ABANDONED: [negative]

We have used only 2 files negatives.yml and positives.yml within total of around 2700 words.

Links to these files are provided at the end of the chapter. But for making a proper usable application we will need a few more files like incrementers, decrementers and polarity flippers for handling more complicated reviews and getting better scores.

Also the accuracy of the results will depend on the no of words in the dictionary as well as the quality of the dictionary therefore for making a proper sentiment analysis application we will need a fairly large dictionaries with all kind of negative/positive words and phrases. (Figures 7 and 8)

Figure 7.

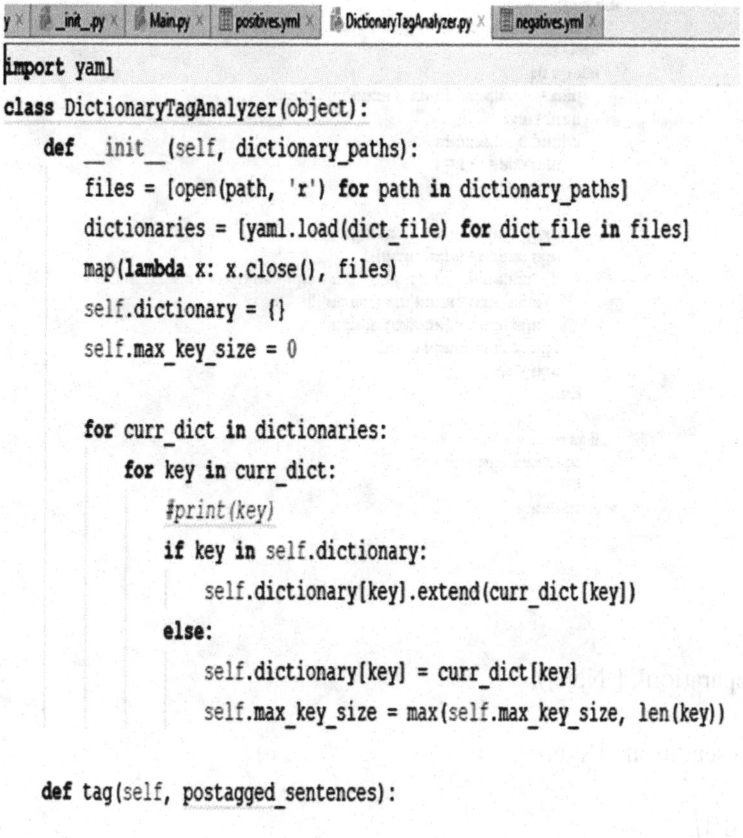

```
y ×  _init_.py ×  Main.py ×  positives.yml ×  DictionaryTagAnalyzer.py ×  negatives.yml ×

import yaml
class DictionaryTagAnalyzer(object):
    def __init__(self, dictionary_paths):
        files = [open(path, 'r') for path in dictionary_paths]
        dictionaries = [yaml.load(dict_file) for dict_file in files]
        map(lambda x: x.close(), files)
        self.dictionary = {}
        self.max_key_size = 0

        for curr_dict in dictionaries:
            for key in curr_dict:
                #print(key)
                if key in self.dictionary:
                    self.dictionary[key].extend(curr_dict[key])
                else:
                    self.dictionary[key] = curr_dict[key]
                    self.max_key_size = max(self.max_key_size, len(key))

    def tag(self, postagged_sentences):
```

Result will be:

Tagged Statements--------------------->
[[('The', 'The', ['DT']),
('food', 'food', ['NN']),
('was', 'was', ['VBD']),
('absolutely', 'absolutely', ['RB']),
('WONDERFUL', ['*positive*', '*JJ*']),
(',', ',', [',']),
('from', 'from', ['IN']),

Figure 8.

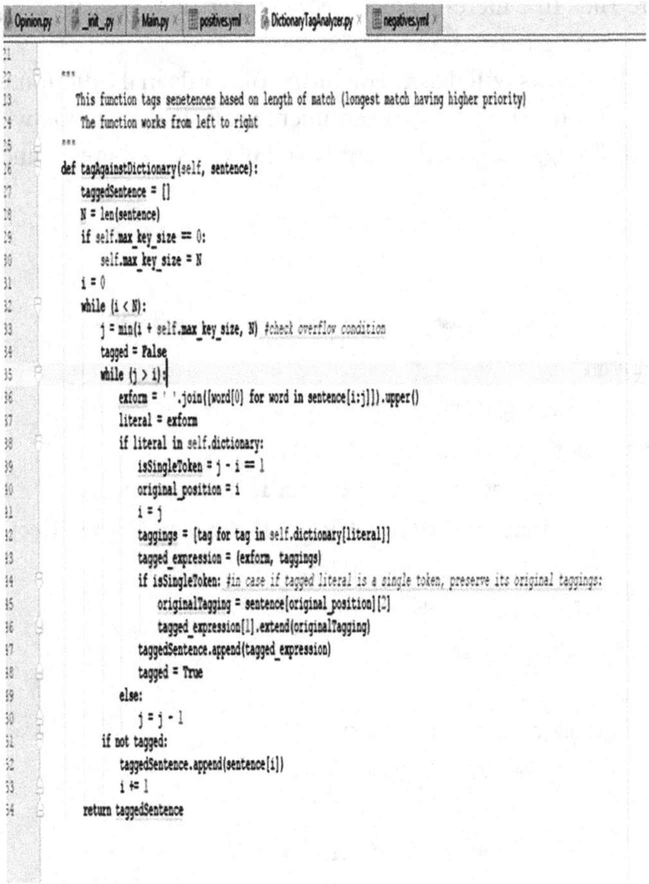

```
Opinion.py    _init_.py    Main.py    positives.yml    DictionaryTagAnalyzer.py    negatives.yml

21
22      """
23          This function tags senetences based on length of match (longest match having higher priority)
24          The function works from left to right
25      """
26      def tagAgainstDictionary(self, sentence):
27          taggedSentence = []
28          N = len(sentence)
29          if self.max_key_size == 0:
30              self.max_key_size = N
31          i = 0
32          while (i < N):
33              j = min(i + self.max_key_size, N) #check overflow condition
34              tagged = False
35              while (j > i):
36                  exform = ' '.join([word[0] for word in sentence[i:j]]).upper()
37                  literal = exform
38                  if literal in self.dictionary:
39                      isSingleToken = j - i == 1
40                      original_position = i
41                      i = j
42                      taggings = [tag for tag in self.dictionary[literal]]
43                      tagged_expression = (exform, taggings)
44                      if isSingleToken: #in case if tagged literal is a single token, preserve its original taggings:
45                          originalTagging = sentence[original_position][2]
46                          tagged_expression[1].extend(originalTagging)
47                      taggedSentence.append(tagged_expression)
48                      tagged = True
49                  else:
50                      j = j - 1
51              if not tagged:
52                  taggedSentence.append(sentence[i])
53                  i += 1
54          return taggedSentence
```

('preparation', 'preparation', ['NN']),
('to', 'to', ['TO']),
('presentation', 'presentation', ['NN']),
(',', ',', [',']),
('very', 'very', ['RB']),
('PLEASING', [*'positive', 'VBG'*]),
('.', '.', ['.'])],
[('We', 'We', ['PRP']),
('especially', 'especially', ['RB']),
('ENJOYED', [*'positive', 'VBD'*]),
('the', 'the', ['DT']),
('special', 'special', ['JJ']),
('bar', 'bar', ['NN']),
('drinks', 'drinks', ['NNS']),
(',', ',', [',']),
('the', 'the', ['DT']),

('cucumber/cilantro', 'cucumber/cilantro', ['NN']),
('infused', 'infused', ['VBD']),
('vodka', 'vodka', ['JJ']),
('martini', 'martini', ['NN']),
('and', 'and', ['CC']),
('the', 'the', ['DT']),
('K', 'K', ['NNP']),
('&', '&', ['CC']),
('P', 'P', ['NNP']),
('Aquarium', 'Aquarium', ['NNP']),
('was', 'was', ['VBD']),
('GREAT', ['*positive*', '*JJ*']),
('(', '(', ['(']),
('even', 'even', ['RB']),
('took', 'took', ['VBD']),
('photos', 'photos', ['NNS']),
('so', 'so', ['IN']),
('we', 'we', ['PRP']),
('could', 'could', ['MD']),
('try', 'try', ['VB']),
('to', 'to', ['TO']),
('replicate', 'replicate', ['VB']),
('at', 'at', ['IN']),
('home', 'home', ['NN']),
(')', ')', [')']),
('.', '.', ['.'])]]
Sentiment Score----------------------> 4

After tagging the sentiment score is 4 which means the system has identified 4 words as positive from the dictionary.

Since the dictionary is having very few words so tagging has identified only 4 otherwise the result would have been better.

Similarly we can analyze and summarize any textual data using NLTK with various data sets.

WEKA

WEKA is the product of the University of Waikato (New Zealand) and was first implemented in its modern form in 1997. It uses the GNU General Public License (GPL). The software is written in the Java™ language and contains a GUI for interacting with data files and producing visual results (think tables and curves). It also has a general API, so you can embed WEKA, like any other library, in your own applications to such things as automated server-side data-mining tasks.

Weka is a collection of machine learning algorithms for data mining tasks. The algorithms can either be applied directly to a dataset or called from your own Java code. Weka contains tools for data pre-processing, classification, regression, clustering, association rules, and visualization. It is also well-suited for developing new machine learning schemes.

Weka contains a collection of visualization tools and algorithms for data analysis and predictive modeling, together with graphical user interfaces for easy access to these functions. The original non-Java version of Weka was a Tcl/Tk front-end to (mostly third-party) modeling algorithms implemented in other programming languages, plus data preprocessing utilities in C, and a Makefile-based system for running machine learning experiments. This original version was primarily designed as a tool for analyzing data from agricultural domains, but the more recent fully Java-based version (Weka 3), for which development started in 1997, is now used in many different application areas, in particular for educational purposes and research. Advantages of Weka include:

- Free availability under the GNU General Public License.
- Portability, since it is fully implemented in the Java programming language and thus runs on almost any modern computing platform.
- A comprehensive collection of data preprocessing and modeling techniques.
- Ease of use due to its graphical user interfaces.

Weka supports several standard data mining tasks, more specifically, data preprocessing, clustering, classification, regression, visualization, and feature selection. All of Weka's techniques are predicated on the assumption that the data is available as one flat file or relation, where each data point is described by a fixed number of attributes (normally, numeric or nominal attributes, but some other attribute types are also supported). Weka provides access to SQL databases using Java Database Connectivity and can process the result returned by a database query. Weka provides access to deep learning with Deeplearning4j. It is not capable of multi-relational data mining, but there is separate software for converting a collection of linked database tables into a single table that is suitable for processing using Weka. Another important area that is currently not covered by the algorithms included in the Weka distribution is sequence modeling.

WEKA User interfaces

Weka's main user interface is the Explorer, but essentially the same functionality can be accessed through the component-based Knowledge Flow interface and from the command line. There is also the Experimenter, which allows the systematic comparison of the predictive performance of Weka's machine learning algorithms on a collection of datasets.

The Explorer interface features several panels providing access to the main components of the workbench:

- The Preprocess panel has facilities for importing data from a database, a comma-separated values (CSV) file, etc., and for preprocessing this data using a so-called filtering algorithm. These filters can be used to transform the data (e.g., turning numeric attributes into discrete ones) and make it possible to delete instances and attributes according to specific criteria.
- The Classify panel enables applying classification and regression algorithms (indiscriminately called classifiers in Weka) to the resulting dataset, to estimate the accuracy of the resulting predic-

tive model, and to visualize erroneous predictions, receiver operating characteristic (ROC) curves, etc., or the model itself (if the model is amenable to visualization like, e.g., a decision tree).

- The Associate panel provides access to association rule learners that attempt to identify all important interrelationships between attributes in the data.
- The Cluster panel gives access to the clustering techniques in Weka, e.g., the simple k-means algorithm. There is also an implementation of the expectation maximization algorithm for learning a mixture of normal distributions.
- The Select attributes panel provides algorithms for identifying the most predictive attributes in a dataset.
- The Visualize panel shows a scatter plot matrix, where individual scatter plots can be selected and enlarged, and analyzed further using various selection operators.

Working With WEKA Explorer

In this book chapter we will be discussing Weka as one of the sentiment classification tool of opinion mining on a movie reviews dataset. The goal is to classify a movie review as *positive* or *negative* (for the reviewed movie). The dataset consists of 1200 user-created movie reviews. The reviews are equally partitioned into a positive set and a negative set.

Each review consists of a plain text file (.txt) and a class label representing the overall user opinion. The class attribute has only two values: *pos* (positive) or *neg* (negative).

Below are the steps:

- Open Weka Explorer (Figure 9)

Figure 9.

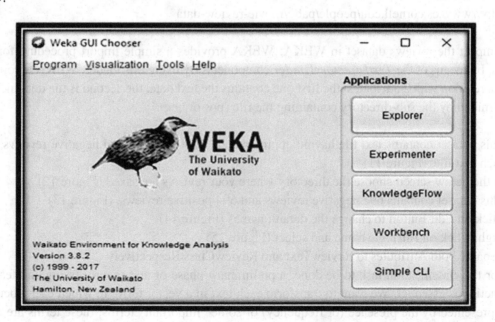

- Click on the open file (Figure 10)

Figure 10.

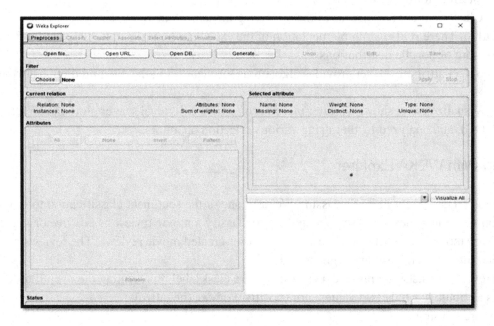

- To perform this experiment we need a dataset of movie reviews, there are a lot of data set available, We are using a dataset of IMDB provided in Cornell university website, link of the data set is given below
  http://www.cs.cornell.edu/people/pabo/movie-review-data

To import the reviews dataset in WEKA; WEKA provides a simple import procedure for textual datasets, by means of the *TextDirectoryLoader* component. By using this loader, WEKA automatically creates a relation with 2 attributes: the first one contains the text data, the second is the document class, as determined by the sub-directory containing the file (pos or neg).

- This dataset contains text file having approximately 1200 positive and negative reviews, one for each text file. (Figure 11)
- In the below screen choose the directory where your reviews are saved (Figure 12)
- This dataset contains 692 negative reviews and 694 positive reviews. (Figure 13)
- Click on Edit Button to change the default names (Figure 14)
- Right Click on Attribute name and select (Figure 15)
- Rename both Attributes to ReviewText and ReviewClass Respectively
- For the classification task to be done, a preliminary phase of text preprocessing and feature extraction is essential. We want to transform each text in a vector form, in which each document is represented by the presence (or frequency) of some "important" terms; these terms are the ones contained in the *collection vocabulary*. Now we need to perform some text preprocessing tasks

such as word extraction, stop-words removal, stemming and term selection. Finally, we run various classification algorithms (naive bayes, k-nearest neighbors) and I compare the results, in terms of classification accuracy.

- To perform the preprocessing in WEKA, we can use the *StringToWordVector* filter from the package *weka.filters.unsupervised.attribute*. This filter allows configuring the different stages of the term extraction. Indeed, you can:

Figure 11.

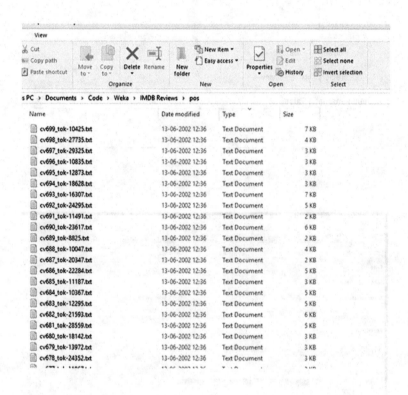

Configure the tokenizer (term separators);
Specify a stop-words list;
Choose a stemmer.

- To perform this step, click on the filter textbox, select *StringToWordVector* from weka->filters->unsupervised->attribute->StringToWordVector (Figure 16)
- In this form keep other settings as default stop words file in stop words handler. It can be any stop words list. After completing the settings clicks on Ok and then click on apply in front of the filter.
- The default text retrieval model used by the StringToWordVector filter is boolean: each document is represented with an n-dimensional boolean vector, where n is the size of the vocabulary, and each value models the presence or the absence of a vocabulary term in the document. One can also choose to use a frequency-based model such as the TF-IDF weighting model by setting to true the *TFTransform* and *IDFTransform* parameters.

Figure 12.

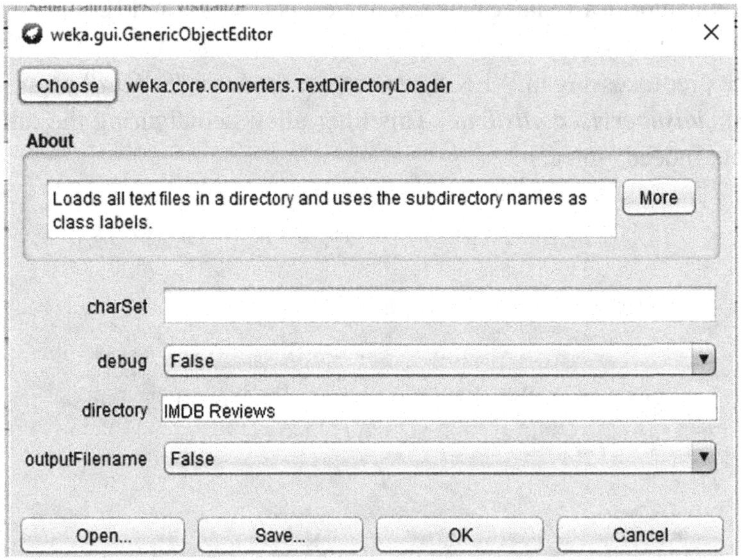

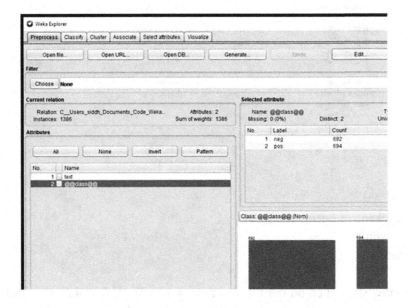

Figure13.

- You can set a stop-words list by clicking on stopwords and setting to true the *useStopList* parameter. In my experiments I used a 630 english stop-words list (whose origin I don't recall) and the Porter's stemmer (for the english language).
- Furthermore, you can set a maximum limit on the number of words to be extracted by changing the *wordsToKeep* parameter (default is 1000 words) and a minimum document frequency for each term by means of the *minTermFreq* parameter (default is 1). The latter parameter makes the filter drop the terms that appear in less than *minTermFreq* documents (Figure 17)

Figure 14.

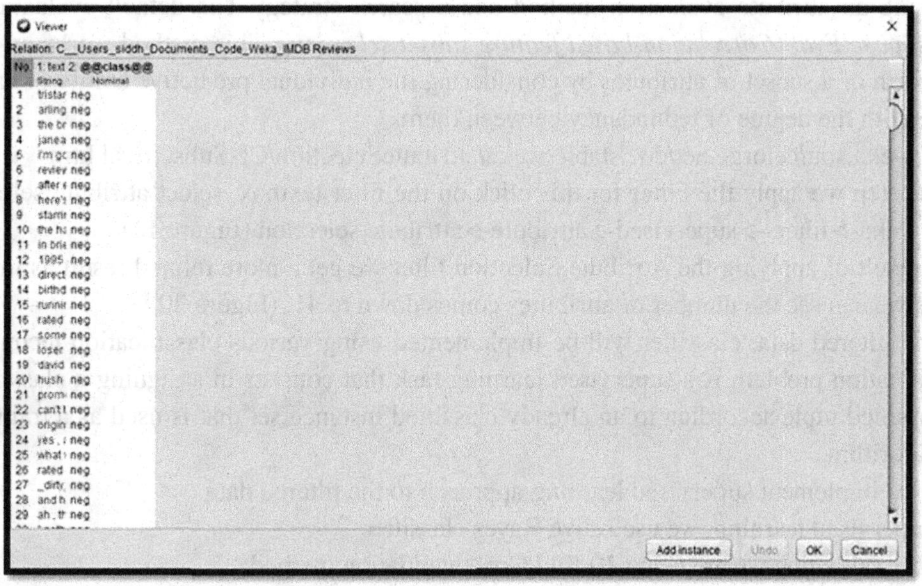

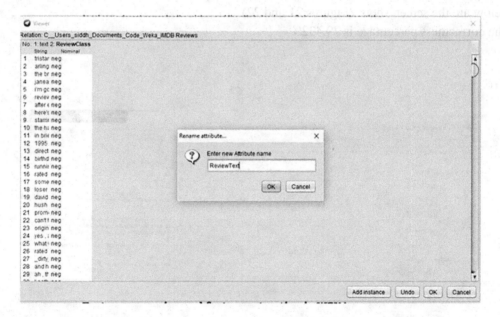

Figure 15.

- We get a relation containing 1272 binary attributes. Below is a histogram for the word awful which features mostly in negative reviews (Blue color is for negative reviews) (Figure 18)
- In the final pre-processing step we have to eliminate the poorly characterizing attribute
- The last preprocessing operation is the attribute selection. Eliminating the poorly characterizing attributes can be useful to get a better classification accuracy. For this task, WEKA provides

the *AttributeSelection* filter from the *weka.filters.supervised.attribute* package. The filter allows choosing an attribute evaluation method and a search strategy The default evaluation method is *CfsSubsetEval* (*Correlation-based feature subset selection*). This method works by evaluating the worth of a subset of attributes by considering the individual predictive ability of each feature along with the degree of redundancy between them.

- http://weka.sourceforge.net/doc.stable/weka/attributeSelection/CfsSubsetEval.htm
- In this step we apply the Filter for this click on the filter textbox, select attribute selection filter from weka->filters->supervised->attribute->attribute selection (Figure 19)
- As a result of applying the Attribute Selection filter we get a more refined result as in the below figure we can see the number of attributes comes down to 41. (Figure 20)
- On the filtered data, classifier will be implemented using various classification techniques. The classification problem is a supervised learning task that consists in assigning a class label to an unclassified tuple according to an already classified instance set that is used as a training set for the algorithm.
- Now we implement supervised learning approach to the filtered data
- For supervised learning, we use Naive Bayes classifier
- And for validation we are using 10-fold Cross validation method
- In WEKA, the Naive Bayes classifier is implemented in the *NaiveBayes* component from the *weka.classifiers.bayes* package. The best result achieved with this classifier has shown a correctness percentage of 79.432%, using a dataset on which only attribute selection was performed. Below are the screen shots. (Figures 21 and 22)
- The correctness percentage is 79.432%

Figure 16.

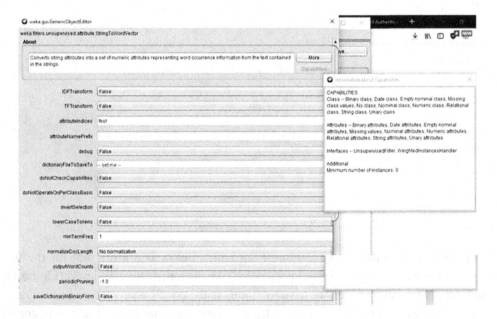

Figure 17.

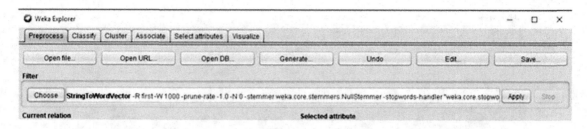

Figure 18.

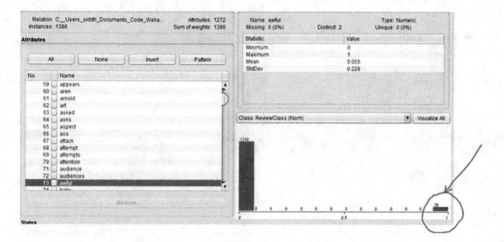

Figure 19.

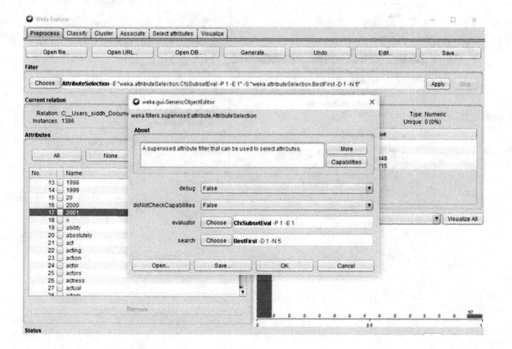

Figure 20.

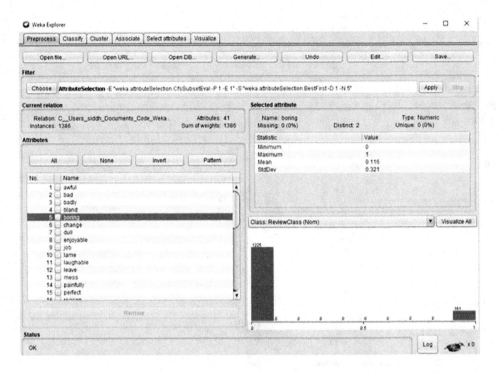

Figure 21.

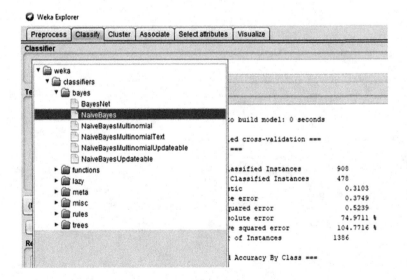

Figure 22.

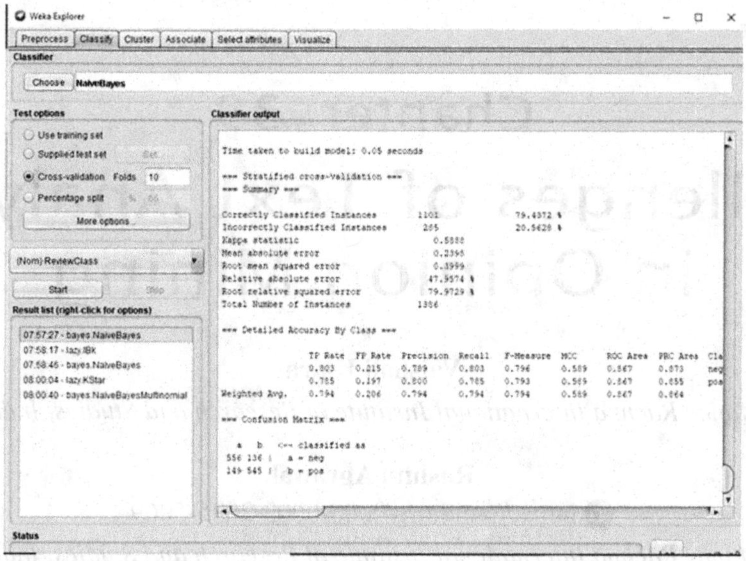

CONCLUSION

The idea of Opinion mining and Sentiment Analysis tool is to process a set of search results for a given item based on the quality and features. In this book chapter we have discussed two opinion mining tools, NLTK and WEKA to classify and analyze the opinion of the datasets. Concepts of these tools have been discussed with all the possible screen shots. User can use any other data set and can implement the opinion mining tool to classify and analyze the data for better decision making.

REFERENCES

Camacho-Collados, J., Pilehvar, M. T., & Navigli, R. (2015). Making sense of word embeddings. A unified multilingual semantic representation of concepts. *Proceedings of the Association for Computational Linguistics*, 741–751.

Huang, E. H., Socher, R., Manning, C. D., & Ng, A. Y. (2012).MaxMax: A Graph-based Soft Clustering Algorithm Applied to Word Sense Induction. *Proceedings of the 14th International Conference on Computational Linguistics and Intelligent Text Processing*, 368–381.

Navigli, R. (2009). Entity linking meets word sense disambiguation: A unified approach. *Transactions of the Association for Computational LinGUIstics*, 2, 231–244.

This research was previously published in Extracting Knowledge From Opinion Mining; pages 179-203, copyright year 2019 by Engineering Science Reference (an imprint of IGI Global).

Chapter 39
Challenges of Text Analytics in Opinion Mining

Vaishali Kalra
Manav Rachna International Institute of Research and Studies, India

Rashmi Agrawal
https://orcid.org/0000-0003-2095-5069
Manav Rachna International Institute of Research and Studies, India

ABSTRACT

Text analysis is the task of knowledge distillation from unstructured text. Due to increase in sharing of information over the web in text format, users required tools and techniques for the analysis of the text. These techniques can be used in two ways: One, this can be used for clustering, classification, and visualization of the data. Two, this can be used for predicting the future aspects, for example, in share market. But all these tasks are not easy to perform, as there are lots of challenges in converting the text into the format onto which various actions can be taken. In this chapter, the authors have discussed the framework of text analysis, followed by the background where they have discussed the steps for transforming the text into the structured form. They have shed light on its industry application along with the technological and non-technological challenges in text analysis.

INTRODUCTION TO TEXT ANALYTICS

In real world, organization needs to take decision every other minute, in order to ensure organizational success. Such decisions may include but not limited to introduction of new product and its potential demand, profitability, market share, competitor's benchmarking etc. In the past, such decisions were taken by the top management based on their experience only but such decisions may not be always good for the organization, however, with the advent of technology the amount of data has increased massively, so now decision cannot be taken easily and requires analytics technique. Using Analytics techniques businesses can take strategic decision which are more reliable compared to decision taken on judgment of single person.

DOI: 10.4018/978-1-6684-6303-1.ch039

Text Analytics is one of the methods to analyze the textual data available on web. Text analytics can be defined as a way for computers to analyze the text using natural language processing to derive the certain facts from raw text. Such analysis can be in form of retrieval of customer opinion regarding any product, hotel reviews, movie reviews, categorization of documents based on the given information, can be used in market analysis and prediction and so many other similar tasks (Irfan et al., 2015).

In order to achieve the above purpose, the users need to follow the text mining process. Generally, Text mining and text analytics are alternatively used but there is thin line difference between the two. Text Mining can be understood as the process to retrieve information from data; however, information can be retrieved from data using text analytics techniques (Agrawal & Batra, 2013)

But both cannot be used in isolation as the end objective is same to take informed decision and taking an informed decision is not possible without using both. To further elaborate, Text analytics can be applied to any text data, which can be in any native language like Japanese, Chinese, English, Hindi etc. and same is available on the web. Such web data is not only the textual content always and it can have images, audios, and videos, which make it completely unstructured data. So the task of text analytics is to extract the text from retrieved real-world information from the web and application of text mining to visualize the text data only.

On the above retrieved text in the past, the text analytics only plays with bag of words, the word frequencies and are used for summarization, clustering the documents and classification of document topic wise (Agrawal, 2014). It does not have the capability of knowing the meaning of the text; it has difficulty in handling the problem of polysemy, homonymy, synonyms and deriving the hidden information that is called semantic analysis or qualitative analysis (Hu & Liu, 2012). Textual data comes with additional challenges such as incorrect spellings, incorrect syntax of the sentences and it leads to challenges for the extraction of the correct information out of that and its processing also. Therefore, researchers are focusing more on handling such data because of above issues (Knoblock, Lopresti, Roy, & Subramaniam, 2007). They are investing quality time in handling the complexities and its high dimensionality of the large corpus of data.

Although the researchers are applying statistical methods and techniques like using singular value decomposition and support vector machine for handling the high dimensionality issues, word sense disambiguation for handling synonyms problems, however, the challenges has not completely resolved and work is still in progress. The intent of this chapter is to study some of the challenges faced by researchers today, let's make a deep dive.

BACKGROUND

Framework of Text Analytics

The text analytics is performed on text documents, so the first step of text analytics should be extraction of text data from the web which is followed by conversion of this text data into an actionable form is shown in Figure 1.

The data source is any repository available for the analysis, for market analysis it can be data available on social media sites like Twitter, Facebook, blogs, etc, it can be the sensors data, academic records, patient history, like this there are various resources are available from where the data can be extracted. Text content available in these repositories is in unstructured format, as there is not only the text data.

There are videos, images audio available on the sites. Using text retrieval functions only text content can be retrieved and this text may not be in same formatting styles then this has to be preprocessed (Abbasi, 2008; Roberts, 2000; Lacity, 1994). The pre-processing has various steps from tokenization to removal of stop words, conversion of words into same formatting styles (Kalra, & Agrawal, 2017). Pre-processing requires the support of NLP, which process the raw string and checks for its syntax, semantic and pragmatic structure of sentence (Sun, Luo, & Chen, 2017). In the next section NLP will be discussed in detail. After pre-processing the data is normalized, normalization is required to reduce the dimension of the data. Once the data is normalized any mining algorithms can be applied. These mining algorithms can be used to extract information which can further be utilized to take informed decisions.

Figure 1. Text analytics framework

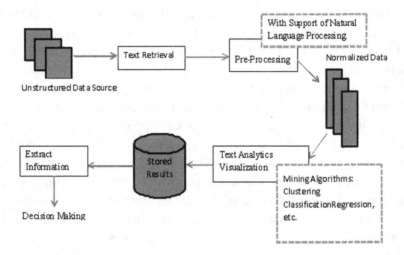

Natural Language Processing

Natural language processing (NLP) is a backbone of text analytics. Text analytics performed before application of any machine learning algorithm. NLP determines the syntax and semantics of the sentence. The NLP is performed on a raw string, which converts the raw string into two forms:

- Set of characters
- Set of Words

Set of characters is the most common and easiest way of representation of text. But it does not play any important role in text analytics; it has the application in text compression only. Whereas the set of words play an important role in text analytics, with the help them you can do topic characterization, opinion mining, sentiment analysis, you can also describe the entities from these words and can give the relationship between them which may be helpful in information extraction. Identification of set of words is not easier to find in all languages, languages like Chinese and Japanese where no boundary is defined for the word characterization it becomes difficult but with the help of specialized tools, the words can be found for such languages also. So, our focus is on the processing of words. NLP on words can be done at three levels: Lexical analysis, semantic analysis, and syntactic analysis (Sun, S., 2017).

Levels of NLP Analysis

As explained above NLP on words can be performed at three different levels as follow:

1.   Lexical Analysis:

This is the first step of text analytics where it breaks the sentence into set of tokens (words). In English language space, comma between the words helps in characterizing the tokens. On these tokens, Part of Speech (POS) Tagger can be used to Tag each word as noun, verb, adjective, determiner, etc. POS helps in determining the right context of the word whether it is an adverb or a noun. For example, in the given sentence: she gives a fire performance on stage, "fire" is an adverb and the POS tagging can correctly determine it. Another measure use of POS tagging is, it helps in determining the relationship between words or entities, for example A cat is chasing a Rat; here POS tagging determines that chase relationship exist between cat and rat (Vyas, 2014).

POS tagging helps in removing language ambiguities known as word sense disambiguation. It assigns the tag to each word by considering its neighboring words also. For example, if the word appears with determiner in the end than it can be a noun or if the same word appears with a determiner in the mid then it can be an adjective or an adverb. This depends on the neighboring words which can give a different meaning to the same word. In support of this, let's take an example of the word back.

She sits at the back. Where back is a noun

I went back to the church. Here it is an adverb.

So, the same word can behave differently and POS tagging helps in identifying the right context of the word which resolves the various ambiguities occurring in the language.

The POS tagger algorithm takes the raw string as an input and produces the words with relevant tags which appear just immediately after the word in the sentence.

While/IN reading/VBG the/DT board/NN she/PRP generally/RB makes/VBZ mistake/NN because/IN of/IN poor/JJ eyesight/NN syndrome/NN

Here in the above example words are tagged like IN is used for tagging a preposition.

- **VBG:** Used for the verbs like playing, eating etc.
- **DT:** Is a determiner a, an, the comes in this category.
- **NN:** Is a Noun
- **PRP:** Is a pronoun
- **RB:** Is an adverb
- **VBZ:** Used for plural verbs
- **JJ:** Is an adjective

These are the few defined categories for English language. For each language there is a different rule for tagging.

2. Syntactic Analysis

Syntactic analysis is the task of identifying the correct grammatical structure of the sentence. After the lexical analysis, you will have the words with tags which determine the correct context of the word in the sentence. Next task is to determine the correct structure of the sentence, and to achieve this chunking is required. Chunking works on tagged words, it starts grouping the tagged words together to create a next higher level of the hierarchy of non-overlapping of tagged words for syntactic check. For example for the English language:

Article + Noun *creates* Noun Phrase Chunk

Verb + Noun Phrase *creates* Verb Phrase Chunk

Now, after creation of the chunks the text parser start parsing these chunks based on the native language grammatical rule, for example:

English Language Grammar Rule states that:

Sentence is made up of Verb Phrase and Noun Phrase, where Verb Phrase should be followed by Noun Phrase.

Let's try to analyze the above grammar rule with the help of below flow diagram shown in Figure 2.

Figure 2. Text parsing

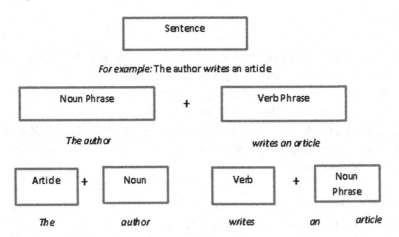

3. Semantic Analysis

Semantic analysis is the task to find out the meaning of the text written by human in their native language. To perform the semantic analysis, the machine required to recognize the tokens correctly in form of context of the complete sentence written by the user in their native language. This can be done with the help of lexical analysis and syntactic analysis. So for semantic analysis, the lexical analysis and syntactic analysis has to be performed first.

The applications of semantic analysis are:

- Helps to remove the semantic ambiguities of text.
- Helps to determine the relationship between words.
- Helps to give the summary of whole document.

To perform the above three tasks of semantic analysis the machine required the support of external dictionaries and statistical approaches. External dictionaries like Wordnet helps in determining the relationship between words. For example, election and politician can have a sense of togetherness. So if in any page the word election appears then it can categorize to the politics text document. The statistical approaches are used to give the whole context of the document, about what the user has stated in his text document. Next is the task how to remove the ambiguities of text. The ambiguities mainly appear due to the words which can infer different meanings. For example bank, the bank has two meanings one is related to a river and another it is a place where we submit our money. The POS tagging determines it as noun in both cases. So here syntactic analysis cannot remove the ambiguity. The semantic analysis can remove it, by going through the whole document to find its correct meaning. The semantic meaning cannot be driven from a single line of the text. For this analysis, the machine has to go through the whole text to find the correct meaning. By keeping in mind the objective of the chapter, The authors have not discussed much about NLP here. This entirely required enough space of discussion otherwise.

APPLICATION IN INDUSTRY

Text analysis has its vast application in industry nowadays, it is used in search engines to give the appropriate results for the query, in banking to make the future planning, movie makers, health care departments, almost at every place it plays an important role (Tated, & Ghonge, 2015).

Several well-known companies are using it, for example, Netflix is making wide use of this technique for the review of their movies and they are trying to do better for their user's, based on their preferences. Bank of England is also using the text analytics, they review tweets and from there they try to find about their clients when they can withdraw their money and based on that, they can make their financial decisions. Similarly in healthcare domain, Memorial Sloan-Kettering Cancer Center is making use of IBM Watson Technology to get the patient case history and use this information for prescribing the medication (Ittoo, Nguyen, & van den Bosch, 2016).

So, let's analyze few applications which are using the text analytics. The next subsequent table explained the use of text analytics in different applications

In Table 1, different broad categories of applications are discussed corresponding to the techniques of text mining. However, all defined applications are somewhere already using these techniques but this also defines scope of improvement in some applications also.

Table 1. Applications corresponding to techniques

	NER	Sentiment Analysis	Opinion Mining	Classification	Clustering
Biomedical	Drugs relationships and genes relationship (Simpson, 2012)			Classification of disease based on the history available in databases and electronic reports	1. Used to develop a system to collect the reports in one repository of similar types. 2. Drugs functioning the same effect can be grouped together
Banking		Banks used sentiment analysis to know their reputation in the market, by getting their clients reviews from social media.	People views shared on Twitter can be helpful for banks in making strategy	Banks can classify their clients based on their investments in bank and their credit can use and can provide benefits accordingly to leverage their customers.	
Search engines	Heavily rely on NER system for giving better search results.			Search Engines used it to automatically classifying the documents into predefined categories for efficient web search, eg: Yahoo	If the predefined category is not given then categories the documents based on their content similarity to improve search results.eg: Google
Q & A System	Helps in finding out the entities relation to give a better match for the asked question.			Classification of documents to the pre-defined category for retrieval of efficient results.	Grouping of documents which are relatively matched with each other for giving the good results of the asked question.
Agriculture		Helps farmer in choosing the fertilizers from the reviews given by the other users and scientists.	Blogs related to the agriculture and climate helps to cultivate the crop to give industry benefit.	Used for classifying the types crops production based on climate behavior, soil type, fertilizers etc.	Used for categorizing various crops production according to the tropical region
Traffic Management			Tweets shared on social media helps in traffic management.		
Product Review		1. Product reviews given by users on e-comers sites helps users for purchasing the product. 2. Helps industries also in production & improvement.			
Education		Reviews of different institutes helps students and parents in choosing the right institute for studies	Students feedback given in natural language required the support of opinion mining can help the management in building a strong system		

Challenges in Text Analytics

There are several challenges for performing Text Analytics and it is difficult to discuss all of them in detail, however, the challenges can be broadly defined in the following two categories:

- Common Challenges: These should be understood challenges faced all the times while performing text analytics for any data set.
- Specific Challenges: These challenges are domain specific challenges which may or may not appear all the time for all datasets.

Common Challenges and Its Classification

The most commonly faced challenges for Text Analytics can fall into any of the following categories:

- Unstructured and Inappropriate data
- Incomplete data (because of cloud-based data)
- Inconsistent data

1. **Unstructured and Inappropriate Data:** Unstructured and inappropriate data cites biggest challenge for text analytics. The data available on the web and repositories may be full of grammatical errors, may have used short forms of words, misspellings. Such erroneous data is the biggest roadblock in achieving the appropriate results.
2. **Incomplete Data:** The data available on the web does not necessarily have the complete information; some attributes may have missing values. In the real-world scenarios the failure of any node of a sensor device may cause some missing values. Although there are various techniques are available for handling the missing data like the attributes can be ignored if doesn't have much weightage or some other value can be substituted in replace based on some. But in some applications, it causes the measurable difference in results. So handling of incomplete data is a challenge (Grimes, 2010).
3. **Inconsistent Data:** Real-time data is a time-variant data and generally it causes inconsistency in the data as Kaisler, Armour and Espinosa(2013, January) mentioned that the data is increasing at rapid growth and the data is integrated from various sources available at different places. The different sources have the different structured formats which cause the inconsistency in the data.

Next, in the Table 2 various challenges are categorized to the specific type mentioned above.

Specific Challenges of Text Analytics

As explained earlier in this chapter, specific challenges may not appear all the time but can be present in any of data sets, so some domain-specific challenges are explained below:

1. **Named-Entity Recognition (NER):** NER is used in various applications like in Information Extraction, Topic analysis, Indexing of full documents, Sentiment Analysis etc. but Marrero, Urbano, & Sánchez-Cuadrado et. al. (2013) have tested this NER results on various tools like MUC-7, AUC-08, CoNLL-03 and they found each tool is having its own boundaries and rules

for defining each entity in different categories. For example, MUC defines the date in Time/ Date category and AUC mentioned this into temporal expression. Some tools determine date mentioned in numeric as an entity but if it is mentioned in words then they do not determine it as an entity. So there are different rules and it's not easy to analyze the results as it can give different annotation to the same entity and sometimes they do not classify into any category of annotation. Although lots of research has been done on this, still various categories remain to sort and the main challenge of NER is to categorise the entity based on their semantic behavior. The new tools must be adaptive in nature so that they can be trained on new words time to time.

Table 2. Common challenges of text analysis

S.No.	Challenge	Type
1	**Handling of unstructured data**: Conversion of unstructured data into the structured form required special skills; this handling is a challenge for the analysts.	Unstructured and inappropriate data
2	**Noisy Data**: Data available on web contains lots of information other than the content which needs to be analyzed, the data may have advertisements along with the information and the textual content itself may be inappropriate structure. So conversion and extraction of relevant information is a challenge for the text analysts.	Unstructured and inappropriate data
3	**Multilingual Data:** Data available on the web is not in a single language, it is in multiple languages. Text analytics tools are language dependent, they cannot work independently. Development of support for each language is a challenging task for the analysts. Sharma, Gupta, Motlani, Bansal, Srivastava et al. (2016) have designed a model for the handling of Hindi-English combined usage of language in social media. For handling of this bilingual model, they have first identified the words that with which native language they actually belong. They have categorized into three classes Hindi, English and Rest. After then they have done normalization POS Tagging of words followed by shallow parsing where they have tagged each word	Unstructured and inappropriate data
4	**Heterogeneous Source of Information:** Data is extracted from different sources and collected at one place. Heterogeneous place of information has its own formatting and structure. Conversion of this heterogeneous information into homogeneous task required lots of efforts of analysts.	Incomplete data
5	**Time-Variant Real-Time Data:** The advancement required a lot from the data available on the web, performing analytics on real-world data required lots of efforts in gathering the information and performing the right prediction from the extracted information to leverage its customers(Sun, 2014)	Inconsistent Data
6	**Reliability of Available Data:** Lot of data is available on the web and in repositories but choosing the right data for analysis and making trust in the available data is difficult. The data available is the reliable one or not cannot be assured easily.	Unstructured and Inappropriate data
7	**Lack of Resources of Data:** Technology advancement is on boost and it is benefitting the companies also. But still, some companies hesitate in providing the data, which lacks in giving a good source of information.	Incomplete data
8	**Quality Results:** Inappropriate data always leads to inaccurate results. When the data available on web source is unstructured and noisy, it could not give appropriate results. The industry expects more from this data. So it's the biggest challenge for analysts to derive the accuracy in results.	Unstructured and Inappropriate data

2. **Sentiment Analysis:** Sentiment Analysis gives a review on a product or on a service in form of positive, negative and neutral. It can be given in form of scores also to help its customers or the market for strategy planning accordingly. But it is difficult to analyze and give a correct opinion about the product or a particular feature. As to collect the sentiments from different places available in different formats and different formats can state differently. There are different yardsticks

used by the different site to measure the customer sentiments or service which creates a bigger challenge as data cannot be statically analyzed. For example, some may rate in the format of 4.1 and some may have rated in form of good, very good product. So reviewing the sentiments from heterogeneous sources of information is difficult (Aggarwal & Zhai, 2012).

Pang & Lee(2008) describe another challenge of sentiment analysis the correct set of documents which only targets the sentiment is a difficult task. If one has managed to choose the right set of documents, then also it is difficult to find the opinion regarding a particular attribute. Pang also mentioned that overall opinion is context dependent, the independent sentence cannot describe the correct opinion about the product. However, the positive words have the more frequency in the description of the product, but if the last line describes the negative review then the product review gets the negative polarity.

So the sentiment analysis has the various challenges from a selection of the documents to the prediction of correct contextual sentiment. And if the sentiment is extracted correctly then applying this information in a right manner for market strategy planning is again a challenge. Although one can say it helps user for choosing the right direction for decision making but sometime it may mislead if they are not correctly classified.

3. **Opinion Mining:** Sentiment analysis and opinion mining suffer from the same kind of problems. They both have to tackle multilingual languages used in users reviews and each language requires the separate training for processing, which is time-consuming and required a lot of effort for the creation of training set. Opinion Mining always required the complete contextual information for giving the complete feedback otherwise it may misinterpret the results. For example, if a sentence has maximum good words than it doesn't mean that it is giving a good feedback, it can be said sarcastically also (Maynard, Bontcheva & Rout, 2012). That can be interpreted correctly only by the complete paragraph or a complete document containing the information. Opinion mining also suffers from the problem of selection of target documents on which the task is needed to be performed. It also has the difficulty in selection of evaluation method because both sentiment analysis and the opinion mining are feature dependent and another person cannot determine easily the other's viewpoint.

Opinion mining can be done on the feedback of the users given on twitter also, and it's a challenging task because tweets are in a microscopic format which does not tell much about the context from which you can determine about the opinion of the user. To perform the task efficiently, (Maynard, et. al. 2012) have used the support of machine learning algorithms and retrieval of entities and their relationships so that correct classification can be made on the user's viewpoint.

4. **Classification:** Classification is the task of categorizing the set of documents to the labeled class. Classification is easy to perform on documents which are having high density of content related to a particular topic. But it is not easy to perform on documents which are having less content. This type of classification is named as short text classification. The challenge of short text classification is lesser relevant content related to a particular labeled class. The example of the dataset is web blog data used for classification or the instant messages, and tweets classification etc. Few words specified in messages are not enough to perform classification accurately. This is the problem on which most research is going on (Aggarwal, 2012).

5. **Clustering:** The most common problem of clustering is to specify the number of clusters manually. Which the researchers resolved by using semi-supervised approaches. Using semi-supervised approaches the researchers can determine the value of k. But the other problem which generally faced is overfitting of documents to the specified number of clusters. Sometimes it's not necessary that all the documents may have the mapping in the available cluster set. But still, clustering will map that document only to specified clusters, which generate the erroneous results (Aggarwal, 2012).

CONCLUSION

The text analysis is an emerged area for the researchers and nowadays it has its vast applications in the market from decision making to prediction, categorization of documents, and sentiment analysis to opinion mining. These all tasks required a dataset, and the source of this dataset is the web. The web information is neither complete nor correct which gives a lot of challenges to the researchers for doing any of the text analytic tasks efficiently. In this chapter we tried to shed light on the basic framework of text analysis, its application and various challenges which occurs due to web information and some domain specific challenges also which occurs while performing the above-defined application.

All the challenges which have been discussed give the future direction for the researchers where more work can be done. What can be concluded from the mentioned challenges that, the task of performing text analytics is not an easy task and this must require the domain knowledge of the application to produce the good results. This domain knowledge is gathered from the expertise and given as input while training the system. This trained system could be able to produce good results.

REFERENCES

Abbasi, A., & Chen, H. (2008). CyberGate: A design framework and system for text analysis of computer-mediated communication. *Management Information Systems Quarterly, 32*(4), 811–837. doi:10.2307/25148873

Agrawal, R. (2014). K-Nearest Neighbor for Uncertain Data. *International Journal of Computers and Applications, 105*(11).

Agrawal, R., & Batra, M. (2013). A detailed study on text mining techniques. *International Journal of Soft Computing and Engineering, 2*(6), 118–121.

Al-Daihani, S. M., & Abrahams, A. (2016). A text mining analysis of academic libraries' tweets. *Journal of Academic Librarianship, 42*(2), 135–143. doi:10.1016/j.acalib.2015.12.014

Hu, X., & Liu, H. (2012). Text analytics in social media. *Mining text data*, 385-414.

Irfan, R., King, C. K., Grages, D., Ewen, S., Khan, S. U., Madani, S. A., & Tziritas, N. (2015). A survey on text mining in social networks. *The Knowledge Engineering Review, 30*(2), 157–170. doi:10.1017/S0269888914000277

Ittoo, A., Nguyen, L. M., & van den Bosch, A. (2016). Text analytics in industry: Challenges, desiderata and trends. *Computers in Industry*, *78*, 96–107. doi:10.1016/j.compind.2015.12.001

Kaisler, S., Armour, F., Espinosa, J. A., & Money, W. (2013, January). Big data: Issues and challenges moving forward. In *System Sciences (HICSS), 2013 46th Hawaii International Conference on* (pp. 995-1004). IEEE.

Kalra, V., & Agrawal, R. (2017). Importance of Text Data Preprocessing & its implementation using RapidMiner. Academic Press.

Knoblock, C., Lopresti, D., Roy, S., & Subramaniam, L. V. (2007). Special issue on noisy text analytics. *International Journal on Document Analysis and Recognition*, *10*(3), 127–128. doi:10.100710032-007-0058-9

Lacity, M. C., & Janson, M. A. (1994). Understanding qualitative data: A framework of text analysis methods. *Journal of Management Information Systems*, *11*(2), 137–155. doi:10.1080/07421222.1994.11518043

Marrero, M., Urbano, J., Sánchez-Cuadrado, S., Morato, J., & Gómez-Berbís, J. M. (2013). Named entity recognition: Fallacies, challenges and opportunities. *Computer Standards & Interfaces*, *35*(5), 482–489. doi:10.1016/j.csi.2012.09.004

Maynard, D., Bontcheva, K., & Rout, D. (2012). Challenges in developing opinion mining tools for social media. *Proceedings of the@ NLP can u tag# user-generated content*, 15-22.

Pang, B., & Lee, L. (2008). Opinion mining and sentiment analysis. *Foundations and Trends® in Information Retrieval, 2*(1–2), 1-135.

Roberts, C. W. (2000). A conceptual framework for quantitative text analysis. *Quality & Quantity*, *34*(3), 259–274. doi:10.1023/A:1004780007748

Seth Grimes. (2010, February 8). *Text Analytics Opportunities and Challenges for 2010, BeyeNETWORK*. Retrieved from http://www.b-eye-network.com/view/12638

Sharma, A., Gupta, S., Motlani, R., Bansal, P., Srivastava, M., Mamidi, R., & Sharma, D. M. (2016). *Shallow Parsing Pipeline for Hindi-English Code-Mixed Social Media Text*. arXiv preprint arXiv:1604.03136

Simpson, M. S., & Demner-Fushman, D. (2012). Biomedical text mining: A survey of recent progress. In Mining text data (pp. 465-517). Springer US.

Sun, S., Luo, C., & Chen, J. (2017). A review of natural language processing techniques for opinion mining systems. *Information Fusion*, *36*, 10–25. doi:10.1016/j.inffus.2016.10.004

Sun, X. (2014). Structure regularization for structured prediction. In Advances in Neural Information Processing Systems (pp. 2402-2410). Academic Press.

Tated, R. R., & Ghonge, M. M. (2015). A survey on text mining-techniques and application. *International Journal of Research in Advent Technology*, *1*, 380–385.

Tated Aggarwal, C. C., & Zhai, C. (Eds.). (2012). *Mining text data*. Springer Science & Business Media. doi:10.1007/978-1-4614-3223-4

Vyas, Y., Gella, S., Sharma, J., Bali, K., & Choudhury, M. (2014, October). *POS Tagging of English-Hindi Code-Mixed Social Media Content* (Vol. 14). EMNLP. doi:10.3115/v1/D14-1105

This research was previously published in Extracting Knowledge From Opinion Mining; pages 268-282, copyright year 2019 by Engineering Science Reference (an imprint of IGI Global).

Chapter 40
Learning Algorithms of Sentiment Analysis:
A Comparative Approach to Improve Data Goodness

Suania Acampa
University of Naples Federico II, Italy

Ciro Clemente De Falco
University of Naples Federico II, Italy

Domenico Trezza
University of Naples Federico II, Italy

ABSTRACT

The uncritical application of automatic analysis techniques can be insidious. For this reason, the scientific community is very interested in the supervised approach. Can this be enough? This chapter aims to these issues by comparing three machine learning approaches to measuring the sentiment. The case study is the analysis of the sentiment expressed by the Italians on Twitter during the first post-lockdown day. To start the supervised model, it has been necessary to build a stratified sample of tweets by daily and classifying them manually. The model to be test provides for further analysis at the end of the process useful for comparing the three models: index will be built on the tweets processed with the aim of detecting the goodness of the results produced. The comparison of the three algorithms helps the authors to understand not only which is the best approach for the Italian language but tries to understand which strategy is to verify the quality of the data obtained.

DOI: 10.4018/978-1-6684-6303-1.ch040

The work is the result of a joint work of the three authors, however the paragraph "Big corpora and Digital Methods: a critical approach to improve data goodness" and "Sentiment Analysis and Main Text Classification Algorithms" are by Suania Acampa; the paragraph "Supervised Learning Algorithms used in the analysis "and" Index Scores and Tweet Characteristics "are by Ciro Clemente De Falco; the paragraph "Data and Methods to compare some Supervised Algorithms" and the paragraph "Analysis. Path, Models and Comparisons" are by Domenico Trezza.

INTRODUCTION

Big Corpora and Digital Methods: A Critical Approach to Improve Data Goodness

The ubiquity of digital technologies and the popularity of opinion-rich platforms such as social media and review sites generates a large and rapid amount of user-generated data encoded in natural language daily. Reviews, tweets, likes, links, shares, texts, posts, tags etc.; these are only part of the billions of digital traces that we leave on the web every day, through which it is possible to accurately trace the tastes, opinions, and attitudes of everyone. Big corpora represent a profitable empirical basis for all those who investigate social phenomena on the net. The production and increasing availability of data offers new possible forms of knowledge of social complexity that social researchers cannot ignore. The data revolution is considered as *"the sum of the disruptive social and technological changes that are transforming the routine of construction, management and analysis of data consolidated within the various scientific disciplines"* (Amaturo, Aragona, 2017, p.1). The new digital technologies and big data allow social research to move from the construction of empirical bases through interrogation to the construction of empirical bases through survey. Big data allows us to measure complex phenomena in detail in real time, thanks to the evolution of IT tools and techniques such as artificial intelligence, machine learning, and natural language processing. This promotes interdisciplinarity between different scientific areas and provides social researchers solid empirical bases for experimenting and integrating new and traditional approaches to social research. These technologies push the social sciences into a scenario in which *"web-mediated research [...] is already transforming the way researchers practice traditional research methods transposed to the web"* (Amaturo and Punziano, 2016, 35, 36).

To be able to describe and analyse this wealth of information, social scientists have also begun to use computational analytical methods to assemble, filter and interpret user generated data encoded in natural language. Text mining is part of this context, a branch of data mining that allows you to analyse vast textual corpora in different languages by extracting high quality information with very limited manual intervention. Natural language processing (NLP) is the area of machine learning dedicated to the meaning of the written word.

A very profitable branch of natural language processing is sentiment analysis: it consists in the extraction and analysis of the opinions that users express on the web towards products, services, topics or characters. With language processing and text analysis, sentiment analysis identifies subjective information in sources. The main objective is to determine the general polarity of a text (whether it is a review or a comment) and classify it into three categories: positive, negative or neutral. Sentiment analysis techniques are divided according to the type of approach used: lexicon based or machine learning approach. The machine learning approach treats sentiment classification as a question of general text classification. This approach to classification is divided between unsupervised and supervised learning models. In supervised models it is necessary to arrange a training set labelled with the indication of the polarity of the feeling (negative, positive, neutral) that the algorithm will use to predict the polarity of other textual content contained in the test set. The machine learning approach has the advantage of not depending on the availability of dictionaries, but the accuracy of the classification methods depends a lot on the correct labelling of the texts used for training and on a careful selection of the features by the algorithm. The results of the three supervised algorithms were adopted and compared through an analysis model that involved the construction of the labelled training on which the three models were tested to evaluate the accuracy of each. The next step involved recoding the processed tweets based on their agreement/discrepancy with the output returned by each of the three algorithms. The tweet analysis allows us to define the components (text, sentiment, and other features) that suggest a plausible relationship with the functioning of the algorithm. These algorithms that work through learning open interesting developments by defining data accuracy parameters in relation to validated benchmarks. Our work examines sentiment in a sample of one-day tweets in Italian (May 4, 2020) related to phase 2 of the post-lockdown. The tweets were processed with the three most widely used algorithms in the literature for this type of analysis (Naives Bayes, Decision Tree and Logistic Regression). The results of the three supervised algorithms were adopted and compared based on the accuracy of each and the predictive ability. To check if there were latent differences in the corpus, it was decided to use a lexical correspondence analysis (ACL) which allowed us to define the components (text, sentiment, and other characteristics) that give us information about the functioning of the algorithm. Although the techniques are advancing rapidly and their performances are improving year by year, the analysis shows that the functioning of the chosen algorithms still present various limits for the Italian language.

SENTIMENT ANALYSIS AND MAIN TEXT CLASSIFICATION ALGORITHMS

What do algorithms look for during the human information processing process?

The basis of the functioning of text analysis (Mostafa, M. M., 2013), is natural language processing (NLP): the area of machine learning dedicated to the meaning of the written word. Machine learning (ML) is the ability of the computer to learn independently thanks to algorithms that improve their performance in an experiential way from the examples that researchers provide to learn.

There are three machine learning approaches (Medhat, W., Hassan, A. e Korashy, H., 2014), that guide text analysis and sentiment analysis in particular:

Supervised approach: from a set of labelled data (training), the goal of the classification algorithms is to predict the class attribute on unlabelled data sets (testing). Classifiers learn from training data to make future inferences. For each document to be classified, the algorithms define a vector of properties (called features) that represent it. The extraction of the features from a text is the process of extrapolating its salient characteristic, the most used are words, parts of speech, opinion words, negations (Deshmukh S.N. and Shirbhate A. G., 2016).

Unsupervised Approach: learning algorithms detect the latent structure of unlabelled data: the techniques consist in providing the computer system with a series of inputs that the algorithm will classify automatically and independently on common characteristics and statistical rules.

Semi-supervised approach: combine a small amount of tagged data with a large amount of unlabelled data. Using this approach is very practical when labelling data requires a lot of human intervention.

A highly productive branch of natural language processing is sentiment analysis.

In academia there is a growing interest in this analysis because it provides useful tools for public opinion analysis by automatically detecting the information contained in a textual corpus and measuring polarity (positive, negative, neutral), emotions (angry, happy, sad, etc.) and intentions (interested, not interested).

To analyse the sentiment of a text it is necessary for it to be pre-processed: we will illustrate the details in the following paragraphs.

Sentiment analysis uses various methods and algorithms for natural language processing, these methods can be divided into:

1. Lexicon based approach.
2. Machine learning approach.

In the lexicon-based approach, the definition of sentiment is based on the analysis of individual words or phrases using dictionaries of opinion words where the words are assigned a weight in terms of positivity or negativity.

Figure 1. Sentiment classification techniques by Walaa Medhatun, Ahmed Hassanb and Hoda Korashy

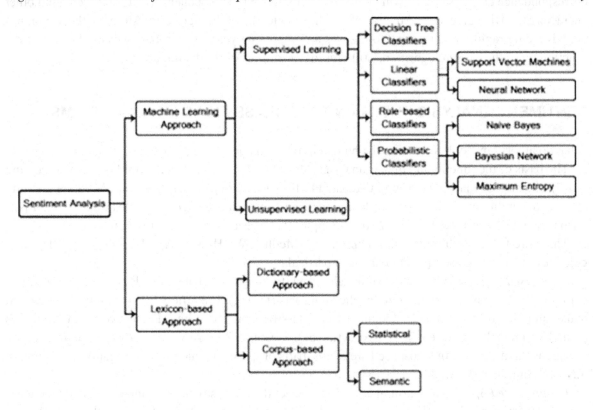

All the words in the document are compared with the words in the dictionary: each time a word in the document matches one in the dictionary, the score associated with that word is added to the overall sentiment score of the document (Taboada M. et al., 2011). The general sentiment of the text will be nothing more than the sum of the scores of the individual words.

The lexical approach can be based on the dictionary or the corpus.

In the dictionary-based approach a comparison is made between the words of the corpus and those of appropriately constructed dictionaries (such as WordNet and SentiWordNet) which contain (in addition to words) syntactic-lexical information such as synonyms and antonyms, with the aim of labelling each semantically relevant term with a sentiment orientation score. The process is iterative and ends when no new words are found in the text.

In the corpus-based approach, the text is compared with a very large collection of already labelled documents.

This approach can be done through two techniques:

a) Statistics. This technique is based on the calculation of occurrences starting from opinion words: if the word occurs more frequently in positive texts then it will have a positive polarity, if it occurs more in negative texts it will have a negative polarity. With this reasoning, the same words within the same concept must have the same polarity.

b) Semantics. This approach is based on the idea that two neighbouring words can have the same polarity by semantic principle, as in the major and most widely used lexical databases present online for sentiment analysis work. Unfortunately, even the largest database will not be able to cover all the words and their possible combinations.

The advantage of the corpus-based approach is that it does not need a previous labelling operation of the incoming texts but is based on already existing dictionaries. This advantage can turn into a limit for the investigation when the availability of dictionaries in the language in which you are investigating is insufficient. The dictionary must be sufficiently large and appropriate to the context we are analysing, since the same dictionary may not have the same effectiveness in different survey contexts. Furthermore, in this approach the comparison takes place with texts written correctly, from a syntactic and grammatical point of view- The texts collected from the Internet, however, are mostly ungrammatical and full of errors.

Machine learning is the other possible approach to sentiment analysis. This approach treats the sentiment classification as a general classification problem.

This approach to classification takes up the division between the unsupervised and supervised learning models described above. In supervised models, a training set labelled with the polarity of sentiment (negative, positive, neutral) is needed, and the classifier will use this to predict the polarity of other textual content. In unsupervised learning only unlabelled texts are used and the analysis is based on the comparison of words in terms of similarity and differences. One example is the Latent Dirichlet Allocation model (Liang, J. et al., 2016). The LDA algorithm attributes a topic to each word of the document through the analysis of co-occurrence. LDA associates each document to the topics most commonly represented by the words that compose it. In this way it is possible to identify the topics of a text only by observing the co-occurrences of the words with respect to a reference knowledge base.

The *machine learning approach* has the advantage of not depending on the availability of dictionaries, but the accuracy of the classification methods strongly depends on the correct labelling of the texts used for training and on a careful selection of the features considered by the algorithm (Basile V., Nissim M, 2013).

For both the supervised and unsupervised approaches, the output always requires careful validation because there is no machine learning model that works better than another. The *"No Free Lunch"* theorem by David Wolpert and William Macready (1997) is famous in the field of machine learning. This says that a model can be good for one problem and bad for another, so you need to test multiple models to find the one that works best for the problem under investigation. Analysing feelings accurately is also difficult for humans and the language (especially the Italian one) has so many nuances that a machine will never be able to understand them all. For this reason it is essential to have a vast knowledge of one's data and the context in which they were collected.

SUPERVISED LEARNING ALGORITHMS USED IN THE ANALYSIS

As previously clarified, in this work the supervised classification approach, an approach that usually involves the use of machine learning techniques, will be used. In the supervised classification the division classes of the statistical units are decided by the researcher. A supervised approach generally requires two phases, regardless of the algorithm used. In the first phase, the model is trained on a training set and its accuracy is studied on a test set. In the second phase, the model is applied to the data to analyse. There are three algorithms and their related R packages that we will use in our work: Naive Bayes (r package "e1071"), Decision trees (R package "Cart") and Logistic Regression (R package "CaTools"). It is necessary highlight that, in line with the "bag of words" model, the starting matrix will be the "Document Term Matrix" for all the algorithms used. The "Document Term Matrix" is a matrix where the number of lines corresponds to the documents present in the dataset while the number of columns corresponds to the significant words in the dataset.

Naive Bayes Classificator

The Naïve Bayes classifier represents a probabilistic approach to solving classification problems. Sentiment analysis is a two- or three-class classification problem. The Naive Bayes classifier is built on Bayes' theorem whose logic is the following: for each possible cause that can trigger a certain - already occurred - event, the probability is calculated. Therefore, the "subjectivist" (Rish, 2001) Bayesian approach allows the scholar to make a priori assumptions, based on their information state, which they enter directly into the model and then these assumptions can be strengthened, rejected or corrected on the basis of the information contained in the data. In Naïve Bayes' technique, the basic idea is to find the probabilities of categories in a given text document by using the joint probabilities of words and categories (Dey et. Al, 2016). In other words, NBC uses maximum a posteriori estimation to find out the class (i.e., features are assigned to a class based on the highest conditional probability) (Samuel, 2020). For sentiment analysis we can use two Bayesian classification models: Bernoulli and multinomial. The first considers the presence of a term in each document. In the multinomial, on the other hand, in addition to the term's presence/absence, its frequency of occurrence in the text is also considered. On the other hand, Bernoulli's NB only considers whether a term is present or not in a document and not how many times it occurs. It should be emphasized that the algorithm is defined as "naive" because it assumes feature independence. In other words, the words within a text have no form of correlation between them. The Bayesian classifier, compared to other algorithms, has the advantage that the training phase can be conducted on a limited number of cases. On the other hand, the assumption of independence between features is difficult to sustain. In the end there is one final aspect to underline related to the use of "Laplace Smoothing", a correction factor used to avoid the documents' classification as an "impossible event". The R package that we are going to use, in addition to giving the choice of reference model (i.e. multinomial or Bernoulli), also gives the possibility of using use "Laplace Smoothing".

Decision Tree

The purpose of the classification and regression algorithms is to describe or predict the class to which a given unit belongs. Classification trees are used when the dependent variable is categorical, while regression trees are used when the dependent variable is cardinal. In the classification trees, as we shall see, the predictive power is calculated on the basis of the percentages of misclassification while in the regression trees it is given by the quadratic difference between observed and expected data. In the case of sentiment analysis, the algorithms used are the classification ones, and the classification tree allows us to identify logical rules to establish the sentiment of a text. (Dey et. Al, 2016). The classification procedure will make it possible to identify the "words", whose presence or absence indicates a certain type of sentiment. Unlike other techniques, in this technique the "predictive variables" (therefore the features) aren't used at the same time but sequentially, and chosen for their ability to produce splits that maximize internal homogeneity between groups and reduce the external one. The aim is to produce a logical path useful for classifying the statistical units. The decision tree construction to carry out sentiment analysis involves three phases:

- choice of subdivision criterion (or split): for each level it is necessary to choose the word that produces the best split according to a given criterion for reducing heterogeneity. The indices usually used to establish the best split are "heterogeneity" or "Gini".
- definition of a stop criterion in the tree construction: the definition of stop criteria is necessary to avoid overfitting problems (i.e. the loss of generality of the model) since the classification can proceed up to the constitution of nodes determined by irrelevant "words". These criteria should be based on two principles: simplicity (trees with as few levels as possible) and discrimination (maximum level of heterogeneity allowed in node
- identification of a rule for assigning one of the J classes of the dependent variable to each leaf: if in each final node there are not all cases with positive or negative sentiment, it is necessary to establish assignment criteria. One of them is establishing class sentiment based on the highest frequency sentiment in the class.

The Curt algorithm we will use in our work uses the Gini index as a measure of heterogeneity. The curt is distinguished by the way it constructs the "tree": first it builds the decision tree of maximum size, after which it carries out a "pruning" phase on the less significant branches. The levels subjected to cutting are linked to the definition of the complexity parameter. Among the possible "subtrees", the one with the lowest misclassification rate will be chosen.

Logistic Regression

Logistic regression is usually used to identify the possible relationship between one or more independent variables and a dichotomous dependent variable, which in the case of sentiment analysis assumes positive (1) and negative (0) values. This technique allows us to understand the explanatory power of the individual independent variables and which independent variables combination has the greatest discriminating power (Samuel, 2020). The term "logistic" is due to the non-linear relationship between x and y that has a binomial distribution described by a logistic curve. In logistic regression the values predicted by the equation are arbitrary and the output regards the probability that a subject or a text, in the case of sentiment analysis, belong to one of the two modalities of the dichotomous variable. The probability is expressed through the odd, which is given by the ratio between the observed frequencies in one class and the observed frequencies in the other. Thus, the reference value of the logistics equation is the odd's natural algorithm, the logit. The logit is chosen instead of the odd for mathematical reasons and specifically because its variation range, which goes from plus to minus infinity, allows us to linearize the relationship between the variables included in the model. To solve the equation, in the logistic regression the OLS method cannot be applied since the assumptions are not verified, so the maximum likelihood algorithm (ML) is used. This algorithm estimates the parameters to maximize the loglikelihood function that indicates how likely it is to obtain the expected value of Y given the values of the independent variables. In the training phase the algorithm, through the analysis of frequencies, identifies which words characterize each modality of the dependent variable.

Model Fit

Confusion matrix, also known as contingency table, is typically used in supervised machine learning techniques for allowing the visualization of algorithm performance on a test set. Usually in confusion matrix, rows are labelled with effective labels and columns are labelled with predicted labels. Starting from confusion matrix it is possible to calculate different types of standard performance metrics: accuracy; precision, recall and F-Measure.

- *Accuracy:* indicates the accuracy of the model and is calculated by dividing the number of correct predictions by the total of the statistical units.
- *Precision*: is the classifier ability to correctly label a certain category. Given a certain category, precision is obtained by dividing the number of correct predictions by the total number of cases labelled in that category.
- *Recall* (or sensitivity): is the classifier's ability to identify all cases of a certain category. Given a certain category, it is calculated by dividing the number of correct predictions by the actual number of cases that fall into that category.

The value of precision and recall range from 0-1, while the value of Accuracy is expressed in percentage. The estimated model works if its accuracy value is larger than the accuracy of the baseline (the model always provides the most frequent value as a forecast). These metrics will help us to evaluate the performance of each algorithm used in the analysis.

DATA AND METHODS TO COMPARE SOME SUPERVISED ALGORITHMS

While the availability of large amounts of data represents the opportunity to build solid analysis paths, on the other hand it poses a non-trivial challenge to the researcher on the methods and strategies of analysis to be adopted when working with large data sets. The recognition of automatic classification techniques in the previous paragraph suggests that supervised machine learning models, although different from each other, are constantly evolving, trying to refine what should be the general objective when doing research: constructing (and returning) reliable data (Marradi, 2007). In this sense, these algorithms, working through learning, open interesting developments by defining data accuracy parameters in relation to validated benchmarks. Our work examines the sentiment of a sample of single-day tweets (May 4, 2020) related to start of the post-lockdown. The results of the three supervised algorithms seen previously were adopted and compared through an analysis model that involved the construction of the labeled training on which the three models were tested to evaluate the accuracy of each. The next step involved recoding the processed tweets based on their agreement / discrepancy with the output returned by each of the three algorithms. The tweet analysis allows us to define the components (text, sentiment and other features) that suggest a plausible relationship with the functioning of the algorithm.

Definition of Dataset to Train the Algorithm

The comparison between the three supervised sentiment algorithms has been conducted on a tweet dataset dated May 4, 2020. The topic was the reopening of activities following the quarantine for the Covid-19 outbreak. Why this day? It responds to the need to test the model in optimal conditions. The hypothesis, in fact, is that the beginning of 'Phase 2' generated mixed feelings (fear of the possible infection resurgence, enthusiasm for the end of domestic confinement, fear for the economic situation, etc.). So, the risk of having a one-way sentiment (and therefore useless for the models to be tested) is not high. For the training of the model, a stratified sample of tweets (corresponding to 1% of the main dataset) was built according to proportional shares for the three daily slots: morning (00:00 - 11:59 am), afternoon (12:00 - 18:59 pm) and evening (19:00 - 23:59 pm). As can be seen in Table 1, users 'tweeted' especially during the first part of the day and in the afternoon (48% and 42% respectively), while only 10% of the tweets were posted during the evening.

Table 1. Tweet by time of day and quote of tweets

	Base	*Quote*	*Training set*
Morning (00:00 - 11:59 am)	9924	*48%*	994
Afternoon (12:00 - 18:59 pm)	8721	*42%*	870
Evening (19:00 - 23:59 pm)	2067	*10%*	207
	20712	*100%*	2071

A sentiment has been assigned for each tweet: positive, negative or neutral. The attribution was stipulated based on criteria shared among the authors of the study. We provided a fourth category, 'non-classifiable', to place tweets of this type: 1. Not containing text but images or links to third party sites; 2. Without any reference to the pandemic, phase 2, or the emergency in general. The distribution in Table 2 shows that only 4% of the tweets in the sample belonged to the latter category. On the other hand, of the 96% of the tweets to which it was possible to attribute a sentiment, most (40.6%) expressed a negative sentiment towards phase 2 and only about 25% were judged to express a positive sentiment. A good percentage of tweets, just over 34%, could not be associated with a positive or negative sentiment, so they were classified as neutral.

Table 2. Tweets by classification and sentiment (v.a. e %)

	v.a.	*%*
Unclassifiable tweets	**90**	**4**
Classifiable tweets	**1981**	**96**
Negative	*805*	*40,6*
Positive	*498*	*25,2*
Neutral	*678*	*34,2*
Tot	2071	100

ANALYSIS. PATH, MODELS AND COMPARISONS

To reduce the elements of possible ambiguity and to test the model better, we decided to only use the tweets with positive and negative sentiment. So the training / testing dataset is constituted by 1303 tweets. The RStudio software was used to analyse this sample of tweets because it is a powerful programming environment with an intuitive interface suitable for the development of scripts for analysing large amounts of data, especially unstructured data. Machine learning algorithms cannot work if applied directly to raw text: first of all, it was necessary to either convert the *"character"* class content into numbers, specifically into numerical vectors in order to reflect the various linguistic properties of the text (Goldberg, 2017). This procedure is called "feature extraction or coding": the *bag-of-word* or the *bag-of-ngram* are the textual analysis and representation models capable of extracting the features from our text to insert them into a textual corpus first, then into a two-dimensional matrix. With the creation of the *BoW Matrix* it was possible to transform each tweet into a vector that will be used as input data for chosen machine learning algorithms. The vector transformation process was carried out on all tweets until the vocabulary of all the words that appear in the entire corpus was obtained with the respective frequency of occurrence of each term for each tweet. Although information on the order, structure of the text and semantic relationship between words is lost, the information content remains intact. For the creation of a vocabulary useful for the extraction of features, what is needed is the set of terms that occur throughout the corpus, because it is the frequency of occurrences of words that is used as a feature to train the text classifiers. What often happens is that a textual corpus contains few words that are useful for analysis, it was therefore necessary to reduce the size of the vocabulary because, while it is true that the language is complex, it is also true that not all the complexity of language is necessary to effectively analyse the texts. (Grimmer and M. Stewart, 2012). The first step was to apply the VCorpus function to create a corpus of 1303 tweets. The second step was to pre-process the corpus, in particular:

1. The text was converted to lowercase so that the algorithm does not include different elements such as "Covid", "covid".
2. Punctuation was removed to prevent the algorithm from considering terms such as "#covid", "co-vid" as different elements.
3. Stop words, very common words with a grammatical function that do not convey meaning, were eliminated from the corpus.
4. A stemming process was activated which returned the inflected form of each word to its root form and then mapped all the words belonging to the same family of meanings.

Stemming is the computational version of the linguistic concept of lemmatization: the lemmatisation algorithms uses dictionaries and the textual context to discover words that belong to the same root.

The Figure 2 shows the words cloud of the most frequent words contained in the corpus following the pre-processing phase. This mode of representation gives us information about our vocabulary. The weight of the tags, rendered with characters of different sizes, is intended exclusively as the frequency of occurrence of the term within the tweets *(tf):* the larger the character, the greater the number of appearances of the word in the textual body. As expected, the most frequent words were those relating to the second phase of the lockdown imposed by the Prime Minister Conte.

Once corpus was pre-processed, the frequency of each single term was extracted by converting the corpus into a documents-terms matrix *(dtm)*. To assess the relevance of the various terms contained in the tweets, it is possible to use the "weighting value" as an indicator, which measures the frequency of occurrence of each word in each tweet and which then weighs its weight within the collection *(tfi-df)*. In the *documents-terms matrix* each column contains the single terms of the tweet corpus; the rows contain the documents (tweet) and the cells contain the number of appearances of that term in that document. The *dtm* contains 1303 documents (tweets) and 7921 distinct terms with 100% sparse. This dispersion index indicates the presence in the corpus of a mass of terms that appear rarely and that therefore most of the cells report a value equal to 0.

We have chosen to set a sparse value = 0.995, only the terms for a sparse value greater than 0.995 have been removed. The sparse topic corresponds to the relative frequency threshold of the document for a term, above which the term is removed. The variable *"sentiment"* has been added to the matrix with sparse at 0.995 and it is ready to be divided into training set and testing set. The training set was built with the first 900 cases and the test set with the remaining 403 cases. At this point it was possible to process the two sets with the three chosen algorithms.

We started the three models (Logistic Regression, Naive Bayes, Decision Tree) for four tests since with the LR algorithm we tried to include 4 quantitative variables in the model, linked to the type of 'engagement' of the tweet - and therefore plausibly linked to sentiment - that is the number of favourites, retweets, the length of the tweet and the author's followers. Tab.3 summarizes the output values of the three supervised algorithms. As we observe, in the four tests we find accuracy values (i.e. the correct percentage of sentiment predicted on the total of tweets) that are lower than the optimal percentage of 90%, ranging from 54.7% of the RL applied only to the text, to a little more than 67% of the Decision Tree algorithm. However, the precision values that calculate the correctness for the single sentiment show us a heterogeneous situation varying from a maximum precision for the positive sentiment calculated by the Naive Bayes model (detects 95% of the total tweets with positive sentiment) to 94% of tweets with negative sentiment detected by the Decision Tree model. This polarization in sentiment prediction suggests that many elements of ambiguity remain in the text of the tweets. Therefore, it is useful to intensify the analysis, this time on the content of the tweets, to explore possible elements of meaning that have conditioned the work of the algorithm. For this reason we decided to build an additive index for each tweet relative to the concordance between the observed and predicted sentiment value for each of the three algorithms.

Figure 2. Words cloud

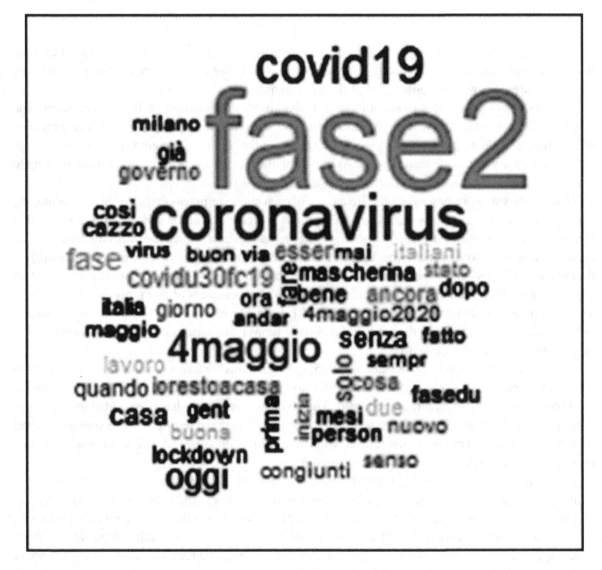

Table 3. Supervised algorithm, values of output

Supervisned Algorithm	R Package	Dataset training	Predictors	Train/test	Accuracy	Precision		Recall	
						Negative	Positive	Negative	Positive
Logistic regression	RL	1303 tweet / pos-neg	text and other variables	2,5	56,5%	59,3%	51,5%	69,0%	40,9%
		1303 tweet / pos-neg	only text	2,5	54,7%	55,6%	53,0%	68,3%	39,5%
NAIVE BAYES	e1071	1303 tweet / pos-neg	only text	2,5	45,0%	17,4%	95,4%	87,5%	38,7%
Decision Trees	CART	1303 tweet / pos-neg	only text	2,5	67,2%	94,2%	18,8%	67,7%	63,1%

INDEX SCORES AND TWEET CHARACTERISTICS

As seen before, the algorithms used have recorded overall different performances and in our case study have shown average high percentages of incorrect classification. Thus, a high percentage of tweets has not always been classified correctly. This partly unlooked-for data suggested an in-depth study aimed at understanding if the wrong classification was attributable to the content of the tweets. To do this, a "correct classification" index was developed. The index ranges from zero to four, where zero indicates that the tweet was not classified well by any algorithm, while four indicates that the tweet was correctly classified by all algorithms. Fig. 3 shows that only 10% of tweets have always been correctly classified, while around 30% of tweets have been correctly classified at least once. The median category is represented by tweets that have been correctly classified twice (23.1%) out of four, while the modal one is represented by tweets that have been correctly classified three times (36.2%). These data are perfectly in line with the accuracy levels seen above.

Regarding the analysis objective, one aspect that partly affects the "correct classification" index is the size of the tweets. Indeed, the analysis of variance shows a significant relationship between the index and the variable "corpus length" ($F = 2.77$; $p <0.05$). The relationship is not linear ($p = 0.122$) but the post hoc test (LSD) evidenced that tweets with an index score of 4 (mean = 193.27; sd = 80.20) are longer than tweets with index 0 and 1 (mean = 155.70; sd; 78.14). In reference to the tweets' content, it is possible to see some interesting differences (in table 4) for each kind of sentiment both the tweets with an index equal to 4 and those with an index equal to 0 are reported.

These tweets are characterized by different lengths, and ones with a high index score, in addition to being characterized by semantically meaningful and unambiguous words, have a discursive structure without particular rhetorical figures such as irony which, as is known, is difficult to understand even for humans sometimes. Indeed, in the second and third sentences with low scores of negative sentiment, it is possible to find irony. Another thing that seems to characterize incorrectly classified tweets is the presence of particular words. In the first two tweets with positive sentiment, we find a lemma like "anticorpo" (antibodies) which is quite transversal with respect to sentiment and semantically not oriented. On the other hand, in tweets with high scores on the index there are well-oriented words to be submitted to the algorithm such as: panico (panic); buona (good); morte (death); cretini (cretins); pagliacciata (clowns); gravità (severity); forti (strong). These lemmas tend to appear only with certain types of sentiment and, therefore, are more easily classified in light of the "bag of words" operating logic underlying the algorithms considered. To check if the background differences recorded on the sample of tweets in the table were present in the entire corpus, it was decided to use a lexical correspondence analysis (ACL) which is a type of exploratory factor analysis, whose purpose is to highlight any latent differences in a corpus of texts (Greenacre, 1984). The check was done through an ACL (documents x words) and by projecting the index variable in Illustrative. The ACL results seem to corroborate the underlying hypothesis: the arrangement of the tweets in the space tends to vary based on the score they have on the index, on both the positive and negative sub-corpus.

As can be seen in Fig. 5 and Fig. 6 the different modalities, which represent the scores, are arranged on different quadrants and this is especially true for positive sentiments where tweets with a score of 4 are on the opposite quadrant to ones with scores of 0 or 1. Regarding negative sentiments, the differences mainly emerge on the second factor.

In both cases, part of the previous discussion on the tweet sample seems to be valid. The results of lexical correspondences analysis highlight that, in addition to the already identified and debated differences, which are partly conceptualized by experts in the field, there may be other differences related to other aspects. These differences could help to understand the reason why there is not always agreement between the algorithms used. This represents an interesting further study that could be made in the future with a larger body of tweets. However, the analysis shows that the incorrect classification of tweets is due to the complexity of the structure of the tweets, and not due to random errors. This complexity, which characterizes the Italian language, can be only resolved through the researcher's intervention.

Figure 3. Tweet for index scores

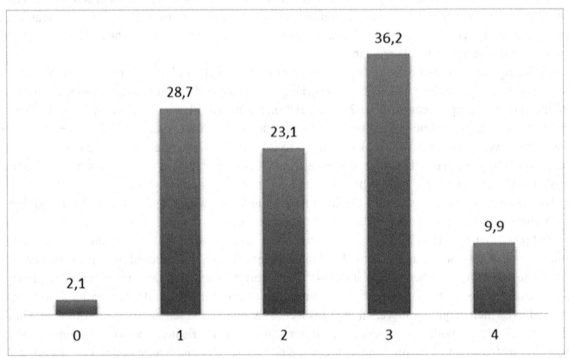

Table 4. Tweet sample for different sentiment and index scores

	Low index score (0-1)		High index score (4)
Positive Sentiment	1) Coronavirus scoperta importante in Olanda: trovato anticorpo monoclonale che blocca linfezione 2) Coronavirus: il vaccino italiano funziona. Anticorpi bloccano il virus - #Coronavirus: #vaccino #italiano 3) Per celebrare la #fase2 un bel giro in #bdc #bicidacorsa sulle colline intorno a #Pescara avevo dimenticato lo sguardo lungo, un orizzonte, i profumi e il vento in faccia #luceinfondoaltunnel #bici #ciclista…		1) #NewProfilePic buongiorno a tutti e auguri a tutti quelli che torneranno alla loro normalità. Riabbracciare i propri cari riprendere il lavoro e avere quel poco di libertà in più #Fase2 2) Oggi inizia la #FaseDue "ora responsabilità, il Paese è nelle nostre mani", rispettiamo le regole e siamo diligenti. Buona #Fase2 a tutti non fate cavolate! 3) Oggi inizia la #Fase2 a cui siamo arrivati grazie al forte senso di responsabilità di tutti gli italiani. Iniziano a chiudere i reparti Covid degli ospedali, sabato scorso è toccato a quello di Parma. Affrontiamo questa fase allo stesso modo e ne usciremo presto e più forti.
Negative Sentiment	1) Ma quale #Responsabilità, il primo giorno di apertura… si ma delle gabbie!!! Se questo è la Fase 2, qualcuno l' ha confusa con la trifase elettrica e ci deve essere rimasto attaccato troppo! #fuoriditesta #sensocivicozero #statobrado 2) "No a party privati" non significa "Sì a party per strada" tutti insieme. Boh… non me pare il caso, no?! #Fase2 3) "Ah che bello, ci voleva proprio una quarantena in pieno agosto.Usate il cervello o finirà davvero cosí. #Fase2"		1) Voi che vi siete messi a far festa per le strade di Milano ma cosa festeggiate che il virus ancora circola!? Ma cosa festeggiate che tanta gente è morta proprio a causa di comportamenti scorretti come i vostri! Ma cosa festeggiate, cretini! #Fase2 2) "non potete pensare che tutti possiamo stare in casa altre due/tre settimane giuro ne va della mia salute mentale, ho attacchi di panico tutti i giorni (mai avuti prima) evitiamo di dire cose a caso se non si conoscono le dinamiche di una persona per favore #Fase2" 3) Hey @GiuseppeConteIT, famo che annulliamo la #Fase2? Visto che nessuno ha capito che non bisogna uscire per ritrovarsi con gli amici, non vedo perchè dobbiamo continuare con questa inutile pagliacciata. La maggior parte del popolo italiano ancora non capisce la gravità della cosa.

Figure 4. Factorial Plan on LCA with Illustrative Variables and Lemmas (positive sentiment)

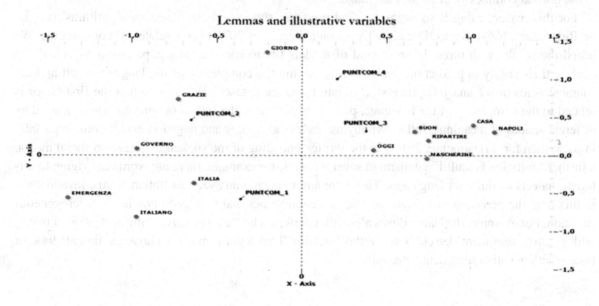

Figure 5. Factorial Plan on LCA with Illustrative Variables and Lemmas (negative sentiment)

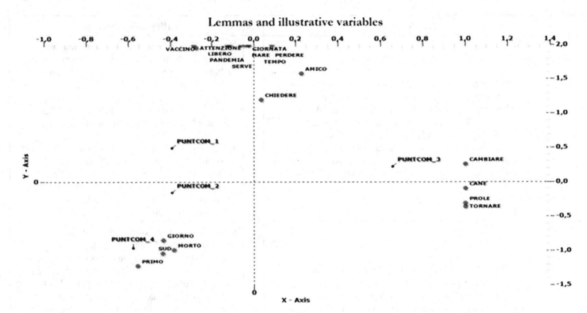

CONCLUSION

There are two main approaches that guide text analysis and sentiment analysis: the *Lexicon based approach* and the *machine learning approach*. Most studies have focused on the second approach and are particular engaged with the comparison between the performances of supervised algorithms, testing the different models' goodness and leaving questions concerning the control of the returned outputs in the background. The rationale behind this study is that despite the rapid advances in natural language processing techniques that improve their performance year by year, some strong limitations remain due to the normal complexity of natural language.

For this reason, using R software, we first ran three supervised classification algorithms' (Logistic Regression, Naïve Bayes, Decision Trees) on a sample of 2071 tweets related to coronavirus,. We tested the results with three different kind of models fits metrics (accuracy, precision and recall) to explore their ability to predict the limitations regarding the complexity of the language itself and the characteristics of the analysis process on Italian language datasets. We believe that the first factor is related to the complexity of the language, particularly because the Italian language is characterized by different shades of meanings, full of synonyms, rhetorical figures and negation expressions, especially in its written form (Dalmonte, 2016). In the written encoding of the spoken language on social media, a further limitation is multilingualism: in several tweets, for example, there are words belonging to different dialects or different languages. These are automatically analyzed as Italian words, invalidating, in this way, the precision of inferences. The precision values that emerged underline a heterogeneous situation. For example, the Naive Bayes algorithm performs better on positive sentiment (95% of tweets with positive sentiment detected) while the Decision Tree algorithm on negative sentiment (94% of tweets with negative sentiment detected).

The second limit that emerged is related to the analysis process, characterized by inaccuracies both in the pre-processing phase and in the processing phase. Firstly, during the preprocessing phase there were difficulties in attributing meaning to certain Italian linguistic clauses, secondly during the elaboration phase (the stemming) all the derogatory words and the pet names, which in Italian have a high emotional value have been reduced to the original root of the word. As seen before from the tweets' analysis with different scores on the index, the ambiguity of some words - whose polarization depends on the syntactic context in which they are used - affects the prediction and classification in a negative way. The different algorithms' performances and the big differences in the sentiment's prediction made it necessary to return to the tweets' content to consider the contextual elements that characterize them. Thus, from this need what emerges is the limit of an Italian language sentiment analysis (maybe also of other languages), reduced exclusively to an automatic classification and that doesn't take into account the human factor that allows us to grasp all those nuances of the context that, inevitably, affect the decision making of the algorithms. In our view, in fact, the researcher's role is fundamental for obtaining better results. Human intervention could be multilevel, *in the formulation of algorithms* and *in progress*.

1) *In the formulation of algorithms*: starting from a conception of algorithms as cultural products (Gillespie, Seaver, 2016), with relevant consequences on the results, these could be better calibrated with the results of research aimed at the identification of the elements of the tweets' contents that affect the classification in a negative way.

2) *In progress*: the algorithm could be set in such a way that if the probability of attribution to a class (and therefore to a sentiment) does not exceed a certain critical threshold, this stops the process requiring the intervention of the researcher.

Such solutions would require greater use of time and an interdisciplinary team, but the results might be worth the effort. In the end, the best accuracy level was recorded by the "decision Trees" algorithm (par.3). This result might suggest that this algorithm has the best operating logic (par.2) in order to match the complexity of the Italian language; further studies are needed to explore this issue, especially in a comparative key with other languages, to understand whether the problems raised are specific to the Italian language, or if they correspond to more general problems of doing automatic sentiment analysis within NLP.

REFERENCES

Amaturo, E., & Aragona, B. (2016). La "rivoluzione" dei nuovi dati: quale metodo per il futuro, quale futuro per il metodo. *Sociologia del futuro. Studiare la società del ventunesimo secolo*, 25-50.

Amaturo, E., & Punziano, G. (2016). *I Mixed Methods nella ricerca sociale*. Carocci.

Aragona, B. (2017). Types of Big Data and designs of evaluation research. *RIV Rassegna Italiana di Valutazione*, 21(68), 48–62. doi:10.3280/RIV2017-068004

Basile, V., & Nissim, M. (2013). Sentiment Analysis on Italian Tweets. In *Proceedings of the 4th ACL Workshop on Computational Approaches to Subjectivity, Sentiment and Social Media Analysis*, (pp. 100-107). Academic Press.

Blinov, P. D., Klekovkina, M. V., Kotelnikov, E. V., & Pestov, O. A. (2013). Research of lexical approach and machine learning methods for sentiment analysis. *Computational Linguistics and Intellectual Technologies*, 2(12), 48–58.

Delmonte, R. (2016). Complessità sintattica e lessicale nelle strutture non canoniche italiane. *Atti del Workshop sulla linguistica computazionale per la complessità linguistica (CL4LC)*, 67-78.

Denny, M. J., & Spirling, A. (2018). Text Preprocessing for Unsupervised Learning: Why it matters, when it misleads, and what to do about it. *Political Analysis*, 26(2), 168–189. doi:10.1017/pan.2017.44

Dey, L., Chakrabort, A., Bose, B., & Tiwari, S. (2016). *Sentiment analysis of review datasets using naive bayes and k-nn classifier.* arXiv preprint arXiv:1610.09982.

Gillespie, T., & Seaver, N. (2016). Critical algorithm studies: A reading list. Social Media Collective.

Goldberg, Y. (2017). Neural network methods for natural language processing. *Synthesis Lecture on Human Technologies*, 10(1), 1-309.

Greenacre, M. J. (1984). *Theory and applications of correspondence analysis*. Academic Press.

Grimmer, J., & Stewart, B. (2013). Text as Data: The Promise and Pitfalls of Automatic Content Analysis Methods for Political Texts. *Political Analysis*, 21(3), 267–297. doi:10.1093/pan/mps028

Günther, E., & Quandt, T. (2016). Word Counts and Topic Models. Automated text analysis methods for digital journalism research. *Journal Digital Journalism*, 4(1), 75–88. doi:10.1080/21670811.2015.1093270

Handler, A., Denny, M., Wallach, H., & O'Connor, B. (2016, November). Bag of what? simple noun phrase extraction for text analysis. In *Proceedings of the First Workshop on NLP and Computational Social Science* (pp. 114-124). 10.18653/v1/W16-5615

Hota, S., & Pathak, S. (2018). KNN classifier based approach for multi-class sentiment analysis of twitter data. *IACSIT International Journal of Engineering and Technology*, 7(3), 1372–1375. doi:10.14419/ijet.v7i3.12656

Kitchin, R. (2014). Big Data, new epistemologies and paradigm shifts. *Big Data & Society*, 1(1). doi:10.1177/2053951714528481

Lauro, N. C., Amaturo, E., Grassia, M. G., Aragona, B., & Marino, M. (Eds.). (2017). *Data science and social research: Epistemology, methods, technology and applications*. Springer. doi:10.1007/978-3-319-55477-8

Liang, J., Liu, P., Tan, J., & Bai, S. (2014). Sentiment classification based on AS-LDA model. *Procedia Computer Science*, 31, 511–516. doi:10.1016/j.procs.2014.05.296

Liu, B. (2012). Sentiment analysis and opinion mining. *Synthesis Lectures on Human Language Technologies*, 5(1), 1-167.

Marmo, R. (2016). *Social Media Mining: Estrarre e analizzare informazioni dai social media*. HOEPLI EDITORE.

Marradi, A., Pavsic, R., & Pitrone, M. C. (2007). *Metodologia delle scienze sociali*. Il Mulino.

Medhat, W., Hassan, A., & Korashy, H. (2014). Sentiment analysis algorithms and applications: A survey. *Ain Shams Engineering Journal, 5*(4), 1093–1113. doi:10.1016/j.asej.2014.04.011

Mostafa, M. M. (2013). More than words: Social networks' text mining for consumer brand sentiments. *Expert Systems with Applications, 40*(10), 4241–4251. doi:10.1016/j.eswa.2013.01.019

Onan, A., Korukoglu, S., & Bulut, H. (2016). LDA-based Topic Modelling in Text Sentiment Classification: An Empirical Analysis. *Int. J. Comput. Linguistics Appl., 7*(1), 101–119.

Pang, B., & Lee, L. (2008). Foundations and Trends® in Information Retrieval. *Foundations and Trends® in Information Retrieval, 2*(1-2), 1-135.

Porcu, V. (2016). *Guida al text mining e alla sentiment analysis con R: Impara l'analisi dei testi con le tecniche di machine learning in R*. StreetLib.

Rish, I. (2001, August). An empirical study of the naive Bayes classifier. In IJCAI 2001 workshop on empirical methods in artificial intelligence (Vol. 3, No. 22, pp. 41-46). Academic Press.

Samuel, J., Ali, G. G., Rahman, M., Esawi, E., & Samuel, Y. (2020). Covid-19 public sentiment insights and machine learning for tweets classification. *Information (Basel), 11*(6), 314. doi:10.3390/info11060314

Shirbhate, A. G., & Deshmukh, S. N. (2016). Feature Extraction for Sentiment Classification on Twitter Data. *International Journal of Scientific Research, 5*(2), 2183–2189.

Silge, J., & Robinson, D. (2017). *Text mining with R: A tidy approach*. O'Reilly Media, Inc.

Taboada, M., Brooke, J., Tofiloski, M., Voll, K., & Stede, M. (2011). Lexicon-based methods for sentiment analysis. *Computational Linguistics, 37*(2), 267–307. doi:10.1162/COLI_a_00049

Welbers, K., Van Atteveldt, W., & Benoit, K. (2017). Text analysis in R. *Communication Methods and Measures, 11*(4), 245–265. doi:10.1080/19312458.2017.1387238

Wickham, H., & Grolemund, G. (2016). *R for data science: import, tidy, transform, visualize, and model data*. O'Reilly Media, Inc.

Wilkerson, J., & Casas, A. (2017). Large-scale computerized text analysis in political science: Opportunities and challenges. *Annual Review of Political Science, 20*(1), 529–544. doi:10.1146/annurev-polisci-052615-025542

Zhao, Y., Dong, S., & Li, L. (2014). Sentiment analysis on news comments based on supervised learning method. *International Journal of Multimedia and Ubiquitous Engineering, 9*(7), 333–346. doi:10.14257/ijmue.2014.9.7.28

This research was previously published in the Handbook of Research on Advanced Research Methodologies for a Digital Society; pages 176-194, copyright year 2022 by Information Science Reference (an imprint of IGI Global).

Chapter 41
Sentiment Analysis on Social Media:
Recent Trends in Machine Learning

Ramesh S. Wadawadagi

ⓘ https://orcid.org/0000-0002-6669-7344

Basaveshwar Engineering College, Bagalkot, India

Veerappa B. Pagi

Basaveshwar Engineering College, Bagalkot, India

ABSTRACT

Due to the advent of Web 2.0, the size of social media content (SMC) is growing rapidly and likely to increase faster in the near future. Social media applications such as Instagram, Twitter, Facebook, etc. have become an integral part of our lives, as they prompt the people to give their opinions and share information around the world. Identifying emotions in SMC is important for many aspects of sentiment analysis (SA) and is a top-level agenda of many firms today. SA on social media (SASM) extends an organization's ability to capture and study public sentiments toward social events and activities in real time. This chapter studies recent advances in machine learning (ML) used for SMC analysis and its applications. The framework of SASM consists of several phases, such as data collection, pre-processing, feature representation, model building, and evaluation. This survey presents the basic elements of SASM and its utility. Furthermore, the study reports that ML has a significant contribution to SMC mining. Finally, the research highlights certain issues related to ML used for SMC.

OVERVIEW

In recent days, social media applications have emerged as leading mass media, as they allow users to work collaboratively and publish their content (Wadawadagi & Pagi, in press; Anami et al. 2014). Accordingly, large volumetric semantically rich information is being generated and accumulated every day in the form of tweets, posts, blogs, news, comments, reviews, etc. Investigating hidden but potentially useful patterns

DOI: 10.4018/978-1-6684-6303-1.ch041

from a huge collection of SMC is a critical task, due to users struggle with overloaded information (Yang & Rim, 2014). SASM is a practice of collecting data from social networks and automatically identifying whether a phrase comprehends sentiment or opinionative content, and further determines the opinion polarity (Jianqiang & Xiaolin, 2017). However, detecting sentiment in SMC faces several challenges, as they are composed of incomplete, chaotic and unstructured sentences, erratic phrases, ungrammatical expressions, and non-lexical words. Moreover, it is hard to detect correlations among opinion sentences due to the broad range of linguistic issues and drives the SA still more challenging (Choi & Park, 2019). To cope with these challenges a real-time SA system needs to be developed to process a large volume of sentiment data in very little time. Furthermore, knowing the public emotions is very useful in many fields, including marketing, politics, online shopping, and many more (Jianqiang & Xiaolin, 2017). To increase productivity, many business firms encourage their customers to participate in virtual discussions, asking for their feedback, opinions, and suggestions.

SASM is generally operated at different levels-of-granularity varying from coarse-grained to fine-grained levels. The coarse-grained analysis deals with determining the sentiment of a whole phrase, while fine-grained analysis is related to attribute level SA. However, employing the right methodology to any key business will drive SASM as a powerful tool for steering organizations and their individual business units as successful outcomes. After several years of constant development, the methodology of SASM is slowly emerging from a disparate set of tools and technologies to a unified framework. The general framework of SASM is depicted in Figure 1. The framework consists of a series of sub-tasks, in which the first task is data acquisition that acquires sentiment data from different sources and stores using different formats. Soon after data acquisition, the data can either be directly streamed to memory for rapid evaluation of unstructured data (in-memory processing) or can be archived to disk (in-database processing) as messages, files, or any machine-generated content. It is being the case that SMC is generally messed up with inconsistent, incomplete and non-dictionary terms, it needs pre-processing before feature vectors are generated. During pre-processing, a series of techniques (e.g., tokenization, stopwords removal, URL pre-treatment, stemming, replacing emoticons) are employed to decrease the amount of irregularity in the data. Additionally, to facilitate the process of identifying document relevancy, the data need to be transformed from a full-text version to a document vector representation that describes the content of the opinion sentences. Two types of representations are extensively used in the literature, namely feature-based representation and relational representation. Perhaps, the most prevalent feature-based representation technique is a vector space model (VSM) (Salton & Yang, 1975). Deduced from basic VSM, some other representation techniques have been used such as n-gram, key-phrase, and hypernym representations. Recently, an alternative document representation based on distributed representation known as semantic word spaces or word-embeddings has shown great success in capturing fine-grained semantic regularities (Mikolov et al., 2013). These vectors consist of low-dimensional real-valued scores that model syntactic and semantic information of individual words. Eventually, these vectors are used as pre-trained features for many sentiment classification tasks. It is evident from the current research, that the earlier SMA systems were designed to facilitate analysts in writing decision rules, while later systems introduce ML for automatic rule generalization. ML algorithms use an example training set of input data to construct a model to make predictions expressed as outputs. Finally, the business analysts or researchers can make critical decisions based on this rich and high-quality data patterns discovered. The key objective of this chapter is to give a comprehensive survey on recent advances in ML techniques used for SASM and its applications. Investigation and analysis of SMC are potentially useful for many ongoing topics of interest such as identification of topics from social interaction among the folks and grouping members based on their ideologies.

The rest of the chapter is arranged according to the following sections. In Section 2, the methodologies required for information extraction (IE) from social media applications are discussed. However, Section 3 covers the important pre-processing techniques applied for SMC. The different ML techniques employed for sentiment classification are presented in Section 4. Numerous applications based on SASM are elucidated in Section 5. Lastly, Section 6 cites many promising and open issues concerned with SMC analysis research.

Figure 1. A general framework of SASM system

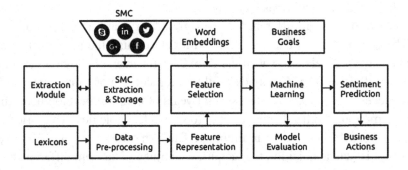

INFORMATION EXTRACTION FROM SMC

The main goal of IE systems is to extract structured data (e.g. events, entities and relationships) from unstructured text present over the social media sites. However, textual content on social media poses several challenges that potentially hinder the task of IE. The use of informal languages in social media posts formed by misspellings, unconventional abbreviations, and grammatically incorrect statements makes IE more difficult. Especially, lack of punctuation and syntax in short sentences place further challenges to disambiguate specified entities and also to resolve co-references among sentences. A typical IE system involves a series of sub-tasks including named-entity extraction (NEE), factual data extraction (FDE), named-entity disambiguation (NED), etc. that need to be applied to the input text. However, rapid developments are seen in more complex tasks such as the extraction of online reviews, opinions, and sentiments.

Web IE and noise removal have been studied in many earlier techniques. In the early systems, programmers are encouraged to write extraction rules; in contrast, contemporary systems adopt ML techniques for automated rule generalization. Taking account of this, Web IE systems can be classified into rule-based extraction; NLP based approaches and based on ML techniques. The rule-based systems depend on knowledge engineering that uses a handcrafted rule set for each work. These systems consider input text as a sequence of characters, and extraction rules are generated using regular expressions over lexical features. For example, ontology-based IE (OBIE) systems have grabbed more attention from the Web mining research community recently. In consequence, an ontology-based IE (OBIE) system to recognize and extract semantic disambiguation of named entities from Twitter data is proposed (Nebhi, 2012). The OBIE systems exhibit different traits by determining the type of entity retrieved and relate them to a semantic description in the formal ontology. This model subsequently combines the problem of named-entity recognition (NER) and a disambiguation component. The empirical study reveals that the OBIE systems exhibit good performance when tested with connected data as free-base and syntactical context for disambiguation. Furthermore, techniques based on NLP are also been addressed by many researchers. These models receive natural language text as input and based on certain criteria they produce structured information relevant to a given application (Singh, 2018). In particular, an open-source NLP pipeline for a micro-blog message extraction model called TwitIE (Bontcheva et al., 2013) is designed. TwitIE is an extended version of open-source software called GATE-ANNIE pipeline (Cunningham et al., 2013) used for news text mining. It consists of two modules, namely, importing Twitter-specific data and handling metadata. The pipeline describes each phase of the TwitIE in the extraction process. The GATE is an open-source IE framework consisting of ANNIE a general-purpose IE pipeline. This further includes essential components of IE such as tokenizer, sentence extractor, POST (Parts-of-Speech tagging) module, lexicon, finite state transducer, orthomatcher, and coreference resolver. The literature study shows that the new open-source TwitIE offers a researcher the best way of dealing with micro-blog extraction challenges. The key benefits of rule-based models include readability, ease of maintenance and ability to transfer the domain knowledge directly into rules. However, the drawbacks of rule-based system are the amount of expertise involved in writing the rules and interoperability of rule languages (Waltl et al., 2018). A paradigm shift in automating IE has unfolded from knowledge-based systems to learning-based extractors. Consequently, a diverse set of ML algorithms have been successfully applied for the task of IE. In the following paragraph, many contemporary ML techniques suggested in the literature for extracting relevant information from social media data are discussed.

Benson et al., (2011) addressed how to extract canonical records of events from Twitter data using conditional random fields (CRF). The CRF is a discriminative model used for predicting sequences in streaming data. The model utilizes a CRF subsystem for extracting aspect values such as event location and performer's name from individual tweets and segregates them according to events with a canonical value assigned for all individual event property. To maintain the internal regularity of each event cluster, the local decisions formed by CRF are regularized according to canonical record values. A factor-graph technique is employed for discovering the relationships between each of these decisions. These variational Bayesian methods appear to be efficient in making predictions on a huge collection of text messages. The extraction of key-phrases from Twitter data for analysis and summarization of tweets is discussed by Zhao et al., (2011). The model employs a three-stage process, namely, keyword ranking, generating cadidate key-phrases, and key-phrase ranking. For keyword ranking, a context-sensitive topical PageRank algorithm is proposed. However, for key-phrase ranking, a probabilistic ranking function that models both relevance and interestingness of key-phrases is used. Furthermore, the model is evaluated over a huge collection of Twitter data, and the experimental results reveal that these methods are very effective in extracting topical key-phrases. The work also studies that the proposed ranking technique can incorporate a user's interests by modeling retweeting behavior. Furthermore, an open-source event extraction and classification model named TwiCal for Twitter data is presented by Ritter et al., (2011). TwiCal is designed to extract a four-tuple signature of events identified as a named-entity, event phrase, event date, and event type respectively. The format chosen resembles the actual event information present on many tweet messages. The model proceeds in three stages. Firstly, the tweet messages collected from streaming are tagged with part-of-speech. Then, the named entities with their associated event phrases and dates involved in significant events are extracted. Further, the temporal expressions involved in events extracted are categorized into different classes. Finally, the proximity of association between each named-entity and date value on which the number of tweets co-occurs is measured to determine whether an event is significant or not.

On the other hand, micro-blogging sites play a critical role in disseminating information among the communities during natural calamities. The size and the speed at which messages are transmitted during crises tend to be very high and needs a real-time extractor. Hence, Meier et al., (2013) presents a system to extract disaster related information from micro-blogs using ML techniques. The model proceeds in two stages, classification of tweets and extraction of tweets. A Naïve Bayesian (NB) classifier is employed to perform fine-grained classification of tweets and later, to extract short messages for analysis. The efficiency is measured on a real-life disaster-related dataset containing a huge collection of micro-blog messages. However, the dataset for training the model is prepared through crowd-sourcing. Empirical results show that ML techniques are well suited for structured data extraction from unstructured short messages. In recent days, user profile extraction on social media has grabbed more attention from the research community. For instance, to extract user profiles from Twitter using a weakly-supervised learning method is illustrated by Li et al., (2014). Interestingly, user profiles from other social networks like Facebook and GooglePlus are utilized as a remote source of supervision. In addition to linguistic features, the model takes into account the network information as a unique feature offered by social media. The proposed model is tested on three user attributes including education, profession, and marital status. The experimental results reveal that the model yields accurate predictions for extracting user attributes on tweets data. Yet another important task of IE from social media is to extract arguments from discussions. Goudas et al., (2014) discussed a two-stage process for argument text extraction from a corpus of social media discussions on a topic of "renewable energy sources". During the first step, k^{th} nearest neighbor (kNN) is employed for the classification of sentences into sentences containing arguments and sentences containing no arguments. In the second step, the model identifies fragments of sentences containing arguments using CRF. The results are quite promising and the model outperforms several baselines. The task of IE is not restricted to those techniques discussed above; however, researchers are trying to develop new IE systems that are more accurate and scalable. Nevertheless, web documents are often incorporated with extra information such as emblems, advertisements, redundant pages, feeds, copyrights, etc., which are irrelevant to the true content and are considered as noise. A framework to remove noise and extract subjective content from online reviews based on the document object model tree (DOM-tree), SMOG readability and linguist tree kernels is addressed by Wadawadagi & Pagi (2019). Firstly, the content of each DOM-tree node is analyzed to predict the perplexity of vocabulary and syntax using SMOG readability test. Then, the semantic tree kernels (STK) embedded with word vectors are employed for the classification of nodes into subjective or objective content. Finally, the nodes carrying subjective content are extracted from the DOM-tree. Table 1 depicts the summary of various IE techniques based on ML and their merits.

PRE-PROCESSING TECHNIQUES

SMC itself is noisy and hence needs pre-processing before ML algorithms are applied productively. Many scholarly approaches have been reported in the literature, and the survey reveals that the most widely accepted techniques for pre-processing SMC include, lexicon-based approaches and techniques based on computational linguistics.

Lexicon-based approaches exploit the features of dictionaries that prepare the data suitable for learning algorithms. For instance, the most commonly used pre-processing technique for sentence-level cleaning is the removal of stopwords (Zhang et al., 2009). Stopwords consist of inferential terms, pronouns, and other lexical terms that do not carry much semantic information alone. The basic idea of removing stopwords is to eliminate terms that carry less or no content information, such as articles, prepositions and conjunctions. Stopwords removal helps in retrieval engines to focus on searching documents that contain relevant keywords. Similarly, morphological and deflective endings from words in English can be removed using a simple pre-processing technique called stemming. Stemming reconstruct the words to its base form, e.g., eliminating 's' from plural nouns, the 'ing' from verbs, or any other affixes. A stem is a natural group of words with identical meanings. Hence, after stemming, each word is delinated by its base word. Porter (2006), originally proposed a set of production rules that perform iterative transforms over English words into their stems called Porter stemmer. In (Pappas et al., 2012), a process called lemmatization is used to extract term scores from SentiWordNet (Baccianella et al., 2010) that converts each token to its dictionary equivalent. Lemmatization maps each verb form to several tenses and nouns to a singular form. Both, stopwords removal and lemmatization will enhance the recall by automatically truncating word endings to their base words, which also help in indexing and searching. Key-phrase extraction algorithms have a critical role in the automatic extraction of topical words and phrases from opinion content (Zhao et al., 2011; Turney, 2000). They provide a concise description of a document's content and are useful in many SASM tasks.

Furthermore, pre-processing techniques based on computational linguistics are utilized to characterize the data, which increases the learning capabilities of ML algorithms. The following are some approaches used frequently with SMC. Word sense disambiguation (WSD) is one among those techniques extensively used in SASM, to address the issue of choosing the most suitable meaning for a term concerning the given context (Tsatsaronis et al., 2010). WSD employs semantic models to recognize the context of a word used in a sentence when the occurrence of a word has multiple meanings. This is essential in several applications such as discourse analysis, anaphora resolution, and improves the relevance of search engines (Wadawadagi & Pagi, in press). Another important pre-processing technique termed, named-entity recognition (NER) (Nadeau & Sekine, 2007) can be applied as a pre-processing technique to locate and classify the information units from given text content into predefined categories. NER task labels sequence of words in a sentence that are the names of things, such as person and company names, or city and country. Additionally, techniques from NLP such as POST and word-net semantic categories are used as augmented features. Given each word in a sentence, POST assigns the proper part-of-speech tags, like noun, verb, adverb, adjective, etc. (Charniak, 1997). This helps to disambiguate homonyms and assigns linguistic information to sub-sentential units. Nevertheless, the above list is not exhaustive, but also includes many other techniques such as negation phrase identification (NPI), bi-term extraction, URL pre-treatment, removal of replicated characters from fancy words, replacement of emoticons, substitute abbreviations by their full names and many more. The comparative study of different IE tasks and pre-processing techniques, and their applicability to various SMC analysis tasks is presented in Table 1.

Table 1. Comparative study of IE tasks and pre-processing techniques

Task domain	Applicability	Process domain	Utility
Arguments extraction	IE task	Identifies and extracts the conflict statements from social media feeds.	Beneficial in fine-grained analysis of sentiments in social media posts.
Bi-term extraction	Pre-processing	Generates the word co-occurrence patterns and learns the topics directly from social media posts.	Improves topic learning by modelling word co-occurrence patterns.
Canonical and event records extraction	IE task	Learns the hidden set of records and record-message alignment.	Useful for converting unstructured text to structured format.
Key-phrases extraction	IE task & Pre-processing	Identifies a set of words and phrases that indicates the topical relevance of a social media post.	It provides a concise description of text content and quantifies semantic similarity between them.
Negation phrases detection	IE task & Pre-processing	Identifies and extracts the negative phrases in the SMC for a given context.	Often useful in polarity detection of and content filtering.
User profiles extraction	IE task	Extracts users's profile information in social networking websites.	Frequently used in grouping of users based on their profile.
Subjective content extraction	IE task	Identifies and extracts the subjective information from social media posts.	Beneficial in subjective content analysis and summerization.
Named-entity extraction	IE task & Pre-processing	Labels each word in a social media post to denote the name of a person, place, object, organization and some times numerical expressions such as date, time and currency.	Useful in finding and categorizing expressions of special meaning in blog posts.
Part-of-speech tagging	Pre-processing	Labels each word in a sequence of text content as mapping to a specific part-of-speech based on definition and context.	It helps to disambiguate homonyms and assigns linguistic information to sub-sentential units and also useful in authorship detection.
Replacement of emoticons	Pre-processing	Removes non-letter symbols and punctuation from feeds, and replacing emoticons with single words and abbreviations by its corresponding full form text.	It improves content representation and makes it suitable for learning algorithms.
Stemming and lemmatization	Pre-processing	Reduces deflective and morphological endings of a word to a common base form.	Helps in indexing and searching and other sentiment classification tasks.
Stopwords removal	Pre-processing	Removes the words that are commonly used in a given language.	Helps retrieval engines to actually focus on searching pages that contain the important words.
URL pre-treatment	Pre-processing	Models navigational and behaviour patterns of users by extracting relevant information from a link and URL.	Useful in web personalization, web log analysis, content filtering and objectionable content detection.
Word sense disambiguation	Pre-processing	Identifies the context for a given word used in a sentence when the occurrence of a word has multiple meanings.	Useful in discourse analysis, improves relevance of search engines and anaphora resolution.

MACHINE LEARNING TECHNIQUES

In this section, several contemporary ML techniques applied for SASM are discussed and evaluated from the perspective of the underlying concepts used. There are different ways that an ML algorithm can model a problem based on its interaction with the input data. Following this trend, we can classify ML techniques into three main categories: (1) Supervised learning, (2) Unsupervised learning, and (3) Semi-supervised learning.

Supervised Learning

In ML paradigm, supervised learning is being referred as classification or inductive learning. This kind of learning is similar to human learning from past evidences to obtain new knowledge, and to improve our ability to solve real-life problems. Thus, in supervised learning techniques, all classes obtained are meaningful to humans, and can easily be applied to discriminative pattern classification. There has been a significant amount of contribution to supervised learning available in the literature to address the challenges of SASM.

In the first place, the naive Bayes classifier (NBC) is the simplest probabilistic classifier derived from Baye's theorem with strong (naive) independence assumptions between the features is utilized (Russell & Norvig, 2003). In connection to sentiment classification, NBC estimates the posterior probability of a class based on the distribution of lexical terms present in the opinion sentence (Medhat et al., 2014). The NBC is consistent with bag-of-words (BOW) feature representation that does not include positions of the words in the sentence. Furthermore, NBC could be employed for both coarse-grained (binary) and fine-grained (multi-class) sentiment classification tasks. For instance, fast and efficient methods of monitoring public sentiments over social media are discussed in (Anjaria & Gudetti, 2014; Alkhodair et al., in press; Chen, et al., 2014). Here, the models have utilized unigram, bigram, and hybrid (unigram and bigram) word vectors as features for NBC. A specific type of NBC known as a multinomial naive Bayes classifier (MNBC) is also used effectively in SASM (da Silva et al., 2014; Vermeer et al., in press). Unlike NBC, MNBC follows multinomial distribution across the feature values instead of features to be conditionally independent of each other. The distribution is estimated through the generative NB principle with the assumption that features are distributed multinomially for computing the probability of the sentence for each class. Classifiers based on NB are known to be computationally efficient in terms of computational time and memory. In addition to NBC, a probabilistic classifier that refers to a group of exponential models known as maximum-entropy (MaxEnt) classifiers are also utilized. The MaxEnt classifiers in no case consider the features to be conditionally independent; however, it is based on the principle of maximum-entropy (Li et al., 2014). The MaxEnt principle asserts that the probability distribution of available information represented in an optimal manner leads to distribution with highest information entropy. In the context of sentiment classification, MaxEnt transforms labelled feature sets to vectors using encoding schemes (Anjaria & Gudetti, 2014; Alkhodair et al., in press). These encoded vectors are utilized to compute the weights for each feature, and are further combined to obtain the most likely label for that feature set. In contrast to MaxEnt, Bayesian network (BN) or probabilistic directed acyclic graph (PDAG) is a probabilistic graph model that represents a set of random variables and their conditional dependencies through a directed graph (Russell & Norvig, 2003; Medhat et al., 2014; Arbelaitz et al., 2013). In such a graph, each vertex corresponds to a random variable $p(x)$, and the edge between the vertices $p(y|x)$ represents the conditional dependency between the variables. The vertices and edges define the structure of the BN, while the conditional probabilities are the parameters for this graph. Inference and structure learning are two main learning tasks for BN. In the simplest case, network structure can be specified manually instead of learning it from data. Once the structure is obtained, classification can be conducted through inference. Similarly, conditional random fields (CRF) are a genre of the discriminative models often used for sentence structure prediction (Pang et al., 2002). CRF utilizes contextual information from previous labels to enhance the amount of information required for making optimal predictions. They find numerous applications in SA including shallow parsing, key-phrase identification, and named-entity recognition.

An alternative to probabilistic classifiers, yet another group of classifiers named as linear classifiers are extensively used in sentiment classification. Linear classifiers carry out classification based on the values of a linear combination of the feature vectors (Medhat et al., 2014; Li et al., 2009). In the case of binary classification task, a linear classifier can be visualized as a hyperplane that separates a high-dimensional input space into two partitions: all points on the one side are classified as *'true'*, and the other side as *'false'*. Linear classifiers are more suitable for specific problems in pattern recognition such as document classification and importantly for data objects comprising more features, reaching high accuracy levels comparable to non-linear classifiers while consuming less time for training. Two of the most important linear classifiers used in SASM are support vector machines (SVM) (Cortes & Vapnik, 1995) and artificial neural networks (ANN) (Wasserman, 1993). The SVM classifier generates an optimal hyper-plane form a given set of labelled training samples, and further categorizes new samples based on the hyper-plane obtained, making it a non-probabilistic binary linear classifier. The hyper-plane is a reference line obtained to best separate the data points in the input space through their class labels into *'true'* or *'false'*. Furthermore, SVM constructs a non-linear decision surface in the original feature space by mapping the data objects non-linearly to an inner product space, where the class labels can be separated linearly with a hyper-plane (Aizerman et al., 1964). The SVM classifier is ideally suitable for handling user-generated content present on the web, this is due to the sparse behavior of textual content in which certain features are not relevant, but they often tend to be correlated with each another. Consequently, SVM is efficiently used in several sentiment classification tasks (Anjaria & Gudetti, 2014; Alkhodair et al., in press; da Silva et al., 2014; Vermeer et al., in press), as this is highly reliable for traditional text classification. A variation of SVM, called passive-aggressive model (PAM) is also used for solving numerous SA related problems (Vermeer et al., in press). PAM models are similar to SVM, but they use margin to update the parameter values of a classifier. In simple words, if the prediction is correct then it will be passive, otherwise, when the prediction goes wrong then weights are updated for correct classification.

On the contrary, ANN is composed of artificial neurons that imitate the biological neurons of the human brain (Medhat et al., 2014; Ruiz & Srinivasan, 1999; Schultz & Reitmann, 2018). These neurons are connected by links and are capable of interacting with each other. The inputs of neurons are represented by the feature vector X_i which denotes the term frequencies of the ith document. Each edge of the network is associated with certain weights for computing the input function. The output of each neuron is then transferred to other neurons in a sequence. The output at each node is referred to as its activation or a node value. They are capable of learning through updating the weight values of each link. Furthermore, multi-layer neural networks which are also called as deep neural networks (DNN) solve the classification problem for non-linear sets by employing hidden layers, to induce multiple piecewise linear boundaries, that are used to approximate enclosed regions belonging to a particular class (Pandey & Solanki, 2019). Accordingly, the output of neurons in the previous layers is fed into the neurons of next layers. The additional hidden layers can be interpreted geometrically as extra hyper-planes, which improve the separation capability of the network. The training process of DNN is more complex because the errors need to be back-propagated over different layers.

Random forest (RF) is one of the other ML techniques that is frequently used in sentiment classification (Alkhodair et al., in press; da Silva et al., 2014; Vermeer et al., in press). It is an ensemble learning method that constructs a multitude of decision trees while training and returns the class with the mode of the classes or mean prediction of the individual trees (Wan & Gao, 2015). The strength of RF classifier is that, it creates a huge number of random classification trees. That is, it randomly resamples the data to train a new classifier for each subsample with a random subsample of available variables. Furthermore, it exhibits robustness against overfitting, and is easy to use, as it needs only two arguments, the number of variables for building the individual trees and the number of trees.

Unsupervised Learning

In several cases, the class labels are unknown to the classification algorithms. However, the analyst wants to investigate the data for mining some interesting patterns underlying the dataset. Unsupervised learning techniques are advantageous to address the issues of identifying hidden patterns in unlabelled data. Many researchers have been tried to explore this phenomenon to provide the solution for sentiment classification problems. For instance, a framework based on unsupervised TRI-clustering is proposed for analyzing both user-level and tweet-level sentiments (Zhu, 2014). The TRI-clustering mechanism exploits the property of duality for both sentiment clustering and tripartite graph co-clustering. However, co-clustering is an unsupervised learning technique and it does not require labelled data. But, the model uses high quality labelled data for experimentation in view of achieving improved performance. Finally, a non-negative matrix co-factorization technique is used to compute the best co-cluster of a tripartite graph. Further, the model uses emotion consistency regularization to generate the clusters of features that are relevant to the feature lexicon, and closer to the sentiment classes. Similarly, an unsupervised and distributed model for twitter data that uses different domain-independent sentiment lexicons, namely, SentiWordNet, SenticNet, and SentiSlangNet is proposed (Pandarachalil et al., 2015). In this technique, a sentiment score for each tweet in a corpus is determined using the SENT_SCORE algorithm. The n-grams of tweet messages are obtained through pre-processing and are input to the algorithm. The results prove that SenticNet yields better polarity scores for several n-grams which are frequently used in tweets and hence, improves the performance of the model. In (Lim et al., 2017), an unsupervised learning technique to discover the real-world latent infectious diseases from social media data is discussed. The model investigates the public's expressions about symptoms, body parts, and location information present in SMC. The emotion detection algorithm called SentiStrength (Thelwall et al., 2010) is efficiently employed to perform the unsupervised SA task. The SentiStrength algorithm receives social media text as input and generates a sentiment score that ranges between -5 to 5. Subsequently, a weight vector of symptoms and a period of individual sentiments can be recorded. Finally, the weight vectors obtained are used to discover the latent infectious disease-related information. In addition to this, a novel approach for predicting sentiments in Twitter messages using unsupervised dependency parsing-based text classification that jointly works with NLP techniques and sentiment lexicons is presented (Fernández-Gavilanes et al., 2016). The sentiment lexicons are created through a semi-automatic polarity expansion algorithm, enabling them for domain-specific applications. Further, NLP techniques are applied to capture the linguistic peculiarities from the tweets that improve detection performance. The list mentioned above is however not exhaustive, but suggestive of a wide range of ML techniques used for SASM.

Semi-Supervised Learning

Recently, semi-supervised learning techniques have been extensively used to address the problem of insufficient labelled data readily available for training. Hence, semi-supervised learning techniques use limited amount of labelled data with a huge amount of unlabelled data to train an accurate model. For example, in (Khan et al., 2017), a semi-supervised model that combines a lexicon-based (SentiWordNet) approach with a SVM to perform sentiment classification is proposed. The model utilizes two statistical techniques namely, information gain (IG) and cosine similarity to update the sentiment scores defined in SentiWordNet, and further they are termed as Senti-IG and Senti-Cosine respectively. The subjective features are then extracted using Senti-IG and Senti-Cosine for processing. Interestingly, nouns are treated as semantic words when combination with adjectives, verbs and adverbs. Finally, a context-specific hybrid learning model coupled with SVM is developed to achieve desirable performance. Furthermore, a model based on non-negative matrix factorization (NMF) termed as constrained-NMF (CNMF) that imposes labelled information constrain and sparseness constrain for social media spam detection is presented (Yu et al., 2017). The learned representation presents highly distinguishable features through the data provided by a few labelled samples and a large amount of unlabelled samples. The performance of the model is estimated through the iterative update rules (IUR) and optimization of the CNMF-based social media spammer detection. In addition to this, an emerging semi-supervised learning technique for the task of emotion recognition in social media posts using multi-dimensional scaling (MDS) through random projections and biased-SVM (bSVM) is presented (Hussain & Cambria, 2018). The above model uses biased regularization that provides an easy way to implement an inductive bias in kernel machines. This aspect carries great importance in ML theory and characterizes the generalization capability of a learning system.

Gupta et al., (2018) presents a new approach based on semi-supervised and transfer learning for the task of sentiment classification. This model is designed based on the principle of coherent implementation of several technologies will yield good results. Hence, this model uses dense feature representations, pre-training, and manifold regularization. In the first stage, the model learns dense representations for opinion sentences with *doc2vec* word-embeddings, and later performs classification with pre-training and manifold regularization. The research records significant improvements in results for supervised learning techniques when a good amount of data is available. Similarly, an ensemble semi-supervised learning technique that blends label propagation and transductive-SVM (TSVM) with Dempster–Shafer theory is presented for accurate prediction of social lending in unlabelled data (Kim & Cho, 2019). Label propagation is a technique used to assign class labels to previously collected unlabelled data so that data with similar features are mapped to the same class. The TSVM classifier is responsible for discriminating data with different features, and Dempster–Shafer fusion method measures whether unlabelled data can be classified on the basis of results obtained for semi-supervised learning methods. The effectiveness of the proposed model is illustrated with the experiment being conducted over the social loan data comprising two-third unlabelled data.

CHALLENGES OF APPLYING ML TECHNIQUES TO SMC

The application of ML techniques to SMC exhibits several intellectual challenges. In the following paragraph, many issues and challenges of applying ML techniques to social media data are presented. In the first place, the unique qualities of SMC, which is being formed by short text messages, pose a major challenge (Sapountzi & Psannis, 2018). It is seen that short messages carry sparse data and often depends on the context in which they are stated. Accordingly, they differ substantially from other sentiment data such as online reviews. Hence, the feature vectors obtained on a specific corpus of SMC may not yield sufficient productivity for document similarity. Furthermore, social media platforms support informal writing, where people use idiomatic and creative phrases in their posts. This causes ML algorithms hard for them to build automated models for large-scale SA. Additionally, short messages streaming over the social media in large quantities, leads to labelling problems when used for supervised training. Finding adequate techniques for real-time analysis of streaming data is a potential problem (Ji et al., 2015). However, unsupervised training does not require labelled data and hence, clustering has become a promising ML approach for real-time analysis of social media data.

Table 2. Different learning models and their merits

Learning model	Methodology	Merits
Artificial neural networks	Based on biological neural networks that learns to accomplish tasks through instances without being explicitly programmed with any task-specific rules.	A robust data-driven, flexible and self-adaptive learning model resilient to capture non-linear and complex underlying characteristics with a high degree of accuracy.
Naive Bayes	A probabilistic model originated from Bayes theorem with strong independence assumptions among the features.	Highly scalable and fast model construction with linear predictors and row scoring scales. Effectively used for both binary and multi-class problems.
Support vector machines	A classifier learns from labelled data and generates optimal hyper-planes that categorize new examples.	Merits includes kernel based model, absence of local minima, sparseness of the solution, and capacity to control the margin by optimization.
Maximum entropy	The probability distribution that best represents the current knowledge will be the one with the largest entropy subjected to precisely stated prior data.	The facts used to model the data are linguistically very simple, but yet succeed in approximating complex linguistic relationships.
Bayesian networks	A probabilistic graphical model that characterizes a set of random variables and their conditional dependencies through a directed acyclic graph.	Readily handles incomplete data, and facilitates use of prior knowledge. Also provides an efficient method for preventing the over-fitting of data.
Random forests	Constructs a forest of decision trees during training and results a class with mode of the classes or mean prediction of the individual trees.	Highly accurate classifier for scalable dataset and also useful in estimating prime attributes in the classification process.
Passive aggressive models	This model is streaming ML technique used for classification and regression.	A fast classification model for big streaming data and easy to implement, but does not guarantee global parameters observed in SVM.
TRI-clustering	It uses an automatic boundary searching algorithm based on a divide-and-conquer technique capable of identifying statistically significant REV values that correspond to a 3D region in the whole data space.	Provides an explicit representation of the regulatory effects in the dataset and identifies transitions in the network from condition-to-condition implicit in the boundaries of the identified TRI-clusters.
Non-negative matrix factorization	Factorizes a iven matrix into two matrices based on non-negative constraints, which allow learning parts from objects.	Efficiently extracts features from the text contents, and generates feature-document matrix that describes clusters of related documents.

Secondly, SMC is inherently noisy, consisting of unconventional words, misspells, grammatical errors, acronyms, spammers, and even slang. A considerable amount of pre-processing is required before applying ML techniques to social media data (Goswami & Kumar, 2017). Formulating business strategies with inaccurate and noisy data leads to distortion in the results of analytics. However, pre-processing is still a time-consuming process. Moreover, processing and analysis of privacy-preserved data is another critical challenge in SASM (Bello-Orgaz et al., 2016). Many social media data providers vend their data to various third party customers such as companies and analysts. To prevent data from privacy breaching and attacks, it is often protected with privacy-preserving techniques. It is hard to evaluate and test privacy-preserved data using traditional ML techniques. Therefore, it would be interesting to design and develop specialized techniques and benchmark datasets to address this issue. Finally, each research problem in SASM adopts a different ML technique; many researchers are concerned about how some ML techniques can hardly be validated (Wadawadagi & Pagi, in press). Although most researchers use popular validation techniques such as confusion matrix, precision and recall, area under curve (AUC), etc. for their models, some researchers do not use any measurements. Hence, much of the debate on validating techniques for automated SASM is misguiding. Further, automated SASM methods are incorrect models of languages. This means that the performance of any technique on a new dataset cannot be guaranteed, and therefore validation is important when applying these methods.

APPLICATIONS

Investigation and analysis of SMC have potential advantages over several ongoing topics of interest such as investigating how topics evolve along with the underlying social interactions between participants, and to distinguish vital members who have a great influence on various topics of discussion. Based on the study of current literature, the following paragraphs present several application areas of SASM.

Brand Sentiment Analysis

Social media messages are extensively used to investigate consumer's sentiment towards a brand. They offer a unique repository of customer reviews in the world of brand sentiment. Popular brands and celebrities receive opinions and comments directly from consumers or members in real-time through a public forum. Both the targeted and competing brands have the opportunity to interpret the opinions for bringing transformation in consumer sentiments towards their brand (Ghiassi et al., 2013). For example, TripAdvisor is America's biggest tourist web portal providing reviews of travelers about their experiences in flights, hotels, and restaurants. These customer opinions may have a positive or negative influence on brand perception, loyalty, and promotion. Thus, SA on large-scale user opinions will help enterprises to tap into customer's insight for improving their quality of product, services, or even anticipate new business opportunities and other activities accordingly.

Political Ideology Detection

The identification of political ideology from micro-blog contents is extremely useful in analyzing one's affinity towards a political movement. This brings an ideal environment for advertising political thoughts during the heat of election campaigns (Chen et al., 2017). Though political ideologies follow diverse and complex phenomenon, yet they can be approximated through the utilization of NLP and ML techniques. The basic concept of discovering ideologies is to understand the difference of opinions toward certain topics. Then, based on the distribution of opinions quoted different ideologies can be grouped (Gu et al., 2016). Most of the research work on ideology detection has been discussed as a binary classification problem, i.e. grouping people into liberal or a conservative. However, this ignores the fact that people's ideology always lies in a broad spectrum (Larsen, 2015). Every individual carries different ideology which differs his stand on political matters. Hence, it is important to infer ideologies not only based on opinions but also the target entities or topics on which the sentiment is expressed. Further, this may also help in exploring and tracking electoral preferences (political trends) of citizens in the country.

Emotion Detection

Emotion detection in SMC is beneficial for several applications such as recommendation systems, personalized advertising, developing automated counseling systems, emergency response systems, etc. It deals with the investigation of emotional state of individuals or communities who are participating in online campaigns. Emotion detection systems are instrumental in disaster management, where people use social media to report emergency service agencies (Ceron et al., 2015). These messages often carry not only sentiments related to disaster management, but also contain status information. Hence, specialized models need to be designed to address sentiment prediction infused with other emotion-related traits. In addition to this, social media offers an opportunity to acquire insights through which the emotional pulse of the nation can be determined, and hence, to discover web communities (Bügel & Zielinski, 2013; Kanavos et al., 2017). Web communities are created through the identification of associated clusters based on similar emotional behaviors.

Implicit Sentiment In Financial News

The exploitation of sentiments in financial news enables business analysts to study the impact of news on the company's growth (Kauter et al., 2015). However, the term sentiment in financial domain is used in a different perspective as "the expectations of stakeholders relative to some standards". Essentially, this kind of analysis helps in predicting the effect of financial news on stock markets. In practice, business analysts carry out manual predictions of the stock exchange based on comments and reports in the news articles. Through advanced language models and machine intelligence, the activity of stock market prediction can be performed with better accuracy over a huge collection of text content. Recently, the formulation of domain-specific ontology enabled automatic processing of information through knowledge representation. There is a growing demand for the construction of precise and powerful ontology in the financial domain.

Monitoring Public Health

Surveillance of communicable diseases (epidemics) caused by viruses or bacteria, which spreads among the people can be a challenging problem (Ji et al., 2015). Keeping records of infectious diseases in the interest of public health and identifying its causes are therefore important. On the other hand, monitoring emotional changes of the public after being affected by diseases is also a prime concern of the public health department. In view of this, SASM offers a better tool for public health inspectors and concerned authorities to take the measure of concern expressed by the public. For instance, Twitter as a micro-blog service alone generates 400 million tweets every day, directly received from the public. Tweets expressing concerns about certain diseases may not have a direct emotional impact of that disease on the public. However, messages that are re-tweeted with emotional expressions might be directly affected.

Sarcasm Detection

The term sarcasm refers to a kind of irony broadly used in social media and micro-blogging posts. It is sophisticated form of opinon statement used to express implicit information of a person such as criticism or mockery (Bouazizi & Otsuki, 2016). However, identification of sarcasm is difficult even for human beings. Hence, recognition of sarcastic phrases could be beneficial in improving the automated SA of data collected from micro-blogging or social media posts. The use of aggressive, violent or offensive language, hateful comments, targeting a specific group of people sharing common property, whether this property is their gender (i.e., sexism), their ethnic group or race (i.e., racism) or their believes and religion are considered as hate messages. However, most of the online social networks and micro-blogging websites forbid the use of hate content. The size of these networks and websites makes it almost impossible to control all of their content.

CONCLUSION

This chapter focused on numerous state-of-the-art ML techniques used in the domain of sentiment analysis on social media (SASM) and its applications. The research sheds light on several techniques used for extracting relevant information from social media content (SMC). Further, the work studied important pre-processing techniques employed to filter out the noise from SMC. Subsequently, many issues and challenges of applying ML techniques to SMC are also presented. Finally, the chapter discussed several application areas that assert the importance of ML techniques in SASM. Despite, the continuous evolution of SASM techniques, still there are ample opportunities and challenges for researchers. Interest in SMC for regional languages other than English is growing as there is still a lack of tools and technologies concerning these languages. Lexicons similar to WordNet which supports many regional languages other than English need to be developed. In many cases, opinions are very much dependent on the context. Hence, it is beneficial to study the context of the opinion and research needs to be focused on context-based SASM systems.

REFERENCES

Aizerman, M., Braverman, E., & Rozonoer, L. (1964). Theoretical foundations of the potential function method in pattern recognition learning. *Autom. Rem. Cont.*, 821–837.

Alkhodair, S. A., Ding, S. H. H., Fung, B. C. M., & Liu, J. (in press). Detecting breaking news rumors of emerging topics in social media. *Information Processing & Management*. doi:10.1016/j.ipm.2019.02.016

Anami, B. S., Wadawadagi, R. S., & Pagi, V. B. (2014). Machine learning techniques in web content mining: A comparative analysis. *Journal of Information & Knowledge Management*, *13*(1), 1–14. doi:10.1142/S0219649214500051

Anjaria, M., & Gudetti, R. M. R. (2014). A novel sentiment analysis of social networks using supervised learning. *Social Network Analysis and Mining*, *4*(3), 181–193. doi:10.100713278-014-0181-9

Arbelaitz, O., Gurrutxaga, I., Lojo, A., Muguerza, J., Maria, J., & Perona, P. I. (2013). Web usage and content mining to extract knowledge for modeling the users of the Bidasoa Turismo website and to adapt it. *Expert Systems with Applications*, *40*(18), 7478–7491. doi:10.1016/j.eswa.2013.07.040

Baccianella, S., Esuli, A., & Sebastiani, F. (2010). Sentiwordnet 3.0: an enhanced lexical resource for sentiment analysis and opinion mining. *Proc. of the Annual Conference on Language Resources and Evaluation*, 2200–2204.

Bello-Orgaz, G., Jung, J. J., & Camacho, D. (2016). Social big data: Recent achievements and new challenges. *Information Fusion*, *28*, 45–59. doi:10.1016/j.inffus.2015.08.005

Benson, E., & Haghighi Barzilay, R. (2011). Event discovery in social media feeds. *Proc. of the 49th Annual Meeting of the Association for Computational Linguistics: Human Language technologies*, *1*, 389-398.

Bontcheva, K., Derczynski, L., Funk, A., Greenwood, M. A., Maynard, D., & Aswani, N. (2013). TwitIE: a fully-featured information extraction pipeline for microblog text. *Proc. of the International Conference On Recent Advances In Natural Language Processing*, 83-90. *doi:*10.6084/m9.figshare.1003767.v2

Bouazizi, M., & Otsuki, T. (2016). A pattern-based approach for sarcasm detection on twitter. *IEEE Access: Practical Innovations, Open Solutions*, *4*, 5477–5488. doi:10.1109/ACCESS.2016.2594194

Bügel, U., & Zielinski, A. (2013). Multilingual analysis of twitter news in support of mass emergency events. *International Journal of Information Systems for Crisis Response and Management*, *5*(1), 77–85. doi:10.4018/jiscrm.2013010105

Ceron, A., Curini, L., & Iacus, S. M. (2015). Using sentiment analysis to monitor electoral campaigns: Method matters-evidence from the United States and Italy. *Social Science Computer Review*, *33*(1), 3–20. doi:10.1177/0894439314521983

Charniak, E. (1997). Statistical techniques for natural language parsing. *AI Magazine*, *18*(4), 33–44.

Chen, W., Zhang, X., Wang, T., Yang, B., & Li, Y. (2017). Opinion-aware knowledge graph for political ideology detection. *Proceedings of the Twenty-Sixth International Joint Conference on Artificial Intelligence (IJCAI-17)*, 3647-3653. 10.24963/ijcai.2017/510

Chen, X., Vorvoreanu, M., & Madhavan, K. (2014). Mining social media data for understanding students learning experiences. *IEEE Transactions on Learning Technologies*, *7*(3), 246–259. doi:10.1109/TLT.2013.2296520

Choi, H. J., & Park, C. H. (2019). Emerging topic detection in Twitter stream based on high utility pattern mining. *Expert Systems with Applications*, *115*, 27–36. doi:10.1016/j.eswa.2018.07.051

Cortes, C., & Vapnik, V. N. (1995). Support-vector networks. *Machine Learning, 20*(3), 273–297. doi:10.1007/BF00994018

Cunningham, H., Tablan, V., Roberts, A., & Bontcheva, K. (2013). Getting more out of biomedical documents with gate's full lifecycle open source text analytics. *PLoS Computational Biology*, *9*(2), e1002854. doi:10.1371/journal.pcbi.1002854 PMID:23408875

da Silva, N. F. F., Hruschka, E. R., & Hruschka, E. R. Jr. (2014). Tweet sentiment analysis with classifier ensembles. *Decision Support Systems*, *66*, 170–179. doi:10.1016/j.dss.2014.07.003

Fernández-Gavilanes, M., Álvarez-López, T., Juncal-Martínez, J., Costa-Montenegro, E., & González-Castaño, F. (2016). Unsupervised method for sentiment analysis in online texts. *Expert Systems with Applications*, *58*, 57–75. doi:10.1016/j.eswa.2016.03.031

Ghiassi, M., Skinner, J., & Zimbra, D. (2013). Twitter brand sentiment analysis: A hybrid system using n-gram analysis and dynamic artificial neural network. *Expert Systems with Applications*, *40*(16), 6266–6282. doi:10.1016/j.eswa.2013.05.057

Goswami, A., & Kumar, A. (2017). Challenges in the Analysis of Online Social Networks: A Data Collection Tool Perspective. *Wireless Personal Communications*, *97*(3), 4015–4061. doi:10.100711277-017-4712-3

Goudas, T., Louizos, C., Petasis, G., & Karkaletsis, V. (2014). Argument extraction from news, blogs, and social media. In A. Likas, K. Blekas, & D. Kalles (Eds.), Lecture Notes in Computer Science: Vol. 8445. *Artificial Intelligence: Methods and Applications. SETN 2014*. Cham: Springer.

Gu, Y., Chen, T., Sun, Y., & Wang, B. (2016). *Ideology detection for twitter users with heterogeneous types of links*. ArXiv:1612.08207

Gupta, R., Sahu, S., Espy-Wilson, C., & Narayanan, S. (2018). *Semi-supervised and transfer learning approaches for low resource sentiment classification*. arXiv:1806.02863

Hussain, A., & Cambria, E. (2018). Semi-supervised learning for big social data analysis. *Neurocomputing*, *275*(31), 1662–1673. doi:10.1016/j.neucom.2017.10.010

Ji, X., Chun, S. A., Wei, Z., & Geller, J. (2015). Twitter sentiment classification for measuring public health concerns. *Social Network Analysis and Mining*, *5*(13).

Jianqiang, Z., & Xiaolin, G. (2017). Comparison research on text pre-processing methods on Twitter sentiment analysis. *IEEE Access: Practical Innovations, Open Solutions*, *5*, 2870–2879. doi:10.1109/ACCESS.2017.2672677

Kanavos, A., Perikos, I., Hatzilygeroudis, I., & Tsakalidis, A. (2017). Emotional community detection in social networks. *Computers & Electrical Engineering*, *65*, 449–460. doi:10.1016/j.compeleceng.2017.09.011

Kauter, M. V., Breesch, D., & Hoste, V. (2015). Fine-grained analysis of explicit and implicit sentiment in financial news articles. *Expert Systems with Applications*, *42*(11), 4999–5010. doi:10.1016/j.eswa.2015.02.007

Khan, F. H., Qamar, U., & Bashir, S. (2017). A semi-supervised approach to sentiment analysis using revised sentiment strength based on SentiWordNet. *Knowledge and Information Systems*, *51*(3), 851–872. doi:10.100710115-016-0993-1

Kim, A., & Cho, S. (2019). An ensemble semi-supervised learning method for predicting defaults in social lending. *Engineering Applications of Artificial Intelligence*, *81*, 193–199. doi:10.1016/j.engappai.2019.02.014

Larsen, M. E., Boonstra, T. W., Batterham, P. J., O'Dea, B., Paris, C., & Christensen, H. (2015). We feel: Mapping emotion on Twitter. *IEEE Journal of Biomedical and Health Informatics, 19*(4), 1246–1252. doi:10.1109/JBHI.2015.2403839 PMID:25700477

Li, J., Ritter, A., & Hovy, H. E. (2014). Weakly supervised user profile extraction from twitter. *Proceedings of the 52nd Annual Meeting of the Association for Computational Linguistics,* 165–174.

Li, X., Nsofor, G. C., & Song, L. (2009). A comparative analysis of predictive data mining techniques. *International Journal of Rapid Manufacturing, 1*(2), 50–172. doi:10.1504/IJRAPIDM.2009.029380

Lim, S., Tucker, C. S., & Kumara, S. (2017). An unsupervised machine learning model for discovering latent infectious diseases using social media data. *Jouranl of Biomedical Information, 66,* 82–94. doi:10.1016/j.jbi.2016.12.007 PMID:28034788

Medhat, W., Hassan, A., & Korashy, H. (2014). Sentiment analysis algorithms and applications: A survey. *Ain Shams Engineering Journal, 5*(4), 1093–1113. doi:10.1016/j.asej.2014.04.011

Meier, P., Castillo, C., Imran, M., Elbassuoni, S. M., & Diaz, F. (2013). Extracting information nuggets from disaster-related messages in social media. *10th International Conference on Information Systems for Crisis Response and Management,* 1-10.

Mikolov, T., Sutskever, I., Chen, K., Corrado, G., & Dean, J. (2013). *Distributed representations of words and phrases and their compositionality.* Arxiv:1310.4546

Nadeau, D., & Sekine, S. (2007). A survey of named entity recognition and classification. *Lingvisticae Investigationes,* 3–26.

Nebhi. (2012). Ontology-based information extraction from Twitter. *Proc. of the Workshop On Information Extraction And Entity Analytics On Social Media Data,* 17–22.

Pandarachalil, R., Sendhilkumar, S., & Mahalakshmi, G. S. (2015). Twitter sentiment analysis for large-scale data: An unsupervised approach. *Cognitive Computation, 7*(2), 254–262. doi:10.100712559-014-9310-z

Pandey, S., & Solanki, A. (2019). Music Instrument Recognition using Deep Convolutional Neural Networks. *International. Journal of Information Technology.* doi:10.100741870-019-00285-y

Pang, B., Lee, L., & Vaithyanathan, S. (2002). Thumbs up? Sentiment classification using machine learning techniques. *Proc. of the Conference On Empirical Methods in Natural Language Processing (emnlp), Philadelphia, July 2002, Association for Computational Linguistics,* 79-86.

Pappas, N., Katsimpras, G., & Stamatatos, E. (2012). Extracting informative textual parts from web pages containing user-generated content. *Proc. of 12th International Conference on Knowledge Management and Knowledge Technologies, 4,* 1–8. 10.1145/2362456.2362462

Porter, M. F. (2006). An algorithm for suffix stripping. *Electronic Library and Electronic Systems, 40,* 211–218.

Ritter, A., Clark, S., & Etzioni, O. (2011). Named entity recognition in tweets: An experimental study. *Proc. of the Conference on Empirical Methods in Natural Language Processing (EMNLP 2011),* 1524–1534.

Ruiz, M., & Srinivasan, P. (1999). Hierarchical neural networks for text categorization. *ACM SIGIR Conference, Proc. of the 22nd Annual International ACM SIGIR Conference on Research and Development in Information Retrieval*, 281–282. 10.1145/312624.312700

Russell, S., & Norvig, P. (2003). *Artificial intelligence: a modern approach* (2nd ed.). Prentice Hall.

Salton, G., & Yang, C. S. (1975). A vector space model for automatic indexing. *Communications of the ACM, 18*(11), 613–620. doi:10.1145/361219.361220

Sapountzi, A., & Psannis, K. (2018). Social networking data analysis tools & challenges. *Future Generation Computer Systems, 86*, 893–913. doi:10.1016/j.future.2016.10.019

Schultz, M., & Reitmann, S. (2018). Machine learning approach to predict aircraft boarding. *Transportation Research Part C, Emerging Technologies, 98*, 391–408. doi:10.1016/j.trc.2018.09.007

Singh, S. (2018). *Natural Language Processing for Information Extraction*. CoRR abs/1807.02383

Thelwall, M., Buckley, K., Paltoglou, G., Cai, D., & Kappas, A. (2010). Sentiment strength detection in short informal text. *Journal of the American Society for Information Science and Technology, 61*(12), 2544–2558. doi:10.1002/asi.21416

Tsatsaronis, G., Varlamis, I., & Nørvg, K. (2010). An experimental study on unsupervised graph based word sense disambiguation. *Computational Linguistics and Intelligent Text Processing, LNCS, 6008*, 184–198. doi:10.1007/978-3-642-12116-6_16

Turney, P. (2000). Learning algorithms for keyphrase extraction. *Information Retrieval, 2*(4), 303–336. doi:10.1023/A:1009976227802

Vermeer, S. A. M., Araujo, T., Bernritter, S. F., & Noort, G. (in press). Seeing the wood for the trees: How machine learning can help firms in identifying relevant electronic word-of-mouth in social media. *International Journal of Research in Marketing*. doi:10.1016/j.ijresmar.2019.01.010

Wadawadagi, R. S. & Pagi, V. B. (in press). An enterprise perspective of web content analysis research: *A strategic road-map. International Journal of Knowledge and Web Intelligence*. doi:10.1504/IJKWI.2017.10010794

Wadawadagi, R. S., & Veerappa, B. (2019). A multi-layer approach to opinion polarity classification using augmented semantic tree kernels. *Journal of Experimental & Theoretical Artificial Intelligence, 31*(3), 349–367. doi:10.1080/0952813X.2018.1549108

Waltl, B., Bonczek, G., & Matthes, F. (2018). Rule-based information extraction: advantages, limitations, and perspectives. *Jusletter IT, 22*.

Wan, Y., & Gao, Q. (2015). An ensemble sentiment classification system of twitter data for airline services analysis. *IEEE International Conference on Data Mining Workshop (ICDMW)*, 1318–1325. 10.1109/ICDMW.2015.7

Wasserman, P. D. (1993). *Advanced Methods in Neural Computing*. New York: John Wiley & Sons, Inc.

Yang, M. C., & Rim, H. C. (2014). Identifying interesting Twitter contents using topical analysis. *Expert Systems with Applications, 41*(9), 4330–4336. doi:10.1016/j.eswa.2013.12.051

Yu, D. N., Chen, F. J., Fu, B., & Qin, A. (2017). Constrained NMF-based semi-supervised learning for social media spammer detection. *J. Knowledge-Based Systems, 125*, 64–73. doi:10.1016/j.knosys.2017.03.025

Zhang, X., Xu, C., Cheng, J., Lu, H., & Ma, S. (2009). Effective annotation and search for video blogs with integration of context and content analysis. *IEEE Transactions on Multimedia, 11*(2), 272-285.

Zhao, X., Jiang, J., He, J., Song, Y., Achananuparp, P., Lim, E., & Li, X. (2011). Topical keyphrase extraction from Twitter. *Proc. of the 49th Annual Meeting of the Association for Computational Linguistics: Human Language Technologies*, 379–388.

Zhu, L. (2014). Tripartite graph clustering for dynamic sentiment analysis on social media. *Proc. ACM SIGMOD International Conference on Management of Data (SIGMOD 14)*, 1531-1542. 10.1145/2588555.2593682

Chapter 42
Integrating Feature and Instance Selection Techniques in Opinion Mining

Zi-Hung You

Department of Nephrology, Chiayi Branch, Taichung Veterans General Hospital, Chiayi, Taiwan

Ya-Han Hu

iD https://orcid.org/0000-0002-3285-2983

Department of Information Management, National Central University, Taoyuan, Taiwan & Center for Innovative Research on Aging Society (CIRAS), Chiayi, National Chung Cheng University, Taiwan & MOST AI Biomedical Research Center at National Cheng Kung University, Tainan, Taiwan

Chih-Fong Tsai

Department of Information Management, National Central University, Taiwan

Yen-Ming Kuo

Department of Information Management, National Chung Cheng University, Chiayi, Taiwan

ABSTRACT

Opinion mining focuses on extracting polarity information from texts. For textual term representation, different feature selection methods, e.g. term frequency (TF) or term frequency–inverse document frequency (TF–IDF), can yield diverse numbers of text features. In text classification, however, a selected training set may contain noisy documents (or outliers), which can degrade the classification performance. To solve this problem, instance selection can be adopted to filter out unrepresentative training documents. Therefore, this article investigates the opinion mining performance associated with feature and instance selection steps simultaneously. Two combination processes based on performing feature selection and instance selection in different orders, were compared. Specifically, two feature selection methods, namely TF and TF–IDF, and two instance selection methods, namely DROP3 and IB3, were employed for comparison. The experimental results by using three Twitter datasets to develop sentiment classifiers showed that TF–IDF followed by DROP3 performs the best.

DOI: 10.4018/978-1-6684-6303-1.ch042

1. INTRODUCTION

The prevalence of computing and mobile technologies and the proliferation of social media such as Twitter, Facebook, and Google+ have extended the means of human communication (Ellison, 2007; Xiaomei et al., 2018). According to Thelwall et al. (2011), Twitter has more than five hundred million registered users, and more than 80% of them record their daily experiences and events on the Internet. Consequently, certain businesses have paid considerable attention to customer satisfaction with their products and services. In particular, opinions or comments that are based on text messages can be further analyzed.

Opinion mining or sentiment analysis poses a critical research problem (Li and Wu, 2010; Bravo-Marquez et al., 2013; Hu et al., 2017; Kaue & Moreira, 2016; Khan et al., 2014). It is usually based on text mining techniques including natural language processing (NLP), text analysis, and computational linguistics for identifying and extracting meaningful information from online opinions and reviews, news, or other sentences to predict the emotional state of users (Chatterjee et al., 2018; Deshmukh & Tripathy, 2018; Hu et al., 2018; Lee et al., 2018; Nguyen & Nguyen, 2018; Piryani et al., 2017; Tian et al., 2014). In general, useful keywords or terms related to emotions are extracted on the basis of NLP algorithms (Manning and Schutze, 1999) and publicly available resources such as SentiWordNet[1]; conversely, constructed sentiment classifiers can be used to classify the valence of certain selected opinions.

Opinion mining or sentiment analysis is similar to text classification or categorization. However, effective opinion mining poses two challenges. The first one is that the restrictions of writing an opinion differ substantially between different social network websites, which renders extracting the content of an opinion difficult. Consider, for example, Twitter; a single message is restricted to 140 characters. Under this constraint, fully describing a user's opinion can be extremely difficult.

Researchers in related works have attempted to extract representative keywords to describe sentimental statuses (Bravo-Marquez et al., 2013; Hu et al., 2017; Khan et al., 2014; Li & Wu, 2010; Nguyen & Nguyen, 2018; Tian et al., 2014). This feature extraction step can produce representative features for each opinion and thus enable constructing a classifier. However, the number of features extracted to describe an opinion (or text message) is usually very high, resulting in very high-dimensional feature vectors. Certain features in the high-dimensional feature vectors are not beneficial for the classification task, and such features can be considered noisy information. Therefore, performing feature selection to filter unrepresentative features has been widely studied in research on text classification (Aghdam et al., 2009; Lee & Lee, 2006; Rehman et al., 2017; Zheng et al., 2004). Recently, this topic has been considered in studies on opinion mining (Abbasi et al., 2008; Agarwal & Mittal, 2013; Nicholls & Song, 2010), but it has not been fully explored.

The second challenge is that when the volume of text documents is certainly large, certain documents can generally be considered outliers, which may degrade the final classification performance. Performing instance selection for filtering unrepresentative data has been shown to be effective in enhancing the performance of a classifier relative to a classifier without instance selection (Li & Jacob, 2008; Wilson & Martinez, 2000). Recent related studies have considered instance selection in text classification (Tsai & Chang, 2013; Tsai et al., 2014; Vinodhini & Chandrasekaran, 2017). However, few studies have focused on the effect of performing instance selection on opinion mining.

The research objectives of this study were (1) to provide a comprehensive evaluation of performing both feature and instance selections in opinion mining and (2) to develop a novel opinion mining process by integrating feature and instance selection techniques.

This paper examines the classification performance by investigating both feature and instance selection tasks over data sets of opinion mining. Specifically, two ordering strategies exist for performing feature and instance selection for opinion mining. The first strategy entails performing feature selection and then instance selection, whereas the second one involves executing instance selection and then feature selection. The main contribution of this paper is that it describes the most effective ordering strategy as a guideline for future opinion mining studies.

The remainder of this paper is organized as follows. Section 2 reviews the related literature including opinion mining, feature selection, and instance selection. Section 3 describes the two ordering strategies of performing both feature and instance selection. Section 4 presents the experimental setup and results. Finally, the conclusion is provided in Section 5.

2. LITERATURE REVIEW

2.1. Opinion Mining

Opinion mining or sentiment analysis focuses on extracting and analyzing judgments on various aspects of specific items. It also includes many types of evaluative text analysis. Classification is a fundamental process in opinion mining. In general, classification is based on the binary classification task of labeling an opinionated document as expressing the polarity of the opinion (Pang & Lee, 2008).

The first step for effectively mining opinions requires a deep understanding of explicit and implicit, regular and irregular, and syntactical and semantic language rules, which belong to the problem of NLP (Cambria et al., 2013). Therefore, to ensure that a classifier directly interprets texts (i.e., opinionated documents), an indexing procedure based on feature extraction is required; in such a procedure, meaningful terms are extracted from each document as features for document representation. A standard term frequency–inverse document frequency (TF-IDF) function is commonly used for determining weight of each term (Salton & Buckley, 1988). In addition, publicly available lexical resources such as SentiWord-Net can be used for analyzing sets of synonyms and assigning three sentiment scores to them, which are positivity, negativity, and objectivity.

Once each text document is represented as a feature vector, the second step is to collect a selected set of feature vectors and their corresponding sentimental statuses as training examples to construct a classifier on the basis of supervised learning techniques (Mitchell, 1997). In particular, such a classifier is trained to approximate the mapping between input-output examples, and it appropriately labels the training set with a certain level of accuracy. After the classifier is constructed, it can classify an unknown instance into one of the learned class labels in the training set.

2.2. Feature Selection

Because the number of extracted features from text documents is typically extremely high (e.g., >10 000), the problem of dimensionality and overfitting in a high-dimensional feature space used for training a classifier may arise. Specifically, not all of the collected features of a selected data set are informative or provide high discriminative power (Powell, 2007). To solve this problem, feature selection can be considered, which focuses on removing irrelevant or redundant features (or both). After their careful selection, the features can facilitate performance improvement for the classifier learning task (Guyon & Elisseeff, 2003).

Feature selection can be defined as the process of choosing a minimum subset of n features from an original data set of m features ($n < m$) so that the feature space (i.e., the dimensionality) is optimally reduced.

Feature selection has been widely studied in text classification, where numerous unrepresentative unique terms can be filtered (Yang & Pedersen, 1997; Forman, 2003; Azam & Yao, 2012), and feature selection has also been considered in opinion mining (Abbasi et al., 2008; Agarwal & Mittal, 2013; Nicholls & Song, 2010). Among the various feature selection methods in the literature, TF, document frequency, and TF–IDF are the most widely used baseline methods.

2.3. Instance Selection

Similar to feature selection, collected training data might not all be equally informative, and certain data observations can be considered noisy points or outliers, which are likely to degrade the final classification performance. In general, outliers are unusual observations (or unfavorable data points) that are far from the mass of data. Specifically, an outlier is a value further away from the sample mean than what is deemed reasonable.

Although no standard definition of outliers is available, instance selection can be considered a substitute for eliminating outliers; the aim of instance selection is to automatically remove unrepresentative data observations from a selected training data set without human involvement, and the reduced data set can still maintain the integrity of the original data set (Wilson & Martinez, 2000).

Instance selection can be defined as follows. Let X_i be an instance where $X_i = (X_{i1}, X_{i2}, ..., X_{im}, X_{ic})$, meaning that X_i is represented by m-dimensional features and that it belongs to class c given by X_{ic}. Next, assume that there exists a target set TA comprising M instances, which is used for instance selection. Consequently, the subset of selected samples S is produced, where $S \subseteq TA$. Given a testing set TS, we can classify a new pattern T from TS over the instances of S and TA. If the instance selection algorithm has been chosen appropriately, then the performance of a classifier trained by S should be higher than that of a classifier trained by TA.

In the literature, various instance selection methods have been proposed for improving the classification performance. In particular, García et al. (2012) conducted a comprehensive study to compare numerous well-known algorithms, and they found that hybrid–learning-based algorithms, such as DROP3, IB3, GA, and ICF, can determine the smallest subset, which maintains or even improves the generalization accuracy of test data. For the text classification domain problem, Tsai and Chang (2013) and Tsai et al. (2014) have used some of these methods as the baseline to perform instance selection, and their experimental results revealed that the final performance was highly dependent on the chosen algorithms. Specifically, not all of the instance selection algorithms can improve performance. However, based on our research, no study to date has focused on examining the effect of instance selection on opinion mining.

In summary, feature and instance selection are the two major data preprocessing steps in data mining, and they are aimed at filtering noisy or unrepresentative features and data observations, respectively. Therefore, investigating the mining performance associated with executing both feature and instance selection is imperative. Moreover, the order in which feature and instance selection is performed on a data set may affect the mining performance, and this is related to the main objective of this paper: to identify the optimal ordering of combining feature and instance selection.

3. THE PROPOSED TWO APPROACHES

This study proposes two processes of combining feature and instance selection techniques, namely feature selection + instance selection (FSIS) and instance selection + feature selection (ISFS).

3.1. The FSIS Approach

Figure 1 illustrates the first process of the FSIS approach. Given a set of review documents as the data set D, the documents are preprocessed through NLP. Specifically, three processes, namely parts-of-speech tagging, stemming, and extraction of representative terms (i.e. features) based on SentiWordNet, are performed in this step. Therefore, each document is represented by an m-dimensional feature vector D_m.

Figure 1. FSIS process

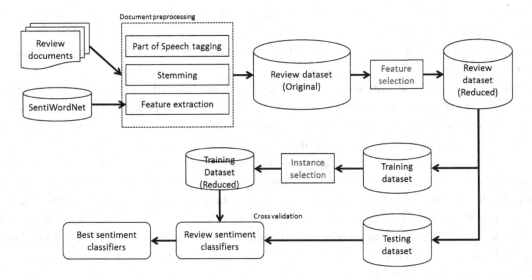

Next, feature selection is executed to reduce the dimensionality of D_m. This step enables representing each document by a lower dimensional feature vector than m, which is denoted as D_n (where $n < m$).

Subsequently, to execute instance selection, D_n is divided into training and testing data sets through the k-fold cross validation method (Kohavi, 1995), in which the training data set is used for instance selection. Suppose that the original training data set contains i documents; performing instance selection yields a reduced training data set D_n^j, which is composed of j documents (where $j < i$).

Finally, the reduced training data set D_n^j is used to train a classifier, and the testing data set is used to test the classifier to examine its classification performance.

3.2. The ISFS Approach

The detail of the ISFS approach is illustrated in Figure 2. After document preprocessing, which is identical to that in the FSIS process, each document is represented by an m-dimensional feature vector D_m.

Figure 2. ISFS process

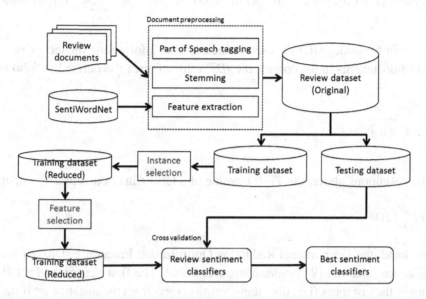

Next, D_m is divided into training and testing data sets through k-fold cross validation. Instance selection is executed to reduce the number of documents in the training data set. Suppose that the original training dataset contains i documents; the reduced training data set is denoted as D_m^k (where $k < i$ and k is not necessarily the same as j in FSIS).

Subsequently, feature selection is performed over D_m^k, yielding a lower dimensional training data set D_o^k (where $o < m$ and o is not necessarily the same as n in FSIS). When each document of the reduced training data set is represented by the o-dimensional feature vector, the documents in the m-dimensional testing data set are also reduced to o-dimensional features. Finally, D_o^k and the o-dimensional testing data set are used to train and test the classifier, respectively.

3.3. The Investigated Feature and Instance Selection Techniques

For feature selection, TF and TF-IDF were adopted, whereas for instance selection, DROP3 (Wilson and Martinez, 2003) and IB3 (Aha et al., 1991) were used. A text d_j is represented as a vector of term weights $\vec{d_j} = \left\langle w_{1j}, ..., w_{|T|j} \right\rangle$, where T is the set of terms (or features) that occur at least once in at least one document of T_r, and $0 \leq w_{i,j} \leq 1$ represents the extent to which term t_i contributes to the semantics of document d_j (Sebastiani, 2002).

Term frequency (TF) is used to calculate the frequency of words in each document. The *TF* value of term t_i in document d_j, denoted as $tf_{i,j}$, is defined as follows:

$$TF_{i,j} = \frac{n_{i,j}}{\sum_k n_{k,j}} \tag{1}$$

where $n_{i,j}$ is the number of times that term t_i occurs in document d_j, and $\sum_k n_{k,j}$ is the number of all words in d_j.

Inverse document frequency (IDF) is used to measure the information the term t_i provides. Assume that D is the set of documents in the corpus, the *IDF* value of term t_i is defined as follows:

$$IDF_i = \log \frac{|D|}{\left|\left\{j : \ t_i \in d_j\right\}\right|} \tag{2}$$

Based on the definitions above, the TF-IDF value of a term t_i in document d_j is calculated as:

$$TF - IDF_{i,j} = TF_{i,j} * IDF_i \tag{3}$$

On the other hand, the Decremental Reduction Optimization Procedure (DROP) is a family of algorithms for instance selection (Wilson & Martinez, 2000). The first version of DROP (i.e. DROP1) iteratively removes the instances (i.e., document term vectors) from the instance set if the removal does not reduce the prediction accuracy of 1-nearest neighbor (1-NN) classifier in the remaining instance set. DROP2, the second version of DROP, was proposed to overcome the order dependency problem in DROP1. The third version of DROP (i.e. DROP3), which is chosen in this study, additionally performs the edited nearest neighbor (ENN) algorithm before the instance selection process in DROP2. This preprocessing step can remove both noisy instances and border points, which can smooth the decision boundary slightly.

IB3 is an incremental instance selection algorithm proposed by Aha et al. (1991). IB3 records and maintains a classification record to summarize the classification performance of an instance in subsequent training instances. Significance tests are performed to classify instances as good or noisy data. The basic concept of IB3 is to select an instance x from the training set and put x into a new set S if the nearest acceptable instance in S has a different class label than x. Acceptability is defined by the confidence interval:

$$\frac{p + \dfrac{z^2}{2n} \pm z\sqrt{\dfrac{p(p-1)}{n} + \dfrac{z^2}{2n^2}}}{1 + \dfrac{z^2}{n}} \tag{4}$$

where z is a user-defined confidence factor, p is the classification accuracy of a given instance to be added to S, and n is the number of classification trials for the given instance (while added to S) (Tsai & Chang, 2013).

Based on the investigated feature and instance selection techniques, each of the FSIS and ISFS processes involves four combinations: TF+DROP3, TF+IB3, TF–IDF+DROP3, and TF–IDF+IB3 for the FSIS process and DROP3+TF, DROP3+TF-IDF, IB3+TF, and IB3+TF-IDF for the ISFS process.

3.4. The Investigated Classification Techniques

For the classifier design, four techniques were employed for comparison: decision tree (C4.5) (Quinlan, 2014), naïve Bayes (NB), logistic regression (LR), and support vector machine (SVM) (Vapnik, 1995). In this study, the Waikato environment for knowledge analysis (WEKA) was used to build the classification models (Liu et al., 2014).

The generation process of decision tree consists of two phases: tree growing and pruning (Quinlan, 2014). In the tree growing phase, C4.5 (J48 in WEKA) adopts a divide-and-conquer approach, which selects a suitable independent variable as an internal-node of the tree and then partition the training set into subsets (i.e., the child-nodes of the internal-node). This process is recursively applied to each internal-node until any of the stopping criteria are satisfied. Once an internal-node stops partitioning, the internal-node is marked as a leaf-node and a class label is assigned to it based on a majority vote. In the pruning phase, the C4.5 adopts a post-pruning approach to reduce the size of the tree and avoid the problem of overfitting.

NB (NaiveBayes in WEKA) is a well-known probabilistic classifier based on Bayes' theorem. The basic concept of NB is that, given a class variable, each input variable is independent to any of other input variables. For each instance, the conditional probability of belonging the target class can be calculated.

LR (simpleLogistic in WEKA) is a statistical method to model the relationship between a binary dependent variable and the independent variables. In addition to using a binary dependent variable, there are other extensions for more than two levels of dependent variables including multinomial logistic regress or ordinal logistic regression.

SVM (SMO in WEKA) was developed by the research team at the AT&T laboratory (Vapnik, 1995). Assume that we have a set of training samples, the SVM algorithm can be used to develop a model for the purpose of classification. Specifically, SVM projects the training samples into a high-dimensional vector space and try to find an optimal hyperplane to separate training samples into two or more classes. Once the hyperplane is determined, it can be used to classify unknown samples into one of the trained class labels.

4. EXPERIMENTS

4.1. Experimental Setup and Performance Measurement

To assess the performance of combining feature and instance selection for opinion mining, three related Twitter data sets were used: Health Care Reform (HCR; Speriosu et al., 2011), Stanford Twitter Sentiment (STS; Go et al., 2009), and Obama–McCain Debate (OMD; Shamma et al., 2009). These data sets were collected from Twitter and contain different tweet topics, and the sentimental statuses of the tweets were identified by experts, which can be used to evaluate sentiment classifiers (Saif et al., 2016). Table 1 shows related information of the three data sets. Notably, we used only the review documents belonging to the positive and negative sentimental statuses.

The FSIS and ISFS processes were compared with the baseline process without performing feature and instance selection to train and test a classifier over the three data sets. In addition, the 10-fold cross validation technique was utilized to partition each data set into the training and testing datasets.

Table 1. Basic information of the three Twitter data sets

Datasets	No. of Data Samples	Sentimental Statuses
HCR	839	positive, negative, neutral, unrelated, others
STS	1600000	positive, negative, neutral
OMD	3269	positive, negative, others

To evaluate the performance of the constructed classifiers, the classification accuracy and F1 score were examined, which can be measured on the basis of the confusion matrix shown in Table 2:

$$Accuracy = \frac{TP + TN}{TP + TN + FP + FN} \tag{5}$$

$$Precision = \frac{TP}{TP + FP} \tag{6}$$

$$Recall = \frac{TP}{TP + FN} \tag{7}$$

$$F1 = 2 \times \frac{precision \times recall}{precision + recall} \tag{8}$$

Table 2. Confusion matrix

		Predicted	
		Negative	Positive
Actual	Negative	TN	FP
	Positive	FN	TP

4.2. Results on the HCR Data Set

Figure 3 shows the classification accuracy of the various classifiers based on the FSIS and ISFS processes applied to the HCR data set. The highest performance (72.4% accuracy) was attained by the LR classifier based on TF-IDF+IB3, IB3+TF, and IB3+TF-IDF. This result is consistent with those of the other three classifiers. That is, TF-IDF+IB3, IB3+TF, and IB3+TF-IDF were the top three processes for combining the feature and instance selection methods.

Regarding the F1 score, the NB classifier based on the IB3+TF process demonstrated the highest performance, with a score of 0.628. Considering the average F1 scores of these four classifiers, IB3+TF-IDF was the optimal combination process, producing a classification accuracy of 71.4% and an F1 score of 0.628.

Figure 3. Classification accuracy of C4.5, NB, LR, and SVM applied to the HCR data set

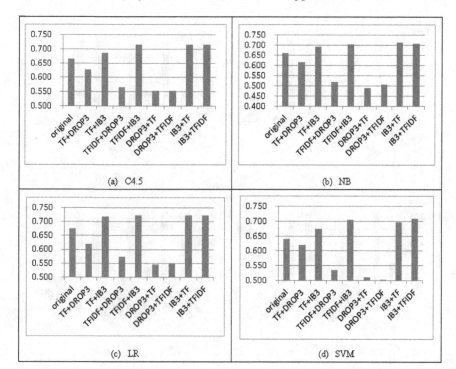

4.3. Results on the STS Data Set

Figure 4 shows the classification accuracy of the various classifiers based on the FSIS and ISFS processes over the STS data set. Among all classifiers, the NB classifiers based on TF-IDF+DROP3, DROP3+TF, and DROP3+TF-IDF attained the same highest rate of classification accuracy, which is 86.6%. Except for the SVM classifier, the C4.5 and LR classifiers applying TF-IDF+DROP3, DROP3+TF, and DROP3+TF-IDF demonstrated higher than those of the other combinations of feature and instance selection methods.

Regarding the F1 score, the results are identical to the classification accuracy results, with the NB classifier based on TF-IDF+DROP3, DROP3+TF, and DROP3+TF-IDF yielding an F1 score of 0.866. For the average classification performance of these eight different combinations of feature and instance selection methods, (i.e., classification accuracy and F1 score), TF+DROP3, TF-IDF+DROP3, DROP3+TF, and DROP3+TF-IDF demonstrated similar performance levels, differing by less than 0.1%.

4.4. Results on the OMD Data Set

Figure 5 illustrates the classification accuracy of the diverse classifiers based on the FSIS and ISFS processes over the OMD data set. In contrast to the previous results, the highest performance (68.8% accuracy) was attained by the SVM classifier executed without performing feature and instance selection. The optimal combination of feature and instance selection methods was associated with the NB classifier applying TF-IDF+IB3, which yielded an accuracy of 66.4%.

Figure 4. Classification accuracy of C4.5, NB, LR, and SVM over the STS data set

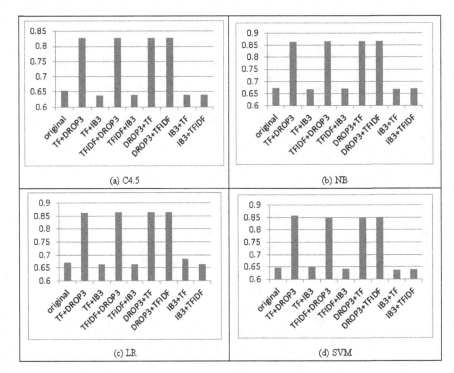

Figure 5. Classification accuracy of C4.5, NB, LR, and SVM over the OMD data set

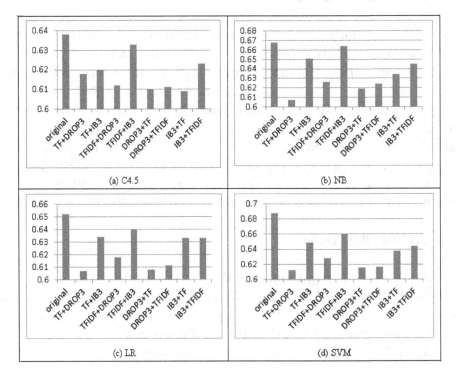

Similar to the classification accuracy, the SVM classifier executed without performing feature and instance selection attained the highest F1 score (0.682). The NB classifier based on TF-IDF+IB3 yielded an F1 score of 0.652. Regarding the average classification performance including classification accuracy and F1 score, the classifiers executed without performing feature and instance selection demonstrated optimal performance over the OMD data set. The second highest average classification performance was based on TF-IDF+IB3.

4.5. Discussion

According to the average classification performance, Table 3 shows a comparison of the optimal combination approaches over the three data sets in terms of their feature dimensionality and the reduction rates after instance selection. The reduction rate is the proportion of the data observations filtered from a given training set.

Table 3. Comparison of the optimal approaches over the three data sets

Datasets	Approaches	Dimensionality	Reduction Rates
HCR	IB3+TF-IDF	227	22.7%
STS	TF+DROP3 TF-IDF+DROP3 DROP3+TF DROP3+TF-IDF	992 2070 629 1549	54.4% 54.3% 54.3% 54.3%
OMD	TF-IDF+IB3	490	50.9%

Table 3 indicates several findings. For the STS and OMD data sets, which are considerably larger than the HCR data set, including the feature dimensionality and sample sizes, these results indicate that the reduction rate is approximately 50% for larger-scale data sets, regardless of the applied instance selection algorithm (i.e., DROP3 and IB3).

TF-IDF should be the optimal feature representation approach to be combined with the instance selection algorithm. In addition, for larger-scale data sets, such as STS and OMD, performing FSIS should be a more favorable approach to data preprocessing for opinion mining. Specifically, because TF-IDF+IB3 and TF-IDF+DROP3 demonstrate highly similar classification performance over the OMD data set, with an estimated performance difference of less than 2%, TF-IDF+DROP3 should be a favorable choice as the baseline data preprocessing process for future studies.

5. CONCLUSION

Opinion mining or sentiment analysis involves several challenges associated with extracting representative textual terms as feature representation to describe an opinion, and with filtering unrepresentative opinions from a given data set for enhancing classification results. In the field of text classification, certain studies have focused on feature selection, whereas others have focused on instance selection. However, few studies have considered performing both data preprocessing tasks simultaneously.

In this paper, we examine the final classification performance associated with executing both feature and instance selection in sequential orders. Specifically, one data preprocessing task can be performed in the first order and the other one can be executed in the second order. Our experiments are based on three related Twitter data sets, and for feature comparisons, two feature and instance selection methods are combined, namely TF and TF–IDF (for the feature selection task) and DROP3 and IB3 (for the instance selection task); combining these methods yields eight combinations for integrating both data preprocessing tasks. In addition, four classifiers are constructed: C4.5 decision tree, naïve Bayes, logistic regression, and SVM.

Our experimental results reveal that performing FSIS should be a favorable approach to data preprocessing for large-scale opinion mining tasks. In particular, performing TF–IDF first followed by DROP3 is recommended as the optimal combination strategy. This can be considered the baseline data preprocessing approach for future studies in this field.

This study contributes to the literature on proposing a new process of sentiment analysis. We are the first to integrate feature and instance selection techniques on the field of sentiment analysis. How to improve the performance of opinion mining by combining these two approaches becomes a possible interesting research topic. In addition, practical implications may also be derived from this study. Our approach can be developed as a meta-learner, which provides an alternative approach to enhance the performance of prediction models in machine learning tools. Companies can apply our proposed opinion mining process to effectively identify customers' preference from online social media.

In future works, several issues can be considered. First, there exist many other feature and instance selection techniques; future research may include these new techniques in our opinion mining process. Second, it is also recommended to perform tests from other datasets collected from different application domains or contexts; this may uncover other possible factors that might be considered in the process of opinion mining.

REFERENCES

Abbasi, A., Chen, H., & Salem, A. (2008). Sentiment analysis in multiple languages: Feature selection for opinion classification in Web forums. *ACM Transactions on Information Systems*, *26*(3), 12. doi:10.1145/1361684.1361685

Agarwarl, B., & Mittal, N. (2013). Optimal feature selection for sentiment analysis. In *Proceedings of the International Conference on Linguistics and Intelligent Text Processing* (*Vol. 2*, pp. 13-24). Academic Press. 10.1007/978-3-642-37256-8_2

Aghdam, M. H., Ghasem-Aghaee, N., & Basiri, M. E. (2009). Text feature selection using ant colony optimization. *Expert Systems with Applications*, *36*(3), 6843–6853. doi:10.1016/j.eswa.2008.08.022

Aha, D. W., Kibler, D., & Albert, M. K. (1991). Instance-based learning algorithms. *Machine Learning*, *6*(1), 37–66. doi:10.1007/BF00153759

Azam, N., & Yao, J. T. (2012). Comparison of term frequency and document frequency based feature selection metrics in text categorization. *Expert Systems with Applications*, *39*(5), 4760–4768. doi:10.1016/j.eswa.2011.09.160

Bravo-Marquez, F., Mendoza, M., & Poblete, B. (2013). Combining strengths, emotions and polarities for boosting Twitter sentiment analysis. In *Proceedings of the International Workshop on Issues of Sentiment Discovery and Opinion Mining*. Academic Press. 10.1145/2502069.2502071

Cambria, E., Schuller, B., Xia, Y., & Havasi, C. (2013). New avenues in opinion mining and sentiment analysis. *IEEE Intelligent Systems*, *28*(2), 15–21. doi:10.1109/MIS.2013.30

Chatterjee, S., Mukhopadhyay, A., & Bhattacharyya, M. (2018). A weighted rank aggregation approach towards crowd opinion analysis. *Knowledge-Based Systems*, *149*, 47–60. doi:10.1016/j.knosys.2018.02.005

Deshmukh, J. S., & Tripathy, A. K. (2018). Entropy based classifier for cross-domain opinion mining. *Applied Computing and Informatics*, *14*(1), 55–64. doi:10.1016/j.aci.2017.03.001

Ellison, N. B. (2007). Social network sites: Definition, history, and scholarship. *Journal of Computer-Mediated Communication*, *13*(1), 210–230. doi:10.1111/j.1083-6101.2007.00393.x

Forman, G. (2003). An extensive empirical study of feature selection metrics for text classification. *Journal of Machine Learning Research*, *3*, 1289–1305.

Garcia, S., Derrac, J., Cano, J. R., & Herrera, F. (2012). Prototype selection for nearest neighbor classification: Taxonomy and empirical study. *IEEE Transactions on Pattern Analysis and Machine Intelligence*, *34*(3), 417–435. doi:10.1109/TPAMI.2011.142 PMID:21768651

Go, A., Bhayani, R., and Huang, L. (2009). Twitter sentiment classification using distant supervision. *CS224N Project Report*.

Guyon, I., & Elisseeff, A. (2003). An introduction to variable and feature selection. *Journal of Machine Learning Research*, *3*, 1157–1182.

Hu, Y.-H., Chen, Y.-L., & Chou, H.-L. (2017). Opinion mining from online hotel reviews – a text summarization approach. *Information Processing & Management*, *53*(2), 436–449. doi:10.1016/j.ipm.2016.12.002

Hu, Y. H., Shiau, W. M., Shih, S. P., & Chen, C. J. (2018). Considering online consumer reviews to predict movie box-office performance between the years 2009 and 2014 in the US. *The Electronic Library*, *36*(6), 1010–1026. doi:10.1108/EL-02-2018-0040

Kauer, A. U., & Moreira, V. P. (2016). Using information retrieval for sentiment polarity prediction. *Expert Systems with Applications*, *61*, 282–289. doi:10.1016/j.eswa.2016.05.038

Khan, F. H., Bashir, S., & Qamar, U. (2014). TOM: Twitter opinion mining framework using hybrid classification scheme. *Decision Support Systems*, *57*, 245–257. doi:10.1016/j.dss.2013.09.004

Kohavi, R. (1995). A study of cross-validation and bootstrap for accuracy estimation and model selection. In *Proceedings of the International Joint Conference on Artificial Intelligence* (*Vol. 2*, pp. 1137-1143). Academic Press.

Lee, C., & Lee, G. G. (2006). Information gain and divergence-based feature selection for machine learning-based text categorization. *Information Processing & Management*, *42*(1), 155–165. doi:10.1016/j.ipm.2004.08.006

Lee, P. J., Hu, Y. H., & Lu, K. T. (2018). Assessing the helpfulness of online hotel reviews: A classification-based approach. *Telematics and Informatics*, *35*(2), 436–445. doi:10.1016/j.tele.2018.01.001

Li, N., & Wu, D. D. (2010). Using text mining and sentiment analysis for online forums hotspot detection and forecast. *Decision Support Systems*, *48*(2), 354–368. doi:10.1016/j.dss.2009.09.003

Li, X.-B., & Jacob, V. S. (2008). Adaptive data reduction for large-scale transaction data. *European Journal of Operational Research*, *188*(3), 910–924. doi:10.1016/j.ejor.2007.08.008

Liu, K. E., Lo, C. L., & Hu, Y. H. (2014). Improvement of adequate use of warfarin for the elderly using decision tree-based approaches. *Methods of Information in Medicine*, *53*(01), 47–53. doi:10.3414/ME13-01-0027 PMID:24136011

Manning, C. D., & Schutze, H. (1999). *Foundations of statistical natural language processing*. MIT Press.

Mitchell, T. (1997). *Machine Learning*. McGraw Hill.

Nguyen, H. T., & Nguyen, M. L. (2018). Multilingual opinion mining on YouTube – a convolutional n-gram BiLSTM word embedding. *Information Processing & Management*, *54*(3), 451–462. doi:10.1016/j.ipm.2018.02.001

Nicholls, C., & Song, F. (2010) Comparison of feature selection methods for sentiment analysis. In *Proceedings of the Canadian Conference on Advances in Artificial Intelligence* (pp. 286-289). Academic Press. 10.1007/978-3-642-13059-5_30

Pang, B., & Lee, L. (2008). Opinion mining and sentiment analysis. *Foundations and Trends in Information Retrieval*, *2*(2), 1–135. doi:10.1561/1500000011

Piryani, R., Madhavi, D., & Singh, V. K. (2017). Analytical mapping of opinion mining and sentiment analysis research during 2000 – 2015. *Information Processing & Management*, *53*(1), 122–150. doi:10.1016/j.ipm.2016.07.001

Powell, W. B. (2007). *Approximate dynamic programming: solving the curses of dimensionality*. Wiley-Interscience. doi:10.1002/9780470182963

Quinlan, J. R. (2014). *C4. 5: programs for machine learning*. Elsevier.

Rehman, A., Javed, K., & Babri, H. A. (2017). Feature selection based on a normalized difference measure for text classification. *Information Processing & Management*, *53*(2), 473–489. doi:10.1016/j.ipm.2016.12.004

Saif, H., He, Y., Fernandez, M., & Alani, H. (2016). Contextual semantics for sentiment analysis of Twitter. *Information Processing & Management*, *52*(1), 5–19. doi:10.1016/j.ipm.2015.01.005

Salton, G., & Buckley, C. (1988). Term-weighting approaches in automatic text retrieval. *Information Processing & Management*, *24*(5), 513–523. doi:10.1016/0306-4573(88)90021-0

Sebastiani, F. (2002). Machine learning in automated text categorization. *ACM Computing Surveys*, *34*(1), 1–47. doi:10.1145/505282.505283

Shamma, D., Kennedy, L., & Churchill, E. (2009) Tweet the debates: understanding community annotation of uncollected sources. In *Proceedings of the ACM SIGMM International Workshop on Social Media* (pp. 3-10). ACM. 10.1145/1631144.1631148

Speriosu, M., Sudan, N., Upadhyay, S., & Baldridge, J. (2011) Twitter polarity classification with label propagation over lexical links and the follower graph. *International Workshop on Unsupervised Learning in NLP*, pp. 53-63.

Thelwall, M., Buckley, K., & Paltoglou, G. (2011). Sentiment in Twitter events. *Journal of the American Society for Information Science and Technology*, *62*(2), 406–418. doi:10.1002/asi.21462

Tian, F., Gao, P., Li, L., Zhang, W., Liang, H., Qian, Y., & Zhao, R. (2014). Recognizing and regulating e-learners' emotions based on interactive Chinese texts in e-learning systems. *Knowledge-Based Systems*, *55*, 148–164. doi:10.1016/j.knosys.2013.10.019

Tsai, C.-F., & Chang, C.-W. (2013). SVOIS: Support vector oriented instance selection for text classification. *Information Systems*, *38*(8), 1070–1083. doi:10.1016/j.is.2013.05.001

Tsai, C.-F., Chen, Z.-Y., & Ke, S.-W. (2014). Evolutionary instance selection for text classification. *Journal of Systems and Software*, *90*, 104–113. doi:10.1016/j.jss.2013.12.034

Vapnik, V. (1995). *The Nature of Statistical Learning Theory*. Berlin: Springer-Verlag. doi:10.1007/978-1-4757-2440-0

Vinodhini, G., & Chandrasekaran, R. M. (2017). A sampling based sentiment mining approach for e-commerce applications. *Information Processing & Management*, *53*(1), 223–236. doi:10.1016/j.ipm.2016.08.003

Wilson, D. R., & Martinez, T. R. (2000). Reduction techniques for instance-based learning algorithms. *Machine Learning*, *38*(3), 257–286. doi:10.1023/A:1007626913721

Xiaomei, Z., Jing, Y., Jianpei, Z., & Hongyu, H. (2018). Microblog sentiment analysis with weak dependency connections. *Knowledge-Based Systems*, *142*, 170–180. doi:10.1016/j.knosys.2017.11.035

Yang, Y., & Pedersen, J. O. (1997) A comparative study of feature selection in text categorization. In *Proceedings of the International Conference on Machine Learning* (pp. 412-420). Academic Press.

Zheng, Z., Wu, X., & Srihari, R. (2004). Feature selection for text categorization on imbalanced data. *ACM SIGKDD Explorations Newsletter*, *6*(1), 80–89. doi:10.1145/1007730.1007741

ENDNOTE

[1]   http://sentiwordnet.isti.cnr.it/

This research was previously published in the International Journal of Data Warehousing and Mining (IJDWM), 16(3); pages 168-182, copyright year 2020 by IGI Publishing (an imprint of IGI Global).

Chapter 43
Deep Learning for Social Media Text Analytics

Anto Arockia Rosaline R.

Department of Information Technology, Rajalakshmi Engineering College, Chennai, India

Parvathi R.

School of Computer Science and Engineering, VIT University, Chennai, India

ABSTRACT

Text analytics is the process of extracting high quality information from the text. A set of statistical, linguistic, and machine learning techniques are used to represent the information content from various textual sources such as data analysis, research, or investigation. Text is the common way of communication in social media. The understanding of text includes a variety of tasks including text classification, slang, and other languages. Traditional Natural Language Processing (NLP) techniques require extensive pre-processing techniques to handle the text. When a word "Amazon" occurs in the social media text, there should be a meaningful approach to find out whether it is referring to forest or Kindle. Most of the time, the NLP techniques fail in handling the slang and spellings correctly. Messages in Twitter are so short such that it is difficult to build semantic connections between them. Some messages such as "Gud nite" actually do not contain any real words but are still used for communication.

DEEP LEARNING APPROACH IN HANDLING THE TEXT

The deep learning is a new learning method of the machine learning, it analyze the neural network through the imitation of the human brain and the interpretation of the appropriate data. In the process of text mining, the application of the deep learning would be suitable for text clustering and text classification, it is easy to find the desired text information, so the application of the deep learning plays an important role in process of handling the text.

The Deep learning architectures are helpful in understanding a number of languages faster. A number of variations such as slang and spellings exist across various languages. The language dependent knowledge can very well be reduced with the help of Deep learning architectures. The mathematical

DOI: 10.4018/978-1-6684-6303-1.ch043

concept of word embeddings can be used to preserve the semantic relationship between words. This kind of representation generally helps to retrieve the deeper semantic meaning of words.

Social media sites such as Facebook,Instagram,Twitter etc. allows users to share lots of photos tagged with text information. The joint understanding of image and text is so important to perceive the user's information. The Deep learning architecture helps in the joint understanding of the text and visual content.

Deep learning allows the algorithms to understand the structure and semantics of the sentence. The model considers the representation of the entire sentence. The result is so meaningful as the entire sentence is based on the arrangement of the words and the interaction between the words.

Deep learning is better than traditional machine learning algorithms because they try to learn high-level features from data in an incremental manner. Deep learning techniques outperform other algorithms in the performance when the data size is very large. Deep Learning really shines when it comes to complex problems such as image classification, natural language processing, and speech recognition.

SOCIAL MEDIA ANALYSIS

Social media is an important communication medium during crisis.The machine has to understand the text by recognizing the words. The task is so challenging in social media because it contains misspellings, abbreviations and moreover social media text does not follow any syntax and semantics. The traditional supervised learning approaches mainly depend on the correctness of the training set. A number of ways the word is misspelled is so large and the traditional supervised learning approaches fail to reach its target (Acharyya,2009).

The traditional supervised machine learning approach has certain limitations on the predefined topics. When text on a new topic i.e some new crisis is presented to the algorithm it will misclassify it as one of the existing topics. In the sequence of semantically related words Deep learning can be used to predict the next word (LeCun,Bengio & Hinton,2015) and thus the Deep learning approach have learnt the semantic representation of words. This approach also predicts the next character in a sequence of characters and is used to generate the text (LeCun,Bengio & Hinton,2015) .Deep learning approach can be used on the normalized text and is used to learn the features for the concepts automatically. The document is decomposed into concepts and the text is segmented into semantically meaningful atomic units (Mehdi Ben Lazreg,Morten Goodwin,& Ole-Christoffer Granmo,2016).A deeper understanding is established by identifying the underlying concepts of a document or a sentence. This is the foundation for the understanding of social media text.

DEEP LEARNING MODELS

Convolutional Neural Networks (CNN)

The Convolutional Neural Network(CNN) comprises of pooling layers and sophistication as it produces a standard architecture to map the sentences of variable length into sentences of fixed size scattered vectors. This CNN framework for the visual sentiment analysis can very well predict sentiments of visual content. The Single one-dimensional convolution layer is followed by a max pooling layer combining neighboring vectors. The final linear classifier for each class selects the class with highest confidence score. The goal is to learn a region based on text embedding.

This architecture consists of convolution and pooling layers followed by fully connected layer. The convolution and pooling layers performs the feature extraction and the fully connected layer does the classification.

It can be successfully applied to NLP applications and recommender systems. It is powerful than many of the previous architectures as it is capable of detecting the various features automatically without any human intervention.

Recurrent Neural Network (RNN)

The traditional neural networks work by assuming that all the inputs and outputs are independent of each other. But this is not a suitable idea for predicting the next word in a sentence.RNNs are called as recurrent because the computation is performed on every element in a sequence and the output depends on the previous computations.

The recurrent neural network has a number of applications. It plays a vital role in classifying the sentiment. For example any social media text can be applied to this architecture and can be categorized into positive or negative affectivity. This architecture helps in the automatic description of an image. The description of the image in varying lengths of text can be produced as output. Thus the RNN architecture helps in a variety of applications where input and output are of different types and lengths.

Bidirectional Recurrent Network

The idea of Bidirectional recurrent network is that the input data need not be fixed. The structure of this network combines the hidden layers of opposite directions to the same output. As a result the output layer gets information from the past and future states. This network helps to reach the future from the current state.

GOAL OF DEEP LEARNING ARCHITECTURE

The following steps are carried out:

1. The training data in the standard format is uploaded by the user. The labels define the task to be solved.
2. The system defines the fundamental architectures such as convolutional or recurrent neural networks.
3. The system trains the architecture and finally optimizes it.
4. The various parameters are used to measure the performance of the architecture.
5. At last the system wraps the optimized architecture into a library and it will be ready for production.

TEXT FEATURE EXTRACTION

Deep learning was a class of unsupervised learning approach (Hinton & Salakhutdinov, 2006). The idea actually originated from artificial neural network. The lower level features are combined to form more abstract, higher level features.The deep learning approach mainly helps to discover distributed feature representation of data. The deep learning learns features from big data on its own, instead of adopting handcrafted features (Wang,Raj,& Xing,2017) and that is the major difference between Deep learning and Pattern recognition. The deep learning is capable of acquiring new effective feature representation from training data quickly.

Several deep learning methods, applications, improvement methods, and steps used for text feature extraction are available.

Autoencoder

An autoencoder (Rumelhart,Hinton,& Williams,1988) is a feed forward network. It usually consists of one hidden layer between input and output layer. Hidden layer is more compact as it contains fewer units than input or output layer. The process of training the autoencoder is the same as traditional neural network with backpropagation.

Restricted Boltzmann Machine

This version of Boltzmann machine comes with a restriction that there are no connections either between visible units or between hidden units (Wang, Raj,& Xing,2017).This network is composed of visible units (visible vectors) and some hidden units (hidden vectors). Visible vectors and hidden vectors are binary vectors whose values can be either 0 or 1. The entire system is a bipartite graph. There are no edge connections among visible units and among hidden units. Edges only exist between visible units and hidden units. The Restricted Boltzmann Machine (RBM) is illustrated in Figure 1.

The training process repeats the following three steps:

1.Each input combines with a weight and bias and the result is transmitted to the hidden layer during the forward pass.

2. Each activation combines with a single weight and bias and the result is transmitted to the visible layer during backward pass for reconstruction.
3. Compare reconstruction and initial input.

The above three steps are repeated using different weights and biases until reconstruction and input are close as far as possible.

Deep Belief Network

Deep Belief Networks (DBN) (Hinton,Osindero,& Teh,2014) is shown that the RBM can be stacked and trained. This class of deep neural networks consists of a number of hidden layers. This set of hidden layers is connected to each other but there are no connections exist between units within each layer.

A Deep belief network is generally obtained by stacking a number of RBM together. The first layer of RBM represents the input of the whole network. The output is obtained from the hidden layer of the last RBM. The input to the RBM at layer 'n+1' is obtained from the hidden layer 'n' of the RBM.The training process of DBM includes various phases such as layer wise pre training and fine tuning.

Figure 1. Restricted Boltzmann machine

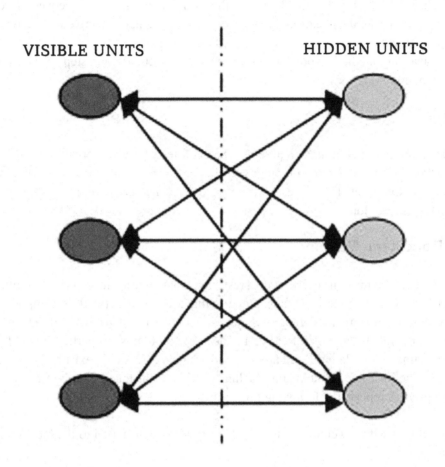

Convolutional Neural Network

Convolutional is one of the artificial neural networks. It is more similar to the biological neural networks because of the weights of the sharing network structure. Because of the characteristics it mainly reduces the complexity of the network model and has a greater adaptability. A machine translation system can translate words, phrases and sentences to another language automatically. A greater performance has been achieved by deep learning in translating words and also words in images automatically.The system is capable of translating the articles contained in the image into another language.

Several typical CNN models (Kim,2014) are applied to feature extraction in text classification. A number of filters with different lengths are used to convolve text matrix. The width of the filters is equal to the lengths of word vectors. Followed by filters max pooling is employed to operate vectors of every filter. Each filter corresponds to a digit and these filters are connected to represent a sentence which is actually a vector. CNN convolves and abstracts word vectors of the original text with filters of a certain length, and thus previous pure word vector become convolved abstract sequences (Zhou,Sun,& Liu,2015).

Recurrent Neural Network

Recurrent neural networks (RNNs) are used to process sequential data. The traditional neural network models operate from the input layer to hidden layer to output layer. There is no connection between nodes of each layer and the layers are fully connected. RNNs (Wang, Raj,& Xing,2017) provide better performance for tasks involving sequential inputs such as speech and language. In this type of neural network the input sequence is processed one element at a time. The history of the past elements of the sequence is maintained in the hidden units of a state vector. The artificial neurons get inputs from other neurons at previous time steps.The Recurrent neural network is illustrated in Figure 2.

The recurrent neuron calculates the current state by combining the current input with the previous state. The steps are repeated for a number of times. The final current state yields the output of the network. The output is then compared with the actual output and the error is generated. The error is then back propagated to the network to update the weights. The network is trained in this way.

SENTIMENT ANALYSIS

Sentiment analysis is one of the main challenges of natural language processing. It generally refers to an attitude, feeling, or emotion associated with a situation, event, or thing. Data mining is the most popular approach in performing sentiment analysis. But still identifying features and selecting the best is the most challenging task especially in a Big Data.

Deep learning and inference improves sentiment analysis in two ways:

- Accuracy can be increased
- Opinion mining is much more useful

It is widely studied in data mining, Web mining, text mining, and information retrieval(Zhang Lei, Wang Shuai,& Liu Bing).When a decision has to be made such as buying the product, review on a movie etc. people often seek the help of other opinions. This is not only applicable for people, it is also suitable for organizations. The organizations often would like to know the feedback of the product launched, reviews on the product released, and would like to know the positives and negatives of the product from other's opinions. Because of this abundance of such information publicly available there is no need for any kind of polling options required. Such opinionated postings have helped the organizations to improve their businesses. It has thus become mandatory to collect and study opinions.

There exists huge number of opinions in web which makes it more difficult for the human to summarize the opinions. Therefore automation on sentiment analysis is required. Enormous techniques are available for sentiment analysis at present which includes both supervised and unsupervised methods.

Sentiment Analysis Tasks

Sentiment analysis can be represented at three levels of granularity. The various sentiment analysis tasks are illustrated in Figure 3.

Figure 2. Recurrent neural network

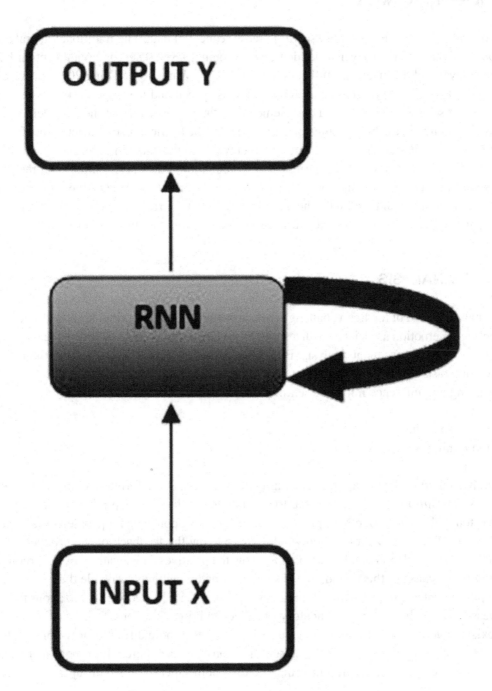

Figure 3. Types of sentiment analysis tasks

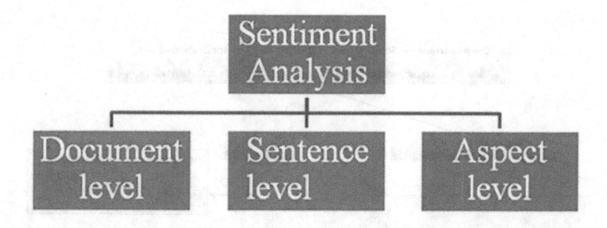

Document Level Sentiment Classification

The document level of classification considers the document as one basic unit and gives the opinion as positive or negative. This level of granularity is used to determine whether the document (review on a movie, feedback on a product say phone etc.) is having an overall positive or negative opinion. The overall opinion for the document could be in the form of stars as as it is observed in most of the products reviews say in the range from 1 to 5 stars.

The traditional methods considered for classifications are Bag of Words and Bag of N grams.The methods are explained in Figure 4. Bag of words considers set of words and their frequency count.The main disadvantage with this approach is that it fails to consider the word order in the document. The Bag of N grams is an approach, extension of Bag of words considering the word order.But it also suffers from data sparsity and high dimensionality(Zhang Lei, Wang Shuai,& Liu Bing).

The deep learning methods for document level sentiment classification are summarized in Table 1.

Sentence Level Sentiment Classification

This approach is used to classify the individual sentences in a document. Subjectivity classification is done to identify whether the sentence has any opinion. If the sentence has opinion, it is further classified into various categories such as Positive, Negative and Neutral.

Sentence level sentiment classification works well than the document level sentiment classification since it deals with sentences. So this classification holds good for handling shorter texts and therefore it handles the twitter data such as tweets effectively.The subjectivity classification is illustrated in Figure 5.

The deep learning methods for sentence level sentiment classification are summarized in Table 2.

Figure 4. Classification using Bag of words and Bag of N grams

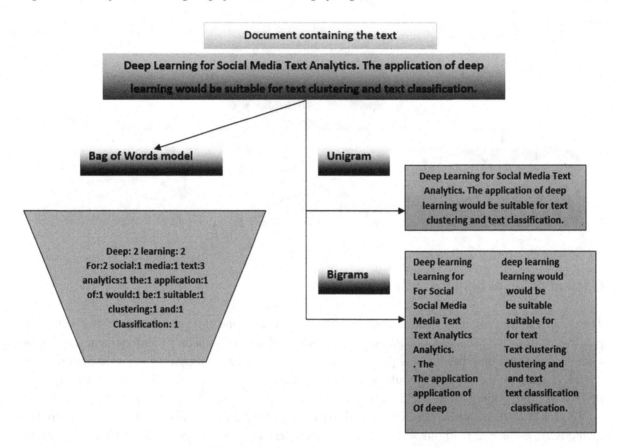

Aspect-Based Sentiment Classification

The aspect based sentiment classification is used to analyse the entities and the aspects of entities expressed in a sentiment. This classification includes the extraction of entities, extraction of aspects and classifying the sentiment of the aspect.

When an organization launches a product it is so important to perform the aspect based sentiment analysis so as to improve their business by understanding the positive and negative aspects of that product. For example consider the sentence "The camera of my mobile is great but the price is so high".In the above sentence "mobile" should be identified as entity during entity extraction, "camera" and "price" should be identified during aspect extraction. Aspect sentiment classification should classify the sentiment expressed on the camera of the mobile as positive and on the price of the phone as negative. The aspect based sentiment classification is illustrated in Figure 6.

The deep learning methods for aspect-based sentiment classification are summarized in Table 3.

A number of deep learning models are available to extract the aspect and entity that are associated with opinions. In the process of aspect categorization same aspect expressions are grouped into a category. For instance, the aspect terms "image", "photo" and "picture" of the mobile can be grouped into one aspect category named camera. The various deep learning models available for aspect extraction and opinion extraction are given in Table 4.

Table 1. Deep learning methods on Document level sentiment classification

Research	Deep Learning Model	Description
Moraes,Valiati & Neto,2013	Artificial Neural Networks (ANN)	In most cases produced competitive results to SVM
Glorot, Bordes & Bengio,2011	Stacked Denoising Autoencoder	sparse rectifier units performs unsupervised text feature/representation extraction
Zhai& Zhongfei (Mark) Zhang,2016	semi-supervised autoencoder	Sentiment information is considered in the learning stage and better document vectors are obtained
Le & Mikolov,2014	Paragraph Vector	Unsupervised learning algorithm that learns vector representations for variable-length texts
Johnson & Zhang,2015	BOW-CNN	Bag-of-word conversion in the convolution layer
Johnson & Zhang,2015	Seq-CNN	sequential information of words by concatenating the one-hot vector of multiple words
Tang, Qin & Liu,2015	CNN/ Long Short Term Memory(LSTM) with Gated recurrent unit (GRU)	CNN/LSTM for sentence representation and GRU for document representation
Dou, 2017	Deep Memory Network	LSTM for document representation, memory network with multiple computational layers to predict the review rating for each document
Yang, Yang, Dyer, He, Smola & Hovy,2016	Hierarchical attention network	document level sentiment rating, prediction of reviews at word level/sentence level
Yin, Song & Zhang,2017	Hierarchical interactive attention-based model	document-level aspect-sentiment rating prediction task
Zhou,Wan & Xiao,2016	Attention-based LSTM network	cross-lingual sentiment classification at the document level, two attention-based LSTMs for bilingual representation (each LSTM is also hierarchically structured)
Li,,Zhang,Wei,Wu & Yang,2017	Memory Network	cross-domain sentiment classification

Table 2. Deep learning methods on Sentence level sentiment classification

Research	Deep Learning Model	Description
Kim,2014	CNN	experimented with several variants: word embeddings are randomly initialized, word embeddings are pretrained and fixed, word embeddings are pre-trained and fine-tuned, multiple sets of word embeddings are used
Wang,Liu,Sun, Wang & Wang,2015	LSTM	Twitter sentiment Classification
Wang, Yu, Lai & Zhang,2016	Regional CNN-LSTM model	Predict the valence arousal ratings of text
Wang,Jiang & Luo,2016	Joint CNN and RNN architecture	Sentiment classification of short texts
Akhtar, Kumar, Ghosal,Ekbal,& Bhattacharyya,2017	Multi-layer perceptron based ensemble models	Sentiment classification of financial microblogs and news
Zhao,Lu,Cai,He & Zhuang,2017	Recurrent random walk network learning approach	Sentiment classification of opinionated tweets

Figure 5. Subjectivity Classification

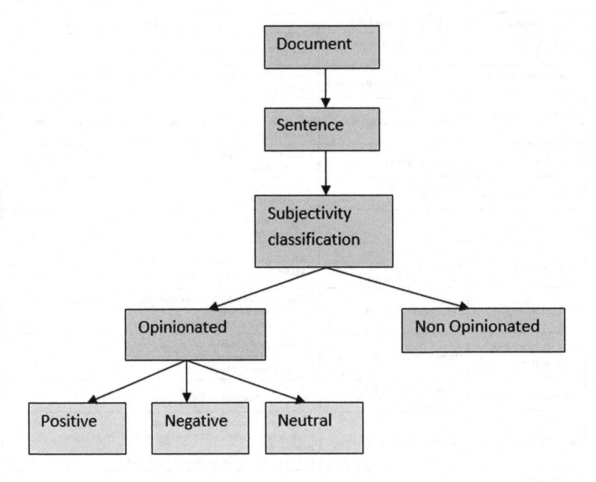

Table 3. Deep learning methods on aspect-based sentiment classification

Research	Deep learning Model	Description
Dong,Wei,Tan,Tang,Zhou, & Xu,2014	Adaptive Recursive Neural Network (AdaRNN)	Twitter sentiment classification, root node representation is used as features and softmax classifier is used to predict the distribution over classes
Vo & Zhang,2015	Twitter sentiment classification	Additional features are obtained using unsupervised learning methods
Wang,Huang,Zhu,& Zhao, 2016	Attention-based LSTM	attend to the related part of a sentence, it helps in attending the important part of the sentence and response to the specific context
Yang, Tu,Wang, Xu,& Chen,2017	Two attention-based bidirectional LSTMs	Improves the classification performance
Liu & Zhang,2017	Extension of attention modeling	Used to differentiate the attention obtained from the left context and the right context
Ma, Li, Zhang & Wang,2017	Interactive Attention Network (IAN)	uses two attention networks to interactively detect the important words of the expression and the important words of its full context

Figure 6. Aspect-based sentiment Classification

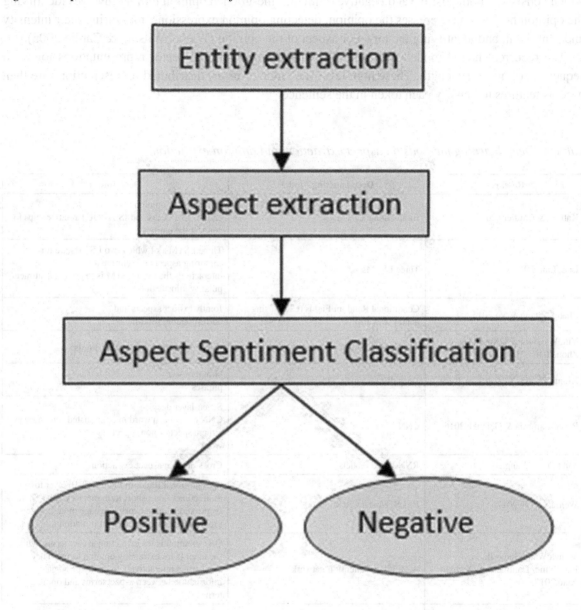

OPINION MINING

Opinion mining is generally used to understand the opinions held by a person. It is generally used to understand the likes and dislikes towards the product features. A number of challenges are faced upon using opinion mining. For example a word takes different meanings depending upon the sentence in which it is used. The sentence "The mobile's battery life is long" expresses the positive opinion and the sentence "The laptop's start up time is so long" expresses the negative opinion. The small change in two sentences should not be assumed to have the same meaning. For example the sentences "I like the phone" and "I don't like the phone" are entirely different sentences where one sentence expresses the positive opinion and the other sentence expresses the negative opinion. Other challenges occur in handling the text which consists of both positive and negative opinion. Fine-grained opinion mining involves identifying the opinion holder who expresses the opinion, detecting opinion expressions, measuring their intensity and sentiment, and identifying the target or aspect of the opinion (Wiebe, Wilson, & Cardie 2005).

The recurrent neural models are used to compute compositional vector representations for word sequences of arbitrary length. These high level (i.e., hidden-layer) distributed representations are then used as features to classify each token in the sentence.

Table 4. Deep learning methods on aspect extraction and opinion extraction

Research	Deep learning Model	Description
Katiyar & Cardiem,2016	Bidirectional LSTMs	Extraction of opinion entities,IS-FORM and IS-ABOUT relationships to connect the entities
Li & Lam,2017	Three LSTMs	Three LSTMs, of which two LSTMs are for capturing aspect and sentiment interactions,the third LSTM is to use the sentiment polarity information
Zhang, Zhang & Vo,2015	Conditional Random Fields (CRF) using a neural network	Jointly extract aspects and corresponding sentiments,
Yin, Wei, Dong & Xu,Zhang & Zhou,2016	Word embedding	Dependency path connecting words
Xiong, Zhang, Y., Ji & Lou,2016	Deep distance metric learning model	Group aspect phrases
Poria, Cambria & Gelbukh,2016	CNN	Seven-layer deep CNN to tag each word in opinionated sentences as either aspect or non aspect word
Ying, Yu & Jiang,2017	RNN-based models	Cross-domain aspect extraction
Wen, Li & Ye,2017	Bi-LSTM and CRF	A Conditional Random Fields (CRF) layer to bidirectional long-short term memory (Bi-LSTM) recurrent neural network language model, which provides sentence level tag information
Wenya Wang,Sinno Jialin Pan,Daniel Dahlmeier & Xiaokui Xiao,2017	A Multilayer attention network	One attention is for extracting aspect terms, while the other is for extracting opinion terms. They are learned interactively to dually propagate information between aspect terms and opinion terms.
Liu, Pengfei & Joty, Shafiq & Meng, Helen,2015	Discriminative models based on recurrent neural networks (RNNs) and word embeddings	Framework is flexible, allows to incorporate other linguistic features

Elman-Type RNN

In Elman-type RNN(Elman,1990), the output of the hidden layer is always computed from the non linear transformation of the current input and the previous hidden layer output. In Figure 7 X, Y and H represents the input layer, output layer and hidden layer respectively. Let w1 and w2 represents the weight matrices between two consecutive hidden layers.Let b be the bias vector.

Figure 7. Elman-type RNN

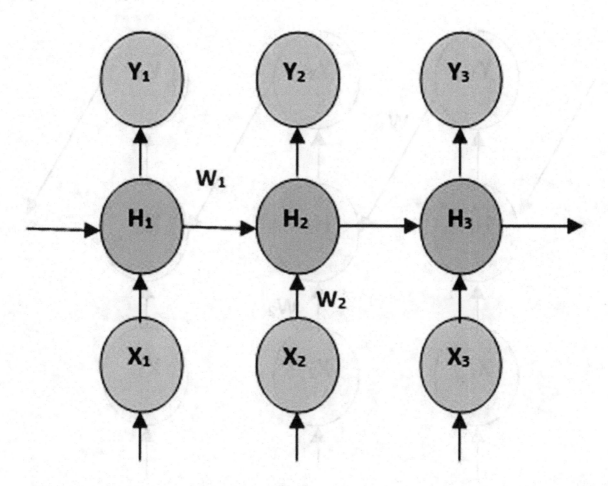

The output of the hidden layer at time t is computed from the current input at time t and the hidden layer output at time t-1. The hidden layer output is defined by the equation as follows:

$$H_t = f\,(w_2\,x_t + w_1\,H_{t-1} + b)$$

Jordan-Type RNN

In Jordan-type RNN(Jordan,1997) the output of the hidden layer is always computed from the non linear transformation of the current input and the previous output layer. In Figure 8 x_i,y_i and h_i represents the input layer, output layer and hidden layer respectively. Let w_1 and w_2 represents the weight matrices between two consecutive hidden layers. Let b be the bias vector.

The output of the hidden layer at time t is computed from the current input at time t and the output layer at time t-1.The hidden layer output is defined by the equation as follows:

$$H_t = f\,(w_2\,x_t + w_1\,y_{t-1} + b)$$

Figure 8. Jordan-type RNN

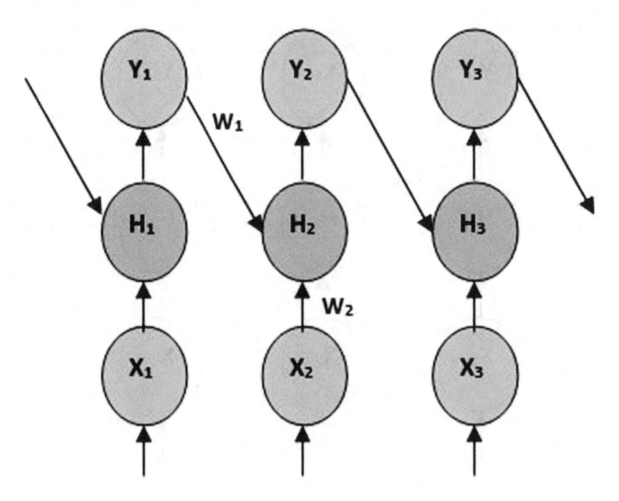

Long Short-Term Memory or LSTM

Long Short-Term Memory or LSTM (Hochreiter and Schmidhuber, 1997) is designed to model long term dependencies in RNNs. The recurrent layer in a standard LSTM is constituted with special (hidden) units called memory blocks.

A memory block is composed of four elements:

1. a memory cell
2. an input gate
3. an output gate
4. a forget gate

The memory cell (i.e., a neuron) is provided with a self-connection,an input gate controls the flow of input signal into the neuron,an output gate controls the effect of the neuron activation on other neurons and a forget gate to allows the neuron to reset its current state through the self-connection.

Figure 9. Long Short-Term Memory

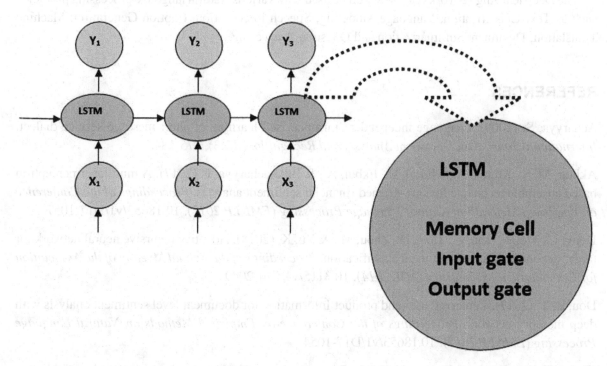

DEEP LEARNING CHALLENGES

Each hidden layer and feature means more number of parameters. It becomes slow and is computationally difficult to train. Human generated text generates very large number of features and thus makes it slow. The solution to the problem is to have distributed vector representations of words. The key concept of this representation is that the words with similar vectors have similar meanings.

CONCLUSION

Deep learning has many advantages when compared to machine learning when handling with unstructured data. Text analytics undergo a number of processing steps such as finding out the sentence boundaries, tokenization, tagging the words using parts of speech and extracting the concept attached with the text. All these steps involved in the feature extraction are done automatically with Deep learning. Deep learning with its architectures will be helpful for a diversity of applications.

One application of deep-learning networks is named-entity recognition. It is a way to extract from unstructured, unlabeled data certain types of information like people, places and things. A deep network is also capable of understanding audio signals. This can be used to identify snippets of sound in larger audio files, and transcribe the spoken word as text. The various applications of Deep learning networks include Sentiment analysis, Theme detection, Fraud detection and Augmented Search.

The Deep learning networks can very well be used with various Natural language processing problems such as Text Classification, Language Modeling, Speech Recognition, Caption Generation, Machine Translation, Document Summarization and Question Answering.

REFERENCES

Acharyya, S. (2009). Language independent unsupervised learning of short message service dialect. *International Journal on Document Analysis and Recognition, 12*(3), 175-184.

Akhtar, M. S., Kumar, A., Ghosal, D., Ekbal, A., & Bhattacharyya, P. (2017). A multilayer perceptron based ensemble technique for fine-grained financial sentiment analysis. *Proceedings of the Conference on Empirical Methods on Natural Language Processing (EMNLP 2017)*. 10.18653/v1/D17-1057

Dong, L., Wei, F., Tan, C., Tang, D., Zhou, M., & Xu, K. (2014). Adaptive recursive neural network for target-dependent Twitter sentiment classification. *Proceedings of the Annual Meeting of the Association for Computational Linguistics (ACL 2014)*. 10.3115/v1/P14-2009

Dou, Z. Y. (2017). Capturing user and product Information for document level sentiment analysis with deep memory network. *Proceedings of the Conference on Empirical Methods on Natural Language Processing (EMNLP 2017)*. 10.18653/v1/D17-1054

Glorot, X., Bordes, A., & Bengio, Y. (2011). Domain adaption for large-scale sentiment classification: a deep learning approach. *Proceedings of the International Conference on Machine Learning (ICML 2011)*.

Hinton, G. E., Osindero, S., & Teh, Y. W. (2014). A fast learning algorithm for deep belief nets. *Neural Computation, 18*(7), 1527–1554. doi:10.1162/neco.2006.18.7.1527 PMID:16764513

Hinton, G. E., & Salakhutdinov, R. (2006). Reducing the dimensionality of data with neural networks. *Science, 313*(5786), 504–507. doi:10.1126cience.1127647 PMID:16873662

Hochreiter, S., & Schmidhuber, J. (1997). Long short-term memory. *Neural Computation, 9*(8), 1735–1780. doi:10.1162/neco.1997.9.8.1735 PMID:9377276

Jeffrey, L. Elman(1990). Finding structure in time. *Cognitive Science, 14*(2), 179–211. doi:10.120715516709cog1402_1

Johnson, R., & Zhang, T. (2015). Effective use of word order for text categorization with convolutional neural networks. *Proceedings of the Conference of the North American Chapter of the Association for Computational Linguistics: Human Language Technologies (NAACL-HLT 2015)*. 10.3115/v1/N15-1011

Katiyar, A., & Cardiem, C. (2016). Investigating LSTMs for joint extraction of opinion entities and relations. *Proceedings of the Annual Meeting of the Association for Computational Linguistics (ACL 2016)*. 10.18653/v1/P16-1087

Kim, Y. (2014). Convolutional neural networks for sentence classification. *Proceedings of the Annual Meeting of the Association for Computational Linguistics (ACL 2014)*.

Le, Q., & Mikolov, T. (2014). Distributed representations of sentences and documents. *Proceedings of the International Conference on Machine Learning (ICML 2014)*.

LeCun, Y., Bengio, Y., & Hinton, G. (2015). Deep learning. *Nature, 521*(7553), 436–444. doi:10.1038/nature14539 PMID:26017442

Lei, Shuai, & Bing. (2018). Deep learning for sentiment analysis: A survey. *WIREs Data Mining Knowl Discov, 8*. doi:10.1002/widm.1253

Li, X., & Lam, W. (2017). Deep multi-task learning for aspect term extraction with memory Interaction. *Proceedings of the Conference on Empirical Methods on Natural Language Processing (EMNLP 2017)*. 10.18653/v1/D17-1310

Li, Z., Zhang, Y., Wei, Y., Wu, Y., & Yang, Q. (2017). End-to-end adversarial memory network for cross-domain sentiment classification. *Proceedings of the International Joint Conference on Artificial Intelligence (IJCAI2017)*. 10.24963/ijcai.2017/311

Liu, J., & Zhang, Y. (2017). Attention modeling for targeted sentiment. *Proceedings of the Conference of the European Chapter of the Association for Computational Linguistics (EACL 2017)*.

Liu, Pengfei & Joty, Shafiq & Meng, Helen. (2015). Fine-grained Opinion Mining with Recurrent Neural Networks and Word Embeddings. 1433-1443. . doi:10.18653/v1/D15-1168

Ma, D., Li, S., Zhang, X., & Wang, H. (2017). Interactive attention networks for aspect-Level sentiment classification. *Proceedings of the Internal Joint Conference on Artificial Intelligence (IJCAI 2017)*. 10.24963/ijcai.2017/568

Mehdi Ben Lazreg. Morten Goodwin,& Ole-Christoffer Granmo.(2016).Deep Learning for Social Media Analysis in Crises Situations.The 29th Annual Workshop of the Swedish Artificial Intelligence Society (SAIS).

Michael, I Jordan. (1997). Serial order: A parallel distributed processing approach. *Advances in Psychology, 121*, 471–495.

Moraes, R., Valiati, J. F., & Neto, W. P. (2013). Document-level sentiment classification: An empirical comparison between SVM and ANN. *Expert Systems with Applications, 40*(2), 621–633. doi:10.1016/j.eswa.2012.07.059

Poria, S., Cambria, E. & Gelbukh, A. (2016). Aspect extraction for opinion mining with a deep convolutional neural network. *Journal of Knowledge-Based Systems*.

Rumelhart, D. E., Hinton, G. E., & Williams, R. J. (1988). *Learning internal representations by error propagation. Neurocomputing: foundations of research*. MIT Press.

Tang, D., Qin, B., & Liu, T. (2015). Document modelling with gated recurrent neural network for sentiment classification. *Proceedings of the Conference on Empirical Methods in Natural Language Processing (EMNLP 2015)*. 10.18653/v1/D15-1167

Vo, D.-T., & Zhang, Y. (2015). Target-dependent twitter sentiment classification with rich automatic features. *Proceedings of the Internal Joi Communicated Communicated nt Conference on Artificial Intelligence (IJCAI 2015).*

Wang, H., Raj, B., & Xing, E.P. (2017). *On the origin of deep learning.* Academic Press.

Wang, J., Yu, L.-C., Lai, R. K., & Zhang, X. (2016). Dimensional sentiment analysis using a regional CNN-LSTM model. *Proceedings of the Annual Meeting of the Association for Computational Linguistics (ACL 2016).* 10.18653/v1/P16-2037

Wang, W., Pan, S. J., Dahlmeier, D., & Xiao, X. (2017). Coupled Multi-Layer Attentions for Co-Extraction of Aspect and Opinion Terms. *Proceedings of the Thirty-First AAAI Conference on Artificial Intelligence (AAAI-17).*

Wang, X., Jiang, W., & Luo, Z. (2016) Combination of convolutional and recurrent neural network for sentiment analysis of short texts. In *Proceedings of the International Conference on Computational Linguistics (COLING 2016).*

Wang, X., Liu, Y., Sun, C., Wang, B., & Wang, X. (2015). Predicting polarities of tweets by composing word embeddings with long short-term memory. *Proceedings of the Annual Meeting of the Association for Computational Linguistics (ACL 2015).* 10.3115/v1/P15-1130

Wang, Y., Huang, M., Zhu, X., & Zhao, L. (2016). Attention-based LSTM for aspect-level sentiment classification. *Proceedings of the Conference on Empirical Methods in Natural Language Processing (EMNLP 2016).* 10.18653/v1/D16-1058

Wen, H., Li, M., & Ye, Z. (2017). Neural Architecture for Negative Opinion Expressions Extraction. In L. Chen, C. Jensen, C. Shahabi, X. Yang, & X. Lian (Eds.), Lecture Notes in Computer Science: Vol. 10366. *Web and Big Data. APWeb-WAIM 2017.* Springer. doi:10.1007/978-3-319-63579-8_35

Wiebe, J., Wilson, T., & Cardie, C. (2005). Annotating expressions of opinions and emotions in language. *Language Resources and Evaluation, 39*(2-3), 165–210. doi:10.100710579-005-7880-9

Xiong, S., Zhang, Y., Ji, D., & Lou, Y. (2016). Distance metric learning for aspect phrase grouping. *Proceedings of the International Conference on Computational Linguistics (COLING 2016).*

Yang, M., Tu, W., Wang, J., Xu, F., & Chen, X. (2017). Attention-based LSTM for target-dependent sentiment classification. *Proceedings of AAAI Conference on Artificial Intelligence (AAAI 2017).*

Yang, Z., Yang, D., Dyer, C., He, X., Smola, A. J., & Hovy, E. H. (2016). Hierarchical attention networks for document classification. *Proceedings of the Conference of the North American Chapter of the Association for Computational Linguistics: Human Language Technologies (NAACL-HLT 2016).*

Yin, Y., Song, Y., & Zhang, M. (2017). Document-level multi-aspect sentiment classification as machine comprehension. *Proceedings of the Conference on Empirical Methods in Natural Language Processing (EMNLP 2017).* 10.18653/v1/D17-1217

Yin, Y., Wei, F., Dong, L., Xu, K., Zhang, M., & Zhou, M. (2016). Unsupervised word and dependency path embeddings for aspect term extraction. *Proceedings of the International Joint Conference on Artificial Intelligence (IJCAI2016).*

Ying, D., Yu, J., & Jiang, J. (2017). Recurrent neural networks with auxiliary labels for cross-domain opinion target extraction. *Proceedings of AAAI Conference on Artificial Intelligence (AAAI 2017)*.

Zhai, S., & Zhang, Z. (2016). Semisupervised autoencoder for sentiment analysis. *Proceedings of AAAI Conference on Artificial Intelligence (AAAI 2016)*.

Zhang, M., Zhang, Y., & Vo, D.-T. (2015). Neural networks for open domain targeted sentiment. *Proceedings of the Conference on Empirical Methods in Natural Language Processing (EMNLP 2015)*. 10.18653/v1/D15-1073

Zhao, Z., Lu, H., Cai, D., He, X., & Zhuang, Y. (2017). Microblog sentiment classification via recurrent random walk network learning. *Proceedings of the Internal Joint Conference on Artificial Intelligence (IJCAI 2017)*. 10.24963/ijcai.2017/494

Zhou, C., Sun, C., & Liu, Z. (2015). A C-LSTM neural network for text classification. *Computer Science*, *1*(4), 39–44.

Zhou, X., Wan, X., & Xiao, J. (2016). Attention-based LSTM network for cross-lingual sentiment classification. *Proceedings of the Conference on Empirical Methods in Natural Language Processing (EMNLP 2016)*. 10.18653/v1/D16-1024

Chapter 44
A Machine Learning–Based Lexicon Approach for Sentiment Analysis

Tirath Prasad Sahu

NIT Raipur, Raipur, India

Sarang Khandekar

NIT Raipur, Raipur, India

ABSTRACT

Sentiment analysis can be a very useful aspect for the extraction of useful information from text documents. The main idea for sentiment analysis is how people think for a particular online review, i.e. product reviews, movie reviews, etc. Sentiment analysis is the process where these reviews are classified as positive or negative. The web is enriched with huge amount of reviews which can be analyzed to make it meaningful. This article presents the use of lexicon resources for sentiment analysis of different publicly available reviews. First, the polarity shift of reviews is handled by negations. Intensifiers, punctuation and acronyms are also taken into consideration during the processing phase. Second, words are extracted which have some opinion; these words are then used for computing score. Third, machine learning algorithms are applied and the experimental results show that the proposed model is effective in identifying the sentiments of reviews and opinions.

1. INTRODUCTION

Sentiment analysis is becoming a trending and popular amongst researchers. Sentiment analysis is a special case of text classification which aims to categorize opinions based on polarities for e.g. positive or negative. People can express their opinions on the web in the form of reviews. The reviews can be extracted from different fields such as product review, movie review, tweets from Twitter, etc. Basically, sentiment analysis is done to express what a person thinks for a particular product, movie, twitter etc.

DOI: 10.4018/978-1-6684-6303-1.ch044

In recent years lots of people are expressing their opinions on the web. Everyday millions of people express what they think in the form of reviews on platform such as blogs, forums, social networking sites like twitter etc. These platforms help people to connect to other people whom they don't even know and get the opinion from them. Basically, these platforms serve as intermediate between the end user and the service provider. From the end users perspective, these platforms are useful to get an idea about the product. From the service provider point of view, it helps to improve the standard of their product and services.

The data on the web is increasing everyday as many people are using it as a platform to express their reviews and opinions. Therefore, it becomes a very hectic task for people to take instant decision about the reviews and opinions. People are confused that on which review they can trust and on which review they cannot. Due to this problem, an automatic system must be designed to make the process of analysis, summarization and classification easy. The general approach for sentiment analysis is the Bag of Word (BOW) Approach (Dave, Lawrence, & Pennock, 2003). In this approach, a document is divided into bag of words to make feature vector which will be used in the classification process. However, BOW approach is failed to generate the desired results as it doesn't capture word sequence and semantic relation. The works have been carried out in the field of sentiment analysis to improve BOW in combination with linguistic knowledge (Dave, et al., 2003; Gamon, 2004; Kennedy & Inkpen, 2006; Na, Sui, Khoo, Chan, & Zhou, 2004; Ng, Dasgupta, & Arifin, 2006; Pang, Lee, & Vaithyanathan, 2002; Whitelaw, Garg, & Argamon, 2005; Xia, Zong, & Li, 2011). However, they failed to improve the classification accuracy.

The polarity shift is an important issue in sentiment analysis. Many approaches have been suggested in the literature to overcome the polarity shift problem (Councill, McDonald, & Velikovich, 2010; Das & Chen, 2001; Ikeda, Takamura, Ratinov, & Okumura, 2008; Li & Huang, 2009; Li, Lee, Chen, Huang, & Zhou, 2010; Wilson, Wiebe, & Hoffmann, 2009). However, most of them required either complex linguistic knowledge or extra human annotations. Such high-level dependency on external resources makes the system difficult to be widely used in practice.

Sentiment Analysis can be carried out at different level such as aspect level, sentence level and document level. The proposed method uses sentiment analysis at sentence level using the lexical resources SentiWordNet3.0 (Baccianella, Esuli, & Sebastiani, 2010) and Affin111 (Zol & Mulay, 2015) to decide the overall polarity of the reviews based on feature vector and machine learning algorithms.

2. RELATED WORK

A lot of research has been carried out on sentiment analysis in recent years. The center research areas are sentiment classification and feature-based sentiment analysis. Sentiment classification explores ways to characterize reviews as positive or negative. The efforts on classification at the document level sentiment analysis have been presented in (Das & Chen, 2001; Dave, et al., 2003; Gamon, Aue, Corston-Oliver, & Ringger, 2005; Hearst, 1992; Pang & Lee, 2005; Pang, et al., 2002; Riloff & Wiebe, 2003; Turney, 2002). Most of the methods are based on sentence and document level classification which involves reorganization of opinion words. Corpus based method and dictionary-based method is the two types of method that are basically used. In corpus based, method co-occurrence patterns of words are found out to determine the sentiments of words. The research efforts (Hatzivassiloglou & Wiebe, 2000; Turney,

2002; Wiebe & Mihalcea, 2006) are the example of corpus-based method. In dictionary-based method, synonyms and antonyms have been used from WordNet to decide sentiments of opinion words. The related works using this approach are presented (Andreevskaia & Bergler, 2006; Fellbaum, 1998; Hu & Liu, 2004; Kim & Hovy, 2004). Lexicon-based approach is being used to decide whether the review expressed is positive or negative. The work presented (Kim & Hovy, 2004) is also based Lexicon-based approach. Further, the approach has been improved in (Popescu & Etzioni, 2007) using a more sophisticated approach called relaxation labeling. In (Hatzivassiloglou & Wiebe, 2000), the authors studied sentence level subjectivity classification which decides whether a sentence is a subjective sentence or a sentence based on facts. The various works (Hatzivassiloglou & Wiebe, 2000; Hu & Liu, 2004; Kim & Hovy, 2004; Nasukawa & Yi, 2003; Popescu & Etzioni, 2007; Wilson, Wiebe, & Hwa, 2004) has been carried out for sentence level sentiment analysis. The presented approach in the current work is different from previous works in the sense that: firstly, the sentence is preprocessed to remove unnecessary data from it; secondly, the polarity detection is performed with the use of lexicon dictionary; and lastly, various features are used to train the classifiers for sentiment analysis.

3. PROPOSED APPROACH

The proposed approach is based on Lexicon based approach for sentiment analysis. In the proposed approach, each word in the sentence is considered to compute the weight of the opinion words in order to compute the overall polarity of the sentence. The lexicon resources SentiWordNet3.0 and Affin111 are used for polarity detection. The focus of the presented work is to determine the polarities of the sentences using the following steps: 1) Pre-processing; 2) Negation-intensifier-punctuation-acronyms (NIPA) handling; 3) Feature extraction; 4) Applying classification algorithms. The publically available review datasets are used for sentiment analysis in order to classify the reviews are into two classes i.e. positive (1) and negative (0). The workflow of the proposed algorithm is presented in Figure 1.

3.1. Pre-Processing

The pre-processing of the dataset is to remove the redundant data in order to speed up the process of categorization of the polarities of the sentences or reviews. The pre-processing consists of the following steps:

- **Tokenization:** It is the process of breaking the textual documents (reviews) into the terms (words) in order to identify the importance of terms and applying the text mining techniques efficiently;
- **Stemming:** It is the process of converting the terms into their root form in order to make the analysis and processing easy. For e.g. argument, argued, argues, arguing all are converted into their root form "argue";
- **Stopping:** It is the process of removing the useless terms called stop words from the documents. Stop words basically includes verbs, articles, preposition, etc. (e.g. a, an, the, I, that, etc.). The stop words do not contribute in analyzing sentiments and therefore these words has to be removed from the reviews. For e.g. the review "Twilight is the best series that I have ever seen," will be processed as "Twilight best series ever seen";

Figure 1. Proposed workflow

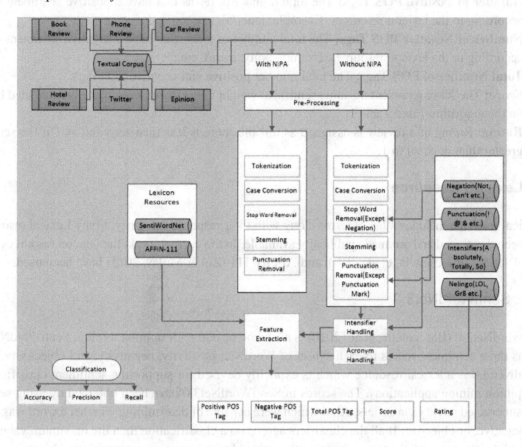

- **Parts of Speech Tagging (POS):** In this process, all the terms in the documents are marked in accordance to their particular POS like verb, adverb, pronoun, noun, determinant and adjective. For e.g. "Berry Alan likes to be the fastest man alive and saves the city from meta humans" is tagged as "Berry (Adverb) Alan (Adverb) likes (Verb) to be (Verb) the (Determiner) fastest (Adjective) man (Noun) alive (Adjective) and (Conjunction) saves (Verb) the (Determiner) city (Noun) from (Preposition) meta (Adjective) humans (Noun)";
- **Case Conversion:** It is the process of converting the reviews into lower case;
- **Punctuation Cleaning:** The presence of punctuation in the text do not gives any useful information. Therefore, the punctuation characters are removed from the reviews.

3.2. Feature Extraction

After pre-processing, next step is to analyze the reviews in order to identify the patterns that affect the polarities of reviews. The lexicon resources SentiWordNet3.0 (Baccianella, et al., 2010) and Affin111 (Zol & Mulay, 2015) are used to find the features w.r.t. the opinion terms for polarity detection. The descriptions of the identified features are as follows:

- **Number of Positive POS Tags:** The total number of terms that have a positive sentiment score according to the lexicon resources. Example: fanciful, awesome, etc.;
- **Number of Negative POS Tags:** The total number of terms that have a negative sentiment score according to the lexicon resources. Example: pity, awful, etc.;
- **Total Number of POS Tags:** The total number positive and negative POS tags;
- **Score:** The score representing some sentiment weight to the documents and it is calculated based on the algorithm 1 and Table 1;
- **Rating:** Rating of a review is assigned as 0 if the score is less than zero and as 1 if the score is greater than or equal to 1.

3.3. Lexicon Resource

A lexical resource includes a list of terms along with their respective polarity. Many Lexical resources have been developed and are made publically available. In the current work, the lexicon resources SentiWordNet 3.0 (Baccianella, et al., 2010) and AFFIN-111 (Zol & Mulay, 2015) have been used.

3.3.1. SentiWordNet3.0

SentiWordNet3.0 (Baccianella, et al., 2010) is a lexicon resource for opinion mining. SentiWordNet3.0 assigns three sentiment scores to each synset of WordNet: positivity, negativity, and objectivity. SentiWordNet 3.0 is a lexical resource which is explicitly devised for supporting sentiment classification and opinion mining applications. The scores in SentiWordNet3.0 have been obtained by using several semi-supervised ternary classifiers, all of which were capable of determining whether a word was positive, negative, or objective. If all the classifiers agreed on a classification then the maximum value was assigned for the associated score, otherwise the values for the positive, negative and objective scores were proportional to the number of classifiers that assigned the word to each class.

3.3.2. AFFIN-111

AFINN-111 (Zol & Mulay, 2015) is a dictionary consisting of English words rated for valence with an integer between minus five (negative) and plus five (positive). The words have been manually labeled by Finn Arup Nielsen in 2009-2011.

3.4. NIPA Approach

In the current work, some assumptions have been made to allocate the polarity Negations, Intensifiers, Punctuations, and Acronyms which are then updated in the lexicon resource in order to compute the polarity.

Algorithm 1. Calculating score, positive POS tag, negative POS tag, neutral POS tag, ratings and evaluation measures

```
INPUT: R- Review Dataset, L- Lexicon Dictionary;
OUTPUT: Score, Positive POS Tag, Negative POS Tag, Neutral POS Tag, Ratings and
Evaluation Measures
For Each term in L do
    Initialize Ws = 0;
    Calculate Ws = Ps- Ns;
End
For each review r=1 to n in R do
    Apply Pre-processing;
    For each word w=1 to i in review R do
        If Ws > 0 then
            PCount++;
        End
        Else if Ws=0 then
            NeuCount++;
        End
        Else
            NCount++;
        End
        TotalPOSCount = PCount + NeuCount + NCount;
End
For each word w = 1 to i till end of review do
    Calculate total word perception Wp of each word in the review r from L;
    Initialize the variables Wsc = 0, Wsts = 0, Wsm = 0, Fss = 0;
    Wsc = Ws/Wp;
    Wsm = 1/Twp;
    Wsts = Wsc/Wsm;
    Fss = ∑ Wsts;
End
For each review assign rating as do
    If Fss > 0 then
        Rating = 1;
    End
    Else
        Rating = 0;
    End
Apply classifier using features calculated
Calculate accuracy, precision, and recall from equations. (1), (2), (3).
```

Table 1. Variables used with their definition

Variable	Definition
WordSense (Ws)	WordSense is the difference between the positive and negative weighted terms in accordance to the number of different perception allocated to that term in the lexicon resource.
WordSenseScore (Wss)	WordSensescore is the aggregation of WordSenseScore to the total number of different perception allocated to a term.
WordSenseSum(Wsm)	WordSenseSum is the weighted average of total number of different perception allocated to a term.
WordSenseSentimentScore(Wsts)	WordSentimentScore is the aggregation of the WordSenseScore to the WordSenseSum of a term.
FinalSentimentScore(Fss)	FinalSentimentScore is the aggregation of all WordSenseSentimentScore of each term that are in a review.

3.4.1. Coping With Negations

While deciding the polarity of a review, the major problem that can arise is polarity shift problem. While performing sentiment analysis coping with negation is a major problem. The negation terms such as not, cannot, would not, etc., are considered as stop words which are often ignored by many researchers. A review can completely change its meaning when negation terms are ignored. If negation terms are completely ignored, a review can be interpreted with a completely different meaning. For e.g. a review

"This movie is not liked by anyone." The polarity of the word 'liked' is positive and the polarity of the word 'not' is negative. It can easily be interpreted that the overall polarity of this review is negative. But many researchers ignored the negative polarity terms. They consider the word 'not', as a stop word and do not include this word while determining the polarity. But they take the review as "This movie is liked by everyone." When the word like 'not' is ignored, the review changes its perception from negative to positive. If the researchers consider the word 'not', the review remains intact with the actual perception i.e. positive. This problem is overcome by the proposed approach. The negation term is replaced by a '^' symbol whenever a review encounters a negation term. A stop words list is made which contains negation words. Review changes its polarity when these negation terms are not considered. For this, modifications are done in the lexicon resource. These negation words are assumed as negative words and hence assigned a negative weight of -1 in the lexicon resource.

3.4.2. Coping With Intensifiers

The sentiment of a review is amplified or diminished by the intensifiers. A critical role can be played by intensifiers while deciding the polarity of a review. The proposed approach considers some intensifiers which have been used by people while giving a review. The intensifiers that are taken are 'So', 'Absolutely', and 'Totally.' In (Dushku), it is inferred that 'Totally' is used along with the negative terms so a negative weight −1 is assigned to it. The term 'So' is used along with the positive term so positive weight +1 is allocated to it. Absolutely gives a neutral perception therefore a neutral weight is allocated.

3.4.3. Coping With Punctuations

In polarity computation, a crucial role can be of Punctuations symbols but this punctuation is often being ignored. The symbol '*Exclamation (!)*' should also be taken into consideration. People use to express a surprise, astonishment and other such strong emotions by using exclamation mark. So, while calculating polarity this measure can play a vital role. Positive weight of +1 is assigned to it as it shows a positive emotion.

3.4.4. Coping With Acronyms

The acronyms are short forms of a complete term. The acronyms are generally used while giving a review in order to save the time and effort. The acronyms should be handled in calculating the polarity of a sentence. In the current work, top 100 acronyms are used from netlingo ("Netlingo, Popular text terms, Top 100 Acronyms,") which are generally used by people when a review is given. The acronyms from netlingo are taken into account to convert it into their actual meaning. For e.g. GR8 is an acronym of term 'Great' which is largely used by the people to express themselves in the form of reviews. The acronyms are generally ignored while calculating the polarity of a review, but it may affects the polarity. In the current work, the acronyms are well handled to calculate the polarity of reviews.

3.5. Classifiers

The two popular classifiers Naive Bayes (NB) (Lewis, 1998) and support vector machines (SVM) (Jain et al., 2017; Joachims, 1998; Wang & Wang, 2014) can be used for sentiment analysis. The prior work

(Pang, et al., 2002) shows the feasibility of these classifiers in sentiment classification. Their results on the movie review dataset shows that the machine learning techniques such as Naïve Bayes, and Support Vector Machine gives a better result than those given by human generated baselines. Therefore, the current work also uses these well-known classifiers namely: Support Vector Machine (SVM) and Naive Bayes (NB) on feature vectors in order to identify the sentiments on different review datasets. The well-known 10-fold cross validation is for binary classification of reviews.

4. OUTCOME AND ANALYSIS

4.1. Dataset Description

In the current work, various product review datasets such as Books, Movies, Hotels, Car, epinion, and Twitter datasets are taken into consideration to evaluate the correctness of the proposed model. The datasets such as Books, Movies, Hotels, and Car are taken from SFU review dataset (Taboada). Positive review and negative review are evenly divided in these review datasets. Movie review dataset has been taken from Pang and Lee ("1382 Ford Automobile Review, Text Analytics, Carnegie Mellon University,"). Datasets from epinions have also been considered which contains reviews for automobiles. The phone dataset is also extracted from Twitter ("479 Twitter Tweets, Text Analytics, Carnegie Mellon University,"). The extracted datasets are evenly divided into positive and negative reviews. The binary classification is used to classify the reviews as positive review or negative review.

4.2. Evaluation Parameters

The conventional evaluation measures for classifier such as accuracy, precision, and recall are taken into consideration. These evaluation measures are defined using confusion matrix of classifier results as shown in Table 2.

Table 2. Confusion Matrix

		Correct Labels	
		Positive	**Negative**
Classified Labels	Positive	TP (True Positive)	FP (False Positive)
	Negative	FN (False Negative)	TN (True Negative)

4.2.1. Accuracy

Accuracy is defined as the ratio of number of correctly classified reviews to the total number of reviews and is given as:

$$Accuracy = \frac{True\,Negative + True\,Positive}{True\,Negative + False\,Positive + False\,Negative + Tru\,Positve} \tag{1}$$

4.2.2. Precision

Precision is defined as the ratio of true positive (TP) to total positives (TP+FP) i.e. the proportion of correctly classified positive reviews and is given as:

$$Precision = \frac{True\,Positive}{True\,Positive + False\,Positive} \tag{2}$$

4.2.3. Recall

Recall is defined as the ratio of true positive (TP) to both true positive (TP) and false negative (FP) i.e. the proportion of positive reviews that is correctly classified and is given as:

$$Recall = \frac{True\,Positive}{True\,Positive + Fasle\,Negative} \tag{3}$$

4.3. Experimental Results

The extensive experiments have been carried out on various datasets with proposed NIPA approach using lexicon resources (SentiWordNet3.0 and Affin111) and classifiers (Naïve Bayes and SVM). The comparison between the proposed NIPA approach and the approach that does not use NIPA has been presented. The various performance measures i.e accuracy, precision and recall of both the approaches are shown in Table 3, Table 4, Table 5, Table 6, Table 7, and Table 8 for Book, Car, Hotel, Phone, Epinion, and Twitter datasets respectively. Similarly, the figures corresponding to the tabular results are also shown in Figure 2, Figure 3, Figure 4, Figure 5, Figure 6, and Figure 7 for Book, Car, Hotel, Phone, Epinion, and Twitter datasets respectively in order to visualize the comparison on various approaches.

Table 3. Comparing results book dataset

	Accuracy With NIPA	Accuracy Without NIPA	Precision With NIPA	Precision Without NIPA	Recall With NIPA	Recall Without NIPA
SentiWordNet and SVM	90.33	61.29	87.50	60.00	87.50	48.00
Affin111 and SVM	81.43	79.43	85.70	80.50	75.00	80.40
SentiWordNet and Naïve Bayes	91.30	54.34	84.00	29.54	95.20	54.34
Affin111 and Naïve Bayes	88.94	86.95	88.33	79.10	86.95	82.60

Figure 2. Results for book dataset

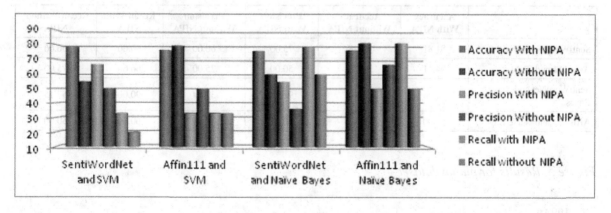

Table 4. Comparing results car dataset

	Accuracy With NIPA	Accuracy Without NIPA	Precision With NIPA	Precision Without NIPA	Recall With NIPA	Recall Without NIPA
SentiWordNet and SVM	78.52	55.00	66.60	50.00	33.00	20.00
Affin111 and SVM	76.47	79.41	33.33	50.00	33.33	33.00
SentiWordNet and Naïve Bayes	76.00	60.00	55.00	36.08	78.57	60.00
Affin111 and Naïve Bayes	76.47	81.25	50.00	66.66	81.25	50.00

Figure 3. Results for car dataset

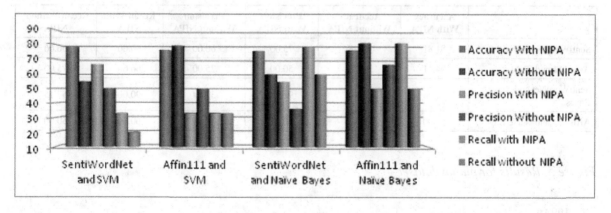

For Book dataset, the highest accuracy is achieved by the approach that uses SentiWordNet3.0 as lexicon resource, Naïve Bayes as classifier, and NIPA. The highest precision is achieved by the approach that uses SentiWordNet3.0 as lexicon resource, SVM as classifier, and NIPA. Similarly, the highest recall is achieved by the approach that uses SentiWordNet3.0 as lexicon resource, Naïve Bayes as classifier, and NIPA. The results of other datasets also reveal that the proposed NIPA approach gives better results than the approach that does not used NIPA approach in all evaluation parameters.

Table 5. Comparing results hotel dataset

	Accuracy With NIPA	Accuracy Without NIPA	Precision With NIPA	Precision Without NIPA	Recall With NIPA	Recall Without NIPA
SentiWordNet and SVM	88.23	58.82	80.00	25.25	80.00	16.16
Affin111 and SVM	85.29	88.23	66.66	50.00	66.60	40.00
SentiWordNet and Naïve Bayes	82.00	62.00	84.21	38.86	96.40	62.00
Affin111 and Naïve Bayes	81.25	87.50	50.00	33.33	33.33	66.66

Figure 4. Results for hotel dataset

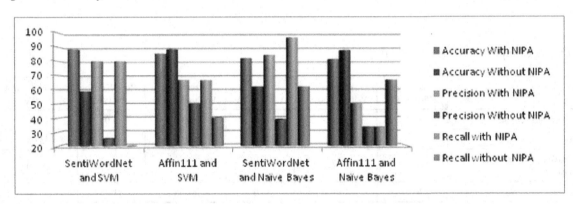

Table 6. Comparing results phone dataset

	Accuracy With NIPA	Accuracy Without NIPA	Precision With NIPA	Precision Without NIPA	Recall With NIPA	Recall Without NIPA
SentiWordNet and SVM	81.81	48.48	75.00	60.00	90.00	66.66
Affin111 and SVM	94.11	88.23	50.00	75.00	66.66	75.00
SentiWordNet and Naïve Bayes	91.83	57.14	96.40	32.74	90.00	57.15
Affin111 and Naïve Bayes	80.00	73.33	50.21	42.85	60.00	50.00

Figure 5. Results for phone dataset

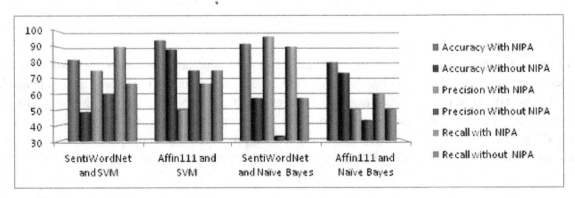

Table 7. Comparing results Twitter dataset

	Accuracy With NIPA	Accuracy Without NIPA	Precision With NIPA	Precision Without NIPA	Recall With NIPA	Recall Without NIPA
SentiWordNet and SVM	94.00	81.38	96.55	80.00	93.00	78.68
Affin111 and SVM	95.26	90.85	97.77	86.31	96.70	92.21
SentiWordNet and Naïve Bayes	91.83	62.42	94.31	39.00	91.55	62.47
Affin111 and Naïve Bayes	92.59	85.80	92.22	85.51	94.31	87.50

Figure 6. Results for Twitter dataset

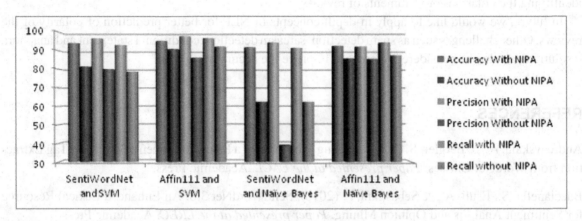

Table 8. Comparing results Epinion dataset

	Accuracy With NIPA	Accuracy Without NIPA	Precision With NIPA	Precision Without NIPA	Recall With NIPA	Recall Without NIPA
SentiWordNet and SVM	97.91	82.14	97.22	82.52	94.54	74.73
Affin111 and SVM	97.59	95.83	96.72	98.46	92.18	93.75
SentiWordNet and Naïve Bayes	91.82	59.40	90.01	35.35	89.85	59.45
Affin111 and Naïve Bayes	88.69	75.00	77.77	75.00	82.30	82.83

Figure 7. Results for Epinion dataset

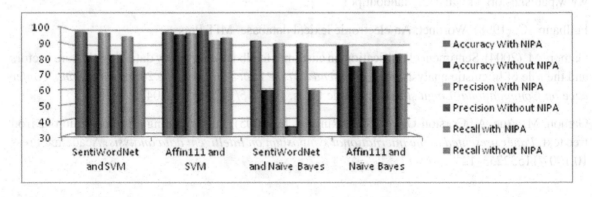

5. CONCLUSION AND FUTURE SCOPE

In the current work, a machine learning based lexicon approach is presented for sentiment analysis. Computation linguistic methods are also applied such as stemming, stopping, Part of speech tagging for the pre-processing of reviews. The problem related to negations, intensifiers, punctuations and acronyms (NIPA) in reviews are effectively handled so as to improve the accuracy. The various features are extracted that have a very strong impact on determining the polarities of review. The feature vectors of various datasets have been maintained to train and evaluate the classifier. The six different review datasets have been used and the results have been reported in terms of evaluation parameters. The experimental results of various datasets suggest that the NIPA handling with lexicon resources are very effective in identifying the polarities or sentiments of reviews.

In future, we would like to apply in-depth concepts of NLP for better prediction of polarity of the reviews. Other challenges such as spam detection, sarcasm detection, conditional statement and anaphora resolution can also be considered in order to improve the accuracy.

REFERENCES

Andreevskaia, A., & Bergler, S. (2006). Mining WordNet for a Fuzzy Sentiment: Sentiment Tag Extraction from WordNet Glosses. *Paper presented at the EACL*. Academic Press.

Baccianella, S., Esuli, A., & Sebastiani, F. (2010). SentiWordNet 3.0: An Enhanced Lexical Resource for Sentiment Analysis and Opinion Mining. *Paper presented at the LREC*. Academic Press.

Councill, I. G., McDonald, R., & Velikovich, L. (2010). What's great and what's not: learning to classify the scope of negation for improved sentiment analysis. *Paper presented at the workshop on negation and speculation in natural language processing*. Academic Press.

Das, S., & Chen, M. (2001). Yahoo! for Amazon: Extracting market sentiment from stock message boards. *Paper presented at the Asia Pacific finance association annual conference (APFA)*. Academic Press.

Dave, K., Lawrence, S., & Pennock, D. M. (2003). Mining the peanut gallery: Opinion extraction and semantic classification of product reviews. *Paper presented at the 12th international conference on World Wide Web*. Academic Press. 10.1145/775152.775226

Dushku, S. (n.d.). Common Intensifiers and Evaluation Phrases in Spoken English. Retrieved from http://www.paulslals.org.uk/Dushku_handout.pdf

Fellbaum, C. (1998). Wordnet: An electronic lexical database. MIT Press.

Gamon, M. (2004). Sentiment classification on customer feedback data: noisy data, large feature vectors, and the role of linguistic analysis. *Paper presented at the Proceedings of the 20th international conference on Computational Linguistics*. Academic Press. 10.3115/1220355.1220476

Gamon, M., Aue, A., Corston-Oliver, S., & Ringger, E. (2005). Pulse: Mining customer opinions from free text. *Paper presented at the international symposium on intelligent data analysis*. Academic Press. 10.1007/11552253_12

Hatzivassiloglou, V., & Wiebe, J. M. (2000). Effects of adjective orientation and gradability on sentence subjectivity. *Paper presented at the Proceedings of the 18th conference on Computational linguistics* (Vol. 1). Academic Press. 10.3115/990820.990864

Hearst, M. A. (1992). Direction-based text interpretation as an information access refinement. In *Text-based intelligent systems: current research and practice in information extraction and retrieval* (pp. 257-274). ACM.

Hu, M., & Liu, B. (2004). Mining and summarizing customer reviews. *Paper presented at the tenth ACM SIGKDD international conference on Knowledge discovery and data mining.* ACM.

Ikeda, D., Takamura, H., Ratinov, L.-A., & Okumura, M. (2008). Learning to Shift the Polarity of Words for Sentiment Classification. *Paper presented at the IJCNLP.* Academic Press.

Jain, D. K., Dubey, S. B., Choubey, R. K., Sinhal, A., Arjaria, S. K., Jain, A., & Wang, H. (2017). An approach for hyperspectral image classification by optimizing SVM using self organizing map. *Journal of Computational Science.*

Joachims, T. (1998). Text categorization with support vector machines: Learning with many relevant features. *Machine Learning, ECML-98,* 137–142.

Kennedy, A., & Inkpen, D. (2006). Sentiment classification of movie reviews using contextual valence shifters. *Computational Intelligence, 22*(2), 110–125. doi:10.1111/j.1467-8640.2006.00277.x

Kim, S.-M., & Hovy, E. (2004). Determining the sentiment of opinions. *Paper presented at the 20th international conference on Computational Linguistics.* Academic Press.

Lewis, D. D. (1998). Naive (Bayes) at forty: The independence assumption in information retrieval. *Paper presented at the European conference on machine learning.* Academic Press. 10.1007/BFb0026666

Li, S., & Huang, C.-R. (2009). Sentiment Classification Considering Negation and Contrast Transition. *Paper presented at the PACLIC.* Academic Press.

Li, S., Lee, S. Y. M., Chen, Y., Huang, C.-R., & Zhou, G. (2010). Sentiment classification and polarity shifting. *Paper presented at the Proceedings of the 23rd International Conference on Computational Linguistics.* Academic Press.

Na, J.-C., Sui, H., Khoo, C. S., Chan, S., & Zhou, Y. (2004). Effectiveness of simple linguistic processing in automatic sentiment classification of product reviews.

Nasukawa, T., & Yi, J. (2003). Sentiment analysis: Capturing favorability using natural language processing. *Paper presented at the 2nd international conference on Knowledge capture.* Academic Press. 10.1145/945645.945658

Netlingo. (n.d.). Popular text terms, Top 100 Acronyms. Retrieved from http://www.netlingo.com/top100/popular-text-terms.php

Ng, V., Dasgupta, S., & Arifin, S. (2006). Examining the role of linguistic knowledge sources in the automatic identification and classification of reviews. *Paper presented at the COLING/ACL on Main conference poster sessions*. Academic Press. 10.3115/1273073.1273152

Pang, B., & Lee, L. (2005). Seeing stars: Exploiting class relationships for sentiment categorization with respect to rating scales. *Paper presented at the 43rd annual meeting on association for computational linguistics*. Academic Press. 10.3115/1219840.1219855

Pang, B., Lee, L., & Vaithyanathan, S. (2002). Thumbs up?: sentiment classification using machine learning techniques. *Paper presented at the ACL-02 conference on Empirical methods in natural language processing*. Academic Press. 10.3115/1118693.1118704

Popescu, A.-M., & Etzioni, O. (2007). *Extracting product features and opinions from reviews. In Natural language processing and text mining* (pp. 9–28). Springer. doi:10.1007/978-1-84628-754-1_2

Review, F. A., & Analytics, T. (n.d.). Carnegie Mellon University. from http://boston.lti.cs.cmu.edu/classes/95-865-K/HW/HW3/FordAutomobile

Riloff, E., & Wiebe, J. (2003). Learning extraction patterns for subjective expressions. *Paper presented at the 2003 conference on Empirical methods in natural language processing*. ACM. 10.3115/1119355.1119369

Taboada, M. (n.d.). The SFU Review Corpus. Retrieved from https://www.sfu.ca/~mtaboada/SFU_Review_Corpus.html

Turney, P. D. (2002). Thumbs up or thumbs down?: semantic orientation applied to unsupervised classification of reviews. *Paper presented at the Proceedings of the 40th annual meeting on association for computational linguistics*. Academic Press.

Tweets, T., & Analytics, T. (n.d.). Carnegie Mellon University. from http://boston.lti.cs.cmu.edu/classes/95-865-K/HW/HW3/Twitter/

Wang, H., & Wang, J. (2014). An effective image representation method using kernel classification. *Paper presented at the 2014 IEEE 26th International Conference on Tools with Artificial Intelligence (ICTAI)*. Academic Press. 10.1109/ICTAI.2014.131

Whitelaw, C., Garg, N., & Argamon, S. (2005). Using appraisal groups for sentiment analysis. *Paper presented at the 14th ACM international conference on Information and knowledge management*. Academic Press.

Wiebe, J., & Mihalcea, R. (2006). Word sense and subjectivity. *Paper presented at the 21st International Conference on Computational Linguistics and the 44th annual meeting of the Association for Computational Linguistics*. Academic Press.

Wilson, T., Wiebe, J., & Hoffmann, P. (2009). Recognizing contextual polarity: An exploration of features for phrase-level sentiment analysis. *Computational Linguistics*, *35*(3), 399–433. doi:10.1162/coli.08-012-R1-06-90

Wilson, T., Wiebe, J., & Hwa, R. (2004). Just how mad are you? Finding strong and weak opinion clauses. *Paper presented at the AAAI.* AAAI Press.

Xia, R., Zong, C., & Li, S. (2011). Ensemble of feature sets and classification algorithms for sentiment classification. *Information Sciences*, *181*(6), 1138–1152. doi:10.1016/j.ins.2010.11.023

Zol, S., & Mulay, P. (2015). Analyzing Sentiments for Generating Opinions (ASGO)-a new approach. *Indian Journal of Science and Technology*, 8(S4), 206–211. doi:10.17485/ijst/2015/v8iS4/62327

This research was previously published in the International Journal of Technology and Human Interaction (IJTHI), 16(2); pages 8-22, copyright year 2020 by IGI Publishing (an imprint of IGI Global).

Chapter 45
Sentiment Analysis of Brand Personality Positioning Through Text Mining

Ruei-Shan Lu
Takming University of Science and Technology, Taipei, Taiwan

Hsiu-Yuan Tsao
National Chung Hsing University, Taiwan

Hao-Chaing Koong Lin
National University of Tainan, Tainan, Taiwan

Yu-Chun Ma
iD https://orcid.org/0000-0003-4904-9844
National University of Tainan, Tainan, Taiwan

Cheng-Tung Chuang
Takming University of Science and Technology, Taipei, Taiwan

ABSTRACT

This article uses text mining and a Chinese word segmentation program developed by the Chinese Knowledge and Information Processing Group in Taiwan's Academia Sinica to analyze Facebook posts from 14 e-commerce companies. In addition, a list of keywords representing brand personalities is analyzed to reveal key factors affecting which social media posts attract consumers' attention. This research uses statistical analysis with a nonmanual questionnaire that is efficient and based on computer science to provide a reference for businesses operating Facebook fan pages and internet marketing.

DOI: 10.4018/978-1-6684-6303-1.ch045

INTRODUCTION

As internet and social media develops, the usage of smart mobile devices increases, the users of internet increases while the user's age bracket decreases. The popularity of Social Networking Site and Instant Messaging lead many business companies to interact and promote its products to consumers via Facebook, Twitter and other social networking sites, sometimes on instant messaging apps such as Line, QQ and WeChat. In the "2013 Taiwan's Internet User Shopping Behavior Analysis" by Market Intelligence & Consulting Institute (MIC) points out that in the category "Which way to buy needed products," "Browse social network sites" takes up 30.1%, which is the second highest in all option. The fan pages in social networking sites always takes up 18.1%. From this statistic analysis, it's clear that the information in social networking sites cannot just only raise Taiwan's internet user's shopping desire, it is also a main source when it comes to comparing products.

According to "Facebook Taiwan Consumer Online Behavior Questionnaire," a research that Facebook commissioned Kantar TNS to conduct points out the fact that Facebook is the most used social network site by Taiwanese people. Consumers, especially students and young professionals spends more time on Facebook than any other websites, TV and printed media. Facebook has a huge influence on Taiwanese consumer, 50% of Facebook Taiwan consumer searched, bought or sold products on Facebook, 22% of Taiwanese that used Facebook will buy the product after getting recommendations from friends. The sales conversion rate is double the 12% of self-search. From this report, it's not hard to realize that Facebook is not just a simple social networking site, but a battleground of business marketing. How to promote and popularize product and corporate identity through Facebook become a something that all business corporate must think about.

This research hopes to use text mining as the main technique, with the data from "Taiwan's Top 10 Online Shopping Sites With The Most Product" provided by EZprice in July 2014, the Facebook fan pages of 10 shopping sites "PChome Online Shopping," "Momo Shop," "Yahoo Shopping Center," "UDN Buy," "Go Happy Shopping Site," "PayEasy Women Shop," "ETMall," "U-Mall," " 7net Online Shopping," "ASAP Flash Online Shopping" as the research objective, using fan page posts from the day the fan page was created until 2016 as the field of research. Through the list of vocabularies that represent brand personality positioning organized from papers and documents, also by calculating the brand personality positioning emotion score, the result can be used in corporate's Facebook fan pages as reference when it comes to marketing and brand market position.

LITERATURE REVIEW

Brand Personality Positioning

Aaker (1997) believes that "Brand Personality Positioning" is the related attribute when business corporates are building product images and consumer's impression, so it is important to understand how consumer feels toward the brand personality positioning. He divides brand personality positioning into five core dimensions: Sincerity, Excitement, Competence, Sophistication, and Ruggedness. These five core dimensions then includes 15 facets and 42 traits. Table 1 shows the brand personality positioning scale.

Table 1. Brand personality positioning scale

Dimensions	Classification	Traits
Sincerity	1. Down-to-Earth 2. Honest 3. Wholesome 4. Cheerful	Down-to-earth, Family-Oriented, Small-town, Honest, Sincere, Real, Wholesome, Original, Cheerful, Sentimental, Friendly
Excitement	1. Daring 2. Spirited 3.Imaginative 4. Up-to-Date	Daring, Trendy, Exciting, Spirited, Cool, Young, Imaginative, Unique, Up-to date, independent, Contemporary
Competence	1. Reliable 2. Intelligent 3. Successful	Reliable, Hardworking, Secure, Intelligent, Technical, Corporate Successful, Leader, Confident
Sophistication	1. Upper Class 2. Charming	Upper Class, Glamorous, Good Looking, Charming, Feminine, Smooth
Ruggedness	1. Outdoorsy 2. Tough	Outdoorsy, Masculine, Western, Tough, Rugged

Building brand personality positioning can bring both the consumer and business itself uniqueness, which brings a lot of benefits, this has led to many scholars to start researching and study brand personality positioning. For businesses, Traci and Lukas (2005) proved with evidence that the hardest part of building a successful brand personality positioning is the diversification. A unique and powerful brand personality positioning can bring the brand a special and outstanding brand positioning. Plummer (2000) believes that Brand Personality Profiles and Brand Personality Statement can represent Brand Personality positioning. Brand Personality Profiles is what the business corporate wants the consumer to feel and think about the brand while the Brand Personality Statement is when business corporate wants to know how consumers really feel about the brand personality positioning. This research will start from the angle of Brand Personality Statement, through the word textual analysis of the comment on each corporate's Facebook fan page and try to analyze the consumer's feeling toward each brand personality positioning.

The Importance of Brand Personality

From the marketing perspective, Brand Personality is the key factor to a successful brand. Bhargava (2008) brought the idea of "Without Brand Personality, marketing is missing it's highlight," which points out the main problem when many corporates are marketing for its brand. Alt and Griggs (1988) also pointed out that the ability to maintain a stable and permanent brand personality will be one of the key factors for a successful marketing. Levy (1999) also states that Brand Personality has the characteristic of consistency, but brand will change according to commercials and change in products. Pierre, Haythem and Dwight (2011) also indicates that from an analysis of the impact on brand equity between a short-term sale promotion and long-term brand personality, it shows that it will impact different consumer group.

For consumers, brand personality can also represent consumer itself, raise the purchase intention if the brand matches its own personality. Keller (2008) believes that when consumer is deciding on a product or making a purchase, they often choose the ones with brand personality close to its own personality traits. Plummer (2000) points out that when consumer decides on a product, it means that "I can see myself in this product" or "This is my brand". Aaker, Fournier and Brasel (2004) states that brand personality is when the brand has characteristic traits like people, which can help consumers to understand its own relationship with the brand. Doyle (1990) mentions that once the consumer realizes that the brand personality of a brand is similar to itself, then it will greatly increase their intention to purchase. Pragya, Shailendra and Durairaj (2012) used Implicit Personality Theory to discuss how to impact the determination of brand personality, everyone's judgement of its own personality trait will be different under certain circumstances.

As internet activity and usage rises, internet user then plays a role in shaping brand personality. Opoku (2006) used text mining and statistics and found 833 vocabulary that is the synonym of brand personality's five core dimension, a keyword vocabulary base of brand personality characteristics is constructed to analyze the content of the websites of countries, small and medium-sized enterprises and business schools to distinguish the brand personality differences of different websites.

Sentiment analysis

Accordingly, in the last decade, sentiment analysis techniques have been used to measure the sentiments conveyed through the content of online reviews (Prabowo & Thelwall, 2009; Fan, Che & Chen, 2017). Recently, a huge amount of online user generated data is available, especially customer product reviews (e.g., Amazon.com, Epinions.com), which describe customers' opinions, attitudes, and user experiences on products they bought. While such information is highly valuable to producers, online marketers, and potential buyers (Jin, Ho, & Srihari, 2009; Zhou, Jiao, & Lei, 2017). Sentiment analysis is also known as opinion mining and/or subjectivity analysis. It is used to extract opinions, sentiments, and subjectivity in unstructured text, that is, to identify whether the expressions indicate positive (favorable) or negative (unfavorable) opinions toward the subject. Sentiment analysis normally deals with detecting polarity, i.e., only positive or negative sentiment, rather than discrete emotions (e.g., happiness, sadness).

Sentiment analysis include determining subjectivity, degree and valence of opinion (positive or negative), and classifying the subject matter and author. Sentiment analysis, through the monitoring of social media or online discuss forum, can change the way firms measure consumer opinions. Pang and Lee (2008) also presented a detailed and comprehensive review on affective computing and computer technology for emotion and expression recognition. Thus, sentiment analysis is a useful research method in text or review mining. The results deriving from sentiment analysis represent a first step towards a better understanding of the nature of reviews.

Text Mining

Text Mining, also known as text data mining, is a process of organizing, editing and analyzing large unstructured text information to discover the association between certain features and to meet the specific information needs of the user, to explore the key information in the text, including people, time, land, and objects. The purpose of text mining is to find and mine available knowledge or relevant potential information, similar to data mining, which is mainly used in spam mails, news materials, marketing, patent documents, etc.

Text mining and data mining have similar process procedure, the difference is the part before processing the information. Before processing the data information, text mining would require the unstructured text data to be stored in advance. The structured numerical data, which is converted by the word pre-processing process into a numerical field similar to that in the database, includes file features, lexical frequency, characteristic matrix, characteristic vector and other important information. As for data mining, it will gather the structured data before processing and proceed with data cleaning, data integration, data conversion, data reduction and other processes, no need to go through the extra step of unstructured text conversion.

Before gathering the structured data before the data processing, text mining needs to process the text information, process like stemming, comparing synonyms, keyword comparison, judging unknown word etc. Later, from the Term, Pattern, Association Degree, finding Keyword and Key Phrase, the use of Concept Hierarchy, Semantic Networks, Classification or Prediction Rule and other that text mining presents, so the follow classification can continue.

In Chinese language system, the sentence structure and the way of expressing through word is different from English. While processing, the biggest difference is that there is a clear gap between a single word and a single word in the English language system, while in Chinese language system, there is no interval between words in a sentence. Therefore, it is necessary to use segmentation to confirm the contents of the Chinese document. Taiwan Academia Sinica's Chinese Knowledge Information Processing Group (CKIP) has developed a Chinese word segmentation system. By using syntactic extraction and structural analysis to process segmentation, role assigning, Chinese language analysis on Chinese sentence, then mark every word's part-of-speech (POS), and provide it to the public (http://ckipsvr.iis.sinica.edu.tw/).

This research uses CKIP to process Chinese Segmentation, by selecting Facebook fan page's posts and process it with CKIP Chinese Word Segmentation System.

RESEARCH METHOD AND DESIGNING THE SYSTEM

First of all, this study establishes the brand experience dictionary, then uses the web crawler technology to obtain the message and comment on the E-commerce's Facebook fan pages. Secondly, analyze the information obtained with text analysis to determine the brand experience part of the sentence, and then uses the emotion analysis to give out the emotion score. By doing so, it is possible to use the keywords and predict the content of fan page posts, concluding the key factors that affect the number of times that the fan page posts are shared among internet users, and the classify the brand personality by using classification of brand personality on the research target to find the research target's product position and advertising strategy. Lastly, the final results are presented in visualization, then ready to be analyzed and discussed.

This research continues to use the WordStat used by Opoku (2006) to find the characteristic key words and synonyms of the five core dimensions: Sincerity, Excitement, Competence, Sophistication, and Ruggedness, then use the results as the vocabulary database. All the text data needed in this research are the Facebook fan page posts obtained by using online web crawler. The preprocessing of text data is organized by web questionnaire platform and web crawler tool into semi-structured data. The text analysis will compare and track all predefined characteristic keyword, all the sentences containing the characteristic keyword will be cut out and classified according the five core dimensions.

AFINN Emotional Word List rated for valence a word's positive and negative integer, it can range from 1-5, so if the text analysis captures any keywords with emotional words will be given an emotion score. After transferring qualitative text data into quantitative data by using emotion analysis system, it can find the research target's product position and advertising strategy and visualize the result to analyze and discuss.

SYSTEM DESIGN

The research adopting sentiment analysis is a hot topic for the past decade. However, simply citing the number of positive and negative mentions is insufficient to capture the complexity of written thought, and relying on a single positive or negative global judgment of open-ended text online is not recommended (Gunter, Koteyko, & Atanasova, 2014). In general, a customer may be satisfied with one aspect of a product but dislike other aspects (Collins, Hasan, & Ukkusuri, 2013). A better and more suitable method is to perform sentiment analysis on a variety of dimensions (Berger & Milkman, 2012). Hence, in this study we propose using the dimensions of existing, documented and accepted marketing scales to categorize free response text data. We demonstrate this technique by doing so using the brand personality construct (Aaker, 1997).

Currently, some of the lexicon/dictionaries-based word list of sentiment f as AFINN, SentiWordNet, WordNet-Affect, MPQA and SenticNet, the AFINN is the only one words list ranging from negative five to positive five, which is the more accurately reflected the polarity of the sentiment.

We keep the individual-level data of single user comments and extract their opinion in term of existed marketing scale of Brand Personality. Thus, school of existed tradition statistics analysis methods could be applied for further analysis. It implies that we demonstrate an example combining the qualitative and quantitative method to reveal the consumer opinion and attitude via online text mining.

Supervised machine learning techniques have shown relatively better performance than the unsupervised lexicon-based methods. However, Supervised sentiment classification is widely known as a domain-dependent task (Glorot, Bordes & Bengio, 2011). However, these unsupervised methods neglect the domain information of the input and are not specialized for the classification task. The sentiment classifier trained in one domain may not perform well in another domain. This is because sentiment expressions used in different domains are usually different (Pang & Lee, 2008). Most domains except movie reviews lack labeled training data the unsupervised methods are important too because supervised methods demand large amounts of labeled training data that are very expensive whereas acquisition of unlabeled data is easy in this case unsupervised methods are very useful for developing applications.

This research uses R (programming language) to integrate the above process and analysis into PHP, so it can turn qualitative text data into quantitative data, after conversion, it can find the research target's product position and advertising strategy and visualize the result to analyze and discuss.

This research uses two different databases for the affective computing system, which are AFINN Lexicon and Brand Personality Dimension Database. AFINN Lexicon is used to determine the polarity of a word (positive, negative, neutral) and a score to rate the valence (it can be positive/negative, ranging from negative five to positive five). Version AFINN- 111 is used for the research, and there is a list of 2477 English word and phrases, and to create phrase polarity database V2.0. Many scholars already repeated data training and classified the brand personality.

CREATE CHARACTERISTIC KEYWORD DATABASE

This research uses the 833 dimension characteristic keywords and its synonym that Opoku (2006) extended from Aaker (1997)'s five core dimension of brand personality. Words related to Sincerity takes up 21%, Excitement 17%, Competence 20%, Sophistication 21% and Ruggedness 21%. This research classifies all the characteristic keyword and synonym according to the core dimension, building the characteristic keyword database.

Web Crawler

To use the Facebook post needed for this research, this step mainly uses Microsoft Excel's plugin Web Crawler Tool called Power Query to browse the E-commerce's official Facebook fan page's comments, and other data like: Post ID, Content of the post, time posted, Reviewer's ID and Review content...etc. In the end, only the Reviewer's ID and its comment is saves as CSV format and input into the emotion analysis system.

Text Analysis

This research uses php program to design a Two-Part Classification Rule, the first part compares the dimension characteristic keyword vocabulary database. The second part is to set up to capture sentences, so when the data is being analyzed by the system, any sentence containing the dimension characteristic keyword will be captured, forming the crucial characteristic sentence. All these sentences will then be classified into the five core dimension to proceed to the next stage, which is emotion analysis. By using a user's review in the momo shopping site:

I've never gotten any prize (^_^;), but still trying my luck with the raffle! But every time I see the winner I feel shocked (O_O) Because it is always the same people! I wonder if that's because they repeatedly comment?

After hyphenation and text analysis, we can make a conclusion as follows in Table 2:

Table 2. Example of text analysis

Dimension	ID	Content of the Comment
Ruggedness	18,387	I | have | never | gotten | any | prices | f | but | still | trying | my | luck | with | the | raffle | But | every | time | I | see | the | winner | I | feel | shocked | oo | because | it | is | always | the | same | people | I | wonder| if | that's | because | they | repeatedly | comment |
Ruggedness	18,387	I | have | never | gotten | any | prices | f | but | still | trying | my | luck | with | the | raffle | But | every | time | I | see | the | winner | I | feel | shocked | oo | because | it | is | always | the | same | people | I | wonder| if | that's | because | they | repeatedly | comment |

In the comment left by reviewer with ID 18,387, after Jiebar Hyphenation, two words were found to be classified under ruggedness, so two sentences were captured and become a crucial dimension sentence.

Emotion Analysis

During text analysis, every comment is already classified into the five core dimension, now the emotion score will also be given to every sentence. The emotion score is given according to Nielsen (2011) AFINN

Lexicon, manually labeled 2478 word's positive or negative emotion, rating each word a positive 1 to 5 or negative -1 to -5. The calculation used is the number system of Collins and others (2013). (For more information, please refer to http://www2.imm.dtu.dk/pubdb/views/publication_details.php?id=6010)

After capturing the crucial characteristic sentences, the system will compare if there is emotion words according to the emotion lexicon, then proceed to find the word's polarity to find the corresponding positive or negative emotion score ranging from positive 5 to negative 5. The AFINN emotion lexicon used have a total of 2478 emotion words ranging from negative 5 to positive 5. The consumer's review text data is processed by comparing with the characteristic keyword vocabulary database, classified into the five core dimension, given an emotion and polarity score, and last, add up all the score, then the final number will be the overall emotion score. Table 3 shows the example of emotion analysis.

Table 3. Example of emotion analysis

Dimension	Emotion Score	Content of the Comment
Ruggedness	+6	I I have I never I gotten I any I prices I f I but I still I trying I my I luck I with I the I raffle I But I every I time I I I see I the I winner I I I feel I shocked I oo I because I it I is I always I the I same I people I I I wonderI if I that's I because I they I repeatedly I comment I
Ruggedness	+6	I I have I never I gotten I any I prices I f I but I still I trying I my I luck I with I the I raffle I But I every I time I I I see I the I winner I I I feel I shocked I oo I because I it I is I always I the I same I people I I I wonderI if I that's I because I they I repeatedly I comment I

The emotion analysis of the comment by reviewer ID 18387's score is +6 points, so under the core dimension of ruggedness, it can get a point of +12.

Collecting Data on Social Media

Power Query, a Microsoft Excel's add-on plugin is used as web crawler tool, gather review and comment data from the official Facebook fan pages of 10 E-commerce: sites "PChome Online Shopping," "Momo Shop," "Yahoo Shopping Center," "UDN Buy," "Go Happy Shopping Site," "PayEasy Women Shop," "ETMall," "U-Mall," " 7net Online Shopping," "ASAP Flash Online Shopping". The reviews are processed with emotion analysis system to find how reviews can help build brand personality. Then, with a visualized E-commerce Brand Perceptual Mapping, then this can be helpful when it comes to marketing.

RESULT AND ANALYSIS

This section collects questionnaire after being processed by the above steps and analyze procedure. Hyphenation and system implementation, uses correspondent analysis to analyze data to further provide analysis' result and visualize the results. The purpose of studying the analysis, besides statistical analysis of data collected, most importantly, to interpret the analysis's result.

This research collected reviews and comment data from Taiwan's 10 E-commerce's official Facebook fan page, then uses the emotional analysis to analyze brand personality's competence, a brand perceptual chart for the 10 E- commerce is created according to the analysis. The results show that the horizontal axis covers 76.08% degree of variation while the vertical axis have 14.61%. The two axis's overall explanatory power is at 90.70%. It shows the distance between the 10 E-commerce brand, suggesting that there's a big difference between each brand.

After processing the review and comments with the emotional system, the brand closest to "Sincerity' in brand personality is Momo Shop and PChome Online Shopping, the closest to "Excitement" is ETMall and Go Happy Shopping Site, "Competence" is Yahoo Shopping Center and UDN Buy, "Sophistication" is ASAP Flash Online Shopping and PayEasy Women Shop, the closest to "Ruggedness" will be U-Mall and 7net Online Shopping. Overall, 7net Online Shopping, UDN Buy. ASAP Flash Online Shopping and Yahoo Shopping Center will be the four with extinguishing brand personality that outstands the other brands.

As a result, there is about three clusters, cluster formed by 7net Online Shopping, Momo Shop, PChome Online Shopping, and U-Mall have the brand personality of "Sincerity" and "Ruggedness," ASAP Flash Online Shopping forms a cluster of "Sophistication," ETMall, Go Happy Shopping Site and Yahoo Shopping Center forms a cluster of "Excitement". Yahoo Shopping center can also be "Competence" while UDN Buy is not in any cluster and leans toward "Competence".

CONCLUSION AND SUGGESTION

This research uses text mining technology to collect Facebook fan page's comment and review data and analyze, combining internet, data mining, statistic and other fields of research. This research uses keyword vocabulary predicts online shopping site's fan page's sharing and number of likes, and use brand personality keyword to conduct prediction on the five-core dimension. In the comments, it is noticeable that users feel "sincerity" with Momo Shop and PChome Online Shopping, "excitement" with ETMall and Go Happy Shopping Site, "Competence" is Yahoo Shopping Center and UDN Buy, "Sophistication" is ASAP Flash Online Shopping and PayEasy Women Shop, lastly "Ruggedness" is U-Mall and 7net Online Shopping. This research converts qualitative text data (comments and reviews) into quantitative data. In the end, present the E-commerce brand with perceptual mapping so it can provide competitor in similar position, then provide reference in marketing and brand strategy. According to the research, 3 clusters of E-commerce is found. UDN Buy is more of a "Competence," it is the most distant one from the other three clusters, which means different marketing strategy.

Since Momo Shop and PChome Online Shopping is closest to Sincerity and Ruggedness, enhancing the difference between two brands and raise customer's attachment will be important. In Sophistication, PayEasy Women Shop's position also includes sincerity, it is not as clear as ASAP Flash Online Shopping, so it is important for them to create a good shopping experience for consumers. As for ETMall and Go Shopping Site are similar in brand position, so they should enhance their difference or improve consumer relationship. There were 4 unique brands, as 7net Online Shopping is closest to Ruggedness, in the outdoor, masculine, Western characteristic are shown in the consumer's reviews. As for UDN Buy (Competence), trustworthy, unique is shown. For ASAP Flash Online Shopping (Sophistication), upper-class, glamour is shown. Since Yahoo Shopping Center is Competence plus Excitement, so there is also trustworthy, hard-working, leadership...etc.

PChome Online Shopping and Momo Shop are similar in brand personality, from the financial report from 2016, PChome Online Shopping's profit is 247.71 billion (NTD), and Momo Shop, online only, is

205.8 billion. Momo Shop's online sales growth went up to 20% comparing to previous year, higher than PChome's 12.51%. In the other hand, ETMall and Go Happy Shopping Site are close in Excitement, and their sales rate in 2016 are about the same, so if they tries to enhance their difference, it might help with their business. ASAP Flash Online Shopping and PayEasy Women Shop are both in "Sophistication," but they're still different, PayEasy Women Shop leans more toward "Sincerity," it might be because they focus on women when it comes to marketing, creating a more sincere and sophisticated brand personality. Even though U-Mall belongs to "Ruggedness," it it's not obvious, maybe because its brand personality position is not distinct. After it was acquired with ETMall, but they still operate separately, so there is still competition. U-Mall can focus on enhancing its brand position to maintain customer retention. From a corporate's point of view, using characteristic brand personality vocabulary can help find Facebook fan page's notable brand personality, so corporates can differentiate with others when it comes to running the fan pages and marketing, it can also become an indicator for increasing customer's loyalty.

FUTURE RESEARCH

Time should be considered in the future researches. Since this research did not consider the time, time period and when the system analyzes the data, some comments and reviews were captured and analyzed short after it was posted. After processing the data, the number of posts of many marketing posts such as news, pictures and other types of post is actually higher than the product's review. In the future, it is better to first organized the posts into categories. The amount of the characteristic brand personality vocabulary base affects the accuracy of brand personality classification, so it is better to expand the vocabulary in the future. There are many internet slangs and emoticons used in the posts, so future researchers should also consider classifying them into the five core dimension of brand personality to increase the classification accuracy. Whether a sincere brand personality can attract more customer should be discussed in the future, just like the two major e-commerce brands: PChome and momo Shop, and see if changing brand personality's position will affect their profit.

REFERENCES

Aaker, J., Fournier, S., & Brasel, S. (2004). When good brands do bad. *The Journal of Consumer Research*, *31*(1), 1–16. doi:10.1086/383419

Aaker, J. L. (1997). Dimensions of brand personality. *JMR, Journal of Marketing Research*, *34*(3), 347–356. doi:10.2307/3151897

Alt, M., & Griggs, S. (1988). Can a brand be cheeky? *Marketing Intelligence & Planning*, *4*(6), 9–16. doi:10.1108/eb045776

Berger, J., & Milkman, K. L. (2012). What makes online content viral? *JMR, Journal of Marketing Research*, *49*(2), 192–205. doi:10.1509/jmr.10.0353

Bhargava, R. (2008). *Personality not included: Why companies lose their authenticity and how great brands get it back*. New York: McGraw-Hill.

Boyd, D. M., & Ellison, N. B. (2007). Social network sites: Definition, history, and scholarship. *Journal of Computer-Mediated Communication, 13*(1), 210–230. doi:10.1111/j.1083-6101.2007.00393.x

Chen, K. J., & Liu, S. H. (1992). Word Identification for Mandarin Chinese Sentences. In *Fifth International Conference on Computational Linguistics* (pp. 101-107).

Collins, C., Hasan, S., & Ukkusuri, S. V. (2013). A novel transit rider satisfaction metric: Rider sentiments measured form online social media data. *Journal of Public Transportation, 16*(2), 21–45. doi:10.5038/2375-0901.16.2.2

Doyle, P. (1990). Building successful brands: The strategic options. *Journal of Consumer Marketing, 7*(2), 5–20. doi:10.1108/EUM0000000002572

Fan, Z. P., Che, Y. J., & Chen, Z. Y. (2017). Product sales forecasting using online reviews and historical sales data: A method combining the Bass model and sentiment analysis. *Journal of Business Research, 74*, 90–100. doi:10.1016/j.jbusres.2017.01.010

Feng, Z., Jianxin Roger, J., & Xi Jessie, Y., & Baiying, Lei. (2017). Augmenting feature model through customer preference mining by hybrid sentiment analysis. *Expert Systems with Applications, 89*(15), 306–317.

Glorot, X., Bordes, A., & Bengio, Y. (2011). Deep sparse rectifier neural networks. In *Proceeding of the Conference on Artificial Intelligence and Statistics* (pp. 315-323).

Gunter, B., Koteyko, N., & Atanasova, D. (2014). Semantic analysis: A market-relevant and reliable measure of public feeling? *International Journal of Market Research, 56*(2), 231–247. doi:10.2501/IJMR-2014-014

Keller, K. L. (2008). *Strategic brand management: Building, measuring and managing brand equity.* New Jersey: Prentice Hall.

Landauer, T. K., Foltz, P. W., & Laham, D. (1998). An introduction to latent semantic analysis. *Discourse Processes, 25*(2), 259–284. doi:10.1080/01638539809545028

Levy, S. J. (1959). Symbols or sales. *Harvard Business Review, 37*(4), 117–124.

Opoku, R., Abratt, R., & Pitt, L. (2006). Communicating brand personality: Are the websites doing the talking for the top South African Business Schools? *Journal of Brand Management, 14*(1-2), 20–39. doi:10.1057/palgrave.bm.2550052

Pang, B., & Lee, L. (2008). Opinion mining and sentiment analysis. *Foundations and Trends in Information Retrieval, 2*(1-2), 1–135. doi:10.1561/1500000011

Pierre, V. F., Haythem, G., & Dwight, M. (2011). The impact of brand personality and sales Promotions on brand equity. *Journal of Business Research, 64*(1), 24–28. doi:10.1016/j.jbusres.2009.09.015

Plummer, J. T. (2000). How personality makes a difference. *Journal of Advertising Research, 40*(6), 79–83. doi:10.2501/JAR-40-6-79-83

Prabowo, R., & Thelwall, M. (2009). Sentiment analysis: A combined approach. *Journal of Informetrics, 3*(2), 143–157. doi:10.1016/j.joi.2009.01.003

Pragya, M., Shailendra, P. J., & Durairaj, M. (2012). Consumers' implicit theories about personality influence their brand personality judgements. *Journal of Consumer Psychology, 22*(4), 545–557. doi:10.1016/j.jcps.2012.01.005

Traci, H. F., & Lukas, P. F. (2005). An empirical analysis of the brand personality effect. *Journal of Product and Brand Management, 14*(7), 404–413. doi:10.1108/10610420510633350

Chapter 46
Deep Learning Based Sentiment Analysis for Phishing SMS Detection

Aakanksha Sharaff

National Institute of Technology, Raipur, India

Ramya Allenki

UnitedHealth Group, India

Rakhi Seth

National Institute of Technology, Raipur, India

ABSTRACT

Sentiment analysis works on the principle of categorizing and identifying the text-based content and the process of classifying documents into one of the predefined classes commonly known as text classification. Hackers deploy a strategy by sending malicious content as an advertisement link and attack the user system to gain information. For protecting the system from this type of phishing attack, one needs to classify the spam data. This chapter is based on a discussion and comparison of various classification models that are used for phishing SMS detection through sentiment analysis. In this chapter, SMS data is collected from Kaggle, which is classified as ham or spam; while implementing the deep learning techniques like Convolutional Neural Network (CNN), CNN with 7 layers, and CNN with 11 layers, different results are generated. For evaluating these results, different machine learning techniques are used as a baseline algorithm like Naive Bayes, Decision Trees, Support Vector Machine (SVM), and Artificial Neural Network (ANN). After evaluation, CNN showed the highest accuracy of 99.47% as a classification model.

DOI: 10.4018/978-1-6684-6303-1.ch046

INTRODUCTION

Text Classification

Text classification is one of the most important parts of text analysis. It is defined as the process of interpreting and extracting important information from the present textual data this data can be of any type like SMS, Twitter data, emoji, and short messages while talking about classification which is one of the major parts of sentiment analysis; which occurs to be the measuring people's attitude from the piece of text through which they are sharing their views. Views can be of different types based on user intent this can be understood through various examples, we saw over the internet sometimes inappropriate like abusive language and pornographic content; sentiment analysis also deals with classifying those data which helps the policymaker to understand the trend that is running in a market that solely depends on users' reviews, feedbacks, and ratings. From a research point of view, some of the major challenges that could be solved through sentiment analysis like spam filtering, phishing attack, categorization, and summarization well over the decades, spamming and phishing based classification has been some of the most researched topics based on techniques like machine learning and deep learning. A good text classifier is a classifier that efficiently categorizes large sets of text documents in a reasonable amount of time with acceptable accuracy. Many techniques and algorithms for automatic text categorization have been devised.

Applications

There are various applications of text classification:

1. **Document Organization:** Document organization is also known as Document classification. (Rinaldi et al., 2021) discuss the documents that were collected through the different platform in huge amount, but from the information retrieval point of view, not all the data was always relevant, so sometimes the issue of information overloading may generate, for solving this issue the new concept of document classification is introduced while using the text present in the document, we illustrate it through an example given below; here document belongs to a different class (class 1, class 2 and class 3) in the training set as given in Table 1 and associated feature is retrieved from each document class and vector is created from these words of class in Table 2. As we can see "Some" belongs to one class, "Yellow" belong to another based on the specified documents, while testing the new data this labeling helps to understand which word vector belongs to which class.

Table 1. Documents

Document Class 1	Document Class 2	Document Class 3
Some Lion live in the jungle	Yellow is a color	Go to Manhattan city

Table 2. Classes of each word

Some	Lion	Live	In	the	jungle	Yellow	is	A	color	Go	To	Manhattan	City	Class
1	1	1	1	1	1	0	0	0	0	0	0	0	0	Class 1
0	0	0	0	0	0	1	1	1	1	0	0	0	0	Class 2
0	0	0	0	0	0	0	0	0	0	1	1	1	1	Class 3

Now when any unlabelled data came, like "Blue is a color" then a new word vector will be created by taking labeled data from the previous table and match it as we see that some word vector matched with class 2 word vector of *Table 2* so we assign unlabelled data with an unknown class as well as 1 as an assigned value for the matched word vector as shown in *Table 3*;

Table 3. Test Data classification

Some	Lion	Live	In	the	jungle	Yellow	is	A	color	Go	To	Manhattan	City	Class
0	0	0	0	0	0	0	1	1	1	0	0	0	0	Unknown

2. **Spam Filtering:** Spam is more likely related to malicious content or comes with suspicious intent mainly through mails and most of the time without the receiver's consent. Initially, this spam comes as a promotion or advertising mail but soon after hackers used it as a mask for attacking a system because it is one of the cheapest ways to get through the user's system. So different researchers after doing rigorous study gave the approach called spam filtering, (Chetty et al., 2019) proposes the idea of detecting and classifying spam mails by using deep learning models, and this model was used to learn the features of text documents, not only deep neural model has been used for spam detection there are various other models like (Jain et al., 2020) suggested the machine learning model which used for smishing attack with a combination of SMS and phishing attack; (Jain et al., 2020) goes one step ahead i.e., by classifying smishing messages from spam messages.

3. **Filtering non-suitable content:** The Internet is a very vast and different type of data move all around over the internet some of these data are harmful for an organization like marketing policies used by different companies is completely confidential, some data comes with an intent to harm society like pornographic content (Garcia et al., 2018) gives the approach to remove or suspend this type of source from the internet; some data is for harming the economy of a country like false message spreading about person or government. So this type of data needs constant monitoring and sometimes the government takes legal policies for stopping such type of content like; recently JIO reliance for its users restrict the pornographic content to access over the network because a large no. of users are using the internet amongst these small aged children are present for them this type of content is inappropriate, also; YouTube is monitoring the content and it is done through YouTube users only when you are seeing any video in YouTube and you don't find that content suitable then you can report that video and if too many reports are there then the server will block owners uploaded a video in similar way twitter suspend the ids for spreading false messages. The server uses the filtering technique while training the model and uses the classification model for a specific type of text or visuals to get restricted.

4. **Summarization Evaluation:** This is nothing but extracting the content from the various informatics source and presents the most important content in a very precise way to the user while understanding summarization most important part is data which is sensitive towards the information on a user, topic, and query asked by the user. So it aims at user-specific classification. In summarization, there is another concept called evaluation which deals with the serious issues of doing automation in summarization. (Lloret et al., 2018) handles the evaluation issues like output that comes using summarization is either correct or incorrect it hard to arrive the conclusion because it completely depends on the user. Another issue is compression, in which evaluation of compression rates increases the complexity of evaluation

5. **Web Page Prediction:** Web page prediction is an area of web mining and this prediction works in the recommendation system. While understanding the prediction (Rajeswari & Nisha, 2018) focuses on weblog files which were generated whenever user access the internet over the network and approach behind this prediction is the previous navigation data to understand the owner's access behavior and is based on the access pattern. This approach works on various parameters like session, time, and frequency of visiting the same page again and again this prediction use for classifying patterns which helps the algorithm to provide the next suggestion to the user. (Rajeswari & Nisha, 2018) provides the different ML models like SVM, Adaboost, c4.5 as well as also suggested the other advanced techniques that can be used for prediction.

6. **Mobile SMS Classification:** While ago, the researcher thought spam messages is associated with e-mails only and can be deployed through promotional advertisements while sent through e-mails but nowadays, a message is passed from one person to another in seconds through mobile. Mobile is a mode through which anyone can send false or obscene messages to someone without understanding the consequences. Several riots and other illegal work take place through messaging only and this type of attack is known as SMS spam and for this monitoring is done through various detection methods. Some detection methods are (Marsault et al., 2020) implemented by using the feature engineering on the lexical extracted text or words, and put the classifier to train the model so that prediction can be done by the model.

Spamming

Initially spamming is an unwanted digital communication that mostly takes place through emails, mostly it is a marketing strategy like a promotion of a product but with time it becomes a weapon for hackers with malicious intent. Hackers take over the ISPs (Internet Service Provider) and send cheating/malicious emails to the users over the network.

There are different types of Spamming is there which are as follows:

1. **Bulking Message:** A message sent to a group of people over a very small period. For example, a Google job offering message in the year 2006 was an example of spam messages spread over mass. There is some other advertising malware is present over the system.

2. **Spreading Malicious links:** When the user's device gets damaged through a malicious link opened by him/her. This malware takes the personal information of the victim and uses it in a harmful way.

3. **Fraudulent reviews:** Today many reviews that you see on youtube, on Twitter fake reviews of products through fake ids that are also one type of spam and comes under fraudulent reviews but in our country for online platforms there are no strict rules for this type of forgery.

4. **Sharing undesired or excessive content:** Insults, threats, and other important, as well as confidential information that is shared by a hacker or sent by a hacker to others, are threatening and it comes under spamming.

Phishing

Phishing is a process of making people visit a duplicitous website and tell them to enter their personal information. These types of websites are not new rather it is some of the known organization's mocked website. Hacker injects these fake websites into the user's system. Phishing is spread through technical teams and send through false mails generally forged by attackers to gain the information of user's system mostly sensitive data, credential data, and some of the highly confidential data. Phishing is one of the most common types of attack as well as a cheaper way to enter one's system but sometimes this phishing attack becomes a ransomware attack. The phishing attack is not something that attacker sends a file and attacks to the user system rather when a phishing attack happens then at that point, the attacker runs the whole life cycle of the attack and when a user came to know about the attack, the damage has been already done. The steps of the lifecycle for Phishing attacks as shown in Figure 1.

Step1: Proper Planning with Setup: In this step, an attacker or hacker finds his/her target organization there is no specific reason for attacking a particular target but most of the time money as well as accessing confidential information is the prominent reason for the attack. Also, the phisher makes some technical strategies to get confidential information.

Step2: Construction of Phishing/false Site: Phisher creates a false website that looks similar to the official website; several tools are available for creating the replica of well-known websites. Once the site is developed, the phisher uploads the files to a web-hosting server.

Step3: Phishing Deployment: The proper distribution method is used to deploy the link of the phishing website.

Step4: Installation: It is a process where a fake link redirects to the fake website created by the phisher and after this; malicious software has been installed to the user system.

Step5: Data Collection: The information filled in by the user over the internet is available to the phisher.

Step6: Breaking-away: After getting all the information from the user, the phisher deletes all the traces or web footprints that work as evidence like phisher accounts, websites, and all other files.

Figure 1. Lifecycle of phishing attack

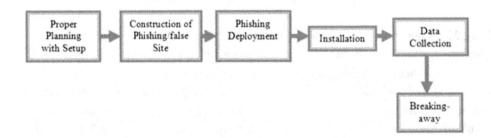

Now we need to understand, various motivations for a phisher to attack the user; some of them are as follows:

1. **Financial Gain:** A ransomware attack is an example of a phishing attack while entering the user's system and corrupt all the data and ask for ransom; nowadays cryptocurrency is one of the ways to give the amount to a phisher or attacker.
2. **Identity Theft:** By taking another person's identity you can do any illegal task like accessing a user bank account, also you can send mails to other users as a valid sender.
3. **Internet Sensation:** Some people did it to become famous and some did it for recognition but it is a serious offense and one can go to jail for it.

Taxonomy of Phishing Attacks

The phishing attack has two environments, which are as follows:

1. Desktop
2. Mobile

First, we need to discuss the desktop environment, (Jain & Gupta, 2021) tells about the phisher who uses the social engineering and technical evasion technique. By using a malicious website that appears legitimate, accessing the whole system became much easier. The technical evasion method does the installation of malware and gains the information from the user's system. The second one, the mobile environment is very vulnerable to a phishing attack in mobiles this attack is done through SMS and WiFi. For a brief understanding of the taxonomy of phishing attacks, one requires knowledge of each area as shown in Figure 2, where these attacks do the major damage.

1. **Social Engineering:** A psychological control over user so that user discloses the secret information. A forged mail looks like a real one and the user relies on and gives all the credentials that are known as Social Engineering.
2. **E-Mail Spoofing:** The fake URL redirects the user to the malicious web page and does the attack.
3. **Website Spoofing:** The attacker doesn't create the whole website because it can be detected by the anti-phishing software. So phisher creates only a login page and embeds the legal contents in the frame of a malicious webpage to avoid the anti-phishing technique.
4. **Spear phishing:** This attack works on the target individuals and sent emails. The attacker regularly monitors the user's activities on the websites or on WhatsApp to acquire the user's information. After collecting the information, the attacker writes an email, which looks like the real mail that comes from any legitimate source like the manager, and takes the organizational details and other personal information.
5. **Trojan horse:** The attack happens from the backdoor and deploys the victim's malicious code and installs the applications like worms to the user's device.
6. **Ransomware:** Ransomware is software or malware which is considered to be a kind of malicious. The concept of Ransomware is that the attacker demands from the victim a particular amount (it can be a different form like Bitcoin is one of the examples.) to restore access to the data upon payment.

Figure 2. Taxonomy of Phishing Attacks

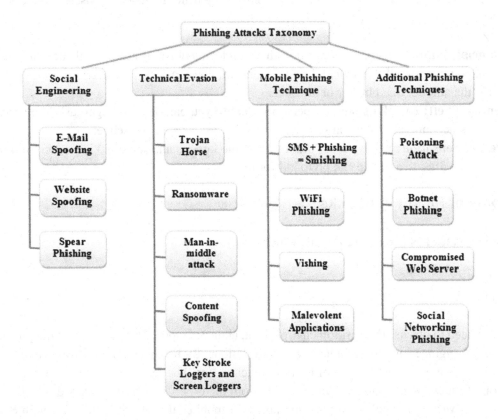

7. **Man-in-middle Attack:** An attack that doesn't manipulate it just does observing and monitoring the traffic between the sender and receiver. Sometimes the whole network is controlled by an attacker and the user doesn't know about it.

8. **Content Spoofing:** Content injection is also used for this attack. There are two types of spoofing used:
    a. **Text Injection:** A vulnerable web application in which URLs get modified. The fake page request link is sent to the attacker server.
    b. **HTML Injection:** The attacker sends the modified URL to the user by any means, by clicking on the URL user is navigated to the attacker's webpage, which looks like a legitimate one.

9. **Keystroke Logger and Screen Logger:** Key logger is malicious software through which attackers can observe the keystroke of the user's system. This is used for getting the password and through that confidential data.

10. **Smishing:** Through phone-text messaging using SMS phishing is performed. Through SMS the user gets the link and if the user accesses the link and shares his personal information with the attacker.

11. **Wi-Fi Phishing:** The associated vulnerable hotspot, the authenticated interface presented to users looks like a genuine one used by the legitimate access point. Creating an authentication interface that looks legitimate may increase the chances of the attack.

12. **Vishing:** "Voice+Phishing" has been more successful over other networks. It is an attack over the phone where someone calls and tells the user that he is from this bank and there is some account details required for updating and user gives the detail of his/her bank account.

13. **Poisoning Attack:** It is the attack where the genuine website is diverted from a fake website. An attacker takes the control to change the data in the DNS cache. Once the cache is poisoned, the data is sent to a malicious URL.

14. **Botnet Phishing:** Botnet word comes from the combination of words i.e. "robot" and "network" and it takes the whole control of the network it uses for various scams and cyberattacks. It works on the steps

    a. **Preparation:** The hijacker uses the malware to exploit the victim.

    b. **Infection:** Once the malware damage the system or hacker takes control through a botnet.

    c. **Activate:** Hacker prepares the infected devices to do further attacks.

15. **Compromised Web Server:** It means that a hacker hijacks the server and sends the fake web pages to the user through the server.

16. **Social Networking Phishing:** This type of phishing can be done through social networking site and sharing the fake URL, this type of URL usually comes through fake advertisement or fake invitation link. Another way of phishing is Masquerading through URLs it can be done by asking on behalf of social networking site ask for a login id and password through a false link. Fake profile creation and asking for credentials is one of the most common types of social networking phishing sometimes the people create a fake profile and ask for money from the friends of that person through messenger and in this way sometimes people got trapped.

RELATIVE STUDY

In this section, we discuss the different ML (Jupin et al., 2019) & DL (Annareddy & Tammina, 2019) techniques that are used for detecting phishing attacks. Now for detecting an attack, one needs to know a phishing attack with its features; so there are mainly 4 features in phishing attack as shown in Figure 3. Feature 1 is based on URL, Feature 2 is based on Page-based, Feature 3 Domain-based, and Feature 4 relies on Content-Based.

While discussing the existing spam and phishing-related applications as shown in Table 4 we understand the different levels in which we can detect phishing as well as which algorithm provides the appropriate classification for phishing and spam detection.

After studying a while on classification; we came to know about different methods that are used with a specific purpose and we try to understand it through Table 5 with all utilities and shortcomings of different method that comes under ML & DL technique.

As per the further discussion through an algorithmic point of view as shown in Table 6, gives the comparison of a different technique with different accuracy this helps in understanding which classifier approach works better for which detection technique.

Figure 3. Phishing Attack Features

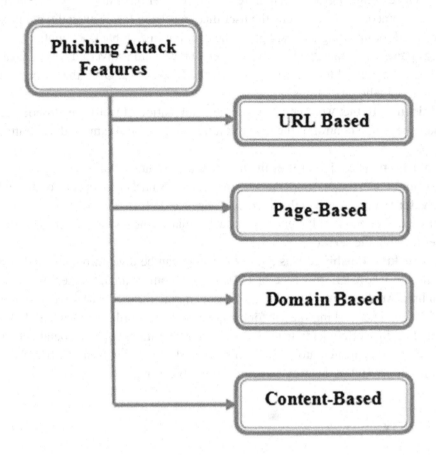

RESEARCH METHODOLOGY

In a follow-up experiment, we will study the implementation in different stages for understanding the role of different classifiers that came under the ML and DL technique and also, which classifier works better and give a higher performance for phishing detection. So through the architecture of this paper as shown in Figure 4 first we analyze the SMS corpus and then classify the message by using different models; it also measures the performance of different algorithms.

Data Collection

The ham and spam SMS messages were collected from the "SMS-spam-collection" dataset from Kaggle. It consists of 5574 messages of which 4287 are ham messages and 747 are spam messages. The dataset was collected in a CSV file where each line represents one message and a label has been presented for each message as either spam or ham. The initial steps of preprocessing is very similar in text mining as we can see for finding positive, negative and neutral tweets for better sentiment analysis.

Table 4. Summary of existing phishing & spam techniques

References	Level	Technique Used	Application	Dataset
(Rinaldi et al., 2021)	Semantic-Based	1. Semantic textual analysis	It helps in textual topic detection	DMOZ a multimedia dataset.
(Chetty et al., 2019)	Document-Based	1. CNN	E-mail filtering, movie reviews, Twitter message classification	UCI repository.
(Yerima et al., 2021)	Application Based	1. CNN 2. DNN 3. Long Short Term Memory (LSTM) 4. Gated Recurrent Units (GRU) 5. CNN-LSTM 6. CNN-GRU	Android device apps	ISCX botnet dataset
(Zhu et al., 2020)	URL based	1. Decision Tree 2. ANN	Spam filtering and fake emails with malicious content	UCI Library, Phishtank, and Alexa records.
(Jain et al., 2020)	SMS Based(Text Level)	1. Naïve Bayes 2. Neural Network 3. Logistic Regression	WhatsApp message system, messenger applications any fake information does not get spread.	SMS dataset contains 5574 messages
(Garcia et al., 2018)	Image(or video) based	1. Segmentation 2. Texture Filtering 3. For classifying confusion matrix is used	A measure for stopping inappropriate content through different platforms.	Multimedia files data set (1239, Images=986, Videos=253)
(Kalaharsha & Mehtre, 2021)	Site Based	1. ML techniques 2. DL techniques	URL based emails, In banking application,	UCI repository
(Shirazi et al., 2017)	Site-based	1. SVM with stratified K-fold	Helps in detecting fake websites, a measure for blacklisting some sites, fake E-mails	From the Alexa database, 6000 online phishing sites were collected.
(Arshey & Angel, 2020)	E-mail Based	1. Classification: Deep belief network(DBN) 2. Training: Earthworm optimization algorithm.	For SMS, spam emails, spoofing	Enron Dataset
(Saha et al., 2020)	Webpage based	1. Feed Forward network	Detecting the fake pages asking for money(mostly in health care)	Kaggle dataset
(Soykan et al., 2021)	EV charging based	1. SMS attack was done through EV charging by using the power grid by creating the testing simulation tool	Helps in the future where EV charging becomes the tool and attack detection is necessary when power grid collapse	IEEE European Low Voltage Feeder Test System.
(Gupta et al., 2021)	SMS based	1. TF-IDF vectorizer algorithm	SPAM SMS detection, spam mails detection, spam with phishing detection	Kaggle repository
(Zhang et al., 2017)	Semantic-based	1. Adaboost 2. Bagging 3. Random forest	Word-based helps in detecting copyright text, URLs, and contents.	Legimitate URLs taken from DirectIndustry web guides a search engine.

Table 5. Methods advantages and disadvantages of ML & DL techniques

Methods	Advantages	Disadvantages
ANN	1. ANN works in distributed memory and benefits in parallel processing. 2. ANN generates the precise model by taking experimental data only 3. ANN can work with incomplete knowledge and with noise. 4. ANN allows defining the attribute as well as types of learning.	1. The result may alter the order of data attributes. 2. ANN is very slow in learning rate. 3. It is difficult to understand the result produced by ANN. 4. Hard to predict the model.
Decision Tree(DT)	1. The classification process takes less time. 2. It is easy to implement. 3. It is simple to interpret the feature relationships.	1. It is low as compared to another ML technique. 2. When no of features increased then DT implementation becomes more complex. 3. Each time a new sample came, the tree rebuilding for each sample becomes quite complex.
RF	1. The efficiency of RF is very high 2. The overfitting problem is handled by RF.	1. A large no of trees is quite a problem of processing. 2. It works only for predictive modeling, not for descriptive modeling. 3. The result produced by RF is not consistent.
Naïve Bayes	1. A less no of data required for the feature classification process. 2. NB handles the missing values. 3. It is a direct method	1. A large amount of data is necessary for higher accuracy. 2. Due to its instance-based nature, NB requires a large space to store the data. 3. Regarding data, NB is not sensitive.
SVM	1. It handles the high-dimensional data better than the other algorithms. 2. It is known for higher accuracy. 3. It handles a large amount of data 4. It helps in finding the optimum solution and memory efficiency. 5. It maximizes the margin and therefore it is one of the robust models.	1. The classification process is time-consuming. 2. Interpretation is difficult. 3. It works for binary classifiers and for other types it needs some modifications. 4. Each set should be correct because SVM is sensitive to the data.
CNN	1. CNN doesn't require feature engineering 2. It works well with complex background.	1. It takes a long time to train a model. 2. Poor labeling is one of the problems. 3. While using pre-trained models and small datasets optimization issues may be generated.
LSTM	1. It dealt with larger data 2. It is efficient and faster 3. No need for a finite number of states 4. It handles the vanishing gradient problem.	1. The sample size is quite small 2. LSTM needs high memory and bandwidth. 3. Past information is not taken for a larger time. 4. The overfitting problem is not solved by LSTM.
GRU	1. For long sequencing training samples. 2. It is more efficient. 3. With less training data GRU works faster. 4. It is simple and modification is easy.	1. Efficiency is very less. 2. Accuracy is very less

Table 6. Comparative Analysis of existing algorithms

Authors	ML technique	DL technique	Spam Detection	Phishing Detection	Classification Algorithm	Accuracy Achieved
(Mishra & Soni, 2020)	✓	✗	✗	✓	Naïve Bayes Classifier	96.29
(Bagui et al., 2019)	✓	✓	✗	✓	Naïve Bayes, SVM, DT, LSTM, CNN, Word Embedding	98.89
(Popovac et al., 2018)	✗	✓	✓	✗	CNN	98.4
(Sonowal, 2020)	✓	✗	✗	✓	The ranking algorithm, AdaBoost, RF, DT, SVM	98.4
(Maurya & Jain, 2020)	✗	✓	✗	✓	Adam, Deep learning algorithms.	97.51
(Makkar & Kumar, 2020)	✗	✓	✓	✗	LSTM	95.21
(Zhu et al., 2020)	✓	✗	✓	✗	Decision Tree and optimal features based ANN	97.5
(Chakraborty et al., 2020)	✗	✓	✗	✗	Gaussian membership function based fuzzy rule	81%
(Basheer et al., 2021)	✗	✓	✗	✗	CNN with RELU activation and also Squash a special type of activation function used for capsule network	92.39%

Pre-Processing

1. **Removal of Punctuation:** It splits the word and checks if it contains any punctuation characters. If yes, it replaces with a blank or else does nothing.
2. **Word Tokenization:** To tokenize the sentences into words based on whitespaces and put them in a list for applying further process.
3. **Converting Words to lowercase:** Converting all the upper, lower, proper case words into lowercase. This reduces the duplicity of words in the corpus.
4. **Stop Word Removal:** To remove the words that do not carry much weight in understanding the sentence. They are mostly used as connecting words.
5. **Keeping Words of At least Three:** To remove words having a length less than 3. These words don't have much meaning to carry.
6. **Stemming Words:** To stem the extra suffixes from the word.
7. **POS Tagging:** pos tag function return the parts of speech for each word. There are four formats for nouns and six formats for the verb.
8. **Lemmatization of Words:** It is the process of grouping together the different inflected forms of a word to analyze as a single item.

Figure 4. Architecture of this paper

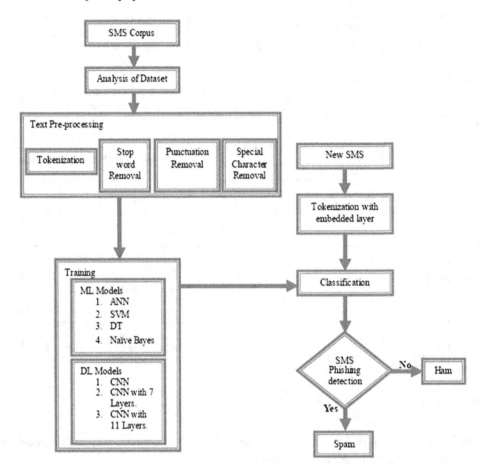

Tf-IDF Conversion

The input to any neural network is in the format of numbers. So the conversion of the text into vector format is very important. So, Tf-IDF conversion is used here. Tf-IDF stands for **"Term frequency-inverse document frequency"**. Firstly the sentences will be converted into tokens and the frequency of each word is found and divided with the number of words in that document for normalization. This is the term frequency. Idf is the logarithm of the ratio of the number of documents to the no of documents containing that word. We multiply tf and idf to find the weight of each word. This gives weights to each word that explains the importance of word in document.

Tf (t,d) = frequency of term / number of words in document
Idf(t,d) = $\log_2$ total no of documents / no of documents containing that word.

MACHINE LEARNING TECHNIQUES

For detecting all these features various techniques are used. First is Machine learning; ML is one of the study areas that belong to artificial intelligence.ML works on the principle of computation that can be done directly from the data, by identifying a pattern and make decisions from observed data. ML trains a model by taking known input and predicting the data as output. In phishing attack ML model is useful; as we can see the attack is based on features these features can be trained through ML models because ML converts the detection problem into classification, once the classification task is completed then detection of attack can be done easily. For detecting the attack, ML uses different models which comprise of;

1.   Artificial Neural Network (ANN)
2.   Decision Tree
3.   Naïve Bayes
4.   Random Forest
5.   Support Vector Machine(SVM)

1. Artificial Neural Network

ANN is a simulated model as shown in Figure 5 of the biological human brain and it works in layers, each layer represents the artificial neurons that are connected. In Figure 5, X1, X2,......, Xn is the input vector of the neuron, W1, W2,........, Wn represented weights which represents the neuron of the input layer. Σ represents the sum of all input with the bias (b), and Activation Function (f) and output (Y) is used in the model.

Figure 5. Basic elements of ANN

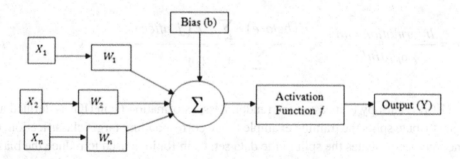

2. Decision Tree (DT)

A Decision Tree is a type of supervised learning algorithm. It works on the root node and leaf node. It is a classification algorithm categorized into two types:

1.   Categorical Variable DT
2.   Continuous Variable DT

Decision trees classify data from the root node to the leaf node in sorting order. Based on the type of target variable DT algorithm suggested other two algorithms which are as follows:

1.   Iterative Dichotomiser(ID3)
2.   C4.5

ID3 works on the "top-down" approach and creates the decision tree. C4.5 is also a DT that handles the problem of missing, large and continuous data. The DT algorithm works on expressions given below (1) to (6) which are as follows

$$E(S) = -\sum_{i=1}^{m} p_i log_2 p_i \tag{1}$$

$$E(T,X) = \sum_{c=X} P(C) E(S) \tag{2}$$

Information Gain(T, X) = $E(T) - E(T, X)$. $\tag{3}$

$$Information\ Gain = E(before) - \sum_{j=1}^{k} E(j, after) \tag{4}$$

$$Gini\ Index = 1 - \sum_{i=1}^{m} (p_i)^2 \tag{5}$$

$$Gain\ Ratio = \frac{Information\ Gain}{SplitInfo} = \frac{E(before) - \sum_{j=1}^{k} E(j, after)}{\sum_{j=1}^{k} w_j log_2 w_j} \tag{6}$$

Now here E(S) is entropy to measure the randomness, Information Gain (IG) is defined as how correctly a given attribute splits the training example to the corresponding target classification. Gini Index is a cost function that evaluates the split in the data set. Gain Ratio is used to reduce the bias.

3. Naïve Bayes Algorithm

An NB algorithm works on the Bayes theorem. Bayes Theorem approach is on probabilistic classification and every character is being independent when classified. The equation (7) is

$$P(a|B) = \frac{P(B|a) P(a)}{P(B)} \tag{7}$$

Here, P (a|B) is an independent probability of a prior probability; P (B) is an independent probability of B, P (B|a) is a conditional probability of a given B. Naïve Bayes is widely used for spam detection in e-mails by computing the probability of e-mails that e-mails are spam or not based on words used in spam and non-spam emails.

4. Random Forest Algorithm (RF)

Random forest is related to a decision tree, it means that RF generates the individual DT at training and then the prediction is done by combining all trees to make the final output of prediction. Through equations (8) to (11), we understand the basic principle of RF.

$$ni_j = w_j C_j - w_{left(j)} C_{left(j)} - w_{right(j)} C_{right(j)}. \tag{8}$$

$$fi_i = \frac{\sum_{j:node\ j\ splits\ on\ feature\ i} ni_j}{\sum_{k \in all\ nodes} ni_k} \tag{9}$$

$$norm\ fi_i = \frac{fi_i}{\sum_{j \in allf\ eatures} fi_j} \tag{10}$$

$$RFfi_i = \frac{\sum_{j \in all\ trees} norm\ fi_{ij}}{T} \tag{11}$$

Here in equation (8) to (10), ni_j is the importance of node j, w_j weighted samples reached node j, $C_{left(j)}$ impurity value of left split child node j and similarly $C_{right(j)}$ is impurity value of right node j. Normalization is the process of converting any value into a range of 0 to 1.

5. Support Vector Machine Algorithm (SVM)

SVM is a type of supervised learning method and helps in classification, outlier detection, and regression techniques. SVM uses specific methods for a specific problem like Support Vector Classifier (SVC) and Support Vector Regression (SVR). For understanding these methods; we need to know the working principle of SVM. So SVM works on few hyperparameters like kernel, hyperplane, and decision boundary. Kernel helps to identify the hyperplane in higher dimensional space without elevating the cost. Sometimes it is difficult to identify the separating hyperplane when there is an increase in dimension so at that point higher dimension space is needed. Now, a hyperplane is nothing but a separating line between two data classes in SVM but for SVR it derives the continuous output for regression. Decision Boundary is defined as the simplification of classes through which positive and negative data class can be distinguished. In SVM optimization the concept of hard margin, and the soft margin is highly popular. Soft margin is flexible and it also handles the large value through regularization; this margin is one of the most useable methods for a dataset with a large no. of values.

DEEP LEARNING TECHNIQUES

In previous sections, we talk about the ML models like SVM, RF, Decision tree, and ANN. In this entire model of ML, the first step is feature extraction and the next step is classification but the feature extraction process is quite complex because it needs the whole knowledge of the problem domain and tested again and again for the better and optimized result. So researcher suggested the new approach called a Deep learning technique which is a subset of ML techniques but with the difference that here feature extraction and classification is combined and gives more abstract and compressed data than the classical ML techniques previously used. DL is quite fast to implement and because a combined version of testing or training requires less cycle while implementing it became one of the widely used approach.

Different models are defined under DL;
In Supervised;

1. Convolutional Neural Network (CNN)
2. Recurrent Neural Network (RNN)
3. Classical Neural Networks (Multilayer Perceptron)

In Unsupervised;

1. Self-organizing maps
2. Boltzmann Machine
3. AutoEncoders

1. Convolutional Neural Network (CNN)

CNN works on two major components i.e. Feature extraction and another one is classification. CNN works in layers, for example, an image of animals or birds needs to classify through CNN, then in the first layer, the pattern and edges get defined and sent to the next layer where shape, size, and color get defined and all this data go to the next layer which is final layer tries to classify the image. The overall structure is given in Figure 6. So these layers are as expressed from equation (12) to (23)

a. **Layer 1:** Convolutional Layer: In this layer, kernel or filter is used to convert the input matrix to an output matrix which is known as convolution. For this, a mathematical equation is there;

$$conv\left(o^{(l-1)}, K^{(n)}\right)_{x,y} = \psi^{[l]}\left(\sum_{i=1}^{n_H^{[l-1]}}\sum_{j=1}^{n_W^{[l-1]}}\sum_{k=1}^{n_C^{[l-1]}}K_{i,j,k}^{(n)}o_{x+i-1,y+j-1,k}^{[l-1]} + b_n^l\right) \tag{12}$$

$$\dim\left(conv\left(o^{[l-1]}, K^{(n)}\right)\right) = \left(n_H^l, n_W^l\right) \tag{13}$$

Output;

$$o^{[l]} = \left[\psi^{[l]}\left(conv\left(o^{[l-1]}, K^{(1)} \right) \right), \psi^{[l]}\left(conv\left(o^{[l-1]}, K^{(2)} \right) \right), \ldots, \psi^{[l]}\left(conv\left(o^{[l-1]}, K^{\left(n_C^{[l]} \right)} \right) \right) \right] \tag{14}$$

$$\dim\left(o^{[l]} \right) = \left(n_H^l, n_W^l, n_C^l \right) \tag{15}$$

Here, $\psi^{[l]}$ is activation function, $o^{[l]}$ is output with size $\left(n_H^l, n_W^l, n_C^l \right)$. n_C^l represents the no of filters where each K has dimensions. With:

$$n_{H/W}^l = \begin{cases} \dfrac{n_{H/W}^{[l-1]} + 2p^l - f^l}{s^l} + 1; s > 0 \\ n_{H/W}^{[l-1]} + 2p^l - f^l; s = 0 \end{cases} \tag{16}$$

b. **Layer 2:** Pooling Layer; Downsampling of features has been done in this layer we observe through equation

$$o_{x,y,z}^l = pool\left(o^{[l-1]} \right)_{x,y,z} = \Phi^{[l]}\left(\left(o_{x+i-1, y+j-1, z}^{[l-1]} \right)_{(i,j) \in \left[1,2,\ldots, f^{[l]} \right]^2} \right) \tag{17}$$

$$\dim\left(o^{[l]} \right) = \left(n_H^l, n_W^l, n_C^l \right) \tag{18}$$

$$n_{H/W}^l = \begin{cases} \dfrac{n_{H/W}^{[l-1]} + 2p^l - f^l}{s^l} + 1; s > 0 \\ n_{H/W}^{[l-1]} + 2p^l - f^l; s = 0 \end{cases} \tag{19}$$

$$n_C^l = n_C^{[l-1]} \tag{20}$$

Where, $\Phi^{[l]}$ represents the pooling function.

c. **Fully Connected Layer:** It takes a finite no of neurons as an input vector and returns another vector.

$$z_j^i = \sum_{l=1}^{n_{i-1}} w_{j,l}^{[i]} o_l^{[i-1]} + b_j^{[i]} \tag{21}$$

$$o_j^i = \psi^{[i]}\left(z_j^i\right) \tag{22}$$

After this we need to seal it with a fully connected layer we have to use flatten function by converting it into 1-dimension

$$n_{i-1} = n_H^{i-1} \times n_W^{i-1} \times n_C^{i-1} \tag{23}$$

Figure 6. Workflow of CNN algorithm

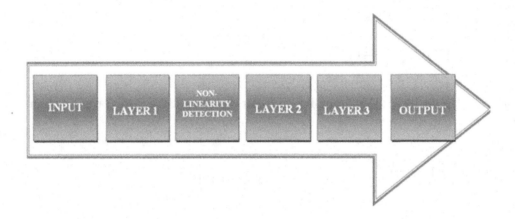

CNN is majorly used for phishing detection because of fast implementation as we discussed above in advantages and disadvantages.

2. Recurrent Neural Network (RNN)

RNN is one of the variants of neural networks and one of the main features of RNN is that it can memorize the previous layer and also helps to train the model with better and more precise output. One of the similar working models is a feed-forward network in which every output is dependent on the specific input. RNN takes input x= (x1,x2,...,xt), the RNN contains the hidden layer h=(h1,h2,....,ht) and the output sequence y=(y1,y2,...,yt) as expressed in equation (24) to (25) where; f(.) and g(.) is an activation function and W_{hx} is input hidden weight, W_{hh} is hidden-hidden weight, W_{yh} is hidden-output weight, b_h is a hidden bias, b_y is output bias, h_t is hidden state to recall over the network over the time step t.

$$h_t = f(W_{hx}x_t + W_{hh}x_{t-1} + b_h) \tag{24}$$

$$y_t = g(W_{yh}h_t + b_y) \tag{25}$$

3. Multilayer Perceptron(MP)

Perceptron defines as a linear classifier in which two categories are present, and are linearly separable through a margin which is mathematically formulated as y=wx+b, where w is the weighted value that may affect the two classes directly. Also, perceptron works with the single output with a single layer but in real life, with real data, this implementation doesn't go too far and as a solution, the next suggested approach is multilayer perceptron which comes under the deep neural network, MP composed of two perceptrons in which one as input and the other as output to take decisions. It comes under the supervised learning technique via a correlation between inputs and outputs. It works in two ways, Forward pass when the signal flows from the input to the output layer, and backward pass, in which bias is backpropagated through the multilayer perceptron.

4. Self Organizing Maps

In previous sections, we saw supervised learning now we have to understand deep learning models in unsupervised learning. So as we know that in unsupervised networks learning is done through their classification no class labels are present in this type of learning. SOM works on the principle of competitive neuron, which means that all the neurons that came as output does competition to get activated and the result of this competition activates one neuron and that neuron known as winner neuron. The purpose of SOM algorithms is to change the arbitrary to two-dimensional maps. For the various input patterns, neurons get selective. Self-organization has four components as expressed as below;

1. **Initialization:** With small random values all the weights are initialized.
2. **Competition:** By using the discriminant function, the winner neuron gets decided with an x input vector of n-dimensional space, between input "i" and neuron "j" the connection weight is present.
3. **Cooperation:** The winning neuron is used to determine the spatial location, providing the basis of cooperation with other neighboring neurons.
4. **Adjusting Neighbors/Adaptation:** The exciting neurons decrement its value of the discriminant functions and adjust the other values associated with that neuron.

5. Boltzmann Machine (BM)

The BM is also unsupervised learning. It is used for an optimization problem; here fixed weights are present that's why we can't train the model. We test the network by using a function called Consensus Function (CF). Boltzmann has a fixed unit called with a bidirectional connection between them.

6. Autoencoders

An auto-encoder is used to copy the input to its output. It works in two parts one is the encoder and the other is the decoder. When we talk about autoencoder then stochastic mapping (a probability space between functions from X to Y as elementary events) is the concept which prominently works. It is a type of unsupervised learning but more it is called self-supervised learning because Auto Encoder requires small information to encode the data.

RESULTS & DISCUSSION

In this section, as we showed the % distribution of the dataset in Figure 7; also find the frequency of words in spam and ham messages helps to count the overall occurrence of each word as shown in Figure 8, and message length of ham and spam with punctuation count is evaluated in Figure 9 we also classify the text that comes under spam and ham in Figure 10 this is the very first step of detecting the phishing attack through SMS.

Figure 7. (A) % wise Distribution of Spam & Ham Message, (B) frequently occurring words graph form,

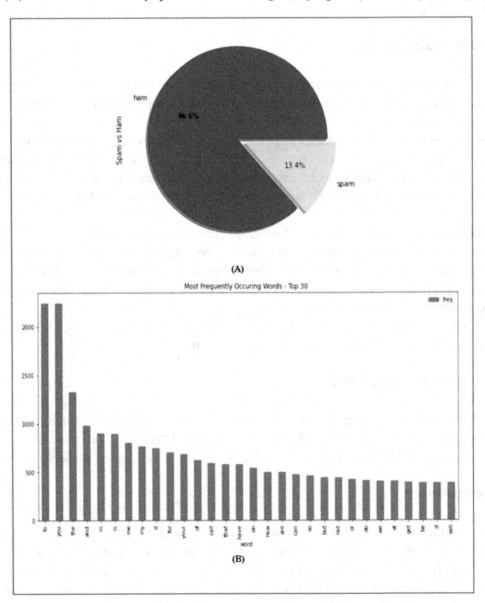

Figure 8. (A) Frequency of Spam word occurrence, (B) Frequency of ham word occurrence

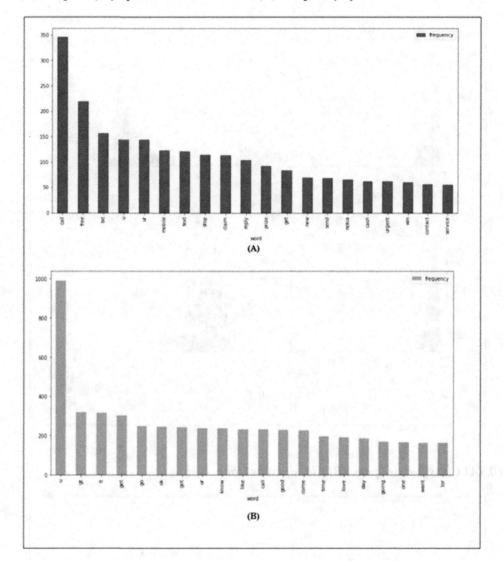

Evaluation Measures

All the evaluation measures used for classification works on the confusion matrix after implementation we also get the confusion matrix which is given in Table 7.

Table 7. Confusion Matrix

		Predicted	
		spam	**ham**
Actual	spam	957	6
	ham	9	143

Figure 9. (A) Message Length ham & spam, (B) Punctuation count in ham & spam

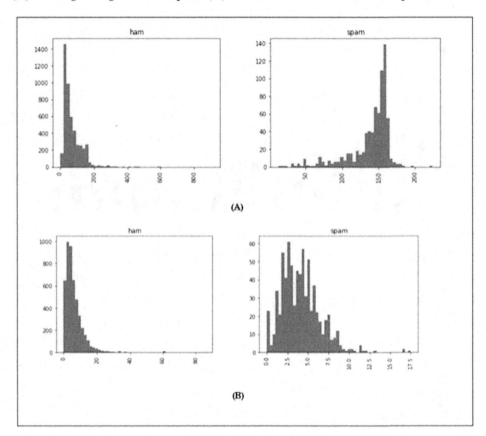

Figure 10. (A) Classified as Spam, (B) Classified as Ham.

Testing Sample:

    The message [Thanks for your Ringtone Order, Reference T56.   ] has been classified as spam

                                    (A)

    The message [Can you say what happen] has been classified as ham

                                    (B)

A confusion matrix generalized as true positive (TP), false positive (FP), false negative (FN), and true negative (TN), and this is calculated between the actual and predicted value and once confusion matrix is evaluated we can find the other measures that we discussed below.

1. **Accuracy:** Ratio of Correctly predicted observation to total no of observation as expressed in equation (26)

$$Accuracy = \frac{\text{Correctly Predicted}(TP + TN)}{\text{Total no.of observations}(TP + TN + FP + FN)} \quad (26)$$

We implemented the only accuracy but other evaluation parameters can be computed based on confusion matrix-like precision, sensitivity (recall), and f1 score

2. **Precision:** It is defined as the rate of correctly predicted positive values to the total no of predictive positive observations as expressed in equation (27)

$$precision = \frac{Correctly\ predicted\ positive\ values\,(TP)}{total\ no\ of\ predicted\ positive\ observation\,(TP + FP)} \quad (27)$$

3. **Sensitivity:** Ratio of predicted observations to the actual observations as expressed in equation (28)

$$Sensitivity = \frac{Correctly\ predicted\ positive\ obsevations\,(TP)}{Actual\ observations\,(TP + FN)} \quad (28)$$

4. **F1 Score:** A weighted average of precision and sensitivity as expressed in equation (29)

$$F1Score = \frac{2*(Sensitivity*Precision)}{Sensitivity + Precision} \quad (29)$$

Training

Various training algorithms are implemented in which SVM, Decision tree, Naïve Bayes, ANN, Convolutional Neural Networks (CNN), 7-layer CNN, 11-layer CNN. The architecture of a CNN has an input layer, hidden layers, and the output layer. The number of hidden depends on each shallow and deep CNN.

1. **Convolution:** The hidden layers in CNN are generally used for pooling and convolution. In each convolution layer, we take a small filter and move that filter across the input matrix or the image and convolution operations will be done. These operations are nothing but the multiplication of the filter values with the matrix values and summing up those values. The filter values will be adjusted as the iterations on the corpus increase. As the epochs increase they start recognizing better features.
2. **Pooling:** It helps in reducing the number of parameters thereby reducing the computation. It prevents the problem of overfitting. There are two types of pooling functions. They are:
    a.   Max pooling function – selects the maximum values.
    b.   Average pooling function – an average of all the values
3. Activation Functions:

a. **ReLU:** The activation used at hidden layers is the ReLU (Rectified Linear Unit) activation. This is a widely used activation in deep learning techniques nowadays.

$$f(x) = \begin{cases} 0 & for \ x < 0 \\ x & for \ x \geq 0 \end{cases} \qquad (30)$$

b. **Softmax:** This activation is used at the output layer. This is a wonderful activation that outputs a vector that represents the probabilities of the list of possible outcomes. The probabilities always sum to 1.

$$f(z_i) = \frac{e^{z_i}}{\sum_{j=1}^{K} e^{z_j}} \qquad (31)$$

c. **Dropout:** It is a technique of regularization. In each iteration, it drops out some neurons randomly and doesn't use these neurons either in forwarding or backpropagation. That is the reason it forces the learning algorithm to spread the weights rather than focusing on specific features.

d. **Flatten:** It flattens the input.

As per the above discussion and implementation of all the training algorithms; we compared these models by using a measure called accuracy as shown in Table 8, for both ML and DL techniques. ANN gave higher accuracy of 97.36% among all ML models. On the other hand, CNN of the DL technique gave an accuracy of 99.47%.

Table 8. Comparative Analysis of ML & DL technique over accuracy

Technique	Classifier Used	Accuracy
ML techniques	**ANN**	**97.36**
	Decision Tree	96.42
	SVM	92.14
	Naiye Bayes	90.07
DL Techniques	**CNN**	**99.47**
	CNN with 7 Layers	97.64
	CNN with 11 Layers	92.14

CONCLUSION AND FUTURE DIRECTION

The proposed work demonstrates that the deep learning method using CNN can get the best results of SMS classification. This deep learning model not only learns high dimensional representations but also performs efficient classification tasks. The test comes about on SMS spam dataset demonstrates that CNN can learn a better generative model and perform well on SMS spam recognition task. The deep learning algorithms provide new design ideas and strategies for future research on SMS phishing discovery. In the future, other deep learning algorithms like Recurrent Neural Networks, LSTM, and GRU can be used in the detection of SMS phishing messages.

ACKNOWLEDGMENT

This research received no specific grant from any funding agency in the public, commercial, or not-for-profit sectors.

REFERENCES

Annareddy, S., & Tammina, S. (2019, December). A Comparative Study of Deep Learning Methods for Spam Detection. In *2019 Third International conference on I-SMAC (IoT in Social, Mobile, Analytics and Cloud)(I-SMAC)* (pp. 66-72). IEEE. 10.1109/I-SMAC47947.2019.9032627

Arshey, M., & KS, A. V. (2020). An optimization-based deep belief network for the detection of phishing e-mails. *Data Technologies and Applications*.

Bagui, S., Nandi, D., Bagui, S., & White, R. J. (2019, June). Classifying phishing email using machine learning and deep learning. In *2019 International Conference on Cyber Security and Protection of Digital Services (Cyber Security)* (pp. 1-2). IEEE. 10.1109/CyberSecPODS.2019.8885143

Basheer, S., Bhatia, S., & Sakri, S. B. (2021). Computational Modeling of Dementia Prediction Using Deep Neural Network: Analysis on OASIS Dataset. *IEEE Access: Practical Innovations, Open Solutions*, 9, 42449–42462. doi:10.1109/ACCESS.2021.3066213

Chakraborty, K., Bhatia, S., Bhattacharyya, S., Platos, J., Bag, R., & Hassanien, A. E. (2020). Sentiment Analysis of COVID-19 tweets by Deep Learning Classifiers—A study to show how popularity is affecting accuracy in social media. *Applied Soft Computing*, 97, 106754. doi:10.1016/j.asoc.2020.106754 PMID:33013254

Chetty, G., Bui, H., & White, M. (2019, December). Deep learning based spam detection system. In *2019 International Conference on Machine Learning and Data Engineering (iCMLDE)* (pp. 91-96). IEEE. 10.1109/iCMLDE49015.2019.00027

Garcia, M. B., Revano, T. F., Habal, B. G. M., Contreras, J. O., & Enriquez, J. B. R. (2018, November). A pornographic image and video filtering application using optimized nudity recognition and detection algorithm. In *2018 IEEE 10th International Conference on Humanoid, Nanotechnology, Information Technology, Communication and Control, Environment and Management (HNICEM)* (pp. 1-5). IEEE. 10.1109/HNICEM.2018.8666227

Gupta, S. D., Saha, S., & Das, S. K. (2021, February). SMS Spam Detection Using Machine Learning. *Journal of Physics: Conference Series*, 1797(1), 012017. doi:10.1088/1742-6596/1797/1/012017

Jain, A. K., & Gupta, B. B. (2021). A survey of phishing attack techniques, defence mechanisms and open research challenges. *Enterprise Information Systems*, 1–39. doi:10.1080/17517575.2021.1896786

Jain, A. K., Yadav, S. K., & Choudhary, N. (2020). A Novel Approach to Detect Spam and Smishing SMS using Machine Learning Techniques. *International Journal of E-Services and Mobile Applications*, *12*(1), 21–38. doi:10.4018/IJESMA.2020010102

Jupin, J. A., Sutikno, T., Ismail, M. A., Mohamad, M. S., Kasim, S., & Stiawan, D. (2019). Review of the machine learning methods in the classification of phishing attack. *Bulletin of Electrical Engineering and Informatics*, *8*(4), 1545–1555. doi:10.11591/eei.v8i4.1344

Kalaharsha, P., & Mehtre, B. M. (2021). *Detecting Phishing Sites—An Overview*. arXiv preprint arXiv:2103.12739.

Lloret, E., Plaza, L., & Aker, A. (2018). The challenging task of summary evaluation: An overview. *Language Resources and Evaluation*, *52*(1), 101–148. doi:10.100710579-017-9399-2

Makkar, A., & Kumar, N. (2020). An efficient deep learning-based scheme for web spam detection in IoT environment. *Future Generation Computer Systems*, *108*, 467–487. doi:10.1016/j.future.2020.03.004

Marsault, B., Gigot, F., & Jagorel, G. (2020). *Sms Spam Detection*. Text Analysis And Retrieval 2020 Course Project Reports, 42.

Maurya, S., & Jain, A. (2020). Deep learning to combat phishing. *Journal of Statistics and Management Systems*, *23*(6), 945–957. doi:10.1080/09720510.2020.1799496

Mishra, S., & Soni, D. (2020). Smishing Detector: A security model to detect smishing through SMS content analysis and URL behavior analysis. *Future Generation Computer Systems*, *108*, 803–815. doi:10.1016/j.future.2020.03.021

Popovac, M., Karanovic, M., Sladojevic, S., Arsenovic, M., & Anderla, A. (2018, November). Convolutional neural network based SMS spam detection. In *2018 26th Telecommunications Forum (TELFOR)* (pp. 1-4). IEEE. 10.1109/TELFOR.2018.8611916

Rajeswari, B., & Nisha, S. S. (2018). *Web Page Prediction Using Web Mining*. Academic Press.

Rinaldi, A. M., Russo, C., & Tommasino, C. (2021). A semantic approach for document classification using deep neural networks and multimedia knowledge graph. *Expert Systems with Applications*, *169*, 114320. doi:10.1016/j.eswa.2020.114320

Saha, I., Sarma, D., Chakma, R. J., Alam, M. N., Sultana, A., & Hossain, S. (2020, August). Phishing Attacks Detection using Deep Learning Approach. In *2020 Third International Conference on Smart Systems and Inventive Technology (ICSSIT)* (pp. 1180-1185). IEEE. 10.1109/ICSSIT48917.2020.9214132

Shirazi, H., Haefner, K., & Ray, I. (2017, August). Fresh-phish: a framework for auto-detection of phishing websites. In 2017 IEEE international conference on information reuse and integration (IRI) (pp. 137-143). IEEE. doi:10.1109/IRI.2017.40

Sonowal, G. (2020). Detecting Phishing SMS Based on Multiple Correlation Algorithms. *SN Computer Science*, *1*(6), 1–9. doi:10.100742979-020-00377-8 PMID:33163974

Soykan, E. U., Bagriyanik, M., & Soykan, G. (2021). Disrupting the power grid via EV charging: The impact of the SMS Phishing attacks. *Sustainable Energy, Grids and Networks*, 100477.

Yerima, S. Y., Alzaylaee, M. K., Shajan, A., & P, V. (2021). Deep Learning Techniques for Android Botnet Detection. *Electronics (Basel)*, *2021*(10), 519. doi:10.3390/electronics10040519

Zhang, X., Zeng, Y., Jin, X. B., Yan, Z. W., & Geng, G. G. (2017, December). *Boosting the phishing detection performance by semantic analysis. In 2017 IEEE international conference on big data (big data).* IEEE.

Zhu, E., Ju, Y., Chen, Z., Liu, F., & Fang, X. (2020). DTOF-ANN: An Artificial Neural Network phishing detection model based on Decision Tree and Optimal Features. *Applied Soft Computing*, *95*, 106505. doi:10.1016/j.asoc.2020.106505

KEY TERMS AND DEFINITIONS

Activation Function: It is one of the important functions in the neural network through which the output of the network is decided. Different activation functions present for a different type of network.

Frequency: Occurrence of no of times word appear during the text processing.

Gated Recurrent Unit: It is an advanced version of RNN. GRU uses the Gates for the information flow, and it is a two-step process with the Reset and Update gate.

Long Short-Term Memory: It comes under the field of deep learning and works on the feedback connection and especially of this network is the whole sequence of data.

Message Length: It shows no. of messages present in ham as well as spam messages which later helpful for finding maximum length.

Pooling: It is used to decrease the resolution of the feature map while preserving the features that are required for classification.

Punctuation Count: It is used to find the total no of punctuation present in ham and spam messages.

This research was previously published in New Opportunities for Sentiment Analysis and Information Processing; pages 1-28, copyright year 2021 by Engineering Science Reference (an imprint of IGI Global).

Chapter 47
Improvisation of Cleaning Process on Tweets for Opinion Mining

Arpita Grover

ⓘ https://orcid.org/0000-0001-5273-686X

Kurukshetra University, India

Pardeep Kumar

ⓘ https://orcid.org/0000-0003-3755-1837

Kurukshetra University, Kurukshetra, India

Kanwal Garg

Kurukshetra University, Kurukshetra, India

ABSTRACT

In the current scenario, high accessibility to computational facilities encourage generation of a large volume of electronic data. Expansion of the data has persuaded researchers towards critical analyzation so as to extract the maximum possible patterns for wiser decisiveness. Such analysis requires curtailing of text to a better structured format by pre-processing. This scrutiny focuses on implementing pre-processing in two major steps for textual data generated by dint of Twitter API. A NoSQL, document-based database named as MongoDB is used for accumulating raw data. Thereafter, cleaning followed by data transformation is executed on accumulated tweets related to Narender Modi, Honorable Prime Minister of India.

DOI: 10.4018/978-1-6684-6303-1.ch047

1. INTRODUCTION

Social media brings people together so that they can generate ideas or share their experiences with each other. The information generated through such sites can be utilized in many ways to discover fruitful patterns. But, accumulation of data via such sources create a huge unstructured textual data with numerous unwanted formats. Henceforth, the first step of text mining involves pre-processing of gathered reviews.

The journey of transforming dataset into a form, an algorithm may digest, takes a complicated road. The task embraces four differentiable phases: Cleaning, Annotation, Normalization and Analysis. The step of cleaning comprehends extrication of worthless text, tackling with capitalization and other similar details. Stop words, Punctuations marks, URLs, numbers are some of the instances which can be discarded at this phase. Annotation is a step of applying some scheme over text. In context to natural language processing, this includes part-of-speech tagging. Normalization demonstrates reduction of linguistic. In other words, it is a process that maps terms to a scheme. Basically, standardization of text through lemmatization and stemming are the part of normalization. Finally, text undergoes manipulation, generalization and statistical probing to interpret features.

For this study, pre-processing is accomplished in three major steps, as signified in Figure 1, keeping process of sentiment analysis in consideration. Foremost step included collection of tweets from Twitter by means of Twitter API. Captured data is then stored in a NoSQL database known to be MongoDB. Thereafter, collected tweets underwent cleaning (Zainol et al., 2018) process. Cleaning phase incorporated removal of user name, URLs, numbers, punctuations, special characters along in addition to lower casing and emoji decoding. The first two phases of data collection and clean ing were demonstrated in previous research. Also, it was shown that application of cleaning process still left data with anomalies and that is why the endmost stage of data transformation is introduced in this research. Data transfor-

Figure 1. Preprocessing steps

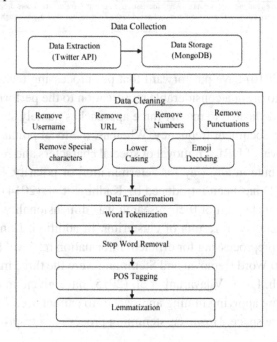

mation comprise of tokenization (Mullen et al., 2018), stop word removal (Effrosynidis et al., 2017), part-of-speech tagging (Belinkov et al., 2018) and lemmatization (Liu et al., 2012).

The remaining paper is organized as follows: Section 2 includes discussion of various author's work in concerned arena. Further, entire methodology for preprocessing of data opted for this research is postulated in Section 4. Then, the results generated through implementation of algorithms mentioned in Section 4 are scrutinized utterly in Section 5. Thereafter, Section 6 provides conclusion of entire work.

2. RELATED WORK

Many studies centered around the issue of preprocessing for text mining are scrutinized in this section.

Figure 2. Errors left in cleaned data

S.No.	Errors Left in Cleaned Data
1.	if bjp had less than lok sabha seats then im sure nitish kumar would have kicked modi amp nda but now out of frustration hes bound to remain shut amp wait for the right moment at least they have a rebellion in nda now for the next years which will help our democracy
2.	pm narendra modi and indias most wanted first week box office collection pmnarendramodi indiasmostwanted
3.	in washington post i profile the very controversial amit shah who is now running india a man with an equally checkered past on human rights as his mentor narendra modi
4.	he lives in a small two room mud house owns a bicycle and nothing else salute to this social worker of odissa who defeated a billionaire and is now a minister in the council of ministers he is mr pratap sarangi mp from balasore folded hands medium light skin tone modi sure picks his ministers well raised fist india
5.	follow recommendation if there is one voice in the government which gives you such a clear account of things is the person such a great article so insightful on the unemployment being at its highest issue
6.	if modi can visit a temple we can visit our mosques if modi can go sit in a cave we muslims can also proudly say our prayers in mosques said
7.	farmers and poor have always been a priority for modi government as promised pm has extend the pm kisan yojana to all farmers cabinet has also approved a new scheme pradhan mantri kisan pension yojana to provide pension to crores of small amp marginal farmers
8.	tn was is and will fight against the hindi imposition at any cost modi govt is playing with fire federal structure must be respected as per the constitution tnagainsthindiimposition stophindiimposition
9.	while we read modi govt data showing joblessness at yr high here a data shows drop in farmer suicides in karnataka credit to lead govt for giving confidence to the farmers a lot to be done though interesting thread

Srividhya and Anitha (2010) have put forward that pre-processing techniques play a major role in reducing the feature space to bring a considerable rectification to the performance metrics for final text classification. The work is dedicated to mainly three approaches namely stop word removal, stemming and term frequency-inverse document frequency. Whereas, the focal points of Hemalatha et al. (2012) in their research were removal of URLs, removal of special characters and removal of questions as these form of texts do not contribute in any way for determination of polarity. Further, a hybrid algorithm combining TF-IDF and SVD has been introduced by Kadhim et al. (2014) for pre-processing the text document in 2014. The ultimate goal of their research was dimensionality reduction of feature vector space so as to intensify accuracy in results of clustering. In addition, Kannan and Gurusamy (2014) have acknowledged role of preprocessing for efficient information retrieval from text document in their scrutiny. Tokenization, Stop Word Removal and Stemming were the three major techniques which were spotlighted in their research. Later, Vijayarani et al. (2015) have given an overview of techniques for pre-processing the text before applying mining approaches to extract useful information so as to reduce the dimensionality of feature space. However, stemming process of pre-processing technique has been centralized by Nayak et al. (2016) MF Porter and Krovetz algorithms of stemming have been analyzed. The survey has put forward some areas of improvement for both algorithms. Moreover, Krouska et al. (2016) have empirically visualized the impact of distinct pre-processing approaches over ultimate classification of tweets using four well known classifiers viz Naive Bayes (NB), C4.5, K-Nearest Neighbor (KNN) and Support Vector Machine (SVM).

All these studies focus a very little on overall implementation of cleaning and transformation steps as whole in context to sentiment mining. Therefore, the focal point of this research is integrated administration of entire procedure for preprocessing of textual data in respect to sentiment analysis.

3. PREPROCESSING OF TWITTER API

The procedure initiates by collection of tweets using Twitter API. Though collected data passed through process of cleaning yet, it left data with some anomalies. These outliers are demonstrated in Figure 2. The presented anomalies still leave data unsuitable for classification. Henceforth, process of data transformation is presented in this research. Data transformation helps in removal of neglected noise and identification of logical words from lump of alphabets.

4. RESEARCH METHODOLOGY

To carry out present research work, a primary dataset generated through Twitter API is gathered so as to perform an analysis on live tweets. Thereupon, entire coding is done in python3.7 on jupyter notebook. In addition to this, nltk toolkit for data transformation and Entropy Model trained on tagset of Penn Treebank for POS tagging were used which are mentioned in sections 4.3 and 4.3.3 respectively.

4.1. Data Collection

Data is collected in form of tweets from twitter using Twitter API in a NoSQL environment, named as MongoDB. Algorithm mentioned for data collection in Algorithm 1 is used for retrieval of complete text.

Algorithm 1. readTweetText(item)

Input: Item with tweet information in json format

Output: text

```
1:  if "extended tweet" in item then
2:      return item['extended tweet']['full text']
3:  else if 'retweeted status' in item then
4:      if 'extended tweet' in item['retweeted status'] then
5:          return(item['retweeted status']['extended tweet']['full text'])
6:      else
7:          return(item['retweeted status']['text'])
8:  else
9:      return(item['text'])
```

4.1.1. Twitter API

One sort of Twitter API called as streaming API (Das et al., 2018) is used to collect data for this study as it benefits with retrieval of huge amount of recent data. Moreover, it helps in real time inspection, such as, ongoing social discussion related to a particular entity. The twitter streaming access has a keyword parameter which restricts domain of collected data. For this work, that keyword parameter was set to Narender Modi, Hon'ble Prime Minister of India. Furthermore, streaming access has a language parameter whose language code was set to "en" for fetching only English tweets. It uses streaming response of HTTP to accommodate data.

4.1.2. Database

Tweets streamed through Twitter API are stored in MongoDB. MongoDB is an open source NoSQL document database (Kumar et al., 2018). To capture tweets into MongoDB collections, foremost step is to set up an environment. "Pymongo" module was installed for this intent. Thereupon, MongoClient was instantiated to establish connection with MongoDB. Then ultimately, a database named "TwitterAPI" and a collection entitled "Tweet" were created. Data streamed with Twitter Streaming API was stored in object of this collection named as "col".

4.2. Data Cleaning

Social media sites like twitter generate a huge volume of data. This raw data can be scrutinized to interpret many interesting facts. But, study of such bulky data can prove to be a nasty piece of work without right procedure. Henceforth, for mining propitious patterns out of this huge pile of textual data, foremost obligation is to have an insight into collected data. It is a crucial step so that characteristics of dataset can be explored justly. The concrete understanding of data helps in identification of incompetent content in correspondence to the patterns that need to be mined. In reference to sentiment analysis this research focuses on emoji decoding, lower casing, removal of user name, URLs, punctuations, special characters and numbers. Following algorithm represents integrated implementation of cleaning process which was discussed, taking each methodology individually.

4.3. Data Transformation

Even after execution of cleaning process data is not in a form that can be passed for classification. It is just a lump of characters. Sentiment retrieval from this pile of text requires identification of logical words. Also, it comprise of anomalies that still need attention. For these reasons, the process of data transformation is implied next. The phase of transformation was implemented in four sequential parts: Tokenization, Stop word removal, Part-of-speech tagging and Lemmatization. A view of implementation for transformation is presented underneath and its resultant is demonstrated in Figure 3.

Figure 3. Output of transformation process

S.No.	Output of Cleaning Process	Removed Stop Words
1.	if bjp had less than lok sabha seats then im sure nitish kumar would have kicked modi amp nda but now out of frustration hes bound to remain shut amp wait for the right moment at least they have a rebellion in nda now for the next years which will help our democracy	bjp less lok sabha seat im sure nitish kumar would kicked modi amp nda frustration hes bound remain shut amp wait right moment least rebellion nda next years help democracy
2.	pm narendra modi and indias most wanted first week box office collection pmnarendramodi indiasmostwanted	pm narendra modi indias want first week box office collection pmnarendramodi indiasmostwanted
3.	in washington post i profile the very controversial amit shah who is now running india a man with an equally checkered past on human rights as his mentor narendra modi	washington post profile controversial amit shah running india man equally checkered past human rights mentor narendra modi
4.	he lives in a small two room mud house owns a bicycle and nothing else salute to this social worker of odissa who defeated a billionaire and is now a minister in the council of ministers he is mr pratap sarangi mp from balasore folded hands medium light skin tone modi sure picks his ministers well raised fist india	lives small two room mud house owns bicycle nothing else salute social worker odissa defeated billionaire minister council ministers mr pratap sarangi mp balasore folded hands medium light skin tone modi sure picks ministers well raised fist india
5.	follow recommendation if there is one voice in the government which gives you such a clear account of things is the person such a great article so insightful on the unemployment being at its highest issue	follow recommendation one voice government gives clear account things person great article insightful unemployment highest issue
6.	if modi can visit a temple we can visit our mosques if modi can go sit in a cave we muslims can also proudly say our prayers in mosques said	modi visit temple visit mosques modi go sit cave muslims also proudly say prayers mosques said
7.	farmers and poor have always been a priority for modi government as promised pm has extend pm kisan yojana to all farmers cabinet has also approved a new	farmers poor always priority modi government promised pm extend pm kisan yojana farmers cabinet also approved new scheme pradhan mantri kisan pension yojana provide

Algorithm 2. Clean(text)

Input: "text" from "col" collection

Output: txt

1: for x in col.find() do

2:     txt   x['text']
3: end for

4: for i in txt do

5:     txt   userRemove('@[^ns]+',i)

6:     txt   uRemove("http?://[A-Za-z0-9./]+",i)

7:     txt   nJoin(i in txt if not i.isdigit())

8:     txt   pJoin(string.punctuation, i)

9:     txt   sRemove(r"[^a-zA-Z0-9]+",i)

10:    txt   cJoin(i.lower())

11:    txt   eJoin(emoji.demojize(i))

12: end for

13: return txt

Algorithm 3. Transform(text)

```
Input: Clean(text)
Output: txt
1:  txt    Clean(text)
2:  words tokenize.word tokenize(txt)
3:  stopWords    set(stopwords.words('english'))
4:  WordsFiltered []

5:  for w in words do
6:      if w not in stopWords then
7:          wordsFiltered.append(w)

8:      end if
9:  end for
10: nltktagged    pos tag(wordsFiltered)
11: wordnet lemmatizer    WordNetLemmatizer()

12: for word in wordsFiltered do
13:     ss    wordnet lemmatizer.lemmatize(word,pos="v")

14:     if ss.strip() == word.strip then
15:         sss    wornet lemmatizer.lemmatize(word,pos="a")

16:         if sss.strip() == word.strip then
17:             w n    wordnet lemmatizer.lemmatize(word,pos="n")

18:             op.append(sss.strip())

19:         else
20:             op.append(sss.strip())

21:         end if
22:     else
23:         op.append(ss.strip())

24:     end if
25: end for

26: txt    " ".join(op)
27: return txt
```

4.3.1. Tokenization

In the beginning phase of data transformation, there is a need of parser for tokenization in document. Henceforth, goal of tokenization step in pre-processing is to explore existent words in a phrase. Accordingly, it can be termed as a process of working on a streamed text to convert it into worthwhile elements known to be tokens. A token may comprise of a phrase, an idiom or a symbol. These tokens are then passed on for next level pre-processing. From tokenize class, word tokenize() function is used to carry out this step. Although, tokenization is the first essential step of data transformation yet there has to be further scrutiny of resultant text to make it suitable for final analysis.

4.3.2. Stop Word Removal

Prepositions, articles, connectors, pronouns etc. are the most frequently used word forms in a textual document. All such words are considered to be stop words. Abundant occurrence of these words make a document bulkier and gradually lowers its importance for analysts. Therefore, dictionary of nltk toolkit is used to rip these words out of the document. Consequently, dimensionality of text is reduced considerably.

Figure 4. Output of stop word removal

S.No.	Removed Stop Words	Processed(Cleaned) Data
1.	bjp less lok sabha seat im sure nitish kumar would kicked modi amp nda frustration hes bound remain shut amp wait right moment least rebellion nda next years help democracy	bjp less lok sabha seat im sure nitish kumar would kick modi amp nda frustration hes bind remain shut amp wait right moment least rebellion nda next years help democracy
2.	pm narendra modi indias want first week box office collection pmnarendramodi indiasmostwanted	pm narendra modi indias want first week box office collection pmnarendramodi indiasmostwanted
3.	washington post profile controversial amit shah running india man equally checkered past human rights mentor narendra modi	washington post profile controversial amit shah run india man equally checker past human right mentor narendra modi
4.	lives small two room mud house owns bicycle nothing else salute social worker odissa defeated billionaire minister council ministers mr pratap sarangi mp balasore folded hands medium light skin tone modi sure picks ministers well raised fist india	live small two room mud house own bicycle nothing else salute social worker odissa defeat billionaire minister council minister mr pratap sarangi mp balasore fold hand medium light skin tone modi sure pick minister well raise fist india
5.	follow recommendation one voice government gives clear account things person great article insightful unemployment highest issue	follow recommendation one voice government give clear account things person great article insightful unemployment high issue
6.	modi visit temple visit mosques modi go sit cave muslims also proudly say prayers mosques said	modi visit temple visit mosques modi go sit cave muslims also proudly say prayers mosques say
7.	farmers poor always priority modi government promised pm extend pm kisan yojana farmers cabinet also approved new scheme pradhan mantri kisan pension yojana provide pension crores small amp marginal farmers	farmers poor always priority modi government promise pm extend pm kisan yojana farmers cabinet also approve new scheme pradhan mantri kisan pension yojana provide pension crores small amp marginal farmers

4.3.3. Part-of-Speech Tagging

Part-of-Speech tagging is a process of characterizing each word in textual data to its reciprocal PoS. This correspondence of words is established not solely on the basis of its definition, but the context with which it is used in a sentence is also taken into consideration. Part of speech tags include verbs, nouns, adjectives, adverbs etc. The non-generic trait of POS tagging makes it more complex than basic mapping of words to their POS tags. In correspondence to different context, there is fair probability that a word has more than one PoS tags for distinct sentences. For this scrutiny, PerceptronTagger employing Maximum Entropy Model was used. It implements probability model for tagging. Further, the Entropy Model was trained with a tagset named Penn Treebank.

4.3.4. Lemmatization

Lemmatization is a method used for reduction of inflected words to its root. While, reducing inflections of words to its lemmas, lemmatization takes into consideration the morphological meaning of text. Therefore, unlike stemming, lemmatization maps inflected words to only those root words which correspond to the language.

5. RESULT ANALYSIS

The raw data collected through Twitter API underwent cleaning process whose results were demonstrated. Now, it can be clearly seen from Figure 2 that the resultant of cleaning process still had some impurities which need to be considered for better results. Section 4.3 specifies the process for data to further deal with these anomalies. Figure 3 postulates output of stop word removal. Then ultimately, Figure 4 delineates output of data transformation.

All these results are represented in tabular format for better visualization, though in real, data is stored in json format within MongoDB collections.

6. CONCLUSION

The foundation or premise for sentiment analysis is pre-processing of textual data. Only the qualitative data can produce accurate and precise results for legitimate decision making. The paper presents cleaning and transformation steps on data collected in MongoDB database via Twitter API. Subsequently, results sketch out the impact of cleaning process on different anomalies encountered in assembled data. Further, it is delineated that the step of cleaning still leaves data with many impurities which need attention for accurate results in later stages of sentiment analysis. Consequently, cleaned data is passed for transformation phase. Therefore, for this research raw data collected through Twitter is filtered with fine sieve of two processes i.e. cleaning and transformation.

REFERENCES

Belinkov, Y. Marquez, L., Sajjad, H., Durrani, N., Dalvi, F., & Glass, J. (2018). *Evaluating layers of representation in neural machine translation on part-of-speech and semantic tagging tasks*. arXiv preprint arXiv:1801.07772

Das, S., Behera, R. K., & Rath, S. K. (2018). Real-time sentiment analysis of twitter streaming data for stock prediction. *Procedia Computer Science*, *132*, 956–964. doi:10.1016/j.procs.2018.05.111

Effrosynidis, D., Symeonidis, S., & Arampatzis, A. (2017). A comparison of pre-processing techniques for twitter sentiment analysis. In *International Conference on Theory and Practice of Digital Libraries*, (pp. 394–406). Springer. 10.1007/978-3-319-67008-9_31

Hemalatha, I., Varma, G. S., & Govardhan, A. (2012). Preprocessing the informal text for efficient sentiment analysis. *International Journal of Emerging Trends & Technology in Computer Science*, *1*(2), 58–61.

Kadhim, A. I., Cheah, Y.-N., & Ahamed, N. H. (2014). Text document preprocessing and dimension reduction techniques for text document clustering. In Artificial Intelligence with Applications in Engineering and Technology (ICAIET), 2014 4th International Conference on, (pp. 69–73). IEEE. doi:10.1109/ICAIET.2014.21

Kannan, D. S., & Gurusamy, V. (2014). Preprocess-ing techniques for text mining. *International Journal of Computer Science & Communication Networks*, *5*(1), 7–16.

Krouska, A., Troussas, C., & Virvou, M. (2016). The effect of preprocessing techniques on twitter sentiment analysis. In *Information, Intelligence, Systems & Ap-plications (IISA), 2016 7th International Conference on*, (pp. 1–5). IEEE. 10.1109/IISA.2016.7785373

Kumar, P., Kumar, P., Zaidi, N., & Rathore, V. S. (2018). Analysis and comparative exploration of elastic search, mongodb and hadoop big data processing. In *Soft computing: Theories and applications* (pp. 605–615). Springer. doi:10.1007/978-981-10-5699-4_57

Liu, H., Christiansen, T., Baumgartner, W. A. Jr, & Ver-spoor, K. (2012). Biolemmatizer: A lemmatization tool for morphological processing of biomedical text. *Journal of Biomedical Semantics*, 3(1), 3. doi:10.1186/2041-1480-3-3 PMID:22464129

Mullen, L. A., Benoit, K., Keyes, O., Selivanov, D., & Arnold, J. (2018). Fast, consistent tokenization of natural language text. *Journal of Open Source Software*, 3, 655. doi:10.21105/joss.00655

Nayak, A. S., & Kanive, A. P. (2016). Survey on pre-processing techniques for text mining. *International Journal of Engineering and Computer Science*, 5(6). doi:10.18535/ijecs/v5i6.25

Srividhya, V., & Anitha, R. (2010). Evaluating preprocessing techniques in text categorization. *International Journal of Computer Science and Application*, 47(11), 49–51.

Vijayarani, S., Ilamathi, M. J., & Nithya, M. (2015). Preprocessing techniques for text mining-an overview. *International Journal of Computer Science & Communication Networks*, 5(1), 7–16.

Zainol, Z., Jaymes, M. T., & Nohuddin, P. N. (2018). Visualurtext: A text analytics tool for unstructured tex-tual data. In Journal of Physics: Conference Series, vol-ume 1018, page 012011. IOP Publishing.

Chapter 48
Machine Learning in Sentiment Analysis Over Twitter:
Synthesis and Comparative Study

Kadda Zerrouki
Tahar Moulay University of Saida, Algeria

ABSTRACT

Social networks are the main resources to gather information about people's opinions and sentiments towards different topics as they spend hours daily on social media and share their opinions. Twitter is a platform widely used by people to express their opinions and display sentiments on different occasions. Sentiment analysis's (SA) task is to label people's opinions as different categories such as positive and negative from a given piece of text. Another task is to decide whether a given text is subjective, express-ing the writer's opinions, or objective. These tasks were performed at different levels of analysis rang-ing from the document level to the sentence and phrase level. Another task is aspect extraction, which originated from aspect-based sentiment analysis in phrase level. All these tasks are under the umbrella of SA. In recent years, a large number of methods, techniques, and enhancements have been proposed for the problem of SA in different tasks at different levels. Sentiment analysis is an approach to analyze data and retrieve sentiment that it embodies. Twitter sentiment analysis is an application of sentiment analysis on data from Twitter (tweets) in order to extract sentiments conveyed by the user. In the past decades, the research in this field has consistently grown. The reason behind this is the challenging format of the tweets, which makes the processing difficult. The tweet format is very small, which generates a whole new dimension of problems like use of slang, abbreviations, etc. The chapter elaborately discusses three supervised machine learning algorithms—naïve Bayes, k-nearest neighbor (KNN), and decision tree—and compares their overall accuracy, precisions, as well as recall values; f-measure; number of tweets correctly classified; number of tweets incorrectly classified; and execution time.

DOI: 10.4018/978-1-6684-6303-1.ch048

INTRODUCTION

Sentiment analysis is the Natural Language Processing (NLP) task dealing with the detection and classification of sentiments in texts. Usually, the classes considered are "positive" and "negative", although in some cases finer-grained categories are added (e.g. "Very Positive" and "Very Negative") or only the "Positive" and "Negative" classes are taken into account. Another related task - emotion detection concerns the classification of text into several classes of emotion, usually the basic ones, as described by Dhande & Patnaik (Dhande, 2014). Although different in some ways, some of the research in the field has considered these tasks together, under the umbrella of sentiment analysis.

This task has received a lot of interest from the research community in the past years. The work is regarded the manner in which sentiment can be classified from texts pertaining to different genres and distinct languages, in the context of various applications, using knowledge-based, semi-supervised and supervised methods, as noted by Liu Bing (Liu, 2011). The result of the analyses performed have shown that the different types of text require specialized methods for sentiment analysis, as, for example, the sentiments are not conveyed in the same manner in newspaper articles and in blogs, reviews, forums or other types of user-generated contents, as noted by Balahur Alexandra and al (Balahur, 2013).

The Sentiment found within comments, feedback or critiques provide useful indicators for many different purposes and can be categorized by polarity, as noted by Kalaivani and Shunmuganathan (Kalaivani, 2013). By polarity we tend to find out if a review is overall a positive one or a negative one. For example:

Positive Sentiment in subjective sentence: "I loved the movie Mary Kom": This sentence is expressed positive sentiment about the movie Mary Kom and we can decide that from the sentiment threshold value of word "loved". So, the threshold value of the word 'loved' has positive numerical threshold value.

Negative sentiment in subjective sentences: "Phata poster nikla hero is a flop movie" defined sentence is expressed negative sentiment about the movie named: "Phata poster nikla hero" and we can decide that from the sentiment threshold value of a word: "flop". So, the threshold value of a word: "flop" has negative numerical threshold value.

Sentiment Analysis is of three different types: Document level, Sentence level and Entity level (Kiritchenko, 2014).

In this paper for Sentiment Analysis we are using three Supervised Machine Learning algorithms: Naïve Bayes, K-Nearest Neighbor (KNN) and Decision Tree to calculate the accuracy, precisions (of positive and negative corpuses) and recall values (of positive and negative corpuses), F-Measure, Number of tweets correctly classified, Number of tweets incorrectly classified and Execution Time. The difficulties in Sentiment Analysis are an opinion word which is treated as positive side may be considered as negative in another situation. Also the degree of positivity or negativity also has a great impact on the opinions. For example: "good" and "very good" cannot be treated same. Although the traditional text processing says that a small change in two pieces of text does not change the meaning of the sentences (Kalaivani, 2013). However the latest text mining gives room for advanced analysis, measuring the intensity of the word. Here is the point where we can scale the accuracy and efficiency of different algorithms (Fan, 2006).

The rest of the paper is organized as follows: Section 2 deals with the related works of our study, Section 3 presents the techniques used for Sentiment Analysis (SA), Section 4 presents our proposed work (Data sets used in our study along with the models and methodology used), Section 5 presents all our experimental results, Section 6 presents the conclusion and future works.

RELATED WORKS

Go Alec, Richa Bhayani, and Lei Huang used the first studies on the classification of polarity in tweets was (Go, 2009). The authors conducted a supervised classification study on tweets in English, using the emoticons (e.g. ":)", ":(", etc.) as markers of positive and negative tweets.

(Read, 2005) employed this method to generate a corpus of positive tweets, with positive emoticons ":)", and negative tweets with negative emoticons ":(". Subsequently, they employ different supervised approaches (SVM, Naïve Bayes and Maximum Entropy) and various sets of features and conclude that the simple use of anagrams leads to good results, but it can be slightly improved by the combination of unigrams and bigrams.

In the same line of thinking, Pak Alexander and Patrick Paroubek (Pak, 2010) also generated a corpus of tweets for sentiment analysis, by selecting positive and negative tweets based on the presence of specific emoticons.

Subsequently, they compare different supervised approaches with n-gram features and obtain the best results using Naïve Bayes with anagrams and part-of- speech tags.

Another approach on sentiment analysis in tweet is that of (Ley Zhang, Riddhiman Ghosh, Mohamed Dekhil, Meichun Hsu and Bing Liu) (Zhang, 2011). Here, the authors employ a hybrid approach, combining supervised learning with the knowledge on sentiment-bearing words, which they extract from the DAL sentiment dictionary, used by Whissell Cynthia (Whissell, 2009). Their pre-processing stage includes the removal of retweets, translation of abbreviations into original terms and deleting of links, a tokenization process, and part-of-speech tagging.

They employ various supervised learning algorithms to classify tweets into positive and negative, using n-gram features with SVM and syntactic features with Partial Tree Kernels, combined with the knowledge on the polarity of the words appearing in the tweets. The authors conclude that the most important features are those corresponding to sentiment bearing words. Finally, (Vo Duy-Tin and Yue Zhang) (Vo, 2015), classify sentiment expressed on previously-given "targets" in tweets. They add information on the context of the tweet to its text (e.g. The event that it is related to). Subsequently, they employ SVM and General Inquirer and perform a three-way classification (positive, negative and neutral).

TECHNICS USED FOR SENTIMENT ANALYSIS

Several techniques were used for Sentiment Analysis. A few related works are as follows:

Rambocas Meena and João Gama (Rambocas, 2013) used the keyword based approach to classify sentiment. He worked on identifying keywords basically an adjective which indicates the sentiment. Such indicators can be prepared manually or derived from Wordnet.

Fan Weiguo and al (Fan, 2006) used a different machine learning algorithms such as Naïve Bayes, Support vector machine and maximum entropy.

Vanitha, Sumathi and Soundariya (Vanitha, 2018) performed document and sentence level classification. He fetched review data from different product destinations such as automobiles, banks, movies and travel. He classified the words into positive and negative categories. He then calculated the overall positive or negative score for the text. If the number of positive words is more than negative, then the document is considered positive, otherwise negative.

Jalaj S. Modha, Gayatri S. Pandi and Sandip J. Modha (Modha, 2013) worked on techniques of handling both subjective as well as objective unstructured data.

Theresa Wilson, Janyce Wiebe and Paul Hoffman (Wilson, 2009) worked on a new approach on sentiment analysis by first determining whether an expression is neutral or polar and then disambiguates the polarity of the polar expression. With this approach the system is able to automatically identify the contextual polarity for a large subset of sentiment expressions, hence achieving results which are better than baseline.

In (Ayetiran, 2012) Eniafe Festus Ayetiran and Adesesan Barnabas Adeyemo designed a predictive response model to identify the customers who are more likely to respond to new product offers. The Naïve Bayes algorithm is applied in constructing the classifier system. Both filter and wrapper feature selection techniques are used in determining inputs to the model.

METHODOLOGY

Figure 1 shows the overview diagram of this research (see Figure 1).

Figure 1. Research overview diagram

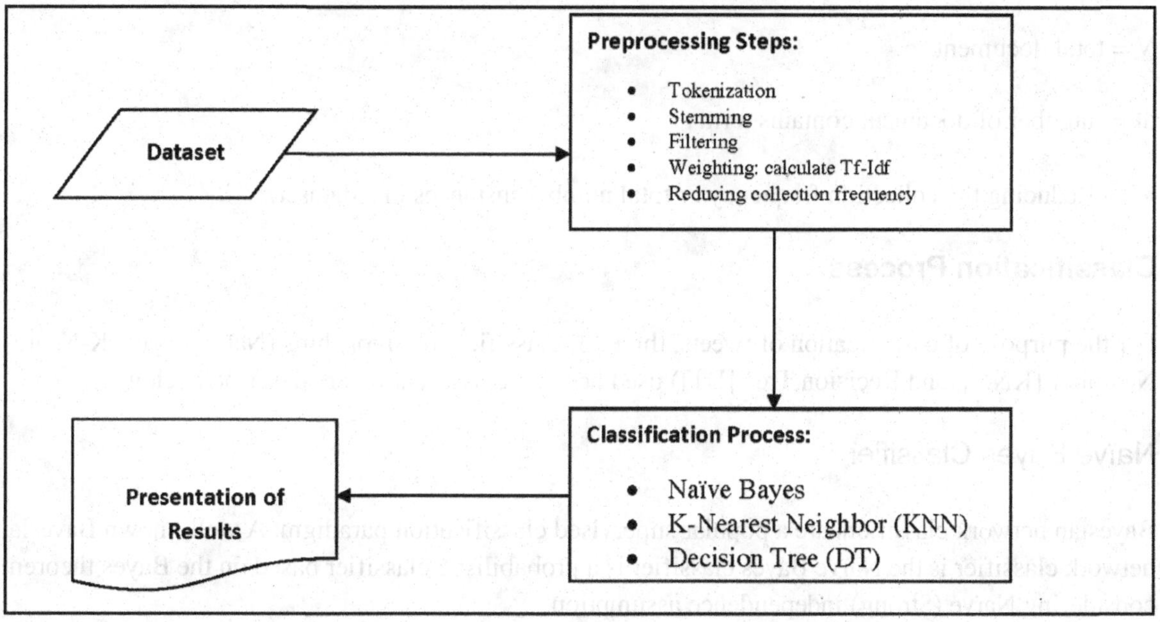

DATASET

The dataset has been prepared by taking 1059218 Instances (Sentiment140).

Preprocessing Text

In text classification, text data will be represented in the vector space model (Garnes Øystein Løhre) (Garnes, 2009). The steps in preprocessing text are as follows:

- Tokenizing: change sentence into a collection of a single word.
- Stemming: returns a word in basic form (root word) by eliminating existing additive. Stemming algorithm used is Porter Stemmer for English language and Nazief-Andriani for Indonesian language (Nazief Bobby and Mirna Adriani) (Nazief, 1996).
- Filtering: eliminating stop words. Stop word is a common word that has little or no meaning, but required in the structure of grammatical language.
- Weighting: calculate TF-IDF for each word, is defined by equation (1).

$$TF - IDF_t = f_{t,d} * \log \frac{N}{df_t} \tag{1}$$

$TF - IDF_t$ = weight of term t

$f_{t,d}$ = occurrences term t in document d

N = total document

df_t = number of document contains term t

- Reducing the collection frequency or total number instances in a dataset.

Classification Process

For the purpose of classification of tweets, three (3) classifiers or algorithms (Naïve Bayes, K-Nearest Neighbor [KNN], and Decision Tree [DT]) used here for classification are described below.

Naïve Bayes Classifier

Bayesian network classifiers are a popular supervised classification paradigm. A well-known Bayesian network classifier is the Naïve Bayes classifier is a probabilistic classifier based on the Bayes theorem, considering Naïve (Strong) independence assumption.

Naïve Bayes is a classification algorithm based on the application of Bayes theorem (Melucci, 2015) (Pratama, 2015). For the purpose of classification of tweets, we make use of Naïve Bayes classifier. Naïve Bayes is a probabilistic classifier based on Bayes" theorem. It classifies the tweets based on the probability that a given tweets belongs to a particular class. We consider two classes namely, positive and negative. We assign class **C** to tweet **d** where, is defined by equation (2):

$$C = \arg \max_c P_{NB}(c|d) \tag{2}$$

The probability of each of its attributes occurring in a given class is independent, is defined by equation (3), we can estimate the probability as follows:

$$P_{NB}(c \mid d) = \frac{\left(P(c) * \sum_{i=1}^{m} P(f \mid c)^{n_i(d)}\right)}{P(d)} \tag{3}$$

f = represents a feature

$n_i(d)$ = represents the count of feature f_i found in tweet d

m = represents the total of feature.

$P(c)$ and $P(f|c)$: are obtained through maximum likelihood estimates, and **add-1** smoothing is utilized for unseen features.

K-Nearest Neighbor Classifier (KNN)

K-Nearest Neighbors (KNN) is a classification algorithm that uses a distance function between the train data to test data and the number of nearest neighbors to determine the classification results. Distance function used in this experiment is the cosine similarity. Cosine similarity is one of the functions that are widely used in the document classification to find similarity between some documents (Pratama, 2015). Scoring function of KNN shown in equation (4). Determining document class is done by voting on a K nearest neighbor. The nearest neighbor is the K-document with the highest similarity value. KNN as a vector in **document-i**/VD_i.

$$Score(C, D_1) = \sum_{D_2 \in S_k D_1} I_C(D_2) \cos(VD_1, VD_2) \tag{4}$$

$Score(C,D_1)$ = scores of test document

D_1 = test document

D_2 = train document

VD_1 = vector test document

VD_2 = vector train document.

I_C = 1 if D_2 is in class C, 0 otherwise

$S_k D_1$ = set of K nearest in test document

K-NN is a type of instance-based learning, or lazy learning where the function is only approximated locally and all computation is deferred until classification. It is a non parametric method used for classification or regression. In case of classification the output is classed membership (the most prevalent cluster may be returned), the object is classified by a majority vote of its Neighbors, with the object being assigned to the class most common among its K-Nearest Neighbors. This rule simply retains the entire training set during learning and assigns to each query a class represented by the majority label of its k-Nearest Neighbors in the training set. The KNN classifier is given in Figure.2 (see Figure 2).

Figure 2. KNN Classifier

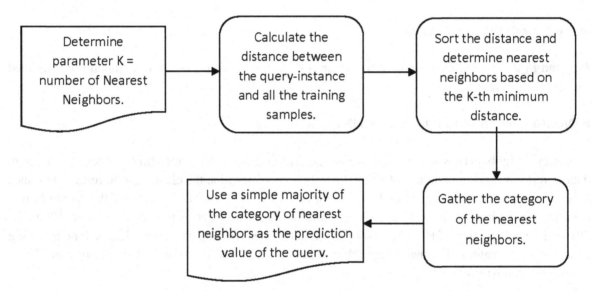

Decision Tree Classifier (DT)

The decision trees are used as an embedded method of feature selection. In the proposed decision tree based feature ranking, a Decision Tree induction selects relevant features and ranks the features. Decision Tree induction is decision tree classifiers learning, constructing a tree structure with internal nodes (non-leaf node) denoting an attribute test. Each branch represents a test outcome and external node (leaf node) denotes class prediction (Jotheeswaran, 2015), (Suresh, 2016).

The algorithm at each node chooses best attribute to partition data into individual classes. Information gain measure is used to choose the best partitioning attribute by attribute selection. Attribute with highest information gain splits the attribute, is defined by equation (5). The attribute's information gain is found by (Jotheeswaran, 2015), (Suresh, 2016):

$$\text{info}(D) = -\sum_{i=1}^{m} P_i * \log_2 * P \tag{5}$$

Where P_i is the probability that an arbitrary vector in D belongs to a class c_i. A log function to base 2 is resorted to as information is encoded in bits. info(D) is average information needed to identify the vector D class name. Before constructing trees, base cases are considered with the following points:

A leaf node is created if all samples belong to a same class.

When no features provide information gain, it creates a decision node higher up the tree using the expected class value.

The decision tree induction algorithm in general checks for base cases and/or each attribute (a), locates information gain of each attribute for splitting. Let a-best be attributed with highest information gain. Create decision node that splits a-best. Return with sub lists obtained by splitting a-best, adding nodes as children for tree.

The proposed method defines a threshold measure to choose relevant features. The threshold measure is based on the information gained value and the proposed Manhattan distance for selecting of the features.

The proposed decision tree method searches heuristically for relevant features. The features are ranked by computing the distance between the hierarchical clusters.

The proposed Manhattan distance for **n** number of clusters is given as takes after, is defined by equation (6) (Jotheeswaran, 2015), (Suresh, 2016):

$$M_{anhattan}D_{istance} = \sum_{i=1}^{n}(a_i - b_i) \tag{6}$$

A cubic polynomial equation is derived using the Manhattan values and the threshold criterion is determined from the slope of the polynomial equation. The features are assumed to be irrelevant for classifying if the slope is zero or negative and relevant when the slope is positive (Jotheeswaran, 2015), (Suresh, 2016).

EXPERIMENTAL RESULTS

Accuracy, Precision, Recall, F-Measure, Number of tweets correctly classified and Number of tweets incorrectly classified are the method used for evaluating the performance of tweets (Instances). In this section, based on the result of Naïve Bayes, KNN (K=1; K=3; K=5; K=7 and K=9) and Decision Tree. Here we give the Accuracy, Precision, Recall, F-Measure, Number of tweets correctly classified and Number of tweets incorrectly classified of Naïve Bayes, different versions of KNN and Decision Tree on 1059218 tweets (Instances). All the experimental results (accuracy, Precision, recall, number of correct classifications, number of incorrect classifications and Execution Time (Seconds)) are measured according to the Table 1 (see Table 1). The performance of Naïve Bayes is compared with different versions of KNN (K=1; K=3; K=5; K=7 and K=9) and Decision Tree are used for the classification of positive and negative tweets. The formula of Accuracy is given by equation 7, Precision is defined with equation 8, Recall is defined by equation by formula 9 and F-Measure is defined by equation 10 (Prabowo, 2009).

$$\text{Accuracy} = \frac{\text{Number of tweets correctly classified}}{\text{Total Number of tweets}} \tag{7}$$

$$\text{Precision} = \frac{\text{True Positive}}{\text{True Positive} + \text{False Positive}} \tag{8}$$

$$\text{Recall} = \frac{\text{True Positive}}{\text{True Positive} + \text{False Negative}} \tag{9}$$

$$\text{F} - \text{Measure} = (2*\text{Precision}*\text{Recall}) / (\text{Precision} + \text{Recall}) \tag{10}$$

Table 1. Results of Accuracy, Precision, Recall, F-Measure, Number of tweets correctly classified and Number of tweets incorrectly classified.

Algorithm	Accuracy	Precision	Recall	F-Measure	Number of tweets correctly classified	Number of tweets incorrectly classified	Total Number of tweets
Naïve Bayes	0.550	0.562	0.67	0.61	582824 (55.024 %)	476394 (44.976 %)	
KNN (K=1)	0.557	0.623	0.41	0.49	590443 (55.7433 %)	468775 (44.2567 %)	
KNN (K=3)	0.577	0.619	0.51	0.56	611708 (57.7509 %)	447510 (42.2491 %)	
KNN (K=5)	0.585	0.616	0.57	0.59	620524 (58.5832 %)	438694 (41.4168 %)	1059218
KNN (K=7)	0.590	0.614	0.60	0.61	625422 (59.0456 %)	433796 (40.9544 %)	
KNN (K=9)	0.593	0.613	0.62	0.62	628666 (59.3519 %)	430552 (40.6481 %)	
Decision Tree	0.528	0.528	1.0	0.69	559826 (52.8528 %)	499392 (47.1472 %)	

The figure 3 (see Figure 3) shows the comparison of accuracy of Naïve Bayes, KNN(K=1), KNN(K=3), KNN(K=5), KNN(K=7), KNN(K=9) and Decision Tree.

From Figure 3, we see that the accuracy of different versions of KNN is always higher than the accuracy of Naïve Bayes and of Decision Tree. From the accuracy, we see that KNN performs better than of Naïve Bayes and better than of Decision Tree for the dataset.

The figure 4 (see Figure 4) shows the comparison of Precision of Naïve Bayes, KNN(K=1), KNN(K=3), KNN(K=5), KNN(K=7), KNN(K=9) and Decision Tree.

As the precision of different versions of KNN is higher of Naïve Bayes and is higher of Decision Tree (from Figure 4), we can conclude that based on precision, KNN performs better than Naïve Bayes and better than Decision Tree.

Figure 3. Comparison of accuracy of Naïve Bayes, KNN(K=1), KNN(K=3), KNN(K=5), KNN(K=7), KNN(K=9) and Decision Tree

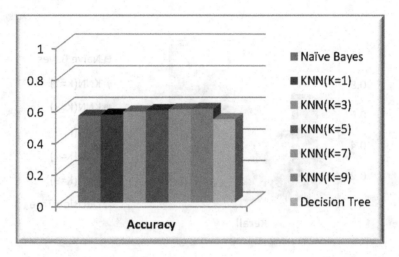

Figure 4. Comparison of Precision of Naïve Bayes, KNN(K=1), KNN(K=3), KNN(K=5), KNN(K=7), KNN(K=9) and Decision Tree

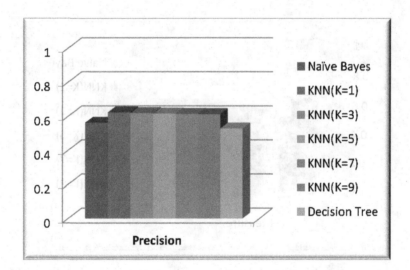

The figure 5 (see Figure 5) shows the comparison of Recall of Naïve Bayes, KNN(K=1), KNN(K=3), KNN(K=5), KNN(K=7), KNN(K=9) and Decision Tree.

From Figure 5, we see that the recall of Decision Tree is always higher than the recall of Naïve Bayes and of different versions of KNN. From the recall, we see that Decision Tree performs better than of Naïve Bayes and performs better than of different versions of KNN.

The figure 6 (see Figure 6) shows the comparison of F-Measure of Naïve Bayes, KNN(K=1), KNN(K=3), KNN(K=5), KNN(K=7), KNN(K=9) and Decision Tree.

Figure 5. Comparison of Recall of Naïve Bayes, KNN(K=1), KNN(K=3), KNN(K=5), KNN(K=7), KNN(K=9) and Decision Tree

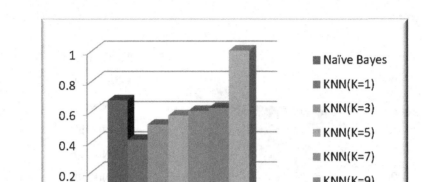

Figure 6. Comparison of F-Measure of Naïve Bayes, KNN(K=1), KNN(K=3), KNN(K=5), KNN(K=7), KNN(K=9) and Decision Tree

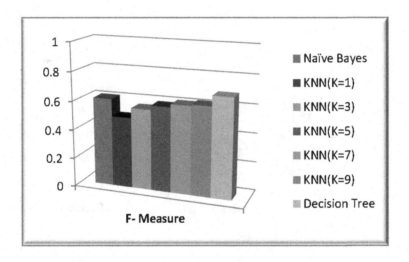

As the F-Measure of Decision Tree is higher of Naïve Bayes and is higher of different versions of KNN (from Figure 6), we can conclude that based on F-Measure, Decision Tree performs better than Naïve Bayes and performs better than of different versions of KNN.

The figure 7 (see Figure 7) shows the comparison of Number of tweets correctly classified of Naïve Bayes, KNN(K=1), KNN(K=3), KNN(K=5), KNN(K=7), KNN(K=9) and Decision Tree.

From Figure 7, we see that the Number of tweets correctly classified of different versions of KNN is always higher than the accuracy of Naïve Bayes and of Decision Tree. From the Number of tweets correctly classified, we see that KNN performs better than of Naïve Bayes and better than of Decision Tree.

Figure 7. of Number of tweets correctly classified of Naïve Bayes, KNN(K=1), KNN(K=3), KNN(K=5), KNN(K=7), KNN(K=9) and Decision Tree

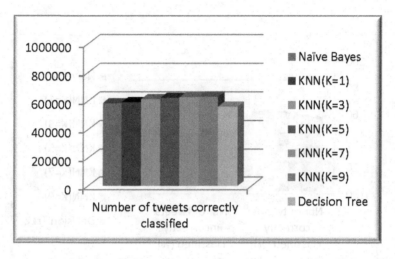

The figure 8 (see Figure 8) shows the comparison of Number of tweets incorrectly classified of Naïve Bayes, KNN(K=1), KNN(K=3), KNN(K=5), KNN(K=7), KNN(K=9) and Decision Tree.

As the Number of tweets incorrectly classified of Decision Tree is higher of Naïve Bayes and is higher of different versions of KNN (from Figure 8), we can conclude that based on Number of tweets incorrectly classified, the different versions of KNN and Naïve Bayes performs better than Decision Tree.

The figure 9 (see Figure 9) shows the comparison of number of tweets correctly classified (%) and number of tweets incorrectly classified (%) of Naïve Bayes, KNN(K=1), KNN(K=3), KNN(K=5), KNN(K=7), KNN(K=9) and Decision Tree.

Figure 8. Comparison of Number of tweets incorrectly classified of Naïve Bayes, KNN(K=1), KNN(K=3), KNN(K=5), KNN(K=7), KNN(K=9) and Decision Tree

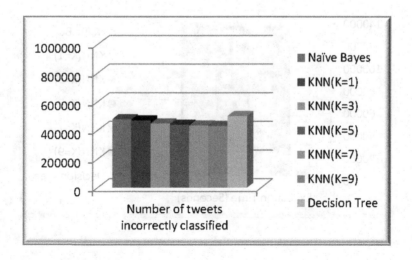

Figure 9. Comparison of Number of tweets correctly classified (%) and Number of tweets incorrectly classified (%) of Naïve Bayes, KNN(K=1), KNN(K=3), KNN(K=5), KNN(K=7), KNN(K=9) and Decision Tree

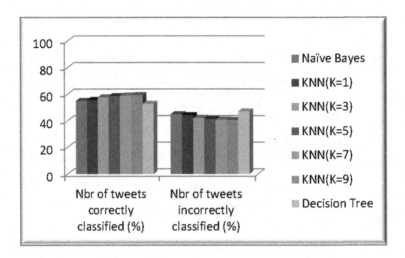

From Figure 9 which indicates the comparison (%) among Naïve Bayes, different versions of KNN and Decision Tree, we see that the different versions of KNN are very is higher that Naïve Bayes and Decision Tree, and the percentage are very good.

The figure 10 (see Figure 10) shows the comparison of execution time (seconds) of Naïve Bayes, KNN(K=1), KNN(K=3), KNN(K=5), KNN(K=7), KNN(K=9) and Decision Tree.

As the Execution Time (Seconds) of different versions of KNN is higher of Naïve Bayes and is higher of Decision Tree (from Figure 10).

Figure 10. Comparison of execution time (seconds) of Naïve Bayes, KNN(K=1), KNN(K=3), KNN(K=5), KNN(K=7), KNN(K=9) and Decision Tree

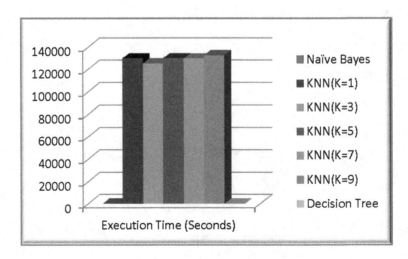

CONCLUSION AND FUTURE WORKS

Sentiment analysis based on micro-blogging is still in the developing stage and far from complete. As an example a positive sentiment is "It is a nice Day!" and a negative sentiment is "it is a horrible day!" In this paper, we will try to find out the positive and negative sentiment on Twitter data.

Sentiment analysis is essential for anyone who is going to make a decision. It is helpful in different field for calculating, identifying and expressing sentiment.

In this paper, we compared three algorithms Naïve Bayes, different versions of KNN (K=1, K=3, K=5, K=7 and K=9) and Decision Tree on 1059218 tweets (Instances). The experimental results show that the Decision Tree approach, giving above 90% accuracy and recall than the Naïve Bayes approach and the different versions of KNN approach.

And show that the different versions of KNN approach, giving above 80% precision and Number of tweets correctly classified than the Naïve Bayes approach and Decision Tree approach.

And finely show that the Decision Tree approach, giving above 85% F-Measure than the Naïve Bayes approach and different versions of KNN approach.

FUTURE WORKS

In this paper, we work with only the English tweets. So our next plan is to work with other language tweets. Apart from this, we will also try to detect another sentiment label of human being. From this, we can say that our future work list may contain the following actions:

- Accuracy calculation and performance evaluation: In current work, we use confusion matrix for calculating accuracy, precision recall and F-Measure. In future Apply others algorithms (meta-heuristics) to calculate accuracy, precision, recall and F-Measure, to improve current results.
- Focusing on detecting another sentiment label of human being: We only work with positive and negative sentiment label. We will extend our work to consider other sentiment labels (Neutral).
- Working with real world problems: Given an efficient sentiment label, we will try to see how it can be applied to solving real-world problems. As, for example, predicting presidential election, estimating product reputation, etc.

In this paper, we are mainly focusing on a general sentiment analysis like the positive and negative sentiment. There is the potential of work in the field of sentiment analysis and we will try to use our knowledge in this field. On the other hand, we would like to compare sentiment analysis with other domains.

REFERENCES

Ayetiran, E. F., & Adeyemo, A. B. (2012). A data mining-based response model for target selection in direct marketing. *IJ Information Technology and Computer Science*, *1*(1), 9–18. doi:10.5815/ijitcs.2012.01.02

Balahur, A., Steinberger, R., Kabadjov, M., Zavarella, V., Van Der Goot, E., Halkia, M., . . . Belyaeva, J. (2013). *Sentiment analysis in the news*. arXiv preprint arXiv:1309.6202

Dhande, L. L., & Patnaik, G. K. (2014). Analyzing sentiment of movie review data using Naïve Bayes neural classifier. *International Journal of Emerging Trends & Technology in Computer Science*, *3*(4), 313–320.

Fan, W., Wallace, L., Rich, S., & Zhang, Z. (2006). Tapping the power of text mining. *Communications of the ACM*, *49*(9), 76–82. doi:10.1145/1151030.1151032

Garnes, Ø. L. (2009). *Feature selection for text categorization* (Master's thesis). Institutt for datateknikk og informasjonsvitenskap.

Go, A., Bhayani, R., & Huang, L. (2009). Twitter sentiment classification using distant supervision. CS224N project report, Stanford, 1(12), 2009.

Jotheeswaran, J., & Koteeswaran, S. (2015). Decision tree based feature selection and multilayer perceptron for sentiment analysis. *Journal of Engineering and Applied Sciences (Asian Research Publishing Network)*, *10*(14), 5883–5894.

Kalaivani, P., & Shunmuganathan, K. L. (2013). Sentiment classification of movie reviews by supervised machine learning approaches. *Indian Journal of Computer Science and Engineering*, *4*(4), 285–292.

Kiritchenko, S., Zhu, X., & Mohammad, S. M. (2014). Sentiment analysis of short informal texts. *Journal of Artificial Intelligence Research*, *50*, 723–762. doi:10.1613/jair.4272

Liu, B. (2011). Opinion mining and sentiment analysis. In *Web Data Mining* (pp. 459–526). Springer. doi:10.1007/978-3-642-19460-3_11

Melucci, M. (2015). *Introduction to information retrieval and quantum mechanics*. Springer Berlin Heidelberg. doi:10.1007/978-3-662-48313-8

Modha, J. S., Pandi, G. S., & Modha, S. J. (2013). Automatic sentiment analysis for unstructured data. *International Journal of Advanced Research in Computer Science and Software Engineering*, *3*(12), 91–97.

Nazief, B., & Adriani, M. (1996). Confix Stripping: Approach to Stemming Algorithm for Bahasa Indonesia. Internal publication, Faculty of Computer Science, University of Indonesia, Depok, Jakarta, 41.

Pak, A., & Paroubek, P. (2010). Twitter as a corpus for sentiment analysis and opinion mining. In *LREc* (Vol. 10, pp. 1320–1326). Academic Press.

Prabowo, R., & Thelwall, M. (2009). Sentiment analysis: A combined approach. *Journal of Informetrics*, *3*(2), 143–157. doi:10.1016/j.joi.2009.01.003

Pratama, B. Y., & Sarno, R. (2015). Personality classification based on Twitter text using Naive Bayes, KNN and SVM. In *2015 International Conference on Data and Software Engineering (ICoDSE)* (pp. 170-174). IEEE. 10.1109/ICODSE.2015.7436992

Rambocas, M., & Gama, J. (2013). *Marketing research: The role of sentiment analysis* (No. 489). Universidade do Porto, Faculdade de Economia do Porto.

Suresh, A., & Bharathi, C. R. (2016). Sentiment classification using decision tree based feature selection. *IJCTA*, *9*(36), 419–425.

Vanitha, V., Sumathi, V. P., & Soundariya, V. (2018). An Exploratory Data Analysis of Movie Review Dataset. *International Journal of Recent Technology and Engineering.*, *7*(4S), 380–384.

Vo, D. T., & Zhang, Y. (2015). Target-dependent twitter sentiment classification with rich automatic features. *Twenty-Fourth International Joint Conference on Artificial Intelligence.*

Whissell, C. (2009). Using the revised dictionary of affect in language to quantify the emotional undertones of samples of natural language. *Psychological Reports*, *105*(2), 509–521. doi:10.2466/PR0.105.2.509-521 PMID:19928612

Wilson, T., Wiebe, J., & Hoffmann, P. (2009). Recognizing contextual polarity: An exploration of features for phrase-level sentiment analysis. *Computational Linguistics*, *35*(3), 399–433. doi:10.1162/coli.08-012-R1-06-90

Zhang, L., Ghosh, R., Dekhil, M., Hsu, M., & Liu, B. (2011). *Combining lexicon-based and learning-based methods for Twitter sentiment analysis*. HP Laboratories, Technical Report HPL-2011, 89.

Chapter 49
Effectiveness of Normalization Over Processing of Textual Data Using Hybrid Approach Sentiment Analysis

Sukhnandan Kaur Johal
Thapar Institute of Engineering and Technology, India

Rajni Mohana
Jaypee University of Information Technology, India

ABSTRACT

Various natural language processing tasks are carried out to feed into computerized decision support systems. Among these, sentiment analysis is gaining more attention. The majority of sentiment analysis relies on the social media content. This web content is highly un-normalized in nature. This hinders the performance of decision support system. To enhance the performance, it is required to process data efficiently. This article proposes a novel method of normalization of web data during the pre-processing phase. It is aimed to get better results for different natural language processing tasks. This research applies this technique on data for sentiment analysis. Performance of different learning models is analysed using precision, recall, f-measure, fallout for normalize and un-normalize sentiment analysis. Results shows after normalization, some documents shift their polarity i.e. negative to positive. Experimental results show normalized data processing outperforms un-normalized data processing with better accuracy.

1. INTRODUCTION

Natural language processing is a field of computational linguistics and artificial intelligence. It is the key to unlock various decisions using narrative web content. The automation of decision support system widely relies over the performance of natural language processors. Data available over the web sphere in various forms such as text, audio, video or pictures. Due to the arbitrary nature of the language, this data

DOI: 10.4018/978-1-6684-6303-1.ch049

is unstructured in nature. Efficiency of decision support system also gets affected by this unstructured data processing. This may sometimes hinder the performance of sentiment analyzer thus affecting the decision support system. As shown in Figure 1, initially, data is collected from the various social sites for automation of the decision support systems. Then data is pre-processed to get the structured content which includes removing the redundant content, cleaning and normalization. Later, various language processing tasks are carried out. Depending on the requirement, the results of the language processor are filtered out for the automation of decision support system. In this work, the result of sentiment analyzer (SA) is considered.

Figure 1. Automation of decision support system

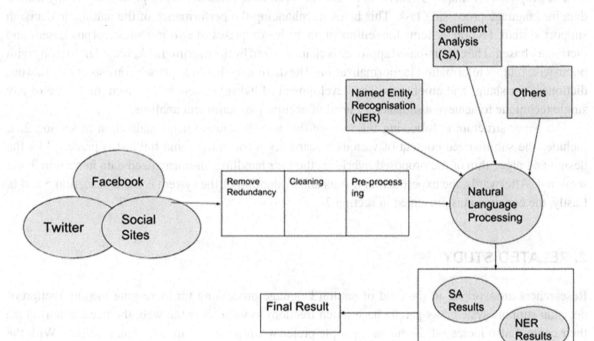

The proliferation of web data primarily as communication medium give rise to the existence of un-structured content in the form of posts, blogs, reviews, etc. This web data is rich indicator of people's reaction for any entity. This reaction of people is analyzed and termed as sentiment analysis in the field of natural language processing.

Classification of this web data into predefined categories, i.e. positive, negative or neutral is the task of sentiment analyzer. The web content is usually the raw data which is taken as an input by the senti-ment analyzer. To reduce the performance degradation, it is necessary to pre-process data efficiently. Given the importance to minimize the human intervention in sentiment analysis and to get better results, systematized and efficient mechanisms is the need of the hour. Normalization is the basic task to handle performance degradation of various natural language processing tasks. The term normalizes in past is taken as to just make the content in a well-structured format. These days normalize has broader term in the field of natural language processing. It includes handling slangs, spell correction, finding missing words, cleaning the text, etc. In this manuscript, the presented system design and algorithm is used to handle unstructured or noisy data for sentiment analysis.

1.1. Motivation and Contribution

The most important source of texts is undoubtedly the Web. The web content is full of unstructured content and slangs. The motivation behind our work is to process the semantically correct and methodologically useful content for sentiment analysis. To find the significant meaning or the replacements of each and every slang is the key concern of the work presented. It is a general methodology which can be embedded into various natural language applications to enhance their performance.

The proposed technique is generic in nature. This can be applied to the pre-processing of any textual data for language processing task. This helps in enhancing the performance of the automatic decision support system. Hybrid systems for sentiment analysis comprises of two modules: corpus based, and dictionary based. The corpus-based approach is characterized by the maximum likelihood ratio along with point-wise mutual information for normalization. The dictionary-based approach consists of a crossword dictionary for slangs and emoticons. The development of hybrid system stems from the failure of any single technique to achieve a satisfactory level of accuracy in sentiment analysis.

The paper structure is following the state-of-the-art algorithms for normalization in section 2. It includes the summarized content of various researchers work in the same field. It is preceded by the design and algorithm of the proposed hybrid method for handling un-normalized data in section 3 and section 4. Afterwards, the experimental results and evaluation of the system is done in section 5 and 6. Lastly, the conclusion is presented in section 7.

2. RELATED STUDY

Researchers are working in the field of natural language processing for increasing the automation of decision support system. As people have much freedom to write over the web, the need to normalize their content also increased. In the past, people prefer writing the text in the formal manner. With the rise in the web content, people prefer writing in short form, slangs, mistaken words, etc. It is needed to normalize the web content.

2.1. Pre-Processing

Nikola et al. (2014) have normalized the text using character-level statistical MAchine translation system and training through a manually annotated dataset. From their work, it is proved that automated normalization of data is more efficient than manual normalization. Dealing with slangs, was still in question. Their results were further modified by Francois et al. (2010). They have worked over the normalization of the textual data using weighted finite state transducers by using the phonemes. Results have shown that their system outperformed the state of art machine translation. Later, due to the growth in the free choice of writing over the internet people started writing in short forms. These short forms were taken as misspelled words by various language analyzers. Alistair et al. (2009) have used the variations in spellings written by people. For normalization training through the tool over human annotated dataset was used. They were also focused for correcting spelling for specific word i.e. keyword. Further, Deana et al. (2012) has proved the effectiveness of normalized text over the performance of text to speech system. Their research also helped normalization in gaining more attention. Pidong et al. (2013) presented an approach for normalization using machine translation. Correction of mistaken punctuation along with filling up with the missing words was included in their work. Results of proposed approach outperformed but its performance was completely depending over the translators effectiveness. Tyler et al. (2015) said in their work that normalization was not the matter of just replacing the words, but it actually depends on the target application. System was designed by them to handle domain dependent normalization. Congle et al. (2013) worked for performing all the necessary steps to have the formal structured content and have used the corpus-based technique for short message normalization. In their work, translation of the short messages to formal English language was handled. Hai et al. (2002) and Tetsuya et al. (2007) both normalized the text independent to the discipline in which it was used. Our approach is also based on this fact to have a normalized text for general purpose. Apart from the above-mentioned researchers, there are many other researchers who are working in the same field and a lot many to come.

2.2. Sentiment Analysis

Sentiment analysis is at the crossroads of Automatic Decision Support Systems, aims at finding the opinion regarding any entity by the web users. This work is proliferated with the rise in social media content and availability of writing freely over the internet. After efficient pre-processing of the text, it is applied for sentiment analysis over the given documents. In literature two kinds of approaches are conferred i.e. Corpus based and Dictionary Based. Both of these approaches have their own pros and cons. Corpus based approaches are basically depends upon the term frequency (Lopes et al., 2016) value for positive and negative terms appeared in any document. Yanyan et al. (2015) used fine gained corpus for not only detecting the sentiment but also the implicit aspect and the global entity about which the sentiment is generated. They have used camera and mobile phone reviews for their work. This also enhanced the work of implicit entity detection in sentiment analysis. In their work they have shown the importance of corpus-based sentiment analysis. Dictionary based approach is very significant in case of domain dependent sentiment analysis. The only drawback is to large volume of dictionary items gives better results. Basant et al. (2015) used domain dependent semantic orientation for sentiment analysis. Lexicon based approach for sentiment analysis was used by them. The investigation of the feature importance and contextual information in deducing the sentiment has done by them. Out performance of the results of their system with respect to the state of art sentiment analyzers was shown in their work. Chloe et al. (2016) have identified the circumstances for the growth of individual advancement for cross-disciplinary work. Dictionary based approach was included. In their work, they have primarily embedded artificial intelligence in the form of neural networks for opinion mining. Different agent-based approaches are employed for their work. Their work results are significant in some areas but are not generic in nature. Later, people work in finding the relation of various entities in the field of sentiment analysis. This further increases the need of having efficient sentiment analyzers. Basant et al. (2015) used random walk and iterative regression for first building concept level lexicon. They have used commonsense for the annotation of the lexicons. Later, Desheng et al. (2013) have found the correlation between stock price and the reviews of stock finance through sentiment analysis. Their work highlights the need of accessing the reviews efficiently for automation of decision support system. Desheng et al. (2014) developed a strategy to extract sentiment from textual as well as visual web data in a combined way. The results are better as compared to state-of-art sentiment analysis in Chinese language as well as visual sentiment analysis individually. In the field of linguistic analysis, emoticons are considered important as another context by Yuhai et al. (2016). Lipika et al. (2017) highlight various issues in sentiment analysis. Monireh et al. (2017) have used sentiment analysis in presidential election to check the popularity of the candidate. From the recent studies, it is analyzed people use social data for various natural language processing tasks such as named entity recognition, text summarization, sentiment analysis, etc. This raised the need of effective processing of the data. Data over the web is very noisy i.e. contains emoticons, slangs, misspelled words, etc. For effective results this noisy data needs to be normalized. Researchers use either dictionary-based technique or corpus based approach to deal with the noisy data. This paper proposes a novel hybrid approach which uses lexicon and corpus-based approach in a combined manner.

3. METHODOLOGY

The hybrid framework of the proposed system for sentiment analysis primarily consist pre-processing and sentiment strength calculation as shown in Figure 2. Pre-processing further includes tokenization, cleaning of data and normalization. Out of these, normalization affects the results to a great deal. It consists two stages for normalization:

- Handling emoticons or slangs using pre-defined list of positive and negative emoticons along with cross word dictionary.
- Handling slangs using maximum likelihood ratio.

For normalization, a corpus-based module and a dictionary-based module as a pre-processing of the textual data is included. It is composed of rich vocabulary of slangs in the form of crossword dictionary and a corpus-based term frequency vector for bigrams and trigrams. The maximum likelihood of the next word is calculated using maximum likelihood ratio. The proposed system is discussed in detail as follows:

3.1 Pre-Processing of the Text

Pre-processing of the unstructured web contents is the major task to enhances the performance of sentiment analyser. It includes tokenization, normalization, stemming, etc.

3.1.1 Tokenization

It is the process of breaking down the input into small units. The delimiter used for the text based on space between words. It can be at word level, character level or sentence level. In this manuscript, word level tokenization is used. As shown in Table 1 which tokens need normalization.

Table 1. Tokenization

This is very gud phone and btry life is very long. Tokenized text: This(1), is(2), very(3), gud(4), phone(5), and(6), btry(7), life(8), is(9), very(10), long(11). Input = 1 document. Output = 11 tokens with their respective index values.

Figure 2. Proposed system design

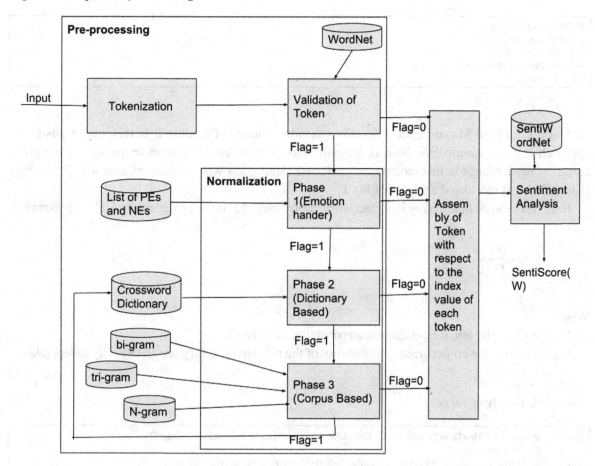

3.1.2 Normalization

Normalization of the web content basically includes 2 modules. These modules are explained in further sections individually. For an instance, Table 2 shows the list of tokens which need to be normalized.

Module 1: Phase 1 and Phase 2 from Figure 1 are included in module 1. Tokens are processed using normalized dictionary-based approach. In this phase, the validity of the word is calculated using English WordNet. The slangs, emoticons or noisy text is replaced using cross word dictionary. Here, positive and negative emoticons are replaced with their respective meaning i.e. means happy, means sad and many more. If the replacement is found in the pre-defined dictionary, then the whole text is assembled in assembly phase.

Table 2. Segregation of Un-Normalized tokens

Input: Tokenized text: This(1), is(2), very(3), gud(4), phone(5), and(6), btry(7), life(8), is(9), very(10), long(11).
Output 1(valid words as per wordnet): This(1), is(2), very(3), good(4), phone(5), and(6), life(8), is(9), very(10), long(11).
Output 2(invalid words as per wordnet): btry(7), gud(4)

Table 3. Normalization based on PMI

PMI(life—battery) = 0.32 PMI(life— animal) = 0.31 PMI(life—the) = 0.01 Maximum likelihood value = 0.32 Output: battery(7)

Module 2: Phase 3 from Figure 2 describes the functionality of module 2. In this, the corpus-based approach is used to normalize the text. Bigrams and trigrams based on term frequency for the given corpus is used. Slangs in this module are corrected using point-wise mutual information (PMI). PMI (Khan, 2016) is calculated using Equation 1.

If 't1' is the word followed by incorrect word or the slang. 't2' is the predecessor of 't1' in bigram list,

$$\text{PMI}\left(\frac{t1}{t2}\right) = log\frac{\Pr\left(t1 \wedge t2\right)}{\Pr\left(t1\right)\Pr\left(t2\right)} \tag{1}$$

Where,

Pr(t1 ∧ t2) is the actual co-occurrence probability of t1 and t2.

Pr(t1)Pr(t2) is the co-occurrence probability of the two terms, if they are statistically independent.

Table 4. Assembly of Tokens

Input (From module 1): This(1), is(2), very(3), good(4), phone(5), and(6), life(8), is(9), very(10), long(11). (From module 2): battery (7), Output: This(1), is(2), very(3), good(4), phone(5), and(6), battery(7), life(8), is(9), very(10), long(11)

Maximum likelihood is calculated using PMI. Maximum likelihood (Jae, 2003) can be defined as a method to find the value of one or more parameters for a given statistic which makes the known the likelihood distribution a maximum. After calculating the maximum likelihood, the misspelled word is replaced with the word having maximum value of PMI. For this OvA (one-vs-all) strategy is used to handle the slangs. As an example, it is shown in Table 3. Both of the modules are implemented using Algorithm 1.

Algorithm 1. Normalization

Input: Document(D)containing noisy data, where $D = d_1, d_2, d_3, \ldots\ldots, d_n$

'n' is the total number of documents Initial list of Bi-grams and tri-grams

Initial list of Positive emoticons (PE) and negative emoticons (NE) with their corresponding meaning

List of Stopwords 'SW'

Standard English Dictionary (Wordnet) 'W'

Crossword Dictionary containing normalized slangs (C_d)

List of assembled Words (L_w)

```
Set i ← 1
for d∈ (d₁, d₂, d₃, ....., dₙ) do
Tokenization
for tᵢ ∈ (t₁, t₂, t₃, ....., tₙ) do
if tᵢ ∈ SW then
Discard
else if tᵢ ∈ W then
append tᵢ to L_w
Appnd tᵢ with respective index value to (L_w)
else if tᵢ ∈ (PE ∪ NE) then
Replace tᵢ with normalized word from PE or NE
Appnd tᵢ with respective index value to (L_w)
else if tᵢ ∈ C_d then
Apply maximum likelihood ratio based on pointwise mutual gain of bigram and
trigram for slang replacement
Appnd tᵢ with respective index value to (L_w)
end if
end for
end for
Apply SentiStrength(L_w)
```

3.2. Assembly of Tokens

In this phase, ensemble of tokens is the key concern according to their respective index values. This is very important part of the system to retain the semantic orientation of the words. As if any negative pointer such as not is misplaced, it may produce wrong results. So, the words are needed to be studded as per their original index values illustrated in Table 4.

Algorithm 2. SentiStrength()
   INPUT:
   Document(D)containing noisy data,
   where $D = d_1, d_2, d_3 \ldots\ldots\ldots d_n$.
   'n' is the total number of documents
   OUTPUT:

```
Ws(Weighted SentiStrength of each document)
// Token list(T) = t₁,t₂, t₃,.........tₘ.
// Word list(W) = w₁,w₂, w₃,.........w_q.
// 'q' is the total number of words in a document
// 'm' is the total number of tokens in a document
// 'Lₙ' is the list of Positive words in a document
// 'L_p' is the list of Negative words in a document
// 'P_w ' is the weight of positive term as per SentiWordNet
// 'N_w' is the weight of negative term as per SentiWordNet
```

```
Set j← 1
for d_i ε D do
Stemming
Normalization
Tokenize(T)
for t_i ε t_1,t_2, t_3,.............. t_m do
if (t_i ε W) ∩(t_i ε L_p) then
W_pos(i) = P_w(t_i)
else if (t_i ε W) ∩ (t_i ε L_n) then
W_neg(i) = N_w(t_i)
else if ((t_i ε W) ∩ (t_i ε L_n) ∩(t_i ε L_p)) then
W_neu(i) = 0
end if
end for
```

$$Ws = \sum_{j=1}^{n} Wpos(j) \pm \sum_{j=1}^{n} Wneg(j)$$

```
end for
```

3.3. Senti-Strength Calculation

After the completion of normalization of the whole document text, the standard sentiment analysis algorithm is applied to it. SentiWordnet (Stefano,2010) is used for the experimental work. Senti-Strength Algorithm (Algorithm 2) is used to find the exact classification i.e. positive or negative with the magnitude calculated using Senti-WordNet.

4. EXPERIMENTAL RESULTS

4.1. Dataset

For the experimental setup, a dataset from the SMS Spam Collection v.1 corpus and blogs of 134 customers (Lipika, 2009) is used. The corpus is a collection of 5,574 English messages. The corpus is representative sample for public data available over the web sphere. To build the dataset, a manual filtration was done to the data by removing hash tags, hyperlinks, etc. For the analysis of results Gold standard of the dataset is built by the linguistic experts.

4.2. Evaluation

In this section, the results are explored based on the automatic normalization of the content using hybrid approach. To examine the results, a common evaluation method was used as described in performance matrix i.e. recall, precision, accuracy, fallout and measure. All the documents used for experimentation contained short messages. Due to which, there is no need to apply the dimension reduction approach to it. In Table 5, the results are presented based on supervised approach, like SVM, Naive Bayes and k-NN.

Table 5. Results based on normalized and un-normalized datasets

Dataset	Model	Precision	Recall	Accuracy	F-measure	Fallout
Un-normalized	SVM	66.74	64.91	79.55	65.81	40
Un-normalized	NB	55.69	56.14	68.57	55.91	2.68
Un-normalized	k-NN	51.38	50.91	73.33	51.14	59.18
Normalized	SVM	67.95	66.14	79.55	66.79	24.77
Normalized	NB	59.93	60.68	73.44	60.33	2.45
Normalized	k-NN	53.29	52.05	75.16	52.66	59.02

These results are divided into two categories: Normalized dataset and Un-normalized dataset. The results obtained by the proposed method are graphically shown in Figure 3. On comparison, it is found that results are better for the normalized dataset than un-normalized. This shows the importance of normalization for any natural language processing task. Another significance of normalized data is reduction in fallout in case of SVM. For Naive-Bayes and k-NN, less significant results are found in fallout for normalized and un-normalized dataset. On the contrary, it is found that the recall and precision values are raised in normalized data processing. Figure 4 shows the performance of various supervised approaches. Results are better using SVM. It is noticeable that there is a trade-off between recall and fallout, precision and fallout. Naive Bayes gives minimum fallout. The highest value of fallout in k-NN reduces its performance in some cases wherever there is a need for less fallout value. It depends on the application and domain to choose the learning algorithm.

Figure 3. Comparison of performance based on un-normalized (UN) and Normalized(N) Data

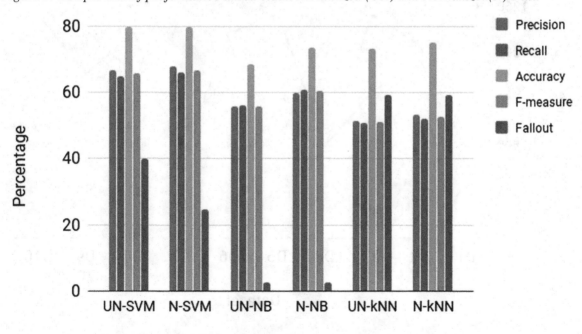

Figure 4. Performance evaluation based on supervised learning

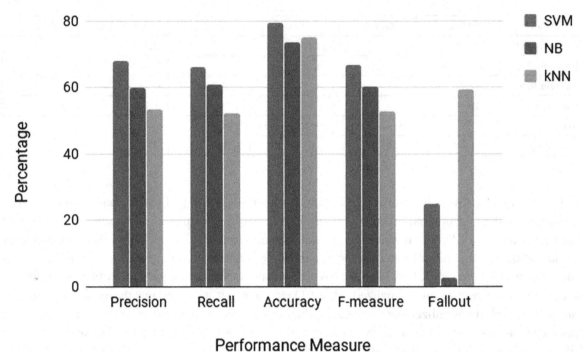

Figure 5. Classification of reviews in positive and negative category using baseline approach

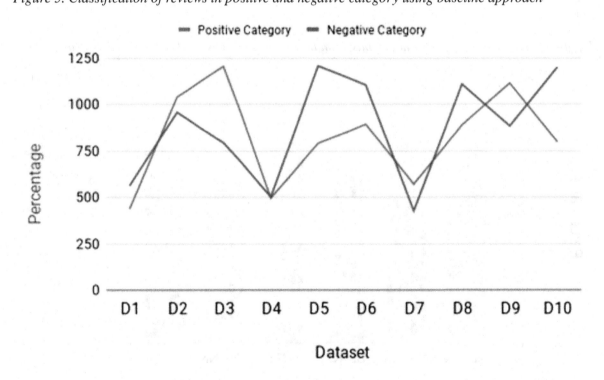

Figure 6. Classification of reviews in positive and negative category using proposed approach

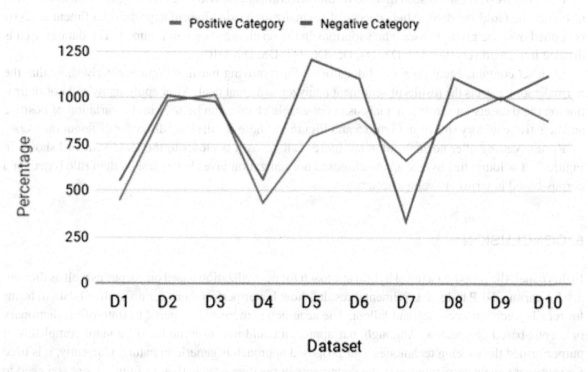

Figure 7: Effectiveness of proposed approach

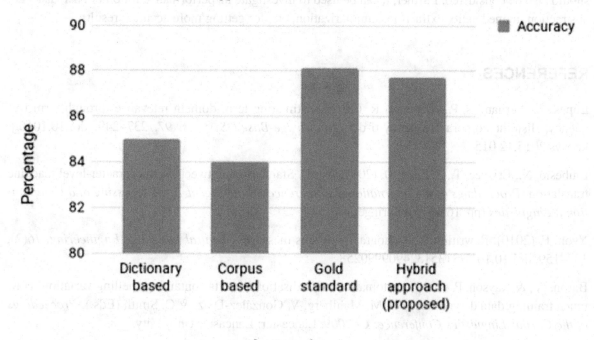

From Figure 7, it can be seen that the results are comparable with the rule based, corpus-based and also with the Gold standard. After successful normalization using hybrid approach, sentiment analysis is applied over the given dataset. The variations in the result are shown in Figure 3. The dataset used is divided into small sets (D1, D2, D3, D4, D5, D6, D7, D8, D9, D10).

Each set contains equal number of documents for removing biasing. Figures clearly show that the normalization affects the results of sentiment analyzer to a great deal. After applying hybrid normalization on the datasets for sentiment analysis, a noticeable change can be seen in the variation of positive and negative category shown in Figure 5 and Figure 6. These results may differ for different dataset.

Results getting after normalization are more realistic as it is closer to the Gold standard shown in Figure 7. It is found that hybrid approach-based normalization gives better results than rule based, and corpus-based in terms of average accuracy.

5. CONCLUSION

In this paper, the proposed a novel hybrid approach for normalization based on corpus as well as dictionary for various NLP tasks. Experimental results show better performance for normalized data in terms for recall, precision, accuracy and fallout. The accuracy is more as compared to state-of-art dictionary or corpus-based approaches. Although, our approach could not meet the Gold standard completely, it outperformed the existing techniques. Our proposed approach is generic in nature. Currently, it is used for sentiment analysis to categorize the documents in positive or negative. In future, there is a need to employ sentiment analysis using proposed approach over bigger dataset. In addition, neutral opinion should also be considered. Further, it can be used to investigate its performance for other NLP tasks i.e. abstraction, named entity extraction, summarization, etc. for getting more accurate results.

REFERENCES

Lopes, L., Fernandes, P., & Vieira, R. (2016). Estimating term domain relevance through term frequency, disjoint corpora frequency-tf-dcf. *Knowledge-Based Systems*, *97*, 237–249. doi:10.1016/j.knosys.2015.12.015

Ljubešić, N., Erjavec, T., & Fišer, D. (2014, April). Standardizing tweets with character-level machine translation. *Proceedings of the International Conference on Intelligent Text Processing and Computational Linguistics* (pp. 164-175). Springer.

Yvon, F. (2010). Rewriting the orthography of sms messages. *Natural Language Engineering*, *16*(2), 133–159. doi:10.1017/S1351324909990258

Baron, A., & Rayson, P. (2009). Automatic standardisation of texts containing spelling variation: How much training data do you need? In M. Mahlberg, V. González-Díaz, & C. Smith (Eds.), *Proceedings of the Corpus Linguistics Conference: CL2009*. Lancaster: Lancaster University.

Pennell, D. L., & Liu, Y. (2012), Evaluating the effect of normalizing informal text on tts output. Proceedings of the Spoken Language Technology Workshop SLT 2012 (pp. 479–483). IEEE Press. doi:10.1109/SLT.2012.6424271

Wang, P., & Ng, H. T. (2013, June). A beam-search decoder for normalization of social media text with application to machine translation. *Proceedings of the 2013 Conference of the North American Chapter of the Association for Computational Linguistics: Human Language Technologies* (pp. 471-481). Academic Press.

Baldwin, T., & Li, Y. (2015). An in-depth analysis of the effect of text normalization in social media. Proceedings of the 2015 Conference of the North American Chapter of the Association for Computational Linguistics: Human Language Technologies (pp. 420-429). Academic Press. doi:10.3115/v1/N15-1045

Zhang, C., Baldwin, T., Ho, H., Kimelfeld, B., & Li, Y. (2013, August). Adaptive parser-centric text normalization. Proceedings of the 51st Annual Meeting of the Association for Computational Linguistics (Vol. 1, pp. 1159-1168). ACL.

Chieu, H. L., & Ng, H. T. (2002). A maximum entropy approach to information extraction from semi-structured and free text. *Aaai/iaai*, 786-791.

Nasukawa, T., Punjani, D., Roy, S., Subramaniam, L. V., & Takeuchi, H. (2007). Adding sentence boundaries to conversational speech transcriptions using noisily labelled examples. *Proc. of AND07 Workshop in conjunction with IJCAI*, Hyderabad, India. Academic Press.

Zhao, Y., Qin, B., & Liu, T. (2015). Creating a fine-grained corpus for Chinese sentiment analysis. *IEEE Intelligent Systems*, *30*(1), 36–43. doi:10.1109/MIS.2014.33

Agarwal, B., Mittal, N., Bansal, P., & Garg, S. (2015). Sentiment analysis using common-sense and context information. *Computational Intelligence and Neuroscience*, *2015*, 1–9. doi:10.1155/2015/715730 PMID:25866505

Clavel, C. & Callejas, Z. (2016). Sentiment analysis: from opinion mining to human-agent interaction. *IEEE Transactions on affective computing, 7*(1), 74–93.

Tsai, A. C.-R., Wu, C.-E., Tsai, R. T.-H., & Hsu, J. Y. (2013). Building a concept-level sentiment dictionary based on commonsense knowledge. *IEEE Intelligent Systems*, *28*(2), 22–30. doi:10.1109/MIS.2013.25

Wu, D. D., Zheng, L., & Olson, D. L. (2014). A decision support approach for online stock forum sentiment analysis. *IEEE Transactions on Systems, Man, and Cybernetics. Systems*, *44*(8), 1077–1087. doi:10.1109/TSMC.2013.2295353

Yu, Y., Lin, H., Meng, J., & Zhao, Z. (2016). Visual and textual sentiment analysis of a microblog using deep convolutional neural networks. *Algorithms*, *9*(2), 1–41. doi:10.3390/a9020041

Cambria, E., Poria, S., Gelbukh, A., & Thelwall, M. (2017). Sentiment analysis is a big suitcase. *IEEE Intelligent Systems*, *32*(6), 74–80. doi:10.1109/MIS.2017.4531228

Ebrahimi, M., Yazdavar, A. H., & Sheth, A. (2017). Challenges of sentiment analysis for dynamic events. *IEEE Intelligent Systems*, *32*(5), 70–75. doi:10.1109/MIS.2017.3711649

Khan, F. H., Qamar, U., & Bashir, S. (2016). Sentimi: Introducing point-wise mutual information with sentiwordnet to improve sentiment polarity detection. *Applied Soft Computing*, *39*, 140–153. doi:10.1016/j.asoc.2015.11.016

Myung, I. J. (2003). Tutorial on maximum likelihood estimation. *Journal of Mathematical Psychology*, *47*(1), 90–100. doi:10.1016/S0022-2496(02)00028-7

Baccianella, S., Esuli, A., & Sebastiani, F. (2010, May). Sentiwordnet 3.0: An enhanced lexical resource for sentiment analysis and opinion mining. *Lrec*, *10*, 2200–2204.

Dey, L., & Haque, S. M. (2009). Opinion mining from noisy text data. *International Journal on Document Analysis and Recognition*, *12*(3), 205–226. doi:10.100710032-009-0090-z

This research was previously published in the International Journal of Grid and High Performance Computing (IJGHPC), 12(3); pages 43-56, copyright year 2020 by IGI Publishing (an imprint of IGI Global).

Chapter 50
Chatbot Experiences of Informal Language Learners:
A Sentiment Analysis

Antonie Alm
University of Otago, New Zealand

Larian M. Nkomo
University of Otago, New Zealand

ABSTRACT

In 2016, a number of language applications released chatbots to complement their programmes. Used primarily in informal learning settings, chatbots enable language learners to engage in conversational speaking practice, which can be perceived as less threatening than face-to-face interactions with native speakers. This study takes a closer look at four second language (L2) chatbots—Duolingo, Eggbun, Memrise, and Mondly—and analyses the experiences which informal language learners expressed on various online platforms (e.g., Duolingo forum, Memrise community, Reddit). Results indicate a degree of curiosity and a willingness to engage in conversation with chatbots. However, learners expressed frustration if the dialogues did not correspond to their learning goals or if they were excluded from using the bots because of technical or payment issues, or discontinuation of services.

INTRODUCTION

Chatbots have come a long way since *Eliza*, the computer program developed in the 1960s, that gave users the (short-term) illusion of conversing with a Rogerian psychotherapist. Weizenbaum's (1966) aim was to study the "natural language communication between man and machine" (p. 36), yet it is the appealing idea of virtual personal assistants that has prevailed, having led to successful applications in business, personal development and education. Language learners, in particular, can benefit from this development to increase opportunities for conversational practice, starting with talking to their smartphone's voice assistant, or by using any general app in their second language (L2). For example, *Luka*

DOI: 10.4018/978-1-6684-6303-1.ch050

advises on restaurants, weather and news; *Lark* is a pocket coach and nutritionist; *Penny*, a virtual bank manager; or *Hello Hipmunk*, a reactive travel consultant. These virtual assistants not only provide good language practice if used in the L2, they also have real-life relevance.

In technology circles, 2016 has been named the year of the chatbot (Olson, 2016). As Dale (2016) points out, a lot has changed in 50 years of chatbot history. The contemporary AI-powered therapy chatbot *Woebot* illustrates the advances in chatbot development, and in people's attitudes towards the virtual assistants. Unlike *Eliza*, who relied on pre-programmed responses (such as: *Can you elaborate on that?*), *Woebot* uses natural language processing to adapt and personalise its replies, providing advice based on principles of Cognitive Behavioural Therapy (CBT). With the development of technology, people have changed their modes of communication, and short typed interactions have become an everyday occurrence (Dale, 2016). Significantly, people are comfortable turning to a machine to talk about their problems. It is not only the convenience of accessibility; people seem to feel less judged talking to a bot rather than talking to a human (Lucas, Gratch, King, & Morency, 2014).

A keen learner of English might well make use of *Woebot* to get additional speaking practice. For learners of other languages, a range of L2 chatbots became available in 2016, either as stand-alone apps or as add-ons for language applications. Similarly, these bots enable language learners to engage anytime in language practice, also providing a safe space to hone conversational language skills. Accessible as apps on smartphones, L2 chatbots are not only available to language learners in educational settings, but to anyone who seeks to practise an L2. Godwin-Jones (2017) sees smartphones as the principal enabler of the growth of informal language learning, that is self-initiated and self-directed learning outside a formal institutional setting (Lai, 2019; Lange, 2019). The rise in informal online learning, also referred to as the *digital wilds* (Sauro & Zourou, 2019) is a topical issue in Computer Assisted Language Learning (CALL) (Dressman & Sadler, 2020). The use of language chatbots in informal language learning, however, is underexplored.

L2 Chatbots

Chatbots are software programs that simulate human conversations (Berns, Mota, Ruiz-Rube, & Dodero, 2018; Fryer, Ainley, Thompson, Gibson, & Sherlock, 2017; Wang & Petrina, 2013). Stewart and File (2007) assert that language learners often struggle in social conversations in the early stages of learning a language as they have little opportunity to practice. However, computer dialogue systems which expose learners to social conversations could offer a good environment for L2 learners to practice their social conversation skills (Stewart & File, 2007). Such systems can be seen as earlier versions of language learning chatbots. Some criticism has centred on the inability of bots to simulate natural conversations, as responses were frequently selected from a list of options (see Chiu, Liou, & Yeh, 2007; Coniam, 2008a; Sha, 2009). Stewart and File (2007), however, argued that conversations in real life are formulaic and that systems allowing users to select responses therefore do not deviate much from normal conversation. Coniam (2008b) highlights the convenience factor of using chatbots for L2 speaking practice, as they are more accessible to many language learners, especially beginners, than human conversation partners. Chatbots provide a convenient platform for written or spoken conversations (Macayan, Quinto, Otsuka, & Cueto, 2018). Fryer and Carpenter (2006) found that language students enjoyed using chatbots. They expressed being more comfortable in conversation with the chatbots than with human partners. Chatbots also provide a dialogue partner that is patient, can handle multiple learners and is not too critical (Kessler, 2018; Stickler & Hampel, 2015). Furthermore, chatbots can support those who may be attempting to overcome shyness and anxiety associated with learning a new language (Fryer et al., 2017).

Coniam (2008a) investigated the potential linguistic value of chatbot programs as a resource for L2 learning. The study evaluated the ability of several chatbots to hold a conversation and how they handled grammatically incorrect user inputs. The study found the chatbots worked best when input sentences were simple everyday sentences, however, some of the evaluated chatbots had the ability to deal with misspelt phrases, although in an erratic manner. In a further study, Coniam (2008b) looked at the pedagogical potential of six chatbots that could be utilised in the context of English as a second language (ESL). The selection of the six chatbots was based on their ability to interact from a language perspective and the attractiveness of the interface. The appearance and functionality evaluations were based on six features: screen design and layout, quality of sounds and graphics, appearance and attractiveness of chatbot, program's speed of response, ease of use of the program, and features offered. As in Coniam (2008a), evaluators were ESL trainees. The study identified similar findings to Coniam (2008a) in that while holding great potential, the chatbots were not that smart, as they functioned better in straightforward conversations.

Coniam (2014) looked at the linguistic accuracy of five notable chatbots. The study found the grammar of the chatbots to be generally acceptable, however, in most cases the answers provided by the bots had no meaning, with the study concluding that chatbots as tools for conversation practice were not yet robust chatting partners. Fryer et al. (2017) found that novelty influences technology-enhanced tasks, and therefore tasks that first appear to be stimulating may not have a sustained appeal to users. This was done through an experimental study to understand the long-term effects of technology on students' task and course interest where students were involved in different speaking tasks with a human and with a chatbot partner. In a recent study, Fryer, Nakao, and Thompson (2019) indicated chatbots were a solution to learners' difficulty in obtaining conversation practice, however, they have not realised their potential as practice partners. The study found that interest in chatbot communication was linked to prior interest in human conversation partners and language competence. Furthermore, communication difficulties were overcome by those learners who had a strong interest in chatbot conversations.

There is an indication that previous, related studies have used somewhat subjective measures to understand the abilities of chatbots as a resource for language learning. Furthermore, most studies related to language learning situations in formal settings. However, chatbots provide opportunities for language learning outside formally structured learning environments. Without the academic and emotional support typically found in a classroom setting (teachers providing guidance and feedback, peers enabling L2-related and social interaction), informal language learners are in charge of creating their own learning environment. This study investigates the role of chatbots in this process. It utilises sentiment analysis and thematic analysis of user data in relation to four L2 chatbots to address the following research question:

What are the experiences of informal language learners when engaging with L2 chatbots?

Methods and Data Collection

This study utilises data collected from various online platforms where language learners discussed their experiences of chatbots for language learning. The applications are *Duolingo*, *Memrise*, *Eggbun* and *Mondly*. *Duolingo* bots were powered by artificial intelligence and, according to the developers, offered learners real life conversations to help with conversational practice without the anxiety and awkwardness associated with face-to-face conversations (*Duolingo*, 2016; Von Ahn, 2016). *Mondly* launched a version of their application that helped learners practice their speaking skills through conversational chatbots. The chatbots combine chatbot technology, speech-recognition platforms and object recognition systems (Iliescu, 2016). The vocabulary app *Memrise* launched what it termed a 'grammarbot' to help learners with their grammar (Rawlings, 2017). The app provided interaction with the chatbots by constructing text-based conversations through selecting words from a list (Kreisa, n.d.). It also had a conversational chatbot for speaking practice. The chatbots appeared randomly as users progressed through the vocabulary app. *Eggbun* is a stand-alone chatbot app. It provides a platform for learners to achieve conversational fluency in languages with a tutor named Lanny (*Eggbun* Education, 2017; Moon, 2017). The *Eggbun* tutor chatbot offers text-based dialogues as well as audio examples, and helps with grammar and vocabulary (Kreisa, n.d.).

The aim of this study was to analyse data generated by users from various online platforms where language learners discussed their experiences of using chatbots for language learning. The platforms identified for data collection were social media networks, blogs as well as website forums. As a result, different size datasets were obtained and analysed in this study. When the population in a study is not well defined, non-probability sampling can be utilised (Etikan, Musa, & Alkassim, 2016). Therefore, purposive sampling was employed.

To collect the user comments from each of these platforms, web data scrapping techniques, that is the automated process of compiling data from web pages (Bonifacio, Barchyn, Hugenholtz, & Kienzle, 2015; Landers, Brusso, Cavanaugh, & Collmus, 2016), were utilised. A summary of the data sources is provided in table 1. Furthermore, a comparison of the respective bots based on their linguistic sophistication, autonomy, and features is provided in table 2.

Data Analysis

The data collected from the web pages were mostly qualitative. Therefore, two types of analysis were conducted. The data was first compiled and thematically analysed using *NVivo* software. The process involved reading and re-reading the reviews (Braun & Clarke, 2006) to identify themes within segments of text associated with the reviews and coded for prevalence as well as the frequency of occurrences. The qualitative data were further analysed using sentiment analysis, natural language processing (NLP) text analysis and a computational technique for the automation of the classification of sentiment (Hussein, 2018).

Table 1. Data Sources

Application	Data Source	Topics of discussion
Duolingo	*Duolingo* Forum	User experience with the bots
Memrise	*Memrise* community, Reddit	User experience with the bots
Mondly	Facebook, Reddit, Blogs, Google Play (Sensor Tower), Appstore (Sensor Tower)	User experience with the bots
Eggbun	Facebook Reviews Reddit, Google Play (Sensor Tower), Appstore (Sensor Tower)	User experience with the bots

Table 2. Comparison of Chatbot abilities

Name	Linguistic sophistication	Autonomy	Features
Duolingo	Recognises different input	Accepts some alternative answers Suggests alternative (better) responses Offers several pathways	Speech recognition Help me reply option Offers translation
Memrise	Words and emojis are selected from a list	Only recognises predefined answers (words or emojis) User must start again after making a wrong selection Offers more than one pathway	Voice recording
Mondly	Alternates questions in scenarios	Recognises different input and accepts some alternative answers Three different replies for wrong answers Offers only one pathway	Voice Recognition Offers translation
Eggbun	Recognises only a narrow range of input	Is not able to respond to unexpected input Gives a standard reply for wrong answer Offers only one pathway but user can change path through answers (yes, no) to enter different selections	Uses voice recordings, prompts user to pronounce words

Sentiment analysis can be used to examine semantic relationships and meaning in people's experiences. It provides an understanding of their feelings towards a particular entity; therefore, sentiment analysis is used in reviews of products, movies and politics, among others. Services such as *Twitter* and online feedback forums are increasingly used to express opinions, so it has become of interest to identify the sentiment of the generated messages (Kiritchenko, Zhu, & Mohammad, 2014; Veletsianos, Kimmons, Larsen, Dousay, & Lowenthal, 2018). In the context of language learning, sentiment analysis has been used to identify sentiments of students in Massive Open Online Courses regarding elements such as peer assessment as well as sentiments that scholars may face online (see Veletsianos et al., 2018; Wen, Yang, & Rose, 2014). In language learning, though the application of sentiment analysis approach is limited, it is essential because identifying L2 learners' experiences with features such as chatbots may enable platform providers to understand how these chatbots support language learning in informal learning settings.

To better understand the experiences of users, data were collected to reflect experiences with the respective applications over several years, from when they were launched to their most recent versions. Some of the comments harvested were in languages other than English. Therefore, comments in languages that could not be analysed through the tools, were translated into English through *Google Translate*. The translation service has been found to have some errors (Groves & Mundt, 2015) and therefore it is possible that some translated text lost context. However, a recent study by Tsai (2019) indicated that English as a first language students were happy to utilise *Google Translate* for their English writing. This can be an indication that the service is improving its accuracy.

Sentiment Analysis

Sentiment is mainly rated on a scale between 0 and 1, with scores closer to 1 indicating positive sentiment and scores closer to 0 indicating negative sentiment (Barga, Fontama, Tok, & Cabrera-Cordon, 2015), however, sentiments can also be expressed in an n-point scale, e.g., very good, good, satisfactory, bad, very bad (Prabowo & Thelwall, 2009).

In this study *Microsoft Azure Cognitive Services* text analytics API was utilised. The service utilises a machine-learning classification algorithm that is trained with a large text dataset with records that are labelled for sentiment from 0 to 1. This is done by tokenising the input text into individual words and by stemming.

The features used to train the classifier are then constructed from those words. N-grams, part-of-speech tagging and word embedding were used so that the classifier could predict the sentiment of any new text after it was trained (Nagender, 2015). N-grams represent all occurrences of *n* consecutive words in the input text, parts-of-speech tagging identifies words that relate to a particular part of speech, and word embedding represents assigning words or phrases that are syntactically similar closer together. When determining the sentiment, the text goes through an objectivity assessment phase, where the model determines whether the text is objective or contains sentiment.

The text does not advance to the sentiment detection phase if it is highly objective, and will result in a .50 score (neutral), with no further processing. If the text advances, the next phase generates a score above or below .50, depending on the degree of sentiment detected in the text (Hill et al., 2019). A sentiment score > 0.7 indicates high positive sentiment, whereas < 0.4 indicates low negative sentiment, with a sentiment score range between 0.4-0.7 indicating neutral sentiment (Chatterjee & Perrizo, 2016). The sentiment analysis tool used in this study does not provide the user with the ability to pre-train the dataset, therefore making the researcher reliant on the pre-trained classifier provided by the service. Furthermore, the service does not consider the context of the text. It is also more accurate with shorter sentences and less accurate on larger blocks of text (Hill et al., 2019). Due to these factors, some of the results may not have been accurately scored for sentiment as they do not consider the context of the text. However, the service outperforms other services such as the *Stanford NLP Sentiment Analysis* engine (using its pre-trained sentiment model) on short as well as longer blocks of text (Chatterjee & Perrizo, 2016) making it a viable option for performing sentiment analysis. Further, a significant number of the sentiment scores were accurate.

Results

The findings from this study indicate that learners' experiences with chatbots for language learning are mixed. Learners were generally intrigued with the idea of using chatbots for language learning, although the bots were perceived to have their limitations.

The results of the sentiment analysis in table 3 indicate user experiences with the *Duolingo* chatbots from the introduction of the chatbots in October 2016 until they were removed by the providing company in April 2018. In relation to topic 1, there was a general positive sentiment of 65.58% towards the introduction of the bots, as users were optimistic regarding the possibilities of the chatbots as language-learning tools. Mostly positive sentiments were also obtained from users discussing topic 2 (56.25%). In topic 3, comments were mostly positive (71.4%). Most of the comments in relation to testing the bots were positive (78.85% and 55.36%), as illustrated in topics 4 and 5 respectively. The sentiment towards the idea of bringing back the bots after they were removed was mostly positive, as users seemingly mostly enjoyed their experiences with the bots. This is indicated through the positive sentiment (53.06%, 56% and 66.13%) in topics 6, 7 and 8 respectively. An example of the text and sentiment scores is shown in table 4.

Table 3. Duolingo (Source: Duolingo Forums)

Code	Question	Sentiment	Frequency (%)	Year
Topic 1	*Meet your new language tutors: the Duolingo Bots*	Negative	264 (24.63)	
		Neutral	105 (9.79)	2016
		Positive	703 (65.58)	
Topic 2	*iOS users, what do you think of Duolingo's new "Chat Bots" feature?*	Negative	5(31.25)	
		Neutral	2 (13.50)	2016
		Positive	9 (56.25)	
Topic 3	*Spanish Bots; What Do You Think?*	Negative	3 (14.3)	
		Neutral	3 (14.3)	2016
		Positive	15 (71.4)	
Topic 4	*Help test the Duolingo Bots in English!*	Negative	5 (9.62)	
		Neutral	6 (11.54)	2017
		Positive	41 (78.85)	
Topic 5	*Help us test Duolingo Bots!*	Negative	20 (35.71)	
		Neutral	5 (8.93)	2017
		Positive	31 (55.36)	
Topic 6	*I want the bots back*	Negative	18 (36.73)	
		Neutral	5 (10.20)	2018
		Positive	26 (53.06)	
Topic 7	*Bring back the bots!!!!!*	Negative	10 (40)	
		Neutral	1 (4)	2019
		Positive	14 (56)	
Topic 8	*Please bring back the Duolingo Language Bots!*	Negative	14 (22.58)	
		Neutral	7 (11.29)	2019
		Positive	41 (66.13)	

Table 4. Duolingo Sentiment Score Examples

Text	Score	Sentiment
I agree! I loved the bots. They weren't perfect, but they were fun to use and practice speaking skills with.	0.87	Positive
Waiting for other languages coming soon on *Duolingo* iPhone app!!	0.5	Neutral
no desktop bots?!? .... c'mon guys:-(	0.02	Negative

In table 5, the results of the sentiment analysis indicate the sentiments users experienced regarding the use of *Memrise* chatbots, since their introduction until September 2019. With regard to data collected from the community, there was generally positive sentiment towards the use of chatbots with 47.50% of the comments voicing positive sentiment. The general sentiment around the chatbots, however, turned negative over the following year, as 54.49% of the comments reveal negative sentiment. More positive sentiment was noted in 2019 with 44.4% of the sentiment being positive. However, the general sentiment over the three-year period from the *Memrise* community data was negative (46.19%). The results from reddit, although from a relatively much smaller dataset, indicate a 50% positive and 50% negative sentiment in 2017. The sentiment around the chatbots in 2018 was slightly more positive (48.15%) than it was negative (44.44%). A single comment in 2019 had positive sentiment. The general sentiment from the reddit data was positive (50%) with 43.33% being negative. An example of the text and sentiment scores is shown in table 6.

Table 5. Memrise

Source	Sentiment	Frequency (%)	Year
Memrise Community	Negative	11 (27.50)	2017
	Neutral	10 (25.00)	
	Positive	19 (47.50)	
	Negative	85 (54.49)	2018
	Neutral	13 (8.33)	
	Positive	58 (37.18)	
	Negative	7 (25.93)	2019 September
	Neutral	8 (29.63)	
	Positive	12 (44.44)	
	Negative	103 (46.19)	2017- September 2019
	Neutral	31 (13.90)	
	Positive	89 (39.91)	
Reddit	Negative	1 (50.00)	2017
	Neutral	0 (0.00)	
	Positive	1 (50.00)	
	Negative	12 (44.44)	2018
	Neutral	2 (7.41)	
	Positive	13 (48.15)	
	Negative	0 (0.00)	2019
	Neutral	0 (0.00)	
	Positive	1(100)	
	Negative	13 (43.33)	2017- September 2019
	Neutral	2 (6.67)	
	Positive	15 (50.00)	

Table 6. Memrise Sentiment Score Examples

Text	Score	Sentiment
… hoping the bots recently introduced will spread through all levels and that the course continues beyond level 7 in the future.	0.95	Positive
I am not sure where the differences are for the bots or grammar bots between non-pro and pro-mode.	0.5	Neutral
The chat and grammar bots are very annoyingly repetitive.	0.05	Negative

For the *Eggbun* chatbot. The results in table 7 indicate slightly more negative sentiments (52.63%) in comparison to the positive (47.37%), in the early stages of the application based on the *reddit* data. With regards to the *Facebook* data, the sentiment was mostly positive (81.82%) in 2017. In 2018, the sentiment was generally more negative (52.38%) than positive (38.10%). In 2019, 71.43% of the sentiment was positive. The overall sentiment from 2017 to 2019 was mostly positive (56.41%). From the *Google Play* data in 2016, there was overwhelmingly positive sentiment (85.34%) towards the application. The positive trend continued in 2017 and 2018, as 79.03% of the sentiment was positive with 70.58% of the sentiment being positive in 2018. However, in 2019, 48.90% of the sentiment was positive with 47.68% of the sentiment being negative. The overall sentiment from the *Google Play* data indicated a strong positive sentiment of 80.90%. For the *Appstore* data, in 2016, 79.91% of the sentiment was positive. For the 2017 data, 80.97% of the sentiment was positive. In 2018, a decline in positive sentiment was noted as only 52.46% of the sentiment was positive. In 2019, there was a general decline into negative sentiments as most of the sentiment was negative (57.86%). The overall sentiment, however, from 2016 to October 2019, was generally positive (72.69%). An example of the text and sentiment scores is shown in table 8.

Table 7. Eggbun

Source	Sentiment	Frequency %	Year
Reddit	Negative	10 (52.63)	2016
	Neutral	0 (0.00)	
	Positive	9 (47.37)	
Facebook	Negative	2 (18.18)	2017
	Neutral	0 (0.00)	
	Positive	9 (81.82)	
	Negative	11 (52.38)	2018
	Neutral	2 (9.52)	
	Positive	8 (38.10)	
	Negative	2 (28.57)	2019
	Neutral	0 (0.00)	
	Positive	5 (71.43)	
	Negative	15 (38.46)	2017- September 2019
	Neutral	2 (5.13)	
	Positive	22 (56.41)	
Google Play	Negative	669 (12.98)	2016
	Neutral	87 (1.69)	
	Positive	4400 (85.34)	
	Negative	390 (19.71)	2017
	Neutral	25 (1.26)	
	Positive	1564 (79.03)	

continues on following page

Table 7. Continued

Source	Sentiment	Frequency %	Year
	Negative	151 (25.68)	2018
	Neutral	22 (3.74)	
	Positive	415 (70.58)	
	Negative	195 (47.68)	2019
	Neutral	14 (3.42)	
	Positive	200 (48.90)	
	Negative	1405 (17.28)	2016- October 2019
	Neutral	148 (1.82)	
	Positive	6579 (80.90)	
AppStore	Negative	85 (18.97)	2016
	Neutral	5 (1.12)	
	Positive	358 (79.91)	
	Negative	118 (17.96)	2017
	Neutral	7 (1.07)	
	Positive	532 (80.97)	
	Negative	81 (44.26)	2018
	Neutral	6 (3.28)	
	Positive	96 (52.46)	
	Negative	81(57.86)	2019
	Neutral	7 (5.00)	
	Positive	52 (37.14)	
	Negative	365 (25.56)	2016- October 2019
	Neutral	25 (1.75)	
	Positive	1038 (72.69)	

Table 8. Eggbun Sentiment Score Examples

Text	Score	Sentiment
Fun and Educating:D	1	Positive
The only thing I'd add on would be more review at the end of each lesson and romanisation to see the pronounced word	0.5	Neutral
I love it, but some lessons not free that's make me sad [crying emojis]	0.0002	Negative

For the *Mondly* chatbot. Table 9 indicates positive (100%) sentiment for the chatbot feature in 2016 from the product hunt data source. For the *reddit* data, there was an indication of mostly positive sentiment (53.13%). From the *Google Play* data in 2016, 57.14% of the sentiment was negative with 42.86% being positive. However, in 2017 the sentiment turned positive, as 53.85% of the sentiment was positive. In 2018, there was an even split of 46.88% positive and 46.88% negative sentiment. In 2019, 59.09%

of the sentiment was positive. The overall sentiment, from the *Google Play* data, was mostly positive (52.84%), from 2016 to October 2019. From the *Appstore* data in 2016, 62.50% of the sentiment was positive with 37.50% being negative. The positive trend declined from 2017 to 2019, as the sentiment was 73.33%, 62.22% and 61.54% positive in 2017, 2018 and 2019 respectively. The overall sentiment from the *Appstore* data, from 2016 to October 2019 was positive (63.55%). An example of the text and sentiment scores is shown in table 10.

Table 9. Mondly

Source	Sentiment	Frequency (%)	Year
Product hunt	Negative	0 (0)	2016
	Neutral	0 (0)	
	Positive	14 (100)	
Mondly Reddit	Negative	12 (37.50)	2016
	Neutral	3 (9.38)	
	Positive	17 (53.13)	
Google Play	Negative	4 (57.14)	2016
	Neutral	0 (0.00)	
	Positive	3 (42.86)	
	Negative	15 (38.46)	2017
	Neutral	3 (7.69)	
	Positive	21(53.85)	
	Negative	30 (46.88)	2018
	Neutral	4 (6.25)	
	Positive	30 (46.88)	
	Negative	25 (37.88)	2019
	Neutral	2 (3.03)	
	Positive	39 (59.09)	
	Negative	74 (42.05)	2016- October 2019
	Neutral	9 (5.11)	
	Positive	93 (52.84)	
Appstore	Negative	3 (37.50)	2016
	Neutral	0 (0.00)	
	Positive	5 (62.50)	
	Negative	4 (26.67)	2017
	Neutral	0 (0.00)	
	Positive	11 (73.33)	
	Negative	16 (35.56)	2018
	Neutral	1 (2.22)	
	Positive	28 (62.22)	

continues on following page

Table 9. Continued

Source	Sentiment	Frequency (%)	Year
	Negative	13 (33.33)	
	Neutral	2 (5.13)	2019
	Positive	24 (61.54)	
	Negative	36 (33.64)	
	Neutral	3 (2.80)	2016- October 2019
	Positive	68 (63.55)	

Table 10. Mondly Sentiment Score Examples

Text	Score	Sentiment
Very happy that there is a chat bot with the ability to record your own voice, everything is intuitive.	0.88	Positive
Mondly - the Siri for learning languages.	0.5	Neutral
Not very good chat bots and lessons are hard and difficult not fun. Voice recognition may be faulty.	0.001	Negative

DISCUSSION AND CONCLUSION

The year 2016 has seen the launch of a range of L2 chatbots, which unlike their predecessors are readily available to informal language learners. In the absence of teachers and peers, the users of chatbots often turn to online communities to discuss their reactions and issues with their learning situations. Prior studies have shown that concerns regarding L2 chatbots centred around the inability of the bots to hold a natural conversation, meaningless responses and not having met their full potential as language practice partners (see Chiu et al., 2007; Coniam, 2008a, 2014; Fryer et al., 2019; Sha, 2009). However, communicating with chatbots, as opposed to face-to-face communication, can create a safe space in which the learner can take time to respond and react at their own pace, thus reducing language speaking anxiety.

This study looked at four chatbot applications for language learning. For *Duolingo*, the sentiment was generally positive. Throughout the bots' lifespan, users of the bots were enthusiastic about the idea of having a bot as a conversation partner. However, there was negative sentiment regarding a lack of some advanced functionality in the bots as well as the lack of bot features in different versions of the application. Enthusiasm for the idea of learning with chatbots was further illustrated by themes relating to the lack of an android platform and the bot feature in other languages. Furthermore, users expressed various ways in which they utilised *Duolingo* bots, suggesting that the bots facilitated informal language learning. When the bots were removed there was a generally positive sentiment toward bringing the bots back as most users likely found them to have been an intriguing way of learning a language.

The results about *Memrise* were mixed. The users were generally eager when the grammar bots were introduced, however, over time sentiment toward the grammar bots tended to be negative as indicated by the *Memrise* community data. Although the reddit data-set was smaller, it showed mostly positive sentiments. Users indicated the bots were not always accurate, were not available for many languages and that the bots were only available in the pro version. Furthermore, the bots seemingly had few tasks, as users indicated a constant repetition of tasks. These drawbacks gave the impression of users not having an effective platform to learn grammar.

The *Facebook* and *reddit* datasets indicated mostly positive sentiment for *Eggbun* at an early stage and negative sentiment at a later stage, although most concerns referred to access to premium accounts and some concerns with the content of the bots. The sentiment toward the conversation chatbot was overwhelmingly positive in the larger datasets from *Google Play* and the *Appstore*. Learners identified the app's possibilities for language learning, particularly for users in Korean. For *Mondly,* the datasets (2016-2019) indicated mostly positive sentiment. Users indicated that good interaction with chatbots promoted a good language learning experience.

Overall, the general idea of chatbots was welcomed as an enjoyable way of language learning in informal learning contexts. Furthermore, chatbots allow users to practice their target languages without the pressure of real-life human conversations. However, in most cases, users had to pay for the pro version of the app to enjoy the full features of these chatbots, payment which users found to be a burden. Generally, chatbots can improve as they become smarter and more useful. However, Coniam (2014) indicated that ability to interact with a chatbot is a motivating factor for ESL learners, even if the user is aware they are interacting with a machine and not a real person. Although these results may be seen as a novelty effect (see Fryer et al., 2017), other studies have indicated that interest in the bots eventually resumes (Fryer et al., 2019). In conclusion, chatbots have the potential to foster a non-threatening learning environment, where informal learners may experience learning a second language without the anxiety and shyness frequently associated with classroom-based language learning. Although chatbots have not reached their full potential yet, it can be assumed that they will continue to improve along with other interactive technologies, opening realistic alternatives to human to human conversations for informal language learning practice.

REFERENCES

Barga, R., Fontama, V., Tok, W. H., & Cabrera-Cordon, L. (2015). *Predictive analytics with Microsoft Azure machine learning.* Springer. doi:10.1007/978-1-4842-1200-4

Berns, A., Mota, J. M., Ruiz-Rube, I., & Dodero, J. M. (2018). Exploring the potential of a 360° video application for foreign language learning. *Proceedings of the Sixth International Conference on Technological Ecosystems for Enhancing Multiculturality.* 10.1145/3284179.3284309

Bonifacio, C., Barchyn, T. E., Hugenholtz, C. H., & Kienzle, S. W. (2015). CCDST: A free Canadian climate data scraping tool. *Computers & Geosciences, 75,* 13–16. doi:10.1016/j.cageo.2014.10.010

Braun, V., & Clarke, V. (2006). Using thematic analysis in psychology. *Qualitative Research in Psychology, 3*(2), 77–101. doi:10.1191/1478088706qp063oa

Chatterjee, A., & Perrizo, W. (2016). *Investor classification and sentiment analysis.* Paper presented at the 2016 IEEE/ACM International Conference on Advances in Social Networks Analysis and Mining (ASONAM). 10.1109/ASONAM.2016.7752388

Chiu, T.-L., Liou, H.-C., & Yeh, Y. (2007). A study of web-based oral activities enhanced by automatic speech recognition for EFL college learning. *Computer Assisted Language Learning, 20*(3), 209–233. doi:10.1080/09588220701489374

Coniam, D. (2008a). Evaluating the language resources of chatbots for their potential in English as a second language. *ReCALL, 20*(1), 98–116. doi:10.1017/S0958344008000815

Coniam, D. (2008b). An evaluation of chatbots as software aids to learning English as a second language. *The Eurocall Review, 13*.

Coniam, D. (2014). The linguistic accuracy of chatbots: Usability from an ESL perspective. *Text & Talk, 34*(5), 545–567. doi:10.1515/text-2014-0018

Dale, R. (2016). The return of the chatbots. *Natural Language Engineering, 22*(5), 811–817. doi:10.1017/S1351324916000243

Dressman, M., & Sadler, R. W. (Eds.). (2020). *The Handbook of Informal Language Learning*. Wiley-Blackwell.

Duolingo. (2016). *Say hello to the Bots. The most advanced way to learn a language*. Retrieved October 17, 2019, from http://web.archive.org/web/20161007172736/http://bots.duolingo.com/

Eggbun Education. (2017). *Learn Korean/ Japanese/ Chinese*. Retrieved October 17, 2019, from https://www.facebook.com/eggbun.edu/

Etikan, I., Musa, S. A., & Alkassim, R. S. (2016). Comparison of convenience sampling and purposive sampling. *American Journal of Theoretical and Applied Statistics, 5*(1), 1-4.

Fryer, L., & Carpenter, R. (2006). Bots as language learning tools. *Language Learning & Technology, 10*(3), 8–14.

Fryer, L. K., Ainley, M., Thompson, A., Gibson, A., & Sherlock, Z. (2017). Stimulating and sustaining interest in a language course: An experimental comparison of Chatbot and Human task partners. *Computers in Human Behavior, 75*, 461–468. doi:10.1016/j.chb.2017.05.045

Fryer, L. K., Nakao, K., & Thompson, A. (2019). Chatbot learning partners: Connecting learning experiences, interest and competence. *Computers in Human Behavior, 93*, 279–289. doi:10.1016/j.chb.2018.12.023

Godwin-Jones, R. (2017). Smartphones and language learning. *Language Learning & Technology, 21*(2), 3–17.

Groves, M., & Mundt, K. (2015). Friend or foe? Google Translate in language for academic purposes. *English for Specific Purposes, 37*, 112–121. doi:10.1016/j.esp.2014.09.001

Hill, A., Erickson, D., Sharkey, K., Ericson, G., Wells, J., Steen, H., . . . Farley, P. (2019). *Sentiment analysis using the Text Analytics from Azure Cognitive Services | Microsoft Docs*. Retrieved April 25, 2019, from https://docs.microsoft.com/en-us/azure/cognitive-services/text-analytics/how-tos/text-analytics-how-to-sentiment-analysis

Hussein, D. M. E.-D. M. (2018). A survey on sentiment analysis challenges. *Journal of King Saud University - Engineering and Science, 30*(4), 330–338. doi:10.1016/j.jksues.2016.04.002

Iliescu, A. (2016). *Mondly launches first voice chatbot for learning languages*. Retrieved October 17, 2019, from https://www.mondly.com/blog/2016/08/25/mondly-chatbot-press-release/

Kessler, G. (2018). Technology and the future of language teaching. *Foreign Language Annals, 51*(1), 205–218. doi:10.1111/flan.12318

Kiritchenko, S., Zhu, X., & Mohammad, S. M. (2014). Sentiment analysis of short informal texts. *Journal of Artificial Intelligence Research, 50*, 723–762. doi:10.1613/jair.4272

Kreisa, M. (n.d.). *5 Resources for Chatbots to Be Your Language Learning BFFs*. Retrieved October 21, 2019, from https://www.fluentu.com/blog/language-learning-chatbot/#

Lai, C. (2019). Technology and Learner Autonomy: An Argument in Favor of the Nexus of Formal and Informal Language Learning. *Annual Review of Applied Linguistics, 39*, 52–58.

Landers, R. N., Brusso, R. C., Cavanaugh, K. J., & Collmus, A. B. (2016). A primer on theory-driven web scraping: Automatic extraction of big data from the Internet for use in psychological research. *Psychological Methods, 21*(4), 475–492. doi:10.1037/met0000081 PMID:27213980

Lange, P. G. (2019). Informal Learning on YouTube. The International Encyclopedia of Media Literacy, 1-11.

Lucas, G. M., Gratch, J., King, A., & Morency, L.-P. (2014). It's only a computer: Virtual humans increase willingness to disclose. *Computers in Human Behavior, 37*, 94–100. doi:10.1016/j.chb.2014.04.043

Macayan, J. V., Quinto, E. J. M., Otsuka, J. C., & Cueto, A. B. S. (2018). Influence of Language Learning Anxiety on L2 Speaking and Writing of Filipino Engineering Students. *3L: Language, Linguistics, Literature®, 24*(1).

Moon, F. (2017). *The Origin of Eggbun Education*. Retrieved October 17, 2019, from https://medium.com/story-of-eggbun-education/the-origin-of-eggbun-education-1b63baa23f59

Nagender, P. (2015). *Introducing Text Analytics in the Azure ML Marketplace*. Retrieved April 25, 2019, from https://blogs.technet.microsoft.com/machinelearning/2015/04/08/introducing-text-analytics-in-the-azure-ml-marketplace/

Olson, P. (2016). *Get Ready For The Chat Bot Revolution: They're Simple, Cheap And About To Be Everywhere*. Retrieved October 20, 2019, from https://www.forbes.com/sites/parmyolson/2016/02/23/chat-bots-facebook-telegram-wechat/#3bbda2dc2068

Prabowo, R., & Thelwall, M. (2009). Sentiment analysis: A combined approach. *Journal of Informetrics, 3*(2), 143–157. doi:10.1016/j.joi.2009.01.003

Rawlings, A. (2017). *Introducing Memrise's Brand New Grammar Chats*. Retrieved October 17, 2019, from http://web.archive.org/web/20171027094549/https://blog.memrise.com/2017/05/23/introducing-memrises-brand-new-grammar-chats/

Sauro, S., & Zourou, K. (2019). What are the digital wilds? *Language Learning & Technology, 1*(23), 1–7.

Sha, G. (2009). AI-based chatterbots and spoken English teaching: A critical analysis. *Computer Assisted Language Learning*, 22(3), 269–281. doi:10.1080/09588220902920284

Stewart, I. A., & File, P. (2007). Let's chat: A conversational dialogue system for second language practice. *Computer Assisted Language Learning*, 20(2), 97–116. doi:10.1080/09588220701331386

Stickler, U., & Hampel, R. (2015). Transforming Teaching: New Skills for Online Language Learning Spaces. In R. Hampel & U. Stickler (Eds.), *Developing Online Language Teaching: Research-Based Pedagogies and Reflective Practices* (pp. 63–77). Palgrave Macmillan UK. doi:10.1057/9781137412263_5

Tsai, S.-C. (2019). Using google translate in EFL drafts: A preliminary investigation. *Computer Assisted Language Learning*, 32(5-6), 510–526. doi:10.1080/09588221.2018.1527361

Veletsianos, G., Kimmons, R., Larsen, R., Dousay, T. A., & Lowenthal, P. R. (2018). Public comment sentiment on educational videos: Understanding the effects of presenter gender, video format, threading, and moderation on YouTube TED talk comments. *PLoS One*, 13(6), e0197331. doi:10.1371/journal.pone.0197331 PMID:29856749

Von Ahn, L. (2016). *Meet your new language tutors: the Duolingo Bots*. Retrieved October 17, 2019, from https://forum.duolingo.com/comment/18155544

Wang, Y. F., & Petrina, S. (2013). Using learning analytics to understand the design of an intelligent language tutor–Chatbot lucy. *Editorial Preface, 4*(11).

Weizenbaum, J. (1966). ELIZA---a computer program for the study of natural language communication between man and machine. *Communications of the ACM*, 9(1), 36–45. doi:10.1145/365153.365168

Wen, M., Yang, D., & Rose, C. (2014). *Sentiment Analysis in MOOC Discussion Forums: What does it tell us?* Paper presented at the Educational data mining 2014.

This research was previously published in the International Journal of Computer-Assisted Language Learning and Teaching (IJCALLT), 10(4); pages 51-65, copyright year 2020 by IGI Publishing (an imprint of IGI Global).

Chapter 51
A Novel Approach to Optimize the Performance of Hadoop Frameworks for Sentiment Analysis

Guru Prasad
SDMIT, Ujire, India

Prithviraj Jain
SDMIT, Ujire, India

Amith K. Jain
SDMIT, Ujire, India

Nagesh H. R.
A.J. Institute of Engineering and Technology, Mangalore, India

ABSTRACT

Twitter is one among most popular micro blogging services with millions of active users. It is a hub of massive collection of data arriving from various sources. In Twitter, users most often express their views, opinions, thoughts, emotions or feelings about a particular topic, product or service, of their interest, choice or concern. This makes twitter a hub of gargantuan amount of data, and at the same time a useful platform in getting to know and understand the underlying sentiment behind a particular product or for that matter anything expressed in twitter as tweets. It is important to note here that aforesaid massive collection of data is not just any redundant data, but one which contains useful information as noted earlier. In view of aforesaid context, Sentiment analysis in relation to twitter data gains enormous importance. Sentiment analysis offers itself as a good approach in classifying the opinions formulated by individuals (tweeters) into different sentiments such as, positive, negative, or neutral. Implementing Sentiment analysis algorithms using conventional tools leads to high computation time, and thus are less effective. Hence, there is a need for state-of-the-art tools and techniques to be developed for sentiment analysis making it the need of the hour to facilitate faster computation. An Apache Hadoop framework is one such option that supports distributed data computing and has been commonly adopted for a variety of use-cases. In this article, the author identifies factors affecting the performance of sentiment analysis algorithms based on Hadoop framework and proposes an approach for optimizing the performance of sentiment analysis. The experimental results depict the potential of the proposed approach.

DOI: 10.4018/978-1-6684-6303-1.ch051

1. INTRODUCTION

In today's digital world social networking sites play a vital role and also have an influential say in modern way of life. Twitter is one among the most popular social networking sites with more than 100 million of daily active users. According to Statista survey, as of year 2017 Twitter had 328 million active users and the number is said to have increased and still increasing day by day (Andreas et al.,2017). In Twitter, registered users can read and post tweets; tweets are limited to 280 characters. They can also upload images and short videos of size not more than 5MB and 512MB respectively. Millions of users express their views, opinions, thoughts, emotions, feelings about different products, events, people, etc., on the twitter platform.

Indian Premier League (IPL) is a popular, professional Twenty-Twenty (T20) cricket league played in India. It ranks sixth among all sports leagues across the world. As we already know cricket in India is not just viewed as a sport, but, a religion in itself. Due to its humungous popularity, unending reach along with an uncanny ability to arouse interest and then being able to follow it up with definite action, it evokes all sorts of emotions, feelings and what not among cricket viewers. The same goes true for IPL, its fans, and in general, viewers of IPL. In Twitter, IPL fans originating from various places express their views, opinions, thoughts, emotions or feelings about their favorite IPL teams and players. During IPL season millions of tweets get tweeted every day on a regular basis. Aforesaid live stream of data is considered to be a rich source of information for Sentiment analysis. Natural Language processing is used to mine people's opinions about IPL teams and players expressed in form of tweets. Sentiment analysis helps in classifying people's opinions as positive, negative or neutral Implementing Sentiment analysis algorithms using traditional data analytics tools seem unable to handle Twitter Big Data as data to be handled is humongous, changing at a fast pace and characteristically complex by nature. Big data analytics has modernized traditional data analytics by introducing new technologies that support distributed storage and processing of large amount of data. Today, Apache Hadoop has become a highly popular and powerful distributed computing framework to process large amounts of data. It is composed of Hadoop Distributed File System (HDFS), Yet Another Resource Negotiator (YARN) and MapReduce parallel programming model. The unique features of Hadoop that make it so attractive are ease of access, robustness, fault tolerance, scalability and ease of parallel programming. Using Hadoop framework, a lot of work has already been proposed on Sentiment analysis in relation to Twitter data. However, some parameters affecting the performance of Sentiment analysis remain a challenge on Hadoop framework. When working with large amounts of data sets, there will be challenges and difficulties such as data sets consuming more HDFS disk space, network related issues and high computation time. In this paper, the author identifies the factors affecting the performance of sentiment analysis algorithm based on Hadoop framework and proposes an approach for optimizing the performance of sentiment analysis. Experimental results obtained show that proposed novel approach effectively optimizes the HDFS disk space utilization, speeds up the data movement in the network and optimizes the computation time.

The rest of the paper is organized as follows: Section 2 comprises of literature survey in relation to the proposed topic; Section 3 presents the proposed framework and associated implementation so as to optimize the performance of sentiment analysis with regard to Twitter data; Section 4 substantiates aforesaid analysis by showcasing comprehensive experimental results; Finally, Section 5 delivers conclusion to the paper.

2. LITERATURE SURVEY

Andreas et al. (2017), has presented that Sentiment Analysis of Twitter data is certainly a challenging problem due to the sheer amount of volume, velocity and variety associated with the same. Sentiment analysis of aforesaid large quantity of information offers extensive potential in terms of sentiments present in this information leaning towards specific topics. Most of the existing algorithms with respect to sentiment analysis are limited to centralized computing platforms, and hence can handle at the most a few thousand tweets. This kind of computing platform is not fully representative when it comes to finding sentiment polarity regarding a specific topic, owing to the fact that huge number of tweets are being posted daily. In aforesaid paper, the authors developed two modules, MapReduce and Apache Spark framework for the purpose of Big Data Programming. Authors implemented Sentiment Analysis technique using Machine Learning algorithms and utilized Apache Spark framework. The proposed systems were trained to collect real-time Twitter Data and process the same in a distributed manner. The experimental results show the quality of sentiment identification as compared with the same in conventional solutions.

Diamantini et al. (2017), has explained that Traditional sentiment analysis based on lexicon technique falters in identifying the right negation as they fail to make use of available efficient methods to identify the right negation window. In aforesaid paper, authors have addressed issues of instinctive resolve of scope of negation and then proposed dependency-oriented parse tree to identify negation. The proposed work is built upon proper utilization of semantical relations that exist between terms necessary for framing of a meaningful statement, and thus emphasis is put on finding out terms which are tormented by negation. Furthermore, aforesaid technique has been combined with semantic disambiguation technique so that sentiment associated with a statement is properly recognized. Based on experimental results obtained on various sample sets, it is found that quality of aforesaid analysis is enhanced in the proposed technique. In future works, authors have planned to advance the correctness of the negation handling approach by determining more features, namely, effect of various conjunctions, or the usage of punctuation marks. Along with this, authors have also planned to address the problem of use of emoticons in sentences, which are being enormously used in social networks, specifically on Twitter.

Araque et al. (2017), has expressed that Sentiment Analysis is in dire need of deep learning techniques so as to facilitate automatic feature extraction, enabling of richer representation capabilities, along with offering better performance than conventional feature-based techniques (i.e., surface methods). In this paper, the authors developed an enhanced, deep learning-oriented Sentiment Analysis system based on a word's embedding method, along with linear machine learning approach. Several experiments were conducted wherein performance of presented technique was analyzed with the baseline deep learning technique, and experimental results depict that the performance of the proposed model is enhanced than the baseline model.

Clavel, et al. (2016), has expressed that Sentiment Analysis has seen an enormous surge in interest owing to the availability of huge amount of Social network data. It is also expressed that Sentiment analysis is instrumental to and is being pursued by lot of emerging research areas. Development of Embodied Conversational Agents (ECA) to interact with humans is one among them. The human-agent interaction communities and opinion mining enthusiasts are presently addressing sentiment analysis from completely different views that consists of, on the one hand, disparate sentiment-related phenomena and procedure representations, and on the opposite side, various detection and dialog management ways. In aforesaid paper, the authors identified, and later discussed the upcoming challenges in multidisciplinary fields. Authors proposed different potentialities for mutual profit, specifying a lot of analysis tracks and presenting open queries and prospects. To conduct proposed experiment, job interviews and conversation with regular visitors who attend museums have been considered as test cases.

Doan et al. (2017) described that most of the times people associated with business regularly want to know customer's opinion regarding standard of their service, so as to improve and hence, increase profit. Sentiment analysis of customer reviews holds and plays important effect on a business's improvement techniques. Sentiment analysis based on offline solutions comprise of training data being collected beforehand, and model being built later. This leads towards model being trained again and again. To avoid retraining of complete model from time to time, incremental learning offers itself as the best alternate solution and is the need for proposed task. In this paper, the authors proposed an alternate online random forests algorithm to accomplish sentiment analysis with regards to respective customers' reviews. The proposed work has been able to achieve more accuracy in comparison to traditional works.

Jose et al. (2015) proposed a Sentiment Analysis system to predict Delhi assembly election result through collection and analysis of twitter data. The author presented that sentiment analysis is the computational learning of information present in opinions, emotions, feelings, attitudes, and views, expressed in the form of text. It denotes a classification problem with major emphasis put on being able to forecast the polarity of words and later classify them as positive, negative or a neutral sentiment. In Twitter, users express their views, opinions, thoughts, emotions, feeling, etc., towards variety of topics, including political party and politicians. In this paper, the authors introduced Sentiment Classifier using Word Sense Disambiguation (WSD), based on lexicon technique. The proposed system is implemented in the data pre-processing step using a negation handling to achieve more accuracy and hence proper classification of tweets as positive, negative or neutral. Experimental outcomes depict that the proposed approach attained high accuracy. However, limitation of the proposed work lies in the fact that collected data size was way too small to come at a meaningful conclusion.

Bharti et al. (2016), has explained that Sarcasm is the kind of sentiment where people express their negative emotions using positive words. While talking, people generally use heavy tonal stress and certain gestural intimations like moving of the eyes, hand movement, and so forth to reveal sarcasm. In textual data, these tonal and gestural intimations of information are missing, making sarcasm recognition exceptionally difficult for a normal human. Because of these difficulties, researchers have shown interest in sarcasm identification of social media text, particularly in tweets. In aforesaid paper, the authors presented a sarcastic sentiment detection model based on the Hadoop framework. Proposed model captured real-time tweets and analyzed it with a set of various approaches, such as TCTDF, TCUF, IWS, PSWAP, PBLGA, and LDC to identify sarcastic sentiment effectively. Aforesaid approaches were implemented with and without Hadoop framework. The experimental result shows that the elapsed time for analyzing and processing twitter data is more significant in the Hadoop framework as compared to conventional methods.

Cunha et al. (2015) described that social media advancements coupled with exponential increase in volume and complexity of data that are being generated by Internet services have made analysis difficult not only technologically, but also in view of emerging trends. In this paper, the authors proposed an all-purpose functional architecture based on Hadoop MapReduce platform and Mahout for storing and distributed processing of large data that can be applied in various situations. To prove its potential, strength, advantages, and applications, authors considered Twitter data related to health as a case study. Experimental outcomes of data analysis on Twitter health data demonstrated the potential of the proposed architecture.

3. FRAMEWORK AND IMPLEMENTATION

In the proposed work, a novel architecture to optimize the performance of sentiment analysis of Twitter data has been proposed. The proposed architecture i.e., SHOC (Sentiment analyzing Hadoop framework Optimized through Compressing data) is as shown in Figure 1, which expands the baseline of Hadoop framework.

Figure 1. SHOC architecture

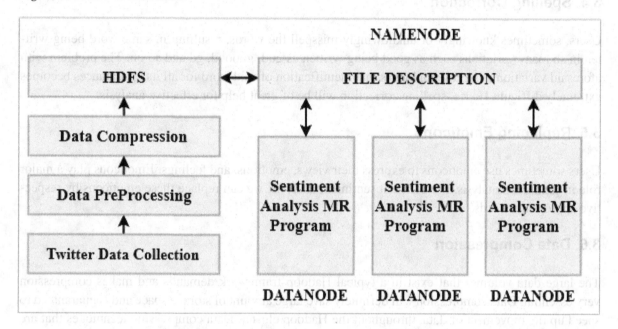

Detailed step by step description of the SHOC is as follows.

3.1. Twitter Data Collection

Using Twitter API, one can collect live data directly from twitter. In order to access such live Twitter data, the developer has to create a Twitter application, and the same has been created. In the proposed work, Twitter data concerning Indian Premier League (IPL)-2017 has been collected in JSON format for the duration 12-March-2017 to 22-May-2017.

3.2. Data Pre-Processing

The raw data so collected from Twitter is often inconsistent, sometimes irrelevant and may comprise of noisy tweets. Hence, data needs to be pre-processed. Data pre-processing is a process that involves transforming raw twitter data into an understandable format. It involves removing URL and hashtags, spelling corrections, and replacing emoticons.

3.3. Removing URL and Hashtags

While tweeting, sometimes a user mentions another user as @username and shares some useful information using URL and hashtags. Most of the times, the URL and hashtags which come along with the information hold little value to the recipient, and thus can be treated redundant. The proposed system eliminates such redundant information in connection with sentiment analysis of tweets like user information, time, date, URL, hashtags, duplicates of tweets, and hence reduces memory consumption.

3.4. Spelling Correction

Users, sometimes knowingly or unknowingly misspell the words, resulting in same word being written in so many variations such as good being written as gud, gooood, gd and so on. The problem with aforesaid variation in representations is that identification of said word for all its appearances becomes extremely difficult. Hence, spelling correction will be of great help for effective analysis.

3.5. Replacing Emoticons

Users sometimes use emoticons to express their views, emotions, and feelings. Emoticons play a major role in sentiment analysis. For efficient sentiment analysis, we can replace these emoticons by respective appropriate words.

3.6. Data Compression

The large data volumes that exist in a typical Hadoop framework demands and makes compression very essential. Data compression will definitely save large amount of storage space and is guaranteed to speed up the movement of data, throughout the Hadoop cluster. Data compression techniques that are supported by Hadoop frameworks are as follows.

3.6.1. Gzip

Gzip is a compression utility used for the purpose of file compression and decompression. It is based on the DEFLATE algorithm, which is a combination of LZ77 coding and Huffman Coding. The Gzip file format comprises of:

1. A 10-byte header providing version number and timestamp;
2. Optional extra headers which provide original file name;
3. A body, containing a DEFLATE-compressed payload;
4. An 8-byte footer, containing a CRC-32 checksum, along with length of the original uncompressed data.

By default, Gzip is supported in Hadoop ecosystem. The file extension of Gzip compressed file is .gz. Gzip does not support file splitting and parallel processing of files.

3.6.2. Bzip2

Bzip2 is an open source data compression technique based on Burrows-Wheeler algorithm. It provides a high degree of compression, with its downfall being low compression speed. Bzip2, as such is naturally supported in Hadoop ecosystem. The file extension of Bzip2 compressed file is .bz2. It supports file splitting and parallel file processing.

3.6.3. Lzo

Lzo is one such data compression technique which provides us with a modest degree of compression, along with high compression speed. Lzo, as such is naturally supported in Hadoop ecosystem. The file extension of Lzo compressed file is lzo. It supports file splitting and parallel file processing.

3.7. Sentiment Analysis

Sentiment analysis has been carried out by implementing SentiWordNet approach in MapReduce parallel programming model. SentiWordNet is a lexical resource for sentiment analysis and is one of the most popular approaches used for sentiment analysis. Aforesaid approach classifies the tweets as positive, negative or neutral, based on the context. The pseudo code of sentiment analysis is as shown below.

Algorithm 1. Sentiment analysis
Begin
- sentiment←0 (If there is no word related to a particular sentiment in current tweet, then)
- ps←0 // positive sentiment
- ns←0 // negative sentiment
- nus←0 //neutral sentiment
- while there are words related to a particular sentiment in current tweet, then
- if positive word is present in relation to the context, then ps++
- else, if negative word is present in relation to the context, then ns++
- else, if neutral word is present in relation to the context, then nus++
- end while
- positive percentage=(ps/(ps+ns+nus)) *100
- negative percentage=(ns/(ps+ns+nus)) *100
- neutral percentage=(nus/(ps+ns+nus)) *100
- sentiment = (ps-ns)/(ps+ns)
End

4. RESULTS AND DISCUSSION

The Performance Analysis of Twitter data using Hadoop MapReduce framework with respect to data compression, time taken to load data from local file system to HDFS System, and data process time was initially benchmarked with original Hadoop and then compared with results obtained using Proposed Compression Approaches i.e. Gzip, Bzip2, Lzo.

4.1. Experimental Environment

Performance analysis is carried out on a test platform which contains Hadoop five node cluster with homogeneous hardware property, i.e.., Each node in the cluster has a 3.8 GB RAM, Intel® Core i5 3470 CPU @3.20GHz * 4 processor. A cluster has been set up on Ubuntu 16.03 with Hadoop 2.6.5 stable release using oracle jdk 1.8 and ssh configuration to manage Hadoop daemons. The cluster setup comprises of 1 NameNode and 5 DataNodes as part of the experiment. Configuration files such as mapred-site.xml, core-site.xml, hdfs-site.xml and yarn-site.xml are setup with default values, i.e.., replication factor of 2 and data block size of 128 MB.

4.2. Sentiment Analysis

The total number of tweets collected for the purpose of sentiment analysis were 18,950 for Mumbai Indians (MI), 18,500 for Rising Pune Supergiant (RPS), 17,940 for Kolkata Knight Riders (KKR), 16,200 for Royal Challengers Bangalore (RCB), 14,000 for Sun Risers Hyderabad (SRH), 12,000 for Kings XI Punjab (PK XI), 13,000 for Delhi Daredevils (DD) and 11,000 for Gujarat Lions (GL). The same is plotted in Figure 2.

Figure 2. Number of tweets collected in relation to IPL teams

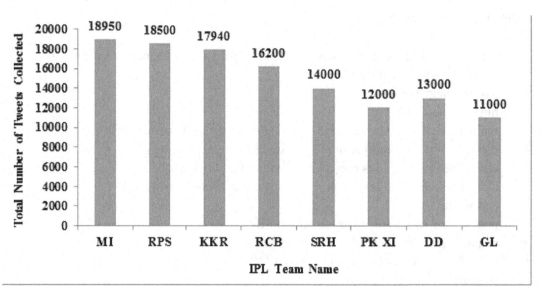

The so collected tweets were analyzed using SHOC. SHOC classifies the tweets as positive, negative or neutral, based on the context of the tweet. Total percentage of positive tweets, negative tweets and neutral tweets are calculated using Equations (1), (2) and (3) respectively. Table 1 demonstrates the percentage of Positive, Negative and Neutral Tweets with respect to IPL teams. Figure 3 depicts a graphical representation of data presented in Table 1:

$$P_{PT} = T_{PT} / T_T \tag{1}$$

$$P_{NT} = T_{NT} / T_T \qquad (2)$$

$$P_{NUT} = T_{NUT} / T_T \qquad (3)$$

where:
PPT = Percentage of Positive Tweets
PNT = Percentage of Negative Tweets
PNUT = Percentage of Neutral Tweets
TT = Total Number of Tweets
TPT = Total Number of Positive Tweets
TNT = Total Number of Negative Tweets
TNUT = Total Number of Neutral Tweets

Table 1. Percentage of positive, negative and neutral tweets with respect to IPL teams

IPL Team	P_{PT} (%)	P_{NT} (%)	P_{NUT} (%)
MI	80.88	12.21	6.91
RPS	78.96	12.94	8.10
KKR	78.62	17.99	3.39
RCB	63.06	33.00	3.94
SRH	69.01	26.05	4.94
PK XI	60.14	32.93	6.93
DD	76.79	20.95	2.26
GL	55.98	38.25	5.77

Figure 3. Percentage of positive, negative and neutral tweets with respect to IPL teams

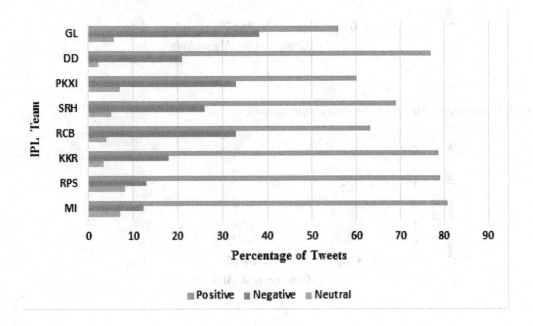

957

4.3. Data Compression

The large data volumes that exists in a typical Hadoop framework demands and makes compression very essential. Data compression will definitely save large amount of storage space, and is guaranteed to speed up the movement of data, throughout the Hadoop cluster. Data compression techniques that are supported by Hadoop frameworks are Gzip, Bzip2, and Lzo.

Experiments were conducted to compress 10 GB of twitter data using SHOC compression approaches i.e. Gzip, Bzip2, Lzo. Table 2 demonstrates the total time taken by proposed approaches to compress files along with compressed file size. Figure 4 depicts a graphical representation of total time taken by the proposed approaches to compress files and Figure 5 depicts a graphical representation of the compressed file size, upon compression.

Table 2. Total time taken by proposed approaches to compress files along with compressed file size

Technique	Original File Size in GB	Total Time Taken to Compress File in Seconds	Compressed File Size in GB
Gzip	10	690	2.2
Bzip2	10	1305	1.4
Lzo	10	285	3.9

Figure 4. Total time taken by proposed approaches to compress files

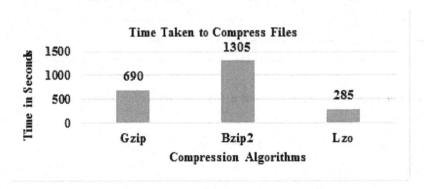

Figure 5. Compressed file size in proposed approaches

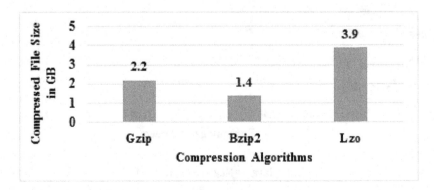

4.4. Data Uploading

To process the input data, user needs to upload the same from local disk to HDFS. Proposed Approach compresses the input data and uploads the compressed data to HDFS. The formula to calculate data uploading time is as follows:

$$T_{DU}^{Total} = T_{CF}^{Total} + T_{MF}^{Total} \qquad (4)$$

where:

T_{DU}^{Total} = Total time taken for data uploading

T_{CF}^{Total} = Total time taken to compress files

T_{MF}^{Total} = Total time taken to move compressed files to HDFS

Experiments were conducted to test the data uploading time in Baseline System (default Hadoop) and Proposed Compression Approaches i.e. Gzip, Bzip2, Lzo. Table 3 demonstrates the time taken to upload data from local disk to HDFS by Baseline System and the Proposed Approaches. Figure 6 depicts a graphical representation of data presented in Table 3. With reference to Table 3, time required for Sentiment Analysis in Proposed Approaches i.e. Gzip, Bzip2, Lzo is optimized than in Baseline System by 61.19%, 29.30% and 80.78% respectively. The result obtained clearly indicates that the performance of Proposed Approaches is better than in the Baseline System.

Table 3. Comparative analysis of total time taken to upload data from local disk to the HDFS

Technique	T_{CF}^{Total} in Seconds	T_{MF}^{Total} in Seconds	T_{DU}^{Total} in Seconds	% Time Optimization
Baseline System	-	1894	1894	61.19%
Gzip	690	45	735	
Baseline System	-	1894	1894	29.30%
Bzip2	1305	34	1339	
Baseline System	-	1894	1894	80.78%
Lzo	285	79	364	

"-" relates to the fact that Baseline System does not compress files

4.5. Data Processing Time

Experiments were conducted to compute total time taken for Sentiment analysis in the Baseline System and Proposed Compression Approaches, i.e. Gzip, Bzip2, Lzo. Later, the same has been compared. The total time taken for Sentiment analysis can be calculated using Equation (5):

Figure 6. Comparative analysis of total time taken to upload data from local disk to HDFS

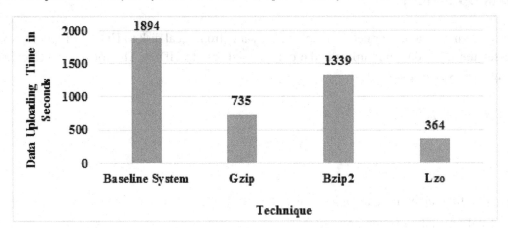

$$T_{SA}^{Total} = T_m^{Total} + T_r^{Total} \qquad (5)$$

where:

T_{SA}^{Total} = Total time taken for Sentiment analysis

T_m^{Total} = Total time required for execution of map phase

T_r^{Total} = Total time required for execution of reduce phase

Table 4 demonstrates comparison of total time taken by Baseline System and Proposed Approaches in relation to Sentiment analysis. Figure 7 depicts the data presented in Table 4 in form of a chart. With reference to Table 4, time required for Sentiment Analysis in Proposed Approaches i.e. Gzip, Bzip2, Lzo is optimized than in Baseline System by 56.43%, 69.38% and 47.90% respectively. The result obtained clearly indicates that performance of Proposed Approaches is better than the Baseline System.

Table 4. Comparison of total time taken by baseline system with proposed approaches in relation to sentiment analysis

Technique	T_m^{Total} in Seconds	T_r^{Total} in Seconds	T_{SA}^{Total} in Seconds	% Time Optimization in Proposed Approaches When Compared With Baseline System
Baseline System	1165	148	1313	56.43%
Gzip	520	52	572	
Baseline System	1165	148	1313	69.38%
Bzip2	385	17	402	
Baseline System	1165	148	1313	47.90%
Lzo	608	76	684	

Figure 7. Comparison of total time taken to execute sentiment analysis by baseline system with proposed approaches

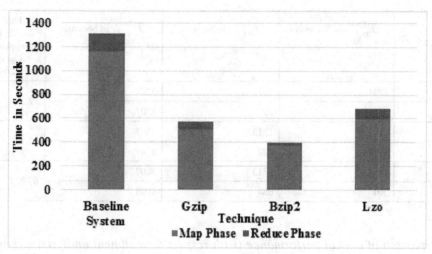

4.6. Overall Performance

Overall performance is defined as total time taken to complete the Sentiment analysis job. Experiments were conducted to compute the overall performance of Baseline System and the Proposed Compression Approaches i.e. Gzip, Bzip2, Lzo. Later, the same has been compared. The total time taken to complete Sentiment analysis job can be calculated using Equation (6):

$$T_{CJ}^{Total} = T_{DU}^{Total} + T_{SA}^{Total} \tag{6}$$

where:

T_{CJ}^{Total} = Total time taken to complete the Sentiment analysis job

T_{DU}^{Total} = Total time taken for data uploading

T_{SA}^{Total} = Total time taken for Sentiment analysis

Table 5 demonstrates the overall performance of Baseline System and Proposed Approaches. Figure 8 depicts a chart showcasing overall performance of Baseline System and Proposed Approaches. With reference to Table 5, overall performance of Sentiment Analysis using Proposed Approaches i.e. Gzip, Bzip2, Lzo is optimized than in Baseline System by 59.24%, 45.71% and 67.32% respectively. The result obtained clearly indicates that overall performance of Proposed Approaches is considerably optimized than in the Baseline System.

Table 5. Comparison of overall performance (with respect to sentiment analysis) of baseline system with proposed approaches

Technique	T_{DU}^{Total} in Seconds	T_{SA}^{Total} in Seconds	T_{CJ}^{Total} in Seconds	% Time Optimization in Proposed Approaches When Compared With Baseline System
Baseline System	1894	1313	3207	59.24%
Gzip	735	572	1307	
Baseline System	1894	1313	3207	45.71%
Bzip2	1339	402	1741	
Baseline System	1894	1313	3207	67.32%
Lzo	364	684	1048	

Figure 8. Comparison of overall performance (with respect to sentiment analysis) of baseline system with proposed approaches

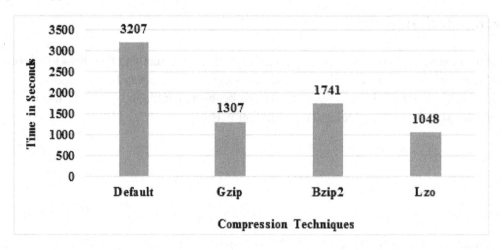

5. CONCLUSION

Twitter is one of the most popular microblogging platforms. Here, user's express their views, opinions, thoughts, emotions, feeling, etc., about any topic, product or service. Sentiment analysis is a good approach to classifying the opinions formulated by individuals into different sentiments such as, positive, negative, or neutral. Because of the exponential growth of Twitter data implementing sentiment analysis algorithms using traditional tools is not an effective way that results in high computation time. New distributed computing frameworks are required for faster computation. Presently, Hadoop is a popular distributed computing framework to process a large amount of data. With a comprehensive set of experiments, we identified that the parallel implementation of sentiment analysis algorithm in Hadoop framework is not best in terms of disk space utilization and execution time. In this paper, we proposed a novel approach to optimize the performance of Hadoop MapReduce framework for opinion mining. The experimental results depict that the proposed approach on Hadoop MapReduce framework provides the best performance in terms of execution time and disk space utilization as compared with the baseline Hadoop MapReduce framework.

ACKNOWLEDGMENT

We would like to thank every member of the faculty at SDMIT, Ujire for their guidance and support, which has helped us, complete this research project successfully.

REFERENCES

Andreas, N. (2017). Nikolaos, D. Tsolis, and G. Tzimas, "Large Scale Implementations for Twitter Sentiment Classificatio. *MDPI Alogorithms*, *10*(1), 1–21.

Araque, I., Corcuera-Platas, I., Sánchez-Rada, J. F., & Iglesias, C. A. (2017). Enhancing deep learning sentiment analysis with ensemble techniques in social applications. *Expert Systems With Applications*, *77*(1), 236–246. doi:10.1016/j.eswa.2017.02.002

Bharti, B., Vachha, B., Pradhan, R. K., Babu, K. S., & Jena, S. K. (2016). Sarcastic sentiment detection in tweets streamed in real time: A big data approach. *Elsevier Digital Communications and Networks*, *2*(3), 108–121. doi:10.1016/j.dcan.2016.06.002

Clavel, C., & Callejas, Z. (2016). Sentiment Analysis: From Opinion Mining to Human-Agent Interaction. *IEEE Transactions on Affective Computing*, *7*(1), 74–93. doi:10.1109/TAFFC.2015.2444846

Cunha, J., Silva, C., & Antunes, M. (2015). Health twitter big data management with Hadoop framework. *Procedia Computer Science*, *64*, 425–431.

Diamantini, C., Mircoli, A., & Potena, D. (2016, October). A negation handling technique for sentiment analysis. *Proceedings of the 2016 International Conference on Collaboration Technologies and Systems (CTS)* (pp. 188-195). IEEE.

Doan, T., & Kalita, J. (2016, December). Sentiment analysis of restaurant reviews on yelp with incremental learning. *Proceedings of the 2016 15th IEEE International Conference on Machine Learning and Applications (ICMLA)* (pp. 697-700). IEEE.

Jose, R., & Chooralil, V. S. (2015, November). Prediction of election result by enhanced sentiment analysis on Twitter data using Word Sense Disambiguation. *Proceedings of the 2015 International Conference on Control Communication & Computing India (ICCC)* (pp. 638-641). IEEE.

This research was previously published in the International Journal of Open Source Software and Processes (IJOSSP), 10(4); pages 44-59, copyright year 2019 by IGI Publishing (an imprint of IGI Global).

Index

M

O

T

Y

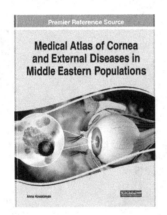

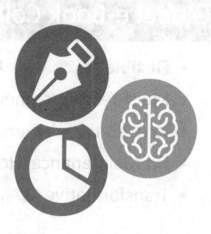

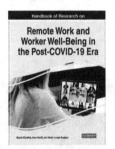

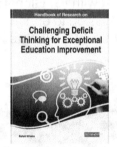

Printed in the United States
by Baker & Taylor Publisher Services